Facilities for Health, Physical Activity, Recreation and Sports:

Concepts and Applications

Tenth Edition

Thomas H. Sawyer
Editor-in-Chief

©2002 Sagamore Publishing
All rights reserved.

Book Design: Janet Wahlfeldt

ISBN: 1-57167-485-3
Library of Congress Number: 2002102278

Printed in the United States of America
10 9 8 7 6 5 4 3

Dedication

The 10th edition of this textbook is dedicated to Edward Turner, writer, educator, and true professional. Dr. Turner was an author in four editions of this textbook. He is enjoying his well-deserved retirement in the great State of Maine. Thanks, Ed!

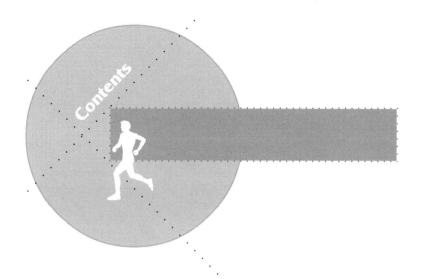

Contents

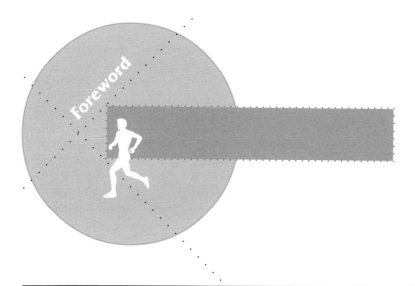

There has never been a time characterized by such a keen interest in sports and wellness-related activities and programs—on college campuses, in schools, within organizations, and in communities. These programs, aimed at improving the quality of life of all individuals, can be best supported by facilities that are well planned, well designed, well constructed, and cost effective.

The book, **Facilities Planning for Health, Fitness, Recreation and Sports: Concepts & Applications (10th Edition)**, represents more than a half-century of work by professionals dedicated to the planning, design, and construction of facilities in support of physical education, sport, recreation, and wellness. The premiere edition of the book, **Guide for Planning Facilities for Athletics, Recreation, Physical and Health Education**, was published in 1946 following the first ever national conference on facilities for health, physical education, and recreation.

In 1945 at the Board of Directors' meeting of the American Alliance for Health, Physical Education, and Recreation (AAHPER) in Washington, D.C., support was given to a proposal submitted by Caswell M. Miles, AAHPER Vice-President for Recreation, to prepare a grant to finance a national workshop on facilities. Subsequently, a request for $10,000 was submitted to and approved by Theodore P. Bank, president of the Athletic institute, to finance the first workshop. The December, 1946 workshop at Jackson's Mill, West Virginia, resulted in the publication of the premiere edition of the **Guide for Planning Facilities for Athletics, Recreation, Physical and Health Education**.

The 1956 edition of the guide was a product of the second facilities workshop held May 5-12, 1956, at the Kellogg Center for Continuing Education at Michigan State University in East Lansing. This meeting also was financed by The Athletic Institute.

The 1965 edition was prepared by the third workshop, which was financed jointly by AAHPER and The Athletic Institute and was held January 15-24, 1965, at the Biddle Continuing Education Center, Indiana University in Bloomington. Two years later, April 29-May 8, 1967, another workshop was held at Indiana University. Among those invited were a number of outstanding college and technical personnel engaged in planning and administering programs of athletics, recreation, outdoor education, physical education, and health education. Other planning authorities and specialists receiving invitations included city planners, architects, landscape architects, engineers, and schoolhouse construction consultants.

The 1974 **Guide** was restructured in such a way that it would serve as a more practical tool for school administrators, physical education heads, architects, planning consultants, and all others interested in planning new areas and facilities or checking the adequacy of those already in use.

The Athletic Institute and AAHPERD Council on Facilities, Equipment, and Supplies initiated the 1979 revision of the **Guide**. A blue-ribbon Steering Committee was appointed by the Council. Edward Coates from the Ohio State University, and Richard B. Flynn from the University of Nebraska at Omaha, were appointed as co-editors and contributing authors.

Professionals well-known for their expertise in facility planning, design and construction, were invited to assist in a complete rewrite, which resulted in **Planning Facilities for Athletics, Physical Education, and Recreation**.

The 1985 edition of **Planning Facilities for Athletics, Physical Education, and Recreation** represented a continuing effort on the part of The Athletic Institute and AAHPERD to keep the text current and relevant. Richard B. Flynn was selected to be editor and contributing author. Many of the contributors to the previous edition updated their chapters and some new material was added.

The American Alliance for Health, Physical Education, Recreation, and Dance published the 1993 edition, entitled **Facility Planning for Physical Education, Recreation, and Athletics,** and Richard B. Flynn again was asking to serve as editor and contributing author. Again, many of the contributors to the previous edition updated their chapters and some new material was added.

The AAHPERD Council on Facilities and Equipment selected Thomas H. Sawyer of Indiana State University to serve as Chair of the editorial committee and Editor-in-Chief of the 1999 edition of **Facilities Planning for Physical Activity and Sport.** Many new contributors were selected to complete a major revision of the text resulting in a great deal of new material and many fresh ideas and concepts.

This revised 2002 edition, with Thomas H. Sawyer again serving as editorial committee Chair and Editor-in-Chief, fulfills the intent of the committee to revise the text on a regular basis. Given the rapidity of change in facility planning, design, construction, and standards, the commitment by the AAHPERD Council on Facilities and Equipment to revise the book at regular intervals is commendable, and represents a major contribution to the profession.

It should be noted that much of the material in this text reflects the composite knowledge of many professionals who have contributed to past AAHPERD text editions, as well as of those individuals who were solicited to serve as authors, editors, and reviewers for the current text. The American Alliance for Health, Physical Education, Recreation, and Dance (AAHPERD), the American Association for Active Lifestyles and Fitness (AAALF), and the Council on Facilities and Equipment (CFE) have endorsed this book as one of the best on the topic of planning facilities for sport, physical activity, and recreation.

Having had the pleasure to contribute to select past editions, I am pleased to offer my strong endorsement for the current text. This highly informative edition of **Facilities Planning for Physical Activity and Sport** contains updated and relevant material that will guide professionals involved in the planning, design, evaluation, and construction of facilities related to physical activity and sport. I believe it clearly represents one of the most comprehensive resources available today.

Richard B. Flynn, President
Springfield College

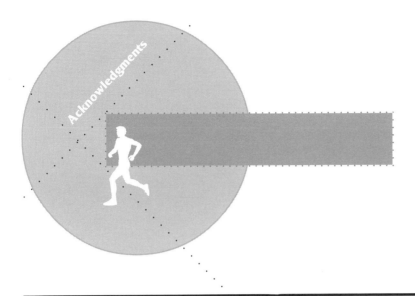

Acknowledgments

Appreciation is expressed to the Editorial Committee members of the Council for Facilities and Equipment (CFE) for assuming initial responsibility for outlining the content and chapters for the text and selection of the chapter authors. While some served as authors/editors for specific chapters in the text, all served as reviewers for assigned chapter drafts. The Editorial Committee members include:

Dr. Thomas H. Sawyer, Chair and Editor-in-Chief, Indiana State University, Chair CFE, 1995-97

Dr. Bernie Goldfine, Kennesaw State University, Chair CFE, 1999-2001

Dr. Michael G. Hypes, Indiana State University, Chair CFE, 2001-03

Dr. Richard LaRue, University of New England, Chair CFE, 1994-95

Dr. Todd Seidler, University of New Mexico, Chair CFE, 1991-92

Dr. Jan Seaman, AAALF Executive Director

We are indebted to a number of authoritative sources for permission to reproduce material used in this text.
- The National Collegiate Athletic Association for permission to reproduce drawings from selected 1997 NCAA rule books. It should be noted that these specifications, like others, are subject to annual review and change.
- Athletic Business for permission to reprint selected drawings.
- Selected architectural firms for supplying photographs, line drawings, artists renderings, and other materials.

Special recognition is due those professionals who served as chapter authors or editors, including: John Gartland, Bernie Goldfine, Thomas Horne, Larry Horine, Susan Hudson, D.J. Hunsaker, James Karabetsos, Richard LaRue, David LaRue, Hervey LaVoie, John McNichols, Arthur Mittlestaedt, Thomas Rosandich, Jr., Todd Seidler, Donna Thompson, Jack Vivian, Hal Walker, and Harvey White. These individuals worked diligently to present chapter material in an informative and useful manner.

Without the great assistance from a number of very special and important folks, this book would not have been possible: Julia Ann Hypes who was responsible for the glossary and author information; Sagamore Publishing, for invaluable advice, counsel, patience, and encouragement during the final edit of the manuscript; Indiana State University's Graphic Arts group, for their graphic design services; and Meghan Sawyer for graphic designs and photographs that enhanced the quality of this manuscript.

Lastly, the editors wish to thank and acknowledge Jan Seaman, Executive Director of AAALF, for her continued encouragement and support during the preparation of this text.

Thomas H. Sawyer, Ed.D. Editor-in-Chief

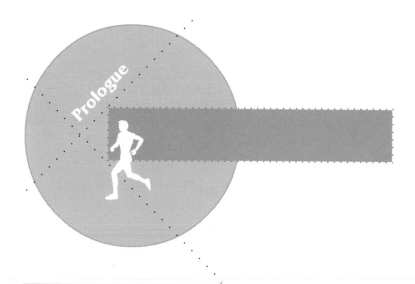

Todd L. Seidler, University of New Mexico
Bernie Goldfine, Kennesaw State University

Have you ever seen a facility with so many design problems that it left you shaking your head in disbelief? Each facility presents its own unique design challenges; if these chal-lenges are not addressed and overcome, the result is a facility with design problems. Typically, the larger a building project, the greater the likelihood that mistakes will be made in the planning and design process. Often, details are overlooked, and sometimes even major mistakes are made in the planning process and not discovered until after the facility is built and opened for use. For example, most of us have seen buildings with poor lighting, ventilation, or access control that could have been prevented with appropriate planning. In particular, one of the most common design flaws in recreational, physical education, and sports facilities is a lack of proper storage space. Surely, we have all visited buildings where hallways, classrooms, and even activity spaces were used for temporary or permanent storage of equipment.

A lack of planning has resulted in countless design flaws in sport and recreation facilities. Can you imagine a high school football team playing on an 80-yard football field? What about a recreation center with access to the locker rooms available only by crossing the gym floor? Do you believe a facility designer would locate a locker room toilet one foot lower than the septic field it was supposed to drain into? How about a gymnasium with large picture windows directly behind the basketball backboards? And how safe is an indoor track that has been constructed as part of a pool deck that has water puddles present in every running lane? Impossible? No.

These "Building Bloopers" are real and are not as uncommon as we would like to believe. Such mistakes can be embarrassing, expensive, amazing, and sometimes humorous (if it is not your facility). These and many other planning and design errors can usually be traced to insufficient planning. An example of an outrageous building blooper is Olympic Stadium in Montreal. Constructed as the track and field site for the 1976 Montreal Olympics, it has yet to be completed satisfactorily. Originally estimated to cost about $60 million, the price thus far is in excess of $1 billion. And to top it off, a large percentage of the seats did not have direct sight lines to the finish line on the track.

Building bloopers are often caused by devoting insufficient time, effort and/or expertise to the planning process. The earlier in the process that mistakes are discovered and corrected, the less they are going to cost to rectify. It is inexpensive to change some words on a paper, somewhat more expensive to change lines on a blueprint, and outrageously expensive or impossible to make changes once the concrete has been poured. Furthermore, the impact of a poorly designed building is staggering when compared with other management problems. Problematic staff or other personnel can be relieved of their responsibilities. Funds can be raised for under-financed programs. However, the consequences of a poorly designed building will have to be endured for decades. Therefore, it is essential to devote all available resources early in the planning process.

All too often, facilities are planned without in-depth consideration of the programs that they will support. Basically, a facility is a tool. The better it is planned, designed, and constructed, the better it will support the objectives of the programs it will house. Strange as it may seem, often sport facilities are designed without a great deal of consideration being given to programming and user desires. Aesthetics, the interests of one sport or program at the time, or the personal desires of decision-makers may, in fact, dictate the design of facility. Implementing a new program in an existing or poorly planned facility often requires designing the programs based on the limitations of the facility. Poorly designed venues may limit or even prevent some activities from taking place. Conversely, a well-designed facility will support and enhance the desired programs. Planning and building a new facility is a great opportunity to ensure that it will optimally support these pro-grams. Furthermore, if done properly, well-planned venues allow for flexibility when the popularity of activities and user demand fluctuate. Planned with an eye toward future trends, these facilities are designed to be easily altered so that new activities can be added as needs change.

This book is intended to provide a basic understanding of the planning and design process as well as the unique features of many different areas and types of facilities. Although there is no such thing as a perfect building, with significant time, effort, and expertise devoted to the planning and design process, future building bloopers can be kept to a minimum. It is hoped that those of you involved with the planning of sports facilities will find this book to be a significant resource.

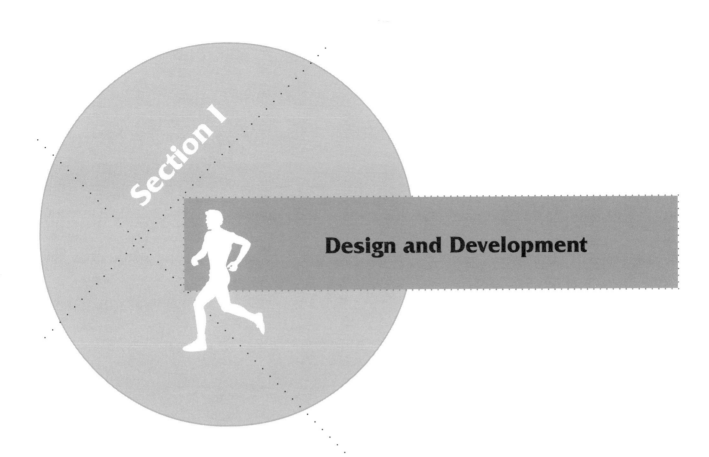

Section I

Design and Development

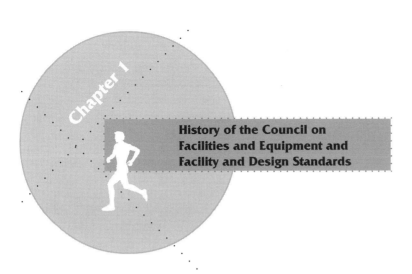

Thomas H. Sawyer, Indiana State University
Michael G. Hypes, Indiana State University

The Council on Facilities and Equipment (CFE) focuses on concerns regarding facilities and equipment in relationship to physical activity and sport. The CFE works to develop policies, standards, guidelines, and innovations to ensure the safest and most effective means for quality health, physical education, recreation, dance, sport, and fitness facilities and equipment for the young through the aging populations. This chapter describes the development of the CFE and facility and equipment standards.

Learning Objectives

After reading this chapter, the student will be able to:
- describe the historical development of the Council on Facilities and Equipment,
- understand the historical evolution of the standards process in the last 50 years,
- discuss the steps taken in developing standards for facilities and equipment,
- describe the difference between standards and guidelines,
- gain insight into the impact on sports and related products and facilities by the emerging standards processes,
- learn the procedures employed in the United States for developing standards,
- identify the varied products and facilities for which standards have been formulated,
- differentiate between a standard and other guidelines, criteria and requirements, and
- understand the difference between mandatory/regulatory and voluntary standards.

Initial Interest in Facilities

Aside from Dr. Edward M. Hartwell's comprehensive report on gymnasium construction in 1885 and occasional articles in *The American Physical Education Review* (the official publication of the American Association for the Advancement of Physical Education [AAAPR]), no concerted effort was made by the profession to consider facilities (Rice, Hutchinson, & Lee, 1958). In the early 1920s the Society of Directors of Physical Education in College (College Physical Education Association) appointed a committee, of which Dr. George L. Meylan was chairman, to consider physical education facilities. Its work was published in booklet form in 1923, entitled *Physical Education Buildings for Education Institutions, Part I, Gymnasiums and Lockers* (Hackensmith, 1966). The committee remained active, and following Meylan in the chairmanship was Harry A. Scott until 1927; A.R. Winters from 1927-28; and Albert H. Prettyman, from 1928-1945 (VanDalen, Mitchell, & Bennett, 1953).

The halt in the construction of facilities during the depression was only temporary, and as soon as the federal government entered the picture, building programs were resumed on a grander scale than before. In its early stages, many obvious and absurd mistakes were made in architectural planning (VanDalen, et al., 1953; Rice, et al., 1958; & Hackensmith, 1966). This led to government provision of expert guidance in planning facilities. In addition, the National Recreation Association and the Recreation Division, Work Project Administration, issued many pamphlets as guides in planning recreation facilities. The College Physical Education Association also initiated the practice of collecting and filing architectural plans of college facilities that were made available to the profession on request (Hackensmith, 1966).

By the end of the 1930s, the degree of interest in the planning and construction of facilities was demonstrated by many publications on the subject, including Herbert Blair's *Physical Education for the Modern Junior and Senior High School* (1938), Emil Lamar's *The Athletic Plant* (1938), George Butler's *The New Play Areas-Their Design and Equipment* (1938), Fredrick W. Leuhring's *Swimming Pool Standards* (1939), and Ruth Eliott Houston's *Modern Trends in Physical Education Facilities for College Women* (1939).

Early Physical Education Facilities

Many gymnasiums were erected after the Civil War, starting with the Dartmouth building of 1867, which cost $24,000. Following that, Princeton replaced its earlier red shack with a $38,000 "gym," the finest of its day. Bowdoin's gymnasium had no heat, and the men dressed for class even in zero weather, changing to cotton shirts and tights and cloth slippers. In 1870, the University of Wisconsin built a $4,000 gymnasium (the first state university to build one). The Yale gymnasium of 1875 had eight long "bathtubes" lined with zinc, which the students used only on payment of a special fee. Then 1879 brought the wonder gymnasium of the age—Harvard's $110,000 Hemenway Gymnasium—followed in 1878 by the University of California's modest $12,000 Harmon Gymnasium. During the 1960s and 1970s, many colleges that could not afford gymnasia fitted up vacant rooms as drill halls (Rice et al., 1958).

In the women's colleges, physical education classwork got underway in this period by using the outdoors, corridors, assembly halls, and storerooms. One school used a privately owned gymnasium in the local community—Radcliffe at Sargent's Gymnasium. Vassar was the only college that started its physical education work with a special building constructed for that purpose. In 1860 it built a "Hall of Calisthenics" with footprints painted on the floor to indicate where the students should stand during their exercise periods. Mt. Holyoke built a gymnasium by 1865 that cost $1,900. Other gymnasiums that were constructed included one at Smith in 1875, Bryn Mawr, by 1885; Goucher, by 1888; and Mills College, by the end of the century. Goucher College constructed the first swimming pool for women in 1888, although it did not list swimming as an activity for students until 1904. Vassar built the second pool in 1889, and Smith installed a "swimming bath" in 1892 that could be used by two to five students at a time and was used for over 30 years; Bryn Mawr built its pool in 1894, and by the end of the century, Radcliffe College had built one. There were no pools for women or men in any coeducational college or coeducational university of this era (Rice, 1929; Rice et al., 1958).

The coeducational colleges/universities lagged far behind the women's colleges in procuring facilities for women students. As a rule, the women were permitted to use the men's facilities on occasion, and in many schools a large room in the women's dormitory was set aside for a women's gymnasium (Hackensmith, 1966).

American Alliance for Health, Physical Education, Recreation, and Dance

The American Alliance for Health, Physical Education, Recreation and Dance (AAHPERD) was founded on November 27, 1885, when William Gilbert Anderson, a physical training instructor in Brooklyn, New York, invited a group of people who were working in the gymnastic field to come together to discuss their profession. These 60 people talked informally of methods of teaching, the best system of measurements, normal-training classes, and the manufacture of apparatus. After a demonstration of new exercise methods, they embarked on the formation of a permanent organization that was named the Association for the Advancement of Physical Education (AAPE). Forty-nine people, all teaching physical education, enrolled as members of the organization with a pledge to meet the next year at the same place. The first convention ran full-circle with discussions, speeches, a demonstration, enrolling members, adoption of a plan of organization, and election of officers.

At the second meeting in 1886, a formal constitution was adopted, and the name was changed to the American Association for the Advancement of Physical Education (AAAPE). The name was later changed to the American Physical Education Association (APEA). In 1937, the APEA and the Department of School Health and Physical Education of the National Education Association were formally amalgamated to form the American Association for Health and Physical Education (AAHPE). The following year, recreation was added to the title, and the American Association For Health, Physical Education and Recreation (AAHPER) continued until 1974 when the American Alliance for Health, Physical Education, and Recreation was reorganized. Dance was added to the title in 1979.

The early years of the alliance focused on defining and exploring the field of physical education and encouraging its inclusion in the schools. By the close of the century, the organization had grown in number of members from 49 to 1,076 and was spreading throughout the nation. As the years went by, the alliance grew in structure, size, and scope as it worked toward the acceptance of the study of physical education.

In late 1896, the AAPE approved a plan to begin publishing a quarterly magazine, the *American Physical Education Review*, which became the *Journal of Health and Physical Education* in 1930 and becoming the *Journal of Physical Education, Recreation, and Dance* in the '70s. The journal is published nine times a year. In 1930 the Association began publishing the *Research Quarterly*, now called the *Research Quarterly for Exercise and Sport*.

The years following World War II saw an emphasis on two key issues. One was the need for adequate and well-planned facilities, and the other was the pressing need for improved professional preparation of teachers. The alliance also continued its interest, which had developed during the War, in federal legislation relating to physical education and health services.

The decade of the 1950s was notable for a prodigious expansion of AAHPER activities, evident in three areas: conferences, consultant services, and publications. During this time, AAHPER also provided significant support and service to the cause of fitness. In 1958, the Alliance developed the Youth Fitness Test, which was the first program of testing with national norms that applied to the fitness levels of America's school-age children.

In 1965, a second national study was conducted, and the norms for the test were revised. It was during this year that the President's Council on Fitness joined with AAHPER, using the Youth Fitness Test, to initiate and promote the Presidential Physical Fitness Award.

In 1980, AAHPERD developed the Health-Related Fitness Test, where the items on the test battery related to major health risk factors. From 1980 through spring 1988, the alliance sponsored its Youth Fitness Test and the Health-Related Fitness Test. The Physical Best Program was developed in 1988 and contains both the health-related test and the teaching of fitness concepts.

The alliance went through growing pains in the late '80s and launched two major initiatives to explore its future. One, the Blue Ribbon Task Force, devoted three years of study to the structure and function of the alliance in an attempt to analyze its effectiveness for meeting member needs. Somewhat overlapping this effort was an experimental project focusing on autonomy. This project, called the AAHE Experiment, used a different method of accounting for cost of doing business and revenue sources. It allowed AAHE to experiment with more autonomous decision-making as well as taking responsibility for those decisions. This experiment, along with the outcome of the Blue Ribbon Task Force, resulted in Model III, a move toward autonomy for all national associations. The American Alliance for Health, Physical Education, Recreation, and Dance (AAHPERD) is an educational organization designed to support, encourage, and provide assistance to member groups and their personnel nationwide as they initiate, develop, and conduct programs in health, leisure, and movement-related activities.

AAHPERD seeks to:
- encourage, guide, and support professional growth and development in health, leisure, and movement-related programs based on individual needs, interests, and capabilities;
- communicate the importance of health, leisure, and movement-related activities as they contribute to human well-being;
- encourage and facilitate research that will enrich health, leisure, and movement-related activities, and disseminate the findings to professionals and the public;
- develop and evaluate standards and guidelines for personnel and programs in health, leisure, and movement-related activities;
- coordinate and administer a planned program of professional, public, and government relations that improves education in areas of health, leisure, and movement-related activities; and
- conduct other activities for the public benefit.

AAHPERD is composed of six national associations, including:
- American Association for Active Lifestyles and Fitness (AAALF)
- American Association for Health Education (AAHE)
- American Association for Leisure and Recreation (AALR)
- National Association for Girls and Women in Sport (NAGWS)
- National Association for Sport and Physical Education (NASPE)
- National Dance Association (NDA)

Association for Research, Administration, and Professional Councils (ARAPC) History 1949-2000

The American Association for Active Lifestyles and Fitness (AAALF) evolved out of the General Division of the American Association for Health, Physical Education, and Recreation. In 1949, the General Division was created as the fourth division of AAHPER, joining the Health Education Division, Physical Education Division, and the Recreation Division. This reorganization plan consolidated the general sections to eliminate duplication of functions and service. At the time of its formation, the General Division included 12 sections, three of which originated in the AAHPER well before 1930.

These 12 sections were:
- Aquatics
- Administration and Supervision
- Athletics Boys and Men
- Athletics Girls and Women
- Camping and Outdoor Education
- Dance
- Measurement and Evaluation
- Professional Education
- Professional and Public Relations
- Research
- Students
- Therapeutics

The General Division's substructures fluctuated in number through the years, beginning with the addition of the Research Council in 1952. General Division councils and sections were differentiated by functions. The sections operated primarily to plan and conduct programs at the annual AAHPER conventions in their specialized interest area.

The General Division 1970 Operating Code stated that "The purpose of the General Division shall be to provide leadership and coordination to those groups developing programs and fostering education activities under its auspices" and to
- Provide an organizational structure to serve groups whose professional interest and activities relate to two or more existing AAHPER divisions or whose professional interests do not readily lend themselves to inclusion in other divisions.
- Promote flexibility in serving the many and varied professional interests and levels of the AAHPER membership by providing opportunity for growth of new and continuing professional interest groups.
- Recognize inter-divisional professional interests and activities and to encourage com- munications and cooperation among the divisions of AAHPER.
- Coordinate and lend intra-divisional support to professional interests and programs.

On April 16, 1973, the AAHPER Representative Assembly approved the Reorganization Committee's Model II to change AAHPER from an association to an alliance. This gave the eight AAHPER divisions and their structure self-determination of association status and placement. The premise was that the alliance would "provide unity with diversity", allowing the associations full control over their professional programs, while being a united structure of related disciplines. It is within these concepts and at that time that the Association for Research, Administration, and Professional Councils (ARAPC) had its origin. In October 1974, the Alliance Board of Governors defined the term "society" as an alliance structure, and further stated that all societies would be housed in

ARAPCS, formerly the General Division of the American Association for Health, Physical Education, and Recreation. The name change took place during the early 1960s. ARAPCS was composed of those councils and a professional society that did not clearly fit into the other national associations—National Association for Sport and Physical Education, National Association for Girls and Women in Sports, American Association for Leisure and Recreation, and American Association for Health Education.

In spring 1994, ARAPCS changed its name to the American Association for Active Lifestyles and Fitness (AAALF). This name change was designed to more clearly define the focus and mission of the association. With its 12 councils and one society, AAALF has a broad range of interests and programs. All professional activities are carried on through the special interest areas of its councils. With this format, most of the income received by AAALF is allocated directly to the councils/society for their professional activities, which maximizes allocations for program content.

American Association for Active Lifestyles and Fitness

The American Association for Active Lifestyles and Fitness (AAALF), formerly ARAPCS, is one of six national associations within the American Alliance for Health, Physical Education, Recreation, and Dance (AAHPERD). The goal of AAALF and its 12 councils (Adapted Physical Education Council, Aquatics Council, College and University Administrators Council, Council on Aging and Adult Development, Council on Facilities and Equipment, Council on Outdoor Education, Ethnic Minority Council, International Relations Council, Measurement and Evaluation Council, Physical Fitness Council, Student Action Council) and one society (School and Community Safety Society of America) is to promote active lifestyles and fitness for all populations through support of research, development of leaders, and dissemination of current information. The membership is provided the latest information in the field, professional development opportunities, career networking and contacts, an annual national convention, regional workshops/ conferences, publication opportunities, advocacy of mission, leadership opportunities, professional recognition, and headquarters support staff.

The Birth of the Guide for Planning Facilities for Athletics, Recreation, Physical and Health Education

At the meeting of the Board of Directors of the American Alliance for Health, Physical Education, and Recreation in Washington, D.C. in April 1945, favorable action was taken on a proposal by Caswell M. Miles, AAHPERD vice-president for recreation, that a grant be obtained to finance a national conference on facilities. Subsequently, a request for $10,000 to finance the first facilities conference was placed before Theodore R. Bank, president of The Athletic Institute. The project was approved and the money appropriated to finance the first conference. The conference was held at Jacob's Mill, West Virginia. As a result of this conference, the *Guide for*

Planning Facilities for Athletics, Recreation, Physical and Health Education was published that same year.

The second conference was held from May 5-12,1956, at the Kellogg Center for Continuing Education at Michigan State University in East Lansing. The second conference, like the first, was financed by The Athletic Institute. The second edition (1956) of the *Guide* was the result of this second conference.

The third edition (1965) was prepared at the third conference, which was financed jointly by AAHPER and The Athletic Institute and held at the Biddle Continuing Education Center, Indiana University, in Bloomington from January 15-24, 1965. The fourth conference was held two years later, from April 29-May 8, 1967, at Indiana University. Among those invited were a number of outstanding college and technical personnel engaged in planning and conducting programs of athletics, recreation, outdoor education, and physical and health education. In addition, invitations were extended to a number of specialists responsible for planning and constructing facilities for these programs. These specialists included city planners, architects, landscape architects, engineers, and schoolhouse construction consultants.

At the 1974 facilities committee meeting, five members were assigned the task of restructuring the *Guide* (fourth edition) in such a way that it would serve as a more practical tool for school administrators, physical education heads, architects, planning consultants, and all others interested in planning new areas and facilities or checking the adequacy of those already in use.

During recent years, there have been many new developments in facility planning and construction. These have been due to a number of factors. The need for improving education, recreation, and fitness opportunities for the youth of the nation has been highlighted by many groups. The extensive work of the President's Council on Physical Fitness is one illustration of the growing national interest in health, physical education, and recreation activities. Much of the research and attention devoted to facility planning and construction during the past three decades has been due to the increased leisure time in society and a growing realization that recreation, and especially physical activity, is a fundamental human need essential to the well-being of all people.

The Athletic Institute and AAHPERD Council on Facilities, Equipment, and Supplies initiated the fifth edition (1979) of the *Guide* following a careful review of the fourth edition (1974). A blue-ribbon steering committee was appointed by the Council. Edward Coates of Ohio University and Richard B. Flynn of the University of Nebraska at Omaha were appointed as co-editors and contributing authors. Professionals well-known for their expertise in facility planning and construction were invited to assist in a complete rewrite.

The sixth edition (1984) of *Planning Facilities for Athletics, Physical Education, and Recreation* represents a continuing effort on the part of The Athletic Institute and AAHPERD to keep the text current and relevant. Richard B. Flynn of the University of Nebraska at Omaha was selected as editor and contributing author. Chapter input was solicited from carefully chosen leaders in the field as well as from outstanding architects. Efforts were made to incorporate the most recent advances in facility planning and construction. Certain program areas, such as planning for the handicapped, were expanded, while outdated or irrelevant materials were deleted.

Richard B. Flynn, who edited the seventh edition, was selected to serve as editor and contributing author for the eighth edition (1993). This edition carried the same title as the seventh edition (1988). Many of the same contributors volunteered to revise their sections. The text was revised but not expanded.

For the ninth edition (1999) a new editorial team was put together by the Council on Facilities and Equipment to do a complete overhaul of the book. The editorial team consisted of Thomas H. Sawyer, Ed.D. (Indiana State University), Editor-in-Chief; Bernie Goldfine, Ph.D. (Kennesaw State University); Michael G. Hypes, D.A. (Indiana State University); Richard L. LaRue, D.P.E. (University of New England); and Todd Seidler, Ph.D. (University of New Mexico); There were 21 authors involved in writing the 29 chapters. The name of the text was changed to *Facility Development for Physical Activity and Sport: Concepts and Applications*, in order to reflect an expanded content aimed at a broader audience.

The 10th edition (2002) used the same editorial team led by Thomas H. Sawyer. This edition was revised and expanded to 37 chapters, including a chapter describing the newest Japanese Olympic Training Center. The book was published by Sagamore Publishing/AAALF publications. The ninth edition was published by Kendall-Hunt Publishing Company. Over 3,000 copies were sold of the ninth edition. The 10th edition is proposed to sell 4,000 copies. The 11th edition will be published in 2005 with the same editorial team as used for the 10th edition. See Table 1.1 for a summary of the Guides development since 1946.

Evolution of the Council on Facilities and Equipment
1955-2000

In 1955, AAHPER established the Council on Equipment and Supplies, with Thomas E. McDonough (Emory University, Georgia) as chairman and Charles Heilman (Drake University, Iowa) as secretary. The purpose of the council was to assist physical educators, athletic coaches, and recreation leaders in the selection, purchase, and care of equipment and supplies. Since its organization, the council has secured the cooperation of manufacturing companies and stimulated professional interest through exhibits of equipment and supplies at conferences and conventions. In 1959, AAHPER and the Athletic Institute cosponsored a third National Workshop on Equipment and Supplies for Athletics, Physical Education, and Recreation at Michigan State University, whose report was made available in 1960. The name of the council was changed (1976) to reflect its work in the area of facilities: Council on Facilities, Equipment, and Supplies.

In 1993 the Council on Facilities, Equipment, and Supplies changed its name to the Council on Facilities and Equipment (CFE). The new name better identified the Council's focus on concerns relating to facilities and equipment in relationship to physical activity. CFE works to develop policies, standards, guidelines, and innovations to ensure the

Table 1.1
Summary of Guide's Development - 1946 - 2002

Organization	Editor-in-Chief	Year	Edition	Title
AAHPER/Athletic Institute	Caswell M. Miles	1946	1st	*Guide for Planning Facilities for Athletics, Recreation, Physical and Health Education*
Council on Equipment & Supplies AAHPER/Athletic Institute	Council	1956	2nd	Same
Council/AAHPER/Athletic Inst.	Council	1963	3rd	Same
Facilities Committee/General Div. AAHPERD/Athletic Institute	Committee	1974	4th	Same
Council on Fac, Equip, & Supplies ARAPCS/AAHPERD/Athletic Inst.	Edward Coates Richard B. Flynn	1979	5th	Same
CFES/ARAPCS/AAHPERD/ Athletic Institute	Richard B. Flynn	1984	6th	Same
CFES/ARAPCS/AAHPERD/ Athletic Institute	Richard B. Flynn	1988	7th	Same
CFES/ARAPCS/AAHPERD Athletic Institute	Richard B. Flynn	1992	8th	Same
Council on Facilities & Equip. (CFE) AAALF/AAHPERD	Thomas H. Sawyer	1999	9th	*Facility Development for Physical Activity and Sport: Concepts and Applications*
CFE/AAALF/AAHPERD	Thomas H. Sawyer	2002	10th	Same

safest and most effective means for quality health, physical education, recreation, dance, sport, and fitness facilities for the young through the aging populations.

The purposes of the CFE are:
- To initiate a national cooperative effort to improve the quality of the facilities and equipment for health, physical education, recreation, and dance;
- To improve the quality of undergraduate and graduate instruction in facilities and equipment design and planning;
- To present research findings and to review needed research projects for possible endorsement and development by the council;
- To prepare and disseminate information to aid members to keep abreast of current innovations, promising practices, comparative data and practical ideas;
- To cooperate with related professions (architecture, engineering, construction, manufacturing), representing the alliance in all matters within its purview and proposing and implementing joint projects with other councils within AAALF;
- To initiate and conduct state, district, and national conferences on facilities and equipment issues;
- To plan and develop needed publications through the alliance; and
- To provide consultant services for referral to potential users and developers of facilities.

Who Should Be a Member:
- Those teaching courses or a unit within a course in facilities planning;
- Any HPERD professional who has an interest in facility planning; and
- Any professional who plans, designs, and manages facilities, and manufacturers of equipment involving fitness, physical activity, and sport.

CFE Membership Services:
- Consultant service for potential users, planners, and designers of physical activity facilities and equipment;
- Research on current trends in physical activity facilities and equipment;
- Programs and site visits of facilities at the annual AAHPERD national conference;
- Newsletter, *Focus on Facilities*, published semi-annually. It contains news about ongoing projects within the council and important happenings in facility and equipment development;
- Awards given to members who contribute significantly to the CFE;
- World Wide Web connection is http://www.aahperd.org/aaalf.html; and
- Publication of state-of-the-art textbook used in educating undergraduates and graduates in the field of facilities and equipment; available from AAHPERD Publications.

The CFE is represented in the districts as follows:
- Six AAHPERD regional district representatives, along with the coordinator, serve our council at the dis-

trict level. Some vital responsibilities of council representatives are:
- To disseminate information within the district about council goals and programs;
- To establish lines of communication with facility and equipment specialists in states within each district;
- To promote facility and equipment workshops, clinics, and seminars to address expressed specific needs within each district;
- To nominate facility and equipment professionals from their district who make outstanding contributions to the field of facility and equipment development for the CFE Professional Service or Honor Awards;
- Membership in the Council on Facilities and Equipment provides automatic membership with AAALF/AAHPERD. In addition to the benefits of the CFE membership, AAALF/AAHPERD benefits include twice yearly AAALF Newsletters, AAHPERD's UPDATE, a choice of four professional journals, discounts at the national convention and other professional events; and
- For membership information about the Council on Facilities and Equipment, please write or call: The Council on Facilities and Equipment/AAALF, 1900 Association Drive, Reston, VA 22091, (703)476-3430 or 1-800-213-7193 or e-mail: aaalf@aahperd.org or FAX (703)476-9527.

Future of the Council on Facilities and Equipment

The CFE sees great potential for its newest version of the facility development book. The expanded book provides greater detail for students, professionals in the field, consultants, and architects than previous editions. Further, the CFE will seek sponsorships to expand its semi- annual newsletter to a quarterly newsletter of eight to 16 pages. Finally, the CFE will continue to update its bi-annual list of consultants for sale to the membership and the private sector.

Standards

Standards are the basis by which fitness, physical activity, recreation, sport products, and facilities can be harmonized between companies, between sports associations, trade associations, and between countries. Standards that have been developed over the past 50 years have provided a uniform approach to producing devices and parts used in fitness, physical activity, recreation, and sport equipment and in the construction elements of a facility. Standards have also provided sports organizations with consistency among levels of a sport and variations of the game itself. This has perhaps been the weakest aspect of standardization, as various sport organizations have similarities and differences that become the competitive edge for control of that market.

A standard is something established for use as a rule or basis of comparison in measuring or judging capacity. A standard applies to some measure, principle, model, etc., with which things of the same class are compared in order to determine their quantity, value, or quality. A standard has a set of criteria used to test or measure the excellence, fitness, or correctness of something.

Standards for facilities and equipment are established by associations, societies, trades, or federal and state governments. The American Society for Testing and Materials (ASTM) is an example of a society that establishes standards. From the work of 132 technical standards- writing committees, ASTM (http://www. astm.org) publishes standard specifications, tests, practices, guides, and definitions for materials, products, systems, and services. ASTM also publishes books containing reports on state-of-the-art testing techniques and their possible applications. These standards and related information are used throughout the world.

Mandatory and Voluntary Standards

Standards may be either mandatory or voluntary. The status of a standard depends on the sponsor's organizational standing (i.e., governmental or voluntary non-governmental). A mandatory standard is developed by a federal agency such as the Environmental Protection Agency (EPA) and Occupational Safety and Health Administration (OSHA). The voluntary standard is developed by a professional non-profit agency. A violation of a mandatory standard carries a penalty. In addition to standards, other written documents control the unity and uniformity of equipment and facility development; including legal codes or regulations, technical specifications, guides, and literature and learned treatises.

Legal codes are developed by elected public officials, such as the National Bureau of Standards, EPA, and OSHA. Further, each state or local government has its own building codes. Technical specifications and guidelines are developed by voluntary organizations such as the American Society of Testing and Materials (ASTM) or American National Standard Institute (ANSI), which create standards through committee or trade group processes. Many other professional, trade, and organizational associations also promulgate standards, specifications, or guides that are used to measure a standard of care. Literature and learned treatises document common knowledge in a variety of ways, including professional journals, magazines, reference books, textbooks, and reports.

Standard of Practice

A standard of practice is a usual practice accepted by the national or local government regarding some aspect of equipment or facility design or usage. It is a usage or practice of the people, which, by common adoption and acquiescence and by long and unvarying habit, has become compulsory and has acquired the force of law with respect to the place or subject matter to which it relates. It is considered a customary practice that prevails within a geographical area.

Standard of Care

In laws of negligence, the standard of care is that degree of care that a reasonably prudent person should exercise in the same or similar circumstances. If a person's conduct falls below such standard, legal or customary, he or she may be liable in damages for injuries or damages resulting from his or her conduct.

Evolution of Standards

The development of standards began in earnest at the conclusion of World War II. The movement was enhanced by the efforts of the National Bureau of Standards to establish partnerships with ASTM, ANSI, and other groups to standardize materials and methods used by private industry and government. During the 1950s and 60s, automation of the workplace increased the need for greater standardization of materials and methods. The computer age has again increased the need for yet greater collaboration between government and the private sector in the development of additional standards as well as the modification of previous ones.

The development of standards in the fitness, physical activity, recreation, and sport area began in the early 1970s. The F-8 Committee on Sports Equipment and Facilities was organized by ASTM. The initial standards promulgated by the F-8 Committee dealt with footwear and football helmets. Ten years after the F-8 Committee was developed, the Committee on Skiing and Amusements was established. Over the years, a wide range of standards has been developed that influence fitness, physical activity, recreation, and sport. These standards have also made equipment and facilities safer for participants.

Though such standards have been through the gauntlet of objections and reservations, they are here to stay. Some fear standards may inhibit creativity, negatively affect the growth of the sport, and increase its cost. When participants are engaged in a sport they seem to want to use something to protect themselves. When they do, that something should meet reasonable and meaningful requirements, demonstrating that it provides the protection. The cost of debilitating injuries is reduced by this common denominator.

Organizations Advancing Standards

American National Standards Institute (ANSI)

ANSI is another significant organization that develops standards. It is a nonprofit, privately funded membership organization that coordinates the development of U.S. voluntary national standards and is the U.S. member body to nontreaty international standards bodies, such as the International Organization for Standardization (ISO) and the International Electrotechnical Commission (IEC) through the Institute's U.S. National Committee (USNC). ANSI serves both the private and public sectors' need for voluntary standardization. The voluntary standards system contributes to the overall health of the economy and the competitiveness of U.S. industry in the changing global marketplace.

ANSI was founded in 1918, prompted by the need for an "umbrella" organization to coordinate the activities of the U.S. voluntary standards system and eliminate conflict and duplication in the development process. The institute serves a diverse membership of over 1,200 companies; 250 professional, technical, trade, labor, and consumer organizations; and some 30 government agencies. The ANSI federation is guided by the national culture and the free enterprise system. For over 70 years, the U.S. voluntary standards system has been administered successfully by the private sector, through ANSI, with the cooperation of federal, state, and local governments. Standards exist in all industries, including telecommunications, safety and health, information processing, petroleum, banking, and household appliances. ANSI's key functions as stated are to:

- Coordinate the self-regulating, due-process concensus-based, U.S. voluntary standards system;
- Administer the development of standards and approve them as American National Standards;
- Provide the means for the U.S. to influence development of international and regional standards;
- Disseminate timely and important information on national, international, and regional standards activities to U.S. industry; and
- Promote awareness of the growing strategic significance of standards technology and U.S. global competitiveness.

A standards board is a standing organization within ANSI, having planning and coordination responsibilities on a continuing basis for a defined scope of activity under the purview of, and advisory to, ANSI's Executive Standards Council (ExSC). Standards boards serve in a purely advisory capacity. They do not develop standards, nor do they have authority over the activities of accredited standards developers. Membership within ANSI is a prerequisite to service on a standards board. The standards board has responsibility for establishing overall planning and coordination for national and international standards activities in the safety and health area. Further, it reviews the standards activity of applicants for accreditation and the initiation of new standards activities by accredited standards developers. It reviews applications for accreditation of International Standards Organization's U.S. Technical Advisory Group (TAG) Administrators and makes recommendations to the ExSO regarding approval of TAG Administrators, TAG membership lists, and accreditation. The board also reviews lists of candidates for American National Standards and recommends the addition of directly and materially affected interests, and it makes recommendations to the ExSO concerning suggested changes to ANSI procedures.

The scope of the standards board includes protection of the health and safety of employees and the public using buildings, machinery, and other equipment; hazardous materials; workplaces (including construction sites); vehicular traffic; public and recreation areas; homes and schools; and occupational and non-occupational hazards. Hazards include such things as explosion; fire; radiation (other than ionizing); mechanical, physical, chemical, and environmental hazards; disease; and inadequate or polluted air. Specifically included are personal protective equipment, including personal protection devices for attenuating noise, practices or devices to prevent or minimize fire, explosion or mechanical hazards, safe work practices, and provision for accident reporting and recording. Specifically excluded are building codes and acoustical (other than personal protective devices), electrical, process industry, and nuclear energy standards.

American Society of Testing and Materials (ASTM)

One of the first materials specifications was found in the Book of Genesis: "Make thee an ark of gopher wood; rooms shalt thou make in the ark, and shalt pitch it within and without with pitch." Prior to the 19th century's industrial revolution, craftsmen told their suppliers in similarly basic language what kinds of materials they desired. Craft experience was indeed key, because artisans had no instruments to measure the tensile strength, chemical composition, and other characteristics of a given material.

The industrial revolution opened a new chapter in the history of material specifications. Locomotive builders, steel rail producers, and steam engine builders who used revolutionary new materials, such as Bessemer steel, could no longer rely on craft experiences of centuries past. Manufacturers encountered numerous quality problems in such end products as steel rails, because suppliers furnished inferior materials. American rails were so poorly made, in fact, that many railroad companies preferred British imports, which were more expensive but reliable.

To avoid such problems, some manufacturers issued detailed descriptions of material to ensure that their supplies met certain quality standards. However, suppliers in many industries, such as construction and metallurgy, objected to standard material specifications and testing procedures, because they feared that strict quality controls would make customers more inclined to reject items and default on contracts.

The Pennsylvania Railroad, the largest corporation of the 19th century, played a key role in the quest for standard specifications. Its efforts in this field were initiated by Charles Dudley, who received his Ph.D. from Yale University in 1874, and who later became the driving force behind ASTM. Dudley organized the railroad's new chemistry department, where he investigated the technical properties of oil, paint, steel, and other materials the Pennsylvania Railroad bought in large quantities. Based on his research, Dudley issued standard material specifications for the company's suppliers.

What is ASTM?

Organized in 1898, ASTM has grown into one of the largest voluntary standards development systems in the world. ASTM is a not-for-profit organization that provides a forum for producers, users, ultimate consumers, and those having a general interest (representatives of government and academia) to meet on common ground and write standards for materials, products, systems, and services. From the work of 132 standards-writing committees, ASTM publishes standard test methods, specifications, practices, guides, classifications, and terminology. ASTM's standards development activities encompass metals, paints, plastics, textiles, petroleum, construction, energy, the environment, consumer products, medical services and devices, computerized systems, electronics, and many other areas. ASTM Headquarters has no technical research or testing facilities; such work is done voluntarily by 35,000 technically qualified ASTM members located throughout the world. More than 10,000 ASTM standards are published each year in the 72 volumes of the *Annual Book of ASTM Standards*. These standards and related information are sold throughout the world.

What Is an ASTM Standard?

As used in ASTM, a standard is a document that has been developed and established within the consensus prin ciples of the society and that meets the approval requirements of ASTM procedures and regulations. Some of the specific standards developed that relate to fitness, physical activity, recreation, and sport facilities and equipment are E-5 Fire Standards, F-6 Resilient Floor Coverings, F-8 Sports Equipment and Facilities, F-14 Fences, F-21 Filtration, F-24 Amusement Rides and Devices, F-26 Food Service Equipment. F-27 Snow Skiing, and F-30 Emergency Medical Services.

What Types of Standards Does ASTM Produce?

ASTM develops six principal types of full-consensus standards. They are:

- Standard test method—A definitive procedure for the identification, measurement, and evaluation of one or more qualities, characteristics, or properties of a material, product, system, or service that produces a test result.
- Standard specification—A precise statement of a set of requirements to be satisfied by a material, product, system, or service that also indicates the procedures for determining whether each of the requirements is satisfied.
- Standard practice—A definitive procedure for performing one or more specific operations or functions that does not produce a test result.
- Standard terminology—A document comprising terms, definitions, description of terms, explanation of symbols, abbreviations, or acronyms.
- Standard guide—A series of options or instructions that do not recommend a specificcourse of action.
- Standard classification—A systematic arrangement or division of materials, products, systems, or services into groups based on similar characteristics such as origin, composition, properties, or use.

Why Are ASTM Standards Credible?

Many factors contribute to the quality and credibility of ASTM standards. Those factors include:

- A voluntary, full-consensus approach that brings together people with diverse backgrounds, expertise, and knowledge;
- A balanced representation of interests at the standards-writing table;
- Intense round-robin testing to ensure precision;
- Strict balloting and due-process procedures to guarantee accurate, up-to-date information; and
- An atmosphere that promotes open discussion.

What is Meant by Full-Consensus Standards?

Full-consensus standards are developed through the cooperation of all parties who have an interest in participating in the development and/or use of the standards. Standards can be developed through varying degrees of consensus. Examples include:

- Company Standard—consensus among the employees of a given organization (principally within such departments as design, development, production, and purchasing).
- Industry Standard—consensus among the employees of a given industry (typically developed by a trade association).
- Professional Standard—consensus among the individual members of a given profession (typically developed by a professional society).
- Government Standard—consensus often among the employees of a government agency or department.

ASTM develops full-consensus standards with the belief that input from all concerned parties in the development of a standard will ensure technically competent standards having the highest credibility when critically examined and used as the basis for commercial, legal, or regulatory actions.

Is the Use of ASTM Standards Mandatory?

ASTM standards are developed voluntarily and used voluntarily. They become legally binding only when a government body makes them so, or when they are cited in a contract.

Who Uses ASTM Standards?

ASTM standards are used by thousands of individuals, companies, and agencies. Purchasers and sellers incorporate standards into contracts; scientists and engineers use them in their laboratories; architects and designers use them in their plans; government agencies reference them in codes, regulations, and laws; and many others refer to them for guidance.

Who Writes ASTM Standards?

ASTM standards are written by volunteer members who serve on technical committees. Through a formal balloting process, all members may have input into the standards before they are published by ASTM.

Anyone who is qualified or knowledgeable in the area of a committee's scope is eligible to become a committee member. ASTM currently has 35,000 members representing virtually every segment of industry, government, and academia.

What Are ASTM Technical Committees?

They are the specific arenas in which ASTM standards are developed. There are 132 ASTM main technical committees, and each is divided into subcommittees. The subcommittee is the primary unit in ASTM's standards development system, as it represents the highest degree of expertise in a given area. Subcommittees are further subdivided into task groups. Task group members do not have to be ASTM members. Many task groups seek non-ASTM members to provide special expertise in a given area.

How Are ASTM Standards Developed?

Standards development work begins when a need is recognized. Task group members prepare a draft standard, which is reviewed by its parent subcommittee through a letter ballot. After the subcommittee approves the document, it is submitted to a main committee letter box. Once approved at the main committee level, the document is submitted for balloting to the society. All negative votes cast during the balloting process, which must include a written explanation of the voter's objections, must be fully considered before the document can be submitted to the next level in the process. Final approval of a standard depends on concurrence by the ASTM Committee on Standards that proper procedures were followed and due process achieved. Only then is the ASTM standard published.

How Long Does It Take to Develop a Standard?

It usually takes about two years to develop a standard, although some committees have produced their standards in a year or less. Progress depends entirely on the urgency of the need, the complexity of the job, and the amount of time committees devote to the work.

How Does Someone Initiate a New Standards Activity in ASTM?

A written request, which describes the proposed activity and lists individuals, companies, and organizations that might have an interest in it, should be submitted to ASTM headquarters. The ASTM staff then researches the project to assess whether there is adequate interest, to discover if parallel activities exist in other organizations, and to determine where the activity would appropriately fit within the ASTM structure.

The process of organizing a new activity includes holding a planning and/or organizational meeting, depending on the activity's complexity. These meetings ensure that all affected interests have an opportunity to determine the need for the activity, participate in the development of a title, scope, and structure, and identify areas that need standardization.

Does ASTM Offer Continuing Technical Education?

ASTM provides continuing education and training in the use and application of ASTM standards through technical and professional training courses. ASTM members propose ideas for the courses, work with staff to establish course outlines, and serve as instructors. Attendees learn the practical application of standards and benefit from the instructors' technical expertise and knowledge of standards development.

Occupational Safety and Health Administration (OSHA)

OSHA (a federal agency) has become extensively involved in standards development. The impetus to develop a new standard can come from a variety of sources: OSHA's own initiative, the U.S. Congress, information from the National Institute for Occupational Safety and Health (NIOSH), a referral from EPA's Toxic Substances Control Act (TSCA), public petitions, or requests from OSHA advisory committees.

The standard-setting process can begin in a number of ways—with publication in the Federal Register of a request for information (RFI), an advance notice of proposed rule-making (ANPRM), or a notice of proposed rule-making (NPRM). Through an RFI or an ANPRM, OSHA seeks information to determine the extent of a particular hazard, current and potential protective measures, and the costs and benefits of various solutions.

Recently, OSHA has begun to develop some new standards through a negotiated rule-making process. Under this process, the agency forms an advisory committee composed of representatives from the various interest groups that will be affected by the new standard. These labor and industry representatives meet with OSHA to hammer out an agreement (consensus standard) that will serve as the basis for a proposed rule. This process is used to resolve long- standing differences that, until negotiated rule making, could not be resolved. OSHA is using this process to draft proposed rules for steel erection in construction and fire protection in shipyards.

Information from these sources, as well as injury and fatality data, is then used to develop a proposal. Formal proposals are published in the *Federal Register* with notice of a public comment period over the next 60 to 90 days. Occasionally, requests are made to extend the comment period or to hold a public hearing.

Finally, OSHA uses all this information to prepare and publish a final standard in the *Federal Register*, or, in some cases, to determine that no standard is needed. Standards usually take effect in 90 days or less, although some provisions (such as requirements for detailed programs) may be phased in over a longer period.

International Environment, Health and Safety (IEH&S) and International Audit Protocol Consortium (IAPC)

New International Environment, Health, and Safety (IEH&S) requirements are also being developed. These requirements include Great Britain's BS7750, the European Union's (EU) Environmental Management Audit Scheme (EMAS), the International Standards Organizations's (ISO) 9000 quality assurance and quality management standards, and the ISO 14000, a global environmental management standard.

Companies are compelled to comply with these environmental management standards for reasons that reach beyond fear of legal reprisal; strong economic and political forces are at work. Consumers are increasingly demanding that companies' products and manufacturing processes be environmentally responsible. One of the goals of the ISO 14000 standards will be to provide a precise "green" measuring tool for a concerned public. Governments, particularly those in the EU, are also favoring the "green" company. Companies without an ISO 14000 certification could be shut out of some international markets.

Fitness, Health, Racquet and Sport Clubs

American College of Sports Medicine (ACSM)

The ACSM has published a second edition of the book entitled *Health Fitness Facility Standards and Guidelines*, which suggests that the "book now sets a clear standard of comparison for use in legal proceedings." These standards are as follows:

"**Standard #1**: A facility must be able to respond in a timely manner to any reasonably foreseeable emergency event that threatens the health and safety of facility users. Toward this end, a facility must have an appropriate emergency plan that can be executed by qualified personnel in a timely manner.

Standard #2: A facility must offer each adult member a preactivity screening that is appropriate to the physical activities to be performed by the member.

Standard #3: Each person who has supervisory responsibility for a physical activity program or area at the facility must have demonstrable professional competence in that activity program or area.

Standard #4: A facility must post appropriate signage alerting users to the risks involved in their use of those areas of a facility that present potential increased risk(s).

Standard #5: A facility that offers youth services or programs must provide appropriate supervision.

Standard #6: A facility must conform to all relevant laws, regulations, and published standards." (ACSM, 5-10)

However, IHRSA, the International Health, Racquet, and Sportclubs Association (see below) has rejected the guidelines. The Association for Worksite Health Promotion (formerly the Association for Fitness in Business) is developing its own standards and certification process in a reaction to ACSM's failure to recognize the AFB's previous contributions to health and fitness certification standards.

There is a veritable alphabet soup of professional certifications from associations wishing to increase their memberships, improve their images, or turn a profit. The ASCM book defers to the state or local codes when it comes to more technical standards.

The ACSM is a medically based organization with a research focus. In the 14 years since the ACSM issued its initial exercise recommendations, the percentage of people complying has not changed substantially. The medical model works in a hospital or testing lab, but not necessarily in clubs or corporate health promotion or municipal fitness programs.

International Health, Racquet, & Sportsclub Association (IHRSA)

IHRSA, is a not-for-profit trade association representing 2,500 health and sports clubs worldwide. It is the largest club association in the world. More than 1,800 IHRSA member clubs offer some form of reciprocal access through the association's "Passport" program, which provides members the opportunity to use another club when they travel.

A club must agree to abide by the IHRSA Code of Conduct and comply with the association's membership standards. A member of IHRSA has the mission to enhance the quality of life through physical fitness and sports. It endeavors to provide quality facilities, programs, instruction, and strives to instill in all those served an understanding of the value of physical fitness and sports to their lives.

IHSRA recognizes the following international certifying agencies:
- Aerobics and Fitness Association of America
- Aerobic Pipeline International
- American Aerobics Association /International Sports Medicine Association
- American College of Sports Medicine
- American Council on Exercise

- Cooper Fitness Institute
- IDEA: The Association for Fitness Professionals
- National Academy of Sports Medicine
- National Association for Fitness Certification
- National Dance Exercise Instructors Training Association
- National Federation of Professional Trainers
- National Strength and Conditioning Association
- Ontario Fitness Council
- Sinai Corporate Health

National Fire Protection Association (NFPA)

The NFPA publishes the Life Safety Codes and will be jointly developing and publishing the first edition of the International Fire Code. This agreement comes after negotiations between the International Code Council (ICC) and NFPA. The ICC's three model code organizations, include the Building Officials and Code Administrators International, the International Conference of Building Officials, and the Southern Building Code Congress International. Representatives have been appointed by the ICC and NFPA to participate in the development of codes. It will be processed through NFPA's International Conference of Building Officials (ICBO).

ICBO is a leading code organization that established a Uniform Building Code (UBC) in 1927. That code contained a little over 200 pages of text, whereas the 1994 version involves three volumes and more than 2,600 pages. Modern codes are steadily moving to performance-type codes rather than the specification type because of the proliferation of types of materials, methods, and machinery used today. Such codes also reflect public policy, which has changed in the past 70 or more years. Contemporary society has looked to codes not only to ensure safety of life and limb, but increasingly to safeguard public welfare or well-being and security. Goals for many public issues, such as air and water quality, energy conservation, recycling, and disabilities, have led to a number of codes that affect recreation, physical activity, and sport facilities.

Codes and standards are sometimes viewed as interchangeable terms. Indeed, a code meets the above definitions of a standard. Codes, or parts thereof, are frequently characterized as being either prescriptive or performance-based. Prescriptive code requirements are definitive and easily measurable, such as the minimum width of an exit corridor, maximum slope for a specific type of roof covering, minimum air gap for back flow prevention, minimum size of grounding conductor, etc. Performance code requirements, on the other hand, use terms that describe the desired result, such as watertight enclosure, smoke removal, safe-for-the-intended-use, etc. Some of these terms have companion standards as part of the code, such as those for smoke dampers, stairway identification signs, and waterproof paper, while others do not. Adopted standards in this context can be thought of as specification codes.

A review of the 1927 Uniform Building Codes reveals that 28 standards were incorporated by reference. These documents were promulgated by various organizations including ASTM, the American Concrete Institute, the National Board of Fire Underwriters, the National Fire Protection Association, and others.

Standards are incorporated into the UBC under a code change procedure involving a proposal, a review by a code change committee in a public hearing, and a vote at a final hearing by the assembled membership at the annual meeting. Anyone can propose a code change and argue for or against any code change.

The Building Officials and Code Administrators International (BOCA) and the Southern Building Code Congress International (SBCCI), the respective publishers of the National Building Code (NBC) and the Standard Building Code (SBC), have similar histories of employing adopted standards in their codes. Together with ICBO, the International Code Council (ICC) has been formed as a consortium of these organizations. The ICC has targeted the year 2000 for the first edition of the International Building Code (IBC), with no further publications of the UBC, NBC, and SBC after 1997.

European Committee for Standardization (CEN)

CEN is the European standards organization that coordinates all European country standards organizations. It has secretariats in various subject areas that in turn relate to ISO Technical Committees. CEN has been the initiator of EC 1992. This is the array of regulatory and standards initiatives that leads to the common European internal market. EC 1992 also requires testing and certifications requirements. It sets forth alternative approaches to testing, certification, and proving conformity with the regulatory directives that are set out. It identifies organizations that will perform conformity assessment functions and U.S. testing and certifying organizations. This has implications on many sports products and ultimately facilities used for international events.

International Standards Organization (ISO) or International Organization for Standardization (IOS)

The ISO is the worldwide body, and ANSI is the member body of this group representing the United States. Approaching the 21st century, ISO sees a world in which global trade between nations continues to grow at a rate three to four times faster than national economies; a world in which the design, manufacture, marketing, and customer service operations of a growing majority of individual enterprises are distributed across many countries; and a world in which electronic communications have dramatically increased technical collaboration between experts in academia, governments, and industries from all countries.

The increasingly rapid development of technology in many sectors will continue to present major opportunities as well as underlying dangers for the general welfare of society It will therefore be incumbent on all social and economic partners to collaborate closely in guiding the applications of appropriate technologies toward sustainable economic development and global prosperity.

In this rapidly evolving scenario, globally applicable standards will play a key role. Such standards, whether developed by ISO or others, will become primary technical instruments supporting international commerce. In this context, ISO intends to be recognized globally as an influential and innovative leader in the developments of globally applicable international standards that meet or exceed the expectations of the community of nations. It will strive at all times to perfect the application of consensus and transparency principles in standardization, and in this way promote the values of rationality, utility, safety, and environmental protection for the benefit of all peoples.

Standardization is essentially an economic undertaking made possible by the achievement of widespread agreements on the coherent and mutually beneficial use of science, technology, and business knowhow. The prime object of ISO and its governance is laid down in the ISO statutes (i.e., to promote the development of standardization and related activities in the world with a view to facilitating international exchange of goods and services and to developing cooperation in the sphere of intellectual, scientific, and economic activity).

National Spa and Pool Institute (NSPI)

The National Spa and Pool Institute has for 30 years been the source of standards for the design, construction, and operation of public as well as residential pools and spas. The organization has a membership of designer-engineers along with manufacturers, builders, contractors, equipment, and chemical manufacturers and suppliers and retailers in every aspect of the pool and spa industry. Many representatives of Health Departments also belong.

In 1996, efforts began to rewrite the ANSI/SPI - 11991 standard for public pools as well as other pool and spa standards. This rewrite has undergone a conflict because of the various concerns for safety. At present, the technical committee of NSPI has assumed the rewrite function and the broad base of interests originally invited to serve are now reviewers.

World Waterpark Association (WWA)

The federal government has had standards for waterparks since they became popular over a decade ago. In 1991, the WWA published *Splash Magazine* as a developer's reference. Concurrently, it established a risk management and safety committee. Representatives of this committee were invited by the National Spa and Pool Institute to sit on the public pool standards rewrite committee. After a year of deliberations, it was decided that water slides and flumes should have a stand-alone standard apart from any public pool standard. As a result, a WWA committee was established in 1997 to write a draft of a standard under the cooperative auspices of NSPI, which is an accredited member of ANSI. This standard is now being circulated.

Sport Indoor and Outdoor Facility Standards

The following organizations establish standards for facilities and equipment for amateur and professional sports in the United States.

Amateur Sports (include, but not limited to):
- National Federation of High School Activities Associations,
- National Collegiate Athletic Association,
- National Junior College Athletic Association,
- Amateur Athletic Union,
- Little League Baseball,
- American Softball Association, and
- United States Olympic Committee and its various National Governing Bodies.

Professional Sports (include, but not limited to):
- National Football League,
- National Basketball Association,
- National Hockey League,
- Major League Baseball,
- Professional Golf Association,
- Ladies Professional Golf Association,
- United States Tennis Association, and
- American Bowling Congress.

Professional Involvement in Standards

Professionals in the fitness, physical activity, recreation, sport, and related fields are not as involved in standards as they could and should be. Standards organizations involve only a small percentage of the professionals directly involved in the teaching, researching, planning, administering, operating, and maintaining of fitness, physical activity, recreation, and sport facilities and activities, regardless of jurisdiction or the type of entity. Many standards applicable to fitness, physical activity, recreation, and sport are developed by manufacturers, medical specialists, businessmen, lawyers, and others.

Professionals have not been aware of these standards organizations nor familiar with how to become involved. Organizations such as the American Alliance for Health, Physical Education, Recreation, and Dance and the National Recreation and Park Association have not specifically designated professionals to serve as their representatives to these organizations. It is imperative that in the future more professionals be appointed or volunteer to lend their expertise to the standards process.

Governmental Involvement in Standards

Governmental agencies have a long history of involvement in standards. Apparently, many of their efforts now tend to be catalytic in evolving standards. This is a significant change over the past 50 years. In most cases they have encouraged producers to regulate their own industries. Where such efforts have failed the government, both state and federal agencies have moved to provide regulations and supportive standards to protect the health, safety, and well-being of the public.

The government usually provides standards in the form of legislation that goes beyond the base line or minimum level of requirement. As a result, industries and professions are becoming more conscious in recognizing that if they themselves do not develop standards, somebody else will.

Guidelines

A guideline is a standard or principle by which to make a judgement or determine a policy or course of action. A guideline is developed after a standard has been established. The guideline is a series of procedures to ensure the maintenance of the standard.

Summary

History is very important, as it tells others about the past experiences of people and organizations. The history of the CFE describes the beginning of an organization composed of professionals concerned about the construction of HPERD facilities. The development of these facilities has improved because of the efforts of the CFE and its leaders and members over the past 50 years.

Standards provide a uniform base by which the requirements for equipment and facilities can be established. Standards are either mandatory or voluntary in implementation. The requirements are set forth as standards, or they can be produced in other forms, such as legal codes, technical specifications, guides, or literature, Standards are also established through legal theories and even case law. They become standards through consistent practice and care.

Standards are created by many different types of organizations, all of which create the standard differently. These organizations are national and international in responsibility and influence trade and governmental relations around the globe. Particularly in sports, recreation, and related fields, standards are more often set by nonprofessionals than by those involved day to day. Government still plays an important role in setting standards, particularly when industry does not pick up on the need to protect the public's health, safety and well-being.

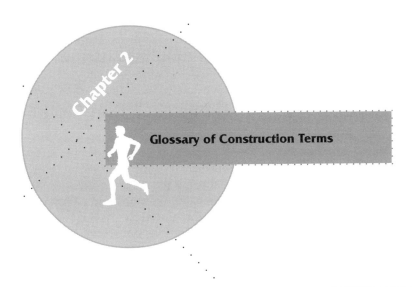

Chapter 2

Glossary of Construction Terms

Access. A way or means of approaching, entering, getting, using, etc.

Acoustical Engineer. Individual responsible for the design of large and small spaces that are appropriate for good sound (i.e., being able to hear in any seat in a large arena or aquatic complex, or not damaging to one's ears while playing racquetball).

Acoustical Treatments. Applications designed to control/absorb sound.

Addendum. A written or graphic instrument issued by the architect prior to the execution of the contract that modifies or interprets the bidding documents by additions, deletions, clarifications, or corrections. An addendum becomes part of the contract documents when the contract is executed.

Advertising Rights. Rights sold to various entities who wish to advertise to the spectators within the sport facility.

Aesthetics. A branch of philosophy dealing with the nature, creation, and appreciation of beauty.

Aggregate. Any hard material (usually sand and rock) for mixing in graduated fragments with a cementing material to form concrete, plaster, and the like.

Alternate Bid. The amount stated in the bid to be added to or deducted from the amount of the base bid if the corresponding change in the work, as described in the bidding documents, is accepted.

Ancillary Areas. Areas that provide support functions for the primary building attractions.

Angle of Reflection. The angle between the reflected ray and the normal or perpendicular to the point of reflection.

Angle of Refraction. The angle between the refracted ray and the normal or perpendicular drawn to the point of refraction.

Annunciator. An electronically controlled signal board that indicates to the building control center which courts/areas are occupied at any time.

Application for Payment. A contractor-certified request for payment of amount due for completed portions of the work and, if the contract so provides, for materials or equipment delivered and suitably stored pending their incorporation into the work.

Appraisal Survey. A method of evaluating the existing community resources, programs, and services in accordance with some established standards or criteria.

Architect. Designation reserved, usually by law, for a person or organization professionally qualified and duly licensed to perform architectural services, including, but necessarily limited to, analysis of project requirements, creation and development of the project design, preparation of drawings, specifications and bidding requirements, and general administration of the construction contract.

Architectural Barriers. Obstacles that prevent parties from entering a facility or any architectural restraint that hampers moving throughout a building.

Area-Elastic Surfaces. Allow for dispersion of impact, where a bouncing object, or an individual jumping, is felt approximately 20 inches around the point of impact.

Area of Deflection. The amount of impact that is felt in the vicinity of the points of contact.

Asset-Backed Securities. Investments secured by expected revenue.

Asphalt. A brown or black solid bituminous substance obtained largely as a residue from certain petroleum and which is insoluble in water. It is used in paving, roofing, and paints and varnishes, and in combination with other materials for floor tiles.

Attractive Nuisance. It is a doctrine that holds if a person creates a condition on his/her premises that may reasonably be construed to be the source of danger to children, he or she must take precautions as a reasonably prudent person would take to prevent injury to children of tender ages whom he or she knows to be accustomed to frequent the area.

Baffles. A mounting or partition used to check the transmission of sound waves.

Base Bid Specifications. The specifications listing or description of those materials, equipment, and methods of construction upon which the bid must be predicated, exclusive of any alternate bids.

Base Bid Sum. The amount of money stated in the bid as the sum for which the bidder offers to perform the work described in the bidding documents, prior to adjustments for alternate bids which are also submitted.

Bearing (azimuth). A direction stated on compass degrees.

Bequests and Trusts. Agreements made with specific individuals that upon their deaths a certain amount of their estates will be given to the organization.

Berm (or dike). A narrow shelf, path, or ledge, as along the top of a scarp or along a road.

Bid. A complete and properly signed proposal to do work or designated portion thereof for the amount or amounts stipulated in the proposal and submitted in accordance with the bidding documents

Bid Bond. A form of bid security executed by the bidder and by a surety to guarantee that the bidder will enter into a contract within specified time and furnish any required performance bond, and labor and material payment bond.

Bid Form. A form furnished to a bidder to be completed, signed, and submitted as the bidder's bid.

Bid Opening. The opening and tabulation of bids submitted within the prescribed bid time and in conformity with the prescribed procedures.

Bid Price. The amount stated in the bid for which the bidder offers to perform the work.

Bidder. A person or entity who submits a bid, generally one who submits a bid for a prime contract with the owner, as distinct from a sub-bidder, who submits a bid to a prime bidder. Technically, a bidder is not a contractor on a specified project until a contract exists between the bidder and the owner.

Bidding Documents. The bidding documents include an invitation to bid, instructions to bidders, the bid form, other bidding and contracting forms, and contract documents, including any addenda issued prior to receipt of bids.

Bond. An interest-bearing certificate issued by a government or corporation, promising to pay interest and to repay a sum of money (the principle) at a specified date in the future.

Bond Period. Most government projects and some larger projects require the contractor to post not only a performance bond, but a one-year (or some other specified time) warranty on the quality of the work.

Brightness. The luminous intensity created by direct emission of light from a source by transmission through a translucent medium or by reflection from a surface. The unit of brightness is the footlambert.

Brightness Balance. Specified limitations of brightness differences and brightness ratios within the visual fields which, if observed, will contribute toward visual comfort and good visual performance.

Brightness Contrast. The relationship between the brightness of an object and its immediate background.

Brightness Difference. The difference in brightness among the various reflecting surfaces and light sources within the total visual field as measured in footlamberts.

Brightness Ratio. The ratio of two brightnesses in the field of view.

Brightness Balance.

British Thermal Unit. The quantity of heat (252 calories) required to raise the temperature of one pound of water one degree Fahrenheit at or near its point of maximum density (620 to 63%).

Broken-Back Track. Track configuration that features a more square track with short straightaways and rounded ends made of double curves.

Builder's Risk Insurance. A specialized form of property insurance that provides for loss or damage to the work during the course of construction.

Building Permit. A permit issued by appropriate governmental authority allowing construction of a project in accordance with approved drawings and specifications.

Bulletin. A document issued by the architect after the contract is awarded. It may include drawings and other information used to solicit a proposal for change in the work. A bulletin becomes part of the contract documents only after being incorporated in a change order. A bulletin may also be referred to as a request for a change.

Bulkhead. An upright partition separating two parts in protection against fire or leakage; as a wall or embankment holding back earth, fire, or water.

Candlepower. The luminous intensity or illuminating capacity of a standard candle, as of a lamp measured in candles.

Cash Allowance. An amount established in the contract documents for inclusion in the contract sum to cover cost of prescribed items not specified in detail, with provision that variations between the established amount and the final amount of the prescribed items will be reflected in change orders.

Cash Discount. The amount that can be deducted from a seller invoice for payment within a stipulated period of time.

Cash Donation. Donation of cash to an organization for a general or specific use in return for a personal tax deduction.

Casing. The act or process of encasing a frame, as of a window or a door.

Caulking. To fill in the seams or cracks with a filler.

Certificate of Insurance. A document issued by an authorized representative of an insurance company stating the types, amounts, and effective dates of insurance in force for a designated insured.

Certification of Occupancy. A document issued by a governmental authority certifying that all or a designated portion of a building complies with the provisions of applicable statutes and regulations, and permitting occupancy for its designated use.

Certificates of Participation. Involves a governmental entity buying a facility. The government entity then leases portions of the facility to the general public.

Certificate of Substantial Completion. A certificate prepared by the architect on the basis of an inspection stating that the work or a designated portion of the work is substantially complete as of a particular date. This establishes the date of substantial completion with respect to the responsibilities of the owner and the contractor for security maintenance, heat, utilities, damage to the work, and insurance.

Chair Rail. An encircling band on the walls around the room at chair height to protect walls from damage by chairs contacting them.

Chamfer. The surface formed by cutting away the angle formed by two faces of timber, stone, or metal; to furrow; to channel; to flute; to bevel.

Change Order. A written order to the contractor signed by the owner and the architect, issued after the execution of the contract, authorizing a change in the work or an adjustment in the contract sum or the contract time. The contract sum and contract time may only be changed by a change order. A change order signed by the contractor indicates the contractor agreement therewith, including the adjustment in the contract sum or the contract time.

Changes in the Work. The changes ordered by the owner within the general scope of the contract, consisting of additions, deletions or other revisions, which result in the contract sum and the contract time being adjusted accordingly. All such changes in the work shall be authorized by a change order, and shall be performed under the applicable conditions of the contract documents.

Checkpoint. An obvious feature shown on the map that helps orienteers determine their progress along the course.

Chlorinate. To combine chlorine with water for purification.

Circuit Breaker. A device that automatically interrupts the flow of an electric current.

Civil Engineer. Individual who is responsible for the following tasks: grading and land movement plans, geometric layout of new improvements, plans for new roads and street pavements, utility plans, and plans for water collection system and sanitary sewers.

Code. It is a legal requirement legislated by federal, state, and/or local government describing legally how a building must be built, including electrical, mechanical, and structural. In many jurisdictions, they are generically titled building codes.

Comprehensive General Liability Insurance. A broad form of liability insurance covering claims for bodily injury and property damage, which combines under one policy coverage for all liability exposures (except those specifically excluded) on a blanket basis and automatically covers new and unknown hazards that may develop. Comprehensive general liability insurance automatically includes contractual liability coverage for certain types of contracts.

Concession. Authority, granted under contract with mutually acceptable provisions by all parties concerned, given by recreation departments to operators permitting them to provide services and/or to sell commodities to patrons of recreation areas and facilities.

Concessionaire Exclusivity. The sale of the exclusive rights for all concessions within a spectator facility for a specified number of dollars over a specified period of time.

Condemnation. To pass an adverse judgment on; disapprove of strongly; censure; to prove guilty of wrong-doing; to declare unfit for service or use; to condemn private property for public use, the processes by which government exercises its rights of eminent domain.

Condenser. That which makes dense, concentrates, or compresses.

Convector. A medium of convection; the transmission of heat or electricity by the mass movement of the heated or electrified particles, such as air, gas, or liquid currents.

Construction Document Phase. This phase is based on the design development phase. The architect prepares final drawings and construction specifications.

Construction Phase. The final phase is the construction phase. The architect shall (1) visit the site at least twice monthly at appropriate intervals at various stages of construction, (2) certify payments for work completed, (3) have the authority to reject work that does not conform to the contract documents, and (4) review.

Contingency Allowance. A sum included in the project budget that is designated to cover unpredictable or unforeseen items of work, or changes in the work subsequently required by the owner.

Contract. A legally enforceable promise or agreement between two or among several persons.

Contract Award. A communication from an owner accepting a bid or negotiated proposal. An award creates legal obligation between the parties.

Contract Sum. The sum stated in the owner-contractor agreement, which is the total amount payable by the owner to the contractor for the performance of the work under the contract documents. The contract sum may be adjusted only by a change order.

Contractor's Liability Insurance. Insurance purchased and maintained by the contractor to protect the contractor from specified claims that may arise out of or result from the contractor operations under the contract, whether such operations are by the contractor or by any subcontractor or by anyone directly or indirectly employed by any of them, or by anyone for whose acts any of them may be liable.

Control. One of several events to be visited by the orienteer.

Control Card. A card carried by orienteers used to verify that the competitor visited the control.

Control Description (Clue Card). A sheet or card with a brief description of the control location, control number, and other clues for locating controls. The International Orienteering Federation control symbols are the internationally recognized symbols for orienteering.

Control Marker. A distinct marker that identifies the control, usually a three-dimensional orange and white nylon marker.

Control Punch. A small clipper used to make a distinctive mark on the control card to verify visiting the control.

Cost Plus Fee Agreement. An agreement under which the contractor (in an owner-contractor agreement) is reimbursed for the direct and indirect costs or performance of the agreement and, in addition, is paid a fee for services. The fee is usually stated as a stipulated sum or as a percentage of cost.

Critical Path Method (CPM). A charting of all events and operations to be encountered in completing a given process, rendered in a form permitting determination of the relative significance of each event, and establishing the optimum sequence and duration of operations.

Crowned Field. A curved field with the summit or highest point (crown) at the middle, running lengthwise. (A football field is crowned for the purpose of drainage.)

Dado. A term applied to the lower portion of walls when decorated separately.

Date of Agreement. The date stated in the agreement. If no date is stated, it could be the date on which the agreement is actually signed, if this is recorded, or it may be the date established by the award.

Date of Substantial Completion. The date certified by the architect when the work or a designated portion thereof is sufficiently complete, in accordance with the contract documents, so the owner can occupy the work or designated portion thereof for the use for which it is intended.

Decibel. The unit for measuring the relative loudness of sounds (as compared with the loudness of a sound that can just be heard by the ear).

Deck. A platform or floor, like a ship's deck or a swimming-pool deck.

Deduction. The amount deducted from the contract sum by a change order.

Deductive Alternate. An alternate bid resulting in a deduction from the base bid of the same bidder.

Desiccant. A substance that absorbs humidity.

Design. The architectural form, pattern, or scheme of construction of health, physical education, or recreation areas, facilities, and their units.

Design-Build Process. A process in which a person or entity assumes responsibility under a single contract for both the design and construction of the project.

Design Development Phase. This phase is based on the results of the schematic design phase. The architect prepares, during this phase, drawings including floor plans, mechanical and electrical systems, and structural design; outline of materials to be used; landscape designs; parking lot designs; and other such documents as may be appropriate.

Dewpoint. The temperature at which moisture will condense out of the air.

Diatomaceous. Containing or consisting of diatoms or their fossils (a number of related microscopic algae, one-celled or in colonies, whose walls consist of two parts or valves and contain silica).

Discomfort Glare. Glare that produces discomfort; it does not necessarily interfere with visual performance or visibility.

District. The district is a large geographical planning unit of a large city, comprising a number of communities.

Drainage. Surface and subsurface removal of water and groundwater. When properly designed, surface and subsurface irrigation eliminates standing water and relieves saturated turf. Further, it will maintain the proper amount of subsurface moisture.

Drawings. Graphic and pictorial documents showing the design, location, and dimensions of the elements of a project. Drawings generally include plans, elevations, sections, details, schedules, and diagrams. When capitalized, the term refers to the graphic and pictorial portions of the contract documents.

Easement. A right or privilege that a person may have on another's land, as the right-of-way.

Eaves. The lower part of a roof projecting beyond the face of the wall.

Economy. Costs are kept at a minimum compatible with program needs, durability of materials, low maintenance, and attractiveness.

Egress. A way out to grade level around a building.

Electrical Contractor. The individual who will provide all electrical wiring, boxes, switches, receptacles, equipment hook-ups, conduit for all telephone wires, computer cable, television cable, security wiring, and public address system.

Elevation. A geometrical projection on a plane perpendicular to the horizon; an elevated place; the distance above or below the zero level or ground level.

Eligible Individuals. Those individuals who have a physical or mental impairment that substantially limits a major life activity.

Eminent Domain. The legal right of federal, state, and local governments to take any property required for public purpose. The right implies that the land must be taken by due process of law, and that the owner from whom the land is taken receives reasonable compensation.

Environment. The aggregate of all the external conditions, surroundings, and influences affecting the place or individual.

Equal Quadrant Track. This type of track configuration features two 100-meter straightaways and two 100-meter curves.

Equipment. Movable furnishings as opposed to stationary property; relatively permanent articles, furnishings, machinery, and devices used in administering, operating, and maintaining recreation programs and services.

Escutcheon. A shield or plate as around a keyhole.

Estimate. It is a forecast of construction cost, as opposed to a firm bid, prepared by a contractor for a project or a portion thereof. A term sometimes used to denote a contractor application or request for a progress payment.

Estimate of Construction Cost, Detailed. A forecast of construction cost prepared on the basis of a detailed analysis of material and labor for all items of work, as contrasted with an estimate based on current area, volume, or similar unit costs.

Extra. A term sometimes used to denote an item of work involving additional cost.

Façade. The face or elevation of a building.

Facilities. Areas, structures, and fixtures essential to accommodate the program.

Fee. A term used to denote compensation for professional ability, capability, and availability or organization, excluding compensation for direct, indirect and/or reimbursable expenses, as an agreement based on a professional fee plus expenses. Sometimes denotes compensation of any kind for services rendered.

Field House. A facility providing enclosed and unobstructed space adaptable to various physical education and recreation activities, services, demonstrations, and meetings. It is often located on, or near, a playfield or athletic field. The term also refers to a service building used by people using the athletic field.

Fixed Limit of Construction Cost. The maximum construction cost established in the agreement between the owner and the architect.

Fixed Turning Radius, Wheel to Wheel. The tracking of the caster wheels and large wheels of a wheelchair when pivoting on a spot.

Fixture. Something firmly attached, as a part or an appendage, such as a light fixture; equipment affixed to the surface of a building in such a manner that its removal would deface or mar the surface. (Legally, it is the property of the building.)

Flashing. Sheets of metal or other material used to waterproof joints and cages, especially of a roof.

Fluid Mechanics. The study of the flow properties of liquids and gases.

Flush. Unbroken or even in surface; on a level with the adjacent surfaces; having no indentation.

Fluting. The vertical channeling on the shaft of a column.

Footcandle. The illumination at a point on a surface that is one foot from and perpendicular to a uniform point source of one candela (candle); a lighting term used to denote quantity.

Footlambert. A unit of brightness of a surface or of a light source. One footlambert equals one lumen per square foot. Candelas (candles) per square inch is an optional term for a unit of brightness of a light source. One candela (candle) per square inch equals 452 footlamberts.

Foot-pound. A unit of energy equal to the amount of anergy required to raise a weight of one pound a distance of one foot.

Force Account. A term used when work is ordered, often under urgent circumstances, to be performed without prior agreement as to lump sum or unit price cost thereof and is to be billed at the cost of labor, materials and equipment, insurance, taxes, etc., plus an agreed percentage for overhead and profit.

Foreseeability. The reasonable anticipation that harm or injury is a likely result from certain acts or omissions.

Fulcrum. The support or point of support on which a lever rotates.

Fullers Earth. A clay-like, earthy substance used as a filter medium.

Function. Measuring satisfaction of purpose, where function is the particular purpose for which a person or thing is specifically fitted or used or for which a thing exists.

Furring. The leveling of a floor, wall, or ceiling, or the creating of air spaces with thin strips of wood or metal before adding boards or plaster; the act of trimming or lining.

Gable. The triangular portion of a wall, between the enclosing lines of a sloping roof.

Gallery. A communicating passage or wide corridor for pictures and statues; upper story for seats.

General Conditions. That part of the contract documents that sets forth many of the rights, responsibilities, and relationships of the parties involved, particularly those provisions that are common to many construction projects.

General Contractor. Individual responsible for constructing and finishing floors, walls, ceilings, steel structure, built-in cabinets, sidewalks, driveways, doorways, windows, and other things not completed by the electrical and mechanical contractors.

General Obligation Bonds. A full-faith and credit obligation bond. Refers to bonds that are repaid with a portion of the general property tax.

Glare. The sensation produced by brightnesses within the visual field that are sufficiently greater than the brightness to which the eyes are adapted to cause annoyance, discomfort, or loss in visual performance and visibility.

Glaze. Any impervious material produced by fire used to cover the body of a tile to prevent absorption of liquids and gases, to resist abrasion and impact, or to give a more pleasing appearance.

Glazed Tile. A hard, dense tile that has been glazed to prevent absorption, to increase its beauty, or to improve ease of cleaning.

Gradient. The grade or rate of ascent or descent; a rate of increase or decrease of a variable magnitude, or the curve that represents it.

Grid. A framework of parallel bars; a grating.

Groundskeeping. The management and maintenance of the outdoor spaces, including landscaped grounds and play spaces.

Guaranteed Maximum Cost. The sum established in an agreement between owner and contractor as the maximum cost of performing specified work on the basis of cost of labor and materials plus overhead expenses and profit.

Gutter. A trough or channel along or under the eaves of a roof to carry off rainwater; also around the upper edge of a swimming pool.

Guidelines. An indication or outline of policy or conduct.

Gymnasium. A building or part of a building devoted primarily to group activities, such as basketball, gymnastics, volleyball, and dancing. It is equipped with gymnastic apparatus, a court area for playing athletic and game activities, dressing-room facilities, and seating arrangements for spectators.

Gymtorium. A combination facility designed to be used as a gymnasium or auditorium. Other combination facilities are cafetoriums (cafeteria and auditorium) and gymnateria (gymnasium and cafeteria).

Header. A wooden beam placed between two long beams with the ends of the short beams resting against it.

Hose Bibb. A faucet with the nozzle bent downward and threaded for hose connections.

Humidity. Moisture content of the air expressed in percent of maximum.

Hydrology. Refers to the study of the patterns of water flow above and below the surface.

Inclusion (Designing for). A concept that supports full facility and full program access to all people.

Indirect Expense. These are overhead expenses (i.e., general office expense) indirectly incurred and not directly related to a specific project.

Indirect Lighting. The act of reflecting light off the ceiling to create a clean and pleasant form of light arrangement in an indoor space.

Indoor Air Quality. A product of the quality of the fresh air introduced into the ventilation system and the quality of the existing indoor air that is recycled.

In-Kind Contribution. An organization, business, or craftsman donates equipment or time to the project in return for a tax deduction.

Instructions to Bidders. Instructions contained in the bidding documents for preparing and submitting bids for a construction project or designated portion thereof.

Integral. The result of integrating parts into a whole; necessary for completeness; essential; whole or complete.

Integration. Functional interrelationship, the process of making whole.

Interior Designer. This individual will assist in selecting paint colors, wallpaper, rugs (color, texture/thickness), furniture, accessories, artwork, and other items to make spaces comfortable, functional and aesthetically pleasing.

IP Telephony. The use of an IP network to transmit voice, video, and data.

Irrigation. Surface and subsurface supplemental watering. When properly designed, surface and subsurface irrigation provides an even distribution of water for plants and turfgrass.

Invitation to Bid. A portion of the bidding documents soliciting bids for a construction project.

Invited Bidders. The bidders selected by the owner, after consultation with the architect, as the only ones from whom bids will be received.

Jam. A side post of a doorway, window frame, fireplace, etc.

Join. A place or part where two things or parts are joined together.

Joint ventures. A joint venture is a project with multiple parties involved in its planning and operation.

Labor and Material Payment Bond. A bond of the contractor in which a surety guarantees to the owner that the contractor will pay for labor and material used in the performance of the contract. The claimants under the bond are defined as those having direct contracts with the contractor or any subcontractor.

Landmark. An easily recognized, obvious feature in the landscape.

Landscape Architect. Individual who provides information such as: specifications and designs for landscaping a building or green area, types of trees to be planted, types of flowers to be planted, number of walkways, specifications and designs for the irrigation system, and types of grass to be planted or sod to be installed.

Landscape Architecture. The art or science of arranging land, together with spaces and objects upon it, for safe, efficient, healthful, pleasant human use.

Latent Heat. The heat liberated or absorbed by a substance as it changes phase at a constant temperature and pressure.

Lease Agreements. A program to lease facilities to other organizations during the off-season or additional spaces within the facility not used for the sporting activity, such as office space or retail space.

Legend. A section of a map that provides an interpretation of map symbols.

Letter of Agreement. A letter stating the terms of an agreement between addressor and addressee, usually prepared to be signed by the addressee to indicate acceptance of those terms as legally binding.

Letter of Intent. A letter signifying an intention to enter into a formal agreement, usually setting forth the general terms of such agreement.

Liability. The responsibility of one who is bound in law and justice to do something that may be forced by action; a condition that gives rise to an obligation to do a particular thing to be enforced by court action; a responsibility between parties that the courts recognize and enforce; an unintentional breach of legal duty causing reasonably foreseeable damage.

Liability Insurance. Insurance that protects the insured against liability on account of injury to the person or property of another.

Life Insurance Packages. A program to solicit the proceeds from a life insurance policy purchased by a supporter to specifically benefit the organization upon the death of the supporter.

License. A formal permission to do something; a document indicating certain permission; freedom to deviate from strict conduct, rule, or practice; generally may be permitted by common consent.

Light. Visible radiation, generally considered to be the electromagnetic radiations of wave lengths between 380 and 780 millimicrons, which are the violet and red ends of the visible spectrum, respectively.

Lintel. The horizontal timber or stone that spans an opening, as over doors or windows.

Louver. An aperture or frame with louver boards fitted in a slatted panel for ventilation.

Low Bid. A bid stating the lowest bid price for performance of the work, including selected alternates, conforming with bidding documents.

Lowest Responsible Bidder. A bidder who submits the lowest bona fide bid and is considered by the owner and the architect to be fully responsible and qualified to perform the work for which the bid is submitted.

Lumen. A unit of measure for the flow of light.

Luminaries. Floodlight fixtures with a lamp, reflector, etc.

Luxury Suites. These areas have been designed for VIP use and leased by large corporations to wine and dine their clients as well as to provide them entertainment.

Magnetic Lines. Lines on an orienteering map pointing toward magnetic north.

Master Map. Large orienteering map near the start line that shows the course and controls.

Mechanical Contractor. Individual who is responsible for all plumbing (hot and cold water, sewage), humidity control, heating and cooling systems, ventilation systems, and pumps.

Mechanical/Electrical Engineer. The individual who provides such information as: specifications for heating and air conditioning equipment, drawings and specification for power and lighting, determinations of plumbing requirements, and the design of any communication system (e.g., security public address, music, closed-circuit television, etc.).

Mechanic Lien. A lien on real property created by statute in all states in favor of persons supplying labor or material for a building or structure for the value of labor or material supplied by them. In some jurisdictions, a mechanic lien also exists for the value of professional services. Clear title to the property cannot be obtained until the claim for the labor, materials, or professional services is settled.

Modification. This is a written amendment to the contract signed by both parties. It is a change order. It is a written interpretation issued by the architect. Finally, it could be a written order for a minor change in the work issued by the architect.

Mullion. A slender, vertical dividing bar between the lights and windows, screens, etc.

Municipal Bonds. Bonds issued by a government or a subdivision of a state.

Named Insured. Any person, firm or corporation, or any of its members specifically designated by name as insured(s) in a policy, as distinguished from others who, although unnamed, are protected under some circumstances.

Naming Rights. Corporations vie for the right to place their name on the facility for a specific sum of money for a specific number of years.

Negligence. The omission of that care which a person of common prudence usually takes of his own concerns.

Negotiating Phase. Phase in which the architect assists the owner in obtaining bids or negotiating proposals and assists in awarding and preparing contracts for construction.

Non-Equal Quadrant Track. This track configuration resembles a stretched or compressed oval shape with two straightaways of one length and two curves of another length.

Non-Guaranteed Bonds. These bonds are sold on the basis of repayment from other designated revenue sources.

Nonslip. Having the tread so constructed as to reduce skidding or slipping.

Nonslip Tile. Incorporates certain admixtures such as abrasive granules in the body or in the surface of the tile.

NorCompass (Thumb Compass). An orienteering compass that attaches to the left thumb of the orienteer.

Nonconforming Work. Work that does not fulfill the requirements of the contract documents.

Opaque. Does not transmit light; substances that will not allow light through.

Open Space. A relatively underdeveloped area provided within or near urban development to minimize feelings of congested living.

Optimal Thermal Environment. Provides conditions that make it possible to dissipate body heat in the most effortless manner. Combines radiant temperature where surface and air temperature are balanced; air temperature between 64 and 72 degrees F, humidity between 40 and 60 percent; and, a constant air movement of 20 to 40 lineal feet/minute at a sitting height.

Orienteer. A person who participates in the sport of orienteering.

Owner-Architect Agreement. Contract between owner and architect for professional services.

Owner-Contractor Agreement. Contract between owner and contractor for performance of the work for construction of the project or portion thereof.

Owner's Representative. The person designated as the official representative of the owner in connection with a project.

Outrigger. Any temporary support extending out from the main structure.

Park. An area permanently dedicated to recreation use and generally characterized by its natural, historic, and landscape features. It is used for both passive and active forms of recreation and may be designed to serve the residents of a neighborhood, community, state, region, or nation.

Park District. A subdivision of state government exercising within its jurisdiction the authority of a municipality. It may operate and maintain parks, recreation programs, police forces, airports, and other such facilities and programs as may be designated in the act establishing the district.

Park-School. The park-school is an area cooperatively planned by school and municipal authorities to provide programs of education and recreation for day-by-day use by the people of a neighborhood or community.

Parkway. Essentially an elongated park with a road running through it, the use of which is restricted to pleasure traffic. The parkway often serves to connect large units in a park system and is rarely found except in large cities.

Parking Fees. Fees generated from parking lots that surround the spectator facility.

Performance Bond. A bond of the contractor in which a surety guarantees to the owner that the work will be performed in accordance with the contract documents. Except where prohibited by statute, the performance bond is frequently combined with the labor and material payment bond.

Permeable. That which can be permeated; open to passage or penetration, especially by fluids.

Pert Schedule. An acronym for project evaluation review technique. The pert schedules the activities and events anticipated in a work process.

Pilaster. A rectangular feature in the shape of a pillar, but projecting only one-sixth of its breadth from a wall.

Plan. A two-dimensional graphic representation of the design, location, and dimensions of the project, or parts thereof, seen in a horizontal plan viewed from above.

Playfield. A recreation area designed to serve the needs of a community or neighborhood having a population of 10,000 to 15,000 persons. Its essential features are a community recreation building, areas for sports and games, a playground for children, picnic areas, public parking, and, occasionally, a swimming area.

Point Elastic Surfaces. Maintain impact effects at the immediate point of contact on the floor, with the ball, object, or individual.

Point-to-Point Orienteering. A type of orienteering where controls must be visited in a specific order and speed in completing the course determines the winner.

Post Sleeves. Metal pipe, installed at ground level or slightly below, which receives posts to facilitate various activities.

Preconstruction Conference. A meeting between the contracting agency and the contractor(s) prior to the commencement of construction to review the contract items and make sure there is an understanding of how the job is to be undertaken.

Preferred/Premium Seating. VIP seating located within the luxury suites or in the club areas of the stadium that are the most expensive seats in the facility.

Prequalification of Bidders. The process of investigating the qualification of prospective bidders on the basis of their experience, availability, and capability for the contemplated project and approving qualified bidders.

Prime Contract. Contract between owner and contractor for construction of the project or portion thereof.

Progress Payment. Partial payment made during progress of the work on account of work completed and/or material suitably stored.

Project. The total construction of which the work performed under the contract documents may be the whole or a part, or it could also include the total furniture, furnishings, and equipment.

Project Cost. Total cost of the project including construction, professional compensation, real estate, furnishings, equipment, and financing.

Property Damage Insurance. Insurance coverage for the insured's legal liability for claims for injury to or destruction of tangible property, including loss of use resulting therefrom, but usually not including coverage for injury to or destruction of property which is in the care, custody, and control of the insured.

Property Insurance. Coverage for loss or damage to the work at the site caused by perils of fire, lightning, extended coverage perils, vandalism, and malicious mischief and additional perils. Property insurance may be written on (1) the completed value form in which the policy is written at the start of a project in a predetermined amount representing the insurable value of the work and adjusted to the final insurable cost on completion of the work, or (2) the reporting form in which the property values fluctuate during the policy term, requiring monthly statements showing the increase in value of work in place over the previous month.

Public Accommodations. A facility operated by a private entity, whose operations affect commerce. The private entity that owns, leases or leases to, or operates a place of public accommodation.

Public Liability Insurance. Insurance covering liability of the insured for negligent acts resulting in bodily injury, disease, or death of persons other than employees of the insured, and/or property damage.

Rabbet. A groove or cut made in the edge of a board, etc., in such a way that another piece may be fitted in to form a point.

Ramps, Ramps with Gradients. Because the term "ramp" has a multitude of meanings and uses, its use in this text is clearly defined as ramps with gradients (or ramps with slopes) that deviate from what would otherwise be considered the normal level. An exterior ramp, as distinguished from a "walk," would be considered an appendage to a building leading to a level above or below existing ground level. As such, a ramp shall meet certain requirements similar to those imposed upon stairs.

Ray. A single line of light coming from a luminous point.

Readily Achievable. Easily accomplishable and able to be carried out without much difficulty or expense. It constitutes a lower standard than undue burden.

Reasonable Accommodations. Requires that employers and facilities make an accommodation if doing so will not impose an undue hardship on the operation of the business or facility.

Record Drawings. Construction drawings revised to show significant changes made during the construction process, usually based on marked-up prints, drawings, and other data furnished by the contractor to the architect.

Reflectance (Reflection Factor). The percent of light failing on a surface that is reflected by that surface.

Reflected Glare. Glare resulting from specular reflections of high brightness in polished or glossy surfaces in the field of view. It usually is associated with reflections from within a visual task or areas in close proximity to the region being viewed.

Reflection Factor. The percentage of light reflected by a given surface.

Refrigerants. Any of the various liquids that vaporize at a low temperature, used in mechanical refrigeration.

Regulations. An order issued by an executive authority of a government and having the force of law.

Reimbursable Expenses. The amounts expended for or on account of the project which, in accordance with the terms of the appropriate agreement, are to be reimbursed by the owner.

Release of Lien. An instrument executed by a person or entity supplying labor, material, or professional services on a project that releases that person or entity for a mechanic lien against the project property.

Resident Engineer. An engineer employed by the owner to represent the owner interests at the project site during the construction phase.

Resilience. The ability to bounce or spring back into shape, position, etc.

Restaurant Rights. The sale of the exclusive rights for all the restaurants within a spectator facility.

Retainage. A sum withheld from progress payments to the contractor in accordance with the terms of the owner-contractor agreement.

Revenue Bonds. A bond that can be backed exclusively by the revenue occurring from the project or from a designated revenue source, such as a hotel/motel tax, restaurant tax, auto rental tax, or a combination of these taxes and others.

Reverberation. Reflection of light or sound waves.

Riser. The vertical distance (and pieces) between the steps in a stairway.

Rolling Load. The capacity of a floor to withstand damage from external forces, such as bleacher movement, equipment transport, or similar activities.

Safety Direction (Panic Azimuth; Safety Bearing). A compass bearing or direction to guide the orienteer directly to a road, major trail, or settlement if lost or injured.

Schematic Design Phase. This phase is based on the program developed by the project committee and submitted to the architect. The architect will prepare, for approval by the owner, schematic design documents, including drawings (floor plans and mechanicals), scale model, project development schedule, and estimated costs.

Schedule of Values. A statement furnished by the contractor to the architect reflecting the portions of the contract sum allocated to the various portions of the work and used as the basis for reviewing the contractor applications for payment.

Score Orienteering. A type of orienteering where controls blanket the course, and each is assigned a point value based on the distance to the controls and how difficult they will be to find. The individual or team with the most points in the prescribed time is the winner.

Service Building. A structure affording the facilities necessary to accommodate the people using recreation facilities such as a golf course, swimming pool, or ice-skating rink. It may contain dressing rooms, lockers, toilets, shower rooms, check and storage rooms, a lobby or lounge, and a repair shop. Also, the term is used in reference to buildings that facilitate the operation and maintenance of the recreation system, such as greenhouses, storage buildings, and garages.

Shadow. The space from which light from a given source is excluded by an opaque object; the area of comparative darkness resulting from the interception of light by an opaque object.

Sheathing. The inner covering of boards or waterproof material on the roof or outside wall of a frame house.

Shelter House. A building, usually located on a playground or playfield, equipped with such features as an office for the director, space for storage, toilets, and a craft or play room.

Shop Drawings. Drawings, diagrams, schedules, and other specific data specially prepared for the work by the contractor or any subcontractor, manufacturer, supplier, or distributor to illustrate some portion of the work.

Sill. A heavy horizontal timber or line of masonry supporting a wall; a horizontal piece forming the bottom frame of a door or window.

Site Analysis. The gathering of information and data about a site and adjacent properties. Its purpose is to find a place for a particular use or find a use for a particular place.

Sleeper. A piece of timber, stone, or steel, on or near the ground to support some superstructure.

Ski Orienteering. Orienteering conducted on cross-country skis.

Soft Space. Space in a facility that requires little or no special provisions (such as plumbing or expensive finishes), and therefore is space that is easily vacated and converted.

Special Authority Bonds. These bonds have been used to finance stadiums or arenas by special public authorities, which are entities with public powers that are able to operate outside normal constraints placed on governments.

Specifications. A part of the contract documents contained in the project manual consisting of written requirements for material, equipment, construction systems, standards, and workmanship.

Sponsorship Packages. Corporate support programs pursued whereby large local and international firms are solicited to supply goods and services to a sporting organization at no cost or at a substantial reduction in the wholesale prices in return for visibility for the corporation.

Staggered. To arrange so that alternate intervals are used, as to space or time.

Stanchion. An upright bar, beam, or post used as a support; one of a pair of linked, upright bars.

Standards. Norms established by authority, research, custom, or general consent to be used as criteria and guides in establishing and evaluating programs, leadership, areas, facilities, and plans; as measures of quantity, quality, weight, extent, or value.

Stile. A vertical piece in a panel or frame, as a door or window; a set of steps used in climbing over a fence or wall.

Stipulated Sum Agreement. A contract in which a specific amount is set forth as the total payment for performance of the contract.

Structural Engineer. Individual concerned with determining possible structural systems and materials, providing cost of preferred systems and materials, and designing final structure to meet architectural requirements.

Sub-bidder. A person or entity who submits a bid to a bidder for material or labor for a portion of the work at the site.

Subcontract. An agreement between a prime contractor and a subcontractor for a portion of the work at the site.

Subcontractor. A person or entity who has a direct contract with the contractor to perform any of the work at the site.

Successful Bidder. The bidder chosen by the owner for the award of a construction contract.

Superintendent. The contractor representative at the site who is responsible for continuous field supervision, coordination, completion of the work and, unless another person is designated in writing by the contractor to the owner and the architect, for prevention of accidents.

Supplementary Conditions. A part of the contract documents that supplements and may also modify, change, add to, or delete from provisions of the general conditions.

Supplementary Lighting. Providing additional lighting on such areas as those containing goals and targets.

Supplier. A person or entity who supplies material or equipment for the work, including that fabricated to a special design, but who does not perform labor at the site.

Survey. A cooperative undertaking that applies scientific methods to the study and treatment of current recreation data, problems, and conditions. The limits of a survey are prescribed before execution, and its facts, findings, conclusions, and recommendations are made common knowledge and provide a base for intelligent, coordinated action.

Synthetic. Artificial; not real or genuine; a substance produced by chemical synthesis.

Tanbark. Any bark containing tannin (used to tan hides) and, after the tannin has been extracted, it is used to cover tracks, circus rings, and dirt floors in field houses.

Template. A short piece placed in a wall under a beam to distribute the pressure; also a beam spanning a doorway, or the like, and supporting joists.

Terra Cotta. Clayware having the surface coated with fine slip or glaze; used in the facing of large buildings for relief ornament or statues.

Terrazzo. A type of flooring made of small chips of marble set irregularly in cement and polished.

Thermostat. An apparatus for regulating temperature, especially one that automatically controls a heating unit.

Thermodynamics. The branch of physics dealing with the transformation of heat to and from other forms of energy, and with the laws governing such conversions of energy.

Threshold. A piece of wood, stone, metal, etc., placed beneath a door; doorsill; the entrance or beginning point of something; the point at which a stimulus is just strong enough to be perceived or produce a response, as the threshold of pain.

Topography. Refers to the surface features of a site including variations in elevation.

Topographical Map. A precise map that designates altitude of the land with contour lines.

Trade (Craft). An occupation requiring manual skill or members of a trade organized into a collective body.

Trade Shows. Expositions that generate sales for a particular industry.

Trail Orienteering (Control Choice). A modified type of orienteering designed for orienteers with disabilities.

Translucent. Transmitting light, but scattering it so that details cannot be distinguished through the translucent medium.

Transparent. Allowing light to pass through so that objects behind can be seen distinctly.

Underpinning. A supporting structure of the foundation, especially one placed beneath a wall.

Undue Hardship. Requiring significant difficulty or expense, considering the employer size, financial resources, and the nature and structure of the operation.

Unglazed Tile. A hard, dense tile of homogenous composition deriving color and texture from the materials of which it is made.

Unit Price. The amount stated in the bid as a price per unit of measurement for materials or services as described in the bidding documents or in the proposed contract documents.

Utility. The degree to which an area, facility, or instrument is designed to serve its purpose, and degree to which it is used; percent of usage during the workday adapted or available for general use or utility.

Vendor/Contractor Equity. Vendor or contractor returns to the owner a specific percentage of the profit generated by the firms during the construction process.

Vestibule. A passage hall or chamber between the outer door and the interior of a building.

Vetting. Checking the orienteering course before competition.

Vinyl Tile. Asphalt tile impregnated with vinyl.

Visual Task. Conventionally, designates those details and objects that must be seen for the performance of a given activity, and includes the immediate background of the details or objects.

Vitreous. Of, pertaining to, or derived from glass; like glass, as in color, brittleness, and luster.

Wainscot. A wood lining or paneling on the lower part of the walls of a room.

Waiver of Lien. An instrument by which a person or organization who has or may have a right of mechanic lien against the property of another relinquishes such right.

Walkway. Because the terms "walk" and "walks" have a multitude of meanings and uses, their use in this text is clearly defined as a predetermined, prepared surface; exterior pathway leading to or from a building or facility, or from one exterior area to another, placed on the existing ground level and not deviating from the level of the existing ground immediately adjacent.

Walk-off Area. The first 12 feet on the inside of an entry doorway that functions exactly as the name implies; it is within this radius that dust, dirt, oil from the parking area and water from rain and melting snow are deposited.

Warranty. Legally enforceable assurance of quality or performance of a product or work of the duration of satisfactory performance.

Workers' Compensation Insurance. Insurance covering the liability of an employer for compensation and other benefits required by workers' compensation laws with respect to injury, sickness, diseases or death arising from their employment.

Weephole. To permit or let drops of water or other liquid exude from inner containers, from such sources as condensation or overflow.

Wilderness. A rather large, generally inaccessible area left in its natural state available for recreation experiences. It is void of development, except for those trails, sites, and similar conditions made by previous wilderness users. (No mechanical transportation permitted).

Zone Heating. To mark off or divide building areas for the purposes of area climate control.

Architectural Drawings

Axonometric Projection. A drawing where the angles can vary depending on the needs of the person drawing it. Axonometric projections tend to offer a view from higher up, and thus are especially helpful in showcasing building interiors with the ceiling pulled away, allowing rooms to be shown within the context of the entire building plan.

CAD Drawings. Computer-aided design has quickly become a staple of building design, as it allows the creation and manipulation of two- and three-dimensional representations of a building. A plan drawn from an eye-level view can be "entered" by the viewer, with perspective automatically maintained by the computer as the client performs the "walk-through." Additionally, the point of view can be changed, allowing architects and clients to immediately see how their designs translate into actual future use.

Cutaway. Similar to an axonometric projection and shows the building from an oblique angle. Where it differs is in its representation of both interior and exterior building elements.

Elevation. A two-dimensional view of a building's external face drawn on a vertical plane; typically, four elevations will be used to show the building from each of four compass points.

Floor plan. A drawn-to-scale overhead view of each floor looking down from an imaginary plan cut three to four feet above the floor. The plans show circulation paths and recreational and support paths as well as doorways, window openings, furniture and counters. Elements located above the plane of the cut are usually shown using dashed lines (e.g., suspended running tracks, balconies, overhead cabinets).

Isometric projection. Drawings drawn with a 30-60-90 triangle, so the subject is always in proportion.

Reflected ceiling plan. Ceilings are detailed on a specific drawing type called the reflected ceiling plan, which is a drawing using a similar cut as the floor plan but higher up the wall looking up, and down.

Rendering. A perspective or elevation drawing, showing building materials, colors, shadows, textures, and natural features of the site.

Section. Similar to a floor plan, except that its imaginary cut is vertical, not horizontal. It is therefore most frequently used to detail arena bowls and stadium grandstands.

Site plan. An aerial view of the entire project site including the facility, parking lots, pedestrian ways, conceptual landscaping ideas, and other site amenities.

Structural Elements

Building walls. Often used to bear loads. However, building walls do not always serve to bear the weight of higher elements. For example, in post-and-beam construction in vertical elements (columns or posts) support horizontal beams or lintels that are beams that bridge an opening such as a door or window.

Cantilevers. A beam that is supported only at one end by means of downward force behind a fulcrum, to eliminate obstructed-view seats but forces stadium decks to be stacked farther from the field, in order to provide support for the extended portion of the beam. Cantilevered beams are also used extensively in the construction of staircases and balconies.

Ceiling. The underside of a roof.

Ceiling plenum. The space between a false ceiling and a structured ceiling.

Clerestories. (Clearstories) are traditionally walls containing windows that are vertically above a low roof line and topped with the uppermost rooftop.

Coffered ceiling. This type of ceiling utilizes sunken square or polygonal ornamental panels.

Colonnade. A colonnade is a series of regularly spaced columns.

Columns, Stanchions (upright structural members), Load-bearing walls. Typically building floors and roofs are supported by columns, stanchions, and load-bearing walls.

Coping. Similar to an eave with a similar purpose, although the term is used liberally to represent a variety of treatments that cover the top of a wall.

Curtain wall. Exterior cladding used as a non-load-bearing wall.

Demi-columns. Half-columns that are half sunk into walls.

Engaged columns. A wall that encases a column or part of a column.

Eave. An overhanging portion of a roof to keep rain from running down exterior walls. An eave is sometimes called a soffit.

Fascia. The horizontal band that joins the roof to the eave.

Fenestration. It refers to the arrangement, proportioning, and design of all openings, including windows, doors, and skylights.

Frame construction. In frame construction, the weight is borne by the framework encased within a facing or cladding of light material.

Inflatable structures. A class of tensile structure supported by difference in pressure between the air inside and the air outside. Air is pumped in using fans, with air escape prevented by the use of airlocks at entrances. Inflatable structures enjoy applications from big-league stadiums to practice football fields to tennis courts, both temporary and permanent.

Long-span spaces. Long-span spaces or large-volume spaces are column-free spaces used for arenas, field houses, and ice rinks, because of the open height required to accommodate sport-specific activities, as well as vertical height for spectator seating.

Parapets. A low wall projection located at the edge of a building's roofline.

Pilasters. A pilaster projects only slightly from walls.

Skylights. Glass structures set into the ceilings to let in light.

Soffit. The underside of any architectural element, including balcony overhangs, and staircases. It also refers to the inner curve of an arch, which is a curved means of spanning an opening, used in place of a lintel.

Span. The horizontal distance between the supports of an upper floor or roof.

Spine. A building spine is the backbone of a building's floor plan. Most often the main circulation pathway in an arena or recreation center.

Suspended ceilings. A false ceiling suspended below a structured ceiling.

Tensile and membrane structures. Flexible systems made of thin, coated fabrics supported by a series of masts and stabilized by cables. These structure are often used as roofs over stadium spectator areas and as domes over stadiums and arenas.

Truss. A rigid frame composed of a series of triangular metal or wooden members that is often used to support flat roofs over long-span spaces. Trusses also support horizontal members in pitched-roof construction, such as purlins, which in turn support rafters, the sloping members that support the roof covering. Rafters are joined together at the apex of a pitched roof.

Vault. An arched ceiling.

Material Elements

Bricks. Bricks are made of fired or sun-baked clay, allow architects to make aesthetic statements by selecting a certain color or by specifying more than one color and setting them in various patterns, sometimes interspersed with concrete blocks and stones.

Brick veneer. Sliced brick pieces affixed with mortar to a concrete load-bearing wall. It is also known as face brick or finish brick.

Concrete. A combination of cement, sand, water, and various sizes of stone. It is used for foundations, structural beams, floors, walls, sidewalks, parking areas, and many other applications.

Note. Structurally, concrete is notable for its high compression capability and for its poor tension characteristics.

Concrete blocks. Concrete masonry units (CMU) can be worked to different textures similar to rustication. Most common texture are split-faced and ground-faced.

Gunite. A popular swimming-pool shell material consisting of cement, sand, and water that is sprayed onto a mold.

Masonry. This refers to work with brick and stone, offers many aesthetic options, both in the variety of colors and textures of natural materials and in the different ways these materials are cut.

Ashlar masonry—hewn blocks of stone, wrought to even faces and square edges, and laid horizontal courses (tiers) with vertical joints.

Quarry-faced masonry—stones left in their quarry state and not made even and square.

Polygonal masonry—masonry utilizing blocks having irregular shaped faces.

Mortar. Similar to concrete, except it does not have stones. It is used to bind bricks and concrete blocks together, to fill interior spaces of concrete-block walls and in some forms, as a ceiling coating.

Reinforced concrete. This type of concrete has rebar (steel reinforcing bars) added to give the concrete slab or beam the ability to withstand tensile stresses. The rebar in reinforced concrete can be put into tension in the factory (e.g., prestressed or pre-tensioned concrete pre-cast) or on-site (post-tensioned concrete or cast-in-place or tilt-up panels).

Rustication. This is a technique used to lend more texture to exterior surfaces, involves the use of large blocks separated by deep mortar joints.

Banded rustication—only the horizontal joints are emphasized.

Smooth or chamfered rustication—smooth faces separated by beveled joints.

Shotcrete. This material is similar to gunite, except it contains stones.

Stucco. This is a plaster made of gypsum (hydrous calcium sulfate), sand, water, and slaked lime.

Terrazzo. This is a floor surface made of cement mortar and marble chips, which after hardening is ground and polished.

Tile. There are three types of tile: ceramic tile (glazed fired clay), quarry tile (unglazed semivitreous tile extruded from shale or natural clay), and composite tile (vinyl).

Who does what?

Aquatic design engineers (pool consultants). S/he designs swimming pools and natatorium spaces.

Architectural designer. This person works with architects and engineers during the initial concept/schematic design phases to integrate building systems (mechanical, electrical, plumbing, and structural) into the building concept.

Building systems. Building systems include electrical, mechanical, plumbing, and structural aspects of a building.

Consultants. S/he are specialists in a specific field employed to assist the architectural team in developing a facility, such as: acoustic (sound and sound barriers), audio/visual, ice rink, and lighting.

Construction manager. S/he supervises all contractors and works with the entire design team to ensure that the project can realistically be built within the allocated budget. Further, this person is charged with keeping costs down and ensuring the project stays on schedule.

Interior architect. This is a licensed architect specializing in interior space design.

Interior decorator. This is a specialist in accessories and color schemes for upholstery.

Interior designer. This is a specialist in space planning, interior casework, furniture, interior finishes, and furnishings.

Landscape architect. This is an architect specializing in vehicular and pedestrian circulation as well as foliage and site grading.

Land use planner. S/he recommends the best spot for a facility and develops site design documents for master plans, and analyzes a site's location and related physical constraints.

Project architect. S/he converts concept, schematic designs into construction documents and coordinates the site, architectural, specialty, and engineering disciplines.

Project engineer. Working with the project architect, the project engineer integrates the building systems with the design.

Project executive (Principal-in-charge). This person provides professionals to complete work in a timely manner and should be contacted regarding legal or staffing questions. S/he may be a licensed architect, engineer, or planner.

Project manager. This person directs all of the personnel assigned to the project, including designers, architects, engineers, and consultants. S/he is heavily involved during the feasibility study phase and manages ongoing financial tasks such as budgets and schedules. The project manager hosts regular project meetings, reviews design details from a cost and buildability perspective, seeks participation of the design team, provides ongoing feedback to the design team, works with the design team to resolve design issues, and ensures that the contract documents become an integral part of the comprehensive design and construction process. Finally, the project manager is a facilitator and mediator.

Design and Construction Overview

Design/Build (turnkey) contracts. Advantages—total cost commitment known in advance, very competitive process, builder responsible for all errors, little administration work required by client, the proposal is a single package, and time frames can be dramatically compressed; Disadvantages—builder is in control of all project actions, unless client produces detailed list of requirements little control over product and process, power of design team reduced as working for builder, liability issues become cloudy as design team, and quality of end product can be compromised.

Change orders. Change orders are formal documents ordering changes in the construction plans. These changes originate from any of the following requested by owner, site conditions, fire marshall, building inspector, contractor, document omission, or document error.

Construction/Project management contracts. Advantages—provides for effective communication, elimination of the general contractor, efficient use of joint expertise in all phases of work, construction may begin early in process, work can be bid sequentially, thus allowing for company expenditures, and high cost of extras potentially reduced; Disadvantages—success of project depends to a great extent on skill of project manager, conflict in control of design and building process, total financial commitment unknown until end of project, procedures result in extra fees to design team, and process necessitates mutual respect of all involved.

Engineering systems. (a) structural—clear span demands, wall projections/pilasters, and internal environmental effects; (b) mechanical—verification of environmental conditions, air conditioning requirements, detect impact on structural, electrical systems, noise generation, and review of operating costs; and (c) electrical—lighting levels, direct, indirect, verification of ceiling heights, and determination of specialized electrical systems.

Master plan. The master plan includes (a) general site master planning—primary objectives, site characteristics (sun, wind, topographic), massing of facilities, functional characteristics, access and transportation characteristics, connection to services and utilities, and zoning; and (b) building specific master planning—primary objective, priorities of development, phasing requirements, and interface with feasibility study.

Needs analysis. The needs analysis consists of technical audit, physical inspection, history and tradition of organization and community, building systems, quality of building finishes, disability access, user requirements, program requirements, safety issues, security issues, and health issues.

Project Cost. The project cost is equal to construction cost + soft costs. Typical construction costs include enclosed building, landscape/sitework, demolition, utility service, fixed equipment, furniture, fixtures, equipment, and art/graphics. Typical soft costs include architect/engineer fees, building permits, testing and inspection fees, special consultants, sewer connection fees, maintenance endowment, parking replacement fund, construction financing, legal fees, in-house administration, other finance fees, and contingency.

Project Team - Design Phase. A project team consists of the following professionals: owner, fund raiser, zoning consultant, legal counsel, surveyor, soils engineer, environmental consultant, special consultants (i.e., programmer, master planner, interior designer, aquatic consultant, acoustic consultant, theater consultant, graphic designer), architect, structural engineer, mechanical engineer, plumbing engineer, civil engineer, estimator, landscape engineer, interior designer, interior decorator, construction manager, and contractors.

Punch list. A list of items that needs to be completed before the project is complete, including aesthetics, quality of construction/finish, code requirements, levels and plumbness, structural deflections, engineering systems, building systems, and maintenance requirements.

Schedule/budget/contingency. This includes (a) identifying total project schedule-design period, bidding phase, contract award, and construction; (b) identifying total project budget-planning and design costs, administration costs, furniture and equipment costs, building costs, and site and utilities costs; and (c) contingencies.

Site influences. The following are the most common site influences during the planning phase: adjacent properties, boundaries of sites, relationships to adjoining streets and roadways, existing trees and vegetation, orientation, wind, sun, shadow and microclimatic control, adjacent building heights, pedestrian and vehicular flow on-site and off-site, utilities and services (water, gas, electricity, sewer, telephone), soils, subsoils, water table, contours, and topography.

Stipulated sum contracts. Advantages—architect in close contact with client, time- tested traditional contract, sequential phasing of design, bidding and construction, best price at time of tender, capital commitment known at time of bid; disadvantages—sequential process, thus time frame longer, creation of powerful adversary with the general contractor, and changes are expensive and time consuming.

Summary

Like the legal and medical fields, the construction field has its on language and unique uses for common words. It is important for students to understand these terms before becoming involved in planning for a facility.

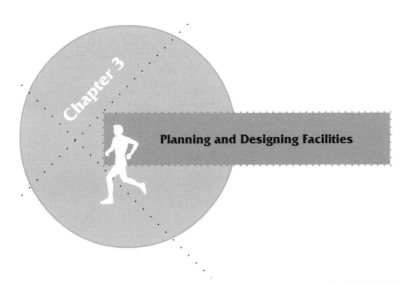

Planning and Designing Facilities

Harvey R. White, New Mexico State University
James D. Karabetsos, Western Illinois University

The sport facilities environment has never been more dynamic. The media are replete with stories of state-of-the-art complexes in both professional and collegiate sports. In recent years the construction costs of such facilities were viewed as stratospheric at $10 million, $15 million, and even $20 million. However, today's premiere sport complexes, for both professional and collegiate sports, have far surpassed those lofty figures, in some cases by as much as ten-fold. Super structures like the Air Canada Centre ($265m) in Toronto; the Staples Center ($330m) in Los Angeles; University of Maryland's Campus Recreation Center ($39.5m) and Oakland University's (Rochester, MI) Recreation-Athletic Center ($32m) are examples. The costs of these and other structures are mind boggling, as the public seems desensitized to the enormity of these huge ticket items and, astonishingly, the continued escalation of the price tags does not appear to be ebbing.

These exorbitant construction costs and the realization that most structures will be used for many purposes have placed extraordinary importance on good planning. The careful analyses of the needs of all facility users have never been more critical. Moreover, these needs must be identified before the actual construction occurs, so that the facility design can effectively support the needs of the programs. For example, the new facility's size or shape, systems specifications, flooring, storage, etc., should not be determined until the size (number of participants or classes) and types of programs that will be offered within the completed facility are known. It is quite obvious that programs that call for rectangular rooms (aerobics, weight rooms, etc.), high ceilings (wall-climbing areas, basketball courts, racquetball courts, etc.), resilient flooring (aerobic rooms, basketball areas) or high HVAC specifications (weight rooms, aerobic rooms) may be seriously impacted if their needs are not considered in the designing phase.

It is an understatement to say the planning of even the less expensive multi-purpose sport facilities is a complex process. Members of facility planning committees play important roles in helping these new facilities become viable and supportive entities. The individuals who serve on these committees must not only understand the present needs of their respective constituents but also understand the importance of considering their future requirements as well. They must take into account anticipated programming trends, predictable societal changes, futuristic technological advances, and any potential regulatory legislation, which could have an impact on the programs or services the structure will be supporting. Although no certainties exist, careful and prudent decision-making by the committees can help take reasonable measures to protect the enormous investments made on new sport structures.

In the past, facility planning frequently occurred in a disconnected fashion. Oftentimes, facility administrators or planning/building committees designed their buildings independently of the other agencies within their organizations. This isolationism frequently led to vacuous areas of non-coverage or duplication of facilities and programs. These facility planners often relied solely on hunches and "guesstimates" to design their edifices. Their intuitions and estimates frequently were off-target, and often the facilities they planned did not adequately serve the programs housed within them.

Even the more conscientious planners of past decades only conducted rudimentary surveys to assist with their planning. The findings of these surveys too frequently were scant at best. On many occasions, the results on which planners predicated their facility designs might not have even included input from user groups or program directors. Consequently, this type of "hard line" planning often resulted in disgruntled reviews and ambivalent acceptance.

Other types of planning approaches commonly found in past decades included political and "grassroots" planning. In the political planning process, the planner made the facility design decisions to influence certain segments of the population. These favors may have resulted in benefits to specific programs or activities but often led to facilities that fell far short of expected standards in other areas. The latter strategy, "grassroots" planning, frequently evolved from negotiations with specific segments of the population and led to a facility geared to support specific services or programs for which respective groups lobbied and were not necessarily based on an assessment of the overall needs of the prospective facility users.

Facility planners today operate in a different environment. The nature of physical education, recreation, and athletics is now characterized by a mix of declining resources, interrelated programs, and shared facilities. These types of complex circumstances, coupled with the enormity of construction costs, necessitate that planning not be done in isolation. The complexity of meeting diverse needs of users and coordinating the efforts of all the agencies using the facility require that all individuals be included who can contribute in a meaningful way. This type of facility planning is called participatory planning. (See Guideline #3)

Learning Objectives

After studying this chapter the student will be able to:
- appreciate the evolution of facility planning.
- understand the composition of a master plan and its importance in the growth of an organization.
- write a program statement.
- understand the role of selected professionals in the planning process (i.e., program specialist, facility consultant, and architect).
- understand the significance of participatory planning.
- understand the planning guidelines.
- select planning professionals.

Technology and Facility Planning

In the 21st century it is not a matter of whether technology will be used in the facility planning process, rather it will be how these new-age tools will be employed. One of the certain ways will be in the designing of new facilities. Architects using CAD (computer-aided design) technology will be able to resolve—with great savings in time and cost—many of the design issues that have been problematic in the past. For example, problems related to pedestrian traffic patterns, color selection, and spatial arrangements of furnishings/equipment can be made with greater certainty. Used today by aerospace firms and automakers, these CAD programs will become less costly to purchase and increasingly more available in the planning and designing phase of sport facility construction. In addition, the use of these valuable planning tools will lead to significant savings in the maintenance of facilities following their construction. These savings will be made possible through the conservation of energy resources and the reduction of manpower that are needed to maintain the completed facilities.

Technology can also be used to enhance education and other services rendered in sport facilities. Most programs, whether they are educational, athletic, or recreational, will be the beneficiaries of advances in technology. These programs may take on different appearances as improvements in communications, scheduling, and the analyses of data become more advanced. "Smart classrooms," distance education, web-based classes are but a few illustrative cases of how this new technology has transformed the educational process. Expedited facility conversions to accommodate different sports, flashy electronic scoreboards that offer limitless information, instant replay, and elaborate special effects are a few examples of how the technology has also changed the way our sport programs are marketed. Future advances in technology will continue to change the way facilities are used to market recreational and sports programs and to meet the academic needs of students.

There is general agreement that facilities should be designed to meet future as well as current programming needs. Program specialists assist in this regard by creating technology plans that consider needs that may be anticipated in the future. This futuristic vision must then be collectively endorsed by members of planning committees who should then adopt a proactive technology plan in an effort to extend the functionality of a facility. In principle, the plan should be guided by the axiom that "form follows function." Therefore, as programs evolve in the future, facility designs will be sufficiently flexible to accommodate the metamorphoses of these programs. If individuals developing technology plans have a clear vision of what forms these future programs will take, then the planning can be done more cogently. With a good technology plan, the committee will be breaking through the paradigms under which planning in the past occurred and facility obsolescence will be impeded for as long as possible.

While not a common practice, some facility planners, in an effort to extend a facility's functional longevity, request that architectural firms employ futurists as consultants. These future-oriented individuals assist planners in foreseeing the services that will be rendered by the facility in three or five years and, in some cases, perhaps longer. The facility planners then factor in these futuristic contingencies, as well as present-day needs, when they design their respective facilities. These futurists are usually available to facility planners without additional charge to the clients.

Individuals responsible for developing the technology plan should:
- Understand the budget restraints
- Acquire input from technology specialists
- Understand the role of technology
- Create a vision of the desired program(s) to be offered
- Consult staff relative to technology needs
- Have a complete understanding of the goals/objectives of the programs that will be supported by technology
- Establish priorities
- Identify a technology plan that will enhance the achievement of the program's goals (understand how people are to function)
- Review, evaluate, and revise the technology plan
- Select equipment that will meet current and future program needs
- If possible, standardize equipment within the organization
- Be careful accepting donated equipment (equipment may be dated and in need of repairs)

- Organize professional development for staff in the use of implemented technology
- Evaluate technology and revise where needed

Planning Guidelines

The Council on Facilities and Equipment (CFE) has adopted the following guidelines for planning facilities:

Guideline # 1: Comply with the Americans with Disabilities Act (ADA)

Title III of the Americans with Disabilities Act (ADA) prohibits discrimination against any "individual with a disability." This federal legislation mandates that services of public entities be extended to all persons in our society including, those with special needs. In order for these services to be available to everyone, architectural barriers limiting access to and mobility within facilities must be eliminated. Those facilities most impacted by this legislation are those belonging to public entities and those viewed as having "public accommodation." As a consequence of this legislation, both accessibility and mobility from one program area to another within a structure must be considered in the designing phase of all public facilities. If any of these standards cannot be met, managers may be required to make reasonable modification to their facility or adopt special policies, practices, and procedures to reach these benchmarks. The ADA applies to all physical education, recreation, and athletic facilities, including gymnasiums, fitness facilities, health clubs, etc.

The planning of a facility to accommodate individuals with special needs is a complex undertaking requiring much thought, cooperation among facility planners and users, and a removal of "attitudinal barriers." To help in measuring up to suggested standards, federal health, education, and welfare regulations recommend that individuals with special expertise be consulted when designing public facilities. Good resource groups for facility designers to consult with are local chapters of national organizations whose primary purposes are to assist individuals who have special needs. A technical manual on the ADA can be found at the following Website: http://www.usdoj.gov/crt/ada/taman3.html This topic is addressed in more detail in Chapter 7.

Guideline #2: Use a Master Plan (Comprehensive Plan)

It is recommended that today's planners use a well-contemplated, systematized strategy that takes into account many variables (present and future) that may have an impact on a facility's functionality. This strategy utilizes personnel who have both facility design and programming expertise, thus helping to prevent debacles in facility construction that can be attributed to slipshod planning. The keystone documents upon which the foundation of all (current and future) facilities are designed is known as the Master Plan, or in municipal agencies, the Comprehensive Plan. This plan is a formal, comprehensive building scheme that identifies all the organization's facility needs and establishes the priority in which construction of new or the renovation of existing facilities will occur.

The process of developing master plans involves the accumulation of vast amounts of information that, directly or indirectly, support the organization's mission. Usually the charge for developing facility master plans resides at the higher administrative levels of an organization and involves high-level administrators and/or their designees. The complexity of developing such a plan is influenced by several factors: the size of the institution or agency conducting the planning; the human and financial resources available to support the planning process; and the master planning skills of the individuals involved. An example of the steps that may be followed in the process of developing a facility master plan for an educational facility is illustrated in Figure 3.1.

The format of facility master plans may differ from one organization to another; however, they are basically composed of all the organization's anticipated long-range and short-range acquisitions, renovations, and/or new constructions. The plans include all possible community and regional developments, areas best suited for expansion possibilities, predicted demographic shifts, and anticipated programmatic needs changes. The long-range projection of the Master (or Comprehensive) Plan is usually five to 10 years, and the short-range projection is generally one to four years. In some instances, organizations also use long-term forecasts that project 10- to 20-year outlooks. The development and maintenance of a master plan is a continuous and ongoing process and is characterized by periods of highly intense planning. The components of the plan are directed toward specific planning goals that are identified in the organization's facility development program (see Figure 3.2). These components of the Master Plan provide an abstract of any acquisitions or changes that are anticipated in the future.

Guideline #3: Use a Participatory Planning Approach

The view that users, organizational units, and occupants of current facilities have primary input into both new construction and/or renovation of existing structures is an essential precept in participatory facility planning. Furthermore, if the data obtained from these principal parties are clearly explained and adequately understood by the designers, the chances of a particular facility meeting the needs of the program constituents are substantially increased.

When designing facilities in this collegial environment, organizations commonly include all persons who are interested in or have a penchant for physical education, recreation, and athletic facility design. The specific thrust varies from one agency or organization to another. Community agencies take into account their large, divergent user groups, and universities and colleges usually focus on the needs of the educational community. However, the importance of receiving input from representative user groups is the common thread that is interwoven into the fabric of this approach to facility planning. A sample participatory, or team planning process, is illustrated in Figure 3.3.

Origination of the Idea (Basic Program Level). The idea typically emanates from individuals intricately involved in the outdated facility and the programs it houses. However, the idea may also originate from higher administration. For example, high-level administrators may be approached by a potential donor who is interested in contributing funds to

**Figure 3.1
Developing Master Plan**

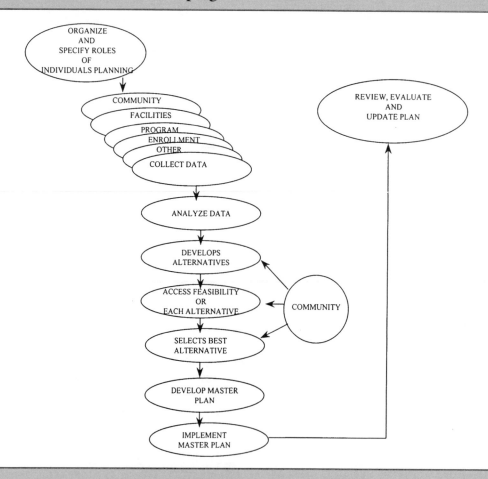

**Figure 3.2
Facilities Master Plan**

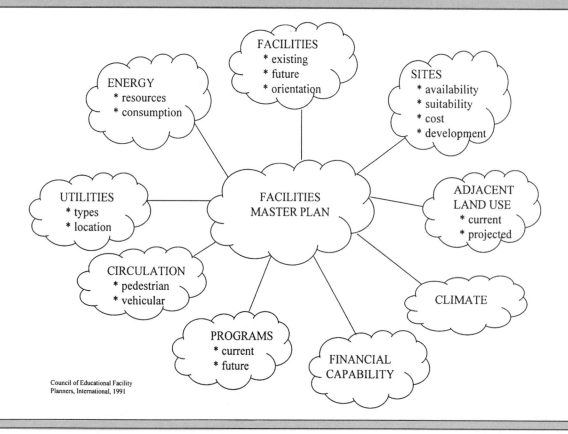

Council of Educational Facility
Planners, International, 1991

Figure 3.3
Sample Planning Process

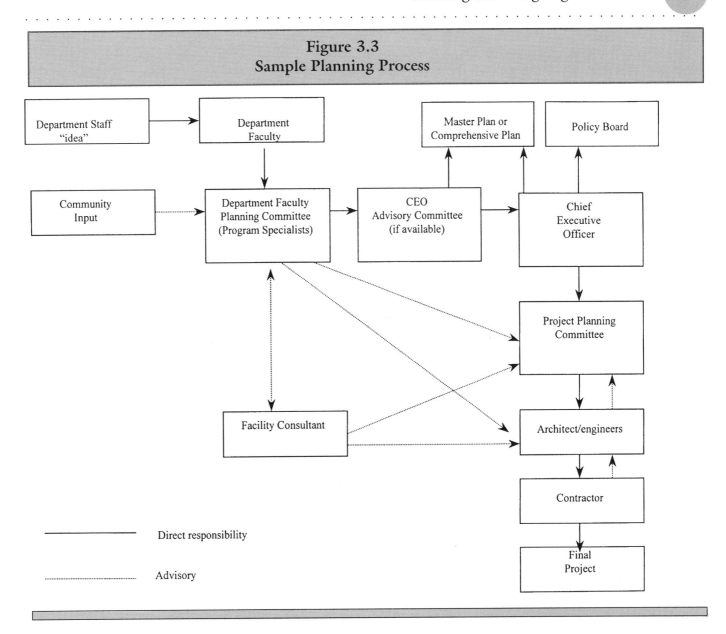

build a facility for a specific purpose. When the impetus for a new building project begins at this level, the respective program directors are notified of the windfall and are brought into the planning stages early to begin the planning process and all preliminary steps, from the "Origination of Idea" through the "Approval of Highest Authority," can be significantly expedited.

Presenting the Idea to Higher Authority. Those conceiving the idea attempt to convince their departmental colleagues of the need for the project, whether it is a new facility or simply remodeling an existing one. If adequate support is generated, a departmental planning committee is selected by the principal administrator of that unit (i.e., department chair, agency head, etc.). The mission of this planning team is to review the initial proposal, modify it, and embellish the substance of the report before presenting it to the next highest authority. If the project is approved, selected department members who possess programmatic expertise will function as program specialists and advise both the project planning committee and the project architect on the facility's user groups' needs. (Projects emanating from the higher administrative level can eliminate this and the next step completely, inasmuch as the project will have already received the necessary high-level approval.)

In Preparation for Highest Authority. Some colleges and universities, school systems, and recreation departments require a succession of complex steps to gain project approval, while others have relatively few and simple procedures. Regardless of organizational differences, a common feature should be the referencing of the organization's Master Plan to determine the reasonableness of the facility proposal. Referring back to the Master Plan will help assure consistency for the programs and facilities within the organization. Gaining project approval from the policy board, the chief executive officer (CEO) appoints a project planning committee (see Guideline #5). This committee has a number of important responsibilities that assist the architect in designing the best facility possible.

Guideline #4: Research Your Funding Options

The single most important requisite when proposing a new or renovating an existing facility is to determine how the project will be funded. The proposal has a better chance of being approved by higher authorities if all available funding sources are researched and a precise funding strategy is developed in advance. This plan should include a listing of the different funding sources (i.e., governmental grants, private organizations, interested philanthropists, etc.) that are available to support the project or identifying parties and/or organizations that have expressed a willingness to help provide the necessary funds (See Chapter 5 for more information on funding).

Guideline #5: Organize a Project Planning Committee

Once a facility project has been approved, a project planning committee may be established to accumulate and organize all information pertinent to the project and to make facility design decisions as they arise. The make-up of this committee usually consists of selective members from the department (program specialists), administrator(s), a principal member of the architectural firm (ex-officio), a facility consultant (ex-officio), representatives from user groups, and maintenance personnel (see Figure 3.4). Engineers are sometimes included as members. When they are not, their input into committee discussions is made by either the project architect or the facility consultant. The facility consultant and architect, whose responsibilities are defined in greater detail later in this chapter, should be ex-officio members of this group.

Among the most important responsibilities of this committee are to gather information from user groups and use it to prepare a final, coherent, and informative document for the architect. This report is called the program statement (see Guideline #7) and is used by the architect to develop a facility design. In order to design an acceptable end product, the project architect must have a program statement that accurately and thoroughly depicts the programs that will be housed in the proposed facility. It is from this document the architect will be seeking guidance in preparation of the design schematic. Therefore, college and university physical education, recreation, and athletic planning committees should seek input from a wide variety of program areas, such as adaptive physical education, aquatics, team/individual/ dual sports, dance, outdoor recreation, exercise science, martial arts, and basic instruction classes. In municipal recreation planning, representation from indoor recreation, outdoor recreation, and therapeutic recreation is germane.

Following the development of the program statement, the project planning committee, in concert with the project architect, makes a majority of the crucial design decisions. This group has the responsibility of reacting to the architect's initial concepts and schematic drawings. It coordinates the design planning with the various users of the facility. In addition, it reacts to questions dealing with program statement interpretation, proposal changes, and possible deletions due to cost or program changes. There should be no deviations in the project design without first having the input from this committee. If immediate decisions should ever become imperative, the chairperson of the committee may be called upon to render some judgments without group consensus; however, to avoid conflict, this option should be minimized.

Guideline #6: Understand when to Renovate, Retrofit, or Replace

By definition, the renovation of an existing facility is the rehabilitation of the physical features of a building, including the rearrangement of spaces within the structure.

Retrofitting, on the other hand, is the addition of new systems, features, materials, and/or equipment to a facility that were not in place at the time the building was constructed. These changes may be minor or they could be significant to the point of changing the primary function of the facility.

The practice of buying, using, then discarding items is unacceptable in today's recycling-conscious society. This conservation mind-set not only applies to the day-to-day management of our facilities, but is carried over to facility improvements as well. Due to the high cost of new construction, upper-level administrators, whether in the private sector, university, municipal agency, or in a public school system, have the responsibility of making prudent decisions regarding the use of existing buildings. In meeting this obligation, it is necessary for administrators to seek input from knowledgeable resource professionals in order to effectively consider the feasibility of either renovating or retrofitting an existing building or constructing a new facility.

Administrators have a myriad of factors to consider to accurately ascertain whether renovation, retrofitting, or new construction is the best alternative. One of the most important considerations is the impact that the construction process will have on ongoing programs. Consideration, for example, must be given to possible program modifications and adaptions that may be necessitated during the construction phase of the project. Some of the other factors that should be contemplated include, but are not limited to the following:

- *Costs.* The costs include construction to provide comparable space, compliance with safety codes, accessibility standards, and maintenance. The "50% rule" can be used as a guide: Do not retrofit/renovate if cost is greater than 50% of replacement.
- *Site selection.* Is there sufficient space for a new building? Would the proposed site be an appropriate location? Is there adequate parking at the old site? Are appropriate utilities available at the site?
- *Architectural and structural standards.* There are many standards to be considered, including aesthetics, meeting current and long-range program goals, energy efficiency, condition of footings and foundations, condition of heating and ventilation, air conditioning, and security system, etc.
- *Educational considerations.* The educational considerations focus upon meeting needs of current and future programs.
- *Community needs and restrictions.* These include population needs, zoning requirements, and the future plans for the area.
- *Life expectancy of the current facility.* Factors that should be considered include the increase/decrease in size of the populations served by the facility, growth and development of nearby areas, and re-zoning implications that may be problematic in the future.

Guideline #7: Develop a Program Statement for the Architect

The program statement, also referred to as the "building program" or "educational specifications," is an extremely important document that provides linkage between the programs and the facility design (also discussed under guide-

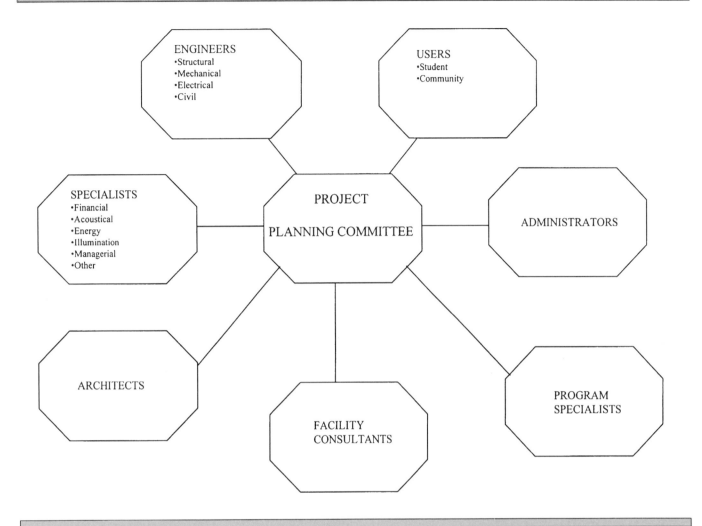

Figure 3.4
Project Planning Committee

line #5). It is a written document describing all the programs current and proposed activities and events, plus their facility and/or space requirements. It describes the programs' goals and objectives and identifies any special facility needs the programs may have (see Figure 3.5).

In the initial section of the program statement, the goals and objectives that are to be achieved in each functional area of the programs are stated. Goals are defined as desirable conditions sought, and objectives are defined as specific means to be achieved in reaching these program goals. The next section of the program statement consists of a conceptualization of the program(s) that are necessary to achieve the previously stated goals. A sample building program statement outline can be seen in Figure 3.6.

It is essential that the program statement be written to accurately reflect the needs of the programs that will be using the completed facility. The statement should address the broader relationship of the physical education, recreation, and athletic programs, as well as the specific needs of each program. Typically, this information is arrived at by critically evaluating the current programs and determining whether new approaches will be used in lieu of old ones or if old and new programs will be combined. All facility needs should be considered, both indoor and outdoor, and the location of

buildings should be addressed in the report in terms of its importance on programming. This statement is the vehicle by which the needs of the organization's programs are communicated to the architect, so its accuracy is extremely important.

Since the program statement reflects the professional opinion of all members of the project planning committee (administrators, facility consultant, specialists, and users), all revisions should be circulated to each member for approval. Once an accurate draft is obtained, it can then be disseminated to those competing architects who are vying for the project. The architects' proposals' (RFPs) are, in turn, submitted to the project planning committee for consideration. Thereafter, the selected project architect uses the program statement for guidance in the designing of the facility schematic.

Guideline #8: Use Planning Professionals

Efficient facility planning requires the expertise and collaboration of many individuals. All participants are important to the planning process; however, their levels of involvement may vary depending on what phase of planning is being undertaken at any particular time. Roles of three professionals and their respective selection process are identi-

Figure 3.5
Program Statement

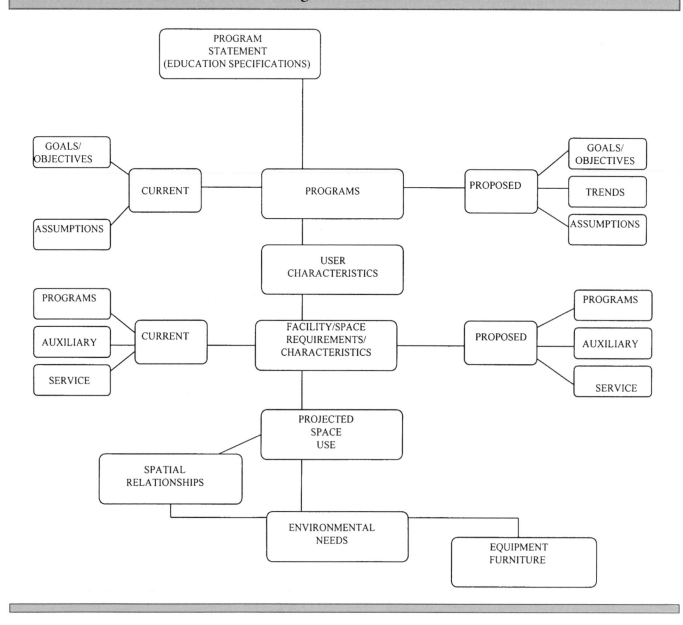

fied in the following sections. It should be understood that each individual's role is predicated on the client's needs. These needs should be understood before the professional is formally hired and the terms for each should be committed to writing when appropriate.

Selecting Planning Professionals

It is a responsibility of the project planning committee, after it has completed the building program statement, to select a facility consultant, project architect, and perhaps engineer(s). This is an extremely important responsibility for the committee; therefore, a careful and judicious selection process should be utilized for each. Before the committee can begin this task, it must first decide what types of professionals are needed to complete the project and then decide on the hiring procedures that will be employed in the selection process. For example, many architectural firms have either their own engineering departments in-house or a work-

ing relationship with an outside firm. Therefore, it may be advisable to allow the firm to select its own engineers to facilitate a more compatible working relationship. Whether to hire a facility consultant for the project is another consideration that the project planning committee may be called upon to decide. This decision is commonly based on the availability of funds for the building project.

Program Specialists

The role of program specialists in facility planning is very important. Program specialists normally are individuals who are actively engaged in the programs for which the facility is being designed. Therefore, these experts are usually key individuals from groups who are viewed as the primary user groups of the project facility. These specialists should be acutely aware of their programs' facility needs and some of the problematic areas that need to be addressed. The involvement of these professionals increases the likelihood that

---

**Figure 3.6
Sample Building Program Statement Outline**

Part I. Objectives of the programs
    a. Instructional (professional service)
    b. Recreational sports
    c. Adapted
    d. Athletics (interscholastic and intercollegiate)
    e. Club sports
    f. Community/school programs
    g. Others

Part II. Basic Assumptions to be Addressed
    a. Facilities will provide for a broad program of instruction,
       adapted activities, intramural sports and other
    b. Demographics of the population who will use the facility
    c. Existing facilities will be programmed for use
    d. Basic design considerations. "What's most important?"
    e. Facility expansion possibilities will be provided for in the planning
    f. Outdoor facilities should be located adjacent to indoor facilities
    g. Consideration will be given to administration and staff needs
    h. Existing problems
    i. Others

Part III. Comparable Facility Analysis
    a. Visit comparable facilities that have been recently constructed
    b. Compare cost, design features, etc.

Part IV. Factors Affecting Planning
    a. Federal and state legislation
    b. Club sports movement
    c. The community education or "Lighted School" program
    d. Surge of new non-competitive activities being added to the curriculum
    e. Expansion of intramural sports and athletic programs
    f. Sharing certain facilities by boys and men and girls and women (athletic training
       rooms and equipment rooms)
    g. Coeducational programming
    h. Emphasis on individual exercise programs
    i. Physical fitness movement
    j. Systems approach in design and construction
    k. New products
    l. Others

Part V. Explanation of Current and Proposed Programming
    a. Instructional
    b. Intramural sports
    c. Club sports
    d. Adaptive programs
    e. Community/school
    f. Recreational programs
    g. Priority listing of programs
    h. Others

Part VI. Preliminary Data Relative to the Proposed New Facilities the project planning committee is both accurate and realistic when developing its program statement. Examples of the type of input the program specialist may provide are as follows:

- Determines the number of activity and/or teaching stations needed to serve the instructional, intramural sports, recreation, athletics, club sports, and adaptive programs.
- Assists in recommending the selection of materials (e.g., hardwood and/or synthetic floors, lighting requirements, acoustical treatments, and maintenance issues).
- Informs all appropriate persons and the general public about the program purposes and needs for the facilities.
- Ascertains the various sizes of teams, classes, and groups that will use the facilities and knows the requirements of their activities and the implications they present in facility design.
- Advises the project planning committee of trends that should be considered when developing the program statement (i.e., changes in synthetic surfaces, all-weather tracks, coed-athletic training rooms, coed and senior citizen classes, programs for the disabled, total community use of recreational facilities, and rapid development of sports clubs).
- Identifies desired and problematic traffic patterns for various individuals and groups, including spectators.
- Provides the architect and project planning committee with examples of facilities that meet desired needs. If the sites are too distant for visitation, slides or pictures may be taken as illustrations for the architect and planning committee.
- Points out areas that represent quality as well as those that represent minimal quantitative standards.
- Points out the special considerations necessary to allow persons with disabilities full use of facilities.

The program specialist may be assisted by facility consultants in identifying specific material needs, dimensions, space relationships, innovations, and other pertinent information.

Facility Consultant

A facility consultant is a professional in the field who is either employed by another organization or is self-employed in the facility-consulting business. This individual usually has had experience with facility planning and is familiar with recently constructed facilities in the country. The consultant is up-to-date with the latest innovations in facility construction materials, building concepts, and general programming. In many instances, this professional will know the location of some recent renovation or construction projects and would be a good resource person to the project planning committee when hiring an architect.

The facility consultant assists the project planning committee, in an ex-officio capacity, by developing alternatives and establishing priorities in the building project. As an objective expert, the consultant normally is looked upon as a person who can exert considerable influence on all members of the project planning committee, including the project ar-

chitect. Also, the consultant can be very helpful as an ex-officio member of the project planning committee, because of his/her objectivity and expertise in designing specific spaces that may be unfamiliar to the architect or the program specialists. This role becomes even more valuable when the architect hired for the project lacks a basic orientation of the specific programs for which the facility is being designed. Although it is always best to hire an architect who possesses sufficient experience, there are times when this does not occur. In these situations, the consultant's contributions to the success of the project become crucial.

Basic considerations in selecting the facility consultant should include the following:

- educational background
- work experience
- planning experience
- proximity to project
- reputation
- ability to work with the project planning committee, architects, engineers, and contractors
- ability to understand and read blueprints and specification documents
- ability to understand the organization's programs and the future needs of such programs

The committee can develop a list of prospective consultants by contacting the American Alliance for Health, Physical Education, Recreation and Dance (http://www.aahperd.org).

Architect

One of the central members of the project planning committee is the architect. Since the architect's role is of paramount importance, a great deal of time should be spent on investigating the firm and/or individuals interested in the project. When selecting an architect, the firm's reputation and experience should be considered. It is desirable that the architect be able to provide examples of work completed on projects similar to that being proposed. The architect's interpersonal skills and ability to establish rapport with members of the project planning committee, consultants and other individuals who will be involved in the planning and construction are very important. Not to be discounted in importance when selecting an architect is the location of the individual's firm. There is a decided advantage in selecting an architectural firm that is located near the proposed project. Besides the obvious political benefits of this selection, close proximity to the construction site allows for frequent visitations to the site necessary for thorough supervision of the construction, thus providing a greater safeguard against the possibility of construction errors. With project supervision as an integral function of the architect's responsibilities, the selection of an individual whose project management skills are well honed is preferred.

Ideally, the entire project planning committee should participate in the selection of the architect. The committee should develop a list of prospective architectural firms who have experience in developing similar facilities in their geographic area. A list of architects can be solicited from the American Institute of Architects *(http://www.aia.org)* or by contacting personnel from other similar sport facilities who have worked with architects on similar projects (also see the section entitled: "Web Site Information" later in this chapter). A common practice used to select architects is to utilize a request-for-proposal (RFP) procedure. Using this approach, firms are asked to submit proposals to the committee that explain how they would address the program statement. The proposals are then analyzed and the selection of the architect is made based on the assessment of all relevant considerations. Once the proposals have been gathered, reviewed, and ranked, the committee selects the top five to 10 firms for an interview. The committee then interviews the firms and selects the one that it deems will provide the best service.

After selecting an architectural firm, a contractual agreement should be completed and signed before proceeding to the next stage of the building process. A legally binding contract between the architectural firm and the client should follow a standard form of agreement. The contract should delineate all the responsibilities of the architect, which are numerous and vital. These responsibilities typically include, but are not limited to:

Pre-design planning, where the architect:
- Solicits facility and equipment needs from all user groups.
- Develops a time schedule for each stage of the project.
- Turns the program statement into an architectural or building program.
  Schematic design, where the architect:
- Translates the written program into a graphic representation of a building plan
- Designs and presents plans regarding space relations of various functions and accessibility to the facility. Shows how the facility will satisfy the needs as identified in the predesign conference.
- Studies the site, its topography, its relationship to the community and to traffic patterns, and the availability of utilities. Determines how the site might be developed.
- Reviews applicable codes and laws to determine their effect on the design.

Design development, where the architect:
- Develops the general design of the facility once approval from the highest authority is secured.
- Prepares sketches of elevations and models to establish the visual character of the project.

- Determines building materials and outlines their specifications along with the utilitarian value, aesthetic qualities, and mechanical and electrical systems.

Bidding, where the architect:
- Assists in enlisting national firms, engineers and consultants specializing in recreation and sports facilities obtaining bids and awarding contracts.
- Determines with the client, how the project will be bid and the contractors who will be qualified to bid.
- Answers questions for bidders and clarifies any aspects of the construction documents.
  Provides copies of specifications, documents, and drawings for contractors, owners, and others who may need them.

Directing construction, when the architect:
- Meets with the client and contractor to outline the project and discuss operating procedures.
- Issues bulletins and change orders to accomplish changes requested by the client or required by field conditions.
- Approves payments to contractors.

Other professionals

Other professionals who will be working on the project include: civil, structural, mechanical, electrical, and acoustical engineers; interior designers; landscape architects; and general, electrical, and mechanical contractors (See glossary for full descriptions). These professionals may be selected by the project planning committee, or that responsibility may be delegated to the project architect.

Web Site Information

Having access to a directory of architects and consultants who work in the sport facilities area, as well as suppliers of materials for these projects, may be a helpful resource for planners. Each year the *Athletic Business Journal* publishes such a list. Their most current directory listing may be viewed at: http://athleticbusiness.com/buy-frame.htm

Summary

Ineffective facility planning often leads to needless expense and frequently produces inadequate results. Therefore, the importance of a properly planned building process cannot be overemphasized.

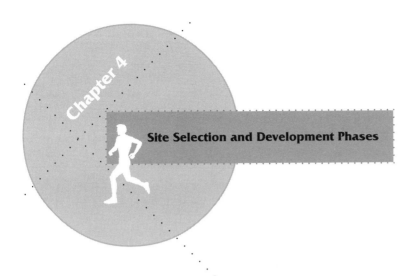

Thomas H. Sawyer, Indiana State University
Michael G. Hypes, Indiana State University

Successful building projects have most likely undergone thorough pre-development reviews, and well-designed site selections and development processes. Projects without these elements are doomed to failure from the outset.

Learning Objectives

After reading this chapter, the student will be able to:
- discuss the function of the pre-development guide,
- describe the process involved in site selection,
- understand the various facility development phases,
- describe what construction documents consist of,
- outline the bidding process, and
- describe the construction phase.

Pre-Development Review

Chapter 3, discussed the planning process that should be employed when developing a building project. Along with the planning process, a thorough review of facility needs should be completed. This review should be completed before an architect or consultant is brought on board. This can save time and money, as well as assuring that the structure will fit the proposed program. It is important to review the following checklist at the beginning, not the end of the planning process. This will help focus and guide the dream and planning process. Combine the specific checklist in Figure 4.1 with the more general checklist found in the Appendices.

Figure 4.1
Physical Activity and Sports Facility Checklist

Lobby/Entrance
- Peak traffic rate entering and exiting
- energy conservation
- door size
- lobby size
- seating arrangements
- public restrooms
- floor surfaces
- lighting
- ADA requirements

Control area
- number of patrons at peak periods
- number of staff at peak loads
- computers, cash registers, automated check-in
- towel service
- locker registration
- TV surveillance

- light controls
- door monitor system/panel
- fire annunciator panel
- public address system
- emergency alarm system/panel
- equipment issue/return/storage; equipment to be stored; storage cabinets; separate issue and return functions; peak load considerations; staffing
- building directory
- phone system

Strength training area
- number of mechanized weight machines
- electrical needs
- flooring considerations
- mirrors
- audio/visual accommodations
- control center

continued

Figure 4.1 continued
Physical Activity and Sports Facility Checklist

- desk and computer
- storage space and cabinets
- clocks
- peak load considerations
- HVAC considerations

Free Weight area
- benches
- weight racks
- dumbbells and racks
- weight platforms
- chalk holders and chalk
- floor considerations
- control area
- desk and computer
- mirrors
- HVAC considerations
- audio and visual considerations
- peak load considerations

Fitness Testing
- treadmill
- exercise bike
- monitoring equipment
- desk and bed
- storage cabinets
- sink and counter space
- computer
- telephone
- tack board

Cardiorespiratory area
- treadmills
- bicycles
- rowing machines
- stair climbers
- arm ergometers
- wall weight racks
- dumbbells
- floor surface
- audio and visual accommodations
- desk and computer
- storage
- HVAC considerations
- peak load considerations

Aquatics center
- competition pool
- teaching pool
- handicapped pool
- diving well
- diving boards
- diving platform
- underwater windows
- underwater sound
- filtration and sanitation
- vacuum
- lane lines
- bulkheads
- moveable floors
- lifeguard stands

- HVAC considerations
- lighting
- handicapped pool lift
- whirlpool for divers
- spectator seating
- rescue equipment
- grab rails and ladders
- acoustic treatment
- wall graphics
- staring platforms
- timing devices, scoreboard, diving scoring, PA system
- deck space and drainage
- corrosion resistant fittings
- emergency telephone or call button
- storage
- control center, desks, computers
- office, desks, computers
- telephones
- automated pool chemical control
- tile or no tile
- pumps and auxiliary pumps
- heater and auxiliary heater
- main drains
- access to pipes

Dependent Care
- number of children
- number of aging adults
- state requirements
- number of staff
- adjacent play areas in and out
- adjacent toilet facilities
- audio and visual accommodations
- office, desk, computer
- storage and storage cabinets

Pro shop
- display windows
- adjustable wall display system
- adjustable display shelving
- adjustable display lighting
- office
- control area, computer, cash register, visual surveillance
- door alarm system for shoplifting

Food Service
- juice bar
- vending
- seating area
- small kitchen with microwave, range, dishwasher, hot water booster, garbage disposal, range hood, refrigeration, sink and counter space
- health requirements
- tiled floor with drains

Gymnasium/Multipurpose Space
- activities to be accommodated
- peak number of people
- floor and wall inserts required

continued

Figure 4.1 continued
Physical Activity and Sports Facility Checklist

- lighting requirements
- folding partitions or dividing curtains, motorized or manual
- baskets and back stops—portable or permanent, motorized or manual
- batting cages
- golf cages
- scoreboards
- seating, portable or permanent
- wall pads
- flooring considerations
- wall graphics
- drinking fountains
- PA system
- large storage area, roll-up doors
- public rest rooms
- concessions
- portable stage
- press box
- press (media) room
- built-in audio-visual hook-ups
- computer hook-ups
- ceiling and wall-mounted projection screens
- video monitoring
- loading dock with roll-up door
- adjacent meeting areas
- adjacent locker rooms
- large janitorial space
- adjacent training room
- climbing wall area
- indoor jumping and throwing areas

Running track (indoor)
- laps per turn
- elevated or floor level
- number of lanes
- type of surface
- adjacent strength training, cardiovascular areas
- radius at turns
- banked curves
- automated banking
- lane markers
- pacer lights

Dance areas
- number of participants at peak loads
- audio accommodations
- acoustics
- ballet bars
- mirrors
- dance floor
- storage
- HVAC considerations
- emergency telephone or call button

Handball/Racquetball/Squash Courts
- number of courts
- competition courts
- spectator seating
- instructor observation area

- type of wall and ceiling system
- type of floor system
- glass or solid walls
- remote lighting
- stripping
- other activities—wall soccer, walleyball, dancercise, etc.
- lighting
- securing valuables
- accessing lighting
- HVAC considerations
- acoustics

Combative/Wrestling Room
- number of participants
- padded walls
- padded floor
- no glass areas
- no protruding fixtures
- remote HVAC sensing
- hanging bag
- hanging rope for climbing

Locker rooms
- number of lockers
- type of lockers and locker system
- tile floor with drains
- grooming area—number of sinks, mirrors, hair dryers, soap dispensers, towel dispensers, waste receptacles, non-slip floor, water resistant electrical receptacles
- handicapped area
- benches or stools—fixed or moveable
- HVAC considerations
- swimming suit drying system
- permanent lockers
- dressing booths

Rest Rooms
- health code requirements
- handicapped area
- non-slip floor
- floor drains
- mechanical exhaust
- diaper changing areas
- toilet partitions
- disposable seat covers
- sanitary napkin dispensers and disposals
- vandal-proof partitions
- corrosion resistant fittings
- automatic flush

Showers
- number of people to accommodate at peak loads
- individual showers
- hose bibb
- soap dispensers
- soap dishes
- handicapped accommodations
- non-slip floor
- floor drains

continued

Figure 4.1 continued
Physical Activity and Sports Facility Checklist

- corrosion resistant fittings
- water-proof membrane as required
- HVAC considerations

Shower drying areas
- number of people
- floor drains
- towel racks or hooks
- non-slip floor surface

Steam Room
- number of people
- steam convector units with cover plates, electric or gas
- waterproof membranes
- observation window
- emergency call button
- remote temperature control
- floor drains
- tiled room
- mechanical exhaust
- shower in steam room
- corrosion resistant fittings
- lighting
- hose bibb
- unisex or separate facilities

Sauna
- number of people
- exterior shower adjacent the sauna
- waterproof membranes
- observation window
- emergency call button
- remote temperature control
- floor drains
- redwood interior, all boards screwed into frame
- mechanical exhaust
- protective covering over rocks
- corrosion resistant fittings
- lighting
- hose bibb
- unisex or separate facilities

Tanning room
- number of units
- type of units
- adjacent a changing area
- wash-up or grooming area

Massage room
- number of massage tables
- heat lamps
- towel storage cabinets

Laundry
- projected volume/required staffing
- number and size of washers
- number and size of extractor units
- number and size of dryer units—gas or electric

- sorting and folding area
- floor drains
- soiled linen area
- carts
- linear feet of linen storage shelving & cabinets required
- HVAC considerations
- office, desk, computer

Administrative areas
- number of offices
- size of offices
- contents

Other miscellaneous areas
- janitorial spaces and break areas
- general storage
- classrooms
- maintenance area
- mechanical areas
- elevators and elevator equipment spaces
- hallways
- stairwells

Outdoor Activity Areas
- sport fields, practice and games
- basketball courts
- sand volleyball courts
- golf course
- tennis courts
- archery and shooting ranges
- ice hockey/skating
- outdoor aquatic center
- playground
- spectator seating
- concessions
- security lighting
- game lighting
- security fencing
- observation areas
- press boxes
- storage buildings and areas
- scoreboards
- ticket booths
- pump houses
- rope courses
- challenge courses
- fitness courses
- picnic areas
- horseshoes
- croquet area
- bocci area
- shuffle board area
- parking—zoning requirements, adjacent existing facilities, surface or garage parking, handicapped spaces, security lighting, landscaping buffers, asphalt or concrete, entering and exiting, pedestrian areas

Site Selection and Development Process

There are 13 common steps that compose a strong site selection and development process, including research, regional analysis, site analysis, program, functional analysis, combined site and function, land use, refinement, site plan/overall design, construction documents, bidding, construction, and review.

Step 1: Research

In its research, the planning committee should be concerned with (1) knowing and understanding the needs and desires of the people who are involved in and/or affected by the proposed project, and (2) knowing everything reasonably possible about the project function and/or activity and the space requirements.

Designers Design for People

At least four groups of people may need to be involved in the research and be eventually satisfied, including clients (board of directors, etc.), users, affected neighbors and/or public, managers and operators, and possibly others. Each of the relevant groups must be identified and its needs, concerns, and desires understood. There will almost certainly be some conflicts between the various groups. Understanding these problems in advance may make it possible to resolve them during the design phase.

Maintenance and Operations

Maintenance and operational needs, small but significant, must be clearly understood. They can make a project successful or doom it to future failure. The following are some specific items to consider:

Maintenance
- Will maintenance be done by in-house labor or by contract?
- Is special equipment used or needed (i.e., riding lawn mowers, etc.)?
- Does maintenance staff have any requirements for any standard equipment requirements (i.e., motors, lights, shower heads, pumps, etc.) used or preferred by the maintenance staff?
- How capable is staff to maintain sophisticated equipment?
- What are maintenance space requirements, such as equipment clearance around mo-tors and pumps so maintenance can be performed, etc?
- Are there any special fire protection requirements?
- What special storage requirements are needed for flammables and chemicals?

Operations
- Security—Is it needed? If so, what type (patrol, electronic, entrance only, dogs)? If patrolled, how—by foot, car, motorcycle, horse, bike, or boat?
- Hours of operation—Is night lighting required?
- Trash pickup—In-house? Contract? Kind of equipment used?
- Deliveries—food, supplies, etc. When are separate entrances and exits needed?
- Communications system—speakers, phone, radio?

- Safety/first aid—Are special facilities needed? Where? Extent? Emergency vehicle access?
- Peak use—How handled? Restrict use or provide overflow capacity?

Special Programs
- Will there be any? If so, what kind? Concerts at noon, employee training, visitor information and/or education, arts and craft shows, special exhibits?
- Any special space requirements for programs? Lighting? Service areas? Other utilities?

Facilities and Their Requirements

Most facilities have specific site requirements. Technical data must be gathered on all the proposed facilities. At a minimum, the following must be known:
- Size—actual dimensions plus any buffer spaces or required accessory space.
- Grade requirements—maximum and minimum.
- Any special construction requirements—tennis courts, ice hockey rinks, etc.
- Utility needs (i.e., type and amount).

Step 2: Regional Analysis

Sufficient data must be gathered about the off-site surroundings to ensure that the project will be compatible with surrounding environments, both man made and natural. This part of the design process is referred to as the regional analysis. It should include:

- Service area of the facility under construction (i.e., major facilities such as parks, large commercial areas facilities, and minor facilities, such as children's playgrounds, senior citizen centers, local library, etc.),
- User demand (i.e., determining the kind of use desired of clients, activity interests, demographic makeup of residents, and local leadership, and calculating the number of users),
- Access routes (i.e., major and secondary routes),
- Governmental functions and boundaries (i.e., contact the local planning agency and local government offices),
- Existing and proposed land uses (i.e., gathering information about abutting land ownership, adjacent land uses, land use along probable access routes, off-site flooding and erosion problems, offsite pollution sources, views [especially of aesthetic and historic interest], and significant local architectural or land use characteristics), and
- Regional influences (i.e., check for anything unusual or unique that could either enhance or cause problems to the project).

Step 3: Site Analysis

The planning committee will need to consider various pieces of information prior to selecting the building site. The considerations for site selection (Fogg, 1986; Miller, 1997) include:
- Access to the site (i.e., ingress and egress, surrounding traffic generators, accessibility via public transportation)

- Circulation within the site (e.g., roads—paved and unpaved, bicycle trails, walks and hiking trails)
- Parking
- Water supply
- Sewage disposal
- Electrical service
- Telephone service
- Other utilities including oil/natural gas transmission lines, or cable TV
- Structures to be constructed
- Environmental concerns and conditions on and off property (e.g., noise, air, water, and visual pollution)
- Easements and other legal issues (e.g., deed restrictions, rights of way, and less-than-fee-simple ownership)
- Zoning requirements. Changing the zoning is usually time consuming and expensive and frequently not possible
- Historical significance
- Any existing uses (activities) on the site
- Climatic conditions prevalent in the area by season (e.g., temperature; humidity; air movement velocity, duration, and direction; amount of sunshine; precipitation—rain, sleet, snow; sun angles and subsequent shadows; special conditions—ice storms, hurricanes, tornadoes, heavy fog, heavy rain storm, floods, and persistent cloud cover)
- Nuisance potentials (e.g., children nearby, noise, etc.)
- Natural features (e.g., topography, slope analysis, soil conditions, geology, hydrology, flora and fauna)
- Economic impact of a site (e.g., labor costs, growth trends, population shifts, buying power index, available work force, property taxes, surrounding competition, utility costs, incentives, area of dominant influence [ADI], designated market area [DMA], and established enterprise zones)
- Natural barriers and visibility
- Supporting demographics (e.g., age, gender, occupation, martial status, number of children, expenditures, education, income, number of earners in the family, race, etc.) and psychographics (e.g., lifestyle data or lifestyle marketing)
- Security concerns (e.g., proximity of police, fire, emergency medical personnel, hospitals)

The most important aspect of site selection is location, location, location. If the site is not in the most accessible location with a high profile for people to recognize, it will have a negative effect on the success of the venture.

Step 4: Program

Program, as used here, is the organization of the information needed for planning a project to provide an appropriate facility to meet the needs of the affected people (client, users, neighbors, and staff). Program needs should include a list of activities, facility needs for each activity listed, number of participants in each activity during peak periods, size of each facility ranging from minimum to ideal, and a description of the relationship between activities and facilities (i.e., can certain activities coexist with other activities at the same time in one facility?).

Step 5: Functional Analysis

Functional analysis is the process of analyzing and organizing the information provided in programming and relationships by translating that analysis into graphic symbols. It establishes the preferred or ideal physical relationships of all the component parts of a project. The process commonly consists of four parts: space diagrams, relationship charts and/or diagrams, bubble diagrams, and land-use concepts. All the elements contained in the activity/program must be considered and their desired functional and physical relationships accommodated.

Steps 6 and 7: Combined Site, Function, and Land Use

Two issues are key relative to land use: people needs and site constraints. At this point, the various constraints and opportunities presented by the site must become integrated with people needs. It is also the time when the reality of the site constraints may require changes in the program. This step combines site analysis (step 3) with functional analysis (step 5). If changes are made in the program, the changes must be incorporated throughout the functional analysis phase. This step in the site design process is where analysis of the site data is most completely utilized.

If the site selected is too small, the following options should be considered:

- Physical modification of the site. This may be the least desirable option, because it is almost always undesirable from an environmental standpoint. It frequently is not esthetically pleasing, and it is usually expensive.
- Expand the site if adjacent land is available. This is frequently not possible and can be expensive.
- Change to another site. This can be expensive, and alternate sites may not be available.
- Cancel the project. This is not usually desirable or possible.
- Creatively look at new ways of solving the problem.
- The location is the most difficult choice. It is always difficult to abandon the proven acceptable way of designing and operating facilities. When successful, however, it can often lead to outstanding innovative solutions.

Steps 8 and 9: Refinement and Site Plan/Overall Design

After the land-use step has been completed, the planning committee needs to refine the focus of the building project before it moves to the site plan/overall design step. After the refinement is complete, then, and only then, should the planners consider site planning and overall design.

A site plan shows all of the existing and proposed site features superimposed on a topographic base map at an appropriate scale. It functions as the coordinating plan that ensures that all the project parts fit together. This is the point in the site design process where imagination and creativity are really important. In addition, this plan is almost always the feature part of any presentation to the client and other interested parties.

Accompanying the site plan will be a number of drawings, including utilities (e.g., water sources, sewer lines, and electricity/communication), grading and drainage, circulation, scale drawings, relationships, and three-dimensional aspects.

Step 10: Construction documents

Construction documents control the actual constructed results. They consist of two separate parts: 1) working drawings and 2) specifications, the written companion to the working drawings. Upon completion of the working drawings and specifications, the project is bid, and if the bids are satisfactory, the contract is awarded.

Schematic Design Phase

In the schematic design phase, the architect prepares schematic design documents, consisting of drawings and other documents, illustrating the scale, and relationship of project components. These are based on the mutually agreed upon program with the owner, the schedule, and the construction budget requirements, and they are submitted to the owner for approval.

Design Development Phase

Based on schematic design documents and any adjustments authorized by the owner in the program, schedule, or construction budget, the architect prepares further design development documents for approval by the owner. These consist of drawings and other documents to fix and describe the size and character of the project as to architectural, structural, mechanical, and electrical systems, materials, and other appropriate elements.

Construction Document Phase

Based on the approved design development documents and any further adjustments in the scope or quality of the project or in the construction budget authorized by the owner, the architect prepares construction documents for the approval of the owner. These consist of drawings and specifications setting forth in detail the requirements for the construction of the project.

Drawings

All working drawings must be clear, concise, and understandable to the people who are going to construct the building. Only as much detail as is necessary to build the project should be included. More detail might give the client more control but will definitely cost more money for design and will result in higher bids. All pieces must be clearly presented in such a manner that will allow accurate building.

All construction drawings must be accurate, clearly labeled, and dimensioned. If in doubt as to the need for a label or a dimension, include it! Normally, written numbers on the plan take precedence over field scaled distances.

A useful tool in outlining the numbers and kinds of construction drawings is a plan control list. Each drawing that is expected to be needed is listed by description. This enables the designer(s) to coordinate work and helps to ensure that all aspects of the project are included.

With the completed list of plans, an estimate of time required to complete the working drawing and the necessary scheduling of work assignments can be carried out. This plan control document will probably be revised during the preparation of drawings. In its final form, it will become the drawing index listing for Sheet 2 of the working drawings package.

The more detailed and elaborate the working drawings, the higher the cost of preparing them, and very frequently, the higher the cost of building the project. A rule of thumb: The smaller the job, the fewer the construction documents. Small contractors do not like excessive control and paperwork. They frequently will not bid on projects with elaborate specifications, and if they do, they bid high. Frequently, too much control will cause bids to be higher, but do not result in an increase in quality.

The construction drawings must be reviewed by the maintenance staff to 1) ensure compatibility of parts with existing facilities, 2) see if the project can be effectively maintained at reasonable cost, and 3) determine if alternative materials or design modifications would reduce the costs and/or simplify maintenance. A detailed cost estimate is almost always necessary at this point in the design process. If costs estimated for the time of construction are too high, then the project may have to be reduced in scope and/or redesigned. Make sure that lifetime operations and maintenance costs are also considered in the estimate.

Specifications

The written portion of the construction documents comes in three parts: bidding and contract requirements (including the bid documents)—Division "0"; general requirements—Division "1"; and construction specifications —Divisions "2-16".

This part of the design process is often most disliked by designers, because of the massive detail required. It is, however, of the utmost importance in ensuring that the design is actually built according to the way it was envisioned.

General Notes

- Include everything in the specifications that you want to see in the final constructed product.
- Make sure that Division "1" includes the contractor providing "as built" drawings, catalogue cuts, and, where appropriate, an operation manual and training of operating and maintenance staff.
- Include only information necessary to the specific project—especially if it is a small one. As with plans, small contractors don't like and frequently don't understand long, involved specifications; therefore, they will not bid or may increase their bids accordingly. The heavier, thicker, and more complicated the specifications, the higher the bid.

- Conversely, the less detail you have in the specifications, the greater the opportunity for misunderstandings between the owner and contractor.
- All phases of specifications are readily adaptable to computerization and/or word processing. Much time can be saved if "canned" specifications are used, thus speeding up this tedious but crucial task. Computerization will probably lead to standardization of details and format.

All designers must keep current on the latest product information available in their field of expertise.

When the plans and specifications are completed, the project is ready for bid.

Step 11: Bidding

Bids are opened in front of witnesses, usually the contractors or their representative(s), and an attorney (normally required by a government agency). The bidding process includes (a) bidding and advertising, (b) opening and review of bids, and (c) award of contract. The bid documents include invitation to bid, instructions to bidders, the bid form, other sample bidding and contract forms, and the proposed documents (e.g., drawings and specifications).

Bidding and Advertising

Bidding is the process of receiving competitive prices for the construction of the project. A bid form should be provided to ensure that all bids are prepared in the same manner for easy comparison. The bids can be received in many ways. The most common are:

- Lump sum (one overall price),
- Lump sum with alternatives (either add-ons or deletions), and
- Unit prices.

All bids on large projects should be accompanied by some type of performance bond, ensuring that the contractor will perform the work as designed at the price bid. This ensures that bidders are sincere in their prices.

The time and place of the receipt of the sealed bids must be clearly shown on all bid packages. NO LATE BIDS CAN BE RECEIVED WITHOUT COMPROMISING THE ENTIRE BIDDING PROCESS.

Small projects (up to $25,000)

A bid of this size can normally be handled informally. The process of calling a selected list of local contractors will usually be sufficient and will probably get the best price.

Larger projects (over $25,000)

A formal bid process is usually necessary to ensure fairness, accuracy, and a competitive result. The process starts with advertising for bids. Advertising frequently is initiated prior to the completion of the plans, with an effective date for picking up the completed plans and specifications. The larger, more complex the project, the wider the range of advertising necessary. Governmental agencies usually have minimum advertising standards. They advertise in the legal advertisement section of the local paper and papers in larger nearby cities, and in professional construction journal(s). In addition, designers or clients frequently have a list of contractors who have successfully built past projects and/or who have indicated an interest in bidding on future projects. As a minimum, the advertisement should consist of

- A description of the project and kind of work required,
- The date and place plans can be picked up,
- The cost of plans and specifications (usually only sufficient to cover printing costs),
- The bid date and time, and
- Client identification.

The approximate value of the project is sometimes included, although some designers and clients do not wish to give out this information. With complex projects, it is desirable to schedule a pre-bid conference to explain the design and bidding process to prospective bidders. During the bidding period, questions are frequently raised by one or more prospective bidders. If the questions require design modifications or clarifications, the questions must be answered in writing in the form of an addendum to all holders of plans.

Opening and Reviewing of Bids

The designers or their representatives are usually present at the bid opening. After the bids are opened and read, it is necessary to analyze them and decide to whom the contract is to be awarded. The technical analysis is usually done by the designers, who consider whether the bid is complete, the prices are reasonable, and the contractor is able to do the work. A recommendation is then made. The legal analysis by the attorney is conducted concurrently examining whether bonds are attached, all necessary signatures are included, and all required in formation is provided.

Award of Contract

Assuming favorable analysis by all involved and that the bids are acceptable to the client, the contract will be awarded. Most contracts are awarded to the lowest qualified bidder. Sometimes, however, the low bidder is not large enough or does not have the expertise to do the work required. Occasionally some bids are improperly prepared. In these situations, they may be rejected, and the next lowest qualified bidder will be awarded the contract, or the project is re-bid. This can lead to problems with the disqualified bids or bidders and is why an attorney should be present.

Step 12: Construction

The architect should visit the site at least twice monthly at appropriate intervals during the construction stage and make the owner generally familiar with the progress and quality of the work in writing. The architect has other responsibilities, including certifying the payments represented to the owner for payment;

The construction step of a project goes through several phases. The number of phases depends upon the scope of the project and the contracting agency. Two general guidelines govern the construction step: (1) the larger the project, the more steps required, and (2) governmental projects usually have more contractual controls. At least some, and perhaps all, of the following steps will be required during construction:

Preconstruction conference

A meeting between the contracting agency and the contractor(s) prior to the commencement of construction to review the contract items and make sure there is an understanding of how the job is to be undertaken.

Construction

Set up or mobilization as well as the actual construction of the facility.

Change orders

Defined as an official document requested by either the contractor or the contracting agency that changes the approved contract documents. These changes usually include an adjustment of the bid price and a benefit to the contractor. It is better to avoid all change orders. Where this is not possible, be prepared to pay a premium price and to accept delays in contract completion.

Pre-final inspection and preparation of punch list

The initial review of a completed construction project. This inspection should have all the affected parties' decision-makers present, including the owner or his or her representative, the architect, the contractor(s), and any subcontractors. At this time, it is also desirable to have the facility operation supervisor present. During this review, a "punch list" is prepared of any work that needs completing by the contractor prior to a final inspection. All items that are not completed or are not completed according to specifications should be included on the list. The punch list is then agreed upon and signed by all affected parties. The contractor must then correct and/or finish all the items on the list. When the punch list is completed, it is time to call for a final inspection.

As-built drawings and catalogue cuts

Defined as the drawings prepared by the contractor showing how the project was actually built. These drawings will be of great value to the operations and maintenance staffs. They must know exactly what facilities were actually built and their locations to be able to maintain the project effectively.

Catalogue cuts are printed information supplied by the manufacturers on materials and equipment used in the project construction. This material is necessary so that the operating staff will be able to learn about the material and equipment. In addition, it is needed for locating necessary replacement parts. It must also be included in working drawings and specifications of future renovations and/or expansion of the project.

Preparation of an operations manual

An operations manual contains written instructions on how to operate and maintain special equipment. The minimum data included should be how to start up, how to shut down, inspection(s) time intervals and what should be inspected, schedule of required maintenance, safety precautions, and whom to contact for specialized repair assistance.

Training on how to operate the project

This contract item is usually included only for larger projects that are unfamiliar to the people who will operate them.

Final inspection

The final inspection should concentrate on items not found acceptable during any previous inspections. The same review team that made the pre-final inspection should be assembled for the final inspection.

Acceptance of completed project

Assuming all the work has been completed as shown on the plans and described in the specifications, the project should be accepted and turned over to the owner or operator. Further, if the contractor has posted a performance bond guaranteeing the work, it should be released by the contracting agency.

If at all possible, avoid partial acceptances. Sometimes it is necessary to take over a part or parts of a project prior to completion of the entire project. If this becomes necessary, the contractor will have the opportunity to blame future problems and/or delays on having to work around the people using the project.

Maintenance period

When living plants are involved, many contractors have a maintenance period included after the acceptance of the project. This can last anywhere from 30 days or more (for lawns) to 90 days for flowers, and frequently one full growing season for ground cover, vines, shrubs, and trees.

Bond period

Most government projects and some larger projects require the contractor to post not only a performance bond, but a one-year (or some other specified period) warranty on the quality of the work. Usually the bond requires the contractor to replace or repair any defective or damaged items during the time covered by the bond. Typical items would be leaking roofs, infiltration of ground water into sewer lines, puddling of water in parking lots or tennis courts, etc.

Bond inspection and final acceptance

At the end of the bond period, another inspection is held by the original final inspection team. Prior to release of the bond, any problems that have been uncovered during this inspection must be rectified at no cost to the contracting agency. It is important to note that when the bond is released, the contractor no longer has any responsibility to the project.

Step 13: Review

The project has been completed and turned over to the client. Does the project do what it was designed to from the standpoint of the (a) client, (b) user, (c) affected neighbors and/or public, (d) manager and operator, and (e) design team? There are two basic kinds of information to be gathered: information on people and on physical conditions.

Summary

A very important process in the construction of a facility is the selection of the most appropriate site. Many variables must be considered when selecting a site, including research, regional analysis, site analysis, program, functional analysis, combine site and function, land use, refinement, site plan/overall design, construction documents, bidding, construction, and review. If the site selection process is successful, the building project will be well established.

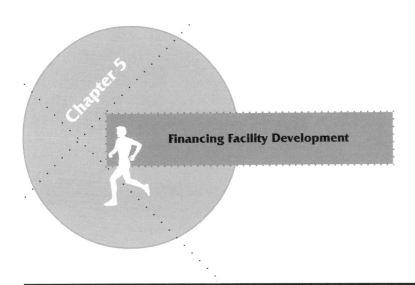

Thomas H. Sawyer, Indiana State University

Recreation and sport facilities are integral parts of communities. Schools, community organizations, teams, leagues, and special interest groups use the facilities for business, entertainment, recreation, and sports. Interscholastic, intercollegiate, and other educational entities, as well as professional teams, use facilities for a variety of entertainment, recreation, sport, and non-sport-related activities.

Sport arenas, stadiums, multipurpose facilities, and parks are financed in one of three common ways: public, private, or joint public/private. This chapter will focus on the financial methods used to build recreational and sport facilities. Several mechanisms are available in structuring public sector involvement in recreation and sport facility development, expansion, and renovation. The financial arrangements of a project are often the foundation for a successful facility. Budgets, cash flow, and financial statements depend on the facility's debt service arrangements. The objective of recreation and sport financial management in the public sector is to minimize public risk, which translates into maximization of municipal cash flow (Regan, 1997). The objective of private sport management is to maximize shareholder wealth, which translates into maximization of stock price (Regan, 1997).

Learning Objectives

After reading this chapter, the student will be able to
- understand the various types of financing options available for construction of facilities, and
- describe the financial team for a building project.

Introduction
Financing Options

Financing recreation and sport facilities requires cooperation between public and private entities. The common types of financing options are public, private, and joint public and private.

Public funding

A variety of taxes can be levied. The most common include hotel/motel tax, restaurant tax, auto rental tax, taxi tax, "sin" taxes (e.g., liquor, tobacco), sales tax, road tax, utility tax, property tax, business license tax, and team tax. The taxes most favorably viewed by local taxpayers are the hotel, restaurant, and auto rental taxes, as they are more likely to be shouldered by tourists (Miller, 1997). Planners should understand from the outset that continual tax increases can generate citizen concern.

Another tax strategy used by governments to stimulate private sector investment and create employment in the community is to offer property tax abatements (Howard & Crompton, 1995). Abatement programs exist in approximately two-thirds of the states (Severn, 1992). Typically, they are awarded whenever they are requested (Wolkoff, 1985); therefore, they often are part of a city's incentive package in negotiations with professional franchises (Howard & Crompton, 1995). A tax abatement will exempt an organization's assets from property taxation for a given period of time. It may be for all or a portion of the tax. The length of time varies according to the state enabling legislation.

The issuing of bonds is the most common way for a city or county to generate the needed money for recreation and sport facilities (Miller, 1997). A bond is defined as "an interest-bearing certificate issued by a government or corporation, promising to pay interest and to repay a sum of money (the principal) at a specified date in the future" (Samuelson & Nordhaus, 1985, 828). According to Howard and Crompton (1995) a bond is "a promise by the borrower (bond issuer) to pay back to the lender (bond holder) a specified amount of money, with interest, within a specified period of time." (58) Bonds issued by a government or a subdivision of a state are referred to as municipal bonds. Municipal bonds are typically exempt from federal, state, and local taxes on earned interest. Bond buyers can include individuals, organizations, institutions, or groups desiring to lend money at a predetermined interest rate. However, according to Miller (1997), bonds are not a panacea for recreation and sport facility development for two primary reasons—debt ceiling or debt capacity, and tax-exemption concerns by the public.

There are basically two types of government bonds: full-faith and credit obligations, and non-guaranteed. A general obligation bond is a full-faith and credit obligation bond. The general obligation bond refers to bonds that are repaid with a portion of the general property taxes. There are two key disadvantages to issuing general obligation bonds—it requires voter approval, and it increases local debt.

Non-guaranteed bonds have been the most common type of bonds used in funding recreation and sport facilities (Howard & Crompton, 1995). These bonds are sold on the basis of repayment from other designated revenue sources. If revenue falls short of what is required to make debt payments, the government entity does not have to make up the difference. There are three main advantages for using this funding mechanism: voter approval generally is not required, debt is not considered statutory debt, and those who benefit the most from the facility pay for it.

Currently, there are three popular types of non-guaranteed funding mechanisms: revenue bonds, certificates of participation, and tax increment financing. Revenue bonds can be backed exclusively by the revenue accruing from the project or from a designated revenue source, such as hotel/motel tax, restaurant tax, auto rental tax, or a combination of these taxes and others.

Certificates of participation involve a government entity buying the facility. The government entity then leases portions of the facility to the general public, and monies generated from the leases are used to pay off the facility's capital expenses. However, there is a moral rather than a legal obligation to appropriate funds if lease payments are inadequate or if the lessee goes out of business.

"Over half the states now have enabling legislation authorizing tax increment financing (TIF)" (Howard & Crompton, 1995, p. 102). TIF is available when an urban area has been identified for renewal or redevelopment. Real estate developed with the use of TIF is attractive to stakeholders, as tax increases are not necessary (Miller, 1997). The tax base of the defined area is frozen, and any increases in the tax base are used to repay the TIF bonds. The economics of any TIF are dependent on the development potential of a chosen site and its surrounding land (Regan, 1997).

Special authority bonds have been used to finance stadiums or arenas by special public authorities, which are entities with public powers (e.g., Niagara Power Authority, New York State Turnpike Authority, or the Tennessee Valley Authority) that are able to operate outside normal constraints placed on governments. Primarily, this has been used as a way to circumvent public resistance to new sports projects (i.e., Georgia Dome, Oriole Park at Camden Yards, or Stadium Authority of Pittsburgh [Three Rivers Stadium]) and construct them without receiving public consent through a referendum. Without having to pass a voter referendum, the authorities float the bonds that are sometimes guaranteed or accepted as a moral obligation by the state (Howard & Crompton, 1995).

Additional sources beyond taxes and bonding available from the public sector include state and federal appropriations and public grants.

Private Funding

Private-sector investment is preferred by most stakeholders as a result of declining public monies and questionable economic impacts (Miller, 1997). Private-sector investments take on a variety of forms and degrees of contribution. The private-sector regularly contributes to financing of recreation and sport facilities, in ways such as the following:

- Donation of cash—Cash is donated to the organization for a general or specific uses in return for a personal tax deduction.
- In-kind contributions—An organization, business, or craftsman donates equipment or time to the project in return for a tax deduction.
- Naming rights—Corporations vie for the right to place their name on the facility for a specific sum of money for a specific number of years (e.g., RCA Dome in Indianapolis, $2 million a year for 10 years; Conseco Fieldhouse in Indianapolis, $2.5 million a year for 10 years; Raymond James (Financial Inc.) Stadium in Tampa, $3.8 million a year for 10 years; Pacific Teleis Corporation—Pacific Bell Park, $50 million over 24 years).
- Concessionaire exclusivity—Companies purchase the exclusive rights for all concessions within a spectator facility for a specific number of dollars over a specific time period.
- Restaurant rights—Corporations purchase exclusive rights for all the restaurants within a spectator facility.
- Sponsorship packages—Large local and international firms are solicited to supply goods and services to a sporting organization at no cost or at substantial reduction in the whole- sale prices in return for visibility for the corporation.
- Life insurance packages—These programs solicit the proceeds from a life insurance policy purchased by a supporter to specifically benefit the organization upon the death of the supporter.
- Lease agreements—These programs lease facilities to other organizations during the off-season or lease additional spaces within the facility not used for the sporting activity, such as office space or retail space.
- Luxury suites—These areas are designed for VIP use and leased by large corporations to wine and dine their clients as well as to provide them entertainment.
- Preferred/premium seating (i.e., club seating—This is VIP seating located within the luxury suites or in the club areas of the stadium, which are the most expensive seats in the facility.
- Permanent seat licenses (PSL)—PSLs provide fans the right to purchase season tickets and actually choose the seat for which they buy the PSL, often for the life of the venue, in return for an upfront payment.
- Parking fees—These fees are generated from parking lots that surround the spectator facilities.
- Merchandise revenues—This income is generated by the sale of shirts, shorts, hats, pants, t-shirts, sweatshirts, key rings, glassware, dishware, luggage, sports cards, balls, bats, etc.

- Food and beverage serving rights—Companies purchase exclusive rights to soft drink, beer, and foods sold to spectators.
- Advertising rights—Rights are sold to various entities that wish to advertise to the spectators within the sport facility.
- Vendor/contractor equity—Vendor or contractor returns to the owner a specific percentage of the profit generated by the firms during the construction process.
- Bequests and trusts—Agreements are made with specific individuals that upon their deaths, a certain amount of their estates will be given to the organization.
- Real estate gifts, endowments, and securities—Agreements are made with specific individuals to give to an organization real estate, stocks, or mutual funds to support an endowment for a specific project. Only the annual income returned by the endowment would be used, not the principal.

The newest private-sector funding strategy, as described by Daniel Kaplan (*Sports Business Journal,* 1998), is called asset-backed securities (ABS). In 1998, Ascent Entertainment, owner of Denver's professional hockey and basketball teams, issued $130 million in asset-backed securities to help pay for the $160 million Pepsi Center arena. Asset-backed securities are investments secured by expected revenue in Ascent's case, contractually obligated fees from arena-naming rights, sponsorships, concession guarantees, and luxury-suite licenses. Unlike such traditional methods of financing as bank loans and bond issues, which generally require the commitment of all revenue generated by a facility, an ABS can be secured with just a portion of the revenue stream. Furthermore, an ABS issue does not require teams or owners to open their financial books to creditors.

The value of private-sector funding is best illustrated by the amount of revenue generated from private sources in the construction of The Ball Park in Arlington, Texas, which included $12.7 million from the ballpark's concessionaires, $6 million from first-year luxury suite revenues, $17.1 million from preferred-seat licenses, totaling $35.8 million (Brady & Howlett, 1996).

Private and Joint Public-Private Funding

Over the past decade, public-private partnerships have been developed to construct large public sport facilities. Typically, the public sector lends its authority to implement project funding mechanisms, while the private partner contributes project-related or other revenue sources. The expanded revenues generated by the facilities and their tenants have resulted in increases in the level of private funding (Regan, 1997). Recent examples of partnerships include the Alamodome (San Antonio), Coors Stadium (Denver), and Big Stadium (Saint Denis, France) (Regan, 1997).

Financial Team

All building projects need to assemble a proper financial team in order to design, organize, and finance a public, private, or public/private facility. A successful financial team should include the owner, facility manager, feasibility consultant, examination accountant, business plan consultant, financial advisor, facility consultant, architect, cost estimator, contractor, construction manager, senior underwriter, bond council, and owner's legal counsel (Regan, 1997). The financial team must work together to develop the goals and objectives of the community and/or owner. Successful facility financing is a partnership between the regional community, the owner, government, the financial institutions, and the investors.

Essential Points of a Financial Plan

The following are essentials in a financial plan. These points should be broken down for each year of the financial plan.

- The mission, goals, and objectives for the overall plan;
- An analysis of the organization's current financial situation;
- An analysis of revenue projections versus expense projections, including dollars obtained through private fund raising and government resources;
- An analysis of capital projections throughout the time period of the plan broken down into needs versus ideals; and
- Specific information regarding the intended financial state at the end of the time period.

Summary

A building project will just be a dream without a financial plan to bring it to reality. The planners need to consider not only the physical facilities but also how they will be financed.

Todd L. Seidler, University of New Mexico

Sports and recreation facilities that are poorly planned, designed, or constructed often increase participants' exposure to hazardous conditions and not only render the facility harder to maintain, operate, and staff, but can also significantly increase the organization's exposure to liability. A poorly designed facility can usually be traced to a lack of effort or expertise of the planning and design team. It is not uncommon for a sport, physical education, or recreation facility to be designed by an architect who has little or no experience in that type of building. For those without the proper background and understanding of the unique properties of sport and recreation facilities, many opportunities for mistakes exist that may lead to increased problems related to safety, operations, and staffing.

Design problems commonly seen in activity facilities include inadequate safety zones around courts and fields, poorly planned pedestrian traffic flow through activity areas, poor access control and security, lack of proper storage space, and the use of improper building materials. Often, safety problems related to design are difficult, expensive, or impossible to fix once the facility has been built. It is essential that these facilities be planned and designed by professionals with activity-related knowledge and experience.

In order to protect themselves from claims of negligence, managers of sport and recreation programs and facilities have a number of legal responsibilities they are expected to perform. In this case, negligence is the failure to act as a reasonably prudent and careful sport or facility manager would act in the same or similar circumstances. In general, facility managers are required to run their programs so as not to create an unreasonable risk of harm to participants, staff, and spectators. One of their specific legal duties is to ensure that the environment provided is free from foreseeable risks or hazards. Unsafe facilities are one of the leading claims made in negligence lawsuits related to sports and physical activity. When discussing facility liability, Page (1988, p. 138) called it "one of the largest subcategories within the broad spectrum of tort law." More specifically, managers of sports

facilities are expected to provide a reasonably safe environment and at least to carry out the following five duties:

- Keep the premises in safe repair.
- Inspect the premises to discover obvious and hidden hazards.
- Remove the hazards or warn of their presence.
- Anticipate foreseeable uses and activities by invitees and take reasonable precautions to protect the invitee from foreseeable dangers.
- Conduct operations on the premises with reasonable care for the safety of the invitee.

According to van der Smissen (1990, p. 235), "The design, layout, and construction of areas and facilities can provide either safe or hazardous conditions, enhancing or detracting from the activity in which one is engaged." A facility that has been properly planned, designed, and constructed will greatly enhance the ability of the facility manager to effectively carry out these legal duties. A look at common safety problems in sports facilities has determined that they can usually be traced to two primary causes: poor facility planning and design and poor management.

When discussing safe facilities, Maloy (2001, p. 105) states, "Most liability problems dealing with safe environment, however, stem from maintenance and operation of the premises, not their design and construction." Even though this may be true, it is important to understand that there are many things that can be done during the planning process that will enhance the sport manager's ability to safely and properly maintain and operate the premises. A well-designed facility makes the management process more effective and efficient. It follows that the easier it is to maintain a facility, the more likely it is that it will be done well. According to Jewell (1992, p. 111) in his book, *Public Assembly Facilities*, "Public safety begins with good architectural design . . . ." Therefore, the majority of this chapter will focus on the planning and design of safe facilities.

Learning Objectives

After reading this chapter, the student will be able to:
- understand negligence and become familiar with the basic legal duties expected of facility managers,
- understand the role that good facility planning has in the design and construction of safe facilities,
- identify at least five methods of controlling access to facilities,
- describe the importance of and identify the minimal guidelines for safety or buffer zones,
- discuss the problem of traffic patterns within facilities and identify alternatives, and
- understand the need for selecting the proper materials for floors, walls and ceilings.

Planning Safe Facilities

In order to plan and build a facility that is safe, efficient, and that optimally supports activities likely to occur in each area, a thorough understanding of those activities is required. During the planning process, each individual space within the facility must be studied in an attempt to identify every activity that will, or might take place in that space. After this has been done, the requirements of the space necessary for each of the activities must be determined. For example, if it is determined that a multi-purpose room will house classes in aerobic dance, martial arts, yoga, and gymnastics, and will also act occasionally as a small lecture set-up with portable chairs, the needs of each of these activities must be met, even though some may be in conflict with others. After the design requirements have been identified for each activity, a master list for each area should be developed. This master list is then used to plan that area in order to reduce the number of design errors as much as possible. The following are areas where errors in planning often create hazardous situations within facilities:

Security and Access Control

When designing a facility, the following two kinds of access will be addressed: controlling access (1) to the facility and (2) within the facility. Controlling access to sport, recreation, and fitness facilities is an important function of facility managers. Legal liability, deterrence of vandalism and theft, member safety and satisfaction, and maintaining exclusivity and value for those who pay for the privilege of using the facility are a few of the reasons it is necessary to deny access to those who don't belong. A properly designed and equipped facility along with the use of computerized controls and a well-trained staff can make access control relatively easy to deal with.

Many facilities, especially older spectator facilities, can be a nightmare to control. Fire regulations require many outside doors for quick evacuation. When limited access is desired, how can these doors be secured, monitored, and controlled without violating fire codes?

When designing a facility, it is often advantageous to plan for one control point through which everyone entering or leaving the building must pass. This control point is usually staffed during open hours so the appropriate fee is paid, ID card checked, or permission given to those who are eligible to enter. If a higher degree of control is desired, a door, gate, or turnstile can also be used.

Recently, many computer software programs have become available to help with access control. If patrons and staff are issued ID cards, such as in a club, school, or corporate setting, systems with magnetic strip or bar code readers can be used to quickly check a person's status. Swiping the ID card through an electronic card reader can determine if the user is eligible to enter. In systems designed for high traffic flow, the computer can be connected directly to a turnstile. If, after scanning the ID, the computer determines that the person should be accepted for entry, it can send a signal to release the turnstile and allow entry. This, however, does not prevent an unauthorized person from using someone else's ID. For increased security, picture ID's are desirable to ensure that the person using the card is the legal owner. Other new systems of access control include software programs that, upon scanning an ID card, display a picture of the patron on a computer monitor. If a higher level of security is desired, some systems actually use biometric identification. These systems may scan a patron's fingerprint, palm print, or even retina and compare it to those in the computer's memory. These systems are not only used to admit members, but can also track attendance and adherence to fitness programs, determine patrons' attendance habits, and set staffing levels to provide services at the proper times of the day and to provide information for marketing efforts.

Example of an illegal
control mechanism.

Another aspect of access control that is improving with advances in technology is the replacement of standard door locks and keys. Systems now exist that place an electronic card reader at each door. Instead of a key, each authorized person is issued a card that can be passed through any of the card readers. A central computer receives the information from the card and compares it with the information stored in memory. The computer determines if the person who was issued that card is authorized to open that particular door and either unlocks it or refuses access.

This type of system has many advantages. The computer can be programmed to allow access only to certain areas for each individual card holder. A part-time employee may have a card that works only on certain doors, while the facility manager's card can be programmed to open them all, like a master key. Also, the computer may be programmed so that certain cards only work during specified hours.

In the case of regular locks, if someone loses a key, it is often necessary to re-key many of the locks in the building. New keys must then be issued to everyone, often at great expense. With the card system, if someone loses an access card, that card can simply be turned off on the computer and a new card issued to the owner. The old card then becomes useless.

Another feature of the card access system is that each time someone uses a card to open a door it can be recorded on the computer. For example, computer records may show not only that a certain door was opened on Tuesday night at 11:05 but also whose card was used and if the person went in or out through the door. This information can be extremely valuable for facility security. The system can also be connected to the fire alarm and programmed to automatically unlock any or all of the doors when the alarm is triggered. Though it may initially be more expensive to install the card reader system than to install standard locks, it will usually pay for itself in increased efficiency, convenience, and long-term cost.

It is often desirable to control access to certain areas within a facility. Most buildings limit access to areas such as equipment rooms, office areas, mechanical rooms, or storage, but when a multi-use facility has more than one event or activity taking place at the same time, it may also be desirable to separate different parts of the building. For example, in a college activity center, it is not uncommon to have a varsity basketball game in the main arena while the rest of the facility is kept open for recreation. With good planning, this can be accomplished by physically separating the spaces through the use of different entrances and exits, different floors, and locking doors, gates, and fences that can quickly restrict passage from one area to another. There are two basic concepts to be familiar with for controlling access within a facility: (1) horizontal and (2) vertical circulation control.

Horizontal circulation control is a common method of managing access to different parts of a facility when there is a need to separate areas on the same floor. In the above example, when the entire facility is open for recreation, an open access plan is utilized. However, when a varsity basketball game is scheduled, certain doors, gates, and fences can be opened or closed in order to restrict spectator access to the arena without having to close down the rest of the building.

Sometimes it may be most efficient to plan for controlling access through vertical circulation control. For example, it may be desirable in a certain arena to have limited access to the lower level. This level may include the playing floor, locker rooms, coaches' offices, training rooms, and storage areas. By limiting public access to the entire floor, it becomes much easier to secure each individual area. In some arenas and stadiums, the luxury suites are located on one floor and access to that floor can be gained only by certain elevators, stairways, or gates. Patrons in general seating areas cannot gain access to the suite level, thereby enhancing security and also providing a feel of exclusivity for suite holders. If vertical circulation is needed for a large number of people, providing non-skid ramps with good hand-rails or escalators usually provides a safer method than stairs.

Safety Zones

Some activities require a certain amount of space surrounding the court, field, or equipment to enhance the safety of the participants. An inadequate amount of space for a safety or buffer zone can present foreseeable risks of injury. A number of lawsuits have been based on claims that an injury occurred as a result of an inadequate safety or buffer zone. Whether it is to separate two adjacent courts or to provide room between the court and a wall or another object, safety zones must be considered.

Failure to provide activity space free of obstruction.

Indoor

Basketball courts should have at least 10 feet (preferred), or six feet (minimum) of clear space around the court that is free from walls, obstructions, or other courts (NCAA, 2001, p. 33). Anything less than six feet presents a foreseeable risk of collision. The area under the basket is especially important. If a full 10 feet of clear space between the end-line and the wall cannot be provided, padding should be placed on the wall to soften the impact where players are most likely to hit if they lose control while going out of bounds. It is recommended that wall padding cover from the floor to a height of seven feet and extend the entire width of the court. When walls are padded, typically it begins six to 12 inches above the floor, rises only to five or six feet and extends only the width of the lane. In these facilities, players diving for a ball and sliding into the wall, those over six feet tall or others outside the lane receive no protection. It is also recommended that wall pads be considered even when the safety zone is greater than 10 feet. One exception to the 10-foot guideline is for competitive volleyball. In this case, it is recommended that a minimum of 15 feet of clear space beyond the end lines be provided. Another problem that is common in basketball is with the scorer's table. These are nearly always placed within three feet of the sideline and often go unpadded. Padded scorer's tables are available, but there are too few in use, especially at the high school level.

Another area where safety or buffer zones are important and often overlooked is in the weight room. Placing weight equipment too close together can present a serious safety hazard. Most weight equipment should be spaced a minimum of three feet apart. This measurement should be made with the movement of the machine or exercise in mind. Some exercises require a horizontal movement, and the safety or buffer zone should be measured from the extremes of this movement. An example occurs with many leg extension machines. As the movement is executed, the legs straighten and extend another two feet or so out from the machine. The safety zone should be measured from the point of full extension. Some exercises require more than a three-foot safety zone. Certain free-weight exercises such as squats and power cleans require more room because of the amount of weight and relative lack of control typically encountered during such exercises.

It should be recognized that an activity area such as a gymnasium may be used occasionally for activities other than those it was designed for. It is not uncommon for outdoor activities such as softball, ultimate frisbee, or track practice to be moved indoors during inclement weather. These activities must be considered when planning a safe gym. The main point is that not all activities will use the traditional court markings for their activity area. This means that the distance from out-of-bounds to the wall is not always a safety

Dangerous overlap of adjacent activity areas.

Activity spaces and surrounding areas should also be designed to be free of obstructions such as doors, poles, columns, and supports. If any such obstruction cannot be moved or eliminated from the activity area or safety zone, it must be padded. All other protrusions that may cause a safety hazard in the gymnasium should be avoided if possible. Common examples of such protrusions include drinking fountains and fire extinguishers, which, during the planning process, can easily be recessed into a wall. Standard doorknobs located in an activity area can also present a hazard, and alternative types of knobs that are recessed in the door are available. Such handles are commonly used on racquetball courts.

factor for those activities that ignore the floor markings. If these activities can be identified and planned for before construction, there is an opportunity to provide a safe environment for them also. Otherwise, it becomes a management concern and a potentially hazardous aspect of the facility that must be compensated for.

Allowing more than one activity to take place in one area can be dangerous. Playing more than one basketball game on two or more courts that overlap, such as using a side basket for one game and an end basket for another, produces a situation in which an injury is foreseeable.

Outdoor

Outdoor fields and courts have many of the same problems. Overlapping fields are a common occurrence and can cause a significant safety hazard if activities are allowed to take place simultaneously. A common example is two softball fields that share a part of the outfields. If games are being played at the same time on each field, the outfielders are at risk of collision. Overlapping courts and fields should be avoided if at all possible. An alternative might be to turn the fields around.

Two activity areas adjacent to each other can be just as dangerous as those that overlap. It is not uncommon to see a baseball field located next to a track. Sometimes this can lead to joggers on the track having to dodge errant baseballs. All adjacent activity areas must be planned with the idea that activities may occur simultaneously, so that foreseeably dangerous situations can be avoided.

Another common design that can produce several hazardous conditions is the typical football field that is surrounded by a track. Very often, facilities for field events are constructed inside the track and include asphalt runways and pit areas in addition to the track and pit areas constructed with concrete curbs. In this situation, there is often little distance between the football sidelines and the inner perimeter of the track, much less the runways, pits, and the commonly used concrete pole vault box.

Ideally, two activity areas, such as a football field and a track, should not be combined in one space. Realistically, there often is not sufficient space to construct the two separately, and they must be combined. If this type of mixed use field is necessary, it is recommended that there be no obstructions within 15 feet of the sidelines or end zone of the football field. At the very least, the jumping and vaulting runways can be placed outside the track. If bleachers on the opposite side of the field are not adequate to accommodate crowds, removable bleachers can be temporarily installed over those runways and pit areas. The high-jump approach as well as the shot put and discus pads can be located more than 15 feet from the end zone without encroaching on the track.

Other common obstructions that can create hazardous conditions are telephone and/or electrical boxes used during football games that are often placed adjacent to the inner perimeter of the track. These are typically metal boxes mounted on poles several inches above the ground. A runner (either track or football) who is bumped, stumbles, or is tackled, can fall and strike the sharp metal receptacle and be severely injured. If such boxes are essential, they should be placed underground with the top flush with the field surface. Any obstructions that are within 15 feet of the field should be padded for safety. The primary problem with padding obstructions is that, even padded, they are still a hazard. Also, the padding deteriorates over time, or disappears, or people get lax about installing it prior to usage of the field. It is better to plan and construct the area without such hazards in the first place.

Another common safety hazard often seen in high school baseball and softball facilities is open dugouts. All dugouts should be screened in front to protect those within from line-drive foul balls and errant throws. Providing protected access to and from the dugout is also important. Water fountains and bat racks should be placed inside or behind the dugout with players being able to gain access to them from the dugout without being directly exposed to the field.

Portable soccer goals that are left out on fields also can create a very hazardous situation. Several children are killed or severely injured each year by climbing on goals that are not anchored to the ground. These goals are often heavy, poorly balanced and tend to tip over when someone hangs on them. Injuries typically occur when a child hangs from the crossbar and is then crushed as it tips over. These incidents can be prevented by either permanently anchoring soccer goals or using a chain or cable to lock them in place.

Pedestrian Traffic Flow

A common flaw in planning a facility that can cause safety problems is failure to properly plan for pedestrian traffic flow from one area to another. Requiring people to walk through an activity area in order to get to their desired destination can result in a needlessly high-risk situation. A very common example is when the main entrance to the locker room can only be reached by walking across the gym floor. The result is people entering and leaving the locker room while an activity is taking place in the same space.

Another example of poor traffic flow planning often occurs when pedestrians are forced to walk across a court or between two adjacent courts to get to another part of the facility. This also puts pedestrians in a situation where a collision with a participant is likely.

Planning pedestrian traffic flow within some activity areas is an important consideration. A weight room can be more hazardous if people do not have good, clear, open pathways to move around to different parts of the room. The design and layout of the weight room should take into account the movement of the users, especially during times of peak occupancy. Laying out the optimal pathways within the weight room that provide users with easy access to the more popular areas or machines will help prevent excess traffic between machines.

Storage

One of the most common complaints that facility managers report when asked about their facility is a lack of adequate storage space. The following is a typical example of how this often occurs. A new facility is planned with plenty of storage space in the early stages of planning. As the design is developed and the estimated cost of construction becomes clearer, it is determined that the project is over budget and something must be cut. Storage areas are often the first spaces to go.

Without proper storage space, equipment will usually be stored in a corner of the gym, in one of the hallways or on the side of the pool deck. Beside the fact that improperly stored equipment is much more likely to be vandalized or stolen, it may also attract children (see attractive nuisance below) or others to use or play with it, usually unsupervised and not in the manner for which it was designed. Equipment such as mats and Port-a-pits, gymnastic apparatus, standards, nets, goals, chairs, hurdles, tables, ladders, maintenance equipment, etc., are often seen stacked in the corner

Example of lack of adequate storage space.

of gyms. No longer a common sight, trampolines were often pushed into a corner and left unattended. This improper storage and poor supervision led to many catastrophic injuries and deaths and has resulted in the elimination of trampolines from most programs today. It is essential that adequate storage space be planned and constructed and that it be readily accessible and easily secured to prevent unauthorized use of the contents.

Lack of sufficient storage space for outdoor equipment is also often a problem. Providing a fenced, lockable storage area for items that are too large to be moved indoors for things such as blocking sleds is recommended. A fully enclosed storage area for pole vault and high-jump pits, hurdles, judge's stands and other moveable equipment will provide protection from the weather, vandals and will prevent creating an attractive nuisance.

Proper Materials

Many factors must be considered during the selection of materials to be used in the construction of a sport or recreation facility. Among these are initial cost, functionality, durability and expected life span, ease, and cost of maintenance and aesthetics. Another often- overlooked factor is safety. Without proper consideration, building and finishing materials can play a large role in the inherent safety of the facility. The potential activities that may take place in every space must be studied thoroughly to ensure that the facility will optimally support each.

Flooring materials must be chosen with great care. Poor selection of the floor surface can contribute to significant safety hazards. One of the most dangerous examples commonly occurs in wet areas, such as locker rooms, shower

Inappropriate use of acoustical panels.

areas, training rooms, and pool decks. The material selected for the floors in these areas should be a long-lasting, easily maintained, non-slip surface. All too often, these wet areas are constructed with a smooth finish, such as smooth or polished concrete, linoleum, or terrazzo. These are excellent surfaces in the proper situation and are usually selected for durability and ease of maintenance. But they all can become extremely slippery when wet. Many excellent non-slip surfaces are available for areas where they may get wet. One of the best surfaces for wet areas is rough finish ceramic or quarry tile. All wet areas should be designed to slope toward a floor drain to avoid standing water.

Wall surfaces also offer opportunities for hazards to be designed into a facility. A major hazard often introduced into a facility is the use of glass in or near activity areas. Glass in doors or windows or covering fire extinguishers is a common cause of injury. Even the use of strengthened glass, such as windows with wire mesh, should be questioned in activity areas. Even though it takes greater force to break this kind of glass, it still occurs and may cause severe injuries.

Another relatively common problem has occurred with the use of glass in what most people think of as a non-activity area. The trophy case in the lobbies of most high school gyms is a good example. Planners often overlook the fact that lobby space is frequently used for activities, whether it's the wrestling team running in the halls during inclement weather, cheerleaders practicing, or just the everyday horseplay that occurs with teenagers. Safety glass of some sort should be used in this area. Mirrors used in weight rooms and dance studios must be selected and located with care. They should be high-strength, shatter-proof glass designed for activity areas. Weight-room mirrors should be mounted about 18 inches above the floor to avoid contact with a barbell that may roll against the wall.

It is also important to select proper ceiling materials. Acoustic ceiling panels can be excellent for classrooms and offices but can become a maintenance headache and safety hazard when used in activity areas such as gyms. Acoustic panels are not meant to withstand abuse from balls and often break or shatter when hit.

The materials selected must be chosen with care in order to withstand the abuse likely to occur in each particular area. Lighting fixtures in activity areas must be appropriate to withstand the activities that will take place. In gyms where balls or other objects may hit the lights, each fixture must be designed to withstand potential punishment. The proper light typically has a plastic cover and a wire screen for protection. If the fixture is struck hard enough to shatter the bulb, the broken glass will be contained by the plastic cover and prevented from falling to the floor. Fixtures without this feature may shower broken glass on the participants below when struck.

Supervision

Designing a facility so that it can be supervised efficiently is a great advantage for two major reasons. First, a lack of proper supervision is one of the most common allegations made in lawsuits alleging negligence in sport and physical activity programs. The design and layout of the facility are often overlooked as a primary reason for poor supervision. Some facilities are easy to supervise and some are not.

Second, a poorly designed facility may require five staff members to properly supervise activities, whereas a well-designed building of similar size and offerings may require only three. Figuring the cost of paying even one extra supervisor, using the number of hours the facility is open each year over the life of the facility, can result in a dramatic increase in cost.

A well-designed facility can be adequately supervised by a minimum number of staff members. Design features that enhance efficiency of supervision include activity areas that are close together and easily monitored. Instead of spreading activity areas around the perimeter of the facility, one efficient method being used is to design a long central hallway or mall off of which are placed the activity areas. With proper windows or other means of observing, a supervisor can view many different areas in a short period of time.

Locker rooms are another area that is often poorly designed for adequate supervision. Concrete floors and walls, steel lockers with sharp corners, and standing water, all make locker rooms perhaps the single most dangerous facility in sport and recreation. In school settings, there is also a lot of unstructured time with classes coming and going, showering and changing clothes. It all adds up to a need for close, active supervision. Most locker rooms are laid out in rows of high lockers, which makes it difficult to supervise the activities and easy for someone to hide. All too often, the teacher/coaches' office is located in a position that does not allow an adequate view of the entire room. Providing the ability to easily and adequately supervise must be considered while planning and designing a locker room.

Another innovation that is seeing increased usage is Closed Circuit Television (CCTV) systems. A well-designed system can allow a supervisor in one location to visually monitor many diverse locations, both within and outside of the facility. Often the supervisor is equipped with a two-way radio in order to stay in constant communication with attendants on duty inside and outside the building. If a problem is observed on the CCTV monitor, the supervisor can direct an attendant to respond immediately. A properly planned system may allow for a smaller staff than is usually required, while actually increasing supervisory coverage of the facility.

Miscellaneous Considerations

All facilities must be planned in compliance with all applicable codes. This includes all Occupational Safety and Health Administration (OSHA), Americans with Disabilities Act (ADA), fire, safety, and health codes that are appropriate for a given situation.

Humidity must be controlled throughout the facility. Excessive humidity not only reduces the comfort level but can cause corrosion and deterioration of building materials. Under the right conditions, high humidity can also condense onto activity floors, steps, walkways, etc., and create a dangerous condition. Lighting levels must be sufficient for the activity. Improper lighting can cause a hazardous situation, especially in areas where participants must visually track fast-moving objects such as in racquetball.

Emergency safety device.

Signage can be an important part of a facility risk management program. Rules, procedures, and warning signs must be developed and posted in proper locations.

Summary

This chapter focused primarily on planning and designing facilities for safety and risk management. It is important to understand that this is only a first step in running a safe program. Once the facility is open, it is essential that a complete risk management program be established and practiced on an ongoing basis.

One of the most common claims made in negligence lawsuits related to sports and recreation is that of unsafe facilities. Managers of sport, physical education, and recreation programs have a legal and moral obligation to make their programs as free from foreseeable risks as possible. As part of this, managers must be aware of how unsafe facilities can increase potential hazards for participants, staff, and spectators alike. In our increasingly litigious society, unnecessary injuries are likely to lead to lawsuits and increased exposure of the program's financial resources to loss. Safe facilities are essential, and a well-planned facility is safer, as well as easier to supervise, manage, and maintain.

Many of the factors that go into making a facility safe are easy to implement if they are planned from the beginning. Once the concrete has been poured and the facility is open, it often becomes much harder or even impossible to make changes. Planning and designing facilities with safety and risk management in mind can help prevent problems, headaches, injuries, and lawsuits in the future.

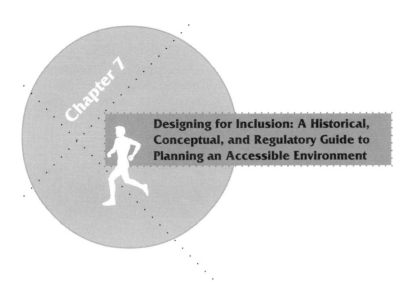

Designing for Inclusion: A Historical, Conceptual, and Regulatory Guide to Planning an Accessible Environment

Richard J. LaRue, The University of New England

Introduction

This chapter presents historical, conceptual, and regulatory information, as well as a comprehensive listing of planning resources related to designing for inclusion. Primary to the regulatory development of accessibility planning today, are the key statutes from the Americans with Disabilities Act (ADA), and information regarding the most recent accessibility guidelines as published by the U.S. Access Board. Many of the ADA statutes have already faced their first test in court, and these cases have resulted in both clearer regulations and improved compliance. Where historically even the government was sometimes slow to respond to early accessibility legislation, such as the Architectural Barriers Act (ABA) and the Uniform Federal Accessibility Standards (UFAS), nearly every organization is now taking strides to meet or exceed the ADA statutes and the Americans with Disabilities Act Accessibility Guidelines (ADAAG).

However, even with published standards and regular updates, it is possible for planners and designers to make serious mistakes. This chapter "designing for inclusion," is also organized to provide serious planners and designers with the accessibility standards, guidelines, and resources necessary to meet with success.

Learning Objectives

After reading this the chapter the student should be able to:
- understand the historical development of constitutional protection and the civil rights of the disabled, including the ADAAG (revised for publication in 2001); ADA of 1990; UFAS of 1984; Sections 502 and 504 of the Rehabilitation Act of 1973 (including amendments); and the Architectural Barriers Act of 1968 (including amendments);
- understand the concept of designing for inclusion and further appreciate the benefits of accessibility implementation for all people;
- understand the legal meaning for—and scope of— ADA terminology, including: architectural barriers, undue hardship, readily achievable, and reasonable accommodation;
- understand the difference between standards and guidelines related to the ADA and other federal accessibility legislation; and,
- understand the legal advantages related to compliance including tax incentives, and the administrative responsibilities related to regulatory enforcement.

The Federal Government and Civil Rights Legislation Related to Persons with Disabilities

The Architectural Barriers Act (ABA) of 1968, authorized four primary agencies: The General Services Administration (GSA), the Department of Defense (DoD), the Department of Housing and Urban Development (HUD), and the U.S. Postal Service (USPS) to issue accessibility standards in accordance with its respective statutory authority. "To ensure compliance with ABA efforts, Congress established the Architectural and Transportation Barriers Compliance Board (ATBCB) in Section 502 of the Rehabilitation Act of 1973" (U.S. Access Board, February 6, 2001, p. 3: *http://www.access-board.gov/ufas/ufas- html/ufas.htm#intro*).

The ATBCB is comprised of representatives from the four initial agencies in addition to seven other governmental agencies: Health and Human Services, Interior, Justice, Labor, and Transportation, and the Veterans Administration; and 11 members appointed from the general public by the President of the United States. A 1978 amendment to Section 502 of the Rehabilitation Act of 1973 added to the ATBCB's functions. This amendment required the ATBCB to issue minimum guidelines and requirements for the standards then established by the four standard-setting agencies (GSA, DoD,

HUD, and USPS). The final rule establishing the Guidelines now in effect was published in the FEDERAL REGISTER on August 4, 1982 " (U.S. Access Board, February 6, 2001: *http://www.access-board.gov/ufas/ufas-html/ufas.htm#intro*).

The four standard-setting agencies determined that the adopted uniform standards would, as much as possible, conform with the 1982 Guidelines of the ATBCB and be consistent with standards published by the American National Standards Institute (ANSI). "ANSI is a non-governmental national organization that publishes a wide variety of recommended standards. ANSI's standards for barrier-free design are developed by a committee made up of 52 organizations representing associations of handicapped people, rehabilitation professionals, design professionals, builders, and manufacturers" (U.S. Access Board, February 6, 2001, p. 3: *http://www.access-board.gov/ufas/ufas-html/ufas.htm#intro*).

It is important to note that ANSI's 1961 standards: "Specifications for Making Buildings and Facilities Accessible to, and Usable by, Physically Handicapped People," formed the technical basis for the first accessibility standards adopted by federal government and most state governments. The development of ANSI's revised standards in 1980 was based upon research funded by HUD. The 1980 ANSI standards were generally accepted by the private sector, including the Council of American Building Officials (U.S. Access Board, February 6, 2001: *http://www.access-board.gov/ufas/ufas-html/ufas.htm#intro*).

In 1984, the Uniform Federal Accessibility Standards (UFAS) became the standard used to enforce the ABA. The UFAS followed the ANSI 1980 standards in format, which as a matter of scope provisions and technical requirements, met or exceeded the comparable provisions of the ATBCB 1982 Guidelines (U.S. Access Board, February 6, 2001: *http://www.access- board.gov/ufas/ufas-html/ufas.htm#intro*).

The Americans with Disabilities Act (ADA) of 1990 significantly expanded the role of the ATBCB, now commonly known as the U.S. Access Board. Under the ADA, the U.S. Access Board became responsible for developing accessibility guidelines for entities covered by the Act and for providing technical assistance to individuals and organizations on the removal of architectural, transportation, and communication barriers.

In 1991 the U.S. Access Board published *The Americans with Disabilities Accessibility Guidelines* (ADAAG), considered more stringent than the UFAS guidelines. The U.S. Access Board maintains responsibility for revisions of the ADAAG as well as the UFAS. In November 2000, the U.S. Access Board published a comprehensive proposal to update both its ADA and ABA accessibility guidelines and to make them more consistent. Changes in these guidelines have been based upon the recommendations from an advisory committee the Board established to review the ADAAG (available online: *http://www.access-board.gov/ada-aba/commrept.htm*). The US Access Board intends to issue the ADAAG in final form in 2001 (US Access Board, February 4, 2001, pp. 2-3: *http://www.access-board.gov/publications/00Annual-Rept.htm*)

Other Related Legislation

Section 504 of the Rehabilitation Act of 1973, as amended, set out the functions of the ATBCB and further: "specified that 'no otherwise qualified handicapped person shall, on the basis of handicap, be excluded from participation in, be denied the benefits of, or otherwise be subjected to discrimination under any program which receives or benefits from Federal financial assistance'" (Lumpkin, 1998, p. 229).

The Education Amendment Act of 1974 "mandated that all children must be placed in the least restrictive environment (LRE), or the setting in which their optimal learning and development could occur" (Lumpkin, 1998, p. 229). The All Handicapped Children Act of 1975 (Public Law 94-142) "mandated that athletics be provided to disabled school students" (Lumpkin, 1998, p. 300). And, the Amateur Sports Act of 1978 "specified that the competitive needs of disabled athletes must be accommodated" (Lumpkin, 1998, p. 300).

The Telecommunications Act of 1996 requires the U.S. Access Board to develop and maintain accessibility guidelines for telecommunications and customer premises equipment (i.e., mandated closed-captioning options on the newest models of televisions). Access standards for electronic and information technology in the Federal sector were issued under Section 508 of the Rehabilitation Act Amendments of 1998 "which requires that such technology be accessible when developed, procured, maintained, or used by a Federal agency" (U.S. Access Board, February 4, 2001, p. 1: *http://www.access-board.gov/publications/00Annual-Rept.htm*).

On October 18, 2000 the U.S. Access Board published a comprehensive set of guidelines as part of the ADAAG that serve to provide access to play areas (available online: *http://www.access- board.gov/play/finalrule.htm*). "The guidelines cover the number of play components required to be accessible, accessible surfacing in play areas, ramp access and transfer system access to elevated structures, and access to soft contained play structures. They address play areas provided at schools, parks, childcare facilities (except those based in the operator's home, which are exempt), and other facilities subject to the ADA" (U.S. Access Board, February 4, 2001, p. 3: accommodation and commercial facilities to be designed, constructed, and altered in compliance with the accessibility standards published in the law. The ADA extends prohibited discrimination beyond state and local governments that were previously prohibited from discriminating under Section 504 of the Rehabilitation Act of 1973. This coverage now includes all services provided by state and local governments, regardless of whether they receive federal money or are privately funded.

The United States Department of Justice is the primary enforcing entity for Civil Rights discrimination under the Americans with Disabilities Act, enforcing Title I, Title II, and Title III. Whereas the ADA uses the term *disabilities* rather than the term *handicaps* used in the Rehabilitation Act of 1973, for purposes of meaning, they are considered equivalent. When considering cases of disability discrimination, the United States Department of Justice will often consider both the ADA and the Rehabilitation Act of 1973, as amended, to achieve formal settlement agreements.

The Five Titles of the ADA

Title I: Title I prohibits discrimination against qualified individuals with disabilities in such areas as job-application procedures, hiring, discharge, promotion, job training, and other conditions of employment. Employers must make "reasonable" accommodations for an individual's disabilities, unless to do so would cause hardship for the employer. Employers must also post notices that explain the act (Miller, 1992, p. 18). The Equal Employment Opportunity Commission (EEOC) is responsible for enforcement of Title I of the ADA. The EEOC is further responsible for issuing interpretative guidance concurrently with title I.

Title II: Title II prohibits exclusion of disabled persons from benefits, services or activities offered by the government. It requires that public transportation be accessible (Miller, 1992, p. 18).

Title III: Title III guarantees persons with disabilities access to privately operated places of business. The title may require changes of policies and practices to accommodate persons with disabilities by removing architectural barriers, making all areas accessible (Miller, 1992, p. 18).

Title IV: Title IV requires telephone companies to provide interstate and intrastate telecommunications relay service, so that hearing-impaired and speech-impaired individuals can communicate with others (Miller, 1992, p. 18).

Title V: Title V refers to the administration and handling of complaints under ADA. Administrative actions may include: awarding of reasonable attorney's fees in any proceeding under the ADA; prohibiting retaliation against, or coercion of any person who makes a charge; allowing insurers to continue to rely on actuarial procedures in underwriting risks; authorizing state governments to be sued under the ADA, providing that state laws offering greater or equal protection cannot be preempted; and, amending the Rehabilitation Act to conform its coverage of drug users to the provisions of ADA (Miller, 1992, p. 18).

Designing for Inclusion

Designing for inclusion is a concept that supports full program access to all people. Two important aspects of this concept must be fully explored by both facility planners and program designers:

- In real terms, the ADAAG (2001) regulations mandate full compliance with the minimum accessibility guidelines, as established under ADA by the U.S. Access Board; regardless of the existing status of the facility. This level of compliance is a major change from earlier requirements that allowed different standards for existing facilities versus new construction.
- "The ADA accessibility requirements apply not only to facilities, but also to participation in certain sports programs. For instance, disabled individuals can only be excluded from intramural or team activities if their participation would result in the likelihood of danger to others" (Munson & Comodeca, 1993, p. 18).

The basis of designing for inclusion, though mandated by law, must transcend the scope of legislated access for equal opportunity. Conceptually, all people might be considered *temporarily able-bodied*. Whether the result of a short-term illness or injury, or the longer term affects of accidental trauma or aging, humans share a common bond that we are subject to a myriad of ills that may leave us disabled. To design space that restricts access and therefore limits appropriate opportunity, for even a few, is wrong. It is also wrong to expect that only able-bodied individuals have the interest and ability to pursue lifespan activity or share in an activity-based experience. Whereas all facilities need to serve a mission, in our society today, we have a moral obligation to be forward thinking, so that our facilities and programs will always best represent the concept of designing for inclusion.

Curb cut.

Automated handicapped entrance.

Handicapped parking.

Sample handicapped accessible ramp,
Science Bldg. Indiana State University.

Handicapped aquatic ramp,
YMCA, Murfreesboro, TN.

Retrofitted aquatic transfer seat,
Indiana State University.

The Application of Title III of the ADA: Public Accommodation, Architectural Barriers, Undue Hardship, Readily Achievable, and Reasonable Accommodation

A place of public *accommodation* is defined as a facility, operated by a private entity, whose operations affect commerce and fall within at least one of the following 12 categories:

- Places of lodging
- Establishments serving food or drink
- Places of exhibition or entertainment (stadium)
- Places of public gathering (auditorium)
- Sales or rental establishments
- Service establishments
- Stations used for specified public transportation
- Places of public display or collection
- Places of recreation (park)
- Places of education
- Social service center establishments
- Places of exercise or recreation (gymnasium, health spa, bowling alley, golf course, orother place of exercise or recreation)

Public accommodation further refers to the private entity that owns, leases or leases to, or operates a place of public accommodation. Thus, the ADA is directed not to the physical location, but to the individual or group that owns or otherwise operates the physical location (Cocco and Zimmerman, 1996, p. 46).

A public accommodation shall remove *architectural barriers* in existing facilities where such removal is readily achievable. Examples of steps to remove barriers include:

- installing ramps
- making curb cuts in sidewalks and entrances
- repositioning telephones
- adding raised markings on elevator control buttons
- installing flashing alarm lights
- widening doors
- eliminating a turnstile or providing an alternative accessible path
- installing accessible door hardware
- installing grab bars in toilet stalls
- rearranging toilet partitions to increase maneuvering space
- repositioning the paper towel dispenser in a bathroom
- installing an accessible paper cup dispenser at existing inaccessible water fountain
- removing high pile, low density carpeting

Priorities for barrier removal: A public accommodation is urged to take measures to comply with barrier removal in accordance with the following order of priorities:

- provide access to a place of public accommodation from public sidewalks, parking, or public transportation. Includes installing entrance ramp, widening entrances and providing accessible parking spaces.
- provide access to those places of public accommodation where goods and services are made available to the public.
- provide access to restroom facilities.
- take any other measures necessary to provide access to the goods, services, privileges, advantages, or accommodations of a place of public accommodation.

Where a public accommodation can demonstrate that barrier removal is not readily achievable, the public accommodation shall not fail to make goods, services, facilities, privileges, advantages, or accommodations available through alternative methods, if those methods are readily achievable (ADA, 1990).

Undue Hardship is defined as requiring significant difficulty or expense, considering the employer's size, financial resources, and the nature and structure of the operation (Miller, 1990, p. 18).

Readily achievable means easily accomplishable and able to be carried out without much difficulty or expense. It constitutes a lower standard than undue burden (Cocco & Zimmerman, 1996, p. 46). In determining whether an action is readily achievable, the following factors are to be considered:

- The nature and cost of the action needed under the Act;
- The overall financial resources of the facility or facilities involved in the action; the number of persons employed at such facility; the effect on expenses and resources, or theimpact otherwise of such action upon the operation of the facility;
- The overall financial resources of he covered entity; the overall size of the business or the covered entity with respect to the number of its employees; the number, type, and location of its facilities; and
- The type of operation or operations of the covered entity, including the composition, structure, and functions of the work force of such entity; the geographic separateness, administrative or fiscal relationship of the facility or facilities in question to the covered entity (ADA, 1990).

To the extent that it is readily achievable, a public accommodation in assembly areas shall provide a reasonable number of wheelchair seating spaces and seats with removable aisle-side arm rests. Further, this wheelchair seating must be dispersed throughout the assembly area seating, provided lines of sight and choice of admission at prices comparable to those for members of the general public; adjoin an accessible route that also serves as a means of egress in case of emergency; and permit individuals who use wheelchairs to sit with family members or other companions (who are not using wheelchairs). If removal of seats is not readily achievable, a public accommodation shall provide, to the extent that it is readily achievable to do so, a portable chair or other means to permit a family member or other companion to sit with an individual who uses a wheelchair (ADA:36.308 Subpart C, 1990).

Reasonable accommodations under the ADA requires that employers and facilities make an accommodation if doing so

Removing architectural barrier in shower.

Removing architectural barrier for drinking fountain.

Removing architectural barrier for sinks.

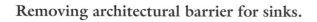

Removing architectural barrier for toilets.

will not impose an undue hardship on the operation of the business or facility (Miller, 1992, p. 18). In general, is [also] an alteration made by the employer or potential employer that puts individuals with disabilities on equal footing with individuals without disabilities" (ADA:29CFR, 1990). Reasonable accommodations include, but are not limited to: "making facilities readily accessible and usable to disabled persons; job restructuring, modifying work schedules and/or reassignment to a vacant position; acquiring or modifying equipment or devices; modifying or adjusting testing processes, training materials and/or policies; providing qualified readers or interpreters" (Miller, 1992, p. 18).

Compliance and Enforcement

"Through lawsuits and settlement agreements, the Department of Justice has achieved greater access for individuals with disabilities in hundreds of cases. Under general rules governing lawsuits brought by the Federal government, the Department of Justice may not sue a party unless negotiations to settle the dispute have failed. The Department of Justice may file lawsuits in federal court to enforce the ADA, and courts may order compensatory damages and back pay to remedy discrimination if the Department prevails. Under title III, the Department of Justice may also obtain civil penalties of up to $50,000 for the first violation and $100,000 for any subsequent violation" (U.S. Department of Justice, February 19, 2001, p.1: *http://www.usdoj.gov/crt/ada/enforce.htm*).

The Department of Justice publishes quarterly reports on its enforcement activities, which include: ADA litigation, formal settlement agreements, other settlements, and mediation (available online: *http://www.usdoj.gov/crt/ada/enforce.htm*). Additionally, the Department of Justice provides technical assistance manuals and publications for state and local governments (available online: *http://www.usdoj.gov/crt/ada/publicat.htm*). Other federal agencies have enforcement authority under the ADA, including The Department of Education, the Equal Employment Opportunity Commission (EEOC), the Department of Transportation, and the Federal Communications Commission.

With regard to reasonable accommodations and compliance, those facilities that are used for both academic and leisure activities will likely be required to provide technology in class or laboratory spaces. Such technology would specifically enhance the academic accommodation of disabled students. *Eligible individuals* are defined as those who have a physical or mental impairment that substantially limits a major life activity. To qualify, individuals with a disability or learning style challenge needing an accommodation, may be required to self-disclose and offer proof of disability to receive some kinds of accommodations. Facilities that are used academically and for sport/recreation should consider permanent installation of computer (online) links, cable (for closed-captioning); multimedia carts (PowerPoint™), slides, etc.) as well as less technologically advanced services, i.e., signers, note takers, etc.

Short- and long-range planning is an integral part of an organization's stated intention to comply with federal accessibility regulations. If an organization claims "undue hardship" to avoid financial strife, it may be only a short-term "fix." It is important to note that the ADA is not passive legislation. As an organization strives to meet existing standards, it is possible that what was considered acceptable in 1998 may not meet future ADAAG specifications. Therefore, if an organization is already out of compliance because of an inability to fund a significant accommodation or barrier removal, etc., they may become hopelessly out of compliance as these guidelines evolve. It is imperative that organizations plan ahead, take advantage of federal tax incentives, and strive to meet or exceed the demands of future accessibility legislation.

Summary

The Americans with Disabilities Act is federal legislation that has been completely enforceable since July 1992. The small business owner and the large corporation have all had ample time to minimally meet compliance through planning. More than this, employers and public accommodations should be following the law because failure to comply is clearly discrimination. For the cost of a postage stamp, an administrative complaint filed against an organization or community may cost thousands of dollars. And, complying with the Act is more than beneficial to all people. If unsure of where to start, consider the resources identified below or consult your state attorney general's office on disability and ask for help. There are countless organizations committed to assisting willing public and private entities with implementation strategies. The burden is clearly ours to make this act more than just words on paper. Designing for accessibility is a concept that understands life's realities: that essentially we are all temporarily able-bodied.

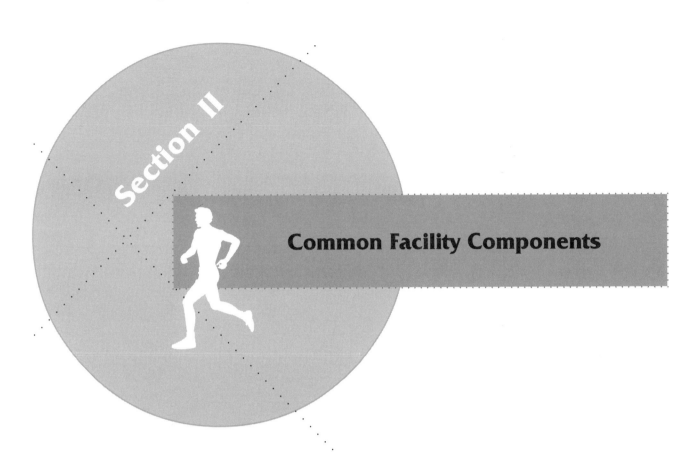

Section II

Common Facility Components

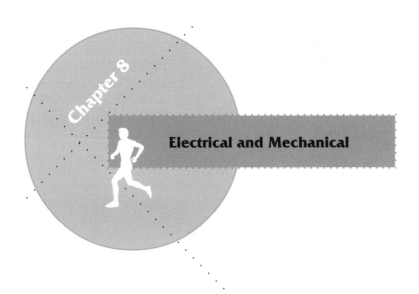

Richard J. LaRue, University of New England
Thomas H. Sawyer, Indiana State University

At its best, technology should conform to the way we work, the way we play, and the way we live. Through electrical and mechanical engineering, we have an opportunity to create extraordinary environments through the manipulation of basic components: lighting, sound, and other electronic technologies; heating, ventilation and air-conditioning; and humidity and air quality control. Advancements in engineering these technologies in both indoor and outdoor spaces require planners to understand the basics and expect unlimited potential for new technologies. Planners must avoid setting limits on how far ahead they look. Only a few years ago, the computer was a luxury. Now computers are a necessity of everyday life, operating everything from membership systems to the building automation and HVAC systems of "intelligent buildings" (Myers, 1997, p. 53). Today's engineering must be about providing for the way we will work, the way we will play, and the way we will live.

Learning Objectives

After reading this chapter, the student will be able to

- understand lighting and sound in terms of functionality,
- understand the challenges of implementing electronic technologies,
- understand climate control concepts in terms of efficiency,
- recognize the administrative responsibilities related to electronic technology and climate control,
- understand the challenges of sick building syndrome, and
- understand both the trends and new technologies in electrical and mechanical engineering.

Electrical Engineering

A theoretical basis of electrical engineering includes an understanding of circuits, electronics, electromagnetics, energy conversion, and controls. Conceptually, when planners intend to consider lighting and sound, they are also considering the broader areas of illumination and acoustics. Therefore, the planning basics of lighting, sound, and other electronic technologies will also include information relevant to the design of electrical systems, which goes beyond electrical engineering in its strictest sense.

Lighting

Lighting is simply a means to illuminate or further brighten an area or space. The two primary lighting options are energy-produced lighting and natural lighting. The product of lighting in combination with other variables, such as the level of darkness, the amount of reflective light (from surfaces), and the color of the lighting, results in illumination. Illumination is measured by the foot-candle. Brightness is the luminous intensity of any surface and is measured by the foot-lambert. Glare, which is an important consideration in physical education and sport facilities, is nothing more than excessive high brightness.

In addition to the amount of light in any given area, the quality of light is of equal importance. Providing efficient illumination is complicated and challenging, and the services of an illumination engineer are recommended in order to obtain maximum lighting efficiency. Gymnasiums, classrooms, corridors, and other specific areas have specific and different lighting requirements. Planning for electric illumination requires that each area be considered relative to specific use.

The foot-candle is a measurement of light intensity at a given point. Light intensity, measured in foot-candles, is one vital factor in eye comfort and seeing efficiency, but intensity must be considered in relation to the brightness balance of all light sources and reflective surfaces within the visual field.

The reflection factor is the percentage of light falling on a surface that is reflected by that surface. In order to main tain a brightness balance with a quantity and quality of light for good visibility, all surfaces within a room should be relatively light, with a matte rather than a glossy finish.

The foot-lambert is the product of the illumination in foot-candles and the reflection factor of the surface. For example, 40 foot-candles striking a surface with a reflection factor of 50% would produce a brightness of 20 foot-lamberts (40 x .50 = 20). These values are necessary when computing brightness differences in order to achieve a balanced visual field. Table 8.1 gives a relative indication as to a comparison of illuminations for specific indoor spaces.

Table 8.1
Levels of Illumination Recommended for Specific Indoor Spaces Courtesy of Illuminating Engineering Society of North America

Area	Footcandles on Tasks
Adapted physical education gymnasium	50
Auditorium	
Assembly only	15
Exhibitions	30-50
Social activities	5-15
Classrooms	
Laboratories	100
Lecture rooms	
Audience area	70
Demonstration area	150
Study halls	70
Corridors and stairways	20
Dance studio	5-50[3]
Field houses	80
First-aid rooms	
General	50
Examining table	125
Gymnasiums	
Exhibitions	50[2]
General exercise and recreation	35
Dances	5-50[3]
Locker and shower rooms	30
Gymnastics	50
Archery	
Shooting tee	50
Target area	70
Badminton	50[2]
Basketball	80[2]
Deck tennis	50
Fencing	70[2]
Handball	70[2]
Paddle tennis	70[2]
Rifle range	
Point area	50
Target area	70
Rowing practice area	50
Squash	70[2]
Tennis	70[2]
Volleyball	50
Weight-exercise room	50
Wrestling and personal-defense room	50
Games room	70

continued

Ice rink		100[3]
Library		
	Study and notes	70
	Ordinary reading	50-70
Lounges		
	General	50
	Reading books, magazines, newspapers	50-70
Offices		
	Accounting, auditing, tabulating, bookkeeping, business-machine operation	150
	Regular Office work, active filing, index references, mail sorting	100
	Reading and transcribing handwriting in ink or medium pencil on good-quality paper, intermittent filing	70
	Reading high-contrast or well-printed material not involving critical or prolonged seeing, conferring and interviewing	50
Parking areas		1
Storerooms		
	Inactive	10
	Active	
		Rough bulky	15
		Medium	30
		Fine	60
Swimming pools		
	General and overhead	50
	Underwater[4]	
	Toilets and washrooms	30

These standards have been developed by a panel of experts on facilities for health, physical education, and recreation after careful consideration of the activities involved. In all instances, the standards in this table are equal to, or exceed, the standards which have been recommended by the Illumination Engineering Society, American Institute of Architects, and National Council On Schoolhouse Construction. [2]Care must be taken to achieve a brightness balance to eliminate extremes of brightness and glare. [3]Should be equipped with rheotstats. [4]Must be balanced with overhead lighting and should provide 100 lamp lumens per square foot of pool surface. Courtesy of Illuminating Engineering Society of North America.

Basic Lighting Considerations

Installation

Lights in arenas, gymnasiums, and other high-ceiling activity spaces need to be a minimum of 24 feet above the playing surface so they will not interfere with official clearance heights for indoor sports. Indoor lighting systems are generally of two types: direct and indirect lighting. Direct lighting systems face directly down at the floor. Indirect lighting systems face in some direction other than the floor, i.e., side walls or ceiling, reflecting the beaming light in an effort to reduce glare. Indirect lighting is more expensive to operate, since with each reflection light is diminished. Therefore, more energy is consumed in indirect lighting compared to direct lighting in order to obtain the same final illumination of an area. Both lighting systems should meet the required level of footcandles without causing glare or shadows on the playing surface. The type of lighting—incandescent, fluorescent, mercury-vapor, metal halide, quartz, and sodium-vapor —will likely depend upon the type of space and the way the space will be used (see Figure 8.1). The style of fixture may have more to do with aesthetics than functionality, though the advantages and disadvantages of aesthetics vs. functionality should always be considered.

Designed for Impact

In spaces where the play may involve hitting, kicking, or throwing balls, etc., lighting fixtures should be designed to absorb their impact. Lighting systems are available that include shock-absorbing characteristics. Perhaps more important is the additional protection these lights require in the event that they are struck and the bulb is broken. Falling shards of glass from broken lights should be avoided at all costs. Lights need to be covered with a transparent polycarbonate sheeting (a screen may not be enough) that will catch broken glass bulbs and also protect the bulbs from direct impact. The sheeting or cover should also keep softer, potentially flammable sport implements (i.e., tennis balls, shuttlecocks, and nurf or wiffle-balls) from lodging within the fixture against a high-temperature bulb (Turner, 1993).

Lighting Types

The incandescent light is instantaneous, burns without sound, and is not affected by the number of times the light is turned on or off. Incandescent lights and fixtures are considerably cheaper in initial cost, are easier to change, and the lamp, within limits, may be varied in size within a given fixture. Incandescent fixtures, however, have excessively high spot brightness and give off considerable heat; a problem when high levels of illumination are necessary.

Fluorescent lamps have the advantage of long life and give at least 2 1/2 times the amount of light that incandescent lamps give for the same amount of electrical current used. They frequently are used in old buildings to raise the illumination level without installing new wiring.

Mercury-vapor lighting is expensive in terms of initial installation. The overall cost of mercury-vapor lighting, however, is cheaper than incandescent lighting. The primary objection to mercury-vapor lighting is its bluish color. However, when incandescent lighting is used in addition to mercury-vapor, a highly satisfactory lighting system results. Mercury-vapor lights are being phased out in favor of metal halide lights.

Metal halide lights do not last as long as mercury-vapor lights but give a better light output and operate more efficiently. Metal halide lights do not have the bluish tint of mercury-vapor lights. Quartz lights and high-pressure sodium lights are outdoor lights. It has been only over the past few years that these lights have been utilized indoors. Quartz lights are not much different than incandescent lights, except they have a slight bronze color and are slightly more efficient. High-pressure sodium lights might well be the indoor activity light of the future. They have long life expectancy; they are highly efficient and give the best light output

of all the lights mentioned. The only problem with high-pressure sodium lights is the yellow-bronze hue associated with them.

Lighting Levels

A number of systems exist that allow different levels of lighting so that special events or lighting requirements can be met. The Jack Breslin Student Events Center at Michigan State University (opened in 1989) affords such variety using an intricate Holophane lighting system.

The lighting levels are turned up or down through a computerized control system, which is pre-programmed for different lighting and uniformity levels. On another control panel, the lights can be adjusted by a single button designated for one of eight different pre-programmed scenes. For example, facility personnel can press one button to set the lighting for televised basketball games, another for non-televised games, another for pre-game set-up, and so forth (Rabin, 1993, p. 6).

When the Dan and Kathleen Hogan Sports Center at Colby-Sawyer College went on line in 1991, the NCAA lighting standard was 60 foot-candles at the water's surface. Today 100 foot-candles of illumination are required for U.S. swimming and collegiate championship events. Because the planners decided upon a higher-than-minimum level for lighting the natatorium at the center, the facility continues to meet required lighting standards without any modification.

Using Natural Lighting

Windows and other translucent materials allow natural light into a facility. Natural lighting can reduce operational costs and enhance the aesthetics of an indoor space. The major problem with windows is that it is very difficult to control the glare that they allow to enter. Avoid windows in any activity area where visual acuity is an important commodity for both learning activity skills and safety. However, other translucent building materials are available that do several things windows cannot:

- provide higher values for insulation reducing both heat loss (during colder seasons) and/or heat gain (during warmer seasons),
- diffuse the light that comes through, reducing glare, and
- provide greater resistance to breaking so they are safer to use in spaces where broken glass is a serious problem, and they are harder to break into from a security standpoint.

Translucent materials are not perfect. Translucent panels or blocks in a high-moisture area will still allow moisture to condense on the inside surface if it is colder outside, and they do not allow clear images to transfer. Windows can also have movable shades, shutters, curtains, or blinds that assist with controlling glare and can improve insulating levels. Skylights are acceptable in "slow movement areas," and vertical skylights are recommended in order to keep both glare and leakage to a minimum. Regardless of the materials used, natural light seems a worthy goal when the facility is designed and used appropriately.

Figure 8.1

COMPARATIVE AVERAGE LUMENS PER LAMP WATT

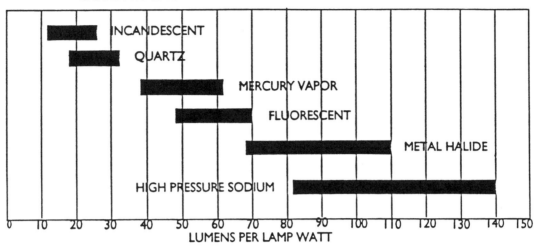

LUMENS PER LAMP WATT

COLOR OF LAMP UNIT

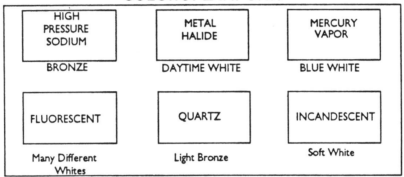

HIGH PRESSURE SODIUM	METAL HALIDE	MERCURY VAPOR
BRONZE	DAYTIME WHITE	BLUE WHITE
FLUORESCENT	QUARTZ	INCANDESCENT
Many Different Whites	Light Bronze	Soft White

ENERGY SAVINGS COMPARISON*

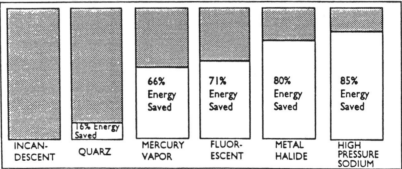

INCAN-DESCENT — QUARZ (16% Energy Saved) — MERCURY VAPOR (66% Energy Saved) — FLUOR-ESCENT (71% Energy Saved) — METAL HALIDE (80% Energy Saved) — HIGH PRESSURE SODIUM (85% Energy Saved)

* Based on Energy Required to Maintain Identical Lamp Lumens

Maintenance

Planning must also take into account the need to change bulbs or replace fixtures. Unless there is a catwalk or crawl space in the ceiling, the lights will need to be changed from the floor using poles, ladders, scaffolding, or hydraulic hoists. Experience informs us that changing all the lights in a space at the same time is the most cost-effective approach to maintenance. However, if your lighting fails to meet required levels whenever a single fixture is out, you will be forced to change your bulbs more frequently. Consider adding a couple of fixtures in each space, more than is required (i.e., if the space/activity standard calls for 50 foot-candles on task, you may wish to exceed this standard by four fixtures, so that you can lose up to four lamps and still meet the minimum). And when four bulbs are gone, it is probably time to replace all the bulbs in the space. As you plan for the need to change bulbs and replace fixtures, remember the characteristics of the space. Even telescoping poles need minimum clearance to get inside a space. Racquetball courts with standard-sized doors may allow the use of a small hydraulic hoist rather than a giant stepladder. Finally, direct-lighting bulbs can sometimes be changed using only a pole (standing on the floor), while indirect lighting can only be changed using a catwalk, crawlspace, or more time-consuming approach.

Therefore, when planning your lighting system maintenance, you should consider designs that will serve the facility without being labor intensive.

Unique Lighting Settings and Issues

Unique settings in sport and recreational facilities require either special lighting systems, special fixtures, or carefully planned designs. In spaces with a higher level of moisture (pool areas, shower and toilet areas, locker rooms, etc.) vapor-proof lighting units are recommended. Remember that broken glass in any such area is a mini-disaster. If a bulb breaks in spaces where participants are often barefooted, extensive cleanup will be required. Locker rooms and athletic training rooms are two examples of spaces where light placement will directly affect the quality of the environment. Fixtures should be placed to enhance the areas between lockers in locker rooms, to afford clear reflections at mirrors, and to brighten places where visibility is critical to the activity in athletic training rooms.

Aquatic Facilities

Lighting indoor swimming spaces has never been the easiest part of natatorium design, although frequently, and with regrettable results, it has been treated that way. With today's multipurpose aquatic centers frequently accommodating diverse programming activities in a shared environment, it has become an even greater creative challenge to get the light right. Natural light is an increasingly attractive option for indoor aquatic facilities. Large windows or open fenestration can be energy-efficient ways to supplement artificial heat and lighting, and they add interest for users and a much appreciated connection to the outside for employees who work all day in an enclosed environment. With all its advantages, however, natural light can be accompanied by an undesirable partner—glare (Hunsaker, 1998, 51).

If windows are used in aquatic areas, the glare trade-off must be addressed during the planning stages. Glare is not an exclusive problem of natural lighting. Glare can result from improperly located artificial lighting when the lights reflect off either the water surface or side walls. With safety a major consideration in aquatic facilities, every effort must be made to control for glare and/or the blind spots caused by glare. Underwater lighting can reduce some of the glare problem and can further enhance visibility in deeper water (underwater lighting is required in some jurisdictions). And in aquatic facilities, there are maintenance issues related to the location of light fixtures over the pool (the preferred location for competitive facilities). The YMCA's Walter Schroeder Aquatic Center in Milwaukee, Wisconsin, was able to locate light fixtures directly over the 50-meter indoor pool after determining that by using the two movable bulkheads, a hoist could be positioned anywhere a fixture required relamping. This avoided the added construction expense of a catwalk or crawl space and the labor intensiveness of using a scaffolding setup in an empty pool to replace bulbs. Finally, artificial lighting in pool areas must consider the variability of water depth.

Outdoor Lighting

Outdoor lighting for sports fields can have some very specific requirements. "Sport lighting should provide a specified quantity and quality of light on the playing surface. For a football field, the quantity (level) of light is determined by

Outdoor lighting on metal poles.

the player's skill level, the number of spectators and any television requirements" (Rogers, 1994, p. 53). Although specific considerations apply when planning illumination of a specific-use field, for the purpose of this chapter, the concepts of outdoor lighting will focus on multipurpose installations.

Multipurpose sports fields are more complicated to light [than single-purpose fields], but you'll save money by combining activities on one field. Several issues need to be addressed when lighting a multipurpose field. Light levels and pole placement become big factors, and design decisions become critical. Controlling spill and glare is also very important. Lighting a multipurpose field is extremely cost-effective. By sharing poles and fixtures among several sports, initial costs can be reduced by 40% or more. At some point, making the decision to use the field for both sports increases the land's productivity, and so will the decision to give it light (Rogers, 1996, p. 51).

Planning steps include the following:

- "Determine the layout of the field and all its potential uses. The most common multipurpose fields combine football with soccer, or football or soccer with softball" (Rogers, 1996, p. 51).
- Determine the quantity (level) as well as the quality needed (Rogers, 1996). The Illluminating Engineering Society of North America (IESNA) publishes light-level guidelines for outdoor sports (see IESNA web site for further information: http://www.iesna.org).
- Determine the type of lamp desired (Rogers, 1996).
- Determine the number of luminaire assemblies (luminaire assemblies consist of lamp reflector, ballast mounting, crossarm and mounting hardware) and poles required to light the playing surfaces while avoiding spill and glare (Rogers, 1996).
- Decide on the type of poles to be used: wood, concrete, and steel are the standard options. Each has advantages and disadvantages.
- Consider all aspects of safety. The lighting system must comply with the National Electric Code as well as state and local codes and use luminaire assemblies that have the Underwriters Laboratory approval (Rogers, 1996).
- Establish switching controls that allow for maximum flexibility and maximum efficiency.
- Recalling that some activities require more lighting than others, switches should afford higher and lower levels of illumination. "Switching capacity becomes even more important with overlapping fields" (Rogers, 1996, p. 54).

Outdoor sports lighting should be:

Safe, simple and efficient. Basic requirements include one transformer and a simple service entrance with a basic feeder and branch circuit. Grounding at the service center and at each pole is needed to ensure the safety of anyone who comes in contact with the pole or electrical equipment. Grounding for lighting protection should be designed and installed according to the National Fire Protection Association (NFPA) Code 780. Safety disconnects on each pole pro-

vide additional protection for service crews. Individual fusing of each fixture avoids gang failure of the lights, eliminating costly emergency repairs (Rogers, 1994, p. 56).

Finally, the planner should consider and compare the warranties offered by different manufacturers: the length of the warranty, the items included, and those not included. "Manufacturers that offer a multi-year warranty are making a strong statement of confidence in their product" (Rogers, 1994, p. 56).

Supplementary and Special Lighting Requirements

It is advisable to provide supplementary lighting on such areas as those containing goals or targets. Supplementary light sources should be shielded from the eyes of participants and spectators in order to provide the proper brightness balance. Other special lighting requirements include:

- Night lighting—lights that remain on 24 hours per day (can be the same circuit as the emergency lighting), lighting large spaces, lobbies, corridors, stairwells, and classrooms.
- Exit lighting—located at all exits (including exit-only locations), should be mounted according to local and state codes. Because these lights remain on 24 hours per day, cost savings can be real ized if fluorescent bulbs are used instead of incandescent bulbs or LED (light-emit ting diode) signs are used as both fluo rescent bulbs or LED fixtures have much longer lives. All exit lighting should be on special circuits that will remain on, even if the power is lost.
- Emergency (white) lighting—should be provided for exits (including exterior open spaces to which exits lead). This light ing should be on a special emergency cir cuit (battery powered) that will power-up whenever power is lost.

Lighting Controls

When planning for lighting, the methods of control are also important to consider. The central light switch box should be located at a major entrance area, and all teaching [or activity] spaces should have individual light switches. A relatively unusual approach to controlling illumination in spaces where lighting is only on as needed (i.e., individual racquetball or squash courts, rest rooms, etc.) is motion sensor or "occupancy sensors" switching. If the sensor detects no movement over a period of 10 to 15 minutes, the lights automatically switch off. The lights come back on as soon as someone enters the room. Light-level sensors are also available for use indoors as well as outdoors. These sensors adjust the lighting level in response to the amount of natural lighting. Replacing the all-or-nothing on/off switch in parking areas or skylit rooms can give just the right amount of artificial light needed as the natural light fades.

Trends in Lighting

On the horizon, if not already here, is the use of Circadian lighting systems in 24-hour operations. Circadian lights facilitate true physiological adaptation to working nights and sleeping during the day. These system installations have proven "entirely successful in providing a means in keeping the shiftworkers awake (industrial settings) and alert while on-shift, improving the safety of the commute home, improving the day sleep of the shift worker, and having a positive impact on family life" (Murphy, 1998, p. 1). In other words, Circadian lighting systems have proven to have a positive biological effect on users in a 24-hour, three-shift environment. More research will be needed to determine the possible use and effects of Circadian lighting in more traditional settings.

Sound

Sound is an important part of everyday life, and subsequently it is an important part of sport and recreation. From the public address system to the telemetric microphone, the ability to hear what is going on is almost as critical as seeing what is going on; frequently, one sense will support another in completing the act of communication. From the sound quality we need in aerobic dance studios to the sound system required for a half-time show at the Super Bowl, technology is advancing the availability of high-resolution sound (Fenton, 1997).

For the sport or recreational facility, sound design starts with creating a suitable sound environment. Beginning in the lobby, where users first enter, several approaches can be utilized:

- Design a small audio/video system that plays videos (either cable or tape), with the audio portion of the videos distributed to other areas as well.
- Building on the first approach, include a video wall in the workout area that receives the same video as the unit in the front lobby.
- Have your sound distribution originate in a workout space such as an aerobics studio, and then distribute this sound or allow it to "drift" to the lobby and/or other areas of the facility (Hall, 1993).

In strength-training spaces, the major sound considerations are:

Even distribution, the ability to overcome background noise, and low-fatigue factors. Correct selection and placement of appropriate speakers will provide even distribution, reduce the impact of background interference, and satisfy low-fatigue requirements. Wall-mounted speakers usually work best, although clubs that have a lot of tall equipment in rooms with low ceilings should use ceiling speakers. Whenever possible, include in your design a dedicated sound system for free-weight areas to increase your flexibility in sound sources and level control (Hall, 1993, p. 42).

In cardiovascular areas, "the most satisfactory approach for most clubs is to supply each exercise station with a headphone outlet and flexibility in source selection, along with one or more video monitors visible to several stations at once" (Hall, 1993, p. 43).

The aerobics room is the one area where your members [users] most expect to hear sophisticated, high-quality sound. Achieving this in a room full of hard surfaces and highly active people is difficult. A well-designed and properly operated sound system will add precision and impact to your classes, establishing a sense of timing and inspiration without fatigue, stress or hearing damage created by distortion and excessive volume levels (Hall, 1995, p. 42-43).

Four categories of components have a very direct effect on these various factors:
- speakers;
- cassette decks/turntables/CD players;
- amplifier, receiver, and equalizer (soft limiter); and
- wireless microphone and microphone mixer (Hall, 1991).

Selecting the correct components is easier when you understand the elements of a high-quality sound system. However, it is important to seek the advice of individuals and/or companies who are familiar with the specific needs of an aerobic studio when choosing components for your new studio or when upgrading your current system (Hall, 1991, p. 40).

Acoustics

Because of the amount of noise and sound that emanates from the activities in physical education and sports, acoustics and sound are of paramount importance in building design. Acoustical treatments in building design are the domain of the acoustical engineer. An acoustical engineer should be consulted when dealing with absorption and reflection qualities of all surfaces within a facility.

Acoustical treatments must both enhance sound so that we can hear easily, and absorb sound. Background noise, basically unwanted sound that originates either in the teaching station itself or intrudes from another area, must be controlled. Internal background noise might consist of "squeaking" chairs sliding on a floor, reverberation or "echoing" of sound, and reflective sound. All sound travels spherically. When a space is to be acoustically treated, walls, ceilings, floors, and other surfaces within that space must be considered for appropriate materials.

Internal Treatments

There are four common modes of internal acoustical treatment of spaces. The use of walls and other barriers is one method of controlling sound. Air space itself is an acoustical treatment. The larger the space, and therefore the farther sound travels, the more it is absorbed. The use of soft acoustical materials on various surfaces is a major means of sound control. Acoustical clouds suspended over large open arenas is still another means of controlling sound. Extending walls beyond dropped ceilings can afford better acoustical control than stopping internal walls at the dropped ceiling height.

External Treatments

External background noise or unwanted sound from outside the teaching space also must be planned for acoustically. Unwanted sound or noise may be transmitted into the room by means of ventilating ducts, pipes, and spaces around pipe sleeves. The transmission of sound through ducts can be reduced by the use of baffles, or by lining the ducts with sound-absorbent, fire-resistant materials. The ducts also may be connected with canvas or rubberized material to interrupt the transmission through the metal in the ducts. Pipes can be covered with pipe covering, and spaces in the pipe sleeves can be filled.

Sound also can be transmitted through the walls, floors, and ceilings. This can be reduced to a desirable minimum by the proper structural design and materials. In conventional wall construction, alternate studs can support the sides of the wall in such a manner that there is no through connection from one wall surface to another. This sometimes is known as double-wall construction. The space inside the walls can be filled with sound-absorbing material to further decrease sound transmission. Sometimes three or four inches of sand inside the walls at the baseboard will cut down the transmission appreciably. Likewise, sound absorption blankets laid over the partitions in suspended ceiling construction frequently can reduce the sound from one room to another.

Machinery vibration or impact sounds can be reduced by use of the proper floor covering and/or by installing the machinery on floating or resilient mountings. "Sound locks," such as double walls or doors, are needed between noisy areas and adjoining quiet areas. Improper location of doors and windows can create noise problems. It is imperative to consider the location of the facility itself and also to consider the placement of internal areas of the facility for sound control. Placing physical education and sport facilities in a semi-isolated area of a school helps control acoustics. This same theory needs to be applied internally within the sports facility. The placement of "noisy" areas such as weight-training areas, aerobic areas, locker rooms, swimming pools, gymnasiums, and spectator areas must be planned for in relation to quiet areas such as classrooms and offices. It is not good acoustical planning to have a weight room above or next to a classroom. Care must be taken in the maintenance of acoustical materials. Oil-base paint reduces the sound-absorbent qualities of most materials. Surface treatment for different acoustical materials will vary. The most common treatment of acoustical-fiber tile is a light brush coat of waterbase paint, but most acoustical materials lose their efficiency after several applications of paint.

Exterior Treatments

Sometimes the exterior of a space or building must be acoustically treated. If a gym is located on the landing flight path of a local airport, or if it is located next to a fairly steep grade on a major truck thoroughfare, exterior acoustical treatment might be needed. Utilize the same acoustical principles as inside, with an exterior twist. Keep hard surfaces such as paved areas and parking lots to a minimum. Use shrubbery, trees, and grass wherever possible. Walls, solid fences, berms, and water are all good exterior acoustical items. It is important to plan for acoustics and sound control in a variety of ways. Think spherical, think internal, think external, and think exterior in order to best acoustically treat a facility.

Whitney and Foulkes indicated that "Many acoustical problems can be avoided from the start if sound transmission concepts are kept in mind at the initial planning stage of a recreational facility. Keeping noisy spaces separated from quiet areas is easy to achieve in the initial design phase; correcting problems due to improper space adjacencies is more difficult. Even the best sound-isolating construction techniques cannot completely solve the problems created by improper adjacencies. The final results will always be more acceptable if serious acoustical issues are solved in the schematic design" (1994, p. 58).

Other Electronic Technologies

Electronic Communication

The standard communication tools in sport and recreation facilities include an intercom system and two-way audio systems to various activity and office spaces. Additionally, telecommunication has advanced tremendously, allowing for the integration of telecommunications devices for the deaf (TDDs), text typewriters (Tts) or teletypewriters (TTYs), and faxing capabilities to standard telephone installations.

Audio and visual communication needs for the 21st century require many facilities to be integrated for computerization and satellite/cable television reception. Any space that might utilize a computer or video connection should be part of this integration. Fiberoptics are the current standard for such integration. However, a thorough planning process will also consider future technologies. Minimally, appropriate conduits should be installed during facility construction to afford the broadest range of future choices.

Within spaces, especially those used for instruction, the planning process should also consider the electronic technologies required for distance education, such as two-way audio and visual communication tools (I see you-you see me, I hear you-you hear me), computer links for internet and computer presentation, conference-call telephones, digital and laser disc players, LCD overhead projectors, keypads for student responses, etc.

Scoreboards and Electronic Timing Systems

The science and technology of scoreboard design has changed the entire sport spectator experience. A scoreboard not only provides spectators with game data, but it can be configured with a giant video screen and message system and integrated with the facility sound system (Bradley, 1994). Large indoor sports arenas are using giant four-sided scoreboards that literally pay for themselves with sponsor advertisement. If timing is your need, recent advances in video systems allow sport races to be judged fairly, regardless of the hundredths of seconds between finish times or the failure of conventional timing equipment (Goldman, 1995).

Elevators and Other Hydraulic Lifts

Elevators and other hydraulic lifts are necessary design features of many sport and recreational facilities. Besides offering physically challenged users federally mandated access to facilities, they enhance the ability of staff to move equipment (possibly reducing the potential for worker-related injury), and they facilitate deliveries. To determine if your facility is required to provide elevators and/or hydraulic lifts, refer to Chapter 7, Designing for Inclusion.

Security

Effective facility security begins with building designs that control access to the facility through a main-desk control area and egress-only doors that do not allow re-entry. A number of electronic technologies can further affect the security of a facility, including:

- entrance/exit (access/egress) controls and alarms such as card systems; electronically controlled doors and gates, check points with metal detectors (magnetometers), and annunciators (egress door alarms). Card access can also be used to gather enlightening and useful data on the facility's clientele (Patton, 1997, p. 64);
- closed ciruit television monitor systems; and
- motion-sensor alarms for controlled areas such as pools (sensor detects water motion).

It is important to remember that as electronic technology is applied to security, any power failure will disrupt such systems unless they are backed up by battery or emergency generator systems.

Emergency Alarms

Facility safety begins with smoke/fire and emergency alarm systems that appropriately warn building users in the event of fire and warn facility staff in the event of a life-threatening emergency. Smoke and fire alarms include those that are user-activated, smoke- or heat-activated, and water-pressure-activated (usually found in wet sprinkler systems). Special alarms for the pool or other exercise area have been designed to notify facility staff in the event of a life-threatening emergency; these are staff activated. Weather or disaster notification will usually utilize an existing intercom system to warn facility users. Emergency alarms, especially those that are designed to warn users, must also be backed up by battery or emergency generator systems.

Emergency Generators

With an increasing reliance upon some of the above electronic technologies and/or the use of air-supported roofs for indoor sport spaces, power outages will require an emergency generator back-up to ensure the safety of facility users and the well-being of the facility. These generators need only provide minimum levels of power (to be determined by the specifications of the facility) to be effective tools. However, where electric energy is at a premium, it is possible that some sport or recreational facilities will plan on a bank of generators to provide unrestricted energy service.

Trends in Electronic Technologies

Illuminated game lines on sport courts and underwater pace lights in swimming pools are two of the more innovative uses of electronic technology. And, with laser tech-

nology, it is only a matter of time before distances in field events, etc. are determined using a laser rather than a tape measure.

Web-to-telephone calling combines the convenience of IP telephony [IP telephony is the use of an IP network to transmit voice, video, and data] with the flexibility of traditional calling. The Web-to-phone interface works via a Web browser plug-in that can be downloaded from a Web site. There is no software to buy. Once call center components are in place, people browsing a company's Web page can use the Web-to-phone plug-in to speak over the Internet directly with someone (Dresner, 1998, p. 42).

Finally, Cable Microcell Integrators (CMIs) are in the news, turning terrestrial television cable systems into communications networks for overcrowded cellular systems. A unique characteristic of CMI technology is the independence of signal coverage from the number of base transceiver stations. In other words, service providers need not build excess capacity to handle occasional, but regular, surges in demand. "Fans and reporters who clog a professional football stadium eight Sundays out of the year might require an additional cell tower/base station to use their telephones, but a CMI system can handle this demand surge without an additional physical plant" (Ackerman, 1997, p. 21). Facility planners may well consider checking with area wireless communication companies to see if a CMI installation is appropriate for their facility. It is fair to say that as technology looks to the 21st century, new ideas will result in wonderful advances.

Mechanical (HVAC)

"Mechanical engineering includes the science and art of the formulation, design, development, and control of systems and components involving thermodynamics, mechanics, fluid mechanics, mechanisms, and the conversion of energy into useful work." An overview of mechanical engineering at Berkley, 1998 [on-line]. Unless facility planners are trained as mechanical engineers, it is likely that the planning process will include one or more of these specialists. Still, there are a number of important concepts that planners should understand as they address a sport or recreational facility. This section provides an overview of those mechanical engineering concepts.

Environmental Climate Control

Environmental climate controls related to heating, ventilation, and air-conditioning affect the quality of our work and play environments. Sport and recreational facilities, specifically, must provide an environment where fresh air is exchanged and effectively circulated, where air temperature and humidity are controlled in a manner that promotes good health, and where the air quality is safe.

There are four factors that, when combined, give an optimal thermal environment:

- radiant temperature where surface and air temperatures are balanced,
- air temperature between 64% and 72% F,
- humidity between 40 and 60 percent, and
- a constant air movement of 20 to 40 linear feet/per/min. at a sitting height.

These factors must all be considered to achieve an optimal thermal environment. However, they are only part of the planning that must go into providing indoor environments that are technically sophisticated and also enhance user effectiveness, communication, and overall user satisfaction—the best definition of an "intelligent building" (Tarricone, 1995). Intelligent buildings link such technologies as "HVAC, fire detection and alarm, access, security, elevator, and communication systems to one computer . . ." (Tarricone, 1995). Although this section deals specifically with HVAC, it is important to consider the advantages of creating the intelligent building with a single computer control. This concept has been implemented in both new designs and retrofits. The key is planning ahead.

Additionally, a number of building design characteristics directly impact the optimal thermal environment in buildings. These interior and exterior characteristics include:

- building envelopes that reduce heat loss and gain through insulation, barriers and thermal mass;
- moisture control through vapor barriers and external shading devices;
- properly glazed windows that have good insulating and glare reduction properties;
- double- or triple-paned glazed windows that prevent condensation on windows. [a facility that is] adequately sized, ventilated, cooled, and designed for easy access, future growth, and reconfiguration; and passive heating, cooling, and lighting methods" (Myers, 1997, p. 52).

And when considering building automation and HVAC systems, there are additional choices to make, including:

- centralized or decentralized HVAC systems; heating systems (such as boilers) and cool-ing systems (such as chillers and cooling towers); ventilation systems; substation sens-ing; humidification and dehumidi-fication control; facility energy management programs such as Night Cycle, Night Purge . . . (Myers, 1997, p. 53).

What used to be simply stated as HVAC has advanced beyond the basics of heating, ventilation, and air-conditioning to environmental air quality.

Dr. James E. Woods, co-chair of the Healthy Buildings/IAQ '97 conference, said, "Building professionals require an understanding of the conditions that contribute to the collection of indoor air pollutants by the design of certain systems or through the operation and maintenance of a building's HVAC equipment and systems" (Giometti, 1997, p. 2).

Facility ventilation is directly tied to the indoor air quality (IAQ). The IAQ is a product of the quality of the fresh air introduced into the ventilation system and the quality of the existing indoor air that is recycled.

Typically, HVAC systems re-circulate as much conditioned air [warm or cooled] as is allowed by health and building codes in order to maximize energy efficiency and reduce the size of mechanical and electrical equipment. In facilities where health and indoor-air-quality issues are paramount [or in facilities where no energy-recovery system exists]

as much as 100% of the conditioned air may be exhausted. Such facilities in climates with significant indoor/outdoor temperature differentials in winter and summer can exhaust tens of thousands of dollars in otherwise reclaimable energy.

Energy recovery in HVAC systems involves transferring heat from one airstream to another. In summer months, intake air at a higher temperature rejects heat to cooler exhaust air prior to being mechanically cooled by the chilled-water or direct-expansion coil [of the air-conditioning process]. Conversely, during the winter, intake air is warmed by transferring heat from exhaust air. Approximately 60% to 65% of the available sensible heat may be recovered; latent heat is not recovered (Fabel, 1996, p. 36).

"Use of mechanical dehumidification systems is an efficient way to manage room humidity and contribute to better air quality" (Flynn & Schneider, 1997, p. 57).

Sick building syndrome is the result of poor indoor air quality. The basics of IAQ seem to minimally require that potential indoor pollutants are controlled at the source and that the building's HVAC system—including all the equipment used to ventilate, heat and cool; the ductwork to deliver air; and the filters to clear air—are well maintained (Anonymous, 1998).

In older or poorly designed HVAC systems that merely recirculate conditioned air without exhausting enough air and/or introducing enough fresh air, the IAQ can become compromised. Indoor air quality can be managed, even in older systems, if a proactive approach is used to address the IAQ issues. This includes controlling pollution at its source, from both indoor and outdoor sources.

One low-cost way to prevent IAQ problems is to stop potential sources of indoor air pollution where they originate. Known as source control, this process manages pollutants by removing them from the building, isolating them from people by using physical barriers, and controlling when they are used (Anonymous, 1998, p. A10).

Another approach is maintaining ventilation systems that include

All the equipment used to ventilate, heat, and cool; the ductwork to deliver air; and the filters to clean air. HVAC systems significantly affect how pollutants are distributed and removed from a building. These systems can even act as sources of pollutants, through dirty or damp air filters or uncontrolled moisture in air ducts or drip pans. Proper maintenance of HVAC systems not only contributes to better IAQ, but can decrease operating costs since properly maintained equipment runs more efficiently (Anonymous, 1998, p. A10)

And, John Spengler of Harvard University, at the same conference, reported that

> ...changes to a building's design during construction often contribute to indoor air pollution. In the process of constructing a building, changes are made at the construction site that affect the design of the HVAC system and produce unrecognized problems which later have implications on the quality of indoor air (Giometti, 1997, p. 2).

All of this does not negate the need for design planning that includes the choice of heat or energy source: fossil fuels (coal and heating oil), and heat or energy alternatives (propane/natural gas, wood, electricity, below grade heat pumps, and solar or wind energy). Factors in these choices include geographic location and heat and energy resource availability. Additionally, the start-up or installation costs of some systems are more expensive, but cost less to operate and/or maintain over the long term; and vice-versa for installation of other systems. If the facility is located in a rural area with clean extended air, make sure windows are openable. In polluted environments such as urban areas, non-openable windows are acceptable.

Propane/natural gas, solar, power wind, heat pump, and nuclear power are all considered "clean" sources of heat or energy and are worth thinking about, considering the depletion of ozone in our atmosphere of fossil fuels. These sources of heat or energy may ultimately reduce operating costs, including the "scrubbing" of exhausted air from your building. Finally, the actual selection and type of heating, ventilation, and air-conditioning should consider the economy of operation, flexibility of control, quietness of operation, and capacity to provide desirable thermal conditions.

Planning for the Future

Jim Moravek (1996) has further complicated the decision-making process with the concept that technologies no longer outlast buildings:

> Designing for flexibility in buildings rather than for specific technologies is the best way to overcome obsolescence of the structure in the future. Buildings often outlast the most current technologies, and new consideration must be given to making buildings and technologies work

together. Flexible design has both structural and system components. Buildings require ample space—both vertically and horizontally—so old systems can be removed and new systems installed quickly, without affecting structure, exits, or life-safety systems. Heating, ventilating, and air-conditioning (HVAC) and power-distribution systems need the capacity to service existing loads and the ability to respond to future requirements (p. 28).

However, no project can be considered without planning for HVAC. And this planning should be done by an engineering professional and based upon the technical data and procedures of the American Society of Heating, Refrigerating and Air-conditioning Engineers, Inc. (ASHRAE) and appropriate federal regulations.

An example of an ASHRAE standard appears in Appendix L. This standard, and others, are in constant review by the ASHRAE based upon various changes in technologies and government regulations. The ASHRAE also issues position statements, e.g., Indoor Air Quality Position Statement (approved by ASHRAE Board of Directors, February 2, 1989). This ASHRAE document states the importance of indoor air quality and energy conservation and its impacts, with the belief that "indoor air quality should be maintained at levels expected to protect occupants from adverse effects and discomfort" (p. 1).

Challenges and Future Trends in HVAC

The challenge of HVAC is clearly to increase energy savings without compromising indoor air quality. The most recent enhancement is mandated "open architecture" under the Building Automation and Control Networks (BACnet) standard. TheBACnet standard, initiated by ASHRAE in 1987 and passed in 1996, establishes a communications protocol to facilitate information sharing between HVAC equipment and controls from multiple vendors. Additional trends in HVAC involve continued research in evaporation cooling and the compliance with ever-changing standards, i.e., federal and ASHRAE.

Summary

The technologies of mechanical and electrical engineering are constantly changing. However, facility planners should become familar with concepts related to the function of HVAC, sound, and lighting, etc.

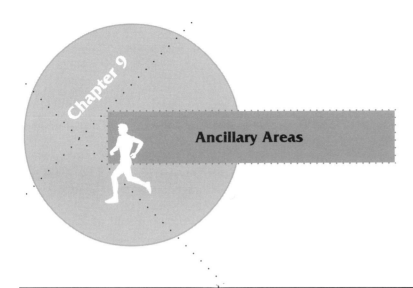

Chapter 9

Ancillary Areas

Hervey Lavoie, Ohlson Lavoie Corporation

The information in this chapter is intended to assist planners, designers, and administrators in their efforts to create superior locker rooms, training, administrative, laundry, storage, and maintenance facilities. This category of uses is referred to as ancillary areas. These are the support facilities for the primary building attractions, such as gymnasiums, pools, and fitness floors. The guidance offered by this chapter will support—not replace—a normal and comprehensive planning and design process.

This chapter will aid the planning and design of ancillary facilities by identifying many of the questions that must be asked, along with the variables that should be considered as the project development team responds to the unique circumstances of each project mission, each site, and each community of users.

Actual design recommendations for specific solutions will not be presented here, because the professional planning/design team that follows the analytical guidelines and considerations brought out in this chapter will be well prepared to reach its own conclusions. Asking the right questions is an essential part of recognizing the best answers.

Learning Objectives

After reading this chapter, the student should be able to:

- Identify the types of ancillary area specialists to be included on the development team,
- Describe design considerations for locker room facilities,
- Explain the concepts of wet and dry areas,
- Describe the various amenities to be included in ancillary areas,
- Identify the major factors to consider in planning a training room,
- Understand the design variables that influence the programming and function of ancillary areas, and
- Gain the ability to critique planning and design work.

The Development Team

Design of ancillary areas will require input from the following specialists who are commonly represented on a facility development team:

- Owner's project manager
- Facility planner/programmer/business planner
- Architect
- Cost authority/construction provider
- Operational consultant
- Component suppliers

Owner's Project Manager

The individual (in-house) or company (out-sourced) who is assigned responsibility to represent the interest of the owner and manage the diverse parties of the development team for the duration of the project.

Facility Planner/Programmer/Business Planner

The individual or company responsible for analyzing the needs of the project owner and producing recommendations as to the mix and magnitude of uses, revenue projections, expense estimates, etc.

Architect

This is the individual or company responsible for taking the work of the facility planner/programmer and creating a building to accommodate the functional requirements and to express the image and style of the building.

Cost Authority/Construction Provider

This is the individual or company responsible for predicting the cost required to create the desired building and site improvements. The same party is often engaged to provide the actual construction of the building.

Operational Consultant

The individual or company responsible for managing the facility, operating the business, hiring staff, creating programs, and providing financial controls. The operational consultant will provide input related to staffing, management, maintenance, marketing, specialized FF&E (fixtures, furnishings and equipment), and other operational issues that impact design of ancillary areas.

Component Suppliers

Providers of facility components (lockers, washing machines, basketball hoops, etc.) are the manufacturers of the special products and equipment that will be included in the facility. They are an essential source of information regarding proper application of their products.

Design Variables

For each ancillary area, the following design variables will be examined and discussed:
- Issues of size, quantity, and dimension,
- Issues of location and relationship (adjacent/proximate, remote),
- Access and circulation considerations for all users—staff, guests, disabled, users and/or members,
- Matters of style, image, and color,
- Issues of materials, finishes and function,
- Engineering issues regarding lighting, HVAC, plumbing and communication systems,
- Gender-specific requirements and other user needs, and
- Requirements for expansion and adaptability.

Facility Types

The most significant variable affecting ancillary areas is that of facility type. As the title of this book suggests, there are many types (and sub-types) including athletics (sub-types for different sports), physical education (sub-types for different age groups: elementary, junior high, high school, and college), recreation/fitness (sub-types for university, municipal, and private).

In addition, many facilities try to wear two or three hats; that is, their mission is to serve the programming needs of a variety of users, varsity athletics, intramural athletics, and physical education, for example. Proper design for ancillary areas will be driven by the particular needs of the overall facility type. For example, the next section will discuss locker rooms in general, and then distinguish between the design of locker rooms for specific types of facilities.

Clearly, planning and design of locker rooms should vary according to facility type. Similarly, other kinds of ancillary areas will vary in use and function for different facility types. The planning and design of training rooms, administrative offices, laundry facilities, storage rooms, and maintenance areas must be viewed in light of their fit to the overall facility mission.

Ancillary, by definition, refers to those functions that are necessary to support the destination program activities for which the facility is created. Users don't come to a facility to use the locker rooms. Rather, they come to use the swimming pool, and the locker room enables them to do so.

Locker Rooms

The term "locker room" encompasses a multitude of components and facilities. More than a room of lockers, the modern locker room accommodates a broad range of functions related to dressing, storage, grooming, personal hygiene, therapy, social exchange, information handling, aesthetics, comfort, safety, and privacy.

Many aspects of locker room planning and design must be considered in light of the overall facility type. However, there are some basic principles that apply to all types of locker rooms, regardless of the facility type. These principles are the planning and design considerations that must be addressed in defining the basic components common to all locker rooms: lockers, toilets, showers, amenities, and grooming stations.

Essential to the accommodation of these functions is the proper location of the locker room within the overall facility and the proper relationship of these components within the locker room itself. Figure 9.1 illustrates the primary relationship that must be considered in properly locating the locker room within the overall facility. Whenever possible, the locker room should be on the same floor level as the aquatic facilities.

One wall of the locker room block is often designed to be a removable wall, located so future expansion also can be accommodated by means of internal conversion of "soft" use spaces that are intentionally located next to the locker room. "Soft" space refers to uses that require little or no special provisions (such as plumbing or expensive finishes), and therefore is space that is easily vacated and converted to locker-room expansion. Examples of "soft" uses include storage rooms, offices, and meeting rooms.

Another approach to expanding existing locker rooms is, for example, to convert the existing women's locker room into an expansion of the men's locker room concurrent with the construction of an entirely new women's locker room as part of a new building addition.

All but the most primitive locker rooms will have lockers, showers, grooming stations, amenities, and toilet facilities. Figure 9.2 provides a conceptual illustration of the proper relationship of these components. Conventional design wisdom has held that consolidation of plumbing facilities to minimize piping runs is a primary consideration in the layout of locker rooms. In truth, the actual economies of clustered plumbing are not significant. The consolidation of plumbing can be quite contrary to the principles of user-friendly design. Toilet facilities backed up to showers will save minor quantities of piping, but can result in a mix of wet bare feet from shower traffic with soiled street shoes from toilet room users. Lavatory grooming counters near toilets and urinals again will save minor amount of piping, but may result in a loss of privacy for toilet users and a compromised atmosphere for personal grooming functions.

Figure 9.1
The relationship of locker rooms to the facility

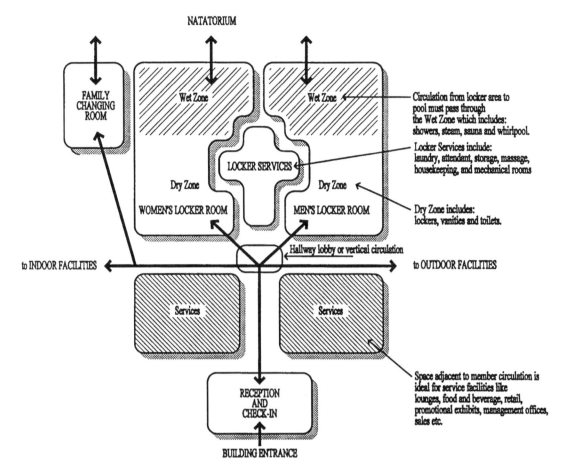

Locker Location

The location of the locker rooms within the facility is important. After going through the reception area, users pass through retail areas, promotional exhibits, and lounges, which help guide them to the locker rooms.

Locker Room Size

The number and size of lockers required will help determine the size of the overall changing room, as will the inclusion of special amenities, such as steam rooms, saunas, massage pools, baths, lounges, or massage rooms. A range of seven to 15-square-feet per locker is possible, depending on locker size and other variables. The best way to accurately program the locker room size that is appropriate for a given facility is to calculate the user capacity of destination attractions (such as gyms, courts, fitness floors, etc.) during peak usage periods. Total occupancy factors are listed below:

Group Exercise Rooms: one person per 45 square feet
Gymnasium: twelve persons per Game Court
Racquet Courts: two persons per Court (four for tennis)
Lap Pools: four persons per Lane
Exercise Pools: one person per 50 square feet
Fitness Floors: one person per 65 square feet
Walk/Jog Tracks: one person per 25 linear feet

When an allowance is made for those who are waiting to participate and those who are finished and showering (an additional 25% to 45% of user occupancy), the total demand for lockers can be predicted. Estimates of the gender ratio of users will allow the total locker count to be distributed between men's and women's locker rooms. Unless special circumstances dictate otherwise, the size of locker rooms for men and women should be the same and each locker count equal to 60% of the total predicted demand. This will account for use patterns that may occasionally result in unequal participation according to gender. On a case-by-case basis, special-use patterns may allow for reasonable reduction of locker count. A university recreation facility that is surrounded by student dormitories may, for example, have many users who shower and change in their dorms. This will cause reduced demand for lockers, showers, and vanities.

The planning objective is to provide a balance between locker-room capacity and the total floor capacity of primary facility attractions, such as fitness equipment, aerobic rooms, and gymnasiums. An imbalance in this ratio will result in

Figure 9.2
Diagrammatic locker area layout, Chicago Athletic Club

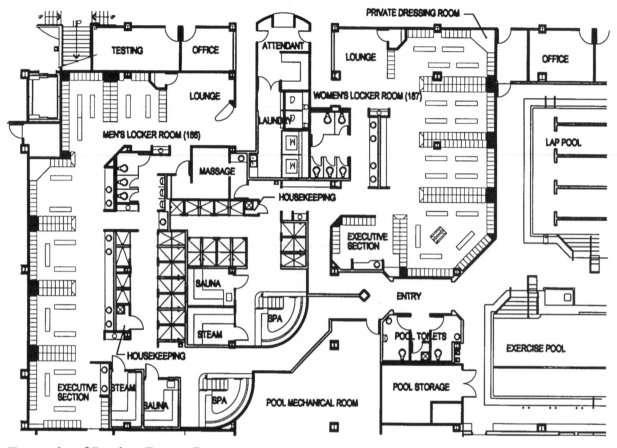

Example of Locker Room Layout

In this Chicago athletic club, the coordination of lockers, wet areas, dry areas, and support facilities can be seen. Maintaining separation between men's and women's facilities while entering and exiting through common gateways and promoting user-friendly flow patterns is key to good locker room layout.

unused capacity or dysfunctional congestion in either the locker rooms or the primary attraction areas. Application of the formula outlined above will ensure properly sized facilities.

Locker Area

The locker area must provide more than securable storage compartments. A good locker layout will allow for a multitude of functional considerations, including:

- Seated dressing space removed from main circulation paths.
- At least one private dressing cubicle for users with special privacy needs.
- At least one dressing/locker cubicle equipped for use by the disabled.
- Size and quantities of lockers determined by analysis of anticipated user groups. In most cases, it is appropriate and sometimes required to provide facilities of equal size for men and women, boys and girls.
- Odor control achieved by means of natural or induced locker ventilation. Management procedures

that encourage proper care of locker contents by users also will be beneficial. Provision of swimsuit dryers can help prevent odors and locker damage caused by storing wet suits. Swimsuit Dryers are compact, self-operated devices that use centrifugal force to "spin" a suit dry in less than one minute.

- Efficiency of locker count can be improved by increasing the height of locker tiers, but caution must be exercised to avoid having lockers so high that they are out of reach of the expected user. It is also problematic to have small lockers located low to the floor where they will be difficult to use without kneeling down.

Figure 9.3 illustrates a range of possible locker and bench configurations with recommended dimensions.

When possible, avoid vast and deep maze-like arrays of lockers. Shallow perimeter layouts around two or three sides of a wet core are more user friendly. This will allow shorter walking distances between locker and shower as well as improved way-finding. Supervision of locker areas may be an important consideration for some facility types where

Figure 9.3
Variations of alcove-type locker arrangements

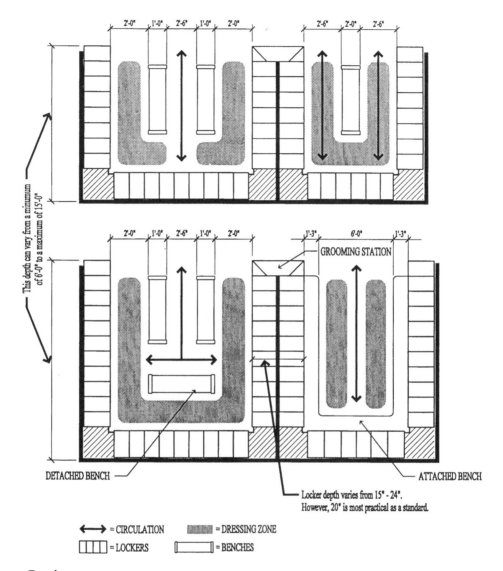

This depth can vary from a minimum of 6'-0" to a maximum of 15'-0"

GROOMING STATION

DETACHED BENCH

ATTACHED BENCH

Locker depth varies from 15" - 24".
However, 20" is most practical as a standard.

⟷ = CIRCULATION   ▓ = DRESSING ZONE
▭ = LOCKERS   ▭ = BENCHES

Locker Alcove Options

To maximize the space available for lockers, alcoves are created as a way to maximize locker count while separating circulation from dressing.

vandalism or victimizing behavior can be expected. Avoid hidden alcoves where unobserved activities can take place.

The main locker-room access will need to accommodate heavy two-way traffic from users carrying bags or equipment. Therefore, locker-room doors should be avoided, and if required for code or security reasons, may be held open with code-approved electro-magnetic devices connected to the fire alarm system. Doorless entries are a commonplace answer to the need for unobstructed two-way circulation in high volume uses such as stadiums and airports. The necessary visual screening of locker room interiors can be provided easily by blocking sight-lines with corners or wingwalls. These visual baffles should be provided even if doors are installed.

Materials and finishes for wet area floors should be selected with maintenance in mind. A variety of impervious floor surfaces are available—ceramic tile, etched terrazzo, vinyl, and synthetics. Considerations should be given to slip coefficients, cleaning techniques, color selection, grout maintenance, aesthetics, and cost. If the daily maintenance program will consist of a hosing down or pressure wash, the best choice of flooring for wet areas is a 1"x1" ceramic tile or a liquid applied synthetic. Such materials should be detailed with coved base.

Floor material options for locker room dressing areas include wood and carpet. Wood floors have been used successfully as an accent in upscale club locker rooms. Carpet is a good choice for locker room dressing areas when a proper maintenance program can be assured. The benefits of carpet (quiet, soil-hiding, colorful, durable) will be lost if it is not vacuumed twice daily and steam cleaned at least four times annually. Odor control of carpet can be enhanced by specifying a factory-applied anti-microbial treatment and taking care in planning of wet area circulation to prevent excessive tracking of water to the carpet.

Ceilings should provide for good light diffusion and acoustic absorption. Moisture resistance is also important. If a lay-in grid ceiling is to be specified, an aluminum grid will resist moisture-induced corrosion. Lay-in panels must have sufficient stiffness to resist "pillowing." The aesthetic impact of ceiling treatment should not be overlooked. Consider the possibility of lighting the locker room indirectly by mounting strip light fixtures on top of lockers. Emergency lighting must be provided. Natural day lighting by means of skylights, glass block, or obscure glazing will enhance the locker-room environment.

Lockers

Locker systems are available in a variety of materials: painted steel, mesh steel, wood panel, and plastic laminate-faced particle board or fiber-resin board. The selection of locker material and construction is a function of several factors. Considerations include:
- Cost,
- Appearance requirements,
- Resistance to abuse,
- Resistance to corrosion
- Availability of desired size, accessories, and locking system, and
- Installation requirements.

Wood may be most suitable in applications where a traditional or luxury image is desired, and the risk of vandalism is small. A variety of wood stains and door designs is available.

Painted steel may be most suitable in non-corrosive environments where the desire for an upscale ambiance does not exist and the risk of abusive behavior is present. A variety of standard and custom paint colors are available. Choice of door styles is somewhat limited, but painted steel lockers have been the standard choice for applications where economy, utility, security, and durability are the prime concerns.

Plastic laminate-faced particle board may be the most suitable choice where economy and upscale design image are both important. A rich variety of colors, textures, and finishes is readily available for door faces. This type of locker is also a good choice for moisture resistance. Many optional accessories, such as shelves, hooks, rods, and mirrors are available. The choice of locking systems must consider the operational challenges and security issues associated with keys, padlocks, cards, and combinations. A new generation of keyless locking systems is becoming available and can offer unique benefits to both users and facility managers. These locks employ a keypad for the user to enter a self-selected code to lock and unlock the device. No key or padlock is required.

Toilets

Careful consideration must be given to location of locker room toilets. Will they be used under wet or dry conditions? Are the locker room toilets intended to serve the nearby aquatic facilities? If so, users will be wet, and toilets must be located in the locker room wet area. In this case, other toilet facilities should be provided for "dry" users in the dry zone of the locker room or in a location outside of the locker room. In any case, mixing of dry and wet toilet room traffic should be avoided. Street shoes on wet slippery floors are a hazard, and the presence of bare feet on wet floors that have been soiled by street shoes is unsanitary and unpleasant. Possible solutions are:
- "Dry" toilets near the locker room entry, and "wet" toilets near the shower area,
- "Dry" toilets near the entry (for convenience of use from outside of locker room), and wet toilets within the natatorium, and
- "Dry" toilets outside of the locker room and "wet" toilets near the shower area.

Other considerations for planning and designing locker room toilets include:
- Sufficient quantities of fixtures (water closets and urinals) should be provided to meet peak user demand. The unique circumstances of each project must be evaluated in making this determination. Rules of thumb suggest that a ratio of one water closet per 60 lockers is sufficient, but this ratio should be modified to account for special circumstances such as large group use or schedule-driven programs that result in surging use patterns.
- Careful attention should be paid to toilet partition materials and construction. Problems with rusting, delamination, warping, and vandalism are common. This is not the place to cut quality for the purpose of reducing cost.
- Lighting of toilet stalls should be placed toward the back of the stall in the form of downlight, wall scone or valance light. This location will provide the best lighting for cleanliness inspections of the water closet.
- Maintenance access to piping and valves must be provided. Access panels in plumbing walls are a common solution to this need. Water-conserving fixtures are often required by code. Auto-activated fittings can also be beneficial for sanitation and user consequence.

Showers

The quantity of showers and the corresponding capacity of hot water-generating equipment together are the most critical components of an athletic facility's ancillary areas. Shortcomings in any other design features can be adapted to or in some way tolerated. Cold showers and/or long lines of people waiting for too few showers will create an extremely negative experience for the facility user.

Figure 9.4
Functional and attractive locker area

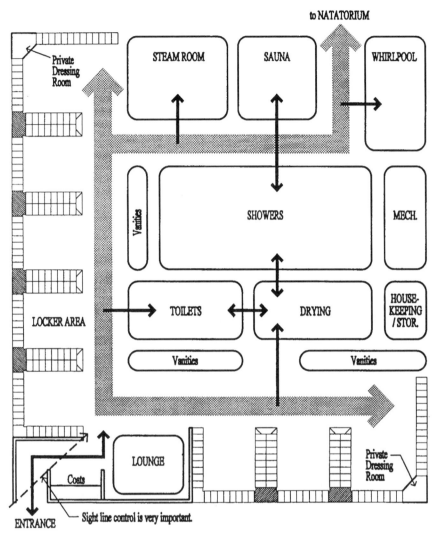

Locker room Flow Patterns

Unfortunately, rules of thumb for shower count are not always reliable. One shower per 20 lockers is a ratio that sometimes is applicable. However, there will be cases when that ratio will result in too many or too few showers. The best approach is for the project planner to conduct an analysis of anticipated overall user capacity (similar to that process suggested above for estimating locker quantities) in the facility as the basis for predicting the peak shower-taking population at any given time. This projection will, in turn, form the basis of the mechanical engineers' calculation of flow rate and duration of hot water that must be supplied for showers.

The selection of a control valve and shower head should be considered carefully to arrive at the balance of shower quality, water economy, and scald safety that is most appropriate for a given facility and the users it serves. Control valves can be specified for automatic shut-off, automatic temperature control, variable or fixed volume, and vandal resistance. It is desirable that shower piping and valves be accessible for maintenance and repair without destruction of the enclosing wall and finishes. Access panels can be provided and detailed to coordinate with the overall decor.

Shower rooms must be ventilated and exhausted to prevent odors and moisture accumulation. Air supply points must be arranged to minimize drafts. In general, ventilation systems must be designated to promote the migration of air from dry areas to wet areas.

A variety of shower types and layouts is possible and is illustrated in Figure 9.5.

Other general guidelines for shower planning and design include:

- Provide a drying area adjacent to the showering facility.
- Provide flush-type recessed hose bibs for cleaning purposes.
- Walls and floors of the shower enclosure must be completely waterproof.

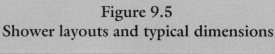

Figure 9.5
Shower layouts and typical dimensions

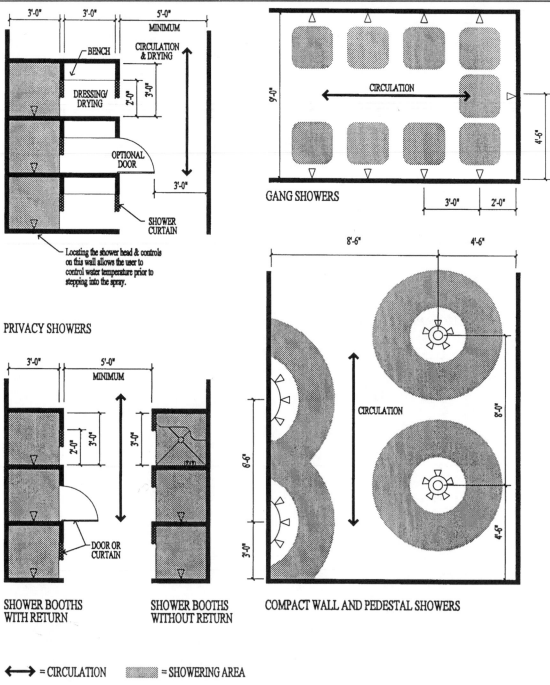

- Shower heads should be self-cleaning and water-conserving. Adjustability of spray and angle should be considered on a case-by-case basis. Locate the shower head where the user can turn on the water and test the temperature without having to stand in the water stream.
- Shower finishes must be impervious to water and easily cleaned. Ceramic tile, stone or etched terrazzo are good choices for floors and walls.
- Ceilings can be finished with ceramic tile or epoxy paint.

- Minimum spacing for gang showers is 30 inches. Shower head heights should be set according to anticipated size of users. A variety of heights can be provided if a mix of users is anticipated. Recommended mounting heights for shower heads depend on pipe configuration. The actual height of the pipe coming out of the wall will be 4" to 8" higher than the head:
- Men: 6'-8" to 7'-0" (from floor to shower head)
- Women: 6'-2" to 6'-6" (from floor to shower head)
- Children: 5'-6" (or adjustable)

Other design issues affecting wet area finishes are:
- Evaluate non-slip characteristics of a floor material when wet. Most manufacturers can provide a slip coefficient for their products. Avoid use of step-over shower curbs, as they can be a safety problem and an access barrier.
- Substrate—a finish material will perform only as well as its underlying support. Of the many options for wet area wall substrate, gypsum board is the least reliable. Concrete masonry and cement boards are preferred, and will stand up to the moisture that will inevitably penetrate the finish material.
- Floor construction of showers and drying areas must be sloped to perimeter or center drains in order to avoid birdbath-like puddles of water on the floor.

Shower planning also must address the inclusion or exclusion of clean towel distribution, towel hooks, foot rests, amenity shelving, consumable dispensers, used towel collection, and provision, if any, of consumables such as soap and shampoo. Inclusion of a drying zone between showers and lockers is important. This area can be equipped with floor mats and drains to prevent tracking of water onto dry area finishes. The shower area often is positioned to serve users of indoor and outdoor aquatic facilities as well as locker room amenities such as steam room, sauna, and jacuzzi bath. Users of these amenities should be encouraged by the layout and flow to shower prior to use. In many jurisdictions, health codes require that all access to pools pass through a showering area.

Amenities

Steam, sauna, jacuzzi, and cold plunge are the amenities most often considered for inclusion in an upscale locker room facility. Each of these features requires careful attention to a host of planning and design considerations.

Steam Rooms

Steam rooms are the most maintenance-intensive of all ancillary facilities and will readily self-destruct if not properly constructed.

- As a guideline, sizing should be based on a capacity factor of one person per 12-square-feet or 2.2 linear feet of bench. Steam generators are sized by the manufacturer according to the volume of the room.
- Entrance doors to steam rooms will release large quantities of steam when opened, and should always swing out and be located where this vapor-laden air will not damage nearby fittings and finishes, particularly on the ceiling.
- Walls, floor, and ceiling of steam rooms must be completely waterproof and finished with non-slip ceramic tile or stone.
- Provision of a glazed door and sidelight will improve supervision and make a more pleasant and open experience for the steam room user.

Figure 9.6
Individual Showers

- Slope the steam room ceiling at 1:12 to a side wall or uninhabited drip point in order to prevent condensation from dripping on users.
- All components of steam rooms (lights, hinges, frames, fire sprinklers, fasteners, etc.) must be corrosion resistant. Plastic and aluminum usually are satisfactory. Stainless steel is not a reliable choice and will likely rust. Avoid painted steel or black iron at all costs.
- Most steam room failures are related to failure of the substrate or wall structures to resist the corrosive effects of the vapor-laden air. Proven steam room construction details are published by the ceramic tile industry and should be followed carefully. Compatibility of components (substrates, membranes, bonding agents, adhesives and finishes) cannot be taken for granted. Any substitutions must be thoroughly researched.
- Maintenance access to the steam generator room should be available from a mixed gender corridor so that servicing of steam equipment can occur without closing the locker room. Even the best steam-generating equipment will require frequent maintenance. Steam-room controls, other than a thermostatic sensor, should be located in a staff-only area to prevent tampering.

The decision to include a steam room must be based on consideration of the operating and maintenance expense, as well as the initial construction cost. Periodic staff supervision also is necessary to prevent misuse. Location of steam jets and sensor must be planned and detailed to minimize risk of burns from steam and metallic fittings and ensure proper temperature control and heat distribution. Accessories usually include thermometer, hose bib, hose, and clock. An overhead shower head sometimes is included. Depending on characteristics of local water supply, a water softener may be required to prevent mineral deposits on the steam heating elements.

Sauna

Saunas are designed to provide dry heat at extremely high temperatures. They are less costly to install than steam rooms but will still require a diligent maintenance program. Planning and design considerations follow: (Figure 9.7)

- Wood-lined walls, floors, and seats are the usual choice, however, tile-surfaced accent walls may be included for ease of maintenance. The high temperatures involved (in excess of 180 degrees F) require that users be protected from contact with metal and other highly conductive materials which could cause burns. Wood hardware, plastic mats, or towels can provide this protection.
- The main problem with wood surface sauna seats is the staining that occurs from accumulated soaked-in sweat and the odors that result. Use of a light-colored wood will reduce the unsightliness of the staining problem. The best approach to odor control is to require use of individual towels for seating, along with daily pressure cleaning and application of disinfectant. For these reasons, a sauna may not be suitable for many types of public facilities where towels and multiple daily cleanings cannot be provided.
- Glazed doors and sidelights will create a more pleasant and more easily supervised sauna.
- As a guideline, sizing decisions can be based on a capacity factor of one person per 12-square-feet.
- Adequate lighting is particularly important for sanitation and maintenance operations.
- Commonly specified accessories are clock, thermometer, and water supply.
- A floor drain can be provided for ease of cleaning, but it may need to be a self-priming type to prevent the sauna heat from drying out the trap and releasing sewer gases into the room.

Figure 9.7
Sauna

Figure 9.8
Jacuzzi bath

Jacuzzi

Also known as a whirlpool bath, this amenity is a communal body of water (100-104 degrees Fahrenheit) equipped with air and water jets to create a turbulent massage effect for the immersed user. Pre-packaged molded fiberglass units generally are unsuitable for the applications addressed in this book and should be avoided. Water quality control is the single most important issue impacting the planning and design of these facilities. Local health regulations will control many aspects of the water purification system, as well as pool and deck materials and configuration.

Other considerations:

- Capacity factors are in the range of 10 to 15 square feet per person.
- Equipment rooms should be located for easy access by maintenance or repair personnel of either gender.
- It is important to encourage users to shower before using the jacuzzi by locating showers convenient to the Jacuzzi.
- Pool basins should be completely tile lined to allow for the frequent draining and cleaning that is necessary to keep a sanitary and attractive body of water. Plaster-lined pools will be more difficult to clean.
- The vapor-laden air of the jacuzzi area will be made more corrosive by the presence of chlorine. Certain grades of stainless steel eventually will succumb to corrosion in this atmosphere. Aluminum, stone, plastic, glass, and ceramic tile are acceptable materials for use in a jacuzzi environment.
- It is essential that air-handling systems for the jacuzzi area be designed to produce a negative air pressure relative to surrounding uses. This will prevent the migration of corrosive vapors and disagreeable odors to other parts of the building.
- Buried piping (which requires jack hammers and shovels to access) is the most economical choice for grade supported pools. However, access points must be provided for cleanouts, valves, and stub-outs.

- For safety reasons it is necessary for the Jacuzzi pool to be surrounded on at least two sides by a non-slip deck at least four feet wide.

Grooming Stations

Sometimes called a vanity, a grooming station is a place in the locker room where users brush teeth, comb hair, wash hands, shave, apply makeup, etc. The fit out for a wet grooming station includes a sink with hot and cold water, a mirror, and a ground fault-protected power source. Minimal facilities for a dry grooming station are a mirror, a power source, and a small shelf. Optional enhancements of grooming provisions can include such niceties as hand-held hair dryers, wall-mounted hand/hair dryers, make-up mirrors, stools, soap or lotion dispensers, face towel, paper towels, waste receptacles, and disposable grooming aids, such as razors and combs. The management of each facility must develop its own policy regarding provision of these optional services. Will they be supplied by building management or by each individual user?

General considerations for user-friendly planning and design of grooming stations follow:

- The required number of wet and dry grooming stations needed must be analyzed according to the unique circumstances of each project and gender-specific grooming practices. As a rule of thumb, total grooming stations should be approximately the same or slightly less than the shower count. A 20-80 split between wet and dry grooming stations may be varied by some planners to provide more wet stations for men (shaving) and more dry stations for women (make-up).
- Lighting at grooming mirrors should be arranged to illuminate both sides of a person's face. Provide a color of light that enhances flesh tones, such as incandescent or warm white fluorescent. (Figure 9.9).
- Avoid locating grooming facilities with toilets or placing them too deeply into wet areas. For convenience

**Figure 9.9
Wet and dry grooming stations.**

of use, they should be located on the seam between the locker dry zone and the shower wet zone. Users will find it very inconvenient to have long distances to walk between their locker and the grooming station.

- Vanity tops must be designed for standing (36" +/-), stool height (42" +/-) seating, or chair height seating (30" +/-) depending on user preference.
- The design image of grooming stations can be used to convey the intended character of a facility. Up-scale club environments should have luxurious grooming facilities. Public recreation facilities may want to convey a more modest but functional character.
- A full-length wall-mounted mirror should be provided for use somewhere along the locker room exit path.

Locker Room Auxiliary Spaces

Special uses are sometimes incorporated into locker-room plans to meet particular user needs. The specific requirements of each must be identified. Examples including social lounges, attendant services, shoe shine, laundry service, workout clothing service, massage, tanning, private telephone cubicles, and personal storage lockers of various sizes. The Planning Team should consider the arguments for inclusion or exclusion of each amenity.

Locker-Room Accessories

Considerations for a well-equipped locker room include an electric water cooler, clock, scale, automatic swimsuit dryer, telephone, emergency call system, plastic bag dispenser, waste containers, hair dryers, television sets, and vending machines for personal grooming items or beverages.

Special Types of Locker Rooms

Family Locker Room: This is a handy name for an arrangement of changing facilities designed to serve cross-gender couples with special needs, for example:
- Mother and a young son who is too old to join her in the women's locker room and too young to venture into the men's locker room alone,
- Father and a young daughter who is too old to join him in the men's locker room and too young to venture into the women's locker room alone,
- An elderly couple, one of whom needs assistance from the other in dressing for a rehab session or senior exercise program,
- An individual man or women with a special privacy need due to a surgical scar, deformity, or personal preference. Family locker rooms can be used for patient changing rooms in facilities that offer integrated clinical services, such as physical therapy or cardiac rehab.

The family locker room is an array of individual changing rooms, each one equipped with a shower, toilet, sink, and changing space. As many as five or six such changing rooms can be provided. An arrangement of storage lockers and benches are provided in a spacious coed common area adjacent to the changing rooms. Grooming, showering, toilet and dressing functions take place in the privacy of the changing rooms. Storage of clothing and final stages of dressing and grooming take place in the coed locker area. These rooms should be fully accessible to the disabled and could in itself satisfy the legal requirement for a handicap accessible locker facility. Other amenities that can be included in the family locker common area are an electric water cooler, swimsuit dryer, wet vanity, dry vanity, towel station, full-length mirror, scale, diaper-changing platform, coat rack, wet bag dispenser, telephone, waste container, and janitor closet. A selection of full-size and half-size storage lockers works well. Provide at least eight lockers for each changing room. The family locker room generally works best with direct access to aquatic attractions. (Figure 9.10).

Express Lockers: It is true for any athletic/fitness facility that some members prefer to arrive wearing their workout/sports attire. They have no desire to use the changing/shower/grooming facilities. They prefer to return to their homes for that purpose after working out. These users need only a secure place for their purse/wallet, hat, car keys, gloves, coat, etc. There is no need to force these members into a gender-specific locker room and add to the potential congestion.

Express lockers can be provided in an area convenient to the ingress/egress circulation of members. This is a coed environment and should include a variety of locker sizes (and a coat rack in four-season climates) and comfortable benches for those users who need to change shoes. Express lockers have proven in practice to be a very cost-effective way of diverting unnecessary traffic from overcrowded men's and women's locker rooms. An express locker count equal to 10% of the total gender-specific locker rooms will usually be adequate.

Staff Locker Room: The question of staff changing facilities is important. If staff use the main locker rooms, they may, in effect, displace a paying customer. Yet providing a separate dedicated staff locker room can be space consuming and costly. Certainly, there is a legitimate need in an athletic facility for staff changing, showering, and grooming functions, as well as a secure holding area for their personal effects.

Many facilities have found it effective to provide a coed staff lounge with a mini-kitchen, basic furnishings including tables and chairs and an arrangement of storage lockers for clothing and personal effects. A pair of private unisex changing/shower compartments can be included to allow staff to freshen up after work without competing with the membership for limited locker/shower availability. A wet vanity/grooming station can also be included. Some management systems will prefer to have the staff mingling with the membership and thus doing an ongoing quality check as they use the same locker facilities that the members do. Once again, a case-by-case determination must be made in order to fit the facility design concept to the management concept.

Officials Locker Room: Facilities designed for competitive team sport activities will require locker room accommodation for umpires, referees and visiting teams. These facilities are gender specific and require a secure location away from contestant and spectator areas.

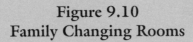

Figure 9.10
Family Changing Rooms

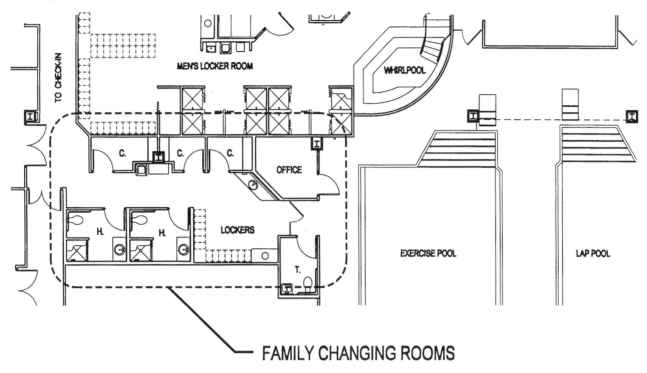

FAMILY CHANGING ROOMS

C. = CHANGING ROOM WITH BENCH
H. = ADA CHANGING ROOM W/TOILET, SHOWER AND SINK
T. = ADA POOL TOILET

Administrative Offices

Staff offices must be barrier free to disabled job candidates and equally accessible to men and women. Staff offices generally fall into two categories of space.

Back office space is required for staff who have little or no regular contact with active facility users. Examples include: accounting, human resources, marketing staff and copy/fax/print functions.

- Front office space is required for staff with supervisory responsibilities and regular contact with active users. Examples include management staff, sales personnel, program directors, and counselors. Other administrative functions that require a mainstream location include:
- Reception, access control, and check-in for the facility at large,
- Supervisory stations for natatorium, fitness floor, gymnasium, racquet sports, and
- Faculty/coaches/instructors' offices.

The size, quantity and furnishings required by each of these staff offices must be determined by the planner in dialogue with department heads and user representatives. Questions to be considered include:

- What are the expected number of full- and part-time staff? What are their titles and work descriptions?
- Which staff members require enclosed private offices? Open but private work stations? Shared work stations (concurrently or alternately)? In-office conference capability?
- Which staff members require frequent contact with each other? With certain activity areas? With certain users?

With answers to these questions in hand, the designer can begin preparation of a space plan for administrative offices. Design considerations include:

- Anticipated circulation patterns for users and staff,
- Type of partition and extent of glass, if any, in walls and doors,
- Need for acoustic privacy,
- Lighting system for both ambient and task lighting,
- Provision of adequate power, communication, and computer hook-ups,
- Provision of year-round heating/cooling and temperature control zones,
- Need for natural daylight or outside view, and
- Computer terminals, computer desks, or computer tables and wiring for main frame and internet access.

Office uses require supplemental spaces that can accommodate the functions necessary to support the working station. The design process should bring these questions to the table for discussion by all appropriate parties. Such spaces include:

- Utility area for facsimile machines, copiers, printers, office supplies, and storage,
- Employee kitchen area with coffee maker, microwave, refrigerator, dishwasher, and (storage, sometimes included as part of a lunch room or staff lounge),
- Conference rooms,
- Coat closets or employee security lockers,
- Designated and specially ventilated smoker's room if operating policies will allow staff smoking on premises,
- Staff-only restrooms and shower/locker rooms may be desired to maintain separation from customer/users,
- Location and type of central telephone reception and distribution must be determined. Many multi-feature phone systems are available,
- Mail and message-handling system should be planned into the administrative component, voice-mail phone systems are now an expected and widely accepted productivity tool for administrative staff.

Laundry

Planning and design of laundry facilities is predicated upon the workload. Just as kitchen design is based on the menu, so laundry design is based on quantity and type of articles to be processed. Towels and athletic clothing are the most common articles needing to be laundered in a recreation facility. The unit of measure applicable to laundry equipment is the pound. Therefore, it is necessary to translate the laundry workload from quantity of articles to their weight in pounds, which must be processed per hour. This is a measure of the actual dry weight of articles to be washed. Without reliable information on weight, quantity, and use rates of laundered articles, the planning of laundry facilities is pure guesswork.

Most equipment cycles allow two loads per hour. Thus, it is possible to arrive at a calculation of required laundry capacity by establishing with the facility operator how many hours per day the laundry will be staffed and running. Certainly a double-shift operation will get more production from a given quantity of equipment than a single eight-hour work shift, but a double shift may not be practical for other reasons. Once the workload is determined, the size and quantity of washers and dryers can be set. It generally is advisable to select machine sizes that allow at least two washing units and two drying units. In this way, a malfunction in one machine will not completely shut down the laundry operation.

The location of laundry facilities is of great importance. The best locations are close to the storage/distribution place for cleaned articles or the collection point for soiled articles. A ground level, grade-supported floor slab is preferred for ease of plumbing and control of vibrations from the equipment. Commercial washer extractors work at very high RPM, which can generate destructive vibrations. Most units must be bolted securely to a 24-inch-thick grade-supported concrete slab in order to control vibration. If an on-grade location is not possible, it will be necessary to specify an extraction washing machine with a built-in vibration dampening system. Most manufacturers offer such a unit as an option. Other factors to consider in selecting a laundry location are:

- The need for an outside combustion air supply for gas-fired dryers may suggest a location along an outside wall.
- The need for exhaust flue for both gas and electric dryers may suggest a single-story location with a roof surface immediately overhead. A booster fan may be required if the length of exhaust duct exceeds manufacturer limits. Lint build-up in the exhaust ductwork requires that maintenance access be planned for and used regularly.
- The high volume of waste water discharge for most commercial washers requires a high-capacity trench drain recessed into the floor.
- Consideration should be given to how equipment can be moved into and out of the laundry space. Washer and dryer sizes should be researched carefully prior to sizing and locating access doorways.
- Accessibility by both men and women staff is needed.

The laundry planner must consider how and by what route both soiled and cleaned articles will arrive at their proper destinations. If carts are used, space must be allocated for storage or holding of extra carts at points of collection, cleaning, and distribution. Folding and sorting of laundered articles is a very labor-intensive process. However, the location of the laundry facility can be planned to allow towel-handling personnel to cover other staff functions such as locker attendant or housekeeping. Other planning and design considerations for laundry facilities:

Confirm that adequate utility capacities exist for electric power, water supply, water temperature, sanitary waste, and gas.

- Domestic washers/dryers will prove unsuitable for all but the most incidental, low-volume laundry operation.
- Placement of washers and dryers should be conducive to a logical and efficient work flow.
- Extractor-type washers use centrifugal force to wring maximum moisture from wet articles prior to drying. This will conserve dryer energy and save time in the drying process.
- Laundry room floors, walls, and ceilings should be finished with a smooth, easily cleaned impervious coating that will not trap dust and lint.
- Dryers typically have a greater weight capacity than a corresponding washer. A 35-pound washer normally will be paired with a 50-pound dryer.
- The laundry room must include space for chemical storage, carts, folding counters, a two-compartment sink, and adequate service access space around the equipment.
- The final pieces of the laundry puzzle are the washer and dryer themselves. Numerous manufacturers offer commercial units varying in size, power, quality, durability, design, and cost. Selection of the best manufacturers (washers and dryers are not necessarily made by the same company) requires diligent comparisons of actual cylinder sizes, types of motor control capabilities, automatic detergent injection systems, control cycles, physical construction, warranties, energy efficiency and maintenance schedules.

Storage Facilities

Of course, storage rooms should be sized, shaped, and furnished with racks, shelves, bins, etc., as required to accommodate the items to be stored. However, it is not always possible to predict, over the life of a facility, how much and what kinds of things will need to be stored. Therefore, when it comes to sizing storage rooms, it is best to err on the side of accommodation and provide at least 20% more storage space than can be justified by actual measurement of the volume of articles to be stored.

Designers frequently assign the storage function to odd-shaped leftover spaces that are not necessarily conducive to efficient storage. There are a few simple planning and design guidelines for storage rooms.

- Within the storage room, allow for a double-loaded circulation way between actual storage space on either side. The depth of the storage space must be appropriate to the item stored so that it may be retrieved without repositioning of intervening stored items.
- Storage room doors should open out from the room and swing flat against adjacent walls. Double-door openings should be considered wherever bulky items will be stored.
- Access to certain storage rooms should be configured so that large, long articles such as ladders can be maneuvered in and out of the room.
- Adequate, utilitarian lighting is a must.
- All storage rooms should be mechanically ventilated.
- Provisions must be made for storage of outside field equipment so that access to storage does not result in unnecessary soiling of interior walkways.
- Code restrictions may impose limits on storage room locations. Many codes, for example, do not allow the dead space under a stairway enclosure to be used for storage.

In general, storage rooms should be located close to the point of use for items being stored. The matter of maintaining storage security and limiting access to authorized persons deserves careful consideration by the design team. Proper door hardware and a well thought-out keying schedule will enhance storage security. The use of motion detection alarms or video surveillance may be appropriate for storage of high-cost items such as audio-visual equipment.

Customizing Ancillary Facilities

The remainder of this chapter will examine the ways in which ancillary facilities in general should be customized to meet the unique requirements of each project type: athletic facilities, physical education facilities, and recreation/fitness clubs.

Athletic Facilities

These are the buildings and fields used by educational institutions to conduct competitive, inter-school athletic programs and include facilities for both training and performance. It normally is only at the collegiate level that designated fa-cilities are provided for the exclusive use of the intercollegiate athletic program. High school athletic facilities are generally shared with physical education uses.

Requirements for the ancillary areas of intercollegiate athletic facilities include recognition of the important role such facilities play in recruiting top-level athletes and coaches and the creation of a successful competitive record.

Locker Rooms

Size, quantity, type, and location of team locker rooms will be determined by the number and size of active sports teams, the timing of practice and competitive seasons, the timing of daily practice sessions, and the location of practice and competition facilities. Other design and planning considerations for team locker rooms include:

- Visiting team locker rooms must be provided for competitive events. Planners must analyze scheduling patterns for all sports with overlapping seasons to determine the number of visiting team locker rooms needed. Security for this area is of utmost importance.
- Locker sizes for athletics will be determined by the equipment required for a given sport. Of course, football and hockey lockers will be larger than basketball and track lockers. The amount of dressing space allowed should also increase as locker sizes increase to accommodate the handling of larger equipment. Sports with non-overlapping practice and competition seasons can share the same locker space.
- Direct outside access to practice and/or game fields may be desirable for sports such as football, soccer, lacrosse, and baseball. The soiling of interior hallways thus can be minimized.
- Planning efforts must ensure that locker room facilities provide equal opportunities for both men and women, able and disabled.
- Game day locker facilities also should be provided for coaches and officials.
- Proper locker ventilation for drying stored articles is extremely important in preventing the build-up of unpleasant odors.

Competitive sports will require team meetings and "chalk talks," which can be conducted in one or more lecture rooms ideally located close to the locker rooms. Such rooms should be equipped with chalkboards and audiovisual equipment. Video replay and analysis is a key component of most coaching programs and planning for the location and networking of the hardware for this function is essential.

Administrative Offices

The need for staff work stations for athletic team programs can be quite extensive. This is particularly true for the high-profile competitive sports programs found in Division I universities. Each program must be analyzed for its own unique set of requirements, but it is not unusual for multi-sport programs to require defined working quarters for such staff positions as athletic director and assistants, head coaches and assistants, public relations and media coordinators, sports psychologists, fund-raising and alumni relations director(s), facilities manager, ticket sales staff, recruiting and scholarship coordinator, accounting staff, student advisors, chaplain, transportation coordinator, equipment and supply manager, director of security, secretarial and clerical aides, audiovisual personnel, and part-time or seasonal employees. Allowances should be made for anticipated growth in the scale of the athletic program and the staff to support it.

The planning process must identify all positions requiring a workstation, and itemize the needs of each in a written document that will be approved by the controlling authority prior to the start of the facility design work. In developing a layout of staff offices, the designer will confront the issue of centralized vs. decentralized administrative offices. This matter is best resolved with input from user groups.

Laundry

Requirements for laundry services to athletic team programs goes beyond the provision of clean towels. The laundry service for a team sport facility must deal with the program's need for clean and sanitary towels, practice and game uniforms, protective equipment (shoulder pads, headgear, etc.) personal wear, and miscellaneous items such as floor mats, foul weather gear, equipment bags, footwear, and utility items. Competitive travel schedules require shipping and receiving facilities not unlike a commercial warehouse operation, complete with loading docks and truck berths. The laundry is best located at the distribution/collection point for all materials to be supplied by the institution. If the laundry is to be a large central plant shared with other institutional users, a remote location may be required. However, a convenient and secure distribution center should then be created for the team sport facility.

The use of individual mesh laundry bags is an effective way to simplify handling of personal items. Each bag carries an identification tag and can be filled with soiled personal wear, turned in, washed, dried, and held for later retrieval by the user. A numbered storage rack will be helpful in keeping the bags arranged for speedy retrieval.

Storage and Maintenance

Off-season handling of reusable sports equipment must be provided. Planning and design considerations include:
- Adequate space for storage includes shelving and/or racks appropriate for the items being stored. Helmets and shoulder pads, for example, will have a longer useful life if properly racked instead of being dumped into a bulk storage bin. Provide for receiving incoming equipment and issuing outgoing equipment.
- Adequate space for repair of items before being stored is important. This procedure will allow non-repairable inventory to be identified, discarded, and reordered prior to the next season. Allow cabinet space for tools and spare parts.
- For team sports, the security of stored items is particularly important. Designers must address the issue of lock keying and access control in coordination with the equipment manager.
- Storage areas should be kept ventilated and dry to prevent mildew, mold, and odor buildup.

Physical Education Facilities

These are the buildings and fields used by institutions of learning in the conduct of physical education programs for all ages. Such programs commonly are provided for students of elementary, middle, junior high, and high schools, as well as the university undergraduate level. Programming of physical education generally is organized in a class format with one or more instructors. A wide variety of skill development activities must be accommodated. Special considerations for the planning and design of the ancillary facilities that support the physical education program follow.

Locker Rooms

Because of the scheduled class format, physical education locker rooms must be able to accommodate large influxes of user groups occupying and quickly vacating lockers, toilets, showers, and grooming facilities. Planners must analyze these use patterns in terms of class size, class duration, age, gender-mix, duration of changeover time between classes, and types of activities being conducted. Not all classes will require use of locker rooms. This analysis will guide determinations such as number and size of lockers, number of toilets, showers, and lavatories, types of locker-room accessories provided, and types of finishes to be used throughout. Designers will reference the same analysis as they create and select provisions for towels, soap handling, energy conservation, grooming aids, handling of refuse, and control of vandalism. The design strategy for dealing with each of these issues should be developed from the dialogue among planners, designers, manager, faculty, and users. Other planning and design considerations unique to physical education locker rooms include:
- Height of locker benches, lockers, and locker security devises should be studied carefully, relative to the average height, reach, and eye level of the typical user. This also applies to heights of water coolers, lavatories, toilets, urinals, and counter tops. In case of a wide mix of users, the design orientation should favor the least able user or provide a mix of accommodations.
- Many schools have after-hours programs for community meetings. If the overall facility is going to offer such programs, the toilet facilities portion of the locker room can be positioned to permit access for community users without allowing them to access to the remainder of the locker room.

Locker systems must be customized to meet the special needs of the physical education program being served. The dressing locker and box storage system frequently is used. In this system, a series of small storage lockers is located near a large dressing locker. Security of the storage locker is accomplished with a combination padlock, which is transferred to the dressing locker along with all the contents of the storage locker when the student is in class. Many variations of locker systems have been developed to meet the special needs of physical education facilities. The designer must analyze the unique circumstances of each application before selecting the most appropriate system for a given project.

Because these locker rooms may play host to large groups of unsupervised adolescents, the design of all components and finishes should be as abuse-resistant as practical. Plastic laminate, and glass and wood veneer, for example, are not considered to be abuse resistant. Avoid creating hidden alcoves where unsupervised behavior could lead to facility damage or personal safety problems.

The need for visual inspection by facility managers of locker contents may exist. If this is the case, the use of an expanded mesh locker construction may be the best choice. Otherwise, a means of overriding locker security devices must be planned for.

Staff Offices

The need for physical education staff work stations is limited primarily to faculty office space. The relationship of these offices to those of the athletic teams and administration is the subject of much discussion in schools with both programs. In general, administrative units requiring little or no contact with students may not benefit from close proximity to those with regular involvement with large numbers of students. However, in some cases, interaction and good communication between these groups of staff may produce beneficial results. This is another planning question that defies universal resolution. It must be resolved as a matter of policy, on a case-by-case basis, for each institution.

Laundry

Options for handling the laundry needs of physical education students are:

- Students are responsible for personal laundry needs, including towels and/or gym uniforms.
- School maintains a laundry facility on the premises for towels and/or gym uniforms.
- School contracts to an outside service for towel laundry and/or gym uniforms.

Potential benefits of a school laundry are improved health, reduction of odors, and cleaner uniforms. The feasibility of an on-site laundry must be demonstrated on a case-by-case basis by analysis of all factors of cost such as staff, equipment, floor space, maintenance, utility connections, operating costs, and supplies.

Recreation/Fitness Clubs

This section addresses those buildings and fields created by universities, hospitals, municipalities, and a variety of private entrepreneurs to serve the recreational/fitness needs of their respective constituencies. These constituencies include: student intramural programs, public recreation programs, and individual fee paying user/members. The basic motivation underlying the purpose of these facilities is enjoyment of sporting activities and/or desire for self-improvements and health maintenance through fitness. To be successful, this type of facility must serve the needs of its users members who are not obligated to participate or who can elect to take their business elsewhere. This customer service orientation can exist on many levels of quality, image, and cost, but it is clearly an orientation that must be reflected in the substance and style of a facility's ancillary areas. The following summary of special planning and design considerations is directed toward the ancillary areas of recreation/fitness clubs.

Locker Rooms

Comfort, style, and service are matters of concern in recreation/fitness locker rooms. However, these concerns do not override the basic functional requirements of locker rooms discussed earlier. Depending on the target market of the facility and the operational economics, which are driven by price and volume of user/members, the level of comfort, style, and service must be set by the planning/design team in collaboration with the management group.

The level of comfort is affected by number, size, and spacing of lockers, lavatories, and showers. It also is affected by spaciousness and the kind of seating provided in dressing areas, the lighting, the quality of the heating and cooling systems, and the acoustical ambiance of the space. (Figure 9.11). For a space such as this, where users are in various states of undress, all circulation paths should be a minimum of five feet in width.

Color, texture, finish materials, and furnishings influence the style and image of the locker room. These must be selected to ensure compatibility with the overall facility mission and maintain the consistency of the aesthetic statement being made throughout the building. Whether this statement is spartan and utilitarian, luxurious and rich, or high-tech and polished, the choices made send a message to the user/member. The designer's challenge is to fit that message to the target market.

The service level of the recreation/fitness locker room is conveyed by the choices made regarding the means of providing locker security, the system for collecting and distributing towels, the availability of soap, shampoo, lotions and grooming aids, the means of drying hair, and the availability of such amenities as steam, sauna and jacuzzi, telephone, and shoe shine.

Attention to the details of providing comfort, style, and service at a level appropriate to the target market is the key to creating a successful recreation/fitness locker room. Other planning and design considerations unique to locker rooms of this facility type follow:

- Private shower booths with doors, curtains, or a private changing chamber may be provided.
- It generally is impractical to offer a permanent, full-size private locker to each member. Many facilities of this type have up to 5,000 members, which could require locker rooms of 18,000 to 24,000 square feet if a private locker is provided to each member. Consider offering a mix of small-sized private rental lockers as an extra cost option and providing a full-size dressing locker to each member for day use.
- A ratio of one full-size day locker per 10 members will be sufficient for facilities with average rates of utilization by its members. Adjustment of this ratio up or down can be made by planning on a case-by-case basis to respond to higher or lower frequency of use.

Administrative Offices

In general, the administrative departments of a recreation/fitness club may include the following units: membership sales, management, recreation/fitness programming, accounting, maintenance/housekeeping, personnel, food/beverage, and front desk/check-in. There is little benefit to consolidating these offices into a single administrative block. Management and sales offices should be located near the front desk check-in point. Recreation/fitness programming staff should be located close to the activity areas they serve. Accounting, maintenance/housekeeping, and personnel can be placed in a more remote back office location, because they have little need for direct member contact. The food and beverage office should be included within the restaurant/bar area if provided. The front desk reception station must be equipped to confirm validity of arriving members, control access to the facility, handle telephone reception and routing, confirm activity programming and court reservations, and handle all public inquiries and member service requests. The front desk also may be the best place from which to control lighting throughout the facility and to conduct announcements over the public address system. It is essential that the front desk be positioned to provide clear control of the line separating the public/free access zone of the facility from the member-only zones. This control of access will preserve the value of membership by preventing guests and non-members from using the facilities without proper payment and signing of liability release forms.

Multi-Purpose Facilities

It is not uncommon for a sports facility to be an intercollegiate athletic team center serving student athletics, a physical education center serving all students, and a center for recreation and fitness serving dues-paying alumni and faculty, as well as the student intramural sports system.

Facilities that attempt to accommodate a variety of uses must be planned accordingly. With so many diverse groups competing for space and time, conflicts are inevitable. The economic benefits are obvious. Multi-purpose facilities are utilized more fully by avoiding duplication of facilities that may sit idle during large parts of the day. However, scheduling compromises may reduce access by certain user groups to unacceptably low levels. Institutions without the financial resources to fund independent facilities for athletics, physical education, and recreation/fitness may elect to undertake the planning challenges of a multi-purpose facility. These challenges involve facility planning, curriculum planning, and schedule planning to accommodate as effectively as possible the needs of each constituency. The Loyola University Medical Center in Chicago, Illinois, is one example of a multi-purpose recreation/fitness facility that serves the medical school student body, hospital faculty and staff, and outside community members.

Summary

In general, the key to creating superior ancillary facilities is found in a design process that invites input from users, managers, staff, design specialists, and component providers. Such a process will always examine comparable design solutions with a critical eye in a diligent effort to avoid repeating past mistakes and to learn from past successes. It is the mix of solid experience, careful listening, and open-minded inventiveness that allows an architect to produce successful design solutions.

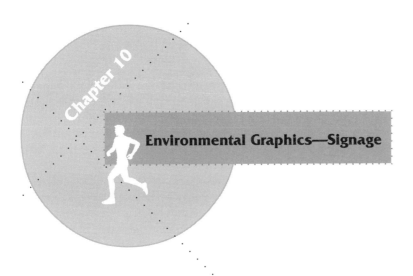

Michael G. Hypes, Indiana State University

Signs and signage have been a part of facilities for years. Until recently, signage, or environmental graphics, has been relegated to a back seat in terms of facility planning. Today's large and complex facilities, great number of sport facility users, guidelines developed through the ADA and OSHA, and a litigation-oriented society, are all moving signage to the forefront when planning a new facility. Increasing use of computer technology, the use of electronic signs, and architectural signage will be the basic areas to rapidly develop in the near future.

Learning Objectives:

After reading this chapter, the student will be able to:
- understand the importance of signage,
- know how to design effective signage,
- know the type of sign needed for a given situation
- understand the cost and maintenance factors of signage, and
- understand the place of graphics in facility architecture.

Type of Signs

The basic purpose of any sign is to impart information. This information varies with the type of sign used. Five categories of signs are identified for use in facilities. These categories include:
- warning, danger, caution, and emergency signs,
- notice and standard operational signs,
- directional signs,
- rules and regulations, and
- sign graphics.

Even though signage is divided into five distinct categories, the groups overlap. A sign could fall into just one category, or it might fall into two or three categories, depending on its purpose and the type of information it is conveying.

When developing signage for a facility or a specific area within the facility, special consideration should be given to the purpose of the signage and the eventual audience for the information. The Occupational Safety and Health Administration identified the following regarding the communication of hazardous conditions:
- comprehensibility,
- readability, and
- standard phrases.

Comprehensibility refers to the ability of the individual reading a sign to understand the information sufficiently to take the desired action. Comprehensibility is different from readability, in that the latter is simply a measure of the grade level of the written information, while the former is a measure of how well the receiver of the information understood it.

Standard phrases refers to the use of "signal words" in signage. The use of the word *Danger* indicates an imminently hazardous situation which, if not avoided, may result in death or serious injury. This signal word should be limited to the most extreme situations. *Warning* indicates a potentially hazardous situation which, if not avoided, could result in death or serious injury. *Caution* indicates a potentially hazardous situation which, if not avoided, may result in minor or moderate injury. It may also be used to alert against unsafe practices.

The importance that professionals attach to signal words may not be shared by the population at large. Many organizations (e.g., ANSI, U.S. Military) have guidelines for the determination of what signal words are to be used with specific hazards, and these are usually unknown to the public. The arousal effects of signal words and accepted organizational guidelines need to be incorporated in the design of effective signage.

Importance of Signs

Signs are an essential part of a facility and should be an integral part of the planning process in a new facility. Signs have come a long way in the last decade. New materials, colors, and graphics have changed the signage world. Many architectural firms now refer to a signage system as the *environmental graphics* of a facility. All recreation and sport facilities include a wide variety of signs. It is important to identify facility entrances and to direct individuals to concourse levels and seating sections. Rest rooms, concession areas, first aid stations, information centers, locker areas, security areas, and exits must be clearly designated. Information concerning parking area locations must be located near the exits. Traffic flow direction information must be imparted by external facility signage. The parking area, if large, will need to be sectioned off by effective signs.

Elevator and room designation signs must have raised-letter markings for visually impaired users. The center of these signs should be placed 60 inches above the floor. Other facility signs should also have raised letters, even though at this time this is not an ADA requirement. Where diverse populations exist, signs must be designed in multiple languages. The use of international graphics (or pictograms) can also help in designing signage for multiple languages.

Designing Signs

If at all possible, design your signs during the planning process of your building and its surroundings. If you are renovating or making additions to an existing facility, this is a prime time to plan for all new environmental graphics in your complex. Make your signs an aesthetically pleasing part of your facility.

Signs need to be simple and understandable, and they need to attract the facility users' attention. Placement, size, shape, repetitiveness, color, and graphics are all important in designing simple, understandable signs that attract user attention.

Placement

Again, signs must attract the facility user's attention. A well-placed sign maximizes its effect on the facility user. Signs need to be placed in the appropriate area and need to be placed at the appropriate place and height to have the greatest impact on the user. For instance, a sign stating, "No Skateboards Allowed in the Building", will not make its point in the interior of the building. This sign needs to be placed at all building entrances, so it can be seen before one enters the building with a skateboard. On the other hand, the sign,

---

Figure 10.1
Americans with Disabilities Act Accessibility Guidelines (ADAAG)
Guidelines for ADA Signage

- Pictograms must be placed on a background with a height of at least six inches. Pictograms must have a text counterpart.
- Raised characters must be at a minimum of 5/8" and a maximum of two inches.
- There are character proportions as well. Letters and numbers must have a ratio of width to height of between 3:5 and 1:1, and a stroke width to height ratio of between 1:5 and 1:10.
- Braille and raised characters have to be raised 1/32", and the font must be either upper-case sans serif or simple sans serif. The font must be accompanied with Braille grade 2.
- There are requirements for the finish and contrast of the characters. The contrast must be at least 70%, and the colors of the background and characters must either be matte, eggshell or some other non-glare finish.
- Signage must be mounted at least 60" above the floor to the center line of the sign.
- Signage must be mounted and installed on a wall that is adjacent to the door's latch side. But, if there is no space for that, then the signage needs to be installed on the nearest adjacent wall. Individuals must be able to approach the signage within 3" without any protrusions, such as the door swinging or any nearby objects.

Many sports facilities are large, sprawling, one- or two-floor facilities. If the facilities have been around for a number of years, there is a good chance additions have enhanced them. Add-ons can create logistic nightmares, and signs become paramount to direct individuals through a facility. It is not uncommon to find sport facilities with interiors of more than 200,000 square feet. Sport facilities are also among the most heavily used facilities on campuses and related sites. Large sport facilities, such as arenas and stadiums, with large numbers of users, call for a well-planned signage system.

"No Food or Drink in the Weight Area" needs to be posted outside the weight area as well as inside the weight area.

It is also important to place signs in normal sight lines. Placing signs too high, too low, or off to the side makes them less viable. It is important to remember that sight lines vary according to the users' height. Signs for young users, six to eight years of age, should be placed lower than signs for adults. Individuals in wheelchairs need signs placed in their sight lines.

Signs may be on a wall, a ceiling, a floor, suspended, free standing, on columns, or on doors. In some instances, a

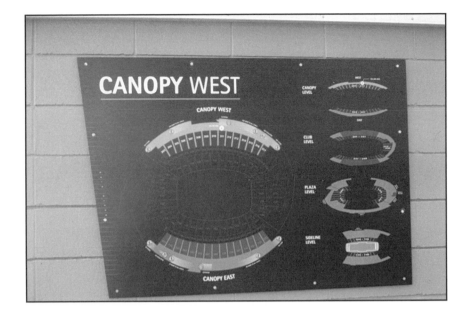

Stadium Seating Signage, Paul Brown Stadium.

sign may be on two or more surfaces. It may be partially on a wall and continue onto an adjacent wall or floor. The effect of a sign on multiple surfaces is eye-catching, thus attracting attention to it.

At times signs must be repetitive within a facility. An example of repetitive signage is in an indoor racquet court battery. If there are eight courts, some signs will need to be repeated eight times, once at each court. An example of repetitive signage is: "Eye Guards Are Mandatory!"

Materials

Signs may be an integral part of the facility as a permanent part of the structure (painted on walls or other surfaces or tiles of different colors that make a sign), or they can be attached to surfaces by a frame or brackets. Architectural or permanent signs are recommended whenever possible. These signs not only impart information, but they are also an aesthetically pleasing part of the structure of your facility. If architectural signage is used, and planned for carefully, few signs will need to be added to your facility. It is paramount to plan in advance for successful architectural signage. If mistakes are made in the planning process, they become permanent mistakes, or at the least costly mistakes to overcome. Even with the greatest of planning of architectural signage, some signs will have to be non-permanent and some signs will have to be later additions. As time and facility use change, signs need to be changed and updated, even though some architectural signage will never need to be changed. Architectural signs are usually made of "like" building material. For instance, a painted wall has a painted sign, or an asphalt tile floor has different size, texture, or color inset tiles to form a sign.

Signs may be made of wood, metal, tile, paper, glass, paint and plastic, or any combination of the aforementioned items. Signs may be electrified, such as lighted signs, billboards, score boards, or "running" sign boards. Electrical signs are more expensive than non-electrical signs. An electrified sign, on the other hand, stands out and attracts attention to itself. Electric signs must be in a secured location, since they are easily broken and are expensive to repair. If

electrical signs are to be used, one must plan carefully for electrical outlets or electrical hookups directly in relation to sign placement.

Extension cords running from signs to an electrical power source is unaesthetic, unsafe, and unacceptable.

Shape, Color, Size, and Graphics

Signs do not have to be rectangular in shape. Rectangular signs do afford maximum use of space if the signs contain only words. Other sign shapes have the ability to be eye-catching and/or informational. Take the eight-sided red sign at the end of the street, attached to a metal post, located on the right hand side of the street. When one sees this sign, it does not need to be read—the shape octagonal, location, and color indicate "STOP." Explicitly shaped signs, for specific information, can be used in facilities to impart information by using sign shape. An example is all pentagonal signs indicate classrooms, all circular signs indicate laboratories, and all diamond-shaped signs indicate offices.

An X-shaped sign in facilities immediately signals not to do something ("No Diving," "Do Not Run") just by the shape of the sign itself. The idea of effective sign shapes follows a recent international trend toward standard pictorial signs. Facility signs now must take on and convey a universal message to many ethnic populations. A sign featuring graphics will not alienate a facility's foreign users as much as a sign in English might.

Color, as the red in stop signs, can also be an important aspect of signage design. All signs of one color can indicate storage and housekeeping areas. Color in signs can be used to attract the attention of facility users. Bright-colored signs on a bland wall surface, in most instances, attract attention. A colored sign will attract a user's attention better than a black and white sign. Think color in your signage theme.

Signs vary in size. The size of a sign, in itself, is a method of drawing the attention of facility users. A very small sign indicating exit, is easily seen suspended from the ceiling or wall. Sometimes a large sign is needed to house important information and to draw the facility users' attention. "No

Handicap accessible signage.

Directional signage.

An example of repetitive signage.

Scoreboard Signage, Paul Brown Stadium.

Example of signage found in swimming areas.

Lifeguard on Duty-Swim at Your Own Risk", is effective as a large sign. Vary the size of your signs depending upon the information to be imparted and make use of sign size to attract attention.

The size of a sign's images and print also are instrumental in how the information is relayed. Words and graphics that are too small make the reader work harder and can result in the sign being ignored.

Just as some signs can be too wordy or hard to comprehend, too many signs posted in a small area also create problems. An overabundance of signs may cause the reader to miss a certain sign that has been lumped together in the busy array of other signs. Separating and isolating signs is important to their overall effectiveness. (Turner, 1994).

The content and message of a sign must be designed for the educational level(s) of the individuals using the facility. Content of a sign for a university will read differently than the content of the same sign for an elementary school. In all cases, it is important to keep signs as *simple* as possible. The simpler a sign, the easier it is to read and understand its content, thus making the sign more effective.

The old adage that a "picture" or graphic is worth a thousand words is still accurate for sign design. Using a clown figure to enhance a "no clowning" sign in a weight area attracts attention to the sign. A facility users' attention is drawn to attractive signs and adding graphics to signs makes them more attractive. A little humor about a serious matter can help to impart important information to facility users.

When there are too many
signs they will not be read.

Using humor to input information.

Bengal Seating,
Paul Brown Stadium.

Signage and the Three Groups It Serves

So far we have directed our attention to signs for facility users. Again, these signs are important to the very large number of individuals who use a facility. They are important to impart information, give direction, indicate warnings and danger, and to state rules. The litigious society that we live in has placed an increased importance on proper and effective signage in our facilities. Effective signage may prevent an injury from occurring, or it may be important in one's defense during a trial. Think of effective signage as both a money and stress saver when it comes to litigation.

All of this aforementioned information is important not only to the facility users, but also to the facility staff. Signs help facility staff acclimate quicker and more safely to their jobs. Good location, direction, and rules signs help new employees adapt more quickly to a new environment.

Hazardous materials are found in many facility laboratories and swimming pools. Bio-hazardous waste, toxic chemicals and gases, and nuclear contaminants must be handled routinely by staff. Signage is paramount in these areas. Signs should first indicate the hazard and second inform the employee how to work safely with the hazard. Containers for hazardous material and waste need effective signage in the form of visible labels. Signage should also be placed in break room and work room areas to inform employees of various performance and safety requirements.

Emergency personnel is the third group of individuals for whom signage must be well planned. All of the aforementioned discussion is also paramount for emergency personnel. Additionally, signs must be planned so that emergency personnel can find their way easily in a complex facility to save lives or deter additional injuries to facility occupants. Emergency personnel should not have to wander around a building before they can complete their jobs. Clear and effective signage in laboratories and pools indicating specifically what hazardous materials were present when an injury occurred can save a life.

Signage Maintenance

Since signs have been placed throughout the facility, they need to be maintained. If you have electronic signs, you will have to replace bulbs and other electronic components. Plan for this in sign placement. Most of these signs can be maintained from the front, however, there are some electronic signs that need to be maintained from the rear or from the top. If the electronic signs are small, they are easy to remove and repair. If the electronic signs are large, heavy, and cumbersome, one needs to plan for this in sign placement. A large rear-entry sign can be placed over a planned opening in a wall so that there is easy access, for repair work to the rear of the sign, without having to remove the sign.

Signs can break. Breakage of signs may be accidental or intentional. Signage in sport complexes takes much abuse. Balls hit them, rackets and bats hit them, and for this reason they need to be protected. If possible, place signs out of the abuse range. Placing signs higher and in areas away from projectiles and hitting devices will help to prolong sign life and reduce maintenance costs. Some signs must be placed in "harm's way". Polycarbonate sheeting works best for signs that need to be encased or covered with a clear material. Be careful, though, because the glossy finish of the sign or its covering can create glare problems and take away from the effectiveness of the sign, as well as provide an unwelcome distraction. Wire mesh (the kind that sometimes covers clocks in school gymnasiums) works as an effective cover on signs whose faces would not be sufficiently protected by plastic sheeting, such as signs that are in the path of balls and other flying objects. If a sign must be covered with a mesh cage, make sure it can still be seen well enough to convey its message (Turner, 1994).

Signs can also be defaced. By placing signs out of reach, one can avoid some defacing. Use materials in the construction and covering of signs that deter defacing. The use of polycarbonate sheeting and other slick surfaces will help keep sign defacing at a minimum.

Signs need to be cleaned on a regular basis. Fingerprints, smudges, dust, and other airborne particles need to be removed from signage as a regular routine. Electronic signs need special attention and regular cleaning so they function at an optimal level. Soiled signage of any type can curtail the amount of information imparted by the sign. Set up a regular cleaning schedule for signage.

Miscellaneous Considerations

Signage cost will vary with materials, size, number of signs, and whether or not the sign is electronic. As mentioned previously, it is suggested to figure your signage cost as a part of your facility construction cost. In some cases, parts of construction costs are bid separately and signage may be bid after the facility is built. This is not recommended. Repetitive signs will reduce costs, since *more* of the same product reduces the cost per sign. The geographic location of your facility will also be a factor in signage cost. It is suggested to purchase high-quality products, even though initially these products may be more costly than low-quality products. Over the lifetime of facility signage, quality products cost less.

The geographic location of the sports complex will dictate which and how many languages will be used in signs. Inner city locations and other locations of high ethnic populations will dictate signage languages.

Signs can be affixed to surfaces either permanently or semi-permanently. The method of affixing will depend on the philosophy of the design and use of the facility. It will also depend on the longevity of the signage. "Exit" signs, for example, are rather permanent, whereas rules and regulation signs may change over time. Signs may be attached flat onto a surface or they may extend out perpendicularly or horizontally from a surface. Protruding signs are sometimes needed for visibility and code adherence. One of the problems with protruding signs is that they are more susceptible to breakage than flush mounted signs.

Keep in mind that the size and shape of some signs might be dictated by local, state, and federal regulations. Check local fire and building codes to make sure a particular facility includes all the required signs. Additionally, check with state and national offices for signage needed to meet ADA and OSHA requirements.

In some instances, a one-sided, flush mounted sign is not sufficient. Signs suspended from the ceiling may impart information on two, three, or four sides. Protruding signs usually give information on two or three sides. As signage is

Example of static
and dynamic
signage.

Information signage.

Fire alarm.

Graphic image, information signage.

Examples of use of graphics.

designed, always think about using signs with multiple sides. Some signs will need to be free standing in order to be moved from one area to another area of the facility. An example of a free-standing sign would be, "Caution: Wet Floor". Free-standing signs can take any shape or form; however, the most common is a two-sided pyramid shape.

Sponsorship in sport complexes is common. Sharing a sign with a sponsor is common in athletics (i.e., rolling sponsorship signs). Score boards and other signs are either purchased by the sponsor or rented by the sponsor so they can advertise on the sign. This concept of sponsorship can be used for signage in other areas—not just for athletics. Sponsorship or sharing of signage is an important concept and should be studied carefully for all signage in a facility. In any case, sign sponsors and sport complex directors can both obtain mutual benefits by this partnership (Turner, 1994).

A rather new area in signage design is the use of art graphics in a sport complex. Art graphics or permanently painted or inset materials that are designed as integral parts of the facility. Various images can be placed on surfaces in the form of sports art, murals or basic signage. These images are color coordinated with the color scheme of the facility. The images can bring "life", "motion", brightness, and attractiveness to an otherwise plain and dull facility. Currently, there are a number of companies that do art graphic work for sport complexes. Computer imagery is now enhancing the appearance of sports art, graphics and murals.

Summary

Effective signage in a sports complex must be well planned. Signage should be an integral part of facility design. There are various types of signs that will be used in any given sports complex. Well planned, easily maintained, well designed, cost effective signs can help prevent injury and related problems.

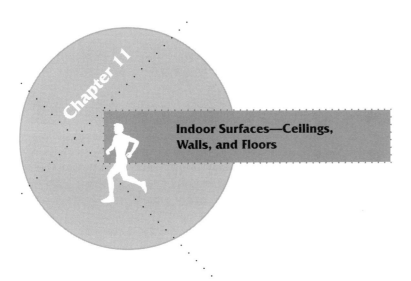

Chapter 11

Indoor Surfaces—Ceilings, Walls, and Floors

Hal Walker, Barry University

Although discussions about indoor surface mate rials seldom elicit excitement, interest, or enthu siasm, these choices are integral to the appearance, utility, and overall success of any facility. The cost, type, installation, and maintenance of these materials are directly linked to facility usage, appearance, longevity, safety, and overall facility "success." Three main categories of indoor surfacing include floors, walls, and ceilings. This chapter will provide useful information to assist in the process of outlining the types of materials available for these surfaces, along with some advantages and disadvantages based on use in specific areas. The importance of planning carefully in the selection of the correct surface material, focusing on needs, available funds, cost of maintenance, and aesthetics will be the focus.

Facility surface choices are generally divided into three distinct areas. These areas are the service/ancillary areas, the main floor, and the office/administrative areas. Planning for and selecting an appropriate indoor surface material, along with the proper installation and maintenance over the facility life span, can profoundly impact facility use. These surface choices can determine optimal facility use features, the activities or functions planned, as well as the incidence of sport injuries. Surface options are extensive with numerous companies offering countless choices of innumerable textures, materials, colors, and performance characteristics. Yet, of the hundreds of products offered currently on the market, no one surface is ideal for all activities a facility plans to offer. There is plenty of room for error in the decision-making process for a surface that meets facility needs, demands, and expectations. As a result, optimal surface choices should be made with extensive deliberation and clear communication among facility planning members. Available budget, planned activity offerings, longevity, maintenance costs, and climate are but a few of the factors that must be considered in making the correct facility surface choices.

Instructional Objectives

After reading this chapter the student will be able to:
- demonstrate knowledge of the primary surface design areas of a facility,
- describe the types of materials available for these surfaces and their characteristics,
- understand the nature of various surface materials, use characteristics, safety issues, aesthetics, and acoustics,
- identify various advantages and disadvantages of surface materials that should be taken into consideration for flooring, wall, and ceiling materials,
- understand the impact of equipment and pedestrian traffic and the impact this has on facility surface life,
- explain recommended maintenance and upkeep practices for various surface materials,
- describe the concept of hardness and how it is measured,
- demonstrate an understanding of an appropriate selection process for facility flooring options, and
- understand the role of a facility manager in the selection of appropriate surface materials for sport facilities

Selection of Indoor Surface Materials

The selection of indoor surface materials must be carefully chosen, considering the nature of the facility and the activities that are planned. As mentioned above, the primary surfaces addressed in this section are floors, walls, and ceilings. The following text will outline the types of materials available for these surfaces, their characteristics, along with some of the factors to consider when going through the planning and decision-making process.

Generally speaking, the planned activity in a given area should dictate the type of flooring surface utilized. Many, if not all surfaces, however, are utilized for more than one purpose. There are three distinct areas of consideration in facilities currently being built. The first of these areas are the service/ancillary areas such as locker rooms, shower rooms, bathrooms, etc. These areas require surfaces that take into account heavy moisture content as well as "slip and fall" concerns. The second area is the main arena or activity center of the facility. This area tends to encompass the majority of time spent on the decision-making process, however, each area should warrant considerable thought and planning. These central activity areas typically require either a hardwood floor or a resilient synthetic material. Offices, administrative areas, and classrooms account for the third facility location (Flynn, 1993).

Special areas require different materials, layouts, and treatments. For example, basketball courts should be made out of a non-slip material, while a dance area should have a finished treatment that allows individuals to slide across the floor (Flynn, 1993). Safety, hardness, absorption, resilience and lateral foot support are each critical in the selection of surfaces for dance floors (*http://www.stagestep.com/whatfl4me.html*).

Durability, flexibility, and cost are three considerations that have allowed synthetic floors to challenge traditional hardwood flooring. Synthetic surfaces take the form of grass or non-grass surfaces. The two most popular synthetic surfacing materials are polyvinyl chlorides (PVC's) and polyurethane. Polyurethane is either poured in place or produced in prefabricated sheets that are adhered on the site, while PVC's are typically prefabricated. The general perception is that polyurethane possesses most of the desirable characteristics sought in a multipurpose facility surface (Flynn, 1993).

It is essential to understand that there are countless types of wooden floors, many floor manufacturers, and the costs can vary dramatically. Costs also vary extensively among other surface alternatives, such as synthetics and carpets. Varying costs often depend on the materials used, the thickness of the surface selected, and the condition of the existing surface. Thicker synthetic surfaces, for example, although they may absorb more shock and offer greater resilience, are generally more expensive (Flynn, 1993). Once again, the planned surface use should be the central factor directing all facility surface decisions.

In the past, the third area—administrative offices and classrooms—have been satisfactorily covered with some type of tile that may include vinyl, vinyl asbestos, asphalt, rubber, or linoleum. Many believe consideration should be given to using carpet in some of these spaces. Hard maple floors are generally the most expensive when looking at initial installation; however, over a long period of time, these flooring options become more than competitive when compared with most synthetic surfaces. Unfortunately, many decisions are made on available finances during initial facility construction, rather than the best surface for long-term facility use. The least expensive flooring surface option, is generally viewed as indoor-outdoor carpeting (Flynn, 1993).

Floors

Sport flooring surfaces, according to Viklund (1995), are categorized as *point-elastic* or *area-elastic*. Point-elastic surfaces maintain impact effects at the immediate point of contact on the floor, with the ball, object, or individual. Area-elastic surfaces allow for dispersion of impact, where a bouncing object or an individual jumping can be felt approximately 20 inches around the point of impact. *Hardness* is another term that is utilized to describe the nature of a flooring surface and its ability to react to surface contact. The term "hardness" is defined readily in the fields of mineralogy, metallurgy, and engineering. In mineralogy, hardness is defined as the ability of the surface to resist scratching, with a softer surface obviously scratching more easily. This is measured by the Mohs scale, after Friedrich Mohs, a German mineralogist. In metallurgy and engineering, hardness is determined by pressing a hard material on a given surface and measuring the size of the indentation made to report the "hardness" of a substance. This is called the Brinnel test, named after a Swedish engineer, Johann Brinell (*http://www.fwkc.com/encyclopedia/low/articles/h/h011000282f.html*).

Viklund (1995) also states that *resilience* is another factor to consider when analyzing performance characteristics of various flooring options. Resilience is the shock-absorption ability of a floor based on the amount of force applied to the surface area. For comparison, concrete is a base value, with no resiliency (zero percent). Point-elastic surfaces (synthetics) have a low absorption level (10 to 50 %), with most in the 25 to 35% range. Resilience is influenced by both the thickness and the hardness of the floor material and the sub-flooring under the surface (Viklund, 1995). When considering carpeting as a surface choice, the quality of the underlay also has a significant impact on the carpet performance as well as the carpet life. According to Driscoll (2000, p.54), "the use of a quality underlay can prolong the life of a carpet from 50 to 75%."

Facility surface choices must also consider the influence of the sub-flooring material. Flooring characteristics on porous or "floating" surfaces will react very differently than others placed on concrete. Flooring choices, in fact, should be carefully considered based on the sub-flooring material that is present. The condition of this sub-flooring can also influence the cost of the project, as this surface may need special preparation for the chosen surface materials to be placed on top. According to Dahlgren (2000), shock-absorption characteristics of wood floors may be more heavily influenced by the sub-flooring than the actual surface material itself.

Area-elastic floors also need to be evaluated based on activities planned for the space. *Area of deflection* must be considered with regard to the primary use of the facility surface. Area deflection is the amount of impact that is felt in the vicinity around the points of contact. With area-elastic flooring, it must be decided that the area of deflection will not adversely impact the activities of other individuals concurrently on the surface. According to Viklund (1995), area of deflection is not a major concern for recreational use; however, it could be a major consideration for competitive or varsity play.

Another important consideration for most organizations in making flooring choices is a concept known as the "rolling load." Rolling load is the capacity of a floor to withstand damage from external forces, such as bleacher movement, equipment transport, or similar activities (Viklund, 1995). Any surface utilized for multi-purpose activities must be able to withstand the movement of equipment or materials over the surface area during transition from one activity to another. Related to this concept are the "walk-off" areas that experience heavy use. Even the most durable surfaces over time, will undergo rapid deterioration under heavy pedestrian or equipment traffic. Mats, padding, or varied traffic patterns can be established by the careful planning of equipment storage areas to extend the life of most facility surfaces. The choices made for the planning of *tear space*, or areas that are not developed for primary activities may also influence the wear and tear on a floor over the life of the facility surface. Decisions for the storage and transport of equipment should not be viewed as unimportant in the facility surface decision process, as this can directly influence the deterioration of a surface with heavy equipment and pedestrian traffic.

There are a variety of floor surface options that can be used successfully as a main gym floor. Once again, this important surface choice is normally dictated by the primary activities planned for this area. Options are generally broken down into three surfaces: hardwood, vinyl, and synthetics. Each surface option has strengths and weaknesses. Many existing athletic facilities have chosen either a hardwood or a standard vinyl tile. According to Bishop (1997), wood flooring with proper maintenance can last 50 years, compared with 20 years for a synthetic surface and 15 years for a vinyl tile. Chart 11.1 illustrates initial cost, life expectancy and annual maintenance cost for vinyl tile, synthetic surface and wood flooring for a 5,000 sq. foot gymnasium (Bishop, 1997).

Vinyl tile floors have a life expectancy of approximately 10 to 15 years, but begin to show their wear after the first few years (Bishop, 1997). Recent technology, however, has significantly improved the quality of sheet vinyl and vinyl composition tile making this flooring choice both more aesthetic as well as more durable (Hasenkamp & Lutz, 2001). Vinyl floors, however, tend to be very hard and have poor absorption qualities. These characteristics can also lead to athletic injuries if high humidity levels are prevalent or if water spills are not managed properly. Unlike other sport surfaces, which require only washing and damp mopping, a vinyl tile floor must be stripped, sealed, and waxed at least three times annually. In contrast, synthetic floors also require regular cleaning, but may require line repainting or a touch-up every five years (Bishop, 1997).

Hardwood floors are generally designed with intricate sub-flooring to provide shock absorption and can be expected to last the life of the school. Wooden floors must always be kept clean to provide proper traction. They must also have the lines repainted or touched up and should be sanded down and refinished every three years. Synthetic floors do not allow for as much sliding as hardwood floors. As a result, if the activities on the floor involve sliding actions, a wood floor is the better choice. Wood floors can also be designed in a number of ways, including sub-floor systems, cushioned systems, and spring systems (Flynn, 1993).

As mentioned above, the nature of the sub-flooring can often be a more significant factor than the actual surface material chosen for a floor (Dahlgren, 2000; Holzrichter, 2001). There are three types of recommended sub-floor constructions. The first is a suspension floor, which is made out of either plywood, foam rubber, or some other type of synthetic material, available in a variety of patterns. The finished floor rests on top of the sub-floor material. The second type of sub-floor construction is a spring floor. This involves coiled metal springs, covered by a plywood sub-floor, with the finished floor resting on the plywood. The third type is referred to as a padded floor. Padded materials, such as foam or other synthetic or porous materials, are laid over concrete or plywood and then covered with the finished floor (Stoll & Beller, 1989). Naturally, the more materials needed to install the floor, the higher the cost. Even though cost is a primary concern, safety should also be considered throughout the decision-making process.

Synthetic floors are softer than wood floors and better acoustically. Wood floors, depending on their suspension systems, can also have "dead spots." Dead spots are areas on the floor that can cause objects impacting the floor surface to perform inconsistently. An example would be a basketball that would have a variable bounce due to a change in the characteristics of the floor. Synthetic floors are evenly laid and are less likely to have "dead spots," although inconsistent ball performance can still occur. Quality installation will maximize optimal surface performance with any surface choice. Upkeep of all gym floors calls for constant maintenance. Rubberized synthetic floors, however, tend to have higher maintenance costs when compared with wooden floors.

There are many different floor covering options related to sport and recreational activities in today's market. Some examples include ceramic tile, cushioned wood flooring, and rubber compound flooring. The selection criteria for certain flooring materials should include:

- Economic feasibility with initial outlay and life-cycle costs. Floor covering choices entail much more than the initial up-front cost. Many now realize that the initial cost for materials and installation is only a small component of the total investment needed. Life-cycle cost considerations not only include the initial expense and installation, but the number of years the flooring is expected to last, cost for removal or disposal of the floor, lost revenues during remodeling or replacement periods, and maintenance costs over the course of the surface life (Hard Questions, Critical Answers, 1998).
- Ease of maintenance and replacement.
- Potential performance capabilities for both intended and possible use.
- Overall compatibility in appearance, according to surrounding surfaces and equipment in the facility (Barkley, 1997; Dahlgren, 2000).

An important factor that is often overlooked when considering floor options concerns: (1) the planned events within the facility, (2) access to electrical outlets, (3) placement of equipment-securing devices (floor plates for volleyball uprights), and (4) the space necessary for intended spectator traffic and equipment movement. If floor plates are to be utilized, they should be taken into consideration early in the process, as well as covered, for ease of maintenance, access, and safety factors. In particular, electrical outlets should be installed in the floor, covered and flush with the floor's surface, as they are commonly associated with safety issues related to traffic flow. Also to be taken into consideration is the time spent in preparing a facility for various activities. Greater planning for both functional and safety factors can

Chart 11.1
Costs for Various Floor Surfaces

Type of Flooring	Life Expectancy	Initial Cost
Vinyl Tile	15 years	$15,000
Synthetic Surface	20 years	$40,000
Wood Flooring	50 years	$65,000

Initial Cost/Life Expectancy	Maintenance Cost Annually	Total Cost Annually
$1,000/yr (vinyl)	$1,210	$2,210
$2,000/yr (synthetic)	$200	$2,200
$1,300/yr (wood)	$2,666	$3,966

save time (equipment set-up and tear-down), reduce costs (tape and mats to cover electrical and media system cords), and reduce accidents (tripping over exposed wires and cords).

When selecting a surface, it is wise to consult other facilities that have similar need and use patterns to explore all flooring options based on performance characteristics. It is also important to consult with individuals who work with and maintain these facilities (i.e., maintenance personnel, students, athletes, publics, etc.), since they will likely have a different perspective regarding the suitability of various facility surfaces. The ultimate choice is made by the planning team, however, all factors should be considered to make the appropriate surface decision.

Although cost tends to be perceived as the overriding factor that drives a facility surface choice, aesthetic factors are being increasingly considered in the decision-making process. Wood flooring, for example, tends to be chosen based on the "quality" or "grade" of the actual wood. Quality is categorized into first, second, and third grades. First-grade wood has the fewest number of defects and deficiencies when inspected prior to sale. "First grade allows for a very modern, clean, and in some minds, sterile, look because it is fairly defect-free. You don't see dark blemishes or a lot of graining" (Dahlgren, 2000, p.78).

Wood flooring options, however, are also chosen based on color, which once again is influenced by visual appeal. Maple tends to be the industry standard and offers good durability due to a "tight grain and density," however, the light color also supports its popularity (Dahlgren, 2000). Second- and third-grade woods tend to offer a darker, more grainy, and "warmer" appearance; however, this choice once again boils down to personal or committee preference. Also a consideration that should not be overlooked is the impact of the floor color or aesthetics on the participant as well as the spectator. A dark or grainy floor, although more appealing to the eye, may be distracting to the participant. As far as performance is concerned, according to Hamar, president of the Maple Flooring Manufacturers Association, "You could blindfold a person and have them dribble a ball on a first-grade floor, a second-grade floor and a third-grade floor, and he or she would never know the difference" (Hamar, 2000, p. 84).

A final consideration in the quest for enhancing the visual appeal of a floor surface is achieved by creative efforts with paint, patterns, colors, and contrast. Tiled flooring can easily be created in various patterns and designs that are very appealing to the eye; however, during the reconditioning process of a wood floor, alterations in surface applications can create a "new" look with the same "old" floor. Again, all these issues need to be addressed by communicating with other facility management personnel and discovering the strengths and weaknesses of the numerous options available before an ultimate decision is made for any facility.

Surface Selection Process

As stated earlier, choosing the appropriate flooring surface is a major decision in the design or renovation process. Floor materials and maintenance patterns can greatly impact athletic performance, determine how well multiple uses are served, and impact the incidence of sports injuries. Floor surfaces come in innumerable materials, textures, colors, and performance characteristics. Yet, of the hundreds of products on the market, no one surface is perfect for all uses, and there is plenty of room to make the wrong choice (Viklund, 1995).

A logical and systematic approach should be followed in conducting a search for the appropriate surface. These guidelines will assist in the decision-making process. According to Viklund (1995, p. 46), the steps in the following "flooring checklist" are recommended:

- Select the room or space to be considered
- Prioritize the sports/activities that will occur within the space
- Decide whether the preferred floor should be area elastic or point elastic
- Review the performance criteria for the selected floor type
- Test flooring options by reviewing samples and comparing costs
- Compare life-cycle costs for flooring options
- Play on the different surfaces
- Check the manufacturers' referenced projects
- Make the final decision

Flynn (1993, p. 77), recommends the following steps in the surface selection process:

Definition

Define the characteristics required to meet specified needs (i.e., bounce characteristics, sunlight effects, etc.). Many of these questions are addressed by manufacturers in their literature.

Solicitation

Cost should not be a limitation for one's initial research and review of possible flooring systems. One should request as much information, from as many manufacturers, as deemed reasonable. The review of this information will allow for a broader knowledge of different systems and a basis for comparison. Material estimates and project costs should be obtained from various manufacturers. Manufacturers should also provide references, a list of installers, and the location of like facilities for comparative analysis.

Comparison

After reviewing manufacturer materials and comparing all possible systems, a categorization of all materials should be performed. Categorize information by type and desirable qualities, i.e., natural vs. synthetic, resiliency, initial cost, longevity, safety, aesthetics, and any additional factors significant to your decision-making process. A table that compares the various positive and negative attributes of each surface option is generally deemed helpful in making the right surface choice for your facility.

Visitation

After the field of choices has been narrowed down based on established criteria, a site visit for each of the facility surfaces being considered should be performed. A closer inspection and discussion with personnel at each facility is also likely to be helpful in making the best choice for your facility. Performance as well as maintenance factors must be explored, as initial cost and utility are only two of numerous factors in making a wise surface choice.

Selection

At this point, select a system based on upon all research efforts. Take into consideration all performance criteria and always keep in mind that surface choices are a significant factor in the overall success of a facility.

Quality

A specific surface may be selected, however, there are numerous levels of quality among any number of surface options. Once more, take into consideration the quality of the materials, workmanship, guarantees, facility use factors, and any other significant considerations when making this important decision.

Manufacturer

Choosing a manufacturer is also important. How long have they been in business? What type of technical support do they provide? What are their methods of quality control, both in the manufacturing process and in the field? What is their reputation? How soon can they provide you with the requested materials? What guarantees do they provide? Many questions should be compiled and asked of each company being considered. Always remember that references are important to obtain, but be careful to do your homework in the inquiry process. One should never rely too heavily on references provided by the company being considered, as they will obviously be more than willing to provide positive references for their own work history. Unsolicited references should be sought for all finalists in the bidding process followed. It is common in the industry that manufacturers will provide products to clients in exchange for positive reviews.

Installer

An installer should be recommended by the manufacturer to help ensure that they are familiar with installation of the manufacturer's product. The installer should be asked questions similar to those asked of the manufacturer. Another key question to ask is the time frame required for completing the installation. Many jobs are started on time; however, seek guarantees for job completion, or factor this item into a reduction in cost for jobs not finished when promised. Facility visits and communication with other clients will once again be helpful in deciding upon an installation company.

Maintenance

Maintenance is a considerable portion of the operating budget, and it is important to define exactly what is involved. What type of maintenance is required? How often will the surface need to be refinished, covered, lacquered, replaced, etc.? Facility planners should not underestimate the expense of properly maintaining facility surfaces and should factor this expense into the overall surface cost and flooring choice.

Kennedy (2000) recommends that maintenance staff should have a thorough knowledge of the various floor surfaces they are maintaining. Cleaning approaches can vary based on the intended use of the surface. Recent research by Agron (2001), describes an overall reduction in expenditures for both maintenance and operations in elementary and secondary schools in recent years. This same author, however, reports an increase in spending for maintenance and operations budgets in higher education facilities. In either case, this concept needs to be factored into the flooring decision process. A less expensive floor may have a very limited life span without proper care. The same can be stated for more expensive flooring that requires more specialized care to attain maximal life-cycle utilization.

Moussatché, Languell-Urquhart & Woodson (2000) provide information that relates life-cycle costs with operations and maintenance considerations for hard flooring, resilient flooring and soft flooring options. As mentioned earlier, the actual cost of the initial flooring is only a portion of the life-cycle flooring expense. "Life-cycle cost analysis allows the evaluator to fully examine each alternative and the true service life cost of the material" (p. 20).

Initial Cost

What is the "total" initial cost of the system? Make sure there are no hidden costs that will arise later. If two systems are considered similar, yet one is more costly than the other, why? Is it the quality of the system? materials? or both? Sometimes product name or reputation is a reason for cost inflation.

Life-Cycle Cost

This comparative analysis considers the initial cost, operational costs, maintenance costs, and if necessary, replacement costs, during the estimated life cycle. These figures will generate the anticipated total costs. Generally, a higher initial cost system will be comparable in the long run, with less expensive systems when all factors are considered.

Bidding

When bidding is required, attention should be directed toward written specifications to ensure the product and installation methods are accurately described to avoid misunderstandings.

Installation

It is in the owner's interest to require the manufacturer to perform periodic on-site supervision of the installer. This will help insure compliance with the manufacturer's specifications.

Chart 11.2
"Evaluated flooring materials' characteristics, appropriate maintenance procedures, and recommended frequency"

Legend:
- ● = Above Average
- ▶ = Average
- ○ = Below Average
- V = Variable
- D = Daily
- W = Weekly
- M = Monthly
- Y = Yearly
- P = Periodically
- S = Semiannually in high traffic areas or yearly in average traffic areas

Material	Strength	Durability	Thermal Insulation	Moisture, oil, chemical resistance	Stain Resistance	Abrasions Resistance Wearability	Mildew Resistance	Heat Absorption	Limited Application Locations	Sweeping or dust mopping	Vacuuming	Damp mopping	Wet mopping	Scrubbing	Stripping	Dry cleaning (chemicals)	Hot water extraction	Waxing	Buffing	Resealing	Regrouting	Sanding & refinishing	Overall Maintenance Ranking
Hard — Ceramic Tile (6"x6"x1/2") Mortar & Grout	●	●	●	V	▶	●	●	○	x	D	x	D	x	S	S	x	x	M	M	x	x	x	High
Ceramic Tile (6"x6"x1/2") Mastic & Grout	●	▶	●	V	▶	●	●	○	x	D	x	D	x	Y	Y	x	x	M	M	x	x	x	High
Quarry Tile Mortar & Grout	●	●	●	●	●	●	●	○	x	D	x	D	x	x	x	x	x	Y	Y	x	x	x	Medium
Exposed Concrete Sealant (2 coats)	●	●	○	○	▶	●	▶	●	✓	D	x	W	Y	x	x	x	x	Y	x	x	x	x	Medium
Terrazzo (1 3/4") Cast in place	●	●	▶	●	●	●	●	●	▶	x	D	x	W	x	Y	x	x	x	x	x	x	P	x	Low
Epoxy resin	▶	○	●	●	●	▶	●	○	x	D	x	W	x	Y	x	x	x	x	x	x	P	x	Low
Laminated wood (synthetic core) vapor barrier & Adhesive	▶	▶	●	▶	▶	▶	●	▶	x	D	x	W	x	Y	x	x	x	x	x	x	P	x	Low
Wood plank (2 1/4") vapor barrier & urethane	●	▶	●	▶	▶	▶	●	▶	x	x	D	x	x	x	x	S	S	x	x	x	x	x	Medium
Resilient — Bamboo flooring vapor barrier & adhesive	●	▶	●	○	▶	●	●	▶	x	x	D	x	x	x	x	S	S	x	x	x	x	x	Medium
Linoleum (.125") - Adhesive	▶	●	●	▶	▶	●	●	○	x	x	D	x	x	x	x	S	S	x	x	x	x	x	Medium
Vinyl Composition Tile (VCT) Vapor barrier and Adhesive	▶	▶	●	○	V	▶	○	○	x	D	x	D	x	x	x	x	x	x	x	Y	x	x	Low
Vinyl Sheet Vapor barrier and Adhesive	▶	▶	●	○	V	▶	○	○	x	D	x	W	x	M	x	x	x	x	x	P	x	x	Medium
Rubber Sheet (1/8") - Adhesive	●	○	●	●	▶	●	▶	▶	x	D	x	W	x	M	x	x	x	Y	Y	x	x	x	Medium
Cork (1/8") - Adhesive	○	○	●	▶	○	○	▶	○	x	D	x	W	x	M	x	x	x	x	x	x	x	x	Low
Soft — Carpet tile (18"x 18", 20oz/syd) Hard back	▶	▶	●	▶	●	▶	▶	●	✓	D	x	D	x	x	x	x	x	x	x	P	x	P	Low
Carpet tile (18"x 18", 20 oz/syd) Cushion back	▶	●	●	▶	●	▶	▶	●	✓	D	x	D	x	x	x	x	x	x	x	x	x	x	Low
Carpet (Nylon loop pile 40oz/syd) Adhesive	▶	▶	●	▶	●	▶	▶	●	✓	D	x	D	x	x	x	x	x	x	x	x	x	P	Low

Source: September 2000, by: Moussatche, Languell-Urquhart, & Woodson, p. 22!

**Wood floor
protective coverings**

Safety

Flooring surface choices clearly need to be assessed based on facility use expectations. Resiliency, slip, traction, absorption, foot support, activities planned for the space, and the age and ability of the intended user are just some of the countless factors to consider when making a flooring choice. A device recognized by the American Society of Testing and Materials (ASTM), called a tribometer, establishes the "slip resistance" of various flooring surfaces and footwear (Di Pilla, 2001). Knowing exactly how slippery each floor surface is enables a determination of appropriate activities for this space, possible shoe requirements, as well as cleaning schedules based on the characteristics of the surface at different times during the day. A simple change in cleaning materials or application method can impact how slippery the surface will be. Although a comprehensive risk management program can address some of these factors, this issue needs to be considered in the planning process to avoid the resultant risks from slips and falls.

Walls and Ceilings

Facility walls serve a greater function than simply serving as a divider or perimeter wall for specific activity areas. Walls function as barriers to sound, heat, light, and moisture. Depending on the location and intended use of the facility, the selection of wall surfaces should be given careful consideration for the acoustical properties of the material as well. Generally speaking, moisture-resistant walls with sound acoustical properties are ideal.

As mentioned earlier with flooring, there remains a trend toward greater aesthetic pursuits on walls and ceilings in the utilization of colors, pictures, and graphics on these surfaces. Banners, sound panels, and other porous materials can be utilized to improve acoustical sound properties of a typical gymnasium. Tasteful color schemes can also have a positive psychological value on the participant or spectator, along with making the environment more aesthetically pleasing (Flynn, 1993; Hasenkamp & Lutz, 2001).

Roof design, local building codes, and the nature of the planned activities should determine ceiling construction.

Ceilings should be insulated to prevent condensation and also be the appropriate height to accommodate all planned and future activities. Painting ceilings can also improve the physical look of the facility, as well as enhance light reflection. Bright white ceilings are strongly advised against in areas where light-colored objects are utilized, i.e., shuttlecocks and volleyballs. It is difficult to visually follow these objects against a bright white ceiling background. A light color is still recommended for ceilings, however, and most facilities find an *off-white* color to work best. A 24-foot minimum distance (lowest suspended object) is required in any teaching station designed for a variety of activities (Flynn, 1993). Whenever possible, facility planners should attempt to exceed this minimum ceiling height, as minimum heights can still contribute to game interference, equipment lodging (i.e., shuttlecocks), and greater ceiling fixture expenses as a result of occasional contact with equipment (i.e., volleyballs).

Acoustical ceiling materials are needed in instructional spaces and areas with many planned activities. Dropped ceiling panels will require considerable maintenance, since they are susceptible to damage by objects or individuals. Since most acoustical instruments are not necessarily made out of the hardest materials, they need to be placed out of range of flying objects. In some cases where there are low ceiling activity areas, dropped ceilings may be equipped with spring-loaded clips that will return the acoustical panel back into place after contact. It should be noted that false ceilings with catwalks above them have been effectively constructed to allow for easier maintenance and the repair of lighting and ventilation arrangements (Flynn, 1993).

Walls in the main gym or activity area should have a minimum height of eight feet and should always be padded for safety reasons. Electrical outlets should be provided every 50 feet and should also be protected by padding (Flynn, 1993). Small inserts can be cut out of the padding and affixed with fasteners for easy removal and replacement for access to electrical outlets. All padding should be checked with regularity, as it can wear and harden with age and still cause significant injury upon contact. Keep in mind that some unobstructed flat wall space should be kept available as appropriate, for teaching and/or lecture space. In some cases, all walls should be kept unobstructed; however, this would be based on the specific activities planned for the space (i.e., indoor soccer).

As mentioned earlier, the ceiling should have a minimum height of 24 feet to the lowest obstacle with an off-white color usually being appropriate. A clear span ceiling design without minimum support pillars and substructure girders should be investigated for safety, viewing, aesthetics, and more open and usable space. If one chooses to mount or store equipment in the ceiling area, structural reinforcement may become necessary at these sites (Flynn, 1993). It is very important to consider all necessary factors when constructing or remodeling the primary features of a facility.

Figure 11.2 provides a guide for floor, wall, and ceiling choices for a variety of rooms within your facility (Flynn, 1993, p. 19).

Windows

The use and aesthetic value of windows are often overlooked in the planning of indoor facilities, as well as within the process of making surface choices. Windows can provide durable and attractive enclosures as well as divisions of space within a facility. Facility planners must keep in mind, however, that windows may face daily exposure to the elements, as well as frequent contact with objects utilized in

Figure 11.2
Suggested indoor surface materials

ROOMS	FLOORS							LOWER WALLS								UPPER WALLS						CEILINGS			
	Carpeting	Synthetics	Tile, asphalt, rubber, linoleum	Cement, abrasive, non-abrasive	Maple, hard	Terrazzo, abrasive	Tile, ceramic	Brick	Brick, glazed	Cinder Block	Concrete	Plaster	Tile, ceramic	Wood Panel	Moistureproof	Brick	Brick, glazed	Cinder Block	Plaster	Acoustic	Moisture-resistant	Concrete or Structure Tile	Plaster	Tile, acoustic	Moisture-resistant
Apparatus Storage Room			1	2				1				2	1	C											
Classrooms		2			1							2		1	2				2	1		C	C	1	
Clubroom		2			1							2		1	2				2	1		C	C	1	
Corrective Room	1				2			2	1			2				2	2	1	2					1	
Custodial Supply Room			1				2																		
Dance Studio					1																	C	C	1	
Drying Room (equip.)				1				2	2	1	2	1	1				1		1						
Gymnasium					1							2	1		2		2	2	1	2	*	C	C	1	
Health-Service Unit			1		1							2	1		2				2	1				1	
Laundry Room				2				1	2	1	2	2			1	C	*						*	*	*
Locker Rooms		3		3		2	1		1	2	2	3	1		*		1	1	2				C	1	
Natatorium				2				1	2	1	3	2			1	*	2	2	1		*	*	C	C	1	*
Offices	1	3			2							2	1		1				2					1	
Recreation Room		2			1			2				2	1		1	2			1	2	*		C	1	
Shower Rooms				3		2	1	1				2	1		*		2	1	2	2	*			1	*
Special-activity Room		2			1							2			1	1			1	1			C	1	
Team Room	1				3	2	1	2	1	2	2	3	1		*		1	1	2				C	1	
Toilet Room				3		2	1	1			2	2	2	1	*		1	1	1					1	
Toweling-Drying Room				3		2	1	1				2	1		*		2	1	2	2	*			1	*

Note: The numbers in the figure indicate first, second, and third choices. "C" indicates the material as being contrary to good practice. An * indicates desirable quality.

the activities planned for the space (Johnson & Patterson, 1997). Climate is also a consideration when deciding on window placement and use, as it can enhance warming features due to sunlight—which can obviously be a benefit or a detriment—depending on the facility's geographical location. Windows can also create glare problems, but with appropriate placement (northern exposure) can greatly enhance the aesthetic qualities and appeal of indoor surfaces (Holzrichter, 2001). Fenestration is the technical term for the natural lighting created by windows.

The selection process for windows, according to Piper (1998), is based on a number of factors, some of which include: 1) Lighting: the three most common ways for controlling the light passing through windows are tinted glazing, heat-absorbing glazing, and low-emissivity coatings; 2) Keeping the elements out; 3) Heat loss; 4) Aesthetics; 5) Security; and 6) View. Windows are often overlooked when making wall surface choices; however, they should be incorporated into the overall building's aesthetic plan, the regional location of the facility, as well as incorporated into the activities scheduled within the facility. Windows also add to the construction costs, but apart from the impact they may have on the activities planned for the space, they can add extensively to the aesthetic appeal of most facilities.

Additional Floor, Wall and Ceiling Considerations

Floors

- an adequate number of floor drains in the proper locations
- proper floor sloping for adequate drainage (if necessary)
- water-resistant, rounded base, where the flooring and wall meet in any locker or shower area
- floor plates are flush-mounted and placed where they are needed
- provision of non-skid, slip resistant flooring in all wet areas (i.e., pool, shower, etc.)
- lines painted as appropriate, prior to any sealers being applied (Patton et al, 1989)

Walls

- an adequate number of drinking fountains, fully recessed into the walls
- a minimum of one wall of any exercise room with full-length mirrors
- all "corners" in the shower and locker room areas are rounded

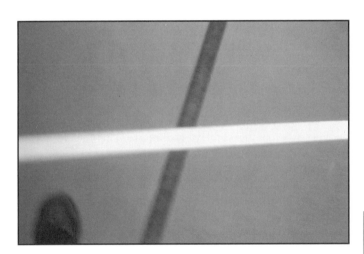

Intersecting lines.

Overlapping and broken lines.

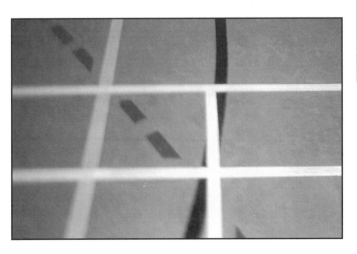

Solid and broken contrasting lines.

- all wall coverings be aesthetically pleasing, as well as matching the decor and color scheme of the facility
- electrical outlets placed strategically within the wall (or floor), firmly attached, and accessible, if the wall is protected with padding
- in wet or humid areas, materials should be easy to clean and impervious to moisture (Patton et al, 1989).

Ceilings

- ensure that ceiling support beams are engineered and designed to withstand stress
- ensure the provision of adequate ceiling heights for all planned facility activities
- all ceilings, except storage areas, are acoustically treated with sound-absorbent materials
- ceilings and access areas are easily accessible for purposes of routine repair and maintenance
- use acoustical materials that are impervious to moisture when they will be used in moisture-dense areas (Patton et al, 1989).

Service and Ancillary Areas

Locker Rooms

Locker area surfaces should possess a combination of maintenance ease along with a strong consideration for hygiene factors. All surfaces should be durable and able to withstand both excessive moisture and humidity, as well as the accumulation of dirt. Aesthetic appeal once again remains a central issue in facility design within locker room areas, as many participants base their attitudes and opinions about the facility as a whole, on their likes and dislikes within the locker-room environment.

Locker room areas should contain hot and humid/wet areas, as well as dry dressing areas, typically within close proximity. Floors in wet areas should always be designed with safety, aesthetics, and maintenance in mind. For obvious reasons, non-slip tile is the best surface for these floors. Since soap and dirt often have a tendency to build up, a beige or brown-colored grout is recommended to keep the tile clean. Some facilities have stopped providing soap, as the resultant slips and falls can create legal problems. Frequently wet areas, such as locker rooms, require greater risk management efforts to readily notice problem areas and reduce potential risks (Di Pilla, 2001).

All wet-area floors within locker rooms should be pitched away from the dry areas and directed towards a drain. Some alternative sources include epoxy sealants over waterproof sheet rock or concrete block. These surfaces have proven in the past to work satisfactorily in the dressing room, sink, and common areas. It should also be noted that all corners of these areas should be rounded so moisture cannot penetrate the seams (Patton et al, 1989).

Moisture is clearly the enemy in any building and even more so where humid or wet areas exist. Precautions during the design process as well as the life span of the facility are important to minimize negative outcomes resulting from humidity, moisture, and microbe growth. Migration of moisture into contiguous areas must also be controlled. Measures must also be taken during the construction process to ensure that all building materials are not moisture damaged prior to installation. An effective and efficient heating, ventilation, and air control system (HVAC), must maintain a balance between humidity control and energy savings (Straus & Kirihara, 1996).

Prevention is the key in controlling microbiological gardens from growing in your building. Clearly, the most eminent hazard is moisture. Moisture can range from large pools of water from roof leaks or broken water pipes, to invisible rain that is absorbed into building materials, or moisture that condenses on facility surfaces. Dust also serves as a nutrient source for microbial growth. Although chemicals are a common method to combat these problems, moisture is the real culprit and should be the primary focus of effective and routine maintenance procedures (Straus & Kirihara, 1996).

In drier areas of the locker room, the floor is a major concern for interior decorators and designers. Mildew and mold are constant problems, and the materials should be able to withstand long periods of moist conditions and show little or no signs of delaminating. A 100 percent nylon carpet is recommended for flooring material in a health and fitness setting. The carpeting provides an aesthetically pleasing appearance and is easily maintained with daily vacuuming and periodic shampooing. It should also be noted that the nylon carpets will have a longer life and will be more easily maintained if they are mildew resistant and Scotch-guarded (Patton et al, 1989). Wear tests have also concluded that appropriate cushioning beneath the carpet surface can greatly enhance carpet life, as well as comfort for the participant (Goodman, 2000).

Wall coverings in locker room areas usually consist of epoxy-coated paint, vinyl, or wallpaper. The chosen material should be strong and not show dirt. There should also be consideration given to the corners and wall-to-wall moldings to reduce the amount of black marks and cuts that often appear, typically with heavy use. Ceilings are typically finished with moisture-proof hand-finished paint. As mentioned earlier, acoustical materials should also be used in conjunction with paint to reduce the noise levels that occur in locker rooms (Patton et al, 1989).

Steam Rooms

Steam rooms require specialized knowledge for construction and care. Building materials utilized and the planned methods of application are critical to minimizing the maintenance efforts in steam rooms. It is highly recommended to hire a contractor with previous experience in the construction of wet areas when considering steam room construction. The floor surface of a steam room should be covered with a liquid rubber material and applied over a concrete slab. A layer of fiberglass fabric is laid over the rubber material, followed with an additional coat of liquid rubber. The floor should also slope toward the drain for proper water drainage. This system both protects against water leaks and expands with floor movement (Patton et al, 1989).

Steam room walls and ceilings should be covered with a cement building board and fiberglass tape. This wall surface should also be placed on galvanized metal studs or treated lumber. It is important to remember to slope ceilings as well, to enable moisture to run-off rather than drip-off.

This system has proven to be durable and helps to prevent against rot and mildew. As with other wet areas, the selected tile should be both attractive and durable. A textured non-slip tile should be used on the floors, whereas many choose to use glazed ceramic tile for the walls and ceilings (Patton et al, 1989).

Aerobic/Exercise Facilities

As aerobic exercise and other impact activities remain popular in fitness, recreational, and athletic centers across the nation, the efforts to reduce impact-related injuries continue. Spring-loaded or "floating" hardwood floors are the most popular surfaces, followed closely by heavily padded carpet surfaces that are sealed and plastic-laminate-bonded to inhibit moisture leaks into the pile textures. This type of flooring allows for regular steam cleaning and avoids the hygiene problems from accumulated perspiration, as with a carpeted and/or padded area. Important considerations are compliance (shock absorption), foot stability, surface traction, and resiliency (energy return). Furthermore, there are synthetic and specially made floors that may be used as alternatives (Patton et al, 1989). Research on various flooring types should be available from most manufacturers that address the specific needs and demands of the activity you plan to offer.

Finding a balance between all facility surface areas is a considerable challenge for the facility-planning team. For example, one of the best shock-absorbing floorings is any type of thick sponge pad. Regular foam may develop dips after prolonged use, but some new synthetics have been specially developed to hold their shape. One such surface is microcell foam, which is available at one-fourth the cost of wood, but it should be noted some difficulties may arise from the interlocking sections. These types of synthetic floors are usually soft enough that individual mats are not needed for floor exercises. It should be noted that cleaning may also present unique problems with these floor types. Bacteria growth may also be a problem, in particular if the surface is textured or not properly maintained (Walker & Stotlar, 1997).

Although the quality of actual polyurethane surfaces continues to improve, these surfaces are not considered resilient enough by some, because they are simply poured directly over concrete. The testing results of a surface may meet all the necessary industry standards; however, the surface "hardness" may still be inappropriate for many activities, again due to the nature of the sub-flooring material. This point was made earlier, however, that it is imperative to consider the sub-flooring material just as vital to the qualities and characteristics of use as the visible surface that is applied, laid, or poured on top. Maintenance issues remain a significant factor, as these surfaces are often plagued with cracking and peeling with age. The life cycle of these surfaces is also much shorter than wood.

Carpeting is relatively easy to install, and newer sport varieties have special shock absorption properties. These should always be used with foam cushioning and never be applied directly over concrete surfaces. Carpet is versatile, inexpensive, and works well, especially in multi-purpose areas. It should be noted, however, that carpets are highly susceptible to staining, can be easily discolored or stretched, and also retain odors. The expected life span of most carpets is two to four years, depending on the use, cleaning methods, and quality of the materials.

Historically, wood floors have been the popular choice. Wood is aesthetically pleasing and provides a high degree of flexibility within most multi-purpose activity areas. Wood floors, however, depending on the sub-flooring utilized, are often extremely hard, not resilient enough for high-energy exercise, and excessive humidity can cause the wood to warp (Walker & Stotlar, 1997).

Strength Training Areas

Another area of continued popularity is the strength training room. The dark and dingy weight rooms of the past are being replaced with colorful new flooring options and light, airy and open spaces. The type of flooring sought depends largely on the nature of the equipment selected, however, the aesthetic appeal is increasingly becoming important in this decision. If a weight area is primarily equipped with machines (Nautilus, Universal, etc.), an easily maintained durable carpet is sufficient. If the room is dominated by free weights, a resilient rubber surface is recommended—tiled, poured, or pre-fabricated. Pre-fabricated options come in the form of sheets or tiles and are simply glued on top of the existing surface or concrete slab.

The desired appearance of the strength training room is an important consideration when selecting a flooring material. The level of supervision over these areas is also a factor, as observed participants tend to be less likely to treat equipment roughly and purposely damage equipment or flooring surfaces. Once again, aesthetic appeal is becoming more desirable, and creative and attractive options are not necessarily more expensive, but they do take more planning (Hasenkamp & Lutz, 2001). The color schemes of the walls, equipment upholstery, and flooring must all be coordinated to appeal to the user. Assistance in this area can be provided by consultants or interior designers (Patton et al, 1989).

Racquetball Courts

The overall playing surface for a racquetball court requires 800 square feet. Traditionally, racquetball courts are covered with a wood floor surface. Maple floors are attractive, provide favorable ball bounce, and absorb shock to the feet, but there is one disadvantage. When moisture enters the wood, it will buckle the system and cause a swelling in the floor. This becomes an important factor to note if subterranean facilities are built in areas with porous soil. The only other viable system is a synthetic one. New polyurethane materials have been implemented with satisfactory results. These floors are poured and trawled over the concrete floor slab (Patton et al, 1989).

The most popular wall systems to choose from are reinforced fiberglass, concrete, plaster, panels, poured-in-place cement slab, and shatterproof glass. Before deciding on a wall system, one should consider the following: material cost, land considerations (moisture and stability), overall appearance, maintenance, and ball action. Plaster is often viewed as a mainstay, as it has been around for years, but maintenance costs usually prove to be expensive. Poured-in-place concrete slabs have not been used very often. The cost is prohibitive, and obtaining a straight wall from a slab that is poured on the ground and then erected is difficult to accomplish. Reinforced fiberglass concrete has a promising future, but many applications have proven inconsistent. Plexiglass walls provide an aesthetic appeal but are too costly for some facilities. Lastly, the floor system with perhaps the best reputation is a panel system designed from compressed wood. The quality of panel systems varies widely, so facility planning members must be careful in selecting a system with a satisfactory quality-to-price ratio (Patton et al, 1989).

Racquetball court ceilings are often constructed from the same materials used for the walls. A popular alternative involves a combination of the wall material for the front half of the ceiling and acoustical tile for the back half. The acoustical tile has been found to be successful in deadening the sound of the ball. Another alternative is the use of sheet rock covered by paint or a glazed material (Patton et al, 1989).

Offices and Teaching Areas

Most offices and teaching stations employ a smooth-surfaced glazed block, or a similar smooth surface on walls ranging from eight to ten feet. Smoother walls are easier to maintain and clean, are more durable, and safer. As mentioned earlier, walls are important aspects of many teaching stations, and must be planned appropriately. Many walls are utilized as rebound areas, barriers for equipment storage, sound barriers, as well as for fitness testing and measurement (Flynn, 1993). Many varieties of wall barriers are available and must be considered based on facility needs and area utilization.

Summary

In summary, facility surfaces are an integral facet of any athletic complex. The primary surfaces within a facility are floors, walls, and ceilings. Activities planned for each area of the facility, the available budget, the life expectancy, and the maintenance and operational costs should dictate surface selection decisions. There are three distinct areas or divisions within facilities. The first of these areas is the service/ancillary areas, such as locker rooms, bathrooms, exercise rooms, etc. These areas require surfaces that are able to withstand heavy moisture content. The second area is the main arena or activity focus within the facility. The third component represents the office and administrative areas within the facility.

Flooring surfaces are categorized into three areas: wood, vinyl, and synthetics. The two most popular forms of synthetic flooring are polyvinyl chlorides (PVC's) and polyurethane. It is important to note that there are countless types of wood flooring, and the costs vary depending on the system that is utilized (the manufacturer), and the installer. Facility walls serve more than simply acting as dividers between given areas. Walls serve as barriers to sound, heat, light, and moisture. Walls also influence the aesthetic appeal of a facility. When selecting wall surfaces, consideration should be given to the acoustical properties of the material, and of course, the planned activities within this space. Moisture-resistant walls with acoustical properties are usually favored. There are also several issues to consider when selecting materials for ceiling construction. The activities planned for the area, roof design, and local building codes should all be taken into account. Ceilings should possess materials that allow for acceptable acoustical standards, be high enough for planned activities, and be insulated to prevent condensation.

Facility surfaces are available in many colors, textures, and materials, and also with varying degrees of performance characteristics. When trying to find the correct fit for your facility, please keep in mind the following concepts in the decision-making process:

- Economic feasibility of the initial and life-cycle costs
- Maintenance and replacement ease
- Performance capabilities for intended use and possible future use
- Overall compatibility in appearance with other surrounding materials within the facility
- Safety and risk management factors

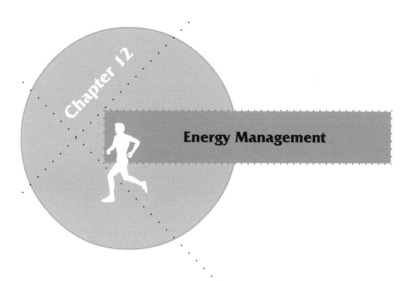

Chapter 12

Energy Management

Jack Vivian, JRV, Inc.

Over the last decade, energy management has moved from being a one-time activity to an on-going and essential part of facility planning and management. Furthermore, energy management has become a widely known applied science with new measures, technologies, and analytic approaches. The importance of energy management to facility planning cannot be overemphasized, especially in sport and recreation facilities that consume large amounts of energy.

The long-range forecasts for the world's energy supplies and price indicate that it is wise to design systems and reduce consumption of energy during periods of shortage and rapidly escalating prices. New technologies and improved heating and air conditioning equipment show that further savings are possible, even during periods of lower fuel prices.

Next to staffing, utilities normally are the second highest cost of operating sport and recreational facilities. This chapter will provide an overview of energy management, outline specific aspects of energy management in the building envelope, building operations and maintenance, heating, cooling, and air-handling systems. We will look at how domestic hot water and air quality affect energy consumption and the impact that lighting and building automation systems have on energy management opportunities. Energy management will be addressed, looking at planning and construction issues as well as maintenance and operating criteria. Finally, the chapter provides reference sources and web sources for the student to further study energy management.

In the planning and construction process for sport and recreation facilities, whether for a new building, a building addition, or major renovation, there are thousands of issues that must be resolved by the owner, the architect, and the construction contractors. Many of these issues deal with design, selection and integration of facilities energy systems (the heating/cooling/ventilation systems, lighting and other energy-consuming equipment). Oftentimes, these issues get very little attention in the design process and end up to be serious and costly mistakes, because over the life of the facility, the energy costs will exceed the initial cost of all the energy systems.

Because many of these issues are quite technical and involve parts of the facility no one usually sees, energy questions may be mishandled in the design process. This results in design professionals being allowed to design the building shell, heating, ventilation, air conditioning (HVAC), lighting, and other energy-consuming systems independently and, to protect themselves from liability or complaints, these systems are typically over-engineered. Energy-efficient buildings should be designed by an integrated design approach in which all of the design professionals work together with energy efficiency as one of their goals.

A second reason energy issues are mishandled in design is the fact that almost everyone makes decisions on the basis of initial cost or first cost rather than on life cycle costs that take into account the initial cost and all of the costs associated with operating and maintaining the facility during its useful life. The most cost-effective time to incorporate energy efficiency into a sport and recreational facility is during construction, when the energy savings need only pay back the incremental cost difference between a "regular" system and a more efficient one. Unless the design team evaluates alternative options on a life-cycle cost basis, sound decisions cannot be made.

Learning Objectives

After reading this chapter, the student will be able to:
- understand terminology related to energy management,
- understand the design, construction, and operating considerations related to energy management,
- identify the various energy savings considerations when planning, operating, and maintaining a sport and recreational facility, and
- learn sources of energy management information and reference materials.

Energy Management as a Process

Initially, energy management was viewed as a one-time application of conservation principles to the building envelope and mechanical systems. Experience has shown that greater savings may be obtained and sustained when energy management is considered an on-going process. It is a process that involves a number of key elements such as:

- An assessment of the building and its operating systems
- A list of appropriate energy conservation measures based on the assessment
- Careful planned implementation
- Regular review of actual energy savings

Once started, energy management is an on-going process that is integrated with building maintenance and operation and with any changes in building occupancy, envelope, or mechanical equipment. Sport and recreational facilities have major changes in occupancy loads during varying periods of the day and seasons of the year, and understanding these impacts on the mechanical system is a critical step to designing systems. Moreover, these facilities are normally large spaces with big building envelopes containing glass entrances and large roofing structures. Under normal circumstances, these characteristics do not lend themselves to being energy efficient.

Energy management as a process also recognizes that buildings are not static. Occupancy changes can affect internal space allocations and patterns of building use, which affect the demands on and performance of mechanical systems. Occupancy codes require a certain number of air changes per hour to satisfy the fresh air needs of the participants as well as the spectators. These requirements directly affect the heating, ventilation, and air conditioning systems.

The three major steps involved in energy management are: conduct an energy audit and analysis, implementation of a strategy, and monitoring of the results.

Energy Audit and Analysis

While a simple walk-through audit will often reveal many opportunities for savings, it is recommended that a full energy audit be undertaken. This will serve as the foundation of the implementation program and as a reference point for partial studies that may be required in future years owing to major changes in building occupancy, envelope, or mechanical systems.

A full energy audit is a complete assessment of the building and its energy use patterns. The physical characteristics of the building shell (e.g., walls, windows and doors, roof, floor, etc.) and the various electrical and mechanical systems (e.g., heating, ventilation and cooling equipment, lights, water heaters, etc.) are inspected (*Energy Ideas*, Feb. 93). Utility bills are reviewed to determine actual energy use. If possible, energy use is allocated to each building system separately.

The energy audit also provides the necessary information for designing an implementation program. A list of energy conservation measures is developed based on the energy analysis and target energy use. The list is usually divided into no-cost housekeeping measures, low-cost maintenance, and upgrading and major retrofit or upgrading projects involving considerable capital expenditure. Capital costs and estimated savings for each measure are summarized in the energy audit report. With the deregulation of electricity, there are numerous energy audit companies available to work with sport and recreational professionals to design conservation plans for facilities.

Implementation

In addition to the building information and recommended measures from the building energy audit, many other practical concerns should be considered in the development of the implementation plan. These include: existing maintenance program for envelope and mechanical system; existing repair and upgrading program for envelope and mechanical system; projected plans for changes in building occupancy; projected plans for major repairs or renovations; available funds; and available staff resources for implementation and program management.

Implementation of specific energy management measures will proceed according to the implementation program. Some key steps in the program are: *allocating* of capital funds and staff resources, *obtaining* estimates and selecting consultants for measures that require professional assistance, *assigning* a project manager or energy manager responsibility for program implementation and monitoring results, and *selecting* contractors and/or internal staff to implement measures.

Monitoring of Results

Monitoring an energy management program is essential in order to measure results and to steer the program with progressive feedback. The simplest monitoring technique involves reviewing energy bills on a monthly and annual basis and comparing them to a previous reference year. However, a more complete monitoring program will include keeping records of factors that affect energy usage. A sample list of the components of a complete monitoring program is noted below:
- measuring energy/usage and costs;
- logging building system performance through indicators such as supply air temperature and boiler efficiency;
- logging weather conditions;
- recording any additions or modifications to the building, recording patterns of building occupancy and use and occupant comments on comfort;
- recording any changes in occupancy patterns and use;
- recording energy management measures as they are implemented;
- logging maintenance of building equipment and systems.

Energy Accounting

Energy accounting is defined as the systematic tracking and analysis of energy costs and consumption in order to better manage and control energy in buildings (*Energy Ideas*,

Feb 93). In energy accounting, the information gathered through monitoring is used to report on the progress of the energy management program. It involves determining where energy is used, how much, and why.

Many factors affect building energy use. These include: weather conditions at the building site; design, quality, and condition of the building envelope; insulation value of walls and roof; number and size of windows, quality and type of windows, air leakage around windows, doors, and other openings. Other factors are: building mechanical systems; heating, ventilating, and air conditioning systems and their operation; process activities inside the building such as lighting, hot water and appliances; maintenance of building equipment and systems, efficiency of systems and components; and patterns of building occupancy and use.

A good energy accounting system can provide tangible benefits that pay for the cost of the system many times over (Goldberger & Jessop, 1994). Some of the most attractive benefits include: verifies monthly invoices, pinpoints problem areas, helps manage budgets, monitors energy management programs, justifies energy conservation investments, provides reports to senior management, and financing options for energy.

Energy management programs can be financed using a number of options.

Operating Funds

Many low-cost/no-cost measures can be funded from existing operating budgets. Energy is an operating expenditure, and energy cost savings can be used to purchase energy retrofits.

Capital Budgets

Energy management retrofit programs can be funded from capital budgets.

Leases

Leases can be used to purchase energy management equipment. Lease payments can be designed to be less than the projected energy cost savings.

Energy Service Agreement

An energy service agreement is a performance contract in which a private company offers to execute efficiency capital improvements in exchange for a portion of the energy cost savings that accrue. Typically, a company enters into a long-term contract and, at its expense, designs, installs, and manages or co-manages an energy efficiency system for the facility.

It is important to evaluate the cost and payback period for each measure as it relates to a particular building. What may be a low-cost measure for a large sports facility would represent a substantial investment for a smaller recreation operation. Each situation has to be looked at separately.

Building Envelope

The building envelope consists of the roof, floor, walls, windows, and doors—all parts of the building that enclose the interior building space and separate it from the outdoor climate. The envelope performs several functions. It provides shelter from the elements, lighting (windows), and in some cases, air changes through natural ventilation (windows), and infiltration. The envelope's success in performing these functions is dependent on the building design, quality of construction, and maintenance of the envelope components.

A building's shape and size will greatly affect its heating and cooling loads. Compact facilities generally require less energy than large seating capacity sports venues that ramble and sprawl all over the site. Proper choice of architectural form and orientation can often reduce energy cost. Large sports facilities should respect the path of the sun and be oriented east/west to minimize solar gain in the summer and maximize solar gain in the winter. Reduced air infiltration and proper analysis for optimum insulation is also critical to study early in the design process.

The role of the mechanical systems and purchased energy is to make up the difference between that which the envelope can provide in occupant comfort and what is required (*Energy Ideas*, Oct 92). The quality of the envelope, then, is a major factor in determining energy used for heating, cooling, lighting, and ventilation. Improvements to the envelope can significantly reduce energy demand.

Uncontrolled air leakage through the building envelope is often associated with moisture damage to building components. An added benefit of energy management attention to the envelope is the resolution and prevention of problems affecting the service life of envelope components. It is important to understand the causes of heat loss through the building envelope and to understand the strategies for upgrading the thermal performance of the building envelope.

Energy to heat interior spaces (in winter) or to cool interior spaces (in summer) is lost through heat transfer and infiltration/exfiltration. Heat transfer refers to the movement of heat through walls, windows, doors, roof, or floors whenever there is a difference between the exterior temperature and the interior temperature. Heat transfer occurs through three natural processes: convection, conduction, and radiation.

Convection is the transfer of heat by the movement of a fluid such as air. For example, cool air moving over a warmer surface picks up heat, carries it and transfers it to a cooler surface. Conduction is the transfer of heat directly through a solid (e.g., wood, brick, drywall, etc). Radiation is the transfer of heat from a surface by electromagnetic waves.

The amount of heat transferred is determined by the temperature difference and thermal resistance factored against the square foot area of the envelope. Poor thermal performance of the envelope puts greater demand on the mechanical systems for heating and cooling. In addition, cold surfaces or excessive solar gain can create comfort problems and decrease the efficient use of the space. Building elements with poor thermal performance such as single-glazed windows can be the site of condensation that can cause deterioration of surrounding finishes. Thermal weak points in the envelope can also contribute to the defacement and/or deterioration of building components.

During cold weather, warm air rises to upper levels, where it leaks out to colder outside air (exfiltration). The air lost at the top is replaced by cold air leaking into the building at the bottom (infiltration). The building mechanical systems can affect the pattern of infiltration/exfiltration through requirements for the combustion and draft air and by operation of ventilation systems.

There are two basic approaches to saving energy through modifications to the building shell. Infiltration/exfiltration may be reduced by air sealing cracks, air barriers, weather-stripping, or adding better-fitting windows and doors. Thermal performance may be improved by adding insulation to the roof, walls, or floor, or by adding double- or triple-glazed windows. Insulated windows, either aerogel or multiple-paned, can prevent conduction of heat through the glass. Low-emissivity (low-E) windows and window films allow windows to reflect heat rather than transmit it, keeping rooms cool in the summer and warm in the winter (*Energy Ideas*).

In general, air sealing and other measures that reduce air infiltration/exfiltration should be implemented before adding insulation. The major areas and extent of air leakage can be determined by means of a complete building audit. The techniques used may include: a walk-through building audit, a fan-depressurization test, an infra-red thermograph scan, and smoke pencil test. Normally, infiltration and exfiltration should be checked at building joints, windows and doors, mechanical penetration areas, and at the top of buildings where the roof structure attaches to the walls. Since sport and recreational facilities are large buildings with roofs spanning long distances, these are important areas to have sealed.

Upgrading the thermal performance of the building envelope can lower demand for heating and cooling. It can also improve occupant comfort and use of space by eliminating uncomfortable drafts and cold spots. Energy conservation measures may also provide effective solutions to serious building damage by correcting thermal weak points that can cause deterioration of building components. A complete energy audit of the building will present a "thermal picture" of the envelope. Furthermore, this will indicate areas of greatest heat loss and cooling load. A thermal picture will be determined by the size, shape of the building, its ages and type of construction. Each part of the building envelope offers unique opportunities and constraints regarding thermal upgrading. The best time to address the thermal performance of a sport facility is during the design phase.

Operation and Maintenance

Proper maintenance is essential to conserving energy in the long term. The building should be designed with future maintenance in mind. Easy access to equipment, having major components of the mechanical and electrical systems labeled and as-built drawings provided are good first steps to making maintenance easier to perform. A manual containing operating instructions and information of all of the components of the mechanical and electrical systems should be turned over to the owner when the systems are commissioned.

A thorough and well-managed maintenance program will directly contribute to reducing energy costs. Equipment that is well maintained operates more efficiently and consumes less energy. If maintenance of heating, cooling, ventilating, or electrical systems is neglected, costs will increase

in the long term. This includes the cost of equipment downtime, emergency repair costs, and the increased energy cost to operate the equipment. Energy costs will also increase, owing to poor operating efficiencies resulting from neglect.

Good operational and maintenance procedures can complement a well-designed energy management program, specifically as they relate to the following systems: heating, cooling, ventilation, water treatment, and lighting. Energy management must become part of daily operations to be effective. All operating procedures should be energy efficient. Operations logs and well-documented operating procedures are essential ingredients of energy management. Keeping operational logs is one activity that is part of the standard operating procedure for a building. Operating logs perform several functions: they provide a permanent historical record of system performance, ensure that systems are inspected frequently, identify problems by providing historical records of changes in operation and/or energy performance and provide a base for evaluating new energy efficient measures and their cost effectiveness.

Heating, Ventilation and Air Conditioning Systems

Sport and recreational buildings incorporate a wide variety of heating, ventilation, and air-conditioning (HVAC) systems. The principal goal of an energy management program is to maximize the efficiency of all systems. Efficiency is a term that describes the relationship between energy input and usable energy output (ASHRAE, 1994).

Air-Handling Systems

Air-handling systems consist of an air-handling unit and distribution equipment such as ductwork, dampers, and air diffusers. The typical air-handling unit refers to a ventilation device that, when installed in a building, may serve a number of purposes. The system should be providing an airflow with adequate pressure and speed to reach all areas served by the unit; filtering and conditioning the air with cooling, heating, and dehumidification processes; and mixing a measured quantity of fresh air with re-circulated air. A typical air-handling unit may contain some or all of the following components: fan(s), filters; heating, cooling, and dehumidification coils; humidifier, dampers to control the direction of the airflow and the mixing of outside and re-circulated air; and control devices to regulate temperature and humidity of the airflow.

Conditioning the Air

Conditioning of the incoming air is generally limited to dehumidification and heating. A room thermostat generally controls the amount of heat required to maintain room comfort. Desiccant systems and heat pipes dry air far more efficiently than causing condensation by super-cooling air. Using a desiccant dehumidifier dries air without cooling it, causing the water to absorb to the surface of the desiccant. The desiccant is recharged using either waste heat from the boiler, from a solar collector, or with gas heat that is returned to the space.

The components of an air-exhaust system include an exhaust fan, ductwork and grilles, and hoods to capture contaminated air as close as possible to the source. In addition, most exhaust systems incorporate a series of controls to regulate the operation of the fan and its accessories, such as motorized damper. Energy management action for exhaust systems will depend in part on the area being exhausted. Fans that exhaust air from locker rooms normally need to operate continuously, especially when athletic equipment needs dried. If this is not the case, then these exhaust fans can be run only when the rooms are occupied.

Heat recovery potential is present in most air-handling systems. However, the use of the recovered heat by a system must be economically justifiable. Return of the recovered heat to the process from which it came should be the first priority, since such systems usually require less control and are less expensive to install.

The hot water heating plant of a building incorporates a number of components that individually are responsible for some form of heat transfer and therefore have their own particular efficiency. Heating systems are made up of three principal components: supply equipment (e.g., boiler); distribution equipment (e.g., supply and return piping); and end use equipment (e.g., heaters and associated controls). Boiler efficiency is indicated directly from temperature and composition of flue gases. The latter indicates the air/fuel ratio at the burner, which is the most important parameter affecting combustion efficiency. Maintaining boiler water quality is essential to maintaining a high system efficiency. In the generation of steam in a boiler, certain impurities (solids) in the water must be purged from the system on a continual basis via an adjustable blow-down valve. Proper adjustment of the blow-down valve must be maintained at all times. Furthermore, energy losses in the heating system can be minimized by ensuring the regular maintenance of distribution piping. Regular maintenance includes an inventory of the system components and documentation of their condition.

End-use equipment in heating systems includes steam and hot water radiators, and heating coils in ventilation units. Conditions that result in excessive energy use in these components include valves that leak or are stuck open and faulty controls. These conditions are often associated with comfort problems in the space that is heated. Proper maintenance will avoid excessive energy use by end-use equipment.

Air Conditioning

All air-conditioning equipment requires regular, planned maintenance to ensure energy- efficient operation. Cooling system maintenance should include periodic inspection of cooling coils (chilled water or direct expansion) for icing or dirt accumulation on the coil. Both will reduce heat transfer rates, reduce airflow to the space, make it difficult to maintain comfort, and waste energy. Cooling system valves and controls should also be inspected periodically to ensure efficient system operation.

Ventilation Systems

Ventilation systems can be large energy users and energy wasters—both directly and indirectly (*Energy Ideas*, Nov 92). Energy is used directly in operation fans. Indirect en-

ergy use takes place in heating or cooling and dehumidifying the fresh air brought in from outside. Damper condition should be checked periodically, because damper efficiency and general condition are directly affected by frequency of use. The damper unit is generally controlled by a damper assembly. A motor mounted at one end of the assembly will control damper positioning. The damper controls how much air is brought in from the outside.

Filter Maintenance

Filter maintenance is another factor that is important in ensuring the energy-efficient operation of air-handling systems. Filter replacement or cleaning should occur on a regular basis according to the rate of the dirt buildup. Clogging of filters does not increase energy use directly. However, a pressure drop increase across a filter, due to dirt buildup, will result in an airflow reduction and fan power increase. The system cannot operate efficiently with dirty filters.

Other Considerations

Other operating and maintenance energy considerations are:

- Dehumidifier Maintenance—Improperly maintained dehumidifiers can increase energy use by maintaining a humidity level higher than required.
- Water Treatment of HVAC Systems—An effective water treatment program should maintain a clean system, free of any hard-water deposits or any corrosion products. A water distribution system that is fouled with deposits has a much lower rate of heat exchange and will reduce the energy efficiency of the entire distribution system.
- Cooling Tower Condenser Water—The most expensive part of an HVAC system to treat is the condenser cooling tower system. A cooling tower has high water losses due to evaporative cooling and requires water make-up to prevent water deposits from forming on the condenser tubes of the chiller. Proper water treatment procedures require the use of water scale control chemicals and corrosion inhibitors.
- Domestic Hot Water Systems—Domestic hot water temperatures should be closely monitored to reduce excessive scaling. Systems can be flushed and descaled at regularly scheduled intervals to improve heat transfer at the heat exchanger.

Heat Pumps

A heat pump is essentially a refrigeration cycle where the heat rejected at the condenser is used for heating purposes. The total heat delivered to the condenser is the sum of the heat extracted in the evaporator and the heat from the compressor work necessary to compress the refrigerant.

The heat pump must have a source of heat to be cooled in order to work. In residential applications, the source of heat is usually outside air, water, or the ground. In large buildings, the source of heat can be waste heat from lighting in interior building areas or heat from computers. The heating requirement must occur at the same time as the cooling requirement if the heat source is inside the building, or thermal storage must be used to transfer the heat to another time period.

Domestic Hot Water

A hot water plant may include one or several hot water boilers, a heat exchanger to produce domestic hot water, circulating pumps, and control devices. A hot water distribution system, sometimes called a hydronic system, is used to circulate hot water between a boiler and the heat transfer equipment located in the various heated areas of the building. A steam distribution system is used to convey steam from a boiler to the heat transfer equipment (*Energy Ideas*, March 93).

Domestic hot water systems provide potable water for handwashing, showers, swimming pools, ice resurfacing, and cleaning. Most sport and recreational buildings incorporate some form of domestic hot water heating system. The domestic hot water system is similar to hot water heating systems, except that the heated water is potable and cannot be chemically treated. Cold water is supplied as make-up to this system from the local water utility.

Domestic hot water systems can be subdivided into unitary and central systems. Unitary systems are point-of-use systems with no distribution piping to serve multiple points of use. Unitary systems, or instantaneous water heaters, eliminate long pipe runs and associated line losses. Central systems are more common in sports facilities and incorporate distribution piping to serve more than one point of use. A central domestic hot water system generally includes: a hot water generator heated by steam, by natural gas, or by an electric element; a storage tank (frequently integrated with the hot water generator); piping (usually copper pipes); recirculating pump(s); plumbing fixtures such as faucets, showerheads; and control devices that regulate the water temperature and occasionally the water flow to the appliances.

The key energy management measures related to various components of the above systems include:
- hot water consumption can be reduced through the use of restricted water flow showerheads.
- consider use of separate boiler for domestic hot water heating if domestic hot water is the only summer load for a large boiler.
- piping losses can be reduced by stopping circulating pumps one hour after occupied periods end. Restart the re-circulation pumps not more than one hour before occupancy periods begin. Computerized energy management systems can be programmed to accomplish these functions based on the activities scheduled in the facility.
- reduce tank losses of the water heater when hot water will not be used for a period of 72 hours or more. Tanks and lines should be insulated to avoid unnecesary losses.

Water, like energy, is an increasingly scarce and expensive commodity whose use has enormous environmental repercussions. Unfortunately, the prices most users pay for clean water do not come close to covering the real cost (Chernushenko, 1994). Moves are afoot in a number of areas, however, to develop pricing mechanisms that transfer the real cost of water to the consumer. Since price can only go up, the sports facility that has taken steps to reduce its water consumption may be only marginally affected.

Large volumes of water are typically consumed by sports facilities for indoor pools, landscaping, and turf maintenance. Artificial snowmaking is another major water consumer. Below are some effective general steps.

Indoor Water Use

The principal areas of indoor water consumption are washrooms, showers, and laundry rooms. Steps to improve water conservation in these areas are:

- Instruct and remind washroom and shower users to shut off taps fully
- Repair drips and leaks promptly
- For automatic flushing systems, check that timing cycles are appropriate for the frequency of urinal use. Shut them down entirely after hours.
- Install low-flow aerators and automatic shut-off valves on tapes
- Retrofit toilets to reduce water consumption

Outdoor Water Use

Facilities such as golf courses and playing fields spend heavily on keeping their turf healthy and green. Watering during dry spells actually works against the health of the ecosystem as a whole by depleting water reserves elsewhere. Sports facilities can reduce demand for irrigation by helping encourage an evolution in the attitudes of users to the point where turf which is less than forest green is acceptable.

Steps to reduce outdoor water consumption:
- Plant only native vegetation or species suited to the climate.
- Limit watering of turf to playing surfaces that receive heavy use.
- Water only during the evening and overnight to reduce evaporation.
- Use trickle or soaker hoses rather than aerial sprinklers.
- Design parking lots and roadways to allow rainwater to return to the soil, streams and ground water.

Air Quality

The air-quality issue in sport and recreational buildings has developed into a significant concern for today's building owners and operators. The public now has greater awareness of health-related concerns, and there is increased research documenting these issues. On the other hand, heating and cooling systems that use excess fresh air also require more energy. To compound this problem, there is no single, accurate method of measuring air quality, and solutions to air-quality problems tend to be building and site specific. The challenge for building managers is to find the optimum levels of fresh air to maintain comfort conditions. Good air quality and energy conservation should be complementary. One should not be achieved at the expense of the other.

Air quality is an evolving issue. Standards and guidelines for air quality in buildings have developed along with an evolving understanding of human requirements for fresh air to support health and of the major air-related contaminants and their effects. The American Society of Heating Ventilation and Air Conditioning Engineers (ASHRAE) was one of the first organizations to establish guidelines for air quality. ASHRAE's research has led to the publication of minimum ventilation rates to maintain the indoor environment within a key range of guidelines.

Air quality is a complex issue that affects occupant comfort, health, and productivity, and acceptance of energy conservation measures. Modern building materials contain many new chemicals that can give off gases or vapor such as formaldehyde and radon. Other organic and inorganic chemicals are introduced to recreation buildings through paints, solvents, and photocopiers. Allergens from airborne particles and dust are also present in these environments.

HVAC designers and building managers in existing buildings, have reduced outside air ventilation rates to lower levels in keeping with energy conservation guidelines. Moreover, outside air quality has generally deteriorated in our major cities due to pollution from industrial plants, automobiles, and other combustion-type processes.

Variable-air-volume systems used in many large spectator facilities often have decreased air-circulation rates compared to conventional constant-volume systems. Air-circulation rates affect the purging of local contaminants such as cigarette smoke and heat from the activity and spectator areas. Many older buildings are undergoing major retrofits to HVAC systems to reduce energy costs. Fans are being modified and generally operated for fewer hours each day. New control strategies call for the conversion from outside air systems to re-circulation-type systems with less outside air delivered to the space. This is especially helpful in settings where the outside air is of poor quality.

Generally, comfort is perceived when physical, chemical, and biological stresses are at a minimum. Quality of air and the perception of air quality can be quite different. The major components influencing each are common and are listed below.

- Physical—physical contaminants in the air
- Chemical—chemical contaminants in the air
- Biological—biological contaminants in the air
- Thermodynamic Characteristics of the Air—air temperature and relative humidity, air velocity

Thermal Factors

Thermal factors affect air quality in two ways. The human perception of air-quality control is related to factors such as air temperature, as well as the actual composition of the air. For example, too high of a temperature or lack of air movement may create a sensation of "stuffiness." Secondly, the thermal characteristics of the air will affect the actions of contaminants in the environment. For example, excessive humidity will promote the growth of microorganisms. A ther-

mally acceptable environment will minimize physical stress. Thermal comfort depends on the factors listed below.

- Air temperature—the temperature set by building operation can vary considerably due to temperature stratification within the space, and such variations can affect occupant comfort.
- Air velocity—air-distribution systems may create the sensation of drafts or conversely of "stuffiness".
- Relative humidity—relative humidity expressed as a percentage varies in the range of 20% to 80% for most buildings. Relative humidity below 20% will result in discomfort for some people.
- Static electricity—static buildup can also occur with low relative humidity. Testing hasshown that most people link dryness or perception of humidity level to air temperature.

Physical Contaminants

Some of the major physical contaminants are listed below.

Contaminant	Source
Dust particles	Outdoor air
Tobacco smoke (particulates & vapor)	Cigarettes
Asbestos fibers	Asbestos building products
Metallic dust	Building materials
Wood particles	Building materials

The particles of smoke, dust, pollen, etc., enter the indoor environment either from outside by infiltration or from activities and processes in the building. The amount of material entering the building from outdoors will depend on the wind velocity and the amount of infiltration. Particles can be generated indoors by smoking, other indoor combustion processes, and existing building materials.

Chemical Contaminants

A number of chemical contaminants can be found in the indoor air of a typical sport or recreation building. These include the products of combustion, namely, Carbon Monoxide (CO), Carbon Dioxide (CO2), Oxides of Nitrogen (NOx), and Sulphur Dioxide (SO2). These chemicals, in some concentrations, can be found in the indoor air whenever a combustion source is within the building. Ice resurfacers and edgers in ice arenas, carpet cleaning, and forklifts on indoor soccer and field-houses and vacuum systems for cleaning seating capacity venues can contaminate the air with carbon monoxide and nitrogen dioxide fumes. Ozone concentrations can increase due to photocopiers and other sources, such as aerosol spray cans. Cleaning agents can give off toxic fumes. Building materials such as paints and particleboards can add to formaldehyde and other hydrocarbon concentrations.

Types of Biological Contaminants

Biological contaminants are microorganisms that can spread through a facility and be inhaled. Constant temperature levels between 60 and 120 degrees in stagnant pools of water provide ideal conditions for the growth of microorganisms. These conditions are found in humidifiers, dehumidifiers, and cooling towers where there is sufficient moisture and appropriate temperature for the growth of bacteria algae and microorganisms. Examples of bacteria-related building epidemics such as legionnaire's disease and humidifier fever have been cited in literature on air quality.

Finding the best solution to an air-quality problem in a specific facility requires knowledge of the building and its mechanical systems as well as its environment and occupancy conditions. As detailed earlier, the design and construction of the building envelope will determine the infiltration rate, i.e., the rate of uncontrolled air leakage into the building. In some buildings, infiltration is depended on as a source of supply for makeup air to replace air removed by exhaust appliances. Any change to the air tightness of the envelope will affect the infiltration rate and the amount of fresh air available to the building.

Air-Quality Checklist

There is no single method for improving indoor air quality. Following is a general checklist that will serve as a reference for air-quality troubleshooting. As a first step, it is always useful to check air temperatures and comfort criteria in problem areas.

Source Removal

- Check for re-circulation of exhaust air into outside air intake.
- Check outside air intakes at ground level to ensure automobile exhaust or other contaminants are not introduced into outside air intake. Since many sports teams travel by bus, it is important to park the buses away from the facility. Motor fumes can be easily sucked into the building by the air-handling systems.
- Check exhaust air systems to ensure toilet exhaust is not re-circulated to return to air systems.

Avoid exhaust air opening near outside air intakes.

- Check proximity of cooling tower to outside air intake. Ensure biological water treatment of cooling tower, especially in summer months.
- Avoid having stagnant pools of water on roof or near outside air intakes.
- Check humidifier pans and sprayed cooling coils for biological contaminants or growths.

Ensure proper water treatment of spray systems.

- Check fan coil units for stagnant water in drip pans. Ensure drip pans drain properly.
- Check flooded carpet areas for biological contamination. Change carpet in contaminated areas.
- Check fan rooms for solvents and other chemicals to ensure no chemical contamination is spread by air-handling system.
- Check chemicals used for rug cleaning, and review concentration of cleaning agents used on rugs and floors.

Exhaust at Source

- Check for exhaust from high humidity locations, smoking rooms, kitchens, photocopy rooms and other process applications.

Dilution

- Check minimum outside air setting, calibrate for normal occupancy.
- Check ambient air concentrations for CO_2 and other contaminants.
- Adjust fan hours of operation and schedule to suit occupancy.
- Check supply air distribution patterns to ensure adequate flushing of occupied space.
- Check for vertical temperature stratification as evidence of poor air distribution.

Lighting

Lighting costs in sport and recreational facilities can account for 30 to 50% of total energy costs (*Energy Ideas*, March 93). Until recently, electrical costs were low and little thought was given in building design to the operational costs of lighting systems. Rather, the selection and design of lighting systems were often based on minimizing capital cost. As a result, there exists a wide range of opportunities to reduce lighting energy use in most buildings.

Lighting systems in recreation and sport facilities serve five distinct purposes: to provide sufficient illumination to enable occupants to see and play in a safe manner; to illuminate safe pathways for the movement of persons in and out of the building; to complement the architectural and interior design by providing a comfortable and pleasant environment; to deter vandalism (outside lighting); and, to enhance or highlight a product or display. A lighting system with higher levels than necessary results in higher first cost and operating expenses.

A well-designed lighting system should provide adequate and safe levels of light for the activities carried out in a space. Often, when a system is designed, the quantity (illuminance) of light is used as the only criterion for providing suitable lighting. However, recent studies have now found that the quality of light installed is also a very important factor to consider when designing or upgrading a lighting system.

Occupant visual comfort and productivity are directly related to the amount of lighting and the way it is provided. Opportunities for reducing lighting energy usage should also be looked upon as opportunities to improve the quality of lighting. Please refer to Chapter 8 for information related to lighting for sport and recreational facilities. We will only deal with conservation strategies in this chapter.

Before developing an energy management plan or program for a building lighting system, an analysis should be undertaken of the existing facilities. Information should be collected that relates to: the amount of light provided in each area, the type of fixtures and their energy consumption, and the occupant activity for specific lighting areas including the time period in use.

Once this information is collected, lighting levels can be compared to recommend levels for the activities involved. Opportunities for energy savings can then be identified. They may include: reducing power consumption of fixtures through modification or replacement of fixtures or through reduced lighting levels, and reducing the operating period of fixtures based on occupant activity. The quality of lighting depends on the following factors as well as the actual level of illumination: geometry of the space to be illuminated, mounting height of lighting fixtures, light-reflecting properties of the ceiling, walls and floor, and color rendering of the particular light type under consideration.

Maintaining adequate illumination levels requires effective lighting system maintenance. An effective maintenance program is comprised of not only lamp replacement but also routine, planned cleaning of lighting fixtures and room surfaces. A regular cleaning and relamping program has definite long-term benefits: more light is delivered per unit cost of electricity, lower-wattage lamps can be installed, fewer luminaries can be installed, and overall labor costs are reduced.

A final factor to be considered before embarking on a lighting energy management program, particularly for large sport and recreational buildings, is the effect of lighting on the heating, ventilating, and air conditioning (HVAC) systems. The lighting HVAC effect refers to the impact of lighting on the heating and cooling load of a building.

Effectively, all of the energy consumed for lighting ultimately ends up as heat. This heat can become a significant part of the cooling load of an air-conditioned space. The energy required to air-condition an interior space includes the energy used by the refrigerating equipment (central chiller or rooftop air conditioners). It may also include pump energy to deliver chilled water to the space, and fan energy to deliver cool air. All of these components can be reduced in size if heat output from lights is reduced. Conversely, reducing the energy use of lights increases the heating load of a space in winter, since the heating effect of lights is reduced. This "HVAC effect" of lighting on heating and cooling must be calculated when planning lighting measures.

Building Automation Systems

Building automation systems can be included in energy management plans both in the planning and design phases of new facilities and with the renovation of older facilities with operating problems, owing to antiquated control systems. Installing a building automation system not only saves money by reducing unnecessary energy consumption, but it can also increase comfort significantly.

The features of an automated control system that can be utilized in conjunction with an energy management program are: sensors to measure, controllers to regulate equipment, and operating equipment. An example of a sensor is a temperature sensor that sends a pneumatic or electronic signal proportional to the temperature back to a controller. Controllers are designed to received sensor inputs, compare the input to a set-point, and send a signal output to a controlled device. The operating equipment is any device connected to and operated by the controller.

Building automation systems include systems that control energy-management functions as well as systems that control other building-management functions, such as security (Cohen, 2000). Building automation systems can be classified by: the number control points, the means of control, and the type of data communication used between the controller and the control points.

There are a number of reasons why a building operator or manager might want to incorporate an automated control system into a building: to improve building operation and comfort, to increase building safety or security, to reduce operating costs, including energy costs, or to provide more efficient building management. Below is a brief description of the various control options that can be incorporated into a computer-controlled, automated system.

- Programmed Start/Stop—Programmed start/stop is a software-based logic that permits the user to schedule starting and stopping of equipment according to a predetermined schedule. In sport facilities when specific occupancy scenarios are known, air-handling equipment can be programmed to increase air volumes when spectators are scheduled in the facility and reduce the volumes during non-use periods. Furthermore, hot water circulating pumps can be programmed to deliver hot water when users are expected to take showers and be turned off otherwise.

- Alarms/Monitoring—This type of software-based logic signals an alarm or initiates a particular action when a upper or lower limit has been exceeded. Sport and recreational facilities have many entry and exit doors to monitor and control. This type of system can be used to signal an unauthorized entry into a space.

- Energy Monitoring—This function allows the recording and accumulation of fuel and electricity consumption data, allowing for improved analysis of the consumption rate of fuel and electricity.

- Demand Control—This software feature reduces electrical power demand by stopping or delaying the operation of certain pieces of non-essential electoral equipment during peak demand periods. Utilities charge a premium to users who consume a lot of electricity at peak periods of time. Staying below this demand rate level will cut electrical cost all year long, since one high-use period sets the rate for the entire year.

- Duty Cycling—This software executes the stop/start cycles for equipment. One can therefore avoid the simultaneous operation of several loads that do not require continuous operation and limit the energy consumption of all the controlled equipment.

- Optimized Stop/Start—This type of program logic calculates the best time to initiate preheating or pre-cooling of the building.

- Optimized Ventilation—This software is used to optimize the blending of outside air and return air based on the enthalpy of the two air streams.

- Optimization of Supply Air Temperature—This software allows the adjustment of supply of air temperature as a function of the heating and cooling loads of the building.

- Chiller/Boiler Optimization—When the cooling system comprises several chillers, this type of logic operates the minimum chilling capacity to satisfy the load.

- Supply Water Temperature Optimization—This type of control can regulate the chilled water and hot water supply temperatures of the cooling/heating systems as a function of the actual demand of the building.
- Temperature Setback/Setup—Temperature setback/setup type of controls provide scheduling of building space temperatures during unoccupied periods.

Other control options available with building automation systems include: controls for exterior and/or interior lighting and security; domestic hot water optimization; cistern flow optimization that modulates water flow to cistern-operated urinals; and options for specialized applications, such as swimming pools and ice arenas. As the technology improves, these systems will change to reflect the additional energy and cost savings available.

Summary

During the design and operation of a sport and recreational facility, one of the most important factors for the management to understand and address is the energy use of the facility. Faced with a future of ever-increasing utility costs, managers must take a fresh look at old operating procedures and install new technologies designed to reduce the amount of energy needed to operate. Building components like the envelope and the infiltration and exfiltration of air through the envelope, the amount and quality of air and the type of heating, ventilation, and air conditioning systems greatly impact energy use. Heating and use of hot water, and the type and amount of lighting to accommodate sport and recreational activities further compound energy consumption. While the computer and its use has automated some of these systems and enabled the operator to study and control energy use, establishing operating procedures that consider energy consumption along with user comfort will be the final ingredient in a total management program.

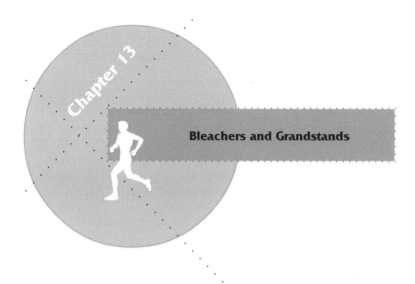

Chapter 13

Bleachers and Grandstands

Michael G. Hypes, Indiana State University

Bleachers and grandstands are part of almost every sport facility. It has been estimated that there are approximately 60,000 facilities with bleachers in the United States. This number includes school facilities, sports facilities, state and local parks, and fitness and recreation centers. Providing safe bleachers and grandstands has prompted the passage of the Minnesota Bleacher Safety Act and the development of the Consumer Product Safety Commission's (CPSC) *Guidelines for Retrofitting Bleachers*.

Learning Objectives:

After reading this chapter, the student will be able to:
- identify the different types of bleachers,
- understand the basic components of a bleacher system,
- discuss ways to improve safety in bleachers,
- understand the place of bleachers in facility architecture.

Type of Bleachers

Bleachers are structures designed to provide tiered or stepped seating and are available in various sizes and configurations. The bleacher system normally consists of a series of seatboards and footboards, generally without any type of backrest. A grandstand is nothing more than a bleacher with a roof attached. The type and number of bleacher components are dependent upon the activity, space requirements, number of spectators, and available financial resources.

Bleachers can be classified into one of four basic categories:
- permanent or stationary bleachers,
- portable or movable bleachers,
- telescopic or folding bleachers, or
- temporary bleachers.

Permanent or stationary bleachers are typically large units that will remain in the same location for the life of the facility. Permanent bleachers can be made of metal or concrete and are usually secured to the ground by an anchor.

Portable bleachers are usually smaller units and are constructed of lightweight materials. The bleachers will have skids or a wheel system that makes them easy to relocate from one site to another.

Telescopic bleachers are typically found in gymnasiums where space is at a minimum. These bleachers can either be pushed in or pulled out for spectator seating. When closed, this type of system takes up relatively little space and can function as a divider.

Temporary bleachers are typically stored in pieces or sections and then constructed together for use during special events (i.e., golf tournaments, parades, circuses, inaugurations). After the event, the bleachers are then disassembled and stored until needed the next time.

Bleacher Components

As mentioned above, a bleacher system has some common elements. These common elements include:
- footboards,
- seatboards,
- risers, and
- guardrails.

Rails are used as a safety feature. They provide security while entering or exiting the bleachers. There are a variety of styles that will lower the exposure to injury. Folding rails are ideal for recessed areas and other obstacles. Rails should be lightweight for easy setup and takedown, yet strong enough to provide adequate support. Guardrails should extend 42 inches above the lowest surface of the leading edge of the bleacher component (i.e., footboard, seatboard, aisle).

Risers and footboards are typically aluminum and should be weather resistant for outdoor use. Seatboards can be aluminum or vinyl-covered metal. Indoor bleachers may have risers, footboards, and seatboards made of wood.

When planning bleachers, it is important to consider any gaps or openings that will be in the final product. Any opening between the components in the seating, such as between the footboard, seatboard, and riser, should prevent passage of a four-inch sphere where the footboard is 30 inches or more above the ground and where the opening would permit a fall of 30 inches or more.

Bleachers usually come in four- to 52-row systems. Local and state building codes should be consulted when planning bleachers. Figure 13.1 provides generalized seating capacity for various row configurations and lengths.

Telescopic or pull-out bleachers should have a wheel or channel system to prevent damage to the floor surface. In addition, these systems are best utilized if they are automated. Electrical systems allow the telescopic bleachers to open or close with the turn of a key. This type of system allows the user to open entirely or partially a section of bleachers without having the section get out of line or damaged. With any mechanical system, a manual override is suggested. For bleachers already installed that do not have an automated system, there is equipment (such as Portable Power System) that is easily handled for convenient movement of bleachers.

The power or automated system provides the user with:
- the ability to open and close bleacher systems quickly and correctly,
- omits and/or reduces maintenance costs,
- solves the problem of broken board ends from manual operation,
- adds stability to the gym bleachers by attaching all sections together to operate as one system,
- omits manual operation by unauthorized personnel, and
- reduces liability exposure on your gym bleacher equipment.

Codes and Regulations

There are several agencies/organizations that have developed codes and/or standards for the construction of bleachers. These organizations include:
- International Building Code (IBC) of the International Code Council (ICC)
- National Building Code (NBC) of the Building Officials and Code Administrators (BOCA)
- Standard Building Code (SBC) of the Southern Building Code Congress International (SBCCI)
- Uniform Building Code (UBC) of the International Conference of Building Officials (ICBO)
- National Fire Protection Association

Figure 13.2 provides a summary of current industry codes and standard requirements for guardrails and openings in bleachers. In addition, state and local codes adopt and modify these codes to develop policy for constructing new bleachers. The local building inspector should be consulted early in the planning phase to avoid expensive and time-consuming errors in the construction of a bleacher system.

Minnesota Building Codes and Standards Division

States (such as Minnesota) develop their own policies regarding construction. The Minnesota Building Codes and Standards Division reviewed the Uniform Building Code, International Building Code, and the National Fire Protection Association Life Safety Code in developing Policy PR-04 (3/00). "Under Minnesota law, reviewing stands, grandstands, bleachers and folding/telescopic seating, whether indoors or out, must be designed, constructed, and installed in accordance with the applicable provisions contained in the *Minnesota State Building Code*." (Minnesota, 2001) This policy addresses the following areas of concern with regard to bleachers and grandstands:
- press box construction,
- number of seats to an aisle,
- required plumbing fixtures,
- aisle width,
- accessibility,
- foundations, and
- use of space below bleachers/grandstands.

Press Box Construction

"According to UBC Section 303.2.2.3, combustible non-rated A-4 occupancies are limited to a height of 20 feet above grade. Except for the press box located on top of most school grandstands serving ball fields, most grandstands are built of noncombustible construction. These noncombustible bleacher structures are permitted to be at least 40 feet in height. However, press boxes are typically built with combustible construction materials (wood framing). This results in classifying the entire structure as combustible, and, therefore, severely limiting the maximum permitted height of noncombustible grandstands with combustible press boxes to 20 feet" (Minnesota, 2001). Minnesota derived the following alternative to part of UBC Section 303.2.2.3. Press boxes located atop open-air bleachers may be built of combustible construction as long as other components of the bleacher system are of non-combustible construction.

Number of Seats to an Aisle

"Prior to the 1997 edition of the Uniform Building Code, the number of seats without backrests between any seat and an aisle could not be greater than 20, for a total of 42 seats in a row with aisles at each end. In general, this is what the bleacher seating industry has used as a standard for the manufacture of their products for years. Now both the 1997 UBC and 2000 IBC only permit a maximum of 14 seats per row with the typical 12-inch wide aisle accessway. In contrast, for indoor bleachers the 1997 UBC permits nine seats between any seat and an aisle, for a total of 20 seats in a row. This is less restrictive than that permitted outdoors. The maximum number of seats permitted between furthest seat and an aisle in bleachers is 20 in outdoor bleacher seating." (Minnesota, 2001)

Required Plumbing Fixtures

Minimum numbers of water closets and lavatories are to be provided for all buildings and structures including ex-

Figure 13.1
Sample number of bleacher seats based on length and number of rows.

Length in Feet	4 Rows	7 Rows	10 Rows	13 Rows	16 Rows
18	48	84	120	156	192
36	96	168	240	312	384
54	104	252	360	468	676
72	192	336	480	624	768
90	240	420	600	780	960
108	288	504	720	936	1152
126	336	588	840	1092	1344
144	384	672	960	1248	1536
162	432	756	1080	1404	1728
180	480	840	1200	1560	1920
198	528	924	1320	1716	2112
216	576	1008	1440	1872	2304
234	624	1092	1560	2028	2496
252	672	1176	1680	2184	2688
270	720	1260	1800	2340	2880
288	768	1344	1920	2496	3072
306	816	1428	2040	2652	3264

Length in Feet	19 Rows	22 Rows	25 Rows	28 Rows	31 Rows
18	228				
36	456				
54	684	792	900	1008	
72	912	1056	1200	1344	1488
90	1140	1320	1500	1680	1860
108	1386	1584	1800	2016	2232
126	1596	1848	2100	2352	2604
144	1824	2112	2400	2688	2976
162	2052	2376	2700	3024	3348
180	2280	2649	3000	3360	3720
198	2508	2904	3300	3696	4092
216	2736	3168	3600	4032	4464
234	2964	3432	3900	4368	4836
252	3192	3696	4200	4704	5208
270	3420	3960	4500	5040	5580
288	3648	4224	4800	5376	5952
306	3876	4488	5100	5712	6324

terior assembly areas, such as bleachers and grandstands. The Standards Division recognizes the following to satisfy this requirement:

- permanent fixtures located either on site or available in an adjacent building, or
- portable temporary fixtures that are available on site when the bleachers are in use.

The use of portable fixtures as acceptable modifications is based on the concept that outdoor bleachers are seasonal in nature. Lastly, the ratio of water closets for women to the total of water closets and urinals provided for men must be at least three to two in accordance with the Minnesota Building Code (1300.3900).

Aisle Width

The Standards Division identified two methods for determining aisle width. Method A identifies that aisles are not required to be more than 66 inches in width nor does it have to be considered a dead-end aisle when the following are satisfied:

- The seating is composed entirely of bleachers.
- The row-to-row dimension is 28 inches or less.
- Front egress is not limited.

Method B is based on IBC Section 1008.5.3. The clear width in inches of aisles shall be not less than the total occupant load served by the egress element multiplied by 0.08

Figure 13.2
Overview of Code and Standard Requirements

2000 International Building Code (IBC) of the International Code Council (ICC)

Guardrails
• required on open sides more than 30 inches above grade
• guardrails must be at least 42 inches high, vertically measured from leading edge
• guardrails shall have balusters to prevent passage of four-inch sphere through any opening up to a height of 34 inches
• from a height of 34-42 inches, should prevent passage of an eight-inch sphere
Openings
• where footboards are more than 30 inches above grade, openings between seat and footboard shall not allow passage of a sphere greater than four inches
• horizontal gaps shall not exceed .25 inch between footboards and seatboards
• at aisles, horizontal gaps shall not exceed .25 inch between footboards

1999 National Building Code (NBC) of the Building Officials and Code Administrators (BOCA)

Guardrails
• guardrails along open-sided surfaces located more than 15.5 inches above grade
• guardrails should be at least 42 inches in height measured vertically above leading edge
• open guardrails shall have balusters of solid material that prevents passage of four-inch sphere through any opening
• guardrails shall not have an ornamental pattern that would have a ladder effect
Openings
• openings between footboards and seatboards prevent passage of four-inch sphere when openings are located more than 30 inches above grade
• horizontal gaps between footboards and seatboards shall not exceed .25 inches

1997 Standard Building Code (SBC) of the Southern Building Code Congress International (SBCCI)

Guardrails
• located along open-sided walking surfaces and elevated seating facilities which are located more than 30 inches above grade
• guardrails shall not be less than 42 inches vertically from leading edge
• open guardrails shall have intermediate rails or ornamental pattern to prevent passage of four-inch sphere through any opening
Openings
• there shall be no horizontal gaps exceeding .25 inch between footboards and seatboards
• at aisles, no horizontal gaps exceeding .25 inch between footboards

1997 Uniform Building Code (UBC) of the International Conference of Building Officials (ICBO)

Guardrails
• perimeter guardrails shall be provided for all portions of elevated seating more than 30 inches above grade
• guardrails shall be 42 inches above the rear of a seatboard or 42 inches above the rear of the steps in an aisle
• open guardrails shall have intermediate rails or ornamental pattern to prevent passage of a four-inch sphere
Openings
• the open vertical space between footboards and seats shall not exceed nine inches when footboards are more than 30 inches above grade

2000 National Fire Protection Association (NFPA) 101 Life Safety Code

Guardrails (applies to both new construction and existing installations)
• guardrails are required on open sides more than 48 inches above adjacent ground
• guardrails must be at least 42 inches above the aisle or footboard or at least 36 inches above the seatboard
• guardrail is exempted where an adjacent wall or fence affords an equivalent safeguard
• openings in guardrails cannot allow passage of four-inch diameter sphere
Openings (applies to both new construction and existing installations)
• vertical openings between footboards and seatboards cannot allow passage of four-inch diameter sphere where footboards are more than 30 inches above grade

continued

> ## Figure 13.2 Continued
> ## Overview of Code and Standard Requirements

• openings in footboards cannot allow passage of .5-inch diameter sphere

Inspections (existing installations)

• annual inspection and maintenance of bleacher/grandstand or folding/telescopic seating required to be provided by owner to ensure safe conditions

• biennially, the inspection is to be performed by a professional engineer, registered architect, or individual certified by the manufacturer

• owner required to provide certification that such inspection has been performed as required by authority having jurisdiction

Modified from U.S. Consumer Product Safety Commission, Guidelines for Retrofitting Bleachers.

where egress is by aisles and/or stairs. The multiplier is 0.06 where egress is by ramps, tunnels, corridors or vomitories (Minnesota, 2001).

Accessibility

Bleacher seating structures must comply with the Minnesota Accessibility Code.

- Access: Exterior access to elevated seating areas in exterior bleachers must be accessible by a route having a slope not exceeding 1 in 20 and a width not less than 48 inches.
- Wheelchair locations are to be provided in the number and location required.
- Alterations to an existing area containing a primary function will not apply if alterations to existing bleacher seating facilities only address compliance with the Minnesota Bleacher Safety Act (Minnesota, 2001).

Foundations

"A foundation plan must be prepared by a Minnesota Licensed Engineer for all open-air bleacher and grandstand facilities. This does not apply to "portable" bleachers of five rows or less" (Minnesota, 2001).

Use of space below Bleachers/Grandstands

Spaces under a grandstand or bleacher shall be kept free of flammable or combustible material. Storage is permitted under bleachers, provided it is separated with fire-resistive construction (Minnesota, 2001).

U.S. Consumer Product Safety Commission (CPSC)

The U.S. Consumer Product Safety Commission has developed Guidelines for Retrofitting Bleachers as a result of a petition by Representatives Luther and Ramstad of Minnesota in 1999. This petition led to the adoption of the first bleacher safety law at the state level. A summary of the CPSC's retrofit recommendations are found in Figure 13.3.

> ## Figure 13.3
> ## Summary of Retrofit Recommendations

• Guardrails should be present on the backs and portions of the open ends of bleachers where the footboard, seatboard, or aisle is 30 inches or more above the floor or ground below.

• The top surface of the guardrail should be at least 42 inches above the leading edge of the footboard, seatboard, or aisle, whichever is adjacent.

• When bleachers are used adjacent to a wall that is as high as the recommended guardrail height, the guardrail is not needed if a four-inch diameter sphere fails to pass between the bleachers and the wall.

• Any opening between components of the guardrail should prevent passage of a four-inch sphere.

• Any opening between the components in the seating should prevent passage of a four-inch here where the footboard is 30 inches or more above the ground.

• The preferable guardrail design uses only vertical members as in-fill between the top and bottom rails. Openings in the in-fill should be limited to a maximum of 1.75 inches. If chainlink fencing is used on guardrails, it should have a mesh size of 1.25-inch square or less.

continued

Figure 13.3 Continued
Summary of Retrofit Recommendations

• Aisles, handrails, non-skid surfaces, and other items that assist in access and egress on bleachers should be incorporated into any retrofit project where feasible.

• The option of replacing as opposed to retrofitting should be considered.

• Retrofitting materials and methods should prevent the introduction of new hazards, such as: bleacher tipover, **bleacher collapse, guardrail collapse,** contact/tripping hazards.

• Bleachers should be thoroughly inspected at least quarterly by trained personnel and problems corrected immediately. Maintain records of these actions.

• Bleachers should be inspected at least every two years and written certification obtained that the bleachers are fit for use. Inspections should be conducted by a licensed professional engineer, registered architect, or company that is qualified to provide bleacher products and services.

• Keep records of all incidents and injuries.

Modified from U.S. Consumer Product Safety Commission, *Guidelines for Retrofitting Bleachers.*

Summary

Bleachers are a part of almost every sport facility. The type and number are dependent upon the activity, space requirements, number of spectators, and available financial resources. The construction of bleachers is an integral part of the overall facility-planning process. Making bleachers safer for spectators should be a priority for anyone involved in planning or managing a facility.

Portable bleachers, Indiana State University.

Permanent bleachers, Rose Hulman Institute of Technology.

Aisle railing.

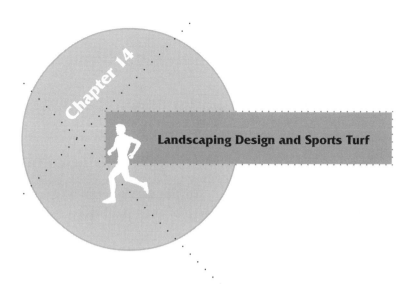

Richard J. LaRue, University of New England
David A. LaRue, Vineyard Gardens, Inc.
Thomas H. Sawyer, Indiana State University

When planning the outdoor spaces of sport and recreational facilities, adjacent "tran-sitional" space and/or sport fields, the process must include individuals who can lend their understanding and expertise to the process. From a design standpoint, a licensed landscape architect or experienced landscape designer should be employed. If a sports field is the focus of, or is included in the plan, then an experienced sports turf manager is important to the process. Finally, as all outdoor facilities and spaces will require maintenance, a logical planning resource will be the maintenance director and/or an experienced representative of the maintenance staff.

Perhaps the most important individual in the early stages of the planning process is the landscape professional. This person will be invaluable when making decisions related to site selection for the facility and utilization of all adjacent outdoor spaces.

More than any of the other major environmental design professions, landscape architecture is a profession on the move. It is comprehensive by definition—no less than the art and science of analysis, planning design, management, preservation and rehabilitation of the land. In providing well-managed design and development plans, landscape architects offer an essential array of services and expertise that reduce costs and add long-term value to a project. While having a working knowledge of architecture, civil engineering, and urban planning, landscape architects take elements from each of these fields to design aesthetic and practical relationships with the land. Members of the profession have a special commitment to improving the quality of life through the best design of places for people and other living things (ASLA, 1998, on-line).

Sport fields are truly special facilities. When natural turf is chosen, a sports turf specialist is needed to oversee the development of a total field management program (Lewis, 1994).

A comprehensive program should include the following: 1) selecting an adapted grass for the locality; 2) mowing this selected grass at proper height and frequency; 3) fertilizing at the proper time and rate according to the turfgrass growth; 4) irrigating as needed to encourage establishment and to reduce stress periods; 5) aerifying to relieve compaction or dethatching according to the turf and the amount of play; and 6) using the appropriate preemergence and post emergence herbicides. The goal is to first produce a vigorous turf that will be competitive to the weeds (Lewis, 1994, p. 28).

Such a program will be served by the design of the field, including irrigation and drainage, and the choice of grass, etc. Careful consideration involves knowing the grass and soil makeup, need for aeration, fertilization, top dressing, seeding, and later, weed control (Mazzola, 1998).

Finally, as the ultimate success of the facility planning process is often measured years later, it is important to consider those aspects of groundskeeping that will be predetermined in the design of the fields and other outdoor spaces. Specifically, the labor and equipment required to maintain these spaces can be controlled with a carefully prepared landscape design. Additionally, the life expectancy of the green and hard goods is directly related to the level of quality afforded. Management of money and resources (capital expenditures, debt load, salaries and wages, existing equipment vs. new equipment, etc.) begins with the planning process and the investment decisions made prior to plan implementation (Hughes, Jr., 1996).

In summary, the planning process must include consideration of both the facility and the adjacent outside or transitional space. Further, the planning process will benefit from the expertise of a certified landscape architect or experienced landscape designer, an experienced sports turf specialist (if planning a formal play space), and a representative of the facilities maintenance staff. The quality of the planning process will be measured against the ability of the facility and all aspects of the plan to meet the goals described in the facility's case statement or building program document.

Sample use of lighting, bench, and garbage can.

Photo by Meghan Sawyer

Instructional Objectives:

After reading this chapter, the student will be able to
- understand landscape design concepts in terms of aesthetics, function, and safety;
- recognize the planning responsibilities related to groundskeeping management; maintenance, and equipment;
- understand the design and operation concepts of surface and subsurface irrigation and drainage;
- understand the concepts related to parking design for aesthetics, function, and safety;
- understand the difference between standards and guidelines related to chemical handling and storage; and
- understand both the trends and new technologies in landscape design and groundskeeping.

Landscape Design: Aesthetics, Function, and Safety

Frequently, when money is tight, and/or the facility costs are exceeding expectations, careful development of the adjacent outdoor space is easily ignored. Experience has demonstrated that this is short-sighted, as there are essential components that must be considered exclusive of the site selection of a facility. The design of this transitional space, whether for an indoor or outdoor facility, should consider the following characteristics:
- the aesthetics of the space relative to all adjacent facilities,
- the funcional characteristics of the space relative to adjacent facilities, and
- the safety of users (including accessibility) within the space, and relative to adjacent facilities.

Aesthetics

The basics of aesthetics in landscape design are sight lines that bring focus to important features of a facility or space, the use of space (especially spatial relationships), and the ability of the "finished product" to enhance the quality of the experience for all users.

Function

There are critical components to a comprehensive design related to function. The way the implemented design reacts to natural and man-made stresses is indicative of the time and resources invested in the planning process. Further, the long-term demand for maintenance will be affected by the design. And the way the design serves the facility program and user needs is a direct result of the planning process.

In addition to the characteristics described above, site selection is an important part of function for an outdoor facility should also include consideration of:
- the orientation of play spaces with respect to the sun angle and predominant wind direction,
- the topography of the developed and undeveloped outdoor space,
- the existing and necessary surface and subsurface irrigation and drainage,
- the appropriate use of natural and man-made barriers,
- environmental concerns, and
- the minimization of normal wear and vandalism (Macomber, 1993).

Safety

It is critical that the planning process for safety results in a landscape design that manages the risk of all adjacent outdoor spaces so that all foreseeable user accidents or injuries can be avoided. This planning for safety and security should include:

- signage in large lettering that clearly identifies pedestrian and vehicular paths, facilities, right-of-way, accessible parking, no parking and fire zones, and any other user-friendly restrictions or expectations;
- perimeter fencing or appropriate use of natural barriers;
- programmable and/or light-sensitive night lighting;
- pedestrian and vehicular circulation that is easy to maintain and has reasonable and unobstructed views of cross traffic at every intersection;
- smooth (yet skid resistant) pavements and other path or road surfaces;
- bollards (permanent and removable barriers) restricting vehicular travel on pedestrian paths; and
- surveillance.

Characteristics of Turfgrasses Commonly used for Sport Turfs

Puhalla, Krans, and Goatley (1999) suggest there are 11 grasses commonly used as turfgrasses. However, of these species, only five are widely used in sports turf situations: bermudagrass, Kentucky bluegrass, tall fescue, perennial ryegrass, and creeping bentgrass. There are two other grasses that are sometimes used: buffalograss and zoysiagrass.

Further, Puhalla, et al. (1999) indicate bermudagrass (monostand) is planted and maintained alone except when overseeded with perennial and annual ryegrass for winter play. Tall fescue, perennial ryegrass, and Kentucky bluegrass are planted and maintained as either monostands or in combination with other cultivars (polystands). Creeping bentgrass is usually planted as a monostand.

Turfgrass selection is usually based upon weather zones (e.g., warm, transition, or cool). In warm weather zones (southern states across the United States), sports turf is generally dominated by bermudagrass, because it flourishes in the hot summers and mild winters, and can withstand occasional summer dryness without damage. In the transitional zone, fields are dominated by tall fescues and specifically developed bermudagrass. Finally, in cold zones (northern states across the United States), Kentucky bluegrass and perennial ryegrass predominate, and a mixture of those species is probably the most popular sports turf (Puhalla, et al., 1999). "Both types tolerate the cold northern winters adequately, and the mixture allows for the aggressive spreading and recovery characteristic of Kentucky bluegrass, along with the stability and wear resistance of perennial ryegrass." (p.8)

Portable Grass

During the 90s, Popke (2000) indicated a number of natural-grass suppliers (e.g., GreenTech(r) Inc-ITM turf modules, Hummer Turfgrass Systems Inc.-Grasstiles™, the Motz Group-TS-II™, Desso DLW Sports International-DD GrassMaster, SportGrass(r) Inc-SportGrass system, Southern Turf Nurseries-STN 2000, Thomas Brothers Grass, a division of Turf-Grass America Co-SquAyers, Southwest Recreational Industries Inc.-AstroGrass(r)) became responsive to facilities' needs for a more durable natural grass product. The suppliers began to use (a) portable grass that unrolls as a cover for concrete floors and parking lots, (b) grass tiles with roots that are reinforced and stabilized with synthetic fibers, and (c) systems that mix grass with synthetic fibers woven or stitched into a backing. These renewed processes allow sections of worn surface (e.g., golf tee-boxes, areas in front of a soccer goal, middle sections of football fields) to be replaced without tearing up the entire area, and the whole surface can usually be removed or installed in less than 24 hours. All of the systems claim to be able to better reinforce the root zone and extend usage.

Often, with these portable systems, grass is grown in trays that allow for drainage and air movement. Synthetic reinforcements play a role in several portable grass surfaces and are considered 100% natural by their suppliers. This can be said because the majority of the additional synthetic material is inserted below the grass surface for root reinforcement and additional wear resistance. However, a better term might be hybrid.

Some of the hybrid systems are a combination of sand-filled, fibrillated synthetic tufts and a dual-component backing of biodegradable fibers and plastic mesh. The matrix shelters the vegetative parts of the grass plant that are essential to rapid growth and recuperation, while the grass roots intertwine with the tufts and grow down through the plastic mesh. If the turf canopy wears away, the sand-filled synthetic matrix continues to provide a consistent playing surface. There are a few systems that do not use a cloth backing, but rather train the roots to grow on top of a plastic barrier, similar to roots in a potted plant.

A Kinder, Gentler Synthetic Turf

Popke (2000) describes three new kinder, gentler synthetic turfs—Astroplay(r), Fieldturf™, and Sofsport™. These synthetic surfaces have been designed to reduce injuries to players. The new synthetic surfaces blend and tuft polyethylene and polypropylene fibers into a permeable surface backing. Each synthetic grass fiber is placed so as to create a pattern of natural grass. The fill is made from sand and ground rubber, which surround each fiber much like soil holds a blade of grass. One supplier does not use sand, but rather uses a combination of rubber and nylon fibers mixed with longer polyolefin strands. This combination enhances drainage, reduces compaction, and adds resilence.

Groundskeeping: Management, Maintenance, Equipment Planning Responsibilities

Appropriate to the review of groundskeeping management, maintenance, and equipment are three concepts related to success in these areas: time management, money and resource management, and machinery and equipment management (Hughes, 1996, pp. 2-3). The responsibility for planning related to groundskeeping should be assisted by a seasoned member of the groundskeeping staff. Efficient use of the staff time can be facilitated in a properly planned landscape design. A significant aspect of the plan will be the re-

Photo by Meghan Sawyer

Tree-lined sidewalks.

Photo by Meghan Sawyer

duction of labor as it relates to maintenance. If by design, you reduce the employee labor required, you are managing time more efficiently. Secondly, if you demand quality green goods when installing your landscape design, then the money and resources for your project will be managed more efficiently. Finally, if your planning process includes a design that can be maintained with existing equipment, you are taking responsibility for the future without ignoring the reality of the present. Groundskeeping management must be considered when designing your landscape. And few people can better assist you with this planning than a knowledgeable representative of your groundskeeping staff.

Surface and Subsurface Irrigation and Drainage

An effective landscape design will consider the operation of surface and subsurface irrigation and drainage. Not having enough moisture can be deadly to your grass and plants. Too much moisture, and no way for the water to drain, can also drown your plants and fields. When rain does not come, appropriate irrigation must be available. Irrigation planning is both an art and science. There are extraordinary examples of how, after large amounts of rain and subsequent flooding, the drainage of a sport field has allowed a contest to be held in an amazingly short time (Smith, 1998; Tracinski, 1998).

Irrigation

The principle of "deep and infrequent" watering remains the norm. This practice over the years has proven to be effective. The physical properties of the soil must be considered in planning any watering program. For example, a clay soil will not accept as much water as a sandy soil, and will require lighter, more frequent irrigation.

Most turfgrasses need as much as 1" to 1 1/2" of water per week during the growing season to support turf growth (Puhalla, et al., 1999, p. 82). The best time to irrigate turf is in the early morning hours, just prior to or after sunrise. This eliminates interference with use, reduces disease incidence and increases the amount of water placed in the soil for plant use.

There are two basic types of irrigation systems available for use—portable and installed irrigation. Portable irrigation systems include traveling irrigators (i.e., rotating sprinkler attached to a hose, propelling itself along a wire), quick coupler systems (i.e., systems are comprised of a series of underground pipes with quick couplers permanently installed flush with the ground), and rain guns (i.e., a huge impact-type sprinkler that is used to irrigate a large turf area).

The price for installed systems is decreasing, while the reliability of operation is increasing. Automatic systems save maintenance labor costs when compared to portable systems, and the even distribution of water is improved.

Drainage

Most landscape architects will use the following rule of thumb relative to drainage: whether designing a single field or a multifield complex, keep in mind that each field should be designed and constructed as an individual drainage unit. A well-designed drainage plan will install interceptor drains to isolate water, cuts and fills, catch basins, swales, and "french" drains.

Further, Puhalla, et al. (1999) suggest field designs for surface drainage fall into one of two categories—crowned or flat. The typical percentage of slope for a sports field runs between 1% and 1.75%. The most common type of crowned field has been a football field. However, now that many football fields are also used for soccer, they have become flat fields because the soccer field overlaps the football field. Most soccer fields are often designed using a lower percentage of slope, and installed drain systems are usually added.

Most flat fields need an installed drain system. Make sure that the field records indicate it is a flat, sloped field. Otherwise, ten years after initial construction, some well-meaning person might try to "recrown" the field, causing a real mess.

Photo by Tom Sawyer

Culvert

Photo by Tom Sawyer

Example of a drainage ditch.

Photo by Tom Sawyer

Example of a French Drain.

Safety

The safety and security of users are the most important characteristics of parking design. Will facility users circulate between the facility and parking areas secure in the knowledge that they will be safe and their vehicle intact? Will the location of the parking areas mandate use of perimeter fencing? Can pedestrian paths be designed that allow users to avoid walking in vehicular areas in the parking lot? Are permanent or removable bollards required to manage vehicular traffic on pedestrian paths? Is lighting adequate for user safety and security at night? How will surveillance in the parking areas be managed: using closed circuit cameras or parking attendant(s)? Will the parking areas have emergency telephone towers or "call stations"? And, if the lot is gated, will the entrance use pedestrian-safe, one-way traffic controllers with below-grade spikes?

Chemical Handling and Storage, Legal Aspects and Recommendations

Besides the Chemical Hazards Act managed under the Occupational Safety and Health Administration (OSHA), both state and federal regulations govern the handling of many of the chemicals used in weed control, insect management, and fertilization. The Chemical Hazards Act requires the employer to properly warn and protect employees using such chemicals. All chemical manufacturers must ship hazardous chemicals with Material Safety Data Sheets (MSDS), which should be kept on file for employees and specifically outline the guidelines for proper use of their products. Other government regulations require groundskeeping staff to be certified in the proper application and handling of chemicals. It is the responsibility of the groundskeeping staff to be knowledgeable in the use and handling of these chemicals and associated equipment. With a knowledgeable resource on the planning committee, the facility can provide for proper storage of chemicals and clean-up of chemical application equipment used in groundskeeping.

Trends and New Technologies in Landscape Design

Finally, the planning process will consider new trends or cutting-edge technologies when designing outdoor spaces. Consider making a significant investment in all aspects of the planning process to reduce short- and long-term mistakes. Once the plan is implemented, the success of the planning process will be easily measured in its ability to meet the needs of the facility program. Include the right people in the planning process. The experts are easy to remember. However, user input is also critical to promote inclusion and a sense of ownership in the process. Users include the people who will manage the facility and outdoor spaces, as well as those who will participate in facility programs, etc. An appropriate number of such people will help build good will and, more important, should serve the planning process effectively because of their unique "user" viewpoint. The long-term reality of maintenance and the cost of labor, materials, and equipment demand that landscape designs provide for low maintenance. A landscape architect or experienced landscape designer as well as a representative member of the groundskeeping staff should provide the expertise to design low maintenance into the outdoor spaces. Finally, the planning process should consider future implementation of the design when it comes to the level of quality selected in green and hard goods. Experience tells us that when purchasing such goods, the better the quality, the better the satisfaction.

Lining Athletic Fields

Steinbach (2000) suggests the primary concern when marking grass fields is to keep the turf in good growing condition. Water-based paints are the preferred choice. Chalk (e.g., limestone or marble) is less friendly to turf due to the accumulated build-up that blocks water's movement to the grass root system. The best paint contains a higher concentration (1 to 2 pounds per gallon) of titanium oxide (TiO_2) which brightens the paint. The other common ingredient is calcium carbonate ($CaCO_2$), a paint filler. Colored paints will have a higher amount of calcium carbonate. White paint can be diluted up to 9 to 1, but colored paints can only be diluted to 1 to 1 ratio. Too much calcium carbonate makes playing fields abrasive, and it can kill the turf grass.

The following are a few painting tips provided by Mike Hebrard, owner, Athletic Field Design:

- Grid method—make an enlargement of the logo to be painted, then drawing a series of lines in a graph format on the drawing at a workable uniform spacing. Lay out the size of the logo, converting inches to feet, and mark dots on the grass at the edges of the design. Use an inverted spray chalk or blue to do the initial layout. Repeat the graph, using string and long nails, going back and forth until the graph is completed. By looking at the drawing, note where each line crosses a grid and duplicate it on the grass by painting a line, gradually connecting the shape of the logo. Use inverted aerosol cans to differentiate colors and features. Once the logo has been completed, you can brighten it using an airless sprayer.
- The most popular method of painting on athletic turf is the stencil on a heavy plastic or trap. These are readily available from most athletic paint suppliers. After use, fold up the stencil and put into a marked duffle bag to store and identify its contents.
- The key to painting dirt is to have it moist enough to take the paint, much like staining wood. If it is too wet, the paint will bleed into the other colors. If it is too dry, the paint will not be very bright and will wear off quickly.

Summary

When planning a sport or recreational facility, it is imperative that the process include the expertise of a licensed landscape architect or experienced landscape planner. The facility manager should have a significant role in the planning process. Other people who may lend their expertise and/or experience include those responsible for facility maintenance and safety, facility users, and program staff.

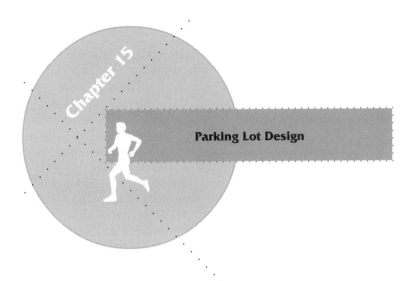

Thomas H. Sawyer, Indiana State University

Parking lot design is a related part of the planning process. A successful parking facility can present an important and positive first image to visitors and to the recreation or sport facility. The parking environment can influence a visitor's first impression of the institution.

Facilities managers are being challenged to (1) develop fair and customer-focused parking strategies, (2) prioritize the use of decreasing parking resources, (3) understand the explosion in parking technology, (4) provide cost-effective parking solutions while catching up with deferred maintenance, and (5) address the widely held perception that safe and convenient parking can only be provided next to the front door. The traditional parking paradigm must be expanded in order to meet the planning challenge. In the past, planning focused on the number of vehicles within given parking parameters. However, as the number of available sites decreases and the cost to develop and operate parking facilities increases, communities are demanding more cost-effective solutions.

Instructional Objectives

After reading this chapter, students should be able to:
- assist in the planning of a parking area for a sport or recreational venue.

Parking Design for Aesthetics, Function, and Safety

Ideally, the parking design should be incorporated into the overall landscape and building design, especially in terms of aesthetics, function, and safety. However, there are some additional design options to be considered, including aesthetics, function, and safety.

Aesthetics

The first experience people have at the facility will likely come when they park their vehicle and approach the facility on foot. What are the sight lines, the use of space, and the placement of parking to the facility that make this experience inviting? Can parking be distributed in a way that avoids a large "car lot" look? Are there natural and man-made barriers that can enhance the aesthetics of the parking space(s) without compromising safety?

Function

Will parking discriminate against users who arrive later in the day? Do plans include large and visible signage, so users understand all allowances and restrictions? Is there adequate parking? Will the facility require a parking garage? Can users exit the parking areas in a timely fashion?

Safety

The parking area should be controlled and monitored for safety. This will require a number of important decisions to be made, including:
- type of parking systems (e.g., ticket and ticketless—magnetic stripe, microwave, etc.);
- type of dispensers (e.g., machines, meters, cards or tags); and
- using a van or shuttle system.

Additional action may be needed to combat a past stereotype that parking structures or areas are not safe. The following strategies may have to be considered:
- installing an emergency telephone system, highly visible, in standard locations;
- adding of glass panels in stairwells to increase visibility;
- installing video cameras;

- adding parking attendants during evening hours;
- providing security personnel walking or driving through the structure;
- increasing lighting level;
- publishing procedures to enhance safety awareness; and
- establishing safety programs such as escort services.

A New Concept for Planning Parking Facilities Customer-Oriented Parking

In the past, planning focused on the number of vehicles within given parking parameters. The new focus should be on consumer needs. Planners and facilities managers should move away from the traditional parking paradigm to one that is consumer oriented.

The Traditional Parking Paradigm

Considerable energy has been focused on the management of vehicles and pedestrians within the boundaries of parking areas. Traditional parking technology contributed to this planning focus, with the "pay-on-foot" approach in parking structures, central pay stations in surface lots, "smart cards," debit cards, proximity cards, and so on. Planners are bombarded with issues, concerns, and solutions within the parking space boundaries. Traditional master planning guidelines for recreation and sport venues have also contributed to this planning focus.

Kirkpatrick (1997) suggests that, "many planners have successfully implemented a pedestrian orientation to the recreation and sport environment, resulting in parking located at perimeter or off-site locations. Typically with this approach, the need for transportation has correspondingly increased." (P. 950) Yet, the planning focus has remained within the boundaries of the parking areas as planners have attempted to match and manage the vehicle demand to the space available. Over the years, many strategies have been developed to manage the increasing demand for limited parking space.

Parking planners have matched various forms and combinations of reserved parking, zoned parking, and open parking to the specific community culture. But the planning focus remained directed at single-occupant vehicles within designated parking boundaries. Regardless of the system that is used to manage vehicles within designated parking boundaries at perimeter locations, customer dissatisfaction with parking systems increased dramatically. Customers lamented that convenient parking space was not available, and that the cost of parking was rising. At the same time, many facility managers were faced with deferred maintenance, escalating costs to operate and maintain a parking system, and increasing customer demand for a decreasing supply of parking.

Weaknesses of Traditional Parking Paradigm

The following factors contribute to the increasing customer and administration dissatisfaction with parking systems that traditionally were perceived as successful:
- New parking structures are costly to build.

- Costs to maintain structures are escalating.
- Surface lots are costly to build.
- Costs to maintain core area surface lots are escalating.
- Deferred maintenance is adding up for many older structures and surface lots where security, aesthetics, and quality construction may not have been a priority in the past.

Thus, it can be seen that costs to build, repair, and maintain parking structures and surface parking lots are escalating. At the same time, customers are not willing to absorb these additional costs by paying higher parking rates, especially when a perceived value may not be present.

A Parking Paradigm Shift—Customer-Oriented Parking

Planning that traditionally started once a vehicle reached a parking area now encompasses options for getting from home to the recreation and sport venue. This has become necessary because:
- many recreation and sport venues cannot cost effectively operate and maintain the traditional expansion of surface lot and structure parking,
- the customer or participant is typically not willing to pay the increasing cost, and
- the traditional parking planning focus of one vehicle per person no longer meets the diverse needs of all customers.

The customer-oriented parking paradigm requires that planners understand and know the customers so as to meet their needs and provide a better service. The parking menu should reflect choices in terms of cost to convenience. For example, the following parking options may be included:
- Reserved space or parking area,
- Core area parking,
- Perimeter area parking,
- Designated motorcycle parking in the preceding four areas if demand requires,
- Carpool/vanpool parking in the first four areas above if demand requires it,
- Bicycle parking, which might include bicycle storage lockers and the traditional hoop,
- Shared parking resources with the surrounding community, such as with park-and-ride programs,
- Economic incentives provided to promote shared bus services with the surrounding community, and
- Walking may be a parking option that needs only to be promoted. Typically, the implementation of many recreation and sport venue master plans has resulted in a pedestrian orientation to the venue, where special attention has been focused on providing appropriately placed sidewalks (seven or eight feet wide for snow removal, which is also a good width for group walking) with excellent lighting, an effective emergency telephone system, and beautiful grounds.

Kirkpatrick (1997) indicates that "the key to implementing a successful menu of parking options, based on the match of cost to convenience, is an understanding of customers' needs and their perceptions of solutions, as well as a willingness by all involved to be receptive to trying new ideas." (P. 953) Another key to success is the flexibility of a parking system to provide multiple options to fit diverse life styles.

Image of the Parking Facility

The parking environment can influence a visitor's first impression of the facility. Many factors will contribute to a positive image. Key factors are the level of maintenance, lighting, signage, and the perception of safety.

Level of Maintenance

An appropriate level of maintenance must be established in the following areas:
- Landscape care
- Striping
- Miscellaneous painting, such as pavement arrows, objects of caution, and structure railing, stairwells, and lobby areas
- Sweeping
- Pavement cleaning, such as of oil spills
- Relamping and cleaning of light fixtures
- Pavement care, such as repair of potholes and cracks
- Replacement of faded, damaged, or missing signs
- Structure window washing
- Trash removal
- Snow removal

Ideally, maintenance should be scheduled during times of low occupancy. However, when this is not possible, prior notification of any closure should be provided for good public relations.

Lighting

Many customers associate safety with lighting level. Incorrect lighting, particularly in parking structures, can create a variety of problems, including shadow zones, sense of insecurity, reduced visibility, loss of direction, and even a sense of claustrophobia. Planners have to be sensitive to the correct illumination, uniformity, color of light, surface colors, and reflectance.

Signage

Most successful signage systems are those that provide as little overall signage as possible. The following ten guidelines will contribute to a successful system:
- Letter size and wording should be standardized throughout the system.
- "Warm fuzzy" wording will contribute to a friendly image. For example, "Please Drive Slowly," rather than "Drive Slowly," may go a long way toward achieving customer cooperation.
- Sign locations should be standardized as much as possible. Customers typically learn where to look for directional signage.
- Signage should be coordinated with lighting locations to further enhance signage visibility.
- High-pressure sodium lighting will distort many colors. If color coding is used as a level indicator, colors should be selected that will not be distorted. For example, red will appear brown, but yellow will not change in appearance.
- Typically, a successful directional system will incorporate multiple approaches. For example, some customers will remember colors better than the printed word. A level or area indicator sign may include the number "2" above the written word "TWO" against a blue background. Such a sign includes numerical and written identifiers, as well as color coding.
- Traditional colors, such as red, brown, yellow, and blue, will probably have a higher recognition level than trendy colors such as mauve, taupe, coral, and cinnamon. Some customers may not know the name of such colors to use when asking for directions.
- Signage located around the perimeter of a surface lot rather than within the parking lot will provide ease of snow removal and sweeping.
- Information panels, campus directories, and "you-are-here" maps should be clustered in pedestrian areas, such as structure elevator lobbies and bus pullouts.
- Standardizing signage, maintaining an inventory, and fabricating and installing in-house typically will provide faster service and a more cost-effective approach.

Funding of the Parking System

Ideally, a parking system should be self-supporting. Typical funding sources are as follows:
- Permits,
- Metered parking,
- Designated visitor parking,
- Parking for special events, and
- Parking tickets.

Budget for the Parking System

Assuming that the parking system is self-supporting, rates should be set to fund the following components annually:
- Administration,
- Maintenance,
- Repair and renovation,
- Deferred maintenance,
- New construction,
- A reserve for new construction, and
- Alternate transportation options.

As the annual budget is itemized for projected expenses and revenue, it is helpful to attach an explanation for each item. For example, why is permit revenue expected to increase/decrease, or why are utility costs expected to increase/decrease? This information may be invaluable in the future for projecting trends.

Parking Systems

Parking administrators have matched various forms and combinations of reserved parking, zoned parking, and open parking to their specific recreation and sport cultures. The following are advantages/disadvantages of each form:

- Reserved parking is typically the most expensive, with the lowest occupancy. As space constraints continue to grow with the projected decrease in core area parking, it may be increasingly difficult to provide reserved parking for large numbers of people.
- Zoned parking typically restricts parkers to an area close to their work site. The occupancy rate is generally higher than that for reserved parking. As core area parking space continues to decline, the demand will typically exceed the supply.
- Open parking, commonly referred to as "hunting license" parking, provides a system of parking on a first-come basis and has the highest occupancy rate. However, as the demand for parking increases, the level of frustration grows as customers perceive wasted time in hunting for a parking space.

Parking Options

The following menu of seven parking options is listed, in order, from the most expensive to the least expensive:

- Reserved space or area

  This option is usually the most expensive and has the lowest occupancy rate. If the demand exceeds the supply, the challenge may be to develop criteria for eligibility that customers perceive to be fair.

- Core area parking

  This option typically provides parking within a reasonably short walking distance to most recreation or sport activities.

- Perimeter parking

  This option generally provides parking that requires a longer walk or a short bus ride to most recreation or sport activities.

- Motorcycle programs

  Space that typically cannot be used for vehicle parking may be promoted for motorcycle parking. Because less space is required for motorcycles than for cars, a lower rate could be charged, whether in a reserved area, core area, or perimeter area parking location.

- Carpool/vanpool programs

  This is a cost-effective approach for those who are willing to contend with the perceived inconvenience of organizing. Payment choices could be offered, depending on whether reserved, core area, or perimeter parking is used.

- Bicycle parking

  A choice of bicycle parking could be offered, from the traditional hoops to bicycle lockers. Because many bicycles are expensive, the provision of lockers may promote the use of bicycles over vehicles. Attended bike corrals are also coming into use.

- Park-and-ride parking

  This option may provide an opportunity to share resources with the surrounding community, to reduce operating costs, to take advantage of parking space that may be underused, and to address a unique need of commuting participants.

Finally, flexibility must be built into the parking system to provide customers with easy access to multiple parking options, based on their own unique needs.

Parking Technology

Like many fields of endeavor, the parking industry is experiencing an explosion in technology. Extensive amounts of data may be tracked and monitored. However, implementation of such technology may be costly. The initial task is to identify the information that is essential to manage a successful parking system. The typical challenge is to fund only the hardware and software that are actually needed, but with expansion capabilities for future growth. Effective strategic planning, together with a total quality management approach, will help to identify the likely future direction for use of emerging parking technologies.

Parking lot security monitors.

Photo by Meghan Sawyer

Photo by Meghan Sawyer

Toll parking entrance and exit.

The following are examples of parking technology that is available:

- Equipment to monitor parking structure activity.

Typically this involves a chip in a card or on a permit, or sensors installed in the pavement. For enforcement purposes, gate equipment may be used. Types of information that may be monitored are as follows:

- Number and time of entry/exit
- Occupancy trends
- Use by permit type, such as student, disabled client, or guest
- Amount of parking used per parker
- Identification of maintenance needs, such as a gate remaining open
- The system may include a "Parking Available/Full" sign at the entrance for customers' convenience. If the system operates close to full occupancy on a daily basis, all structures may be networked so that if a particular structure is full, a message sign will direct customers to the next closest structures that have parking available.
- Central pay stations may be used in structures or surface lots.

Individual parking meters are eliminated, and customers are directed to a central location to pay. Advantages for the customer are that a parking receipt is provided and dollar bills may be used, eliminating the need to carry a large number of coins. Advantages operationally are that 1) enforcement will pull a tape at the central pay station to quickly identify vehicles whose time has expired, 2) collection time is saved, because collection occurs at one location, and 3) audit control is simplified because a tape is provided that identifies the amount of revenue being collected. If multiple locations are added, central pay stations may be networked to an administrative location for on-time identification of all activity in total or per lot. For example, data included could be occupancy, percentage of illegal parkers, and/or revenue collected.

- Debit card systems.

They allow the parker to add value to a card from a central location or multiple locations and pay only for actual time parked. Debit card capability may be added to many systems, such as central pay stations or individual parking meters. The key advantage to the customer is convenience (i.e., not having to carry change). Advantages operationally are that revenue is collected up front, collection costs are reduced, and audit control is simplified.

Photo by Meghan Sawyer

Parking garage.

Referencing the above examples, astute questions must be asked to determine the minimal level of hardware and software needed to operate an effective parking system, but there must be an understanding of future directions to ensure that the system can be expanded.

For example, in monitoring structure activity, is it necessary to know parking use per customer, or is overall occupancy and identification of peak use enough information to operate a parking system successfully? Networking parking structures with a message sign may be costly. Is the cost worth the customer service? Networking multiple central pay station locations provides extensive information at a glance. Does the need for quick information justify the cost of networking and staff time to track and monitor data? Debit cards are a customer convenience. Careful planning must be done to determine whether one solution is better than other options.

Summary

Parking areas should be designed to be multipurpose (i.e., unused parking space as additional recreation space). Provided that vehicular controls are in operation, it is entirely possible to use flat, well-maintained parking surfaces as additional outdoor recreation space or sport courts. However, the best recreation or sport spaces are designed specifically as such a space, and regular use of a parking lot as a play space probably indicates a flaw in the outdoor space planning. Yet, planners must be sensitive to planning for multipurpose uses and maintain flexibility in their plans.

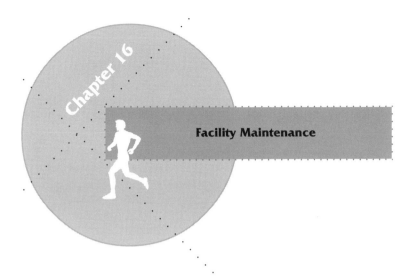

Chapter 16

Facility Maintenance

Thomas J. Rosandich, Jr., United States Sports Academy

M ost maintenance managers will agree that that maintenance requirements are almost never given adequate consideration when facilities are designed. Even when some consideration is given to maintenance during the design phase, changes in design during construction often nullify the original plans. The construction contractor is most usually concerned with completing the building in the manner that will generate the most profit, and as such, is not usually concerned with maintenance and repair requirements once the warranties expire. Further, there is a natural tendency on the part of architects to focus on the visual aesthetics of the design, often at the expense of more utilitarian concerns such as cost efficiency in operations (Beisel, 1998).

Given that the largest cost of a sports facility is borne through the many years of operation following construction and commissioning, maintenance professionals (typically the designated facility maintenance manager) need to participate in the design process. These maintenance professionals should remain involved until the project is completed. So while there should be no question at this point that the maintenance manager can have a lot to offer in terms of the planning of the facility, further discussions are in order as to the practical considerations for operations and maintenance (O&M) in the project planning. This chapter looks at some of the design requirements for the sports facility from the perspective of the maintenance manager. The first part relates specifically to maintenance and support areas and the second to general "generic" maintenance concerns for the facility as a whole.

Learning Objectives

After reading this chapter, the student will be able to:
- provide guidelines for planning maintenance facilities into the sports and recreational facility,
- understand the types of maintenance facilities required in a multipurpose sports facility,
- understand the physical requirements and characteristics for these facilities within the sports facility,
- identify strategies for positioning maintenance facilities within the sports facility, and
- describe maintenance concerns to be considered with the overall design of the facility.

Design Considerations for Maintenance and Operations

Physical education, athletic, and recreational facilities should be maintained in a sanitary and hygienic condition. The very nature of many of the activities conducted within these facilities and the many uses of water within them magnifies the need for consistent, superior custodial care. Unless custodians are provided with adequate and convenient facilities and equipment, the prospects of achieving the desired level of sanitation are significantly diminished.

Among the facilities required by the maintenance and custodian staff for the care and operation of sports facilities include workshops; storage for tools, spare parts, and supplies; janitorial closets; laundry facilities; office and administrative space; and staff break rooms with locker facilities. The following discussion looks briefly at design considerations for these specific O&M areas within the multipurpose sports facility.

Central Custodial Complex

The size and configuration of the custodial complex in any sports facility is contingent upon a number of factors, the first of which is the size of the building and the nature of the programs being conducted. The needs of a small, privately held health club, for example, will vary markedly in both size and scope from those of a multipurpose municipal facility or a university sports complex.

But even between facilities of comparable size, the nature of the organization that owns them will have a significant impact on the size and composition of the custodial complex and the way that it is managed. For example, the physical education, intercollegiate sports, and recreational facilities of a major university can be very similar in size to that of a national sports complex or a municipal stadium.

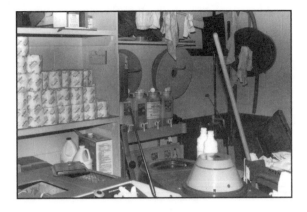

Examples of a central custodial complex.

However, in the university situation, there will typically be less space given over to operations and maintenance within the sports facility itself, because it is likely that elsewhere on campus will be a centralized buildings and grounds operation that will be responsible for the heavy maintenance activities of the entire university. Thus, within the sports facility there may, at most, be a small work space with a storage area for tools and spare parts, which would be totally insufficient for a free-standing, independent operation of comparable size.

Free-standing sport facilities, such as a municipal civic center or a national sports complex, will typically have a self-contained operation for O&M activities. Instead of a small work area for on-site repairs, a free-standing sports facility will need expansive work spaces with a much larger variety of tools and storage for spare parts. Nevertheless, O&M facilities of all types do have a number of elements in common.

One approach for the allocation of administrative and support space for O&M operatives is described by Bronzan (1974). In large facilities, a central custodian headquarters should be planned to include a toilet, shower, lavatory, and dressing area with individual lockers. This unit should also have a separate break and meal area equipped with a sink, hot-and-cold water supply, microwave oven, and a small refrigerator. Additionally, a small, apartment-size breakfast table and chairs should be provided.

While there is no question that a properly furnished break area and locker room facilities for the O&M staff are appropriate, there is a definite need for a separate O&M office. The area for the administrative office in a typical collegiate facility should be about seven square meters. It is im-

portant to note, however, that this space allocation for the administrative office is a minimum, and that the size of the space allocated will grow as the complexity and size of the O&M operation grows. The administrative area should have enough office space to accommodate a desk, filing cabinets, and communications equipment. With today's communication technology capabilities, the administrative office must have a networked computer (either a networked personal computer or a terminal in the case of a mainframe operation) with a printer. Traditionally, the office of the O&M supervisor has been physically located in the workshop or storeroom area. However, because of advances in the application of communications equipment and powerful management tools, such as networked micro-computers, the physical presence of the supervisor in the workshop area is no longer a necessity (de Booij, 1993).

A further case can be made that, because of the coordination required between the different administrators who manage the sports facility, the office of the maintenance supervisor should be located in the same area as other administrators. Regardless, however, of where the office of the maintenance manager is physically located, the office (and those of the other facility administrators) should be hard-wired for communications and micro-computer networking.

There is little point in having the maintenance manager's office hard-wired for data and communications if the work areas of the operatives are not. Thus, each of the main components of the O&M complex, such as the workshop area, storage for spare parts and supplies, and the administrative office, should similarly be hard-wired for data and communications and should have a desk area that can accommodate a micro-computer and communications equipment.

With the exception of the manager's office as outlined above, ideally the rest of the maintenance offices and workshops will be grouped together in one of the service areas of the building. General characteristics of the O&M area include direct or easy access to the exterior of the building, preferably with a loading dock to facilitate the handling of deliveries, which will often arrive by truck. The landing area at the loading dock should be spacious enough to allow the easy movement of cargo pallets and bulky containers and to allow sorting and organization of materials being received before they are moved into storage.

The storerooms and workshop areas should be located close to each other. This will reduce work hours wasted in retrieving parts and supplies before they are used. In addition to easy access to the exterior of the building, the custodial complex should be easily accessed via wide and level (i.e., without impediments) corridors. Wherever feasible, the doors between service and storage areas should "line-up," so custodial operatives do not have to turn corners with cumbersome loads.

Access to the central custodial complex and its various work and storage areas should be through double doors. If some material other than steel is used for these doors (for aesthestic reasons, for example), they should be equipped with kick plates and bumper guards. The service or freight elevator, in the case of a multi-story building, should also be situated in close proximity to facilitate logistic operations. Such elevators should have a ceiling, if possible, of 10 feet and should be as wide as possible. Quite simply, such elevators are going to have to handle the largest pieces of equipment being moved between floors of a multi-story sports facility and should be planned accordingly. Such appropriate logistical considerations will typically yield dividends in the cost-efficient use of personnel and are discussed further below.

However, while easy access to the custodial complex is desirable, the area must still be secured against unauthorized entry. Bear in mind that the typical sports facility will have large numbers of participants and spectators passing through the building and to have them enter service areas, either intentionally or otherwise, is undesirable.

These are the general guidelines for O&M facilities within the building. Each individual area is discussed below.

Maintenance Workshops

Among the most obvious concerns of the maintenance manager during the design phase of the sports facility are the work and support areas that will be utilized by the maintenance crews. The size and location of their work areas will have a significant impact on how well O&M workers can do their jobs. The argument could be made that perhaps the most important of all of the facilities in the custodial complex is the workshop area.

The workshop itself should be situated against an outside wall of the building in the service area, which will allow an exhaust fan to vent outdoors the hazardous fumes and odors generated by activities conducted within. Preferably it should also be situated immediately adjacent to the loading dock entrance and service reception area and have access to the core of the building.

The floor should be of hardened concrete and have a non-corrosive drain. There should also be sufficient open floor space between such permanent fixtures as the storage bins and shelving, work bench, and slop sink to allow free movement around large pieces of equipment that may be brought to the workshop for servicing. The door into the workshop area itself should be a lockable sheet-metal type without a floor sill or threshold. Because of the level of noise generated in the workshop area with power tools, the walls should be of sufficient thickness to inhibit the transmission of sound to surrounding spaces. The walls should also be finished with a stain-resistant and easy-to-clean surface.

As stated earlier, the actual size of the workshop area will depend on whether it is a self-contained operation and how much activity it will be required to handle. Regardless of the size, however, some common characteristics should be considered. The first is a spacious workbench equipped with vises, small mounted power tools such as grinders, and a non-skid surface. The workbench area should be well lit by fluorescent lighting in the 100-lumen range that are mounted directly overhead. There should be sufficient electrical outlets around the room, particularly in the workbench wall near the vises and bench-mounted power tools. Also depending on the type of operation, sufficient floor space may be needed to mount free-standing equipment such as pipe-threaders and certain types of woodworking tools.

The maintenance workshop area should be both air conditioned and well ventilated. Because maintenance personnel use highly toxic and volatile substances such as paint, solvents, and cleaners, the workshop areas and central storage areas have exhaust fans that operate automatically and are vented to the outside.

Another area that needs to be considered is the tool room (also known as a tool crib). While maintenance workers frequently have a set of commonly used tools assigned to them, such as those contained in a lockable tool box, many specialized or very expensive tools and equipment are not assigned to individual craftsmen on a permanent basis. Examples of the specialized tools required for building maintenance may include welding equipment, a variety of metering devices (such as volt meters), and certain power tools. Because these types of tools and equipment are typically high-value items, access needs to be controlled and sign-out procedures employed as with any other inventory item. It is therefore cost effective from a labor standpoint to have the tool room physically located near the workshop area and/or combined with other stockroom activities such as the spare parts store room.

Storage

Storage falls into a gray area between strictly O&M concerns and sports activity and program concerns. On the one hand, storage space is needed for tools, spare parts, and consumables, such as cleaning supplies and dispenser items (toilet paper, paper towels, and hand soap) to support O&M activities. On the other hand, sufficient storage space is needed to support program activities in the building, such as that required for sports equipment, uniforms, and ancillary activities.

Experienced administrators of the various activity programs and experienced supervisors of storage and distribution rooms agree that the most prevalent fault in the planning of these facilities is the failure to allocate sufficient space. As a result, programs suffer in one way or another, and students do not enjoy all of the benefits they should receive. Operations costs increase disproportionately. Thus, it is useful to consider all the storage requirements for a sports facility for both O&M and sports and activity programs concurrently.

Storage for O&M Operations

A wide variety of spare parts and consumable supplies is required to keep any building functioning properly. Examples of spare parts required for a typical sports complex can range from light bulbs, ballasts, filters, and fan belts for air-handling units to replacement modules for scoreboards. Consumables similarly include a wide variety of materials, ranging from equipment lubricants, chemicals such as chlorine for the pool, cleaning supplies required for custodial work, and dispenser items required for the restrooms and locker rooms. Secure tool storage and space for storing bulky maintenance equipment, such as scaffolding and/or hydraulic lifts, are also needed.

There are a number of considerations in determining the size and location of storage and supply rooms to support O&M operation. Obviously, whether the O&M operation is self-contained is one of them. Another is whether the supply room is run on an open-stock or closed-inventory basis and how much inventory is dispersed to other storage locations around the facility, such as in janitorial closets.

If the nature of the organization is such that the sports facilities are a self-contained operation, then the space required for the storage of O&M-related equipment and supplies will obviously be greater. More space must be set aside for larger quantities of tools and supplies and for bulky equipment such as scaffolding. If the sport facilities are, for example, part of a centralized O&M operation on a university campus, it is likely that the high-value tools and equipment, such as lifts and scaffolding, will be kept elsewhere at a central location.

Whether the supplies are run on an open-stock or closed-inventory basis is another consideration. Low-value, high-usage standard stock items such as nails, nuts and blocks, paints, and lubricants are frequently designated open-stock items. Maintenance personnel can obtain them directly from bins without a requisition form, and there is no control over who takes them or what job they are used on. Such items can be stored right in the workshop area, for example, which will further enhance efficiency of the O&M operation. While such an arrangement reduces the need for separate storage space and an inventory clerk, it also invites increased pilferage by employees.

Perhaps the best use of an open-stock situation is in operations where maintenance is centralized, such as on a large university campus. As explained earlier, it is likely that a central O&M complex will serve the whole campus with sufficient volume and value of materials to require a closed-inventory system within the central maintenance complex. Thus, the sports facility, which is at best a peripheral operation, will likely have a smaller workshop area and tool crib with an open stock of standard-issue items.

A self-contained sports facility, such as a municipal stadium or national sports complex, on the other hand, will likely have a closed-inventory system or a combined open-stock, closed-inventory system. Because high-value tools and spare parts required for O&M operation must be retained on the premises, there is a need for access control and accountability and thus for an established inventory system and issue clerk. However, in terms of operational efficiency, it still makes sense in this type of an operation to place some items such as standard issue nuts and bolts in workshop areas and to disperse restroom cleaning supplies and equipment to the janitorial closets. The point is, however, that the space given over to this storage will be markedly greater.

In terms of the physical characteristics of storage areas and supply rooms, these should be situated in close proximity to the areas that they service. For example, tool and spare parts issue should be close to the workshop area, with the space required determined by the criteria discussed above.

The storerooms require temperature and humidity control, as inventory items frequently have specific requirements for storage. The floors should be of hardened concrete with a non-slip surface that is easy to clean. The room should be brightly lit with luminaries located between rows of shelving to ease identification of inventory, which is frequently described on small punch cards or tags affixed to the shelving.

For limited-access storage, there should be a distribution window that can be easily secured when the inventory clerk steps away from the service area to retrieve an item. Near the distribution window should be space enough for a desk and filing cabinet, which should be hard-wired for communications and networked computer equipment (de Booji, 1993). The distribution window should have a counter upon which any transactions can be completed.

Doorway access to the stockroom should be planned to accommodate the largest pieces of equipment or machinery that will enter the area. Unless otherwise indicated, a doorway that is at least 60 inches wide and 84 inches high is recommended, with thresholds that are flush with the floor. The doors will also require good-quality, tamper-proof locks and should be of fire-resistant sheet metal.

Shelving is an obvious requirement for the storage of supplies and inventory. These requirements include adjustable steel shelving with a depth of between 18 to 24 inches and a width of 36 to 48 inches. The first shelf should be at least six inches off the floor and the top shelf no less than 12 inches from the ceiling. So far as possible, shelves should be adjustable and standard sizes used.

Sports Equipment Storage and Repair

In most sports facilities, storage and work areas for sports activity and team equipment is separate from that used for general facility O&M. Regardless, many of the physical descriptions of the space required and fixtures contained in the storage rooms used for spare parts and supplies in the O&M operations are also applicable to storage areas for the sports and activity program. It should be noted that virtually all professional teams and most collegiate programs have professional equipment managers whose responsibility includes inventory control and servicing of team clothing and equipment. Just as a maintenance professional should be included in the design process to review the facilities program from an O&M perspective, so too should the equipment manager be consulted with respect to sport equipment storage and repair areas.

It is recommended that the space given over to the storage of sports equipment include a small area to facilitate the repair of program-related equipment. A well-equipped work area can result in considerable savings over an extended period of time, and sports operations tend to work at a higher level of efficiency with this capability.

Examples of equipment that should be housed in a workshop of this type include a small workbench similarly equipped to that in the main facility workshop area described above. Some of the equipment will vary, because the nature of the work to be done is quite different. Examples of equipment that should be included in this work area are racquet-stringing machines and sewing machines for uniforms. Additionally, the laundry facility will typically be located in or near the equipment manager's facility.

As custodial workers are frequently asked to set up and remove equipment used in various sports activities, of particular interest to the maintenance manager are the location and characteristics of equipment storage rooms situated about the building. Generally, an equipment storage facility should be located adjacent to each major activity area in the building. Each of these auxiliary storage units should be designed to accommodate equipment anticipated to be used in that particular area, such as hydraulic basketball and other game standards in the main gymnasium, racing lanes and recall lines in the swimming pool area, and gymnastics equipment and mats in their specific area. In all cases, design considerations include doors of sufficient size to accommodate bulky equipment (preferably "lined up" to reduce the number of corners to be negotiated when moving equipment), no door sills or thresholds, and appropriate shelving needs.

Janitorial Closets

The janitorial closet is the staging area for all custodial or housekeeping work. If the custodian works out of a room that is disorganized and dirty, it is likely that the cleaning effort will suffer accordingly. Also, much of the damage to custodial equipment occurs in the janitorial closet. An example of this is how mop buckets are frequently wheeled into the closet and not emptied, or floor scrubbing equipment is not cleaned after use. Thus, every effort should be made to design janitorial closets that will facilitate the custodial work (Walker, 1990). In determining the number of janitorial closets, a number of variables need to be considered, such as:
- the number of floors within the facility,
- the type of floor finishes to be maintained,
- the proposed use of the areas, and
- the number of restrooms in the facility.

There should be at least one six-square-meter custodial room for each 930 square meters of floor space, and at least one such room on each floor of the facility. The room should be designed with a large enough open area where equipment can be assembled and checked and janitorial carts properly stocked prior to starting a job (Walker, 1990). Each janitorial closet should have a service sink with a pop-up

drain and a temperature-mixing type of faucet; floor sinks are preferable to large wall sinks for this purpose. Shelves and hanging boards should be constructed in each janitorial closet to facilitate the storage of supplies and tools (Flynn, 1985, 1993). Hanging boards, however, should be designed so that wet mops do not rest flush against the wall. Lastly, the janitorial closet should have a good level of illumination (at least 50 lumens) so that equipment can be properly cleaned after the job and before being stowed, and the fine print on chemical containers can be read (Walker, 1990).

While the foregoing is a general guide to the dimensions required for janitorial closets, the general rule of thumb is that the closet should have sufficient space both relative and particular to the area that is being served. High-volume activity areas with greater traffic flow have greater requirements and will need a larger space to accommodate the supplies and equipment needed to properly service them (Bronzan, 1974). Additionally, areas serviced on a seven-day cleaning schedule will require 35 to 40% more supplies than those cleaned on a five-day schedule, which would suggest a larger space allocation.

As an example of how the size of a janitorial closet should be determined in part by the area being serviced, consider the open floor space required to store floor maintenance equipment. A closet located in a corridor that features tile flooring would require an area large enough for power scrubbing equipment, whereas one in the vicinity of a carpeted office complex could get by with the smaller area required for a commercial-grade vacuum cleaner. Janitorial closets should also be located in or next to restroom and locker room complexes for a number of reasons. First, this location provides a water and sewage source for the mop sink and thus is cost effective from a design and construction standpoint. The second reason is that locker rooms and restrooms typically must be cleaned more often, and work hours are saved if the supplies and equipment are positioned near these areas. And finally, such a location facilitates storage of restroom cleaners, maintenance supplies, and dispenser stock.

As another example of the need to service high-volume traffic areas, a small room should be located near each entrance of the building to store maintenance supplies and tools (Flynn, 1985, 1993). Quite simply, everyone who enters or leaves the building will do so through one or more designated entries, which leads to excessive wear in these areas. The first 12 feet on the inside of an entry doorway is called "the walk-off area" and functions exactly as the name implies: it is within this radius that dust, dirt, oil from the parking lot, and water from rain and melting snow are deposited. Thus, a well-conceived maintenance plan will call for the regular policing of this area to prevent soiling materials from spreading beyond the walk-off area. To facilitate this frequent cleaning, a small custodial storage area should be situated nearby.

The failure to provide janitorial closets in the proper location and of the proper size can be illustrated by the following example. A building was constructed in which the janitorial closets were only 1.5 square meters in size, most of which was taken up by the mop sink. As a result, most of the supplies and power cleaning equipment had to be stored in the basement of the building, and carting supplies and equipment to the place where they were needed each night amounted to 30 hours of labor per five-night workweek. This amounted to an additional three-fourths of a worker-year labor expense, which would have been unnecessary if the facility were properly planned. Additionally, because of operating conditions that arose from this situation, pilferage of supplies and theft of equipment increased, leading to the additional requirements of building a lock-up room in the basement of the building and the administrative controls (and expense) to run it.

Laundry Room

In most physical education, sport, and recreational facilities, it is now more cost effective to establish in-house laundry facilities than to contract out for cleaning uniforms and towel services. As the operation of the laundry most frequently devolves to the custodial staff, and the laundry facility itself is most likely to be situated within the maintenance support areas of the building, it is appropriate to consider planning guidelines for the laundry operation along with the rest of the O&M facilities.

So far as possible, the laundry facility should be physically located on the ground level of the building against an outside wall to facilitate venting of the dryer. Non-skid concrete floors are recommended, since the floors in the laundry should be hardened and impervious to water. Floors should be sloped to a drain trough that leads to non-corrosive drains. The slope should be 1/8 inch per linear foot. The planarity of the floor is important, since puddles can be dangerous. Floor materials should extend up the walls at least 12 inches, with corners rounded or covered. The thickness of the floor should comply with the equipment manufacturer's recommendations, but in any case, the floor should be able to withstand heavy, vibrating equipment.

As with other maintenance and service areas, the laundry facility should have double-hinged, double-doors without a threshold or a sill to facilitate the installation of laundry equipment during construction and the subsequent movement of laundry carts and supplies in and out of the premises. As a laundry is a noisy place, the walls and ceilings should have good sound absorption or non-transmission properties and yet be impervious to water. The wall finish should also be easy to clean and stain resistant.

While the floor space required for the laundry is contingent upon the size of the machines and the projected work load, sufficient space should be included in the plan for the storage of supplies and sorting/folding tables. Lizarraga (1991) provides guidelines by noting that the size of the laundry facility is determined by the size of the workload. The capacity of laundry equipment is determined by weight (pound). To calculate the number and the size of the machines that will be required, compare the anticipated daily quantities of articles to be cleaned multiplied by their respective weights with the poundage capacity of the machines under consideration, which will give the number of loads they can handle per day. Most process formulas will handle two loads per hour. Facilities with multiple goods classifications (i.e., nylon game uniforms and cotton-blend towels) should opt for two or more machines. Drying equipment needs to be matched up with the washers/extractors and typically has a larger capacity. For example, a 50-pound dryer is a good match with a 35-pound washer.

Once the number and types of machines have been determined, it is a relatively simple matter to size them, as the dimensions of the units can be easily obtained from prospective vendors. The machines should be mounted a minimum of two feet away from the walls and with a minimum of 18 inches between machines. Generally, however, sufficient space should be left around them for circulation and work and for equipment servicing as may be required. Combine this with the space required for processing the work and storage to determine the net useable footage required for the laundry.

As with all equipment, access to utilities needs to be considered in the plan. While hot and cold water, sewage, and electricity are obvious, gas driers are the most cost efficient to use, so an appropriate hook-up is in order. The room should also have good ventilation and air circulation in addition to outdoor vents for exhaust generated by the equipment.

In terms of the equipment itself, programmable microprocessor controls on the laundry equipment are highly recommended. Also recommended are liquid detergent supply systems that can provide pre-set, automatic injections of chemicals, as such devices may serve to remove judgement calls by operators, especially if the operators are part-time helpers (such as students) (Lizarraga, 1991).

Generic Concerns for Building Maintenance

While the foregoing discussion focused on the design parameters of the facilities specifically required for the O&M effort, aspects of sports facility design as a whole should be considered from the maintenance standpoint. These are really non-specific issues that can nonetheless produce significant operating costs. Many of these considerations are quite simple, yet because of their very simplicity, they are easily overlooked as more obvious design considerations hold the attention of the architect and design committee.

We have touched on such matters as building logistics in discussing the custodial complex, yet so much staff time is spent moving equipment around the the typical sports facility that further, more specific attention is warranted. Simple accessibility to equipment and fixtures requiring maintenance tends to get short shift in the design process, with potentially disastrous consequences.

Standardizing Building Fixtures and Equipment

By now it should be clear that the variety of building finishes, fixtures, and equipment in a multipurpose sports facility can be staggering. Similarly, the need to inventory and control spare parts and consumable supplies for the maintenance effort can be a very large undertaking. However, by making a conscious effort to standardize building fixtures and equipment during the design phase, the costs of acquiring and carrying building spares can be significantly reduced.

Such reductions are accomplished in two ways. The first is the direct savings realized through a reduction in stocking spare parts. Standardization of finishes and fixtures allows the maintenance manager to reduce the number of items

Emergency lighting.

carried in the spare part inventory, which means a smaller financial burden in carrying costs. As a simple example, consider the effect of standardizing light fixtures. If all the fluorescent light fixtures in the building are the same, the number and variety of ballasts and lighting tubes that must be kept on hand can be considerably smaller than if there were a variety of different fixtures scattered throughout the building. Standardization also prevents the cost of wasted labor that results from bringing the wrong replacement tube to the fixture; the chances of this increase with a wide disparity in fixtures.

The second reduction is more indirect, but significant nonetheless. A smaller inventory requires less room for storage. Additionally, a smaller inventory is easier to administer and control, reducing administrative costs and loss through mishandling and pilferage. Concerted efforts can be made in many areas in standardizing building fixtures, including light fixtures and switches, breaker switches and boxes, bathroom fixtures and dispensers, locker room equipment, door hardware, locks and keys, and moveable equipment.

Logistical Concerns

Operating costs can also be realized by taking into account the needs of the maintenance staff in logistical operations. Logistical operations pertains to the handling of furnishings, equipment, and materials within the facility.

One area that tends to distinguish sports facilities from other types of buildings is the nature of the equipment contained within. A multi-station weight machine is, by its very nature, a very heavy and bulky piece of equipment to move around, particularly without disassembly. Gymnastics apparatus and mats, wrestling mats, and portable basketball goals are other examples of heavy, unusually configured equipment that is frequently moved around the building. An awareness of these characteristics is important during the design phase of the facility. For example (and as stated on several occasions already), the doors between spaces should line up to reduce cornering, and the doors from the loading dock (or main access from the exterior of the building), and equipment storage rooms should be double doors with flush sills and sufficient height to facilitate equipment movement.

Other design considerations from a purely operational point of view include using ramps between levels in the sports hall, provided the change in level is not too significant. Another approach is to ensure that freight or building service elevators are of sufficient size (including height) to facilitate

the movement of equipment between floors. Similarly, making stairwells and landings large enough to handle bulky items, such as boxes of supplies or furniture, will help with logistical concerns.

Lastly, the design phase must recognize all the activities that will take place within the facility. For example, food service or concessions within the building will require the movement of groceries into and garbage out of the building, preferably through service passages.

The author is aware of one sports facility in southwest Asia that was built at a cost in excess of $80 million, in which virtually all of these concerns were ignored in the preliminary plan. Fortunately, once construction was underway, a design review was able to rectify the worst of the errors, but only at considerable additional expense. Had not the design errors been caught, the only access to a second-floor food-service facility would have been via the VIP elevator. A worker seeking to get on board with a bag of garbage when the elevator was already occupied by a member of the Royal Family would have been problematic at best. Similarly, the design included three steps between each wing of the building and no way to move equipment between them. It was a situation rectified by the addition of a ramp after the fact.

Access of Building Operating Equipment

As unfortunate as the logistical situation was in this facility, service access to building operating systems was even worse. There was no way to access light and sound fixtures over the pool or the gymnasium floor because of a novel roof design.

The roof in the facility was a translucent, Teflon-coated fiberglass structure designed as an Arabian tent. But the design did not include access by service passages or catwalks to the fixtures suspended from the ceiling. Lights were changed, for example, by erecting scaffolding or using a personal hydraulic lift, both of which were expensive and time consuming. Unfortunately, the hydraulic lift could not be utilized in the pool area, which necessitated the erection of scaffolding in the swimming pool. Thus, the only way to change the lights was to drain the pool. This is a classic case of the architect's placing aesthetics before the more pragmatic and mundane concerns of operating the building, with quite costly consequences.

The point of this discussion is that maintenance requirements of building operating systems must be considered during the design of a facility. By taking into account such operational requirements as easy access to equipment, particularly control panels and lubrication ports, which require frequent attention, accompanying labor costs can be substantially reduced.

Utilities

In addition to access to control panels and operating systems for routine maintenance, the astute placement of electrical outlets for cleaning equipment and water spigots for hoses can effectively reduce labor hours in the maintenance effort.

Most floor-care equipment requires electrical outlets, whether they are power scrubbers or vacuum cleaners. Therefore, the placement of electrical outlets needs consideration, particularly in corridors, lobbies, and activity areas. Inappropriately situated outlets can cause considerable additional operating expense, both for labor (the need to continually move power cords) and for supplies (the need to purchase excessive numbers of extension cords). Additionally, the need for exterior outlets on the building should not be overlooked. For example, certain types of window-washing equipment require access to power, as do many other types of maintenance and custodial equipment, such as blowers for grass clippings.

Water spigots on the exterior of the building should be treated similarly to electrical outlets on the interior of the building. Water hoses are commonly used for washing down sidewalks and exterior windows, particularly those located near the ground. Thus, careful consideration to the number and placement of spigots similarly warrants close attention in the design phase.

Windows

The whole topic of windows deserves special mention. The arrangement and proportioning of windows is called fenestration. Consideration of the relationships of lighting, color, use of materials, acoustics, and climate control cannot ignore the importance of fenestration. The size and placement of windows cannot be left to chance, personal whims, or merely traditional use.

The generous use of windows has been in vogue in the past few decades, at least in part because of the pleasing visual effects obtained by the architect. But the excessive use of glass in a sports facility may give rise to a host of problems, including high operating costs from heat gain and loss and inordinate cleaning costs.

Glass is a poor insulator. It causes significant heat gain during summer months through the greenhouse effect and a corresponding increase in air-conditioning costs. During the winter, the process is reversed, and large glass areas cause significant heat loss with a similar increase in operating costs. Similarly, large amounts of glass tend to increase maintenance costs as dirt is more visible. Any person who has glass patio doors, for example, can attest to how much attention they require when weather conditions make handprints and streaks more visible. In commercial buildings such as sports facilities, the amount of cleaning required depends on many variables, such as the local environment (rainfall, dust, and pollution) and the extent of the maintenance effort (or, how dirty you are willing to let the glass get?).

Two basic methods are usually used for window cleaning; "over the roof" or "up from the ground." In both cases, special equipment is required for any structure in excess of one story. The cost for these systems can vary from as little as $15 for a garden hose and squeegee with a six-foot handle to as much as $50,000 for a scaffold for "over the roof" work. Regardless of the system used, plans for water and electrical power sources for window-washing equipment should be included in the design phase.

It should be noted that in sports facilities, if windows are to be incorporated in the design, they should be at least 1/16th of the floor area. Additionally, it is recommended that windows be placed nearer the ceiling than the floor. For a multipurpose gymnasium designed to accommodate both international-level volleyball and team handball, the minimum total area of glass windows would be approximately 66 square meters (over 700 square feet) located some 7 to 12 meters (22 to 40 feet) off the ground. Under these circumstances, accessibility and labor costs related to maintaining an appropriate appearance must be considered during the design phase.

Returning to the sports facility in southwest Asia cited earlier, the architect achieved a stunning visual effect with a bank of blue-tinted windows two meters wide and 50 meters long extending the length of the sports hall wall some 15 meters from the ground and cantilevered at an angle of approximately of 140 degrees to the roof line. However, the design made accessing the windows extremely difficult, and in the six years that the author observed the building, the windows were never washed. The result was an originally unique visual effect that was severely degraded because the design did not take maintenance into consideration.

Summary

It is not possible to construct a building that is entirely maintenance free. All the elements of a building deteriorate at varying rates, depending on such matters as component quality, location, degree of exposure to the elements, and use. In this regard, the original design, specification, and construction of a sports facility are all of crucial importance to future performance and maintenance liability. For this reason, it is highly desirable to obtain some appropriate input into the design process from maintenance specialists. Unhappily, this rarely occurs (Roberts, 1996).

A common misconception of many sports administrators is that planning for maintenance and operations (O&M) takes place once the sports facility has been built and the doors are opened for business. However, this approach overlooks the importance of planning for maintenance during the facility acquisition process. It also overlooks the fact that the expense of properly caring for the building and equipment will represent a major portion of the overall life-cycle cost of the facility. Thus, poor planning for O&M will typically result in higher operating expenditures to the facility owner-operator which, in turn, reduces the amount of funding available for conducting programs and activities for which the facility was originally built. It is clear that O&M must be considered during the planning process for the new building.

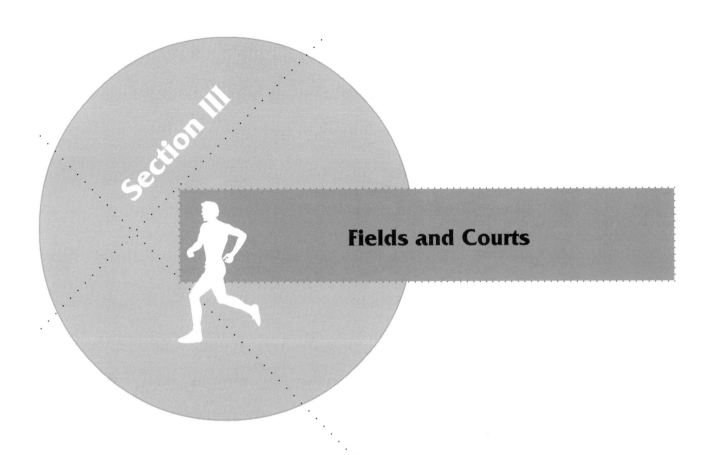

Section III

Fields and Courts

Chapter 17

Indoor and Outdoor Courts

Bernie Goldfine, Kennesaw State University

I ndoor and outdoor courts are popular competition and recreation venues. These venues are continually being modernized and improved. In this chapter, a discussion of 14 of the most popular courts will outline important considerations for planners developing new facilities. Two court areas have benefitted from the dramatic growth of competitive and recreational users over the last decade—racquetball and sand volleyball. The planners of these new courts have taken into consideration many important changes in materials regarding lighting, floor surfaces, wall surfaces, ceiling surfaces, ventilation, and safety.

Learning Objectives

After reading this chapter, the student will be able to
- identify and describe layout, dimensions, and orientations,
- identify and describe various materials used in construction, and
- identify and describe a variety of important specifications and information (e.g., surfacing and lighting) for the courts described in this chapter.

Tennis Courts

Layout, Orientation, Dimensions, Fencing

Tennis was first played in the United States during the mid 1870s. At that time, the game was slow-paced and played on the grass lawns of houses and parks. The game has now changed to a fast-paced athletic sport. As tennis has changed, so too have the courts on which it is played. Today's outdoor courts are laid out in a manner that minimizes the effects of wind, sun, background vision, and the lay of the land. Tennis courts are constructed of grass, clay, soft and hard composition, asphalt, concrete, and various synthetic materials. Many other features such as accessibility, storage, parking, lighting, and fencing need to be carefully planned for in tennis court construction.

In constructing outdoor tennis courts, prevailing winds must be taken into account in the planning process. If prevailing winds exist, courts should be placed near natural barriers, such as woods or hills that act as a windbreak. If no existing barriers are in the area of court construction, a thick stand of staggered trees can be planted to serve as a barrier. Alternately, if existing buildings are near the construction site, they may be used as a wind barrier.

Visual background must be planned for in the layout of tennis courts. The background at both ends of the courts should be natural grass, shrubs, woods, or other natural landscaping. Roads, parking areas, and pedestrian high-traffic areas are not acceptable at the ends of tennis courts. Too many objects moving in front of the tennis player causes lapses in concentration and makes play more difficult. If the busy areas must coexist with tennis courts, they should be at the sides of the courts. Furthermore, tennis complexes should not be placed too far from the remainder of the sports complex or center campus. The more removed the courts are, the more difficult user access will be. Court layout must also meet ADA requirements for all disabled users.

The contour of the land for proposed tennis court construction also needs careful thought. It is much cheaper to construct tennis courts on flat land than on rolling terrain; it is less expensive in terms of both earth moving and drainage concerns. If courts must be on rolling terrain, they should be laid out with the minimum of cost for earth moving and drainage. Also, hills should serve as natural barriers whenever possible.

Outdoor tennis court planning must also include the sun, which can create visual problems for the tennis player. If tennis courts are to be used mostly between April and October, they should be aligned north to south on the long axis of the court. If courts are to be used year round, the long axis should be northwest to southeast at 22° off true north. These orientations minimize the amount of sun-related visual problems for tennis players (USTA, 1997).

If courts are nonporous, provisions must be made for the drainage of water off the courts. Courts may be sloped from 0.5% to 1.5% depending on the type of surface (USTA, 1997). Any slope greater than 1.5% can be visually detected by the players and is not acceptable. Courts may be sloped side to side, end to end, center to end, or end to center. If only one individual court is constructed, either a side-to-side or an end-to-end slope works well. If a battery of courts is being constructed, the slope should be dictated by the fastest way to drain the most courts as quickly as possible. For example, if five courts are built side by side, an end-to-end slope would be best since all courts would drain and dry simultaneously. If a side-by-side slope were used, the courts on the upper end of the slope would dry quickly, but the last few courts would retain water for a much longer period of time, since the water from the upper end slope courts would have to drain across the courts at the lower end of the slope.

Center-to-end and end-to-center slopes are least desirable. When these types of slopes are used, the water remains on the court and court perimeter playing surface much longer than when side-to-side or end-to-end slopes are used. Additionally, an end-to-center slope requires drains at or near the net. Drains on the court itself are not desirable.

When planning to use slope, natural drainage basins should be used whenever possible. Thus, if a small creek basin or lower land is adjacent to the court area, it is worthwhile to slope courts to these areas to limit artificial drainage and minimize drainage costs.

As outdoor tennis courts are planned, the size of the courts as well as the perimeter space around the court need careful attention. A singles court is 78 feet long and 36 feet wide. Including perimeter space, the minimum size for one doubles court would be 122 feet by 66 feet. These dimensions give minimum safety between the court and the fencing on both the sides and the ends of the court (USTA, 1997).

The minimum distance between side-by-side courts is 12 feet. The minimum distance between the court sideline and the side fence is 15 feet. Finally, the minimum distance between the court baseline and the end fence is 22 feet (USTA, 1997). The shortest distance is between courts since a player has open space (the adjacent court) to run to in order to retrieve a ball. There is more distance between the sideline and the side fence since players can run into the fence. Finally, the baseline distance is greatest since this area is essentially a part of the playing area, even though it is not a part of the actual court. Figure 17.1 illustrates these minimum distances, as well as the dimensions of a tennis court.

Tennis courts should be enclosed with chain-link fence. The fence can be either 10 or 12 feet high. The 12-foot-high fence is more expensive than the 10-foot-high fence; however, those additional two feet of fencing keep in a significantly greater percentage of balls (USTA, 1997).

Chain-link fence comes in a No. 6 or No. 9 gauge. The No. 6 gauge is thicker and thus more costly. Either gauge is acceptable. Fence is also available with a polyvinyl chloride (PVC) plastic coating (most often green). Coated fencing is more expensive; however, in addition to its aesthetic qualities, it does not rust, as will galvanized fencing.

Line posts that hold the fencing must be no farther than 10 feet apart, and all corner and gate posts should be stabilized by cross braces. All line posts should be embedded at least three feet into the ground. If a wind/visual screen is attached to the fence, all line posts should be embedded in a concrete footer.

Adequate gates should be placed throughout the tennis court complex. These gates need to meet the needs of both instructors and players. Each set of courts in a complex must have an external gate and internal gates. Gates are expensive, but compromising on the number of gates will compromise accessibility to the courts, both internally and externally.

Types of Courts

Courts are classified as either porous (those that allow water to filter and drain through the court surface itself) or nonporous (those that do not allow water to penetrate the surface). The sloping as previously mentioned is for nonporous courts, but is sometimes used in porous courts to carry penetrated water into the subsurface drainage system. Clay, grass, soft composition (fast dry), porous concrete, and various synthetics are porous courts. Concrete, asphalt (cushioned and non-cushioned), hard composition (liquid applied synthetic), and various synthetics are nonporous courts. As a group, asphalt courts are composed of (a) asphalt plant mix, (b) emulsified asphalt mix, (c) plant and emulsified mix, (d) asphalt penetration mix, and (e) asphalt bound system (cushioned) (USTA, 1997).

Numerous items must be considered when selecting the appropriate type of court. Initial cost, cost of upkeep, amount of use, area of country, maintenance personnel needed, type of players, level of competition, and age of players must be factored in when determining the type of court to be selected.

Clay, grass, and soft composition courts are much easier on the legs of players and allow for a much slower ball bounce than other courts. These courts are superior for young players, beginning players, and older players. However, they need a high level of maintenance, which is costly in both materials and personnel. Clay courts must be leveled, must have clay added periodically, require watering, and must be kept free of vegetation. Soft composition courts must be rolled, require watering, and need to have screen and base components added often. Grass courts are similar to golf greens and need daily maintenance. Additionally, grass courts that receive heavy use should be alternated daily. That is, a court used on Monday should not be used again until Wednesday. Consequently, more court space is necessary for heavily used grass courts. Grass courts give a skidding ball bounce, and sometimes an erratic bounce, because of small divots, excessive wear, and taped lines. Overall, clay, grass, and soft composition courts are recommended for commercial clubs where the cost of upkeep can be packaged into member fees. They are not recommended for schools and recreation programs, because of upkeep costs.

Asphalt, concrete, and hard composition courts need less maintenance but provide a faster ball bounce and cause more stress on the legs of players. Of the three types, asphalt courts are the most inexpensive to construct, and composition courts are most costly. Hard composition courts take a few months to cure and harden, and they should not be used until they cure out completely. Hard composition courts can be constructed with multiple layers of cushioning material. The more layers in the courts, the greater the resiliency of the surface will be, but each additional layer of cushioning

Figure 17.1
Tennis court diagram and dimensions

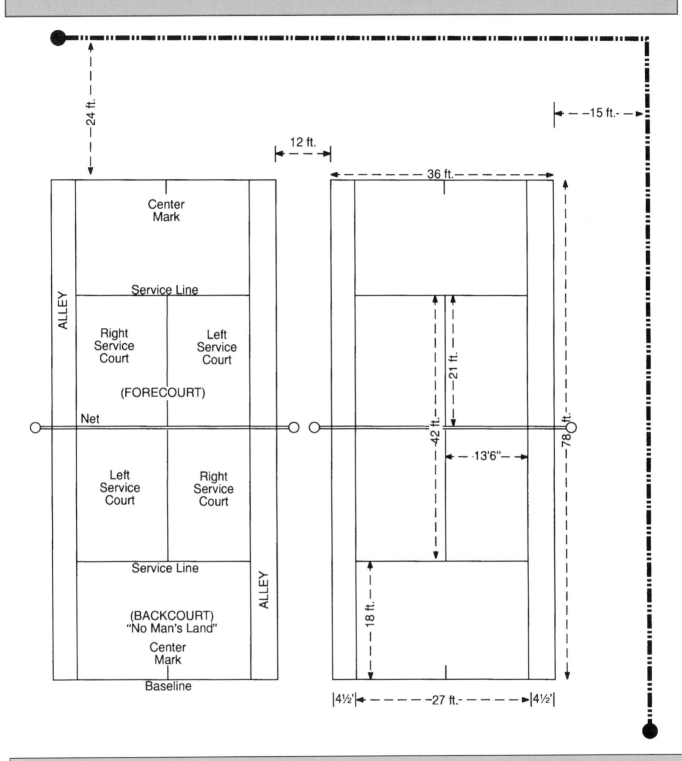

increases the cost. Hard composition courts are smoother than concrete or asphalt; therefore, they cause less wear and tear on balls, shoes, and rackets. Asphalt, concrete, and hard composition courts are recommended for schools and recreation programs. Hard composition is the optimum choice of the three.

Numerous synthetic court surfaces are available. If synthetic outdoor courts are to be constructed, users should be consulted to determine the advantages and disadvantages of

such courts for both players and owners. Also, product descriptions of the material should be studied carefully to help determine which synthetic surface best meets the specific needs of the court under construction.

Regardless of the type of court surface, it is paramount that a tennis court construction firm be employed to build the court(s). A local construction firm, with no tennis court-building experience, should not be permitted to construct the courts. Typically, a builder inexperienced in tennis court construction does not have the expertise to properly build tennis courts. This lack of expertise results in the use of poor construction techniques; more important, it ultimately results in premature (and costly) repairs and renovations.

Costs for an outdoor court surface and base vary, ranging from $10,000 to $15,000 for a clay court to $40,000 to $50,000 for certain synthetic courts. Prices also vary according to the number of courts building (more courts results in a lower cost per court), geographic area of the country, and the amount of grading and drainage required. These costs do not include fencing ($5,000 to $10,000 per court) nor lighting ($5,000 to $10,000 per court). Without a doubt, tennis courts are expensive (USTA, 1997).

Miscellaneous Considerations

All tennis courts should have sufficient secured storage areas, constructed on a concrete base, adjacent to the court complex. The size of the storage area is dictated by the amount and type of equipment to be stored in it. Consider ball hoppers, tennis rackets, fanny packs, ball- throwing machines, and other teaching equipment. The storage area must be waterproof and include shelving, bins, racks, and hooks. If maintenance equipment is needed at the courts, a separate storage area must be built for appropriate machines, rakes, hoses, screens, and materials.

Parking areas need to be built in close proximity to the court complex. The size of the parking area is dictated by the maximum number of user vehicles for the complex in addition to sufficient space for spectator parking. If the tennis complex is lighted, the parking area should be illuminated with high-pressure sodium lights.

Night outdoor tennis is popular in many areas of the country. The recommended surface lighting level for recreational tennis is 38 foot-candles and 63 foot-candles for tournament tennis. Lighting tennis courts is a necessity in some areas. Information as to the number of light standards and how much light will be needed for the complex can be obtained by consulting the local electric company and a manufacturer (e.g., General Electric). A number of outdoor sports lighting companies install quality tennis court lighting systems. If the cost of ongoing high electric use is of concern, coin-operated light boxes can be installed to defray the electricity cost (USTA, 1997).

Although lighting may be optional, water must be provided at each court complex. One water fountain (refrigerated) and one hose connector are recommended for each set of four courts. Electrical outlets must be provided for each court and for any electrical maintenance equipment. All outlets should be located in the fence area and at the storage areas.

Benches need to be provided outside the fencing for those awaiting an empty court. Unobstructed spectator seating should be provided as close to the courts as possible if tournaments or instruction are to be provided on the courts. Courts used for tournaments and high-level competition also require scoring equipment, officials' seating, tables, benches, concession areas, and a protected area for videotaping.

Finally, court surfaces can be a variety of colors. Synthetics can be found in any color, whereas most nonporous tennis courts use a contrasting red and green color scheme. Several factors should be considered when deciding on court colors including: the effect of a color on perception of the ball; how well a color scheme masks or highlights wear and stains; and the color's compatibility with its surroundings (Jones, 1990). Considering ball perspective, single- colored courts are easiest on participants' eyes, due to the fact that multicolored courts promote eye-fatigue as one's vision changes focus from light to dark areas. A subtle difference between actual court coloring (within the lines) and surrounding court coloring (e.g., light green inside the lines, surrounded by dark green) allows for similar reflectivity level and subsequently less eye fatigue. As far as a court's ability to hide stains or wear marks, darker colors are advantageous (Jones, 1990). It should be noted that a variety of colors are available for tennis courts from traditional green to the much-publicized purple courts the Association of Tennis Professionals (ATP) recently experimented with during the Men's Tour of 2000. Choosing a color that is in harmony with the surrounding vegetation (e.g., green courts in an area surrounding by lush green vegetation) provides a nice aesthetic appeal?

Indoor Tennis Courts

Indoor courts can be practical for tennis. Since the weather can affect the ability to play, tennis is a seasonal sport in many parts of the country. Consequently, indoor courts meet a specific need in certain regions.

The number of courts to be enclosed depends on the number of users and the amount of money available for construction. The type of enclosure varies greatly from complex to complex. Prefabricated steel buildings, air structures, tension membrane structures, and standard brick- and-mortar buildings have all been employed successfully. The use of combination structures has some advantages. A translucent tension membrane that allows light onto the courts combined with a turnkey or one standard structure can save roofing costs as well as electricity costs during the day. The following is a cost comparison of three four-court structures:

- sports frame metal building—$561,000 ($140,250 per court),
- tension structure—$422,495 ($105,624 per court), and
- air structure—$366,000 ($91,500 per court) (USTA, 1997).

Lighting should be indirect, so that the tennis ball is not lost in the glare of lights. The background at the end of the courts should be plain. Traffic patterns need careful planning to ensure they do not conflict with play on the courts. Netting must be used between courts since fencing does not exist, and the ceiling height needs to be a minimum of 30 feet. Most indoor court surfaces are synthetic. As with outdoor courts, planning should include storage, parking, water fountains, electrical outlets, seating, concessions, officials' needs, videotaping, and locker/shower facilities.

Paddle Tennis

Dimensions

Paddle tennis courts are 50 feet long by 20 feet wide. The safety space or unobstructed area should be a minimum of 15 feet behind each baseline and 10 feet from each sideline or between each adjacent court. As Figure 17.2 shows, service lines for each side of the court run the entire width of the court, parallel to and three feet inside each baseline. The center service line extends from the service end line, down the middle of the court. The service boxes, therefore, are 22 feet long by 10 feet wide (USPTA, 1996).

An optional restraint line extends the width of the court, 12 feet from the net. These restraint lines are used in doubles play only. All dimensions for paddle tennis court markings

**Figure 17.2
Paddle Tennis Court Dimensions with Restraint Line**

Paddle Tennis Web

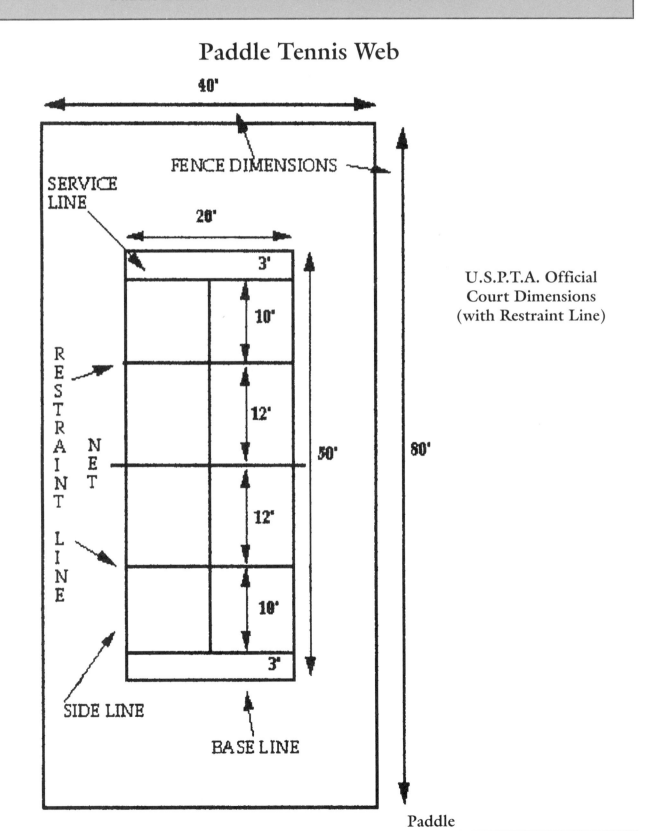

U.S.P.T.A. Official
Court Dimensions
(with Restraint Line)

Paddle

are to the outside of the lines with the exception of the center service line, which is divided equally between service courts.

Miscellaneous Considerations

Paddle tennis net posts are located 18 inches outside of each sideline and are 31 inches in height. Unlike tennis courts, the net is strung taut so that the height measures the same (31 inches) at each post and in the middle of the court. Court surfaces are concrete or asphalt, although competition can also take place on hard-packed sand (USPTA, 1996).

If construction of stand-alone paddle tennis courts is not an option, paddle tennis court markings can be superimposed on a regulation tennis court by using chalk or tape or by painting lighter colored lines, and the net can be lowered to the proper height.

Paddle

Dimensions

The sport of paddle has recently been introduced in the United States and is played in approximately 15 countries. A paddle court is 65 feet, 7 7/16 inches (20 meters) long by 32 feet, 9 3/4 inches (10 meters) wide, with a plus or minus 1% tolerance level. The net, which divides the court in half, extends to the perimeter fence, where it is anchored to the two center posts of this fencing or to an independent anchoring system. Regardless of the anchoring system, the net must coincide with the perimeter fence. The net measures 37 7/16 inches (0.95 meters) at the posts and is two inches lower at the center of the court (35 7/16 inches or 0.90 meters), where it is held down at the center by a central belt that is two inches wide (APA, 1996).

The service lines for each side of the court run parallel to the net and are placed 22 feet, 9 1/2 inches (6.95 meters) from the net. A central service line, two inches wide, runs perpendicular to the net. This line bisects the court, dividing it into equal service zones on both sides of the net. Each service zone measures 22 feet, 9 1/2 inches long by 16 feet, 4 7/8 inches wide. All measurements for the court markings are made from the net or center of the central, perpendicular service line (APA, 1996).

The paddle court is completely enclosed by backwalls, sidewalls, and fencing on the remaining sideline areas. The backwalls, at the end of each court, measure the width of the court (32 feet, 9 3/4 inches) and are between 9 feet, 10 1/8 inches (3 meters) and 13 feet, 1 1/2 inches (4 meters) in height. The partial side or "wing walls" extend 13 feet, 1 1/2 inches (4 meters) from the backwalls. The wing walls decrease in height from 9 feet, 10 1/8 inches (3 meters) to 5 feet (1.5 meters), beginning at the wing wall's midpoint (6 feet, 6 3/4 inches, that is, two meters from the junction of the back and wing walls) to the end of the wall. This decrease in height on the wing wall should be at approximately a 38-degree angle. The remainder of the court perimeter is enclosed with a wire fence measuring 13 feet, 1 1/2 inches (4 meters) in height from the court surface (APA, 1996). (APA, Paddle Tennis Publication and http://virtual.chattanooga.net/paddle/court.htm)

Miscellaneous Considerations

Paddle court surfaces vary from hard courts to artificial grass. The sport can be played on outdoor as well as indoor courts. If played indoors, however, courts must have a minimum ceiling clearance of 25 feet.

Backwalls and partial sidewalls consist of stucco, concrete, or glass and/or a blindex material that provides for optimum spectator viewing of the court from all surrounding areas.

Portable courts (not inclusive of surfacing) are available for purchase for approximately $25,000. Contact the American Paddle Association at 1-800-861-1539 for further information.

Platform Tennis

Dimensions

A platform tennis court is 44 feet long by 20 feet wide. The entire platform surface is 60 feet by 30 feet, which allows for eight feet of space beyond each baseline and five feet of space between each doubles sideline and the fencing. All court markings are two inches wide, and measurements are to the outside of the lines except for the center service line, which is equally divided between the right and left service courts. Service lines running parallel to the net are 12 feet from the net, and doubles alleys are two feet wide (Flynn, 1985).

Net posts are located 18 inches outside of the doubles sidelines, and the net height is 37 inches at the posts and 34 inches at the center of the court. Fencing, which measures 12 feet in height, is 16-gauge hexagonal, galvanized, one-inch flat wire mesh fabric.

Miscellaneous Considerations

The total area needed for construction of a platform tennis court is 2,584 square feet (68 feet by 38 feet). This allows for the foundation beams at the corners and at the locations of the uprights (Figure 17.4). Specifications for a platform tennis court typically call for four-inch-by- six-inch foundation beams across the base of the platform. It is recommended that wood beams be waterproofed with creosote. Each beam rests on four evenly spaced concrete blocks; the blocks should be placed such that the beams rest four feet apart (measured from center to center). The foundation beams at the corners and at the locations of the uprights must project far enough to afford a base for the outer support of the uprights. The deck surface should be constructed of Douglas fir planks measuring two feet by six feet. The planks should be laid 1/8 inch to 1/4 inch apart to allow for drainage. The corner uprights and the intermediate uprights must measure 12 feet from their base (i.e., the deck surface) to their top. The corner uprights should be constructed of four-inch-by-four-inch beams; the intermediate uprights should measure two inches by four inches (Flynn, 1985).

The construction of the backstop is a detailed procedure. The tops of the uprights are connected by "top rails"— bars that measure two inches by four inches. These rails are bolted horizontally to the insides of the tops of the uprights and measure two inches by four inches along the sides. There-

Figure 17.3
Paddle court

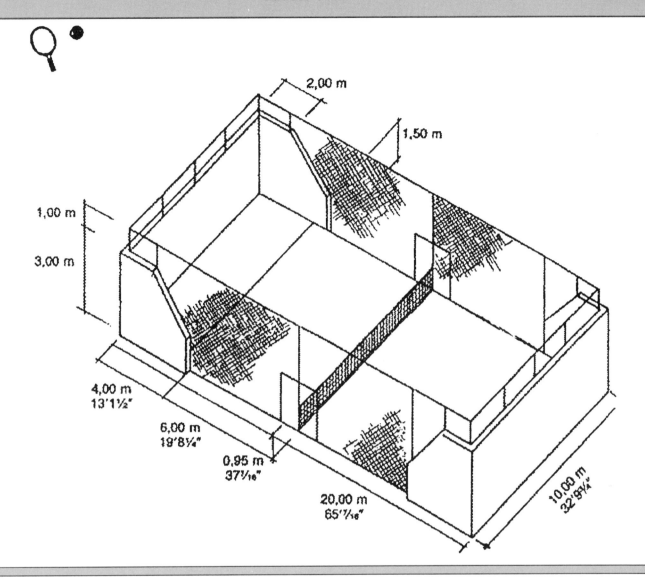

fore, the rails to which the wire fabric is attached project inside the uprights by four inches at the ends and two inches at the sides. All of the space around the platform is covered by wire except 12-foot openings in the center of each side, at least one of which is closed with either netting. This closure is for containing errant balls. All wiring should be attached vertically on the inside of the uprights and stretched in six-foot widths from the top down to the tension rail below (Flynn, 1985).

Badminton

Dimensions

A badminton doubles court is 44 feet in length by 20 feet wide; a singles court is the same length (44 feet), but three feet narrower (17 feet). All court markings, including the center service line, short service lines, and doubles long service lines, are marked in yellow or white and measure 1.5 inches in width. All dimensions are measured from the outside of the court lines, except for the center service line, which is equally divided between service courts.

The court is bisected laterally by a net that is exactly five feet above the ground at the center of the court and five feet, one inch at the net posts. The net posts are placed directly on the doubles sidelines. However, when it is not possible to have the posts over the sidelines, this boundary should be marked with a thin post or strips of material attached to the sideline and rising to the net cord.

The safety distance or unobstructed space behind the back boundary line should measure eight feet behind and four to five feet outside of each sideline or between courts.

Miscellaneous Considerations

Ideally, ceiling clearance for indoor badminton should be no less than 30 feet over the entire full-court area. This is the standard for international play. However, a 25-foot clearance is the recommended minimum and sufficient for other levels of play.

Figure 17.4
Platform tennis court

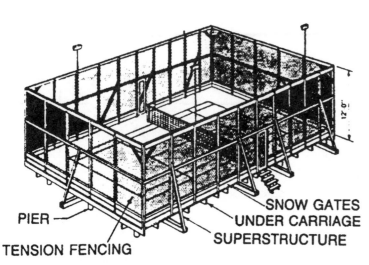

PIER

TENSION FENCING

SNOW GATES
UNDER CARRIAGE
SUPERSTRUCTURE

Isometric showing fence (typical wood construction)

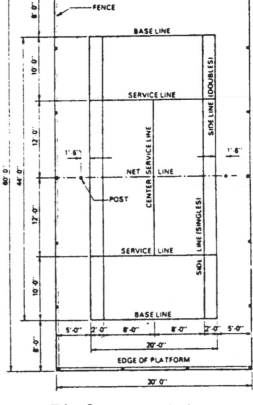

Platform tennis layout

Basketball

Dimensions

Indoor and outdoor basketball courts vary in size depending upon the level of competitive play. It is recommended that courts for junior high, high school, and recreational play be 50 feet wide by 84 feet long. Competitive collegiate and professional basketball requires a 50-foot-by- 94-foot court. Regardless of the level of play, a 10-foot unobstructed or safety space is highly recommended, especially considering today's game and the increased size of the players. However, if a court is constructed with less than 10 feet of safety space (eight feet is a minimum at the end lines and six feet on the sidelines), wall padding should be installed the entire distance of the wall that parallels the side or end line. Another important safety consideration concerns any glass or windows that are part of the surrounding basketball gymnasium. All glass and windows should be shatterproof safety glass. Finally, in a gymnasium setting, especially where other sports can be played, a height clearance of 30 feet is strongly recommended, but a minimum clearance of 23 feet is impera-

tive. Appendix A provides a detailed display of basketball court markings (NCAA, 2000). Concerning the size and colors of the lines, cut several guidelines should be kept in mind:

- All lines must be two inches wide, except for the neutral zones.
- The color of the boundary lines should match the midcourt markings.
- The color of the lane space and neutral zone markings should contrast with the color of the boundary lines (NCAA, 2000).

Note: The three-point arch measures 19 feet, 9 inches from the center of the basket for both high school and collegiate competition.

Miscellaneous Considerations

Collegiate competition requires backboards that are transparent and measure six feet horizontally by four feet vertically. The backboard should have a two-inch white-lined target centered behind the goal. This target should measure 24 inches horizontally by 18 inches vertically. The backboard

Figure 17.5
Badminton court

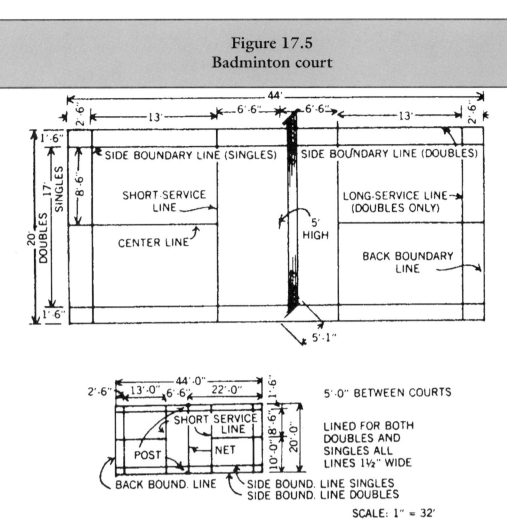

should also have two-inch-thick gray padding on the bottom and up the sides for the players' protection (Head-Summit & Jennings, 1996). Attached to the backboard is an 18-inch (inner diameter) bright orange ring, mounted parallel to and 10 feet above the floor. Although the standard height for a basketball goal (from rim to floor) is 10 feet, adjustable standards that allow the rim to be set at the standard height or lower (i.e., as low as eight feet) provide opportunities for young children to practice shooting at a goal that is more age-appropriate (NCAA, 2000).

The gymnasium flooring is an important consideration. It is imperative that the flooring provide sliding characteristics (the surface friction of a finished floor) and shock absorption that conform to criteria established by the Deutches Institute for Normung (DIN) standards (Table 17.1), to help minimize the possibility of participant injury. Also, the flooring should provide adequate ball bounce or deflection as prescribed under the DIN standards. A final consideration is the placement of padding in appropriate areas, such as the wall directly behind each basketball backboard, especially if the distance between the backboard and wall is less than 10 feet.

Outdoor basketball courts should run lengthwise in approximately a north-south direction. Proper drainage can be insured by slanting courts from one side to the other, allowing "one inch of slant . . . for every 10 feet of court" (Flynn, 1985). If a backboard is mounted on an in-ground pole, the pole should be padded. Additionally, the pole should be off

the playing court, and the backboard should be extended at least four feet onto the court. Fencing is not a necessity; however, if finances allow, anodized aluminum chain-link should be used. The fence height should be a minimum of 10 feet. The fence posts should be placed six inches to one foot inside the hard surface, and the fence fabric should be affixed on the inside of these supporting posts. Posts should be mounted in concrete such that 35% to 40% of the length of the pole is above the surface (Flynn, 1985). Gates or fences should be constructed large enough to allow maintenance equipment to be brought into the court areas.

Volleyball

Dimensions

Although volleyball courts within the United States traditionally measure 30 feet in width by 60 feet in length, the United States Volleyball Rules (which are those of the International Volleyball Federation) call for the court to measure 59 feet by 29.5 feet (18 meters by nine meters). Notably, all court dimensions are measured from the outside edge of the lines, and all court lines should be two inches (five centimeters) wide (Sanford, 1997).

A minimum of six feet, six inches of safety or unobstructed space should surround an indoor court; however, the ideal situation is to provide at least 10 feet from the sidelines and 13 feet from the end lines (NCAA, 1997).

Table 17.1
DIN Flooring Standards

The flooring for a multiuse exercise area should adhere to Deutsches Institute for Normung (DIN) standards. These standards require that a floor meet six criteria:

- Shock absorption—a floor's ability to reduce the impact of contact with the floor surface. The greater the shock absorption, the more protective it is, because it reduces impact forces. An aerobics floor, for example, would need more shock absorption than a basketball court.
- Standard vertical deformation—the actual vertical deflection of the floor upon impact. The greater the deformation, the more the floor deflects downward. Floors with minimal deformation are not good at absorbing impact forces.
- Deflective indentation—the actual vertical deflection of the floor at a distance 50 cm from the point of impact. The greater the indentation, the more likely impact at one spot will cause deflection at a distant point.
- Sliding characteristics—the surface friction of the finished floor. A floor with poor sliding characteristics would be inappropriate for aerobics or basketball.
- Ball reflection (game-action response)—the response of a ball dropped on the floor compared to a ball dropped on concrete.
- Rolling load—a floor's ability to withstand heavy weight without breaking or sustaining permanent damage.
  These DIN criteria are then used to evaluate the effectiveness of a floor. A floor will have one of three functions:
- Sports function—A floor that serves a sports function enhances athletic performance. Surface friction and ball reflection are important here.
- Protective function—A floor that serves a protective function reduces the risk of injury (e.g., from a fall) during activity. Shock absorption is important here.
- Material-technical function—A floor that serves a material-technical function meets the sports and protective functions.

In a health/fitness facility, the gymnasium and multipurpose floors are classified under sports function or material-technical function. The aerobics floor is classified under protective function, with some sports function characteristics.

A floor surface that has a material-technical function should meet the following DIN criteria:

- Shock absorption—53% minimum
- Standard vertical 2.3 mm minimum deformation
- Deflective indentation—15% maximum
- Sliding characteristics—0.5 to 0.7 range
- Ball deflection—90% minimum
- Rolling load—0337.6 lb

Ceiling clearance is a critical issue. Although United States Volleyball Rules call for a minimum or 23 feet (seven meters) of unobstructed space as measured from the floor, 30 feet of overhead clearance is highly recommended (Neville, 1994, p.6). Figure 17.6 provides a detailed display of volleyball floor markings. Notably, in recent years, the service zone has been extended the full width of the court as a result of a rule change permitting players to serve anywhere behind the endline.

Net Height

The volleyball net height is seven feet, 11 5/8 inches (2.43 meters) for men's competition and seven feet, 4 1/8 inches (2.24m) for women's competition, as measured at the center of the playing court. The two ends of the net, directly over the sidelines, must be the same height from the playing surface and may not exceed the official height by 3/4 inch (although a constant height is far more desirable). The net height may be varied for specific age groups in the following ways (Sanford, 1997):

The net itself is 39 inches wide and a minimum of 32 feet long. The posts (supporting standards) are fixed to the playing surface at least 19 1/2 inches to 39 inches from each sideline. Two white side bands, two inches wide and 39 inches long, are fastened around the net vertically and placed perpendicularly over each sideline. Six-foot-long antennas are attached at the outer edge of each side band and extend 32 inches above the height of the net (USVA, 1997).

Miscellaneous Considerations

One of the most important safety factors is to provide poles that are sunk directly below floor level in sleeves or that telescope up from below the floor. Volleyball standards/poles that are on mounted or weighted bases are extremely hazardous. Likewise, volleyball net systems that rely on guy wires are not desirable. If wires are part of an existing volleyball net system, they should be clearly identified and padded. Furthermore, volleyball posts should be padded to a minimum height of six feet, and all official stands should be padded.

Figure 17.6
Volleyball court dimensions

The Playing Court

Design of the Net

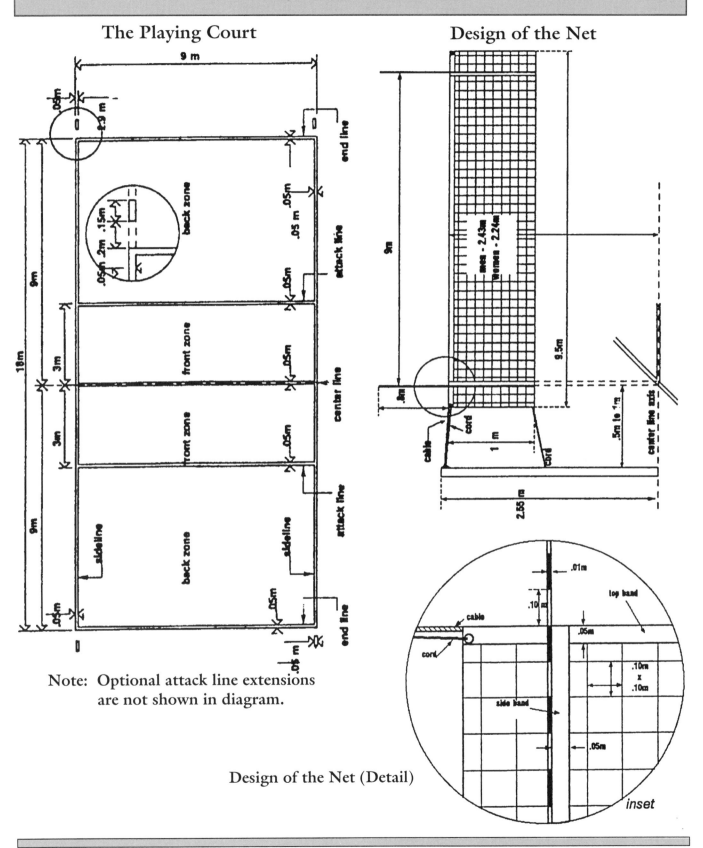

Note: Optional attack line extensions
are not shown in diagram.

Design of the Net (Detail)

Ideally, in a facility built primarily for volleyball, the walls (particularly those behind each endline) should be painted a color that provides some contrast to the color of volleyballs, which are generally white. This contrast in color allows participants to more easily track the flight of the ball during play. Additionally, the ceiling color should be an off-white or other light color that provides a contrasting background for players attempting to follow the flight path of the volleyball.

Light fixtures need to be placed at least as high as the lowest ceiling obstructions to avoid any shadowing effects. Also, lighting needs to be bright (a minimum of 27.9 foot-candles, measured at one meter above the playing surface). The lights, however, should not be closely grouped such that they would create a blinding effect for participants (USVA, 1997).

Outdoor Sand Volleyball Court Guidelines

The dimensions for an outdoor sand court are identical to indoor volleyball court dimensions (i.e., 59 feet (18 meters) long by 29 feet, six inches (nine meters) wide, as measured from the outer edge of the boundary lines). It should be noted that at press time, the Federation Internationale de Volleyball (FIVB), the world governing body, had just approved the reduction of the dimensions of the two-person outdoor sand volleyball court from 16 meters in length to eight meters in width. In non-metric measurements, this particular professional court is six feet shorter, and three feet more narrow than the traditional measurements.

Ideally, the court should be constructed with the net running in an east-west direction so that the morning and evening sun does not face directly into the eyes of one team. Outdoor courts should provide a minimum of nine feet, ten inches or three meters of free space-composed of sand-surrounding the court area. In other words, the complete sand area should measure a minimum of 80 feet long by 50 feet wide. For professional competitions, the court should be centered on an area 93 feet long by 57 feet wide. Standard net heights are the same as for the indoor game: seven feet 11, 5/8 inches (2.43 meters) for men's and coed play, and seven feet, 4 1/8 inches for women's and reverse coed play. Children ages 10 to 16 may have the net height adjusted according to the standards listed above regarding indoor volleyball net adjustments (Sandorti, 1995).

Boundary lines are brightly colored 1/4 inch rope or 1 1/2-inch webbing tied to the four corners with buried deadman anchors. No centerline is required for outdoor play, but approximately 14 feet of rope will be needed, beyond the 177 feet total necessary for court lines, to anchor the corners (Sandorti, 1995).

Net supports should be made of metal, wood, or other material that will withstand tension. The supports should be about 14 feet long and should be buried five feet deep using a concrete footing unless the soil is solid, in which case packing in and washing the soil should suffice. These support standards should be set 39 inches (one meter) from the boundary of the court. Any less space will leave insufficient room for the full net and adjusting cables (Sandorti, 1995).

Suggested specifications for different net supports are as follows. Metal net supports should be four-inch, diameter schedule 40, galvanized steel pipes. Round wood poles should measure eight inches in diameter and should be made of treated, weather-resistant wood. Square wood supports are not recommended because of the potential for participant injury on corner edges. In all instances, padding the support poles is an important safety measure. If the support does not have equal sides, the narrower side should be the net anchor side (facing the court) (Sandorti, 1995).

Hooks, hook-and-eye hardware, and any winch hardware (padded) are necessary to attach the net to the standards. One way to provide for total adjustability of net height is to have four metal collars made that have loops for attaching the net (i.e., the top and the bottom of the net on both sides) that can slide up and down the poles. Holes can be drilled into the collars and set screws inserted, which can be tightened with an allen wrench. Finally, the net should be 10 meters in length with a cable top, although strong rope such as Kevlar also works well. However, the effort of fashioning this system can be avoided by purchasing outdoor standards, now available from a variety of vendors.

Actual sand court construction should start with the excavation of the area with a Bobcat or front-end loader. The court area should be excavated between two and three feet in depth. In low-lying areas, such as shoreline areas of Florida, the court should be excavated only six to eight inches. This will yield an elevated court rather than one that is flush with the ground. Also, the dirt that is excavated should be used to create a slight slope up to the court.

The court perimeter edges can be contained to keep dirt and grass from leaking into the court. Lawn edging material or rubber handrail material from escalator companies seated atop two-inch-by-six-inch wooden boundaries is a good method of providing perimeter boundaries. If railroad ties or similar materials are used, the top edges should be padded to minimize injury potential (Sandorti, 1995).

Drainage of the court under the sand is important. The installation of leaching pipe on the standards with a slant of 14° is highly recommended for a good permanent court. Perforated pipe (approximately two rolls of 250 feet) can be laid perforated side down with the open end at the low point of the court. Each section of the pipe should be wrapped with a flex wrap or "handicap wrap", which can be purchased at plumbing supply houses. This wrap prevents sand from filling up the pipes. Finally, the drainage points should lead away from the court at the lowest point (Sandorti, 1995).

The next step is to set the standards in concrete. Poles should be set at a slight angle outward from the court to allow for any bending caused by eventual net tension. To allow for ease of maintenance or replacement, steel poles should be seated in steel sleeves so that they can be easily removed.

Small pea-sized gravel used for drainage (#56, #57, #2, or #3) should then be placed over the drainage pipe to a depth of about one foot. Approximately 2,600 cubic feet (110 tons) of this gravel is necessary. Plastic landscaping or ground stabilization filter fabric (a woven polyblend that will not deteriorate easily) is placed over the gravel to prevent the sand from washing through (Sandorti, 1995).

The final step in sand court construction is depositing the sand. A good court requires an investment in good sand. Sand comes in a variety of grades; some types are very "dirty" and unsuitable for a court. Washed beach (dune), washed plaster, washed masonry, or washed river sand are the most desirable types of court sand. The most highly recommended sand is silica sand, regionally available by contacting Best Sand at (800) 237-4986. This sand should be deposited and raked level around the court; it should measure one to two feet in depth. The minimum recommended depth of the sand is 19 1/2 inches. In essence, a sand court requires approximately 5,200 cubic feet (205 tons of washed sand). The final price tag for the construction of a good sand volleyball court will range anywhere from $6,000 to $10,000 (Sandorti, 1995).

Racquetball, Handball, and Squash Courts

Dimensions and Design Considerations

Four-wall courts for squash and handball have been in sports facilities for over three quarters of a century. Originally, these courts were made from Portland cement with smaller- than-normal doors. Paddleball and racquetball were first played on these courts in the late 1950s and early 1960s. Today's courts are designed for racquetball, handball, and squash, even though other activities may also be played in these enclosed four-wall courts (such as walleyball and Bi-Rakits). Today's state-of-the-art courts are constructed of laminated panels and/or tempered glass. In the planning of four-wall courts, teaching, competition, accessibility, and amenities need to be considered (AARA, 1997).

The recommended four-wall racquetball/handball court is 40 feet long and 20 feet wide, with a front wall and ceiling height of 20 feet, and a back wall at least 14 feet high (Figure 17.7). The lower back wall provides a space for a viewing or for an instructional gallery, which may be open with a three- to four-foot-high railing. Clear polycarbonate sheeting should be placed under the railing for seated viewing purposes and safety. The gallery may be totally enclosed with clear polycarbonate sheeting and a small four-foot-square open window. An open gallery is recommended for communication purposes between instructors/officials and the players. But an open gallery poses the risk of spectators being hit by a ball; therefore, appropriate signage should be posted to indicate this hazard.

Squash is becoming very popular in some regions of the United States. The international singles squash court is 21 feet wide and 32 feet long. The old North American standard of an 18- foot-6-inches-wide singles squash court is no longer acceptable and should be avoided. North American doubles squash is played on a larger court measuring 25 feet wide and 45 feet long (Figures 17.8a–17.8c). Squash court wall heights vary compared to the standard 20-foot racquetball/handball wall heights (USSRA, 1997).

When more than a single battery of courts is to be constructed, the batteries should be arranged so the back walls of each are separated by a corridor approximately 10 feet wide and 12 feet high. Courts should be located in the same area of the facility rather than being spread out. Courts should be placed on adjacent walls rather than on opposite walls in order to achieve close proximity, thereby aiding in quality instructional time. Corridors and galleries should be illuminated with indirect light. The minimum number of courts for schools should be dictated by maximum class size and total student enrollment. Normally no fewer than six to eight courts are recommended, which can adequately handle 15 to 20 students at a time. The number of courts for clubs and private usage is determined by the number of users and by the popularity of racquetball, handball, and squash in any given area.

Walls may be constructed of hard plaster, Portland cement, wood, laminated panels, or tempered glass. Laminated panels and tempered glass are recommended. The panels are four-by-eight-foot particle board or resin-impregnated kraft papers covered with a melamine sheet. The panels come in different thicknesses, from 13/16 inches to 1 1/8 inches.

The thicker the panel is, the truer the rebound action of the ball will be; however, the thicker panel is also more expensive. Panels are mounted on aluminum channels or metal studs. Screws that hold them to the wall superstructure are inset and covered with a plug. This creates a monolithic surface for the walls. The panels have a high life expectancy and are easily maintained. Glass walls of 0.5- inch-thick tempered, heat-soaked glass are ideal but expensive. All courts are recommended to have the minimum of glass back walls, and one court should have an additional glass side wall. This will offer good instructional and spectator viewing (Figure 17.9). Finally, one-way glass, which provides spectator viewing, but appears to be a solid surface to participants within the court is a relatively new innovation.

If glass walls are utilized, spectator and instructional viewing areas should be planned for carefully. These areas usually are stepped, with carpeted risers along the side wall or back wall of the court. A built-in, two-way audio system should be utilized for this court. Carpet color should not be totally dark and definitely should not be blue or green, since ball visibility through the glass walls is obscured with dark colors as a background. Courts with two glass sidewalls, those with glass sidewalls and a glass back wall, and all glass-wall courts are superior to other courts; however, their cost is prohibitive in most facilities.

Doors are standard size and are placed in the middle of the back wall, not in the corners of the court. The corners are crucial real estate in intermediate and advanced racquet sports, so doors that can cause "untrue" bounces should not be placed there. Door handles should be small and recessed, and all door framing should be flush on the inside of the court. Doors should open into the court, and there should be no thresholds under the doors.

Floors should be hardwood, as in standard gymnasium construction. The more sophisticated the floor system is, the more costly it will be. Resilient wood floors play differently than more rigid system wood floors, but they are more expensive. Any good hard maple floor system is acceptable. Floors should be flush with sidewalls so that no joint is evident. Joints collect dirt, dust, and debris and are a maintenance nightmare. Floors should be resurfaced as needed with a high-grade finish. When floors need refinishing, they become slippery and can be very dangerous. The amount of use, the types of shoes worn during play, and the amount of dirt and grit brought into the courts on shoes will dictate how often refinishing is needed. Floors should be cleaned with a treated mop daily or as needed. Synthetic floors should not be used in racquet courts, because they create too much friction and do not allow feet to slide, which is needed for effective and safe racquet sports.

Court line markings should be a lighter color, rather than a dark color like blue or black, which helps the participants' visual acuity in following a dark ball across lighter lines. Off- white, light pastel yellow, or light grey lines are best. Squash lines are red.

For racquetball and handball courts, the first 12 feet of the ceiling from the front wall should be devoid of any heat or ventilating ducts. This portion of the ceiling must be hard and compatible to the wall surfaces for ball rebounding. Lighting and any other fixtures in the ceiling must be totally flush. The rear eight feet of the ceiling is not as crucial, since this part of the ceiling is used very seldom in play.

Figure 17.7
Four wall handball and racquetball courts and dimensions

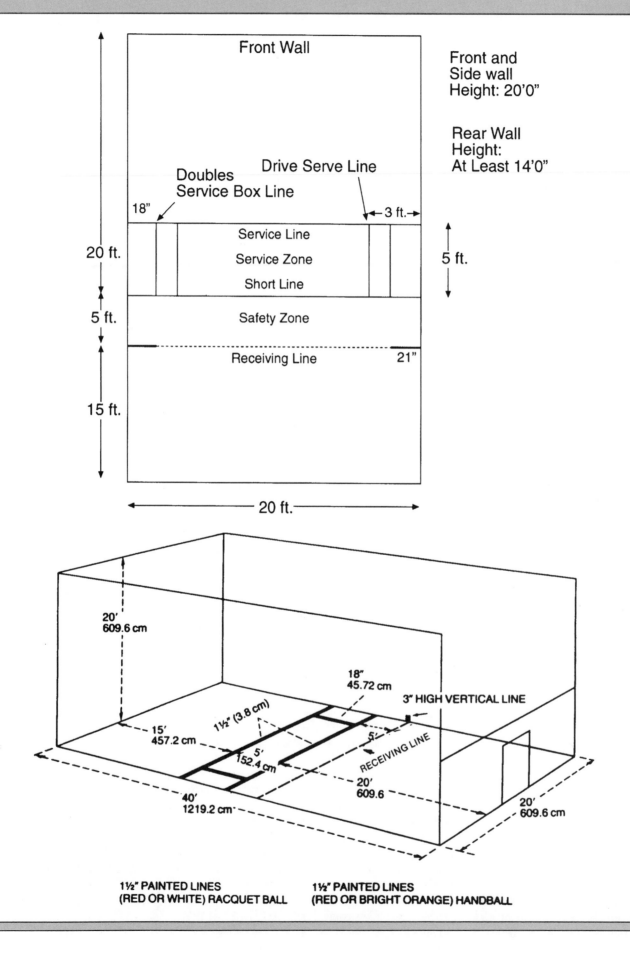

1½" PAINTED LINES
(RED OR WHITE) RACQUET BALL

1½" PAINTED LINES
(RED OR BRIGHT ORANGE) HANDBALL

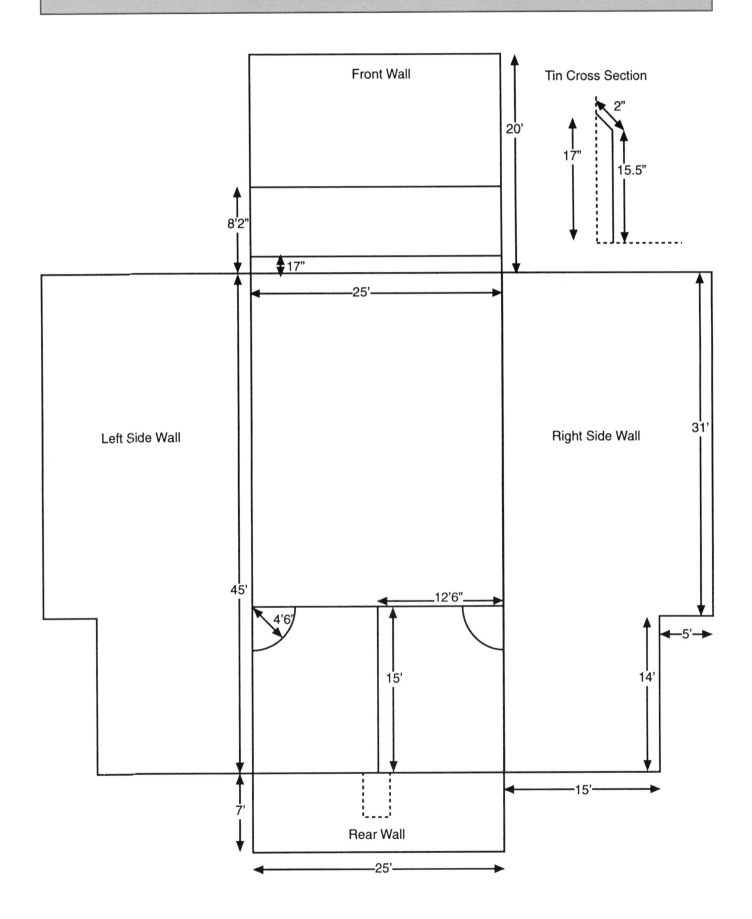

**Figure 17.8a
North American doubles squash court**

Figure 17.8b
International singles squash court

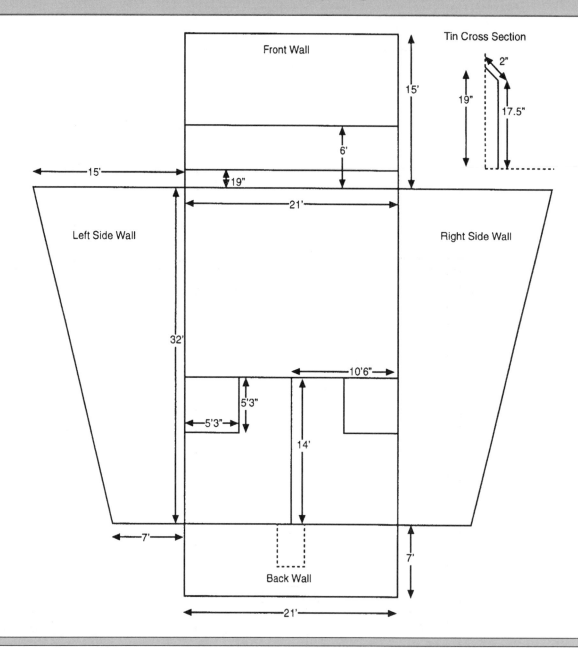

The ceiling is not used in squash, but it should still be made of an impact-resistant material in case errant balls hit it. Panels or Portland cement would be good for the front 12 feet of the ceiling.

If wallyball is to be played in the court, the ceiling must be strong enough to absorb the impact of the volleyball. Panels, but not Portland cement, work well in wallyball courts.

Lighting, Acoustics, and Ventilation

All lighting must be flush with the ceiling. Lights should illuminate all portions of the court equally; therefore, they should be spread throughout the ceiling. Shadows and low-light areas are not acceptable in these courts. Light accessibility for changing bulbs must be planned carefully. Since there is normally a battery of courts, the chore of changing

light bulbs is magnified by the number of courts needing a bulb-changing system. The best lightbulb-changing method for courts is to have a crawl space above the ceiling. This enables maintenance personnel to change bulbs from above. This system eliminates the need to use cumbersome hydraulic lifts and/or "A" frame ladders (AARA, 1997).

A metal halide system of lighting is recommended. Metal halide lights give the most light at the least cost. Metal halide bulbs also have a long life expectancy. However, to garner cost savings and longevity, the court lights must be on at all times. Turning these lights off and on causes a delay (about six to eight minutes) for the bulbs to obtain full brightness. Turning halide lights off and on also increases the cost of lighting and decreases bulb life expectancy. Metal halide lights should be controlled from a central console, not at each court.

Figure 17.8c

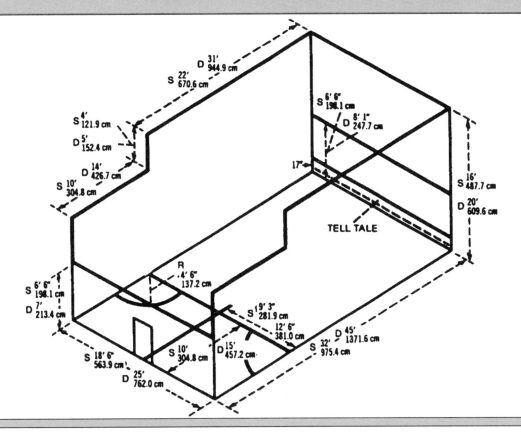

If single courts are not used often, a recommended method of turning the lights on and off is to install switches that are activated by opening or closing the door to the court. This method requires a metal halide lighting system. When the door is closed, lights in the court will turn on. When the door is opened, the lights will turn off automatically, leaving only the night light to burn continuously. Usually, a two- to three-minute delay occurs before the lights go off after the door has been opened, preventing a disruption of lighting during the brief time it takes for players to exit or exchange the court.

A relatively new concept utilizes an annunciator (an electrically controlled signal board) to indicate to the building reservation/control center which courts are occupied at any time. Lights on the signal board are activated by the trip switch on each door as it opens or closes. When lights are to be constantly turned off and on, incandescent bulbs work fairly well. Fluorescent lights should not be used in racquet courts, because they tend to flicker and can cause visual acuity problems during play. If wallyball is to be played in the court, stronger light shields and light fixtures will be needed to absorb the impact of a volleyball.

Court walls and floors are hard surfaces, and much sound reverberates in the courts. For non-glass court surfaces, acoustical treatment is important within the surfaces. Insulation in the walls and ceiling will help to buffer sound within a court and also between courts. The rear eight feet of the ceiling should be constructed of acoustical tiles, because this area is seldom used in racquetball/handball and never used in squash. Although these tiles provide minimal acoustical treatment, it is very important to attempt to control sound, and they should be considered in each court. If wallyball is played in a court, soft acoustical treatment cannot be installed on the ceiling.

Ventilation should be provided by air conditioning. The ventilation of each court is very important so that moisture does not build on wall surfaces, making the courts unplayable. Ample air circulation and dehumidifying the air are major concerns in the ventilation of the courts. Only air conditioning can provide circulation, cooling, and dehumidification. To minimize the potential for moisture, courts should not be built underground with walls exposed to external moisture. Moisture and/or condensation can easily intrude to the interior wall surfaces of the courts. If courts must be built underground, extra waterproofing needs to be completed in this portion of the facility.

All vents for air circulation should be located in the back eight feet of the ceiling for racquetball and handball (Turner, 1992), but squash courts may have vents anywhere in the ceiling. The temperature of each court should be controlled by an individual, jar-proof, flush thermostat that is preset and tamper-proof.

Miscellaneous Considerations

Small storage boxes should be built flush with wall surfaces into side walls near the back wall of each court to house valuables and extra balls. The door to this storage box should be constructed of clear polycarbonate sheeting. Storage areas for students' coats, books, and other gear should be provided in an area near the courts. Extra storage must be provided for rain gear and winter gear where applicable. Se-

Figure 17.9
Racquetball teaching court

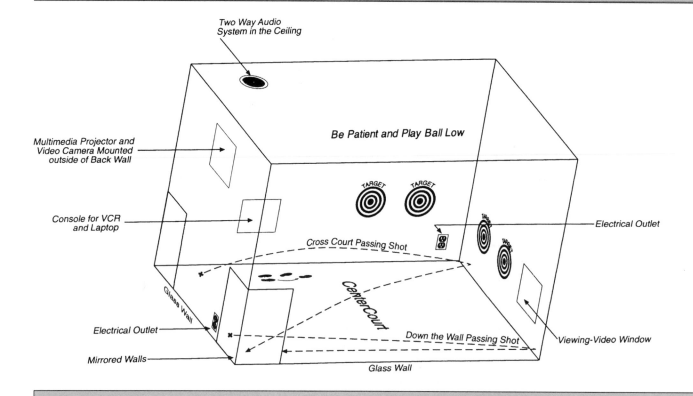

cured storage for racquetball rackets, handball gloves, squash rackets, eye guards, and balls should be provided near the court area.

All courts should have joints, seams, doors, vents, lights, and corners flush with the surrounding surface. Any unevenness in a court will cause untrue ball rebounds, which are unacceptable in court games. Each court should be equipped with a two-way audio system. Access to this system should be housed in the central console. This audio system can be used to make announcements, to provide music, and for instructional purposes between the court user and the instructor.

Effective external signage is important for all courts. Signs for court rules need to be posted near each court entrance. Rule signs such as "Eye guards are mandatory" and "Only non-marking athletic shoes may be worn in courts" are typical for racquet courts. Other signage includes the designation of a challenge court(s) with rules and a daily sign-up sheet. Courts also must be numbered, and a visible wall clock near the courts is important.

Courts and galleries should be accessible to individuals with disabilities. Doors should be wide enough for wheelchair passage and have no barriers, such as thresholds or steps at access points. Additionally, the courts' location within the sport facility and a route from adjacent parking areas must be free of barriers.

University courts should be built at a location with easy access from all points on campus, and ample parking in close proximity of the courts should be carefully planned. Within the sport complex, the courts should be located near the console control area.

In any facility, all courts need to be situated near refrigerated water fountains. In a commercial court complex, an area close to the courts must be designated for a pro shop. This area needs to be large enough to accommodate the types of equipment and apparel to be sold. The pro shop area must also be able to be secured by either lockable doors or a metal mesh gate since it will not be staffed during all operation hours of the court area.

If there is a hallway access to courts and/or galleries, the hallway must have a ceiling height of 12 feet. A lower ceiling height lends itself to damage from individuals jumping up and hitting it with their rackets. Light shields in these hallways should be flush with the ceiling to deter breakage. Skylights above the court ceiling height, in gallery areas only, add a nice aesthetic touch. The use of a translucent glass or polycarbonate sheeting in skylights will alleviate glare problems.

Movable metal "telltales" can be installed across the front of handball/racquetball courts for use in for squash instruction. However, the courts are racquetball size, not squash size. The floors, walls, ceilings, lighting, heating, and ventilation of squash courts are similar to those of four-wall racquetball/handball courts.

One court at any instructional facility should be a permanent teaching court. There should be a three-foot-by-three-foot front-wall viewing and videotaping square. This "window" should be covered with a single sheet of clear polycarbonate sheeting. The window should be three or four feet high from the floor and closer to one side or the other of the front wall. Access to this window from outside the court must be provided. There should be a small lockable area behind the viewing window, preferably five feet by five feet with a ceiling height of eight feet. An adjustable-height table and chair need to be in this small room, and a small area for storage of a portable video camera, videotapes, and speed gun should be provided there as well.

The teaching court also needs two flush, covered, electrical outlets for power sources. A multimedia projector and a video camera should be mounted within the back wall. Both projector and camera need to be protected with a clear polycarbonate sheet. A lockable, flush console should be built into a side wall to house a laptop computer and VCR. This setup allows for slides, videotapes, television, and computer viewing. None of this high-tech equipment ever needs to be moved into or around the courts.

Polycarbonate mirrors, each section measuring six feet long by six feet high, should be placed flush on two adjacent walls. The back wall and a side wall work best for the mirrors. Mirrors are great instructional tools, because they allow the students to view themselves.

Foot templates for various movement patterns should be permanently placed on the floor. Different colors may be utilized along with arrows to indicate foot movement direction. Ball flight path patterns should be painted on the floor, and flight paths for a down-the-wall passing shot and/or a cross-court passing shot should actually be templated onto the floor. Again, different colors should be used for different ball paths. An elliptical circle six feet wide and four feet deep should be painted and labeled "center court" in the center court area of the court. An area three feet square also needs to be painted and labeled in each back corner. The back corners and center court are the two most important areas in racquet courts.

Targets of varying size and height should be placed on both the front wall and side walls to serve as aiming points for various shots. A few targets also need to be placed on the ceiling near the front wall as ceiling shot templates for racquetball and handball. Skill templates should be placed in a few selected areas of the court, such as "Be patient and play the ball low" and "Culminate all sources of power at ball-racquet impact." These become constant visual educational reminders for students.

Ideally, the teaching court should have one glass side wall and a glass back wall. A glass back wall alone will suffice. A two-way communication system must be in place for the instructor, when in the court, to be able to talk to students out of the court and vice-versa (See Figure 17.9).

Good court construction is paramount for teaching, competition, safety, and maintenance. All court surfaces must be flush. The activity that is played in the court will be a determining factor in both the size of the court and the materials used in court construction.

Shuffle Board

Dimensions

The actual playing area of a shuffleboard court is 39 feet long and six feet wide. However, the area outside the court markings includes a six-foot, six-inch standing area at both ends of the court and a two-foot area adjacent to the sideline boundaries. Thus, the entire area for a shuffleboard court should measure 52 feet in length and 10 feet in width (Flynn, 1985).

Figure 17.10
Shuffleboard court

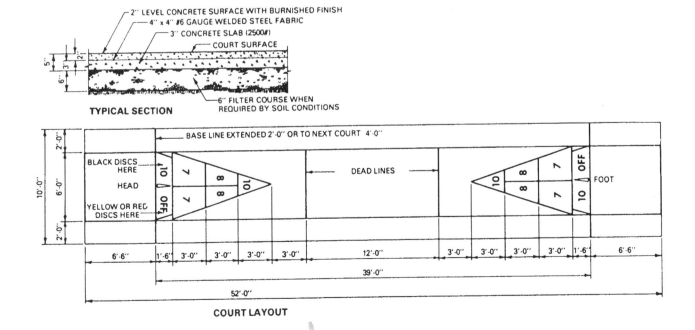

The shuffleboard court is marked off by lines painted with a black dye, white road paint, or white acrylic stain. The lines measure from 3/4 of an inch to one inch in width. The base lines are extended to adjoining courts or two feet beyond the sides of the court (Flynn, 1985).

The separation triangle in the 10/off area measures three inches at the base and extends to form a point in the direction of the scoring area. The outline of the legs of this triangle is 1/4-inch wide, with a clearance of 1/2 inch at both the point and base. Finally, the base of the separation triangle is not marked (Flynn, 1985).

Miscellaneous Considerations

Outdoor shuffleboard courts should be oriented north-south and must be constructed on a level area. A smooth playing surface is essential; therefore, the surface of an outdoor court is typically concrete or asphalt. Furthermore, the courts should be developed over a well-drained area. For proper drainage, a depressed alley should be installed between and at the sides of all courts. The alley must be 24 inches wide and must slope from both base lines toward the center of the court. To ensure proper flow of rainwater, the alley should descend one inch in depth during the first six inches in length (moving along the alley from each base line toward the center of the court) and gradually increase in depth to at least four inches at mid-court, where a suitable drain should be installed. The court can be lit using a 20-inch hinged pole with a 1,500- watt quartzite floodlight. This pole should be erected outside the courts, next to the scoreboard or benches at the base of the courts. Overhead lighting is also an option in recreational areas. Frequently, two-inch-by-two-inch backstops are installed (in a loose fashion) to prevent discs from rebounding back onto the court (Flynn, 1985).

Indoor shuffleboard courts must also be constructed in a level area. Reinforced concrete or any reasonably smooth surface is sufficient. Also, portable courts are available from vendors.

Croquet

Dimensions

The two most common forms of American croquet are six-wicket croquet and nine-wicket croquet. Dimensions, configurations, and layouts are different for each game and are described separately.

The standard croquet court for American six-wicket croquet is a rectangle measuring 105 feet (35 yards) long by 84 feet (28 yards) wide. Boundary lines should be clearly marked, the inside edge of this border being the actual court boundary. If the area is too small to accommodate a standard court, a modified court may be laid out in accordance with the same proportions as a standard court (i.e., five units long by four units wide; for example, a court could be 50 feet long by 40 feet wide). In fact, in instances where the grass is cut high or beginners are competing, a smaller court such as a 50-foot-by-40-foot court is more desirable (USCA, 1997).

The stake is set in the center of the court (Figure 17.11). On a standard full court, the wickets are set parallel to the north and south boundaries, the centers of the two inner wickets are set 21 feet to the north and south of the stake, and the centers of the four outer wickets are set 21 feet from their adjacent boundaries. On a smaller modified 50-foot-by-40-foot court, the corner wickets are 10 feet from their adjacent boundaries, and the center wickets are 10 feet in each direction from the stake (USCA, 1997).

American nine-wicket croquet is played on a rectangular court that is 100 feet long by 50 feet wide with boundaries, although marked boundaries are optional. However, a court may be reduced to fit the size and shape of the available play space. If the court is reduced, a six-foot separation should be maintained between the starting/turning stake and the adjacent wickets (USCA, 1997).

Miscellaneous Considerations

For further information regarding the construction of courts, rules, or equipment, contact the United States Croquet Association, 11585-B Polo Club Road, Wellington, FL 33414 (561) 753-9141, E-mail: uscroquet@compuserve.com

Fencing

Dimensions

The fencing court is referred to as the foil strip or piste, and is constructed of wood, rubber, cork, linoleum, or synthetic material such as plastic. The strip is from five feet, 10 inches (1.8 meters) wide to six feet, seven inches (two meters) wide and 45 feet, 11 inches (14 meters) long. The strip markings include seven lines which cross the width of the entire strip: one center line; two on-guard lines, one drawn six feet, seven inches (two meters) from each side of the center line; two end lines at the rear limit of the strip; and two warning lines marked three feet, three inches (one meter) in front of the end lines (Bower, 1980). Portable strips are also an option for those wishing to avoid permanent floor markings. Finally, ceiling clearance should be a minimum of 12 feet.

Miscellaneous Considerations

For electric foil and epee, a metallic piste must cover the entire length of the strip, including the extension areas. Electrical outlets and jacks should be located at the ends of the strips to provide power for electrical equipment. For safety, any rackets for mounting fencing targets should be either recessed flush with the wall or fastened to the wall at least as high as seven feet.

Summary

Courts, whether they be inside or out, need special planning in relation to playing surfaces, safety issues, playing dimensions, and access. Additionally, planners need to consider storage areas, electrical outlets, lighting, and water fountains.

Figure 17.11
Six-wicket croquet layout

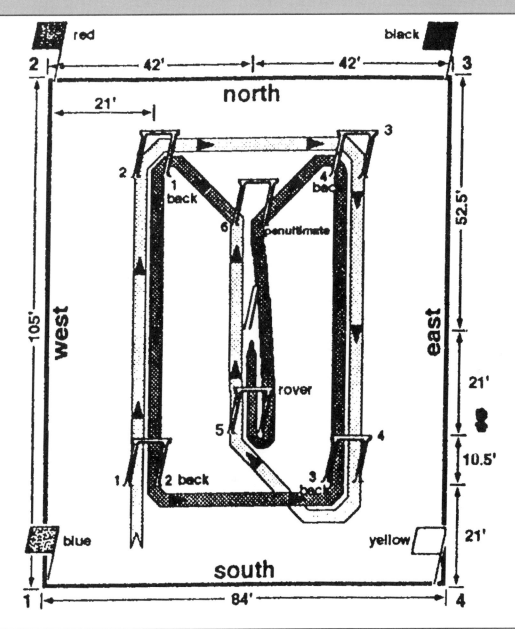

Figure 17.12
Nine-wicket croquet layout

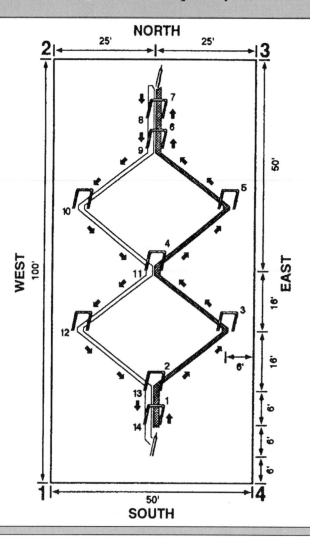

Figure 17.13
Fencing court dimensions

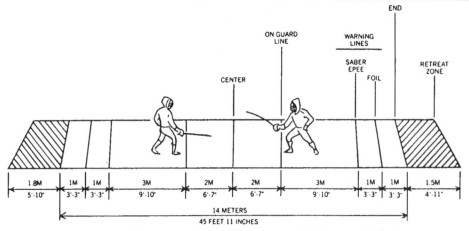

NOTE: The width of the strip shall be a minimum of 1.8 meters (5'10")
and a maximum of 2 meters (6'7"). The length of the retreat zone shall
be a minimum of 1.5 meters (4'11") and a maximum of 2 meters (6'7").
For Foil and Epee, the metallic surface of the strip shall cover the entire retreat zone.

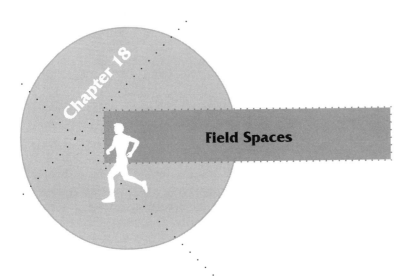

Chapter 18

Field Spaces

**Arthur H. Mittelstaedt, Jr., Recreation Safety Institute
Thomas H. Sawyer, Indiana State University**

Sport fields generally require the largest amount of space in an outdoor complex. The activities that can be conducted are varied and require a variety of sizes. Additional acreage is required for spectators, officials, service personnel, and service areas (i.e., concessions, restrooms, equipment storage, score boards, and press box).

The usability of the areas, particularly at night and after inclement weather, often requires substantial support utilities such as communication, drainage, irrigation, lighting, security, and sewer systems. Further, the surface material, synthetic or natural, and its substructure systems are also critical.

The various sport field venues that will be highlighted in this chapter include baseball/softball, boccie, cricket, crochet, field hockey, football, lacrosse, lawn badminton, lawn bowling, lawn volleyball, rugby, soccer, and team handball. The beginning of the chapter will highlight common planning challenges for all fields, and the latter portion will cover specific needs for the various fields.

Learning Objective

After reading this chapter, the student will be able to
• design a safe outdoor sport field complex.

Safety and Fields

The owner of a potential ballfield property must apply the sound and proven guidelines for planning a facility that are outlined in this text to reduce the athletes' exposure to risks (Chapters 3 and 4). The planning process should include an analysis of the causation of injuries. The following are common causes for injuries on field spaces:

Location

The size of the field area is critical. A field should have 10-yard safety buffers around the perimeter to protect athletes and spectators.

Neither athletes nor spectators should be exposed to any of the following hazards, and planners need to consider each concern when selecting a location for a field:

Streets should not be located any closer than 100 yards to a facility.

Railroad tracks, like streets, should not be any closer than 100 yards to a facility.

Water courses, man-made culverts, or natural streamways can contain deep, fast-moving water that can trap or entangle people who slip, walk, or slide into them. They should not be any closer than 100 yards to a facility.

Trenches or gulleys can be a hazard holding deep muck, hidden snakes, reptiles, or rodents, or containing wires, quicksand, or reinforcing rods that can pierce or entrap a person. They should not be any closer than 100 yards to a facility.

Settlement ponds or basins can contain toxic liquids, silt, or flammable materials and should not be any closer than 100 yards to a facility.

Storage yards, with old concrete or other culvert pipes that can roll and crush, junk cars and machinery that can cut or pierce, old wood and metal junk piles, and hazardous drums of liquids (i.e., lead paint, paints, sealants) or acids that can explode or burn, should not be any closer than 100 yards to a facility.

Climatic noise, odors, smoke, and dust should be avoided.

The protective perimeter of the area should consist of fencing, landscaping, or walls to keep spectators away from the playing field and to keep players within the playing field.

The area must not consist of soils that are toxic, poor-draining, decaying, or of poor structure. They should be free of debris and glass.

In order to protect the athletes and spectators, the field space should be located in an area that has no other activity spaces in close proximity.

The visibility of the entire area should accommodate foot and vehicle security.

The area should be illuminated at critical times to facilitate supervision and security.

Multipurpose fields that are used for baseball or softball as well as soccer, field hockey, or football can, have ruts that create dangerous high-speed bounces on the baseball or softball playing surface.

The games of baseball and softball have three major concerns for spectators and parking areas—foul balls, home runs, and overthrows.

Users

The participants' age, gender, skill levels and/or experience must be considered in creating facilities for all participants.

The area must be accessible to physically and mentally challenged participants and spectators.

Site Conditions

Concealment areas caused by shrubbery or tree canopy or adjacent structures should be eliminated to deter improper activity.

The public comfort for players and spectators must include rest room facilities close to supervised areas, properly designed and positioned litter containers, benches, and drinking fountains.

Space

The safety or buffer zone around the field and its appurtenance and equipment must be large enough to keep players from hitting stationary objects along its perimeter.

The padding or other accepted proven standards, such as releaseable or yieldable devices for outfield fences, stanchions, fences or walls and all other perimeter stationary obstructions, must be used and/or have sufficient buffered perimeter areas.

The safety glazing of nearby windows, observation panels, and doors is a necessity.

The relationship of fields and appurtenance among facilities should be harmonious and complementary in encouraging and facilitating play.

Circulation

The traffic flow of users from one field or appurtenance to another should be designed to be safe.

Materials

The durability and maintainability of the types of appurtenances within and adjacent to the field must be considered.

Access

The pedestrian, player, and spectator traffic around the activity field is important. The field must be located so that there is no interference with the traffic of people, buses, automobiles, service vehicles, vendors, and bicycles. Pedestrian traffic should be routed to have easy access to comfort stations, security, refreshments, lockers, and other related facilities.

The automotive and service (i.e., lawn mowers, maintenance vehicles) driveways should not bisect or parallel open play or human access areas.

Immovable barriers should be installed to separate any automotive traffic routes from all activity areas.

Maintenance vehicle access to fields should have the correct sub-base and surface materials installed so as to limit wear and irregular surfaces.

Utility Lines

The utility lines, above, on, or below ground should be positioned so as not interfere with players, the game, or spectators, nor to be accessible to contact with any person.

Storm drains are frequent hazards, often within the field limits or directly adjacent to them. Players can have their feet entrapped by such street-sized drains.

Irrigation heads for pop-up or quick-couple sprinklers can cause tripping if not designed properly.

Relocatable aluminum irrigation pipes and sports equipment left on the field are also hazardous.

Power lines, poles, transformers and control panels must not be in proximity to playing and/or spectator areas. They should be in remote and inaccessible, secure locations.

Fire hydrants and even drinking fountains must not be placed in the vicinity of the area of play.

Field Turf

Two types of turf are used on sport fields—synthetic and natural. (See Chapter 14 for a complete discussion of natural turf.) Between the late 1960s through the late '80s many natural turf fields were converted to synthetic fields. These conversions were intended to reduce the cost of maintenance and to provide flexibility to sport schedulers without concern about the wear and tear on the natural turf being used by numerous sport teams and "mother nature." Since the late 1980s, the conversion back to natural turf has increased to reduce injuries.

Synthetic Surface

Synthetic materials can be soft or firm. They can be piled, turfed, graveled, or smoothed. They can be rolled or poured, paneled or sprayed. The ingredients of the turf can be rubber, polymer, pigment, PVC, thermset, theromsplastic, and a host of other new high-tech materials. Synthetic products have substrates that are also of varied ingredients.

Synthetic turf is attractive to players for a number of reasons, including that the surface and footwear interact well for better footing, the surface stays in place, it is resilient, balls bounce well, the surface dries rapidly, and it has a cooling effect. It also has distractions for players, including that the surface has little resiliency, balls respond inconsistently, the surface affects the speed of the ball (making it faster), and the surface is very hot on hot days.

Attractions for operators include that the surface is repairable, picturesque, portable, durable, stable, and paintable, and drains rapidly. However, the greatest detractor of synthetic surfaces for the operator is life of the surface, approximately 15 years.

Seating

All fields must have adequate seating for spectators (see Chapter 13 for detailed information regarding bleachers). Numerous types of seating are available, from concrete stands to steel or wood bleachers of various heights, to portable aluminum bleachers. The seating has changed from 18 inches wide to 20 inches to accommodate the spectators' larger backsides. Many of the seats are fiberglass rather than wood, and some are aluminum. The seats are contoured for greater comfort and some areas have soft theater seating. The choice comes down to the size of the purchaser's pocketbook.

The planners need to consider the following safety suggestions when developing seating for spectators for outdoor

Photos by Tom Sawyer

Examples of bleacher seating,
Rose Hulman Institute of Technology.

Photos by Tom Sawyer

events: (1) conforming to ADA guidelines (see Chapter 16), (2) providing railings for each side and the top row to prevent falls, (3) closing areas under each row of seats to prevent children from falling through or climbing, (4) enclosing the structure to gain space for storage, concessions, or rest rooms and at the same time preventing children from playing under the bleachers, and (5) providing aisles with railings for ease of accessing seating.

Lighting

Lighting (illumination) is critical to safety and revenue generation (See Chapter 10 for detailed information). The illumination level for baseball and softball is 20 foot-candles for the outfield and 30 for the infield. The lighting for other team sport fields (i.e., field hockey, football, lacrosse, rugby, and soccer) requires a minimum of 30 foot-candles. If sporting events are to be televised, the lighting requirement will be much different. However, if this happens only occasionally, portable lighting companies can be hired to provide additional lighting requirements. The air should be monitored for contaminants that can cause the reflector surface to change by increasing diffusion and decreasing total reflection. This results in less total light energy leaving the face of the light, with less lumens. There should be no shadows on the field that create unsafe catching, nor should there be any glare or irregular bright patches. All stanchions or poles must be outside the field of play.

Orientation

There are various thoughts as to the orientation of baseball and softball fields. It depends on where the field is and the time games are to be held. One school of thought is that the back of home plate should be set to point south to southwest or have the baseline from home plate to first base run in an easterly direction. The theory is for the batter to look into the sun, which implies the catcher as well. Another thought is for the batter to look away from the sun. Presently, the orientation is probably the least of the safety problems. However, since batter/catcher and pitcher are in the most hazardous positions, they still require consideration. A line through these positions would be the axis for orientation for either position. After locating the axis, locate the sun's position at sunrise, early morning, late afternoon, and sunset. Establish an orientation for the field that avoids the batter/catcher and pitcher from facing directly into the early morning or late afternoon sun.

All other fields should run north to south to avoid the direct movement of the sun from east to west. However, if all contests are played in the evening after sundown, the sun does not become a factor.

Fencing

The entire field must be fenced. The height of the fence ranges from four feet for youth fields to eight feet for interscholastic and up. A number of fields have six-foot fences, which is acceptable but not ideal. The fence should be sturdy enough to withstand an athlete's weight as well as serve as a wind screen. The fence should start at eight feet as it leaves the backstop around the circumference of the field, including in front of the dugouts. The top of the fence should be covered with a colorful vinyl tube to protect the players from injury and as a reference point. The fencing should be attached on the field side of the poles, with all attachments and prongs on the outside of the fence. The fence should be stretched down from the top to the tension rail on the bottom. The fence is meant to protect players as well as spectators. It should be no closer than 25 feet to the sidelines or foul line but preferably 50 to 75 feet.

Drainage and Irrigation (See Chapter 14 also)

A properly constructed sport field has a good drainage system, so that play can resume after a short waiting period, and the turf is not destroyed when played upon in a wet condition. Turf that is too wet or too dry will be compromised. The subsoil of the field should be composed of sand (80-90% sand base) to improve the speed of drainage. The playing field should be crowned to allow the heavy rainwater that cannot be absorbed to drain to the sidelines. The slope on either side of the crown should not exceed 1/4 inch per foot toward the sideline drainage area. The sideline drainage area should be at least five yards from the playing field, contoured and sloped to catch the runoff to direct it to large drains that are approximately 20 yards apart along the sidelines. These drains should be approximately 15 to 20 feet deep with a three- to five-foot diameter filled with gravel and covered with a metal grate. Marketers always say the key to sales is "location, location, location." The key to a great field is drainage, drainage, drainage.

The irrigation of a field is very important in dry climates. There are basically three types of irrigation systems available for fields, including underground with sprinkler heads throughout the field space, underground with sprinkler heads on the perimeter of the field, and above ground with portable piping and sprinkler heads or hoses. The latter option is very labor intensive and requires a lot of equipment storage. The other options are the most convenient and least labor intensive.

The planners of the irrigation system need to consider the following: (1) the safety of the participants (i.e., perimeter or within-field sprinkler layout), (2) type of sprinkler heads, (3) the watering pattern layout (i.e., the number of overlapping zones needed, based on the available water pressure, to reach all areas of the field evenly), (4) the source of water (i.e., wells with a pumping system or government or private water company), (5) a timing system, (6) a plan for winterizing in climates that have temperatures below freezing, (7) tie-ins for drinking fountains and hose bibs, and (8) the possibility of a liquid fertilization option.

Planning Tip for Sport Fields

- Have good construction specifications.
- Have good communications between all parties throughout the project.

- Be able to compromise and solve problems as they develop.
- Use sound agronomics including planning surface and subsurface drainage, doing a good job of soil preparation, and planting turfgrass adapted to the conditions and intended use.
- Follow a good fertilization, irrigation, and mowing program during establishment of the turf.

Sport Field Service Areas

Sport field service areas include concessions areas, press box, restrooms, score boards, and storage. These areas are very important to spectators and support staff. If the service areas are well designed and maintained, they will increase fan loyalty.

Concessions Area

The concessions area should be centralized behind home plate or on both sides of the field. The area can be constructed from wood or concrete block. It should have plenty of counter space for preparation of products and to service the patrons. The floor should be concrete with numerous drains. There should be at least one double sink and ample cabinet space for storage. The area should have numerous electrical outlets and GFI outlets near water sources. The lighting should be florescent. The equipment in the area should include refrigerator, freezer, stove top with at least four cooking elements, microwave, popcorn popper, hot dog cooker/warmer, coffee maker, soda fountain dispenser, ceiling fans, shelving for merchandise, sign board for advertising, and cash register.

Press Box

The press box is important for the press, scouts, scoreboard operator, and those filming games. The press box should be located higher than the highest part of the bleachers. The size will be dependent upon the number of users. It should have an unobstructed view of the playing field. The following should be available for the press: (1) table to write on or broadcast from; (2) comfortable chairs; (3) phone hookups; (4) computer hook-ups; (5) electrical outlets; (6) refrigerator; (7) coffee maker; (8) separate areas for press, radio announcers, scorekeeper, PA announcer, coaches, and scouts; and (9) an area above the press area exclusively for filming games. These facilities are generally constructed of wood with flourescent lighting.

Rest Rooms

There need to be numerous restrooms provided, preferably not portable. The number of facilities for women should be twice as many as that provided for men. Each restroom should provide changing areas for babies, with adjacent waste disposal units. Each restroom area should be handicapped-accessible, or at least an appropriate number of restrooms needs to be handicapped-accessible and so labeled. These facilities are generally constructed of concrete block with concrete floors with drains for cleaning. The lighting should be flourescent. The rooms should be adequately ventilated.

Example of safety considerations for outdoor fencing, DePauw University.

Photos by Tom Sawyer

French Drains.

Scoreboards

There are a number of reliable scoreboard companies. The planners need to consider first what the function of the scoreboard will be—to depict score and time remaining only or to provide entertainment and information as well. Scoreboards can be simple or very complex in nature. The planners need to consider what they want the scoreboard to depict before determining the type of scoreboard to be pur-

chased. The choices include (1) score; (2) periods or innings; (3) injury time or penalty time remaining; (4) times and places by lanes; (5) diving score by judge, degree of difficulty, total points scored, ranking after "x" number of dives; (6) balls, strikes, outs; (7) roster; (8) players vital statistics; (9) advertising; (10) PA system; (11) multiple functions for various sports using the field complex; (12) close-ups of players and spectators; (13) time of day; (14) scores from other games; and much more depending on the planner's imagination.

Storage

As is true with indoor facilities, there is never enough storage. The planners need to consider what items need to be stored. These include, but are not limited to: (1) various types of riding lawn mowers; (2) push mowers; (3) tillers; (4) weed eaters; (5) shovels, rakes; and hoes; (6) utility vehicles; (7) irrigation pipes; (8) hoses and sprinkler heads; (9) field liners; (10) goals; (11) field flags; (12) benches; (13) waste containers; (14) protection screens; (15) pitching machines; (16) tarps; (17) fertilizers, insecticides, and talc; (18) paint; (19) chains, yard markers, and padding for goal post for football; and much more.

Storage areas generally are constructed out of concrete blocks with concrete floors and an appropriate number of drains for cleaning. The space should have flourescent lighting with an adequate number of electrical outlets. There should be a separate work area with a workbench and an adequate amount storage with shelving. The entrance should be an automatic roll-up door at least eight-feet high. The ceiling height should be at least 10 feet. The voids under bleachers should be enclosed (these spaces make inexpensive storage areas). The space for chemical storage must meet OSHA guidelines.

Baseball/Softball Fields

Baseball and softball facilities are important aspects of sport in public schools (grades 5-12), colleges and universities (varsity competition as well as recreation), community recreation programs, Babe Ruth Leagues, Little Leagues, Miss Softball Leagues, corporate recreation programs, and military recreation programs. Due to the alarming number of injuries reported to the Consumer Product Safety Commission (CPSC), safety is a principal concern. This concern places pressure on field operators, turf managers, maintenance managers, and others to have a safe playing field. A "field of dreams" is created from a consistent set of proven guidelines and safety standards to ensure consistency around the country. It is important for the planners to be aware of the field specifications described in the various rules books that govern these two sports (i.e., National Federation of High School Activities Association, National Collegiate Athletic Association, National Intercollegiate Athletic Association, National Junior College Athletic Association, Softball USA, International Softball Federation, National Association for Girls and Women's Sports, Little League Association, and so on). These rule books are the "gospel" in regard to the specific dimensions for the fields, and most rule books are revised annually.

Bases

The base areas must be level, with all irregularities eliminated. The type of base used in either baseball or softball varies, and the rule books stipulate what types are permissible. The planner should contact the American Society of Testing and Materials (ASTM) for detailed information regarding the appropriate standards for bases. Presently, the ASTM F-8 Committee on Sports Equipment and Facilities is establishing standards and classifications for bases.

Bases are intended to be a reference point on a baseball or softball field. They are an integral part of the game.

There are four types of base designs used, including permanent or stationary bases, modified stationary bases, release-type bases, and throw-down bases. The type of base usually refers to how the base is secured to the playing field, or its function.

Stationary Base

This base uses a ground anchor permanently installed in the playing field. The anchor measures either 1 inch or 1 1/2 inches, installed a minimum of 1 inch below the playing surface. The base is designed with a stem that fits into or over the ground anchor and holds the base securely in place.

The base should be constructed of permanently white material, which can be rubber, polyvinyl, polyurethane, or other synthetic material to increase service life. The base top should have a molded tread pattern to increase player traction and reduce slippage. Base size and color should conform to individual governing organizations. Permanent or stationary bases can be used on fields by players with more advanced or higher skill levels only after (1) the players have been thoroughly warned that they can be seriously injured for life if they make a mistake in judgement or miscalculation, and (2) they have been made thoroughly aware of other options (i.e., the tapered side base or low silhouette which tapers to the ground eliminating impact of a sliding player against a vertical surface and uses that momentum to slide over the base). Bases are the number-one cause of injuries to ankles and other body parts, especially stationary, modified-stationary, and poorly designed release-type bases.

Modified Stationary Bases

The flexible base is a one-piece base that uses a fixed anchor system for secure placement. It is constructed with interdependent ribs that allow the base to compress and absorb energy generated by a sliding player. The cover allegedly flexes inward and downward but does not release.

The strap-down base or tie-down base must be held in place by four spikes inserted into the ground. Straps attached to the base are inserted through loops in the spike head and tightened down. The base is constructed of vinyl-coated nylon or canvas filled with a foam or other resilient material. If installed properly, a portion of the base will remain somewhat stable. However, it has a tendency during play to loosen and move. This style is low cost relative to other base styles, which accounts for its popularity.

Release-Type Base

The release-type base is designed to reduce the chance of injury to a sliding player by releasing from its anchor system on the impact of a hard lateral slide. The release base must use a permanent ground anchor securely positioned below ground for installation. There are two-piece and three-piece designs. The release-type must not expose hidden secondary hazards after the primary above-ground base portion releases.

Throw-Down Base

This base is a thin square, sometimes using a waffle design on the bottom, usually constructed of canvas or synthetic material with little or no padding. It is not physically

Example of a structure that contains concessions, press box, restrooms and storage.

attached to the playing surface, and therefore is dangerously subject to moving when a player steps on or rounds a base. Throw-down bases are not recommended for basic skills teaching in a gym, such as a physical education class.

Specialized Bases

The flush or recessed base (except home plate, which is mounted flush with the playing field) is usually not considered for the following reasons: (1) difficulty in keeping the base visible and clean; (2) difficulty for umpire in making a call at the base when the base is not visible; (3) the change in the nature of the game; and (4) the fact that it is not widely used.

Double First Base

The double first base uses a securely positioned ground anchor system. The base is designed to reduce or eliminate the contact between the first baseman and base runner. It is a unit equal in size to two bases side by side, one-half white mounted in the normal first base position, and one-half colored, mounted in foul territory.

Home Plate

The home plate, batter's box, and catcher box and their correct dimensional size and positioning must conform to the game and the rules of the appropriate governing body. The area should be well compacted, properly tapered, and level, with no irregularities. The plate must be firmly anchored and any undermining or ruts corrected before play begins.

The home plate is a reference point on the playing field. It establishes the horizontal limits of the strike zone used by the umpire in calling balls and strikes. It is imperative that all home plates have a white surface that measures 17 by 8 1/2 by 8 1/2 by 12 by 12 inches flush with the surrounding playing surface. Further, all home plates must have a periphery black bevel that does not exceed 35 degrees. The outermost edge of the bevel must be sufficiently below the playing surface. It does not matter how the plates are field mounted as long as they remain flat and flush with surrounding playing surfaces with no sharp corners or sharp nails exposed.

There are four styles of home plate, including buried, staked, anchored, and throw down.

Buried. A rubber or synthetic plate 2 inches or more thick is buried, and the uppermost white surface is installed flush with the playing surface. It can be mounted in a concrete sub-base to provide greater leveling stability.

Staked. A rubber or synthetic plate 3/4 inch to 1 inch thick has an installed white surface flush to the playing surface. It can be mounted in a concrete sub-base for better anchoring.

Anchored. A rubber or synthetic plate has a stem built into the bottom that fits into a permanent ground anchor. The uppermost white surface must be installed flush with the playing surface.

Throw Down. A rubber or synthetic thin mat sometimes using a waffle design on the bottom is laid down on the playing surface and is not mechanically held in place. Throw down home plates are not recommended for basic skills teaching in a gym, such as a physical education class.

Skinned Infield

With an eye to player safety, begin the outfield slope 20 feet back into the outfield, lessening the transition from the infield to outfield (this is for both synthetic and natural fields). The infield slope should be established at 0.5%, the outfield slope at 1.3% all the way around to further speed drainage. The infield should a 80/20 premixed sand to clay material at a depth of three inches. The demarcation between skinned area and turf must be smooth and firm. The skinned areas must maintain the proper pitch to eliminate puddling and erosion. Irregular clumps of turf, uneven edges, and undermining of skinned materials are among some of the causes of ankle and leg injuries in the game.

Skinned areas could be just cut-outs around the bases, home plate, and pitchers mound or include base lines or the entire infield area. In all cases, the skinned areas must be continuously inspected and groomed. All irregularities must be eliminated, particularly around bases where sliding groves the area.

Clay is most often used as such a skinned area; however, other materials and mix of materials have been used depending upon local sources and preference. Most fields should be designed to be playable within 15 to 20 minutes after rain. A higher percentage of sand may be needed to achieve that without underground drainage.

Turf Infield and Outfield

Chapter 14 contains a discussion regarding natural turf as well as irrigation concerns. However, it needs to be noted here that natural turf in the infield and outfield should be Tifway™ Bermudagrass. It should be overseeded (see base paths) with Topflite™ perennial ryegrass.

Pitchers Mound

The pitchers mound and its plate must meet the requirements of the games governing body. The height of the plate, the pitch of the slope within the circle toward home plate, the radius of the circle, the level plate length and width size are all critical to safety in any type of designated and designed fields and must be checked and maintained before any game.

Base Paths

A regular maintenance concern is the rutting of the base path. Like the infield, the base path should be free of ruts and irregularities in the surface. Periodically hand rake the base paths between first and second and second and third to identify any low spots. The base paths between home and first and first and third can be composed of clay and sand like the infield, or natural turf or synthetic material. If the base path is composed of natural turf, it should be overseeded with Topflight™ perennial ryegrass prior to the season, periodically during the season, and at the conclusion of the season, as well as early fall. Prior to overseeding in the early spring and early fall the area should be aerated, then dethatched to provide good seed-to-soil contact. The seeded area should be fertilized first with 10-10-10 fertilizer, and one month later with a slow-release 30-16-10.

Warning Track

The warning track should encircle the entire playing field and provide noticeable surface variations in feel and sound to provide ample warning to players chasing a fly ball who are unaware of the perimeter and any obstacles. The track can be made of clay or crushed (M-10) granite or brick. The crushed brick will add color for enhanced TV coverage. The warning track and/or buffer zone should be equal in width to 5% of the distance from home plate to the deepest part of the playing field and completely encircle the field. Care should be taken than any edge between the track and the turf be smooth and even.

Backstop

The backstop is a key element of a field for safeguarding the players and spectators. The basic purposes of backstop include (1) keeping the ball within the playing area, (2) protecting the spectator, (3) safeguarding others involved in the game (i.e., batters in the on-deck circle, bat persons), and (4) protecting nearby activities from conflict with pop-ups (i.e., adjacent ball fields, concessions areas, rest rooms, parking areas).

When designing the backstop, the planners should consider the following: (1) using small mesh to discourage people from climbing the structure; (2) ensuring the parking and traffic areas are not close; (3) installing a double mesh to prevent fingers, faces, and other body parts of spectators from being crushed by errant balls or thrown bats; (4) keeping the mesh free from any barbs or penetrating parts to ensure safety for players and spectators; (5) ensuring the distance between home plate and the backstop is not less than 25 feet but preferably 60 feet to ensure player safety; (6) using ground materials of either turf with an appropriate warning track composed of clay or crushed granite (M-10) or crushed brick, or no turf with either clay or crushed granite (M-10) or crushed brick; and (7) ensuring the height of the backstop is at least 18 feet, preferably 20 feet, with a four- to six-foot overhang at the top with a 45-degree angle.

The most frequently used backstop consists of three 12-feet wide panels that are 18 to 20 feet high covered with a 1 1/2-inch galvanized wire mesh material. These panels can be made of steel, aluminum, or wood. One panel is placed directly behind home plate and the other two on each side flaring at 30 degrees with the center panel. The fencing on either side of the side panels should gradually taper down to

Warning track, DePauw University.

Photo by Tom Sawyer

Backstop, Indiana State University.

Photo by Tom Sawyer

eight feet behind the players bench area to provide greater protection for the spectators in bleachers on the other side of the fence. The top of the backstop will have three panels, four to six feet by 12 feet, attached to the upright panels and positioned at a 45-degree angle to contain errant balls. This overhang will be covered with the same material as the uprights.

Players' Bench Area

There are two types of player bench areas commonly constructed for baseball and softball. These areas are the dugouts and field-level shelters. The safer of the two is the dugout, but it is also the most expensive to construct. The dugout is usually four feet deep, constructed of poured concrete and concrete blocks with drains to remove water quickly. It has an elevated players' bench area, entrance to locker rooms (if in a stadium complex), drinking fountain, communication, bat rack, other storage space, lights, and electrical outlets. Recently, to better safeguard the players, either shatter-proof plastic or wire mesh has been installed to repel errant balls and bats. The roof is constructed so as to discourage people from sitting or climbing on it.

The field-level shelter is at field level with a poured concrete floor and concrete block walls. It has a wire mesh fence at least six feet high to repel errant balls or bats. The space should have a bat rack, communications, a drinking fountain, additional storage, lights, and electrical outlets. The roof should be constructed to discourage sitting and climbing.

Batting Cage

The batting cage should be located outside the fenced playing field. It should be constructed of either steel, aluminum, or wood. The minimum size for one batter should be 10 feet wide, 100 feet long, and 10 feet high. If more than one batter is going to be hitting, then the cage needs to be wider (i.e., 10 feet wider for each batter) with a separating mesh curtain. The space must be completely covered by mesh netting to protect other players and spectators. There needs to

be a source of electricity and numerous GFI electrical outlets. The floor surface should be similar to home plate for the batters and natural mounds for the pitchers.

Bull Pen

The bull pens should be located either down first and third into the outfield area or in right and left center fields. These areas should be protected from errant balls and the spectators. The area behind the catcher should have a protective fence to protect the spectators. The pitching mounds should be exact replicas of the actual playing field mound. There should also be a home plate area. Finally, there should be benches available for the players.

Size

The area required for a baseball or softball field will vary from 260 to 460 feet depending on the level of play anticipated. Since baseball and softball are now often scheduled on the same fields, the age group and type of activity govern the field size. It is recommended that if multiple age groups are to play on a field, it should be sized for the optimum use. Many fields have been planned for a size for high school play, only to have young adults scheduled for the same field. This creates numerous incidents with players colliding with obstacles or other players. Ideally, if funding is available, there should be separate facilities for the various age groups.

Multi-field Complex

It is common to see multi-field complexes for baseball, softball, and combination baseball and softball. The most common multi-field complex contains four fields. If one were to view the complex from an airplane, it would resemble a wheel with four spokes coming from a central hub.

The central hub would contain a two-story building with each side facing a different backstop and field. The first floor would contain a concession area, rest rooms, storage for game and maintenance equipment, and a first-aid space.

Bull pen area, Indiana State University.

Photo by Tom Sawyer

The second floor would have four large screened windows, four scorer tables, four scoreboard controls, communication center, and field light controls. The pathways leading to the various fields would contain either crushed granite (M-10) or crushed brick. The parking area would be located at least 100 yards from the nearest outfield fence. All fields would be lighted.

Field Hockey, Football, Lacrosse, Rugby, Soccer

Fields for field hockey, football, lacrosse, rugby, and soccer have a number of common requirements. For example, a drinking fountain should be available for each team to use near the team benches. A utility structure should be placed at mid-field, set back from the field 25 feet, to store equipment and house the scorer and controls for the field lights and score board. Shade must be available for the teams at half-time, preferably from a deciduous tree grove at either end or side of the field and about 25 yards away from the playing field.

Specific considerations by sport include the following:

Field hockey

This sport needs sleeves in the ground for corner flags and goal posts. The actual field dimensions are similar to those in Appendix A. Official rule books can be purchased from the NCAA or NAGWS; rules are revised annually.

Football

There should be sleeves in the ground for the end zone flags. The goal posts (usually a single pole with uprights) need to be centered and secured at the end line. Actual field dimensions are similar to the ones inAppendix A. Official rule books can be purchased from the NCAA; rules are revised annually. Planners should review carefully the ASTM publication *Safety in Football*.

Lacrosse

There should be sleeves in the ground to hold the goals. Actual field dimensions are similar to the ones in Appendix A. Official rule books can be purchased from the NCAA or NAGWS; rules are revised annually.

Rugby

There should be sleeves in the ground for the end flags and the goal posts. Actual field dimensions are similar to the ones in Appendix A. Official rule books can be purchased from the United States Rugby Association; rules are revised annually.

Soccer

Sleeves in the ground are needed for the flags for the corner kick area, substitute area, and the goal posts on the end line. Tie-down hooks should be inserted at least one foot into the ground for securing the nets to the ground. There should be a drinking fountain available for each team to use near the team benches. Actual field dimensions are similar to the ones in Appendix A. Official rule books can be purchased from the NCAA; rules are revised annually.

Planning Checklist for Fields

The following is a checklist to be used by field planners when designing field spaces:
- Define the use of the field complex (i.e., single- or multiple-sport users; youth, adolescent, or adult; amateur or professional).
- Pay careful attention to slope on fields to encourage proper and adequate drainage.
- Ensure drainage requirements are met, and the type as well as placement of drainage outlets are well out of the playing area and swales are beyond safety or buffer zones.
- Make sure fences on the perimeter are offset beyond safety or buffer zones. The height of the fence

Photo by Meghan Sawyer

Softball control center, storage, restroom facility, Indiana State University

Softball shelter with drinking fountain and helmet rack

Photo by Meghan Sawyer

should be at least eight feet. Fences should be flexible, resilient, and padded. Further, ensure that fences are placed in front of players (i.e., dugouts and field-level shelters) and spectators. The fence should be sturdy enough to attach a wind- screen or sunscreen. Finally, the mesh on the fences should be of a size to discourage climbing.

- Provide gates for security and for separation of different practice areas.
- Design warning tracks to provide advanced warning of perimeter barriers and ensure they are wide enough and of appropriate material.
- Ensure that light poles, fence poles, and foul poles are not in the field of play.
- Plan that mowing or maintenance strips along fences are inserted so they are not hazardous.
- Place all shrubs and tree plantings well outside the playing area.
- Ensure that the turf (artificial or natural) is suitable for different weather conditions (i.e., hot, cold, dry, or wet).
- Install the scoreboard well outside the playing area.
- Design the irrigation system so that it will not interfere with play and that all valves, distribution boxes, and other utilities are well outside the field of play.
- Make sure that vehicular and pedestrian traffic-flow patterns prevent conflict and interference, and that bike and vehicle parking is marked and controlled.
- Ensure that emergency call stations are placed at strategic locations and emergency vehicle access is available for immediate response.
- Plan the field area so that hazards are not nearby (e.g., major highways, railroad tracks, waterways, culverts, ravines, industries, woods, uncut roughs, and utility lines).

- Create the field area so that security vehicles have easy access and surveillance.
- Understand the importance of field orientation relative to the movement of the sun and prevailing wind patterns.
- Configure spectator seating to ensure the best viewing of the game as well as easy access and exit.
- Ensure each space has the appropriate safety or buffer zones.
- Review the plan to ensure that the field dimensions are accurate and meet the specified association rules.
- Configure all field spaces to include metal sleeves for goal post, goals, and flags.
- Encourage the owners to ensure that regular maintenance and inspections are done to eliminate ruts, ridges, and depressions in the fields after use; remove debris and rocks from the playing area as well as safety zones; ensure all hooks on goal posts, foul line posts, and fencing are recessed; eliminate all sharp edges on posts, rails, and welds; and make sure benches, seats, and bleachers are protected by screening or barriers.
- Create backstops that protect players, spectators, and other game personnel from injury from errant balls or bats.

Summary

Designing safe sport fields is important to athletes of all ages, genders, and skill and experience levels, as well as to spectators and parents. The number of sport fields being built each year has increased dramatically. Sport field complexes with multiple fields will become the norm rather than the oddity.

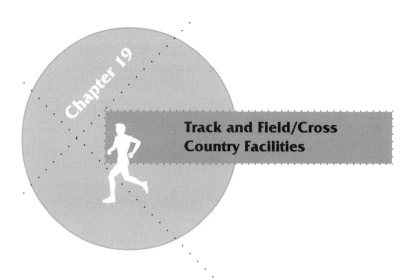
John McNichols, Indiana State University
John Gartland, Indiana State University
Thomas H. Sawyer, Indiana State University

A track and field competition complex is complicated at best when compared to other outdoor or indoor sport spaces, such as an indoor basketball/volleyball court or a base-ball, football, or soccer field. The track and field complex includes areas such as throwing, jumping, running, relaxation and warm-up, spectator, timing and recording, storage, and officials' dressing room. The areas are basically the same for an indoor facility.

A cross-country course (See Appendix J) requires appropriate planning to service both girls and women, and boys and men. The distances differ for genders and level of competition (i.e., interscholastic and intercollegiate).

This chapter will describe the facilities needed for indoor and outdoor track and field and cross country. Further, it will describe various pieces of equipment needed to assist and protect the athletes. The text in this chapter is based on the NCAA Track and Field/Cross Country Men and Women rules.

Learning Objectives

After reading this chapter, the student will be able to
- select an appropriate site for a track and field complex as well as a cross-country course, and
- properly design a track and field complex and cross-country facility.

Site Selection and Planning the Track

Building a running track can be a formidable task, since few athletic facilities are as complex and yet have so many acceptable building options. With so many choices, no two track projects are the same. Each is a product of site constraints, owner preferences, location, budget, and availability of materials and expertise.

Faced with the task of building a track, an owner or facility manager can become overwhelmed by the choices and concerned about the possibility of costly mistakes. The

first step, then, is identifying all decisions that must be made in planning a track facility and learning what to expect from the construction project. The success of the project will depend on proper site analysis, quality design and engineering, expert construction—including construction of proper drainage, a stable, well-built base and a quality synthetic surface—and accurate marking.

The first stage in the construction of a running track is choosing a site and designing a track to fit the site. In calculating the accuracy of a finished 400-meter track, no minus tolerance is acceptable, and a plus tolerance must be no more than 1/2 inch in any lane. These very small tolerances and the numerous design and site factors to be considered make track design extremely complex and demanding. Owners should begin by deciding what size and shape of track is needed. A 400-meter, six- or eight-lane track is the standard for high school and college competition, although a few high school tracks and many large college tracks are 10 lanes wide.

There are two basic shapes. An equal-quadrant track has two 100-meter straightaways and two 100-meter curves, while a non-equal quadrant track has two straightaways of one length and two curves of another length, totaling 400 meters. In the latter case, the result is a track with either a slightly stretched or compressed oval shape.

Recently, a third design—the so-called broken-back track—has come into use. This design features a more square track with shorter straightaways and rounded ends made of double curves. This design creates a larger infield that is large enough for an NCAA soccer field (which neither of the two more common designs can accommodate) and is useful for sites where one of the more common track designs will not work. Generally, an equal quadrant track is desirable, but site factors will determine which design is most feasible.

Will the track have a curb? Most high school tracks are built without curbs, but curbs are required on tracks where NCAA record events will be conducted. The curb will require additional area on the inside perimeter of the track.

How large a site is available? A track will require a site of no less than five acres, a minimum of 600 feet long by 300 feet wide. Additional area must be allowed for grading, curbs and drainage, and for amenities such as grandstands, bleachers, lighting, walkways, and fencing.

Will the track be built around playing fields? Many tracks are built around football or soccer fields. In addition to allowing space for the field itself, space must be allowed for player seating, walkways, and other associated facilities. Artificial turf fields require additional space for anchoring detail at the perimeter.

Will the construction project include field events? Most track projects built today include construction of a high-jump pad; long-jump runway and pit; pole-vault runway and landing area; shot put, discus, and hammer-throwing pads and landing areas; and sometimes a javelin runway and a triple-jump runway and landing pit. It is more economical to construct field event areas at the same time as the track.

It is during the design phase that the design team must consider where the field events will be located. Placing the field events in the infield of the track may facilitate spectator viewing, but may mean more traffic over the runways. Wind must also be considered. Straightaways should be parallel to prevailing winds—which is especially important for dashes and hurdle races. For athlete safety, jumping events should also take place with the wind, since crosswinds are particularly dangerous. Multiple-jump runways should be considered because of the addition of the women's pole vault and time constraints during competition, when there is only one runway for men and women for the long jump and triple jump.

Throwing events should be located so that participants are throwing into the wind. Likewise, for safety reasons, it is essential that high-jump and pole-vault runways be located so that the athlete does not have to look into the sun or artificial lighting.

There are a number of other important considerations in site selection:

- Does a potential site allow for proper drainage and storm water management? Water should drain away from the track. It is best to locate a track on a relatively level plain, higher than surrounding areas. Additional filling or drainage work required by a low site may add substantially to construction costs. Even under the best site conditions, tracks should be constructed with a perimeter drain on the inside of the track to remove storm water that has drained from the track and playing field.

Note: No expense should be spared in developing a good, solid base.

- Is the site reasonably level? While the track will be sloped slightly for drainage, for all practical purposes, the track must be level in the running direction.
- What type of soil exists at the site? Poor soil conditions often lead to excessive settling, heaving caused by freeze/thaw action and drainage problems. The best soil is hard, well-drained, and non-heaving. Locations with peat, clay, topsoil, shear sand, or other organic materials at a depth of eight to 12 inches should be avoided.

- Where are underground utilities located? While the finished facility will require utility service, it is better to avoid constructing the track over underground utilities.

Many track projects are reconstruction or renovation projects. These projects can be even more complex to design than a new facility because of existing constraints.

Track and Field Facilities

Measuring Distances

The distance to be run in any race is measured from start to finish between two theoretical hairlines. All distances not run in lanes are measured 30 centimeters (11.81 inches) outward from the inner edge of the track if a regulation curb is in place. If no curb is used, lane one is measured 20 centimeters (7.87 inches) from the left lane as in other lanes. For all races in lanes around one or more curves, the distance to be run in each lane is measured 20 centimeters (7.87 inches) from the outer edge of the lane that is on the runner's left, except that the distance for the lane next to the curb is measured 30 centimeters (11.81 inches) from the curb. If no curb is used, lane one is measured 20 centimeters (7.87 inches) from the left-hand line as in other lanes (NCAA, 2001).

Visible Starting Line

The visible starting line, 5.08 centimeters (two inches) wide, is marked on the track just within the measured distance, so that its near edge is identical with the exactly measured and true starting line. The starting line for all races not run in lanes (except the 800 meters) is curved so that all competitors run the same distance going into the curve (Figure 19.1).

Visible Finish Line

The visible finish line, 5.08 centimeters (two inches) wide, is marked on the track just outside the measured distance so that its edge nearer that start is identical with the exactly measured and true finish line. Lane numbers of reasonable size should be placed at least 15.24 centimeters (six inches) beyond the common finish line, positioned facing the timing device. The intersection of each lane line and the finish line is painted black in accordance with Figure 19.2. Finally, a common finish line is recommended for all races. Lines in the finish area should be kept to a minimum. If additional lines are necessary, they should be of a less conspicuous color than the finish line, so as not to cause confusion.

Except where their use may interfere with fully automatic timing devices, two white posts may denote the finish line and be placed at least 30 centimeters (11.81 inches) from the edge of the track. The finish posts should be of rigid construction, approximately 1.4 meters (4.59 inches) high, 80 millimeters (3.15 inches) wide and 20 millimeters (0.79 inches) thick (NCAA, 2001).

Note: The white posts have been deleted from new facilities and should be removed from older facilities, because virtually every track has installed automatic timing devices.

The General Track Area (See Figure 19.1-19.3)

Outdoor. In constructing track and field facilities, metric measurements must be used. The construction of track and field areas will follow the International Amateur Athletic Federation rules with respect to grade or slope: "The maximum inclination permitted for tracks, runways, circles, and landing areas for throwing events shall not exceed 1:100 in a lateral direction and 1:1000 in the running and throwing direction." In the high jump, the maximum inclination of the approach and takeoff area not exceed 1:250 in the direction of the center of the crossbar. Prevailing wind conditions should be considered when constructing field-event areas (NCAA, 2001).

Indoor. Tracks, runways, and takeoff areas should be covered with synthetic material or have a wooden surface. These surfaces should be able to accept six millimeter (0.25 inch) spikes for synthetic surfaces and three millimeter spikes (0.13 inch) for wood (NCAA, 2001).

Running Track

*Outdoor.*The running track should not be less than 400 meters in length nor less than 6.40 meters (21 feet) in width, which allows six hurdle lanes of 1.07 meters (42 inches) each. It may be bordered on the inside by a curb of concrete, wood, or other suitable material a minimum of 5.08 centimeters (two inches) in height and a maximum of 10.16 centimeters (four inches) in width (Figure 19.3). The edges of the curb should be rounded (NCAA, 2001).

Indoor

- Straightaways—Maximum lateral inclination in the running direction should not exceed 1:250 at any point and 1:100 overall. Lanes should all have the same width, with a recommended minimum of 1.07 meters (42 inches) and a maximum of 1.25 meters (48 inches) including the white line to the right. There should be a minimum of three meters (9 feet, 10 inches) behind the start line and 10 meters (32 feet, 9.75 inches) beyond the finish line free of any obstruction. It is recommended that clearance beyond the finish line be at least 20 meters (65 feet, 7.5 inches) (NCAA, 2001).
- Oval Track and Lanes—Indoor tracks may vary in size, with 200 meters as the preferable distance. The track consists of two horizontal straights and two curves with consistent radii, which should be banked. The curves should be bordered with a curb of suitable material approximately 5.08 centimeters (two inches) in height (NCAA, 2001).

Where the inside edge of the track is bordered with a white line, it should be marked additionally with cones at least 20 centimeters (7.87 inches) high. The cones should be placed on the track so that the outward face of the cone coincides with the edge of the white line closest to the track. The cones should be placed at distances not exceeding two meters (6.56 feet) on the curves and 10 meters (32.81 feet) on the straightaways (NCAA, 2001).

The track should have a minimum of six lanes. Lanes should have a recommended minimum of 91.44 centimeters (36 inches), including the lane line to the right. Lanes should be marked by lines 5.08 centimeters (two inches) wide (NCAA, 2001).

It is recommended that a maximum angle of banking should not be more than 18 degrees for a 200-meter track. This angle may vary based upon the size of a track. The angle of banking in all lanes should be the same at any cross section. Further, it is recommended that the inside radius of the curves on a 200-meter track should not be less than 18 meters (59 feet, 0.75 inches) and not more than 21 meters (68 feet, 10.75 inches) (NCAA, 2001).

Track Markings

Outdoors

It is recommended that the following color code be used when marking the track: (NCAA, 2001)

- Starting line (white): 55 meters, 55-meter hurdles, 100 meters, 100-meter hurdles, 110- meter hurdles, 200 meters, 300 meters, 400 meters, 1,500 meters, mile, 3,000 meters, steeplechase, 5,000 meters, 10,000 meters
- Starting line (green): 800 meters
- Starting line (red): 800-meter relay
- Starting line (blue): 1,600-meter relay
- Finish line (white): all (A common finish line is recommended for all races.) Except where their use may interfere with fully automatic timing devices, two white posts may denote the finish line and be placed at least 30 centimeters (11.81 inches) from the edge of the track. The finish posts should be of rigid construction, approximately 1.4 meters (4.59 feet) high, 80 millimeters (3.15 inches) wide and 20 millimeters (0.79 inch) thick
- Relay exchange zones: 400-meter relay (yellow), 800-meter relay (red), 1,600-meter relay (blue), 3,200-meter relay (green)
- Hurdle locations: 100 (yellow), 110 (blue), 300 (red), 400 (green), steeplechase (white), break line (green)
- Lanes shall be marked on both sides by lines 5.08 centimeters (20 inches) wide
- The lanes shall be numbered with lane one on the left when facing the finish line
- Relay zones: in all relays around the track, the baton exchange must be made within a 20-meter (65.62 feet) zone, formed by lines drawn 10 meters (32.81 feet) on each side of the measured centerline. All lines and/or boxes or triangles should be inclusive within the zone (NCAA, 2001).

Hurdles

Hurdle lanes should be at least 1.07 meters (42 inches) in width. If no hurdle lanes are marked on the track, they should be judged as equivalent to 2.54 centimeters (one inch) wider than the total width of the hurdles (NCAA, 2001).

Steeplechase (see Figure 19.3)

The standard distance for the steeplechase is 3,000 meters, with 28 hurdle jumps and seven water jumps. The water jump should be the fourth jump in each lap. If neces-

Figure 19.1
Track measurements

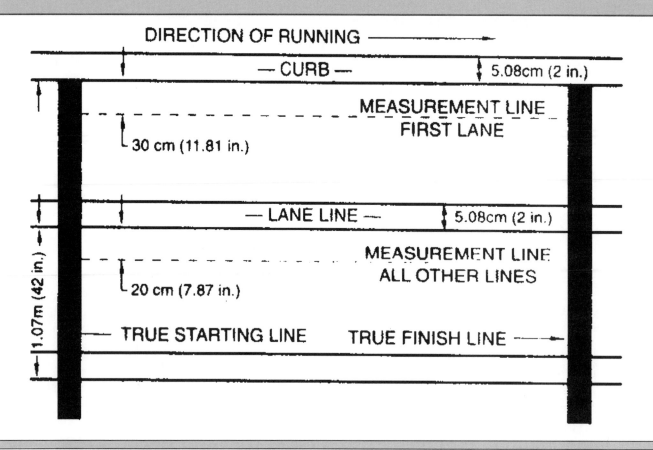

Figure 19.2
Finish-line intersections

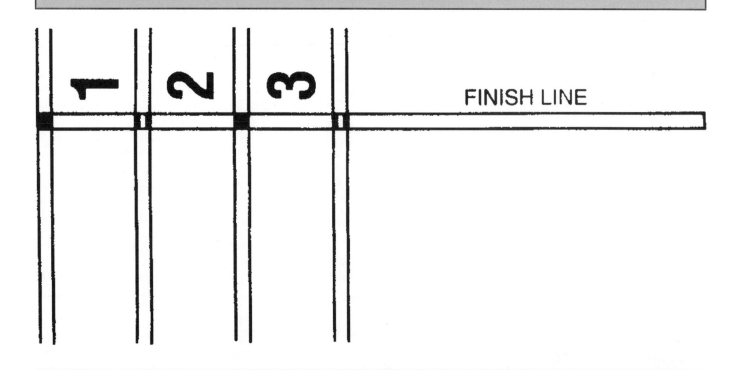

Figure19.3

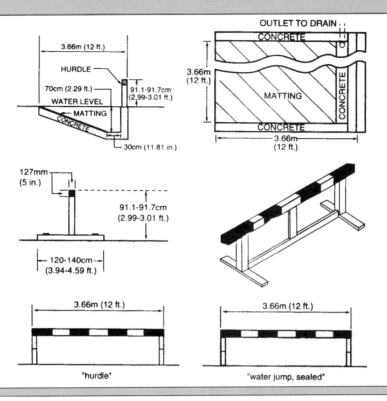

sary, the finish line should be moved to accommodate this rule. The following measurements are given as a guide, and any adjustments necessary shall be made by lengthening or shortening the distance at the starting point of the race. The chart below assumes that a lap of 400 meters or 440 yards has been shortened 10 meters (32.81 feet) by constructing the water jump inside the track. If possible, the approach to and exit from the water-jump hurdle should be straight for approximately seven meters (NCAA, 2001).

Placement of Hurdles on Track—The hurdles, including the water jump, should be placed on the track so that 30 centimeters (11.81 inches) of the top bar, measured from the inside edge of the track, will be inside the track (see Figure 4). It is recommended that the first hurdle be at least five

meters (16 feet, 4.75 inches) in width, and that all hurdles weigh at least 80 kilograms (176.4 pounds) (NCAA, 2001).

Water-Jump Construction—The water jump should be 3.66 meters (12 feet) in length and width. The water should be a minimum of 70 meters (2.29 feet) in depth immediately after the hurdle, and the pit should have a constant upward slope from a point 30 centimeters (11.81 inches) past the water-jump hurdle to the level of the track at the far end. It is recommended that the water jump be placed on the inside of the track. The landing surface inside the water jump should be composed of a nonskid, shock-absorbent material. The area between the vertical uprights of the water-jump hurdle should be sealed with a solid, rigid material or lattice work to provide safety and to aid the athlete with depth percep-

Track press box and control center, Indiana State University.

Photo by Meghan Sawyer

tion. A water source needs to be installed to fill the water-jump and a drain installed to drain the water-jump after use (NCAA, 2001).

- Men and women—The hurdle at the water jump should be firmly fixed in front of the water and be of the same height as the other hurdles in the competition.
- Alternative for Women—The hurdle at the water jump shall be firmly fixed to the water jump 60 centimeters (23.62 in) ahead of the men's hurdle position in the running direction, and be the same height as the other hurdles in the competition. (Note: It is very likely this rule will be changed for the 2002 season, check the NCAA 2002 rules book for clarification.)

Long Jump and Triple Jump

The minimum length of the runway for the long jump and triple jump should be 39.62 meters (130 feet) from the edge nearest the pit of each event's takeoff board. It is recommended that the width of the runway be 1.22 meters (four feet). The construction and material of the runway should be extended beyond the takeoff board to the nearer edge of the landing pit. When the runway is not distinguishable from the adjacent surface, it is recommended that it be bordered by lines 5.08 centimeters (two inches) in width from the start of the nearer edge of the landing pit (NCAA, 2001).

The landing area should be not less than 2.74 meters (nine feet) in width and identical in elevation with the takeoff

Photo by Meghan Sawyer

Water jump,
Indiana State University.

Jumping Areas (Indoor and Outdoor)

High Jump

It is recommended that the approach be an octagon or square with a surface of at least 21 meters (68.909). The minimum length provided should be 15 meters (49.219). The length of the approach run is limited.

The takeoff area is the semicircle enclosed by a three-meter (9.84 foot) radius whose centerpoint is directly under the center of the crossbar. For a record to be approved officially, no point within this area may be higher than the tolerances (NCAA, 2001).

Pole Vault (see Figure 19.4)

The vaulting box in which the vaulting pole is planted should be constructed of wood, metal, or other suitable materials. Its dimensions and shape should be those shown in the accompanying diagram (see Figure 19.4). The box should be painted white and immovably fixed in the ground so that all of its upper edges are flush with the takeoff area. The angle between the bottom of the box and the stopboard (see Figure 19.4) should be 105 degrees. The vaulting runway needs a minimum length of 38.1 meters (125 feet). It is recommended that the width of the runway be 1.22 meters (four feet) (NCAA, 1997).

board. The area should be filled with sand. Figure 19.5 shows an approved device for ensuring proper sand level (NCAA, 2001).

In the long jump, the distance between the takeoff board and the nearer edge of the landing area should not be less than one meter (3.28 feet) or greater than 3.66 meters (12 feet). The distance between the foul line and the farther edge of the landing area should be at least 10 meters (32.81 feet).

In the men's triple jump, the nearer edge of the landing area should be at least 10.97 meters (36 feet) (12.5 meters or 41 feet is recommended) from the foul line.

In the women's triple jump, the nearer edge of the landing area should be at least 8.53 meters (28 feet) (10.36 meters or 34 feet is recommended) from the foul line.

The takeoff should be a board made of wood or other suitable rigid material 19.8 to 20.32 centimeters (7.8 to eight inches) wide, at least 1.22 meters (four feet) long, and not more than 10 centimeters (3.94 inches) thick. The upper surface of the board must be level with the runway surface. This board should be painted white and be firmly fixed in the runway. The edge of the takeoff board nearest the landing pit should be the foul line. For the purpose of aiding the calling of fouls, the area immediately beyond the foul line may be prepared as shown in Figure 19.6. A tray 10.2 centimeters (four inches) wide filled with plasticene or other suitable material may be used. The plasticene or other material should be of a contrasting color to, and level with, the takeoff board (NCAA, 2001).

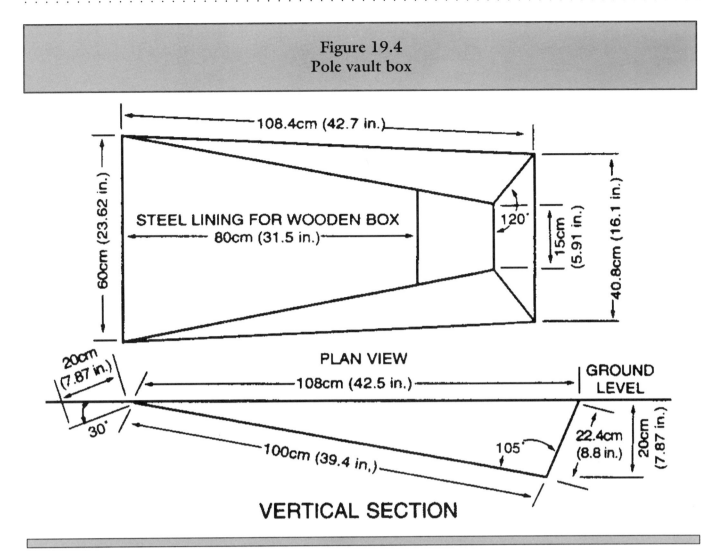

Figure 19.4
Pole vault box

Surfaces for Track and Runways

Once the basic design work is completed, a track surface must be selected. Natural-material track systems, such as cinder and clay, used to be common. These tracks were relatively inexpensive to construct, but they required constant maintenance and were rendered soggy by rains, often causing postponement or cancellation of meets. In recent years, the growing cost of transporting the materials used in these tracks has increased their price to a point where they are nearly as expensive as more modern systems.

All-weather surfaces, the first modern track surfacing systems, became popular in the late 1960s. Their development meant that systems were now available that were relatively durable and unaffected by ordinary weather. Called asphalt-bound, these systems consisted of a combination of rubber with asphalt emulsion, sand and asphalt, or roofing asphalt.

Although many asphalt-bound tracks are still in use, these tracks (like cinder tracks) are no longer being constructed in large numbers because their disadvantages are no longer balanced by a significant cost savings. Asphalt-bound tracks are affected by temperature—they become quite soft in the summer and hard in the winter. More important, asphalt becomes harder as it ages, so that despite its rubber content, an older asphalt-bound track is no more resilient for runners than an ordinary street.

At the same time, the cost of an asphalt-bound track has increased, because it has become increasingly difficult to find an asphalt plant willing to manufacture the special mix required at an affordable price. Existing asphalt-bound tracks in good condition are often sealed to prolong their life. An asphalt-bound track in good condition can be used as a base for a more modern all-weather surface.

Today, most tracks are constructed of rubber particles bound with latex or polyurethane. The latex or polyurethane surface is installed to a depth of 3/8 to 1/2 inch on top of an asphalt or concrete base. The rubber used may be black or colored. Black rubber particles may be granular or stranded and they may be made from natural rubber, styrene-butadiene rubber (SBR), or ethylene-propylene-diene rubber (EPDM), virgin or recycled. Colored rubber particles are almost always made of virgin EPDM rubber and come in granular form only. The relative costs and performance characteristics of the rubber types used are beyond the scope of this article. In general, though, virgin rubber is more expensive than recycled rubber, and colored rubber is more expensive than black rubber (Bardeen, et al., 1992).

Latex-bound tracks provide good performance and durability at an affordable cost. Depending on the specific type of system, color, and location, latex tracks cost from $8 to $25 per square yard (Bardeen, et al., 1992). They can be installed in multiple layers or in a single layer, creating a permeable, resilient surface. In some systems, the rubber is

Figure 19.5
Control of sand level in long jump and triple jump

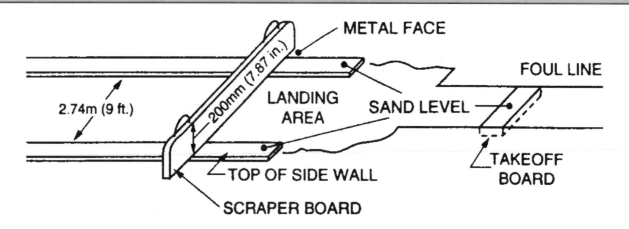

Figure 19.6
Long jump and triple jump takeoff board and foul marker

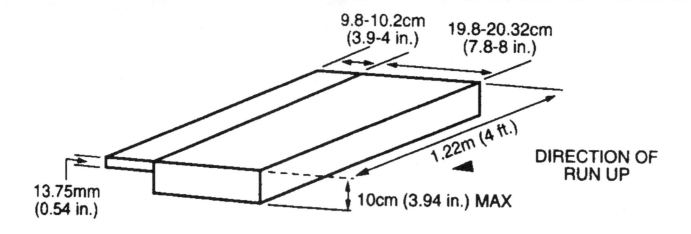

spread over the track surface, which is then sprayed with the latex binder. In other systems, the rubber particles and binder are premixed and then spread. Virtually all latex systems are permeable to some degree.

The basic, and least expensive, system is black, but three types of colored systems are available, including colored binder with black rubber; color sandwich, which has colored rubber and colored binder in the top layers over black rubber/black binder or black rubber/colored binder; or full-depth color, where both the rubber and latex binder are colored throughout the surface.

Polyurethane systems are more expensive than latex systems, costing from $14 to $55 per square yard, but they are considered to be more durable. In addition, their resilient but slightly firmer surface is often preferred by track athletes, so they are often used for world-class competitive tracks. Polyurethane surfaces can be either permeable or impermeable. They are most often mixed and installed on

site, though premanufactured systems are available for locations where on-site mixing and spraying is not feasible (Bardeen, et al., 1992).

Polyurethane surfaces may be colored or black. There are four types. The basic polyurethane-bound system consists of rubber particles bound with polyurethane to form a base mat. The base mat may be used alone, or it may be enhanced by the addition of a structural spray consisting of a mixture of polyurethane and rubber sprayed on top of the mat, which creates a textured surface. Alternatively, the base mat may be coated with a flood coat of polyurethane and rubber, creating an impermeable, textured surface. Or, a full-pour system may be used, where each layer is mixed and poured in place. Full-pour systems are impermeable and textured.

With so many systems available, it is important to consider initial cost, maintenance cost over the expected life of the surface, life expectancy, surface wear, repairability, and performance characteristics of the surface.

In the first step of the construction phase, the track is staked out on the site, and all measurements are carefully checked. Elevations and grades are set. Next, excavation begins. The sod and topsoil are removed, and the track area is excavated to a depth of eight to 12 inches. The area of excavation is wider than the finished track will be. The asphalt courses and synthetic surfacing also will extend beyond the actual dimensions of the track lanes. This pavement extension serves several purposes—it allows for drainage of the track and infield, and serves as a control point for leveling, grading, and establishing the correct length and width of the track (Bardeen, et al., 1992).

In some locations, subsoil must be sterilized after excavation and prior to base construction. If weed growth under or through asphalt surfaces is a problem, herbicides should be considered.

Once excavation is completed, a grader is used to establish the appropriate slope and pitch. Normally tracks are pitched to the inside, with a slope of not more than 1% or 1/8 inch in one foot. (A slope of 2%—1/4 inch in one foot—is acceptable for a high school track.) Finally, a heavy vibratory roller is used to tightly compact the sub-base, which prevents settling that may cause cracking in the finished surface (Bardeen, et al., 1992).

After completion of the preliminary site work, the measurements must be rechecked. The allowable tolerances of the finished track are so small that measurements should be checked at each stage of construction to prevent problems at a later stage.

A base course is then laid. The base course is usually aggregate, but asphalt or penetration macadam also are used. The base course should be no less than four inches thick; more in colder climates. Once spread to uniform thickness, aggregate should be compacted with a tandem roller. After compaction, the grade of the base course must again be verified.

Next are the leveling and finish courses. Asphalt is commonly used for these layers, although concrete can be used. A recent development in track design is the dynamic base track, which uses a rubber, stone, and polyurethane binder mix in place of the solid asphalt or concrete track structure.

A leveling course of hot plant-mix asphalt is applied to the aggregate base to build an asphalt track. This leveling—or binding—layer contains fairly coarse aggregate to provide stability to the finished track. It is rolled and compacted to a thickness of not less than one inch. On top of the leveling course, a surface or finish course of finer asphalt is applied. Like the leveling course, the finish course is compacted to a thickness of not less than one inch. The proper type of asphalt will vary from location to location. State highway department standards can provide some guidance in choosing an asphalt mix.

The finish course is rolled and compacted to complete base construction. Once completed, the asphalt or concrete base must be cured prior to application of the surfacing system. Asphalt is usually allowed to cure for 14 days, while concrete normally cures for 28 to 30 days.

The cured surface is then inspected one last time. The finished surface must not deviate more than 1/8 inch in 10 feet from the specified grade. Its surface may be flooded to check for low areas, called bird baths, to complete the in-spection of the base. The base is then cleaned to remove loose particles, dirt, or oil and, for most surfacing systems, primed.

Next, the synthetic surface is installed. The track surface must be installed in strict compliance with the specifications for that particular type of surface and, for layered systems, each layer must be properly cured prior to the installation of the next one.

The last step in constructing a track is calibration and marking. Various options—such as color code, and design or markings—must be considered in light of the type of competition that will be held on the track. The governing bodies of high school, college, national, and international amateur track have all agreed that the 200-meter race should be marked in such a way that all racers start on a turn. But for some events, the governing bodies differ, so the markings will differ. Once such decisions are made, a track-marking specialist should perform all necessary computations and measurements, marking the required distances on the track. Today, track calibration and marking is frequently computer-assisted to ensure its accuracy.

Permanent markings are then painted on the track, indicating the various distances, start and finish areas, exchange zones, lane numbers, photo timing marks and similar symbols. The track striper then certifies that the marking and striping meet the specifications agreed to by the owner and designer and the requirements of the appropriate governing body. For most high school tracks, certification by the striper is considered sufficient. If the track is to be used for high-level competition, it must be measured and certified as accurate by a professional engineer or licensed land surveyor.

From start to finish, a track project involves many steps. The planning phase of the project can take several months, while actual construction will take at least eight to 12 weeks, without delays caused by weather or other factors. Do your homework—the investment of time and energy now will yield a quality facility in the future.

Throwing Areas (Indoor and Outdoor)

Throwing Circles

The circles in throwing events should be made of a band of metal or suitable rigid material (as described in Figures 7, 9, and 11), the top of which should be flush with the concrete outside the circle. The interior surface should be of concrete or similar material and should 20 millimeters (0.79 inches), plus or minus six millimeters (0.24 inch), lower than the surface outside the circle (NCAA, 2001).

The following is the procedure used for determining a 40-degree sector: The level of the surface within the landing area should be the same as the level of the surface of the throwing circle.

The inside diameters of the shot-put and hammer-throw circles should be 2.135 meters (seven feet), plus or minus five millimeters (0.20 inch), and the diameter of the discus circle should be 2.5 meters (8.20 feet), plus or minus five millimeters (NCAA, 2001).

The circle should be made of metal or suitable rigid material six millimeters (0.24 inch) in thickness and 19.05 millimeters (0.75 inch) in height, plus or minus six millimeters, and be firmly secured flush with the throwing surface.

The insert should be made of metal or suitable rigid material (rubber is not suitable). The top of the insert must be flush with the concrete outside the circle.

All circles should be divided in half by a 5.08 centimeter (two-inch) line extending from the outer edge of the circle to the end of the throwing pad and measured at right angles to the imaginary center of the throwing sector. There should be no lines painted within any throwing circle.

Shot-Put Area

The circle should be constructed in accordance with Figure 19.7. The stepboard is an arc of wood, or other suitable material painted white and firmly fixed so that its inner edge coincides with the inner edge of the shot-put circle. It should measure 1.22 meters (four feet) in length along its inside edge, 112 to 116 millimeters (4.41 to 4.57 inches) in width and 98 to 102 (3.86 to 4.02 inches) in height (see Figure 19.7) (NCAA, 2001).

Radial lines 5.08 centimeters (two inches) wide should form a 40-degree angle extended from the center of the circle. The inside edges of these lines should mark the sector.

The surface within the landing area should be on the same level as the throwing surface. Sector flags should mark the ends of the lines (NCAA, 2001).

Discus Area

All discus throws should be made from an enclosure or cage centered on the circle to ensure safety of spectators, officials, and competitors (see Figure 19.8). The height of the discus cage should be at least four meters (13 feet 1.5 inches). A discus cage is designed to provide limited protection for spectators, officials, and competitors. It does not ensure their safety due to the nature of the event (NCAA, 2001).

The circle should be constructed in accordance with Figure 19.9. The throwing sector for the discus should be marked by two radial lines 5.08 centimeters (two inches) wide that form a 40-degree angle, extended from the center of the circle, and the inside edges of these lines should mark the sector. The surface within the landing area should be on the same level as the throwing surface. Sector flags should mark the ends of the lines.

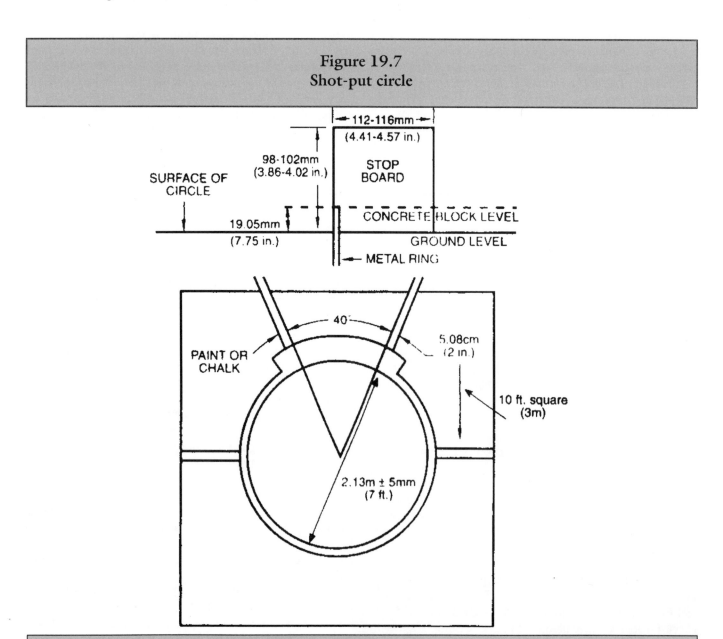

Figure 19.7
Shot-put circle

Figure 19.8
Discus circle

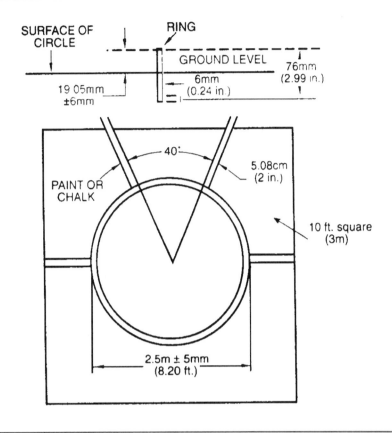

Figure 19.9
Construction for discus cage

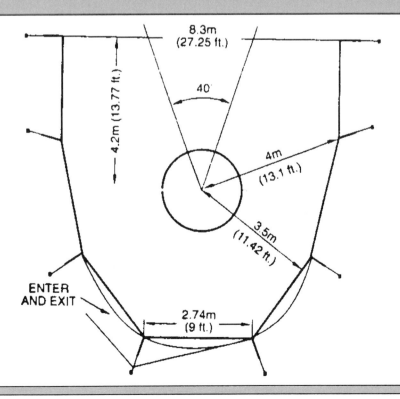

The sector should be centered within the enclosure.

Hammer Area

All hammer throws should be made from an enclosure or cage centered according to the dimensions in Figure 19.10 to ensure the safety of spectators, officials, and competitors. The cage shall be constructed as follows (NCAA, 2001):

- There should be two movable panels at the front of the screen at least 4.20 meters (13.78 feet) but not more than 4.35 meters (14.27 feet) in width.
- These panels should be attached to a fixed vertical support that is 2.85 meters (9.35 feet) away from the sector line and 6.086 meters (20.08 feet) out from the center of the circle. The height of the movable panels should be 6.15 meters (20.18 feet).

The circle should be constructed in accordance with Figure 19.11. The throwing sector for the hammer should be marked by two radial lines 5.08 centimeters (two inches) wide that form a 40-degree angle, extended from the center of the circle. The inside edges of these lines should mark the sector. The surface within the landing area should be on the same level as the throwing surface. Sector flags should mark the ends of the lines. The sector should be centered within the enclosure.

Javelin Area

It is recommended that the runway be constructed of an artificial surface for a width of four meters (13.12 feet) for the entire length of the runway. The minimum length of the runway for the javelin should be 36.58 meters (120 feet). If an artificial surface is used, it is recommended that the runway be extended one meter (3.28 feet) beyond the foul line for safety reasons. The runway should be marked by two parallel lines 5.08 centimeters (two inches) in width and a minimum of 1.22 meters (four feet) apart for 21.34 meters (70.01 feet), widening to four meters (13.12 feet) apart for the 15.24 meters (50 feet) before the foul line (NCAA, 2001).

The foul line should be seven centimeters (2.76 inches) wide and painted white, in the shape of an arc with a radius of eight meters (26.25 feet). The distance between its extremities should be four meters (13.12 feet) measured straight across from end to end (NCAA, 2001).

Radius lines 5.08 centimeters (two inches) wide should be extended from the center of the circle of which the arc of the foul board is a part through the extremities of the arc. The inside edges of these lines should mark the sector. The surface within the landing area should be the on the same level as the throwing surface. Sector flags should mark the ends of the lines (see Figure 19.12) (NCAA, 2001).

Other Structures/Facilities: Finish Line Towers/Press Box

The finish line is the control center for running events. The finish line tower should be directly across from the finish line. There could be up to three towers on a track, one at either end of the straightaway, and another diagonally across from the main tower at the 200-meter start position.

Figure 19.10
Construction of hammer cage

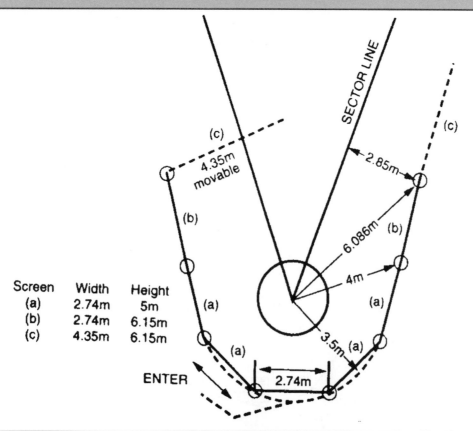

Screen	Width	Height
(a)	2.74m	5m
(b)	2.74m	6.15m
(c)	4.35m	6.15m

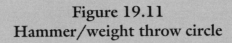

Figure 19.11
Hammer/weight throw circle

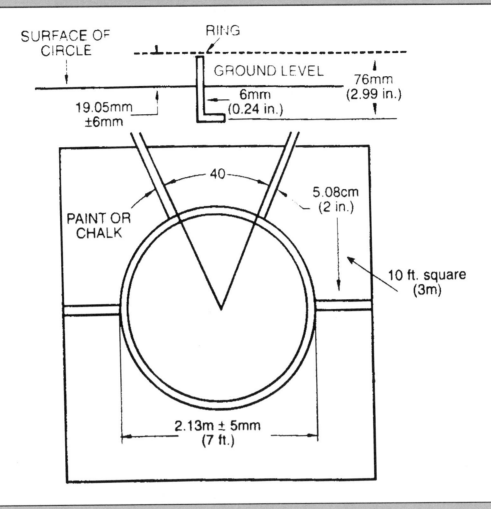

Tower A

It should be a two-story enclosed structure, 20 feet by 40 feet square with eight-foot ceilings and a roof designed as a deck with railings. The first-floor area will contain space for restrooms, a small storage area with a small roll-up door, and concessions. The second floor will have picture windows facing the finish line. The second floor area will have space for the press, announcer, and the automatic timer, computers, and cameras (Flynn, 1993).

Tower B

This will be a duplicate of Tower A, except the first floor will be dedicated to the storage of hurdles, implements, and pads. The first-floor storage area will have a large roll-up door to accommodate the large landing pads.

Both towers should have hot and cold water, sewer connection, communications lines (i.e., telephone, computer, and television), electricity, and appropriate ventilation.

Lighting

The track and field area should be lighted for security at a minimum, but serious consideration should be given to lighting the area for evening competition.

Fencing

The entire facility should be fenced so it can be secured when not in use. The fence should be at least 10 feet high, plastic/vinyl coated, painted to match the surrounding paint patterns. The fence should have gates in appropriate locations for athletes, spectators, and maintenance vehicles (Flynn, 1993).

Fences need to be installed to protect athletes and officials from throwing areas (e.g., discus, hammer, and javelin). These fences need to be at least six feet high. They should also be constructed with plastic/vinyl-coated material.

Spectator Seating

Spectator seating is a necessity. The planners should design seating for both sides of the track. The running track will have two finish lines going in opposite directions. Depending on the prevailing wind, a decision will be made as to which direction the races will be run. Therefore, it is necessary to provide seating on both sides of the track for spectators. (See Chapter 13 for standards relative to new bleachers or retrofitting old bleachers.)

The total number of seats should be based on historical data regarding spectator involvement over the past five

Figure 19.12
Javelin throwing area

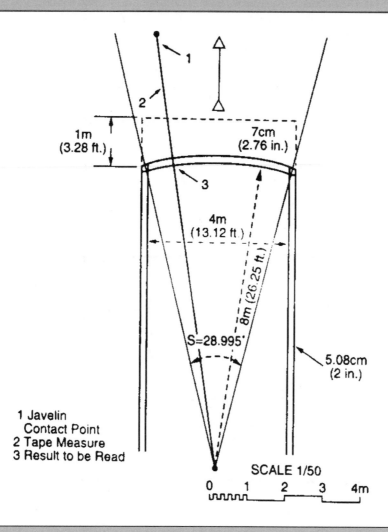

1m
(3.28 ft.)

7cm
(2.76 in.)

4m
(13.12 ft.)

8m (26.25 ft.)

S=28.995°

5.08cm
(2 in.)

1 Javelin
  Contact Point
2 Tape Measure
3 Result to be Read

SCALE 1/50

0   1   2   3   4m

years. The seating can either be permanent, constructed of metal, wood, or other appropriate materials, or be portable aluminum bleachers. The higher the bleachers, the greater the liability concerns. If money is not a problem, construct concrete seating large enough to incorporate storage areas underneath the seats and a press box on the upper level (Flynn, 1993).

Starting System

Modern timing systems are connected to the starter's gun. Therefore, the hard wiring that is required should be placed underground and junction boxes made available at the various starting lines for the races. These junction boxes should be at least four feet off the ground.

Landscaping

There should be an irrigation system designed to provide water to all grass areas, shrubbery, and flowers. When planning the irrigation system, careful consideration needs to be given to providing additional water to drinking fountains throughout the complex and water for the water jump. The track and field area should be large enough to provide at

least a half-acre shaded area for athletes between events. The areas at the end of the straightaways should have trees to provide a wind break for the athletes (Flynn, 1993).

Track and Field Equipment

Starting Blocks

Starting blocks must be made without devices that could provide artificial aid in starting. They may be adjustable but must be constructed entirely of rigid materials.

Hurdles

Hurdles should be constructed of metal, wood, or other suitable material. The hurdles should consist of two bases and two uprights supporting a rectangular frame, reinforced by one or more crossbars. The top crossbar should be wood or other suitable material, with beveled edges, and a height of 70 millimeters (2.76 inches). The center of the crossbar should be directly over the end of the base. The surface facing the starting line should be white in color with two vertical or diagonal stripes. A center chevron should be added to help contestants determine the center of the lane (NCAA, 2001).

Pull-over force refers to the 3.6 kilograms (eight pounds) of steady pulling force required to overturn a hurdle when applied to the center of the uppermost edge of the top crossbar and in the direction of the finish line. If the weights cannot be adjusted to the required overturning force, it is recommended that the next greater setting be used, since records will not be allowed when the overturning force or the weight of the hurdle is less than the required minimum (NCAA, 2001).

When no definite counterweight setting for intermediate hurdles has been made by the manufacturer, it is sometimes possible to attain the correct adjustment by setting one weight as for the 106.7-centimeter (42-inch) height and the other weight as for 76.2-centimeter (30-inch) height. A difference of three millimeters (0.12 inch) above or below the required height will be tolerated (see Figure 19.13) (NCAA, 2001).

Steeplechase Hurdles

Hurdles should be constructed of metal, wood, or other suitable material. The hurdles shall consist of a base and two uprights supporting a rectangular frame, with a single crossbar. The crossbar shall be of wood or other suitable material, without sharp edges or with a 6.35 millimeter (0.25 in) bevel, and have a height of 127 millimeters (five inch) square. The crossbar shall be white in color with stripes of one distinctive contrasting color.

Steeplechase and water-jump hurdles (men) should not be less than 91.1 centimeters (2.99 feet) nor more than 91.7 centimeters (3.01 feet) high and should be at least 3.66 meters (12 feet) in width; and (women) the hurdles shall be not less than 75.9 centimeters (2.49 ft) nor more than 76.5 centimeters (2.51 ft) high and should be at least 3.66 meters (12 feet) in width. It is recommended that the first hurdle be at least five meters (16 feet, 4.75 inches) in width. The section of the top bar of the hurdles and the hurdle at the water jump should be 127 millimeters (five inches) square without sharp edges or with a 6.35-millimeter (0.25 inch) bevel. The weight of each hurdle should be at least 80 kilograms (176.4 pounds). Each hurdle should have on either side a base between 12 meters (3.94 feet) and 1.4 meters (4.59 feet) long (NCAA, 2001).

High Jump

The high jump pad should be a minimum of 4.88 meters wide by 2.44 meters deep (16 feet by eight feet). It should be high enough and of a composition that will provide a safe and comfortable landing. A minimum height of 66.04 centimeters (26 inches), including the top pad unit, is preferred (NCAA, 2001).

The horizontal supports of the crossbar should be flat and rectangular, four centimeters (1.6 inches) wide and six centimeters (2.4 inches) long, and friction-free. Each support should point toward the opposite upright so that the crossbar will rest between the uprights along the narrow dimension (3.81 centimeters [1.5 inches]) of the support (NCAA, 2001).

The uprights should extend at least 100 millimeters (3.94 inches) above the support of the crossbar. The crossbar should be circular and be made of suitable material. The ends of the crossbar should be smooth and not be covered with rubber or any other material that has the effect of increasing the friction between the surface of the crossbar and the supports. The diameter of the bar must be at least 25 millimeters but not more than 30 millimeters (0.98 to 1.18 inches). The crossbar should be constructed in such a way that a flat surface of 25 to 30 millimeters (0.98 to 1.18 inches) by 150 to 200 millimeters (5.91 to 7.87 inches) is designed for the purpose of placing the bar on the supports of the uprights (NCAA, 2001).

Figure 19.13
Hurdle measurements

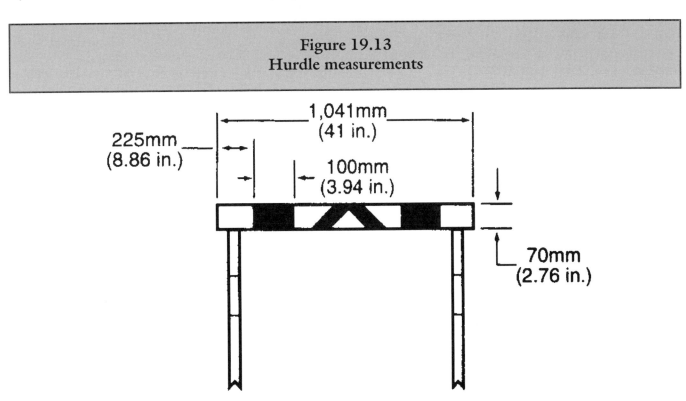

Pole Vault

The pole vault pad measurement beyond the vertical plane of the stopboard should be a minimum of 4.88 meters wide by 3.66 meters deep (16 feet by 12 feet). It is recommended that the front portion of the pad be the same width as the back units, 4.88 meters (16 feet), extending 91.44 centimeters (36 inches) from the back edge of the stopboard to the front edge of the vaulting box. Measured across the bottom of the cutout. The back of the cutout should be placed no farther than 36 millimeters (14.17 inches) from the vertical plane of the stopboard. A height of 81.28 centimeters (32 inches), including the top pad unit, is required. Suitable padding should be placed around the base of the standards (NCAA, 2001).

Any style upright or posts may be used for the pole vault, provided the style is rigid and supported by a base not to exceed 10.16 centimeters (four inches) in height above the ground. Cantilevered uprights are recommended. The distance between the vertical uprights or between the extension arms where such are used should be 4.32 meters (14.7 feet) (NCAA, 2001).

The crossbar should rest on round metal pins that project not more than 75 millimeters (2.95 inches) at right angles from the uprights and have diameters of not more than 13 millimeters (0.512 inches). The upper surfaces of these pins should be smooth, without indentations or aids of any kind that might help to hold the crossbar in place. The crossbar should be circular and made of suitable material. The ends of the crossbar shall be smooth and not be covered with rubber or any other material that has the effect of increasing the friction between the surface of the crossbar and the supports. The diameter of the crossbar must be at least 29 millimeters but not more than 31 millimeters (1.14 to 1.22 inches). The crossbar should be between 4.48 and 4.52 meters (14.7 to 14.83 feet) in length. The maximum weight shall be 2.25 kilograms (4.96 pounds). For the purpose of placing the bar on the supports of the uprights, the ends of the crossbar should be constructed in such a way that a flat surface of 29 to 35 millimeters (1.14 to 1.38 inches) by 200 millimeters (7.87 inches) is provided (NCAA, 2001).

Other Accessory Equipment

The following pieces of equipment will be very useful for both indoor and outdoor track and field facilities (NCAA, 2001):
- Pole vault standards base protection pads,
- Countdown timer,
- Wind gauge—now required for all collegiate 100, 200, 110 & 110 hurdles, long jump, and high jump,
- Implement certification unit,
- Aluminum water jump,
- Foundation tray,
- Blanking lid,
- Take-off board with plasticine insert,
- Long jump/triple jump aluminum pit covers,
- Throwing rings,
- Toe boards,
- Concentric circles,
- Stainless steel or aluminum pole-vault box,
- Pole-vault covers,
- Finish post,

- Aluminum track curbing,
- Rotating track gate,
- Hammer cage,
- Discus cage,
- Indoor throwing event cage,
- Lane markers,
- Distance marker boxes,
- Long jump/triple jump distance indicator,
- Performance boards,
- Lap counter,
- Wind display,
- Awards stand,
- Judges' stand,
- Starter's rostrum,
- Hurdle carts,
- Platform cart,
- Starting block caddy, and
- Implement carts—shotput cart, hammer cart, javelin cart, discus cart, combo cart.

Cross-Country Facility

The Course (see Figure 19.14)

The length of the cross-country course varies as follows:
- Men—The length of a cross-country race should be from 8,000 to 10,000 meters, unless otherwise mutually agreed upon by coaches or determined by the games committee.
- High school—5,000-meter standard, some variations are found between state associations.

Women—5,000 meters; high school—3,000 to 5,000 meters.

Course Layout

The course should be confined to fields, woods, and grasslands. Parks, golf courses, or specially designed courses (see Figure 19.14) are recommended. There should be a control facility constructed at or near the finish line with elevated seating. The turf should be a quality to promote safety and freedom from injury to the runners, keeping the following in mind:
- Dangerous ascents or descents, undergrowth, deep ditches, and in general any hindrance detrimental to the contestants must be avoided.
- Narrow gaps must be no less than two and preferably five meters in width for non- championships courses. Obstacles and other hindrances should be avoided for the first 600 to 800 meters as well as the last 200 to 300 meters of the race.

Note: Championship course must be at least 10 meters wide at all points.
- Continuous traversing of roadways should be avoided.
- The direction and path of the course shall be defined clearly for the runners.
- All turns must be gradual.

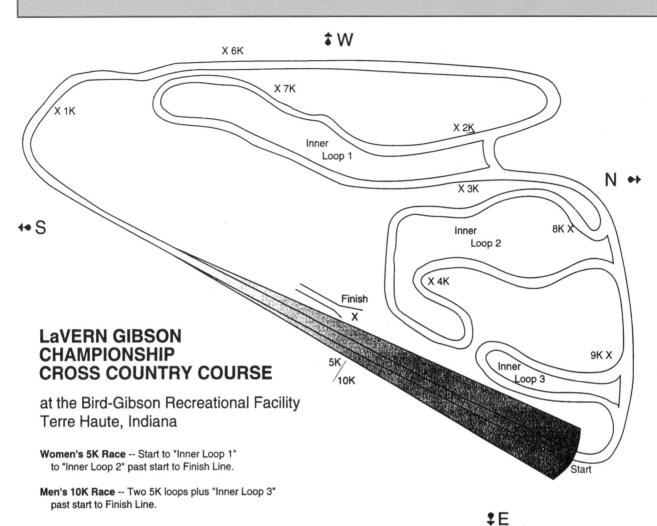

**Figure 19.14
LaVern Gibson Championship Cross-Country Course**

Course Markings

The course should be properly measured along the shortest possible route that a runner may take, and it must be marked clearly by at least two of the following methods, presented in order of preference:

Sign posts not less than seven feet high, with large directional arrows on boards fastened to the tops of the posts so that the arrows will be visible plainly at a distance to competitors approaching the posts. The posts must be placed at every point where the course turns, on the side of the direction of the turn, and wherever there is any doubt as to the direction of travel.

A single white or colored line for directional purposes only—not to be assumed as the measured line—or two lines that mark the outside borders of the course, one on the measured course marking its shortest perimeter and the second such that runners cannot vary from the proper course. In addition, these two lines serve as restraining lines for spectators. Lines on the turns must vary in color from the color of lines approaching the turn.

Flags, sign posts, or stakes that meet the following conditions:

- markers at least seven feet above the ground level,
- a turn to the left marked by a red flag or arrow of direction on a sign post or stake,
- a turn to the right marked by a yellow flag or arrow of direction on a sign post or stake,
- a course continuing straight marked by a blue flag or arrow of direction on a sign post or stake, and
- all flags, sign posts or stakes marking the shortest perimeter of the course.

Finally, all of the above course-marking devices must be placed on the edge of the measured line when lines and flags, sign posts, or stakes are used to mark the course.

Summary

A track and field competition complex is complicated at best when compared to other outdoor or indoor sport spaces, such as an indoor basketball/volleyball court or a baseball, football, or soccer field.

Photo by Tom Sawyer

Cross-Country Control Center,
Indiana State University.

Cross-Country Control Center,
Indiana State University.
Finish line.

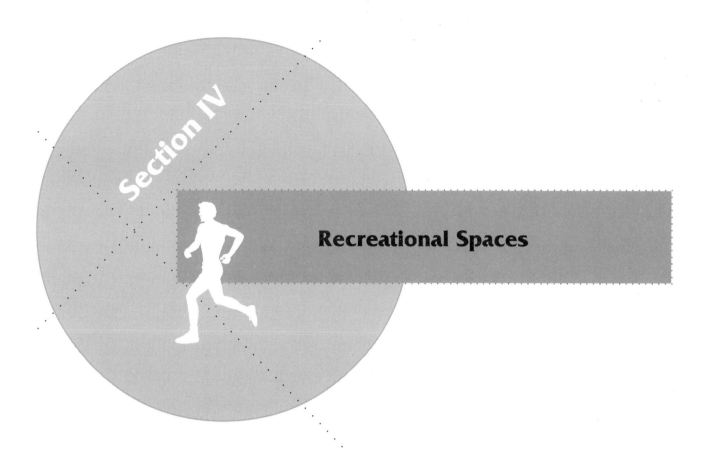

Section IV

Recreational Spaces

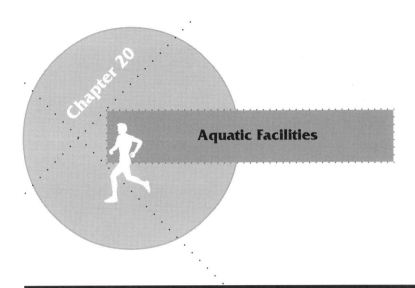

Chapter 20

Aquatic Facilities

D.J. Hunsaker, Councilman/Hunsaker, Natatorium Planners, Designers, & Engineers

The purpose of this chapter is to review current trends in aquatic facilities. The field of aquatics has experienced a broad and comprehensive transition since the early 1980s. From the standpoint of professional programming, activities have been developed for all age groups with attendance increasing mostly among seniors, followed closely by preschoolers. Through the entire age span, North Americans have found aquatic activity in outdoor and indoor swimming facilities to provide entertainment, education, and skill enhancement.

Until the 1970s, swimming/diving activities almost always took place in a rectangular swimming pool that was shallow at one end and deep at the other. The introduction of the wave pool at Point Mallard, Alabama, in the late 1960s demonstrated the opportunity to have more fun and excitement in a manufactured swimming tank that was filled with filtered and hygienically clean water. This new approach led to aquatic entertainment facilities in the commercial sector, called water parks. As private capital underwrote these projects, public agencies at the municipal and county levels began to experiment with non-rectangular pools that featured zero-entry water areas, water slides, and children's water play areas. While most of these initiatives with moving water were cautious, the trend in public aquatic recreation definitely is moving toward the design philosophy that is accepted on a broad front in western Europe, Canada, and resort areas in Asia, the South Pacific, and Africa.

Learning Objectives

After reading this chapter, the student will be able to
- describe aquatic facility trends,
- design and implement a needs analysis for an aquatics facility, and
- describe the technical considerations for designing either a recreational or competitive aquatic facility.

Aquatic Center Leisure Trends

Pool Features

Leisure pool features include water falls, fountains, whirlpools, current channels, lazy rivers, and participatory water play apparatus. They must be designed carefully, considering initial costs, operating costs, life-cycle costs, and long-term popularity.

Falling water can be a dramatic focal point in a natatorium or an outdoor aquatic center. An indoor facility must be designed with acoustical treatment to reduce the reverberation time of the splash noise. An indoor facility also must be designed to minimize atomization of water. Falling water is different from the misting of sprays. The latter will greatly increase the humidity in the space and increase the water vapor inhaled by people in the natatorium.

Current channels, lazy rivers, and water slides must be designed for safety and economy of operation. Since many states do not have regulations that specifically address these new concepts in aquatic recreation features, designers must work with jurisdictional officials to develop systems, designs, and configurations that reflect the philosophy of the agency. Computer technology is a cost-effective component of water features when used to activate and deactivate motors. The motors control the water pumps in an economical sequence that varies at different times of the day, week, and season.

Water slides offer many options for the leisure pool designer. Most installations are engineered by manufacturers based upon the design developed by the architect. The resulting protocol is essentially design/build and allows the configuration to be developed by the organization that is most knowledgeable about this very specialized equipment. In so doing, the manufacturer/designer/constructor accepts the liability for the product.

With few exceptions, the water-slide industry produces only fiberglass flumes. The slides can be open or totally enclosed as tubes. Each year, more elaborate designs are produced for large and small venues.

Children enjoying leisure pool activities.

Current channels and lazy rivers can be designed in a variety of ways. The difference between the two concepts is the velocity of the current and the length of the channel. The lazy river is usually a closed loop that allows participants to float continuously at a slow speed, where the current channel is a part of the leisure pool that provides a relatively short flume with a much faster current.

Therapy Pools and Whirlpool Spas

Another new type of pool that is appearing with frequency in North America is the therapy pool. These pools are being included in the construction of new wellness and fitness centers, many of which are being developed by hospitals. The therapy pool usually features an access ramp, recessed stairs, underwater benches, a deep-water area, and hydraulic lifts or movable floors for the non-ambulatory. These pools can be part of an outpatient facility that specializes in treatment for temporary disabilities (e.g., post-surgical, post-injury or post-trauma, cardiac, etc). Other pools are located in rehabilitation centers for in-patients with permanent disabilities (e.g., paraplegia, quadriplegia, stroke, multiple sclerosis, etc.). Such pools also are in health care facilities that specialize in the treatment and/or care of the physically and mentally disturbed. In many cases, the therapy pools are designed for and serve a variety of user groups.

The whirlpool spa has become a standard water feature in many natatoria at municipal, college, and university sites. However, the spa seldom is seen in high school natatoria. Spas also are popular in health clubs and wellness centers. Their appeal is wide among frequent users of recreation and fitness centers.

Pools and Natatoria

During the mid-1990s, a significant increase in the number of municipalities building leisure pools, both indoor and outdoor, occurred to the degree that the water park industry sees its emerging market being the public sector. This new group of developers creates smaller facilities than commercial developers but in much greater numbers. The result is that manufacturers have designed products and systems for the leisure pool complex, which for many companies is now the major market for their products.

A growing number of indoor natatoria are also being built. These facilities are being created frequently in Canada, with its colder climates, as well as throughout the United States. The reasons are several. The year-round benefits are being recognized along with the justification of higher capital costs for the 12-month programs they provide. Other indoor aquatic centers are being constructed at educational institutions to meet expanding demand on the campus and to meet competition from other schools, colleges, and universities, which are targeting the same prospective students.

These indoor facilities, along with others in health clubs, wellness centers, the YMCA, and the JCCA, etc., are giving their respective populations the opportunity to recreate and develop skills that will enhance the aquatic experience throughout a lifetime. "Moms and Tots" programs introduce infants to the water in the most secure environment (i.e., in the parent's arms). Preschoolers also have the opportunity to learn to swim and be water safe in a way that provides a foundation for lifelong participation in water sports. Competitive swimming and diving is usually the next plateau that the young person will master, although many youngsters find their enjoyment in unstructured recreational swimming. Other skills are learned in aquatic centers. These include advanced swimming techniques, lifesaving, lifeguarding, and scuba. Many of these skills will carry over into family passtimes and fitness regimens. The latter usually take form as fitness lap swimming on a year-round basis.

Regardless of the reason for creating a new swim center, a definite protocol should be followed to produce the most efficient, cost-effective, and programmable facility. This chapter describes the necessary procedure and discipline for creating a facility that will best meet the owner's needs.

Needs Analysis

While many people believe that the first step is to select an architect, two essential tasks really should be executed before an architect is asked to design a building. The first is to analyze the needs of the organization/owner; the second is to develop a design program for the facility. This analysis of needs is executed by identifying current users, potential users, and future users. A description of the activities that these users will want is supplemented by a list of activities and programs that the organization/owner's aquatic staff believes is warranted for the activity program in the new facility.

The analysis of the community's needs is more than a simple list. The data also must show the time and space requirements for proposed activities. This allocation of time and space will reveal potential priorities and demands.

The first step toward the objective is to develop an in-depth understanding of deficiencies in the existing aquatic program and the potential for meeting future demand. This can be carried out best by one or more individuals with experience in this important phase. It is at this time that some organizations/owner groups seek the assistance of a design and planning consultant to help them take the necessary steps toward a commitment to such a complex.

The first phase of the needs analysis is a meeting with staff and administration, followed by meetings with user

As these numbers are developed, it is essential that a distinction be made between construction costs and project costs. This is an area that is often misunderstood, and construction costs are emphasized when, in reality, the total project cost must be determined. A project cost includes the hard cost of construction, plus all of the soft costs of loose equipment, administration, and design required for the end product.

Once the project cost has been established and confirmed, it is necessary to move on to the source of financing. This may be a capital fund drive, the state legislature (university and college), a bond issue, certificates of participation, a capital expansion budget, donations, a build/lease back, or a combination of the above.

After the source of funding has been identified and a commitment received, the next step is to select an architectural team. There is a protocol that should be followed in this phase of the project. The first step is to develop a re-

A leisure pool complex.

groups. As a means of developing an understanding of the true core needs of the community, interviews are conducted, public meetings are held, and existing data are reviewed, including previous programs and efforts. Finally, a consensus must be developed among the various parties interested in the project.

Once the needs have been established and agreed to by all parties, the next step is to develop a design program. The design program is an outline of the features that must be provided in the aquatic center and a designation of the area required for each feature. This process includes not only the natatorium, but also the necessary support spaces for the aquatic center.

After the spaces have been identified and have been given surface area values, it is then possible to develop an estimate of the construction cost. This is done by identifying the square footage involved, estimating a cost per square foot by using a conventional formula, and then comparing it to the industry average for recent construction, and adding an escalation factor to reflect the time frame between completed projects and the date of the bidding for the proposed project.

quest for qualifications, which is a formal communication in letter form that is sent to a number of architectural firms. A formal advertisement is also placed in the newspaper. The firms will determine whether they wish to be considered for such a project. If they do, they will submit by a specified date a package that will reflect information about their selected team, as well as past history and experience with projects of all types, including, presumably, those similar to the proposed project.

These submittals will be reviewed, and a selection committee will choose a limited number of firms for an interview. Interviews of the architectural teams will be scheduled for a specific period of time, and the firms will be given a format for their presentation, which usually includes 60% to 75% of the time for a formal presentation and 40% to 25% of the time for answering questions by the interview committee.

The interview process should follow a certain format, and the interview committee should be experienced or at least prepared for a methodical evaluation of the different teams. The important issue is to create a structure whereby all teams are given the same opportunity and benefit relative to presentation time and question-and-answer opportuni-

University of Georgia aquatic facility.

ties. In addition to the interview, it is suggested that the background and experience of each team be researched with former clients.

The final step is to select the architectural team and to sign agreements between the owner and the architectural firm that will lead the team throughout the project. This firm usually is identified as the project architect or architect of record.

What are the tasks and scope of services of the chosen architectural team? At this point an owner's steering committee should be formed, which is made up of individuals representing the users, the administration, the staff, and the owner's project manager. Together, this group must be qualified to make decisions as the process moves forward.

Programming

Much programming is work done when the design program is developed prior to determining funding needs. Once the architectual team is selected, the owner and the architect will confirm the design program surface area needs and requirements developed in the design program stage. The construction cost estimate will be reviewed and confirmed or changed by the project architect. As a result, there will be a confirmation of the project cost estimate at this time.

An aquatic center or a community center featuring a natatorium is a very complex building. It is helpful if the organization/owner's steering committee understands the situation and the necessary design process. By comparison, a more simple structure is an office building, which basically repeats floor plans floor to floor and has very few special-use areas in the building. The next level of complexity may be a school, which still has redundancy in the classroom requirements plus several special areas, such as a gymnasium, auditorium, lunch room, etc. The next level of complexity is the special-use building, which describes a community center or an aquatic center. In this type of building, there is very little redundancy, and the entire facility is unique unto itself. As a result, the design time is much greater than, for example, the office building. The square foot cost usually is higher because of the special features and characteristics the building must provide.

Once the design program and corresponding budget estimate are confirmed, the architect will develop a series of bubble diagrams and adjacency priorities. This information will be discussed with the steering committee and a consensus reached.

The next step is to develop a schematic floor plan that reflects the data developed in the step above. It is at this point that floor plans, access points, and general operating efficiency are developed.

As these issues are resolved, the schematic plans and elevations (single-line drawings) are developed. The schematics are reviewed by the steering committee, which after discussions and contributions by all members, will arrive at a consensus, resulting in an approved set of schematics. At this point it may be necessary for the architect to create a study model. Some architectural teams prefer to use models as a means of evaluating and studying the total building, both inside and outside. Once the model has been approved, an estimate of construction costs will again be developed.

If the project is on course with budget and program, the design development stage will begin, and more detailed drawings will be created at this time. Outline specifications also will be developed by the architect and various consultants on the design team. These will be reviewed by the steering committee. The outline specifications and design development drawings will be used to provide an update of estimated construction costs. (A constant monitoring of construction cost estimates is necessary to keep the project in line with the budget.)

At this time the steering committee must work closely with the architect until the design development drawings and outline specifications are approved.

Once the design development stage has been completed, the next phase is creation of the construction documents (e.g., drawings, specifications, and general conditions).

When the construction documents are approximately 50% complete, a review should occur again with the various consultants and the steering committee. This is an effective point to again estimate the construction costs to see if there is any necessity for a mid-course correction. When the construction documents reach 90% to 100% completion, they should be reviewed again by the respective consultants and the owner's steering committee. If all team members are in agreement and there are no omissions or errors, the architect will assist the owner in advertising for bids.

When the bids are opened, one of three things will occur:

- The project will be under budget, and the design team will proceed or add any alternatives that may have been called out in the construction documents.
- The budget will be the same as the accepted bid, and the project will proceed into the next stage.
- The low bid will be over budget, and deduct alternates will be deleted.

In the event of a significant over-budget situation, even after deduct alternates, a common process is to submit the overall design for value engineering and develop a priority of deletions. This usually is done in concert with the low bidder.

When the construction contract has been signed between the owner and the general contractor, the project then moves into the construction phase. At this time it also should be noted that there is an alternative to a general contractor protocol, and that is the owner's use of a construction management firm. In construction management, an experienced management team serves as a contract manager for the owner, in which case the construction management firm is paid a fee for its expertise. As the owner's agent, the construction management company negotiates directly with the respective subcontractors. While a relatively new concept, the construction management approach does offer some benefits in certain types of projects.

What Happens During the Construction of the Natatorium?

Site Situations

Ideally the site for an aquatic center is level with good-quality soil. Many times, however, the site is not level and there are subsoil problems, e.g., rock, high water table, undesirable types of soil, cuts and fill, compaction, removal, and replacement with engineered fill.

Design Options

A swimming pool and/or natatorium may feature several below-grade designs. One is a full basement, another is a tunnel around the pool shell, a third is a pool shell backfilled with no below-grade space, and a fourth is a combination of any or all of the above.

Basements

Benefits

The basement can provide a storage area, equipment area, piping and plenum location, access for maintenance repair, and no hydrostatic pressure on the pool shell. (The problem of hydrostatic pressure under a swimming pool is significant. If there is a high water table, and no means have been created for relieving this pressure, it is possible that the swimming pool can float out of the ground when it is empty for construction or maintenance reasons. For this reason, special considerations must be made and appropriate designs engineered.)

Disadvantages.

The below-grade space creates greater costs, delivery problems for mechanical equipment used in the below-grade areas, chemical rooms that are remotely located to filter equipment, and sometimes access problems for maintenance personnel.

Swimming Pool Shell Construction

Cast-in-place concrete (see Figure 20.1)

Benefits

The structure can be built above grade or surrounded by a tunnel/basement, and there is no backfill is required. It can be included in the conventional concrete work by the concrete contractor. Cast-in-place concrete is advantageous for tile and a paint finish.

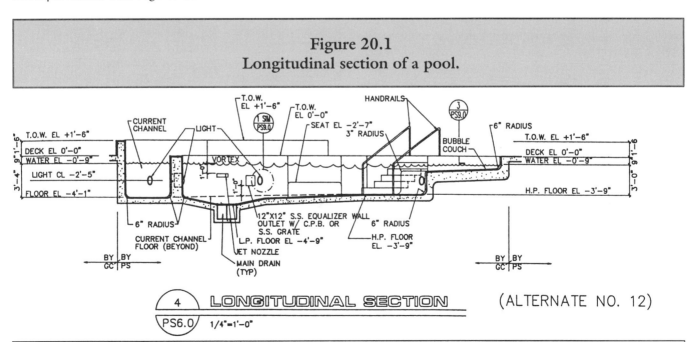

**Figure 20.1
Longitudinal section of a pool.**

Disadvantages

It is costly to create a free-form configuration; water stop and honeycombing leaks are possible, and the wall-to-floor cove is more costly to build compared to pneumatically applied concrete.

Pneumatically Applied Concrete Swimming Pool Shells

Benefits

This is a relatively economical pool shell construction when the pool walls are constructed against a soil embankment or cut. Irregular shapes can be constructed efficiently and at a relatively low cost compared to cast-in-place. The wall-to-floor cove is simple and effective. Monolithic pneumatically applied concrete construction has advantages over the cast components in a cast-in-place pool, which depend upon water stop at joints. It is compatible with tile and marble plaster adhesion.

Disadvantages

It is costly and difficult to build a pneumatically applied pool with no earth cavity. The necessary forms needed for this type of construction erode the cost benefit of the process. Sometimes it is difficult to apply tile to the swimming pool interior. When painting is required, multistep preparation is necessary. Often it is difficult to find experienced and qualified contractors in a local bidding market.

Structural Features In the Natatorium

The first choice is structural steel with concrete and masonry walls, plus a concrete roof system. Because of cost, most natatorium roof structures are made of mild steel beams, joists, and trusses. When these steel components are used, they must be coated with highly effective, long-life coating systems. The roof and ceiling systems must be designed carefully to withstand corrosion created by condensation.

Wooden roof structures are effective if humidity is controlled and air circulation in the space is properly engineered.

A concrete roof structure has many advantages over steel and wood. It is noncorrosive and durable. Its cost, however, is greater than the other two lighter weight options.

Fenestration

Skylights or top lighting are advantageous for location of a natural light source and control of reflective glare on the water. The relation of fenestration to spectator areas, lifeguard locations, and teaching stations is important. Wall and room penetrations for skylights, exhaust ducts, and overhead light fixtures can be the source of problems. As a result, they must be designed, engineered, and constructed with care.

Dehumidification

Relative humidity inside a natatorium should be maintained between 50% and 60%. This can be done in most areas with the use of outside air or refrigerated dehumidification. Such a design must control the dew point, be operated on a 24-hour basis, control condensation, and control the air velocities in the space along with the fresh air mix for needed ventilation. Physical comfort is most noticeable in this phase of the building system.

Materials and Finishes

Because of the high humidity potential and aggressive chloride conditions that may occur in the natatorium space if mechanical systems are shut down either on purpose or by accident, material choices should be tile, epoxy-coated steel (stainless steel used in some swimming pool components), glass, concrete, and anodized aluminum.

Considerations for maintenance tasks are important in the design process. These consist of daily custodial needs, scheduled repair and maintenance, emergency repair and/or replacement, and future repair and replacement (pool filters/HVAC/dehumidification).

During the construction process, a system of inspections and monitoring should be carried out by the owner or his or her representative (e.g., architect/engineer/consultant). This process is necessary to watch for incorrect installation as well as improper components.

Commissioning

This is the important climax to the entire process that has been executed to date. The general contractor, swimming pool contractor, other contractors, the project architect, engineers, and the swimming pool/natatorium consultants coordinate their efforts and put the facility into operation. In this process, notes are made of any and all problems and/or deficiencies. Responsible contractors will make the proper corrections so that the swimming pool and all related systems for the complex will operate according to design and in compliance with all jurisdictional codes and regulations. Likewise, the mechanical HVAC/DH systems will be commissioned.

Because most contracts call for a one-year warranty period, it is recommended that a comprehensive inspection be executed just prior to the expiration of the warranty deadline. An independent and qualified inspector should make this audit, because a swimming pool system or piece of equipment may be operating, but not as it should. Such a situation should be noted, documented, and reported to the owner's representative, who will notify the responsible contractor for corrective action under the warranty.

Upon the completion of the construction phase and after a final check out (punch list), an orientation of the organization/owner's management and operations staff should take place. This is a step that is often overlooked or minimized. With a multimillion-dollar complex, it is understandable that a thorough and professional set of instructions, including start-up procedures, troubleshooting, and daily operation procedures, as well as periodic maintenance tasks, should be provided in a well-documented, written operations manual. In addition, a resource contact should be provided for working with the operator as the owner takes over and puts the new facility into use.

Technical Considerations

Dimensions

The designer of the swimming pool must select the correct dimensions when creating the bounded water volume of the pool(s). Exact dimensions are required for pools used for swimming and diving competitions. These include

- length,
- width,
- depths (minimum and maximum),
- bottom profiles,
- tolerances and allowances (e.g., touchpad, construction, and bulkhead adjustment), and
- perimeter overflow tolerance at rim flow.

There is no exception for these types of pools if they are going to be used for organized competition under the sanction of any one of the rule-making entities (e.g., Federation Internationale de Natation Amateur, United States Swimming, United States Diving, United States Synchronized Swimming, United States Water Polo, National Collegiate Athletic Association, and the National Federation of State High School Associations and Swimming/Natation Canada). The dimensions found in Figure 20.2 are provided as an example, and the reader should contact the appropriate association for accurate and updated information prior to finalizing building plans. Other bodies of water are not as demanding for exact or pre-determined measurements, with the exception of health department safety regulations. These consist of minimum depths in shallow water and in diving areas. Such regulations usually dictate the degree of slope of the pool bottom in the shallow water and in the deep area.

Access for the physically disabled has been a design requirement in swimming pools since the 1970s. Methods of egress for the disabled vary. The most popular is the recessed stair, which is used by all attendees, whether or not they are disabled. Other systems include ramps and hydraulic or mechanical lifts. The latter use permanent or temporary anchors in the pool deck. With the creation of new enforcement powers in 1992, more products will become available in subsequent years. Field experience indicates low use of ramps.

Interior Finishes

Ceramic tile is considered the best choice for the interior of a swimming or diving pool. Its durability, appearance, and longevity cannot be matched by the other options. Marble plaster can develop problems on a large pool and/or one that is exposed to construction dust and wind-blown debris. Because plaster should be applied in one continuous process without interruptions, large pools will require large numbers of plaster finishers working simultaneously. Such a large group of skilled craftsmen may not be available in many market areas in North America.

Another problem that must be solved in plastering a large pool is the filling process. For best results, a pool with a green plaster coating should be filled as soon as possible, preferably in 24 to 48 hours after the completion of the plastering phase. This water fill should be uninterrupted to avoid telltale rings around the pool wall.

A painted pool interior is the least expensive process, but such a finish has a short life. As a result, many painted pool interiors must be repainted every three to five years. In some cases, the repainting is more frequent.

Figure 20.2
NCAA pool diagram, dimensions and equipment requirements

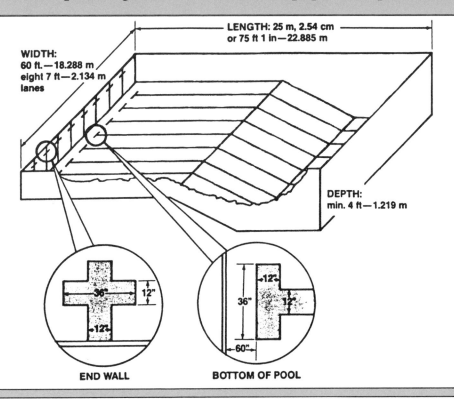

END WALL   BOTTOM OF POOL

Another problem that sometimes develops is peeling, chipping, or oxidizing, which can be unsightly and cause milky water.

Gutter Systems (Perimeter Overflow Recirculation System)

Numerous gutter configurations are used throughout the world. In most cases, the design has been developed by an architect, an engineer, a builder, or a manufacturer. The purpose of the overflow gutter in modern swimming pools is to receive and capture water that flows over the lip. This water is then transferred to the filter plant, usually through a surge chamber, which helps stabilize the water displacement in the swimming pool.

The gutter cross-section can be created in three basic configurations:

Deep Recessed Gutter

This design is often preferred by competitive swimmers and coaches. The pool deck cantilevers over the gutter trough, with the top of the deck approximately 12 to 15 inches above the water. The overhang provides the competitive swimmer with a visual reference plane for the underwater wall. The recessed gutter captures the wave amplitude very effectively and keeps the pool decks relatively dry. The disadvantage is that the high overhang makes egress from the pool rather difficult, and as a result, most people choose to use one of the pool ladders.

Deck Level Gutter

The deck level overflow system features a gutter lip, a flume, and a grate that is very close to the elevation of the pool deck. This design enables even the weakest swimmer to egress over the water's edge with little effort. The disadvantage of the deck level configuration is that the decks around this type of pool usually are quite wet. Competitive swimmers often dislike this gutter profile, because it is difficult to see a reference point above the water that relates to the pool wall under the water. Frequently a swimmer will misjudge the actual location of the turning surface during a race. Backstroke swimmers, in particular, have problems with this situation.

Roll Out

The third concept is the "roll out" gutter profile. This design combines the features of the fully recessed and deck level configurations. It consists of a gutter lip and grate or a very shallow flume at the water level. The pool deck is approximately 7 1/2 inches above the water surface, and it forms a curb at the rear of the gutter grate. This curb contains much of the wave action and keeps the pool deck relatively free of water washing up and over the gutter assembly. The low configuration at the water's edge still allows the swimmers to egress easily. A popular concept is to place the roll out gutter design on the long sides of the pool, with a fully recessed gutter parapet at each end of the race course. This arrangement provides competitive swimmers with a good visual reference at the turning walls of the race course and at the same time provides easy access and egress on the sides of the pool for recreational and student swimmers.

In case of a separate diving pool, a roll out gutter profile should be featured on all four sides of the diving pool. The curb will contain waves created by activity in the pool, as well as those created by the bubble sprayer for platform diving facilities.

A roll out or deck level gutter often is selected for a shallow water recreation pool because of the ease of ingress and egress by users.

Gutter Construction

Any of these gutter profiles can be constructed in several different ways:
- cast-in place concrete with tile, paint, or plaster finish;
- pneumatically applied concrete (gunite or Shotcrete) with tile, plaster, or paint finish;
- stainless steel fabricated with a grate cover made of fiberglass, high-impact plastic, or PVC.

This system contains a return water pressure conduit as well as the overflow to the surge tank and/or filter system.
- a tile finish can produce an attractive appearance, and
- has a long life.
- The cast-in-popular method of construction because it is part of the concrete work on the site and is easily included in that section of work,

Several other factors should be considered with regard to the cast-in-place system. The gutter flume must feature an outfall system. This can require a periodic gutter drain in the trough or a converter drop at one or more locations in the pool perimeter. The return piping inlet system must be located in the pool walls or in the pool floor.

There are several advantages to a 304 low carbon stainless steel overflow recirculation system:
- The gutter segments are fabricated at the factory and shipped to the site. A few days' work by a field welder results in the complete installation of the pool perimeter gutter and return piping system. This is beneficial in regard to the scheduling of trades and phases of work.
- If a floor inlet system is omitted, there is no deep buried piping except that for the main drain. In the event the pressure return conduit, which is part of the gutter assembly, should develop a leak, the water will flow only into the inside of the pool tank. No water will leak into the surrounding soil or into below-grade rooms.
- When a stainless steel system is installed, the filter system usually is provided by the same manufacturer or distributor. This creates the desirable situation of having one manufacturer responsible for the entire recirculation system.
- If a movable bulkhead is specified, it usually is provided and installed by the gutter manufacturer. This single-source responsibility can be a desirable situation and will avoid disputes that might occur if different contractors are involved at the gutter/track.

Figure 20.3
NCAA Pool Dimensions and Equipment Requirements

POOL DIMENSIONS AND EQUIPMENT

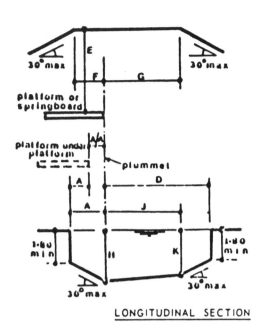

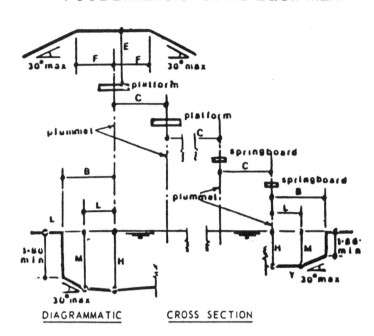

LONGITUDINAL SECTION   DIAGRAMMATIC   CROSS SECTION

NCAA Dimensions for Diving Facilities		Dimensions are in Feet	SPRINGBOARD		PLATFORM		
			1 Metre	3 Metres	5 Metres	7.5 Metres	10 Metres
		LENGTH	16'	16'	20'	20'	20'
		WIDTH	1'8"	1'8"	5'	5'	6'7"
		HEIGHT	3'4"	10'	16'5"	24'8"	32'10"
Revised to 1st Jan. 1987			Horiz. Vert.	Horiz. Vert.	Horiz. Vert.	Horiz. Vert.	Horiz. Vert.
A	From plummet BACK TO POOL WALL	Designation	A-1	A-3	A-5	A-7.5	A-10
		Minimum	6'	6'	4'2"	5'	5'
AA	From plummet BACK TO PLATFORM plummet directly below	Designation			AA5/1	AA7.5/3/1	AA10/5/3/1
		Minimum			5'	5'	5'
B	From plummet to POOL WALL AT SIDE	Designation	B-1	B-3	B-5	B-7.5	B-10
		Minimum	8'3"	11'6"	14'	14'10"	17'3"
C	From plummet to ADJACENT PLUMMET	Designation	C-1/1	C-3/3/1	C-5/3/1	C-7.5/5/3/1	C-10/7.5/5/3/1
		Minimum	8'	8'6"	8'6"	8'6"	9'
D	From plummet to POOL WALL AHEAD	Designation	D-1	D-3	D-5	D-7.5	D-10
		Minimum	29'	34'	34'	36'	45'
E	On plummet, from BOARD TO CEILING	Designation	E-1	E-3	E-5	E-7.5	E-10
		Minimum	16'5"	16'5"	11'6"	11'6"	16'5"
F	CLEAR OVERHEAD behind and each side of plummet	Designation	F-1 E-1	F-3 E-3	F-5 E-5	F-7.5 E-7.5	F-10 E-10
		Minimum	8'3" 16'6"	8'3" 16'6"	9' 11'6"	9' 11'6"	9' 16'6"
G	CLEAR OVERHEAD ahead of plummet	Designation	G-1 E-1	G-3 E-3	G-5 E-5	G-7.5 E-7.5	G-10 E-10
		Minimum	16'5" 16'5"	16'5" 16'5"	16'5" 11'6"	16'5" 11'6"	19'8" 16'5"
H	DEPTH OF WATER at plummet	Designation	H-1	H-3	H-5	H-7.5	H-10
		Minimum	11'	12'	14'2"	15'	16'
J-K	DISTANCE AND DEPTH ahead of plummet	Designation	J-1 K-1	J-3 K-3	J-5 K-5	J-7.5 K-7.5	J-10 K-10
		Minimum	16'5" 11'8"	20' 12'2"	20' 12'10"	26'3" 14'6"	36'2" 15'6"
L-M	DISTANCE AND DEPTH each side of plummet	Designation	L-1 M-1	L-3 M-3	L-5 M-5	L-7.5 M-7.5	L-10 M-10
		Minimum	5' 11'2"	6'7" 12'2"	14' 12'10"	14'10" 14'6"	17'2" 15'6"
N	MAXIMUM SLOPE TO REDUCE DIMENSIONS beyond full requirements	Pool depth Ceiling Ht	30 degrees 30 degrees		NOTE: Dimensions C (plummet to adjacent plummet) apply for Platforms with widths as detailed. For wider Platform increase C by half the additional width(s).		

The stainless steel perimeter overflow system must be approved by local regulatory agencies and be manufactured by a company with experience in similar pool installations. The gutter detail should be a stainless steel prefabricated overflow system featuring a handhold with a gutter profile utilizing a PVC, or fiberglass, grate over the gutter trough. The freeboard on the grate side of the handhold should be 3/40.

The trough of the gutter must have sufficient capacity to meet the requirements of jurisdictional agencies.

The hydraulics of the recirculation system, regardless of construction materials, should be such that the gutter trough develops a surge capacity between swimming races when the static surge is nonexistent. Thus, the gutter trough subsequently will accommodate the dynamic and static surge during the first length of each race. If a stainless steel perimeter system is selected, at least two converters should be provided for a 50-meter pool, while one is sufficient for a 25-yard or -meter pool.

Parapets and Fully Recessed Gutters

The parapets described above can take many forms. The vertical face toward the race course, however, must provide an orientation that indicates the location of the vertical plane of the race course. Parapets may be temporary or permanent. Parapets result when a fully recessed gutter profile is required to match the above water configuration of the movable bulkhead(s).

Swimming Pool Mechanical Systems

Pool Filters

The selection of a filter system is influenced greatly by the limitations created by the volume of waste water that can be removed from the site. The construction of a holding tank is a common solution if sewer capacity is a problem.

Filter Considerations.

There are three basic kinds of swimming pool filtration:
- sand filtration,
- diatomaceous earth filtration, and
- cartridge filtration.

Sand Filters.

Sand pressure systems exist in two forms:
- rapid sand pressure filtration, which operates at a flow rate of three gallons per minute (GPM) per square foot of filter area, and
- high-flow (high-rate) pressure filtration, which operates up to a flow rate of 15 GPM per square foot of filter area.

While many manufacturers rate their systems at 20 GPM per square foot, field experience suggests that the lower flow rate results in better water quality. The system must be designed to completely turn over the pool volume, as required by the jurisdictional health department. Some manufacturers produce a high flow and pressure system the fea-tures a multiple-cell configuration and operates at approximately 7 1/2 GPM per square foot of filter area. These filters are characterized by longer filter runs.

Sand Vacuum Filter Systems

A recent application of sand filter systems to swimming pool water is the vacuum sand system. These units usually require less space than sand systems. While sand systems are very popular because of their simple operation, they have one considerable drawback (aside from their high installation cost). That is the large water volume that is discharged during backwash. A multi-cell filter, however, can backwash in stages, and thus produce less volume at one time.

Diatomaceous Earth Filters

Pressure diatomaceous earth (DE) systems have the same requirement for pressurized backwash as does pressure sand. For this reason, they have no significant advantage over pressure sand systems, except that DE filters can produce a slightly clearer (polished) water quality.

Vacuum diatomaceous earth filtration with 1-1.5 GPM per square foot of filter area is a viable option. The backwash discharge from the open-top filter tank is by gravity, and the filter elements are cleaned by water jet sprays or by manually hosing off the elements. As a result, only a little more than the volume of the filter tank needs to be discharged via the sanitary sewer system.

Some jurisdictional authorities require a reclamation tank between the DE filter tank and the backwash outfall, so that the spent DE is captured and not discharged into the sanitary sewer. This understandably increases labor costs.

One important recommendation with a vacuum diatomaceous earth system is that the top of the tank be slightly above the water level of the pool. The pumps and motors must be below water level for a flooded suction situation.

An open-topped vacuum system should not be installed in a below-grade filter room where the pool water level is above the rim of the filter tank.

A number of quality prefabricated systems are available in the marketplace. Several provide the option of fiberglass or stainless steel tanks, which is essential. Even when coated with special paint systems, mild carbon steel tanks soon can develop corrosion problems, especially if located in the ground with soil backfilled against the walls.

Another common design is for the filter tank to be part of the concrete surge tank with the pump(s) and face piping in the basement level of the natatorium. Such systems usually feature a two-level filter room with open space over both levels.

As a means of avoiding uncontrollable leaks in a fiberglass or metal filter tank below floor level, a concrete well should be built, inside of which the DE tank will sit with space for a person to maneuver around it and be able to look under the tank to locate future leaks. This concrete well must have a floor drain to capture any water that begins to leak from the tank. If the tank walls are backfilled, a subsequent leak can be extremely difficult to repair, especially if multiple leaks develop about the same time.

Chemical Treatment of Pool Water

Swimming pool water must be risk-free for the users. This is accomplished by treating the recirculated pool water with a bactericide. Additional treatment is also required to prevent microscopic plant growth such as algae. Algae, if unchecked, can create an environment that will propagate and harbor organisms that can be harmful to humans in varying degrees.

The most common bactericide and algaecide is chlorine. This chemical has been used for over a century in the treatment of drinking water by municipal water companies. Its application to swimming pools since the early decades of the 20th century is understandable.

Because chlorine creates hypochlorous acid when mixed with water, the product will kill bacteria, and at the same time it will oxidize organic particulant matter in the swimming pool water.

The most popular form of chlorine treatment for public swimming pools historically has been elemental chlorine, which is in gaseous form when it is released from its storage tank and injected into the swimming pool recirculation system. Because chlorine gas can be hazardous if released into the atmosphere and fatal if inhaled in any significant quantity, there is a definite trend away from gas chlorine and toward chlorine compounds. The most popular for public swimming facilities is sodium hypochlorite, which is commonly called liquid chlorine or bleach.

While liquid chlorine does not create some of the risks gas chlorine does, it is not without its disadvantages. The main disadvantages are bulk handling, distribution, and storage, plus the tendency to accumulate total dissolved solids in the pool water. This phenomenon can result in water quality problems.

Dry chlorine products are manufactured and sold in the marketplace and have increased in their share of the public pool demand. The cost of these chemicals is higher than sodium, but their handling and storage advantage is viewed by some owners as worth the premium. These chemicals are usually impractical for large-volume pools, especially outdoor pools.

Because of the problems and limitations of the chlorine treatment of swimming pool water, a search for an alternative is underway in the United States market. The one option is the corona discharge ozone generation system. Widely used in western Europe and parts of Canada, as well as isolated locations around the world, the process can reduce many of the disadvantages of chlorine-only treatment, especially indoors. It must be noted that a chlorine or bromine system is still required for pools in order to provide a free bactericide residual in the pool at all times. This residual chlorine is surplus bactericide that attacks contaminants and germs that are brought into the water by swimmers. Ozone has many qualities, but it has no sustained residual power after the pool water is treated in the contact chamber. Maintenance in the field has been a challenge for many operators.

Both alternative systems (ozone corona discharge and copper and silver ionization) are in the early phases of market penetration. As a result, the supply and field service after the sale are inconsistent in many locations.

Automation

Automation has been a part of modern swimming pool design for several decades. The application has focused on two systems. The first is water chemistry, and the second is filtration.

The water chemistry of the pool is sampled and analyzed electronically by a microprocessor. The analysis is recorded and compared to two set points previously established by the pool operator. One of the set points is the desired level of free chlorine. The other set point is for pH.

When the analyzer samples the pool water (by means of a sample stream that bypasses part of the recirculation piping), he compares the result to the set point for the desired level. If the sample shows that the free chlorine level is above the set point of the analyzer, the unit, which is connected to the chemical feed pump (or a booster pump in the case of chlorine gas), will turn off the chlorine feed pump motor. If the sample reading is below the set point, the analyzer will turn on the feed pump motor if it is off, or it will continue its operation until the pool water in the sample strewn reaches the set point level. In the same way, the analyzer will monitor the sample stream for the pH level and then will energize the chemical feed pump that adds the respective buffer agent (e.g., caustic soda or sodium carbonate [soda ash] to raise the pH, or muriatic acid or carbon dioxide to lower the pH).

There are several benefits to an automated water chemistry feed system. The automated system monitors the pool water constantly, as compared to manual testing by an operator, which takes place anywhere from once an hour to once a day. The analyzer begins and ceases the chemical feed system immediately upon demand, as compared to manual adjustments after each manual testing. With manual adjustment, there is no assurance that the change in the rate of feed by the operator will be of sufficient quantity to change the level of chlorine (or pH) to the desired amount. Quite to the contrary, the likelihood is that the chemical level will exceed the desired level before the next manual test is made.

Another benefit of the automatic chemical feed system is the lower chemical cost to the owner. With the constant monitoring of the water and the subsequent activation of the feeders, both on and off, overfeeding is eliminated, and overall chemical costs are lower. This is due to the tendency of a manual set feed system to overfeed the chemical until the next manual test is taken, and a new adjustment is made to the feed pump rate of feed setting.

Modern automatic water chemistry analyzers can be provided with a remote readout, which usually is located in the pool management office. This allows the management staff to monitor the water chemistry levels in the pool water without having to walk to the filter room to visually monitor the system. The system also can be interfaced with the building's environmental monitoring and control systems, in which case a PC computer in the pool office can display pool water chemical levels. In addition, a recorder will tape readings per minute. The paper tape is stored in the analyzer for review by the operator or maintenance service person. Such data are helpful in understanding the impact of bather loads versus quiescent times in the 24-hour cycle of the pool operations.

Movable Bulkhead

Movable bulkheads became popular during the late 1970s and have continued to be so through the 1990s. There are several reasons. The bulkhead, which is usually three or four feet in width and approximately 4 1/2 feet in depth, can be moved along a horizontal translation. By moving the bulkhead, different course lengths can be created (i.e., with a movable bulkhead, a 50-meter pool can be converted into a 25-yard or 25-meter race course). When two or more bulkheads are used, duplicate or even triplicate courses can be created. In addition to race courses, other aquatic activity areas can be created at the same time, such as synchronized swimming, water polo, instruction classes, or fitness lap swimming.

While United States bulkheads tend to move horizontally over the length of the pool and are stored at the end of the pool when the 50-meter dimension is in use, European bulkheads usually move only vertically, and they are stored in a floor well when the pool is in the 50-meter mode. The reason for these differences is that the U.S. Swimming competition takes place over several configurations of race course (e.g., 25 yards, 25 meters, or 50 meters).

The bulkheads usually are a fiberglass box girder or a stainless steel truss with a skin of PVC or fiberglass grating. The bulkhead is designed to accommodate live loading both from above and from the side (laterally). These design qualifications are needed to provide a rigid training surface for the athletes, and in the case of starts from a bulkhead, mini-

Figure 20.4
Bulkhead Diagram

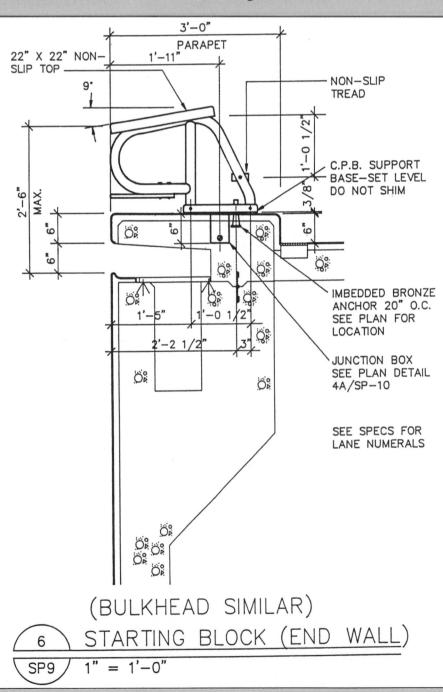

mal deflection from the simultaneous thrust from swimmers diving from starting blocks mounted on the bulkhead. (It is for this reason that many competitive swimmers prefer starting blocks anchored in the pool deck).

The current generation of bulkhead design features a variable buoyancy chamber. This enables the operator to inflate the chamber, which in turn creates a positive buoyancy in the bulkhead off its resting (bearing points) place on the pool perimeter lip or wall. In this position, the bulkhead can be towed to its new position, deflated, and anchored onto the pool perimeter.

Prior to this development, most bulkheads moved on wheels on the pool's perimeter. Difficulty with wheel mechanisms has made some bulkheads difficult to move. It is for this reason that design development has moved toward the variable buoyancy system.

Movable Pool Floors

The hydraulic or mechanically driven pool floor has been popular in western Europe for three decades. Originally developed in Germany, it has the ability to create different water depths, which in turn creates conditions for a greater variety of aquatic activities, making it popular, especially in indoor natatoria. The floor creates a variety of pool configurations, all under the same roof with the same operational costs. This has impressive advantages over building several pools with different depths for different activities.

The "floors," which usually are installed at the time that the pool is constructed, have been used in competition pools, both long-course and short-course, as well as rehabilitation centers, wellness centers, and service organizations, such as YMCAs and JCCAs.

The majority of movable floors installed in the 1970s and 1980s used hydraulic rams for the lift translation. During the 1990s, new movable floor systems use a scissor jack mechanism or a cable tension system activated by a motor and/or hydraulic ram behind the pool wall in a below-grade room.

The approximate maximum size is usually 75 feet by 42 feet and uses four rams. Such a floor section can be used in a 50-meter-by-25-yard pool and create a functional shallow water area for a number of programs.

A frequent addition to the movable floor is a trailing ramp. This is a plane that is hinged to the floor section with the opposite end of the ramp resting on the pool floor with rollers. The ramp extends from pool wall to pool wall and, as such, creates an inclined slope from the edge of the movable floor to the pool bottom. The ramp prevents anyone from swimming underwater beneath the movable floor when it is in a raised position.

The need for movable floors has become more understandable in the past decade, because of the need to locate starting blocks over deep water. A number of young competitive swimmers have been paralyzed when striking the pool bottom with their heads after diving headfirst off a starting platform. If the starting blocks are installed at the deep end of the pool along with the diving board supports, the resulting congestion is not desirable. The historic location of starting platforms at the uncongested shallow end of the pool is hazardous when the starting blocks are used over water five feet deep or less. The movable floor solves these problems by creating an ideal situation for the use of starting blocks, while at the same time avoiding the problems of the combined use of the starting blocks and the diving boards at the deep end of the pool.

Diving Facilities

Diving facilities have evolved out of the development and the requirements of competitive springboard and platform diving. The heights of these respective structures have been standardized at one meter and three meters for springboards and 1, 3, 5, 7.5 and 10 meters for rigid platforms. There are several dimensional requirements, each promulgated by different organizations (e.g., FINA [Federation Internationale De Natation Amateur] and U.S. Diving and National Collegiate Athletic Association [NCAA]).

Springboard diving competition has been influenced greatly by one manufacturer of diving boards, Duraflex International. Since the 1950s, this company has developed three generations of high-performance springboards. Using a patented aluminum alloy and design, Duraflex International has developed a conventional diving board, a double tapered board, and a double tapered board with holes across a section of the board. As a result, the divers are usually lifted higher in the air, allowing them to execute complicated dives at a higher elevation and with a slightly longer time in the air. Both conditions are advantageous to the competitive diver.

The Duraflex board has a reputation for durability and can last for several decades with intermittent resurfacing by the factory. Other diving boards are manufactured by different companies and are sold primarily to the residential pool market, semi-public (motel, hotel, condo, apartment pool market), and the public recreation pool market. These boards usually are fiberglass or vinyl encapsulated wood boards. Other types of diving boards sold to the residential and semi-public market are 100% molded fiberglass.

Diving board supports vary, and the difference is reflected in cost. The least expensive is the cast aluminum stand designed and manufactured by Duraflex International, called Durafirm. The three-meter unit is relatively rigid, is easy to install, requires no underground footing, and needs only a thickened slab beneath the anchored legs.

A more attractive diving board support, in the opinion of many designers and users, is the cantilevered support pedestal with a stainless steel ship's ladder and handrails. The forward-leaning profile creates a dramatic appearance and is often used in public pools, clubs, and schools. Because it has more connected parts, it has a tendency to vibrate and rattle if the bolted connectors are not kept tight by the pool operator. If this type of diving board support structure is specified, it is recommended that the pedestal and flanged ends be 304 stainless steel and painted. It is especially important that the flanges and all bolts not be a mild steel because of the corrosion that will occur. This result is a problem for maintenance personnel who must repaint these components frequently.

The third type of diving board support is a cast-in-place concrete structure for both heights, (i.e., one meter and three meters). This structure has no vibration except from the short stand butt plate and fulcrum base assembly. The overall advantage of the concrete support is the monolithic structure, which will not shake, vibrate, or loosen component connectors. The result is a firm, stable base for the diving board. Understandably, the solid cast-in-place concrete support costs more than the factory-fabricated metal units. This is a result of the labor and materials required and the stair assembly that usually is a part of the design. Because of the greater cost, the concrete supports are usually designed for universities where the budget can accommodate and the diving program justify the expense. Concern over the number of accidents involving children falling down ship's ladders while attempting to climb to a three-meter board has led to the provision of a stair for these high-diving boards. Such a stair follows the typical angle of ascent with handrails.

Consideration of diving boards includes the depth and envelope of the water, which are safety issues. Safety for the diver is paramount, which is complicated by the wide ranges of efficiency and skill possessed by different divers. The trained competitive diver will consistently reach a greater depth after entry because of the streamlined body configuration and disciplined movements. Because of his or her experience, injurious impact with the pool bottom is extremely rare. By contrast, the typical recreational diver almost will always enter the water in an inefficient configuration with little or no streamlined characteristics. As a result, this diver will slow body velocity rapidly after entry and will not plunge to the depths that the experienced competitive diver can achieve at will.

While this describes the typical entry of both experienced competitive divers and inexperienced recreational divers, there can be rare exceptions. To anticipate these potentially hazardous experiences by divers, the depth and envelope of the water below the diving boards must be adequate. Standards and/or requirements are promulgated by local health departments and the governing bodies of competitive diving (i.e., U. S. Diving, NCAA, and FINA). While the competitive rule-making agencies dictate water depths that will accommodate experienced divers, municipal and state regulations allow shallower minimum depths and smaller envelopes. Because there is no way of ascertaining the skill level of a diver before he or she executes a dive or to know the efficiency with which a dive will be executed, shallower water depths may not be appropriate. Another factor that must be considered is the potential for an original low-performance (wood or fiberglass) diving board to be replaced by a high-performance aluminum board. When this occurs, a new set of capabilities is created, and new parameters are required.

The different skill levels and body weights of divers and the different lift characteristics of diving boards suggest that the deeper and larger water envelopes beneath the diving boards (and diving platforms) should be designed for pools that feature regulation aluminum 16-foot diving boards. For this reason, most designers will use the current rules of FINA, U. S. Diving, or the NCAA.

Diving platforms are being built at a noticeably increased rate within new facilities. Most of these are on university campuses and are part of new 50-meter natatoria. This sudden development has been stimulated by the commencement of platform diving at the NCAA Division I Swimming and Diving Championships in 1988. It is anticipated that platform diving will be added to the order of events at conference meets as more platform towers are built at Divi-

sion I campuses. The rationale for this development is to better prepare U.S. divers for international competition. Diving coaches and platform divers are requesting platforms with three center lines instead of the customary two. In the former, the 10-meter, 7.5-meter, and five meter platforms have separate plummet centerlines so that divers can dive from each platform at the same time without conflict. In the latter, the 10-meter platform is directly above the five-meter and one-meter platforms in what is called a stacked configuration. Likewise, the 7.5-meter is stacked above the three-meter platform. The two-centerline design is featured in the great majority of the diving platforms in the world. There are two basic reasons for this. The three-centerline structure is difficult to fit into the desired dimensions of a diving pool, and it is more expensive than the two-centerline design.

Due to budget constraints, tower assemblies sometimes are designed with fewer than the five levels. When this is done, the option most often selected is a single centerline. Other options include a five-meter, 7.5-meter, and a 10-meter. Sometimes a one-meter is added, thus omitting only the three-meter platform.

If a diving tower is specified, the water depth and envelope beneath the tower should meet or exceed the FINA requirements. Diving platforms usually are located over an independent/separate diving pool. This is done for several reasons. The first is to avoid conflict with swimming, which would be the case if the water beneath the platforms (landing zone) was part of the bounded water volume of the racecourse. Such a situation is considered undesirable, because of conflict during meets as well as during practice. Another important reason is the water temperature desired by divers, which is warmer than that preferred by competitive swimmers.

When there is a separate diving pool, the bottom is sometimes finished with a dark blue color. Platform divers find that the dark color helps them with their orientation as they spin and twist in the execution of their dives.

The deck area that surrounds the swimming and/or diving pool(s) provides the medium of access to the water's edge. This space (and material) is the most important element to the user, other than the pool tanks and their contents. A short observation of a pool in use (especially for recreational free swim) will reveal that the swimmers continually interact with the pool deck and the pool water. As a result, the pool deck takes on a number of important functions:

- The deck is the surface over which all users must travel to reach the water's edge or reach a diving facility and then into the water. Because of this function, the deck must be smooth enough to be comfortable for bare feet and yet thorough enough to prevent slipping when the deck is wet.
- Information must be displayed in the deck surface to advise users of potential hazards. This signage will state water depths, warnings, and instructions.
- Because the swimmers and divers are continuously carrying water out of the pool, which drips and splashes into the deck, a workable deck drainage system must be provided.

There are several basic deck drainage systems that are practical around a swimming pool.

Area Drains

This is the most common. The deck area is divided into sections, and the surface in each section slopes to a low point (usually in the center) where a flush, perforated drain fitting is located. This drain is connected to the other drain fittings in the deck, all of which drain the deck surface water to a sanitary sewer.

Slot Drains

There are a number of varieties of the drain configuration. The feature they all have in common is their concentric location with the pool perimeter. Slot drains are usually located approximately three to five feet from the water's edge. Because the deck slopes away from the pool and toward the slot drain, the great majority of the splashed water and the water carried out by swimmers falls on the upside of the slope from the slot drain and the pool's edge and quickly drains away. The slot in the pool deck can be created in several ways. The primary feature is a conduit that is either level or slopes to an outfall where the deck water that has drained into the slot will flow to the sanitary sewer.

In pools with narrow decks, drainage can occur across the deck to a shallow trough along the natatorium wall, or off the edge of the deck into a French drain if the pool is outdoors.

Building Envelope

A natatorium is a room that contains one or more swimming pools. How the room is constructed is of immense importance. The structural components must be such that they will withstand the normal wear and tear of a public space, as well as the unique demands of an enclosed space above (and below) a large body of water that is treated with chemicals and will evaporate tons of water vapor over the period of a year. This, multiplied by 30 or 50 years, underscores the aggression that the building will be subjected to. Mild steel should be avoided where possible and should be limited to large structural components. These components, if exposed to the natatorium environment, should be coated with an industrial-grade epoxy. If the roof decking is mild steel or even galvanized, it must be coated in the same way to protect the metal from corrosion. Non-metallic building components must withstand the impact of high humidity and aggressive chemically laced air. For this reason, concrete, plastic, glass, and stainless steel are appropriate.

In considering stainless steel, it is important to understand that stainless steel has many grades and alloys. The 300 series is usually used for swimming pool equipment. Even so, certain environmental conditions can adversely affect stainless steel over a period of time. For this reason, it is unwise to use this material for small and yet strategic components that are put under stress as structural components (e.g., fasteners that are part of a roof suspension system). Other than pool gutters, bulkhead, and deck equipment, unpainted stainless steel should not be used in natatoria.

The roof sandwich demands scrutiny in its design so as to avoid problems with the air barrier, the vapor retarder, the insulation, and the moisture membrane. The avoidance of thermal bridging is essential, especially in locales with a cold winter climate. Condensation inside the natatorium can cause many problems if not controlled. The most significant is the creation of hydrochloric acid if vapor with chlorine molecules condenses. The same concerns exist for natatorium walls, and design decisions must take these issues into consideration.

The architectural features in a natatorium may vary depending upon the type of owner, the location, the climate, and the activity program.

Fenestration

The decision to use windows in a natatorium will be influenced by its location. If the facility is located in a park setting or has an attractive view (e.g., mountains, ocean, lake, forest, etc.) wall windows can be a major feature. If, on the other hand, the view is an unattractive cityscape such as a parking lot, blank building walls, or unattractive street scene, there is little reason to introduce light through a wall window because of the glare that will likely develop across the surface of the water. This reflected glare can be a distraction to spectators during a swim meet, a safety problem for lifeguards during recreational swimming, and a heat loss or heat gain. It can also create condensation with possible corrosion damage to window casements and walls. All of these problems can be dealt with if justification for the window and natural light can be established.

One means of avoiding many of the negatives named above is the use of translucent skylights. While this technique will avoid many of the negative aspects of wall fenestration, heat gain can still be a problem, but control can greatly reduce the negative effects. Skylights will usually avoid negative glare on the water surface and at the same time reduce the level of needed artificial light. Artificial light is a very important feature in the design of a poolscape, whether it is indoors or outdoors. Indoor light levels are influenced to some degree by standards or rules set forth by the national governing bodies of competitive swimming, diving, synchronized swimming, and water polo. State and local health department agencies will frequently set requirements for outdoor and indoor pools, both for overhead and underwater light sources. A review of the applicable regulations will enable the designer to meet these requirements.

Acoustics is an issue that must be addressed. Often, acoustics will be overlooked, dismissed, or eliminated because of budget. Reverberating sound is a common problem in natatoria. Sound sources include whistles, gunshots, and diving board impact noises, plus shouts, conversation, and the sounds of splashing. Loudspeakers should be selected and specified by an acoustics and sound consultant. Understandably, the size of the natatorium will influence the acceptable reverberation time in the space.

Outdoor acoustics are usually a factor in the overall design of the poolscape. The pool site can be both a source and a recipient of noise. If the pool is near a residential area or some other land use that should not have excessive sound impact, landscape design can provide buffers. If, on the other hand, off-site noise is produced by an adjacent roadway and/or industrial site, protection must be created for the poolscape.

Support Spaces

While the bodies of water are the focal point of the facility, the design, arrangement, and location of the support spaces are factors of the overall design that will influence the efficiency of the operation and the effectiveness of the programs.

The starting point of the adjacency profile is the user's point of entry. A control point must exist at this location. After passing the control point, the user must arrive at the dressing area. The two dressing rooms should have a dry entrance from the control point area and a wet exit to the pool deck. (The reverse applies for users leaving the pool area.)

The pool office should be located with a visual access of the pool deck area and the exits from the dressing rooms onto the pool deck. Other spaces/rooms can be added to the control area, depending upon the size of the pool(s) and programs. The spaces can include an office for lifeguards, a first-aid room, and an office for instructors and coaches. Additional spaces may include a swim meet management office, drug testing room(s), and sports technology research offices. If the facility is a university with a physical education major and post graduate studies, other spaces used for research should be considered.

Functional support spaces include filtration and chemical treatment, storage, circulation, and spectator seating. The issue of spectator seating is somewhat complex. It requires the identification of the type of spectator events that will take place, their frequency, the number of spectators, and the type of facilities that will be provided for the spectators. If there are to be spectator events, is it best to provide permanent or temporary seating? The answer to this question will be influenced not only by the issues listed above, but also by budget, available space, and in some cases, the off-site activities of the owner. The difference of the two basic systems (i.e., permanent and temporary) will be reflected in cost. This applies not only to first costs, but can also influence the construction budget in such areas as exits, stairwells, and even parking spaces. Because of the variables, it is important to have a good understanding (and agreement among members of the owner's project committee) of the true purpose of the spectator facilities.

Both indoor and outdoor access to the seating area can be an important design problem, and it can significantly affect the total construction cost.

HVAC-Dehumidification

The environment in an indoor pool can be comfortable to swimmers and spectators if the relative humidity is controlled and maintained at 50% to 55%. An even greater benefit of this range is the lack of aggressive atmospheric conditions relative to the materials in the space. For many years the soaring humidity in a natatorium was controlled by opening the windows and allowing outside air to dilute the moist atmosphere. In this method, the laws of physics replaced that warm, moist air with cooler, dryer outside air. Understandably, the next improvement was the introduction of motorized exhaust fans that mechanically maintained a constant air flow out of the natatorium with a controlled and strategically located introduction of fresh air louvers. This system, which is still in use, is effective if the outside air is at the appropriate temperature and relative humidity level. In some climatic areas, the appropriate level for outside air is available much of the time. Most locations, however, have

appropriate levels only a small percentage of the time. During the majority of the time, high levels of temperature and humidity in the outside air result in higher temperatures and humidity levels in the natatorium.

During the 1970s, following the fuel crisis and the escalating cost of energy, modifications were made to the conventional mechanical ventilation systems. These modifications captured the heat that previously was exhausted to the outside and used it to raise the heat of the outside air being brought into the natatorium space. Once again, this worked only if outside weather conditions were correct.

In the late 1970s, refrigerated dehumidification was developed. This system is an outgrowth of air conditioning, whereby the warm, moist air is mechanically drawn across an evaporator coil. This lowers the temperature of the air and causes it to condense on the cold coil. The dryer air that exits from the other side of the coil has a lower temperature and a lower relative humidity. This air is then reheated and mixes with the natatorium air. In so doing, it stabilizes the temperature in the natatorium at or near the desired level or set point.

Refrigerated systems use also the heat that has been captured and removed from the processed natatorium air to heat the swimming pool water, heat the natatorium space, or even heat the potable shower water. By using the heat that is taken out of the natatorium air as described above, the overall energy costs of the natatorium are much lower. In spite of a higher first cost for the refrigerated dehumidification, the savings in operating costs create an attractive payback to the owner. This is enhanced if energy costs continue to rise.

Designers must consider the human needs for ventilation and fresh air. While dehumidifiers will control humidity without ventilation, fresh outside air is needed for the occupants of the natatorium. If there is a large number of spectators at special events (e.g., swimming meets, tournaments, water shows, etc.) a separate mode will be required to serve this greater demand for outside fresh air. All modes must meet local building codes and the applicable ASHRAE standards (American Society of Heating, Refrigeration and Air Conditioning Engineers).

There has been a series of complications in natatoria with refrigerated dehumidification beginning in the 1980s that has slowly rectified to some degree since. Those complications have occurred because the recycled air in the natatorium, which is necessary for refrigerated dehumidification, does not mix in sufficient fresh outside air to dilute the accumulation of chloramines off-gassing from the pool water. This problem is not as acute with bromine; however, bromine systems seem to have their own complications that frustrate some operators. As this phenomenon became recognized in the industry, several manufacturers of dehumidification systems have modified their equipment to permit greater make-up air capability. Some feature a 25% minimum fresh air introduction into the system as well as a mode of operation for 100% exhaust at times of chloramine build up in the atmosphere, especially at a time of super chlorination.

The difficulty in some systems has led to significant maintenance cost and/or even replacement of components. The problem seems to be a combination of a chlorine system combined with an air-handling system that recirculates the interior air without sufficient purging of the natatorium's chloramine-laced atmosphere.

Maintenance and Repair

In planning a swimming pool and/or a natatorium, consideration must be given to the ongoing costs of custodial care, maintenance, and repair. Often this aspect of swimming pool and natatorium design is overlooked. The result is a higher operating cost for each day the facility is in operation, all the way to the end of the facility's life.

Custodial care is often taken for granted by the project committee, and little thought is given to the daily chores that must take place to keep the pool and its support spaces at a high level of cleanliness. The result is greater labor hours expended, which affects the annual budget and at the same time may result in a lower level of cleanliness due to a future mandate to cut labor hours because of budget constraints.

Preventative maintenance is always a task that must be executed if the facility is to be maintained as it should be. While budget can have an impact on how well preventative maintenance is carried out, the design of the mechanical systems, support components, working space, and ingress and egress from the mechanical spaces can influence the enthusiasm that physical plant staff will have for practicing preventative maintenance.

The repair of components in the pool and support spaces will be less costly in time and material (and down time of the facility) if parts are available as shelf items. If long lead times are required to obtain some parts, they should be prepurchased and inventoried before the need occurs. This applies to pumps, motors, impellers, chemical feed pumps, air handling units, blowers, and some filter components, etc.

Safety Features

Safety is no accident. It must receive careful consideration by planners, architects, and operators of pools. Many people have been confronted with litigation as a result of an accident in their pools. Lawyers inevitably look for areas of negligence in the operation of the pool or for any defect in the pool's design. Listed below are some essential safety principles, procedures, and policies that should be adhered to in designing the pool and in its operation:

- Rules governing pool use must be conspicuously posted at all points of entry to the pool.
- Special rules should be developed and posted for use at such facilities as diving boards, slides, and towers.
- A lifeguard should be on duty at all times that the pool is open.
- In areas of the pool with less than five feet of water, signs and warnings should be placed at the edge (coping) of the pool that state, "SHALLOW WATER-NO DIVING."
- In shallow-water training pools on the edge of the pool, signs should be posted stating "DANGER SHALLOW WATER-NO DIVING."
- Where springboards and platform diving is provided, the depth of water and other related measurements must conform to the rules of FINA, USD, NCAA, or the NFHSAA.
- Starting blocks for competitive swimming should be installed in the deep end of the pools unless the shallow end of the pool is at least five feet deep.

- Adequate lighting, both underwater and in the pool area, must be provided to ensure the safety of users and meet applicable rules, regulations, and codes.
- Clarity of pool water is essential and must meet applicable rules, regulations, and codes.
- Depth markers at least four inches high must be placed in the interior wall of the pool at or above water level. Larger depth markings must be placed on the pool deck as per health department regulations.
- Never consider the minimum standards for pools promulgated by state governments or the pool industry to be the proper level to achieve in planning a pool. Minimums often become obsolete very quickly.
- Ladders that hang on the edge of a pool and extend into the water represent hazards to swimmers. All ladders should be recessed into the pool wall.
- No safety ledge should ever extend into the pool. Instead the ledge should be recessed into the wall at a depth of approximately four feet.

Checklist for Use by Planning Committee and Owner

Planning Factors

- A clear statement identifies the nature and scope of the program and the special requirements for space, equipment, and facilities dictated by the activities to be conducted.
- The swimming pool has been planned to meet the requirements of the intended program, as well as less frequent special needs.
- Other recreational facilities are nearby for the convenience and enjoyment of swimmers.
- An experienced pool consultant, architect, and/or engineer has been called in to advise on design and equipment.
- The design of the pool reflects the most current knowledge and experience regarding the technical aspects of swimming pools.
- The pool plans reflect the needs of physically disabled people.
- All plans and specifications meet the regulations of both state and local boards of health.
- Provision for accommodating young children has been considered.
- Consideration has been given to provide a room or area near the pool suitable for video/TV and lectures.
- Adequate parking space has been provided.

Design Factors

- The bathhouse is properly located, with entrance to the pool leading to the shallow end.
- The locker rooms are large enough to accommodate peak loads and meet jurisdictional regulations.
- The area for spectators has been separated from the pool area.

- There is adequate deck space around the pool.
- The swimming pool manager's or director's office faces the pool and contains a window with a view of the entire pool area.
- There is a toilet-shower dressing area next to the office for instructors.
- The specifications for competitive swimming set forth by ruling groups have been met.
- If the pool shell has a tile finish, the length of the pool has been increased by three inches over the "official" size in order to permit eventual tiling of the basin without making the pool too short.
- The width of any movable bulkhead has been considered in calculating total pool length.
- Consideration has been given to an easy method of moving the bulkhead.
- All diving standards can be anchored properly.
- Separate storage spaces have been allocated for maintenance and instructional   equipment.
- A properly constructed overflow gutter extends around the pool perimeter.
- Where skimmers are used, they are located so that they are not turning walls where competitive swimming is to be conducted.
- Drains are at the proper pitch in the pool, on the pool deck, in the overflow gutter, and on the floor of shower and dressing rooms as per local jurisdictional regulation.
- Inlets and outlets are adequate in number and located to ensure effective circulation of water in the pool.
- There is easy access to the filter room to permit the transport of chemicals and other supplies.
- The recirculation pump is located below the water level.
- The recirculation-filtration system has been designed to meet anticipated future pool loads.
- Underwater lights in end racing walls have been located 3 1/2 feet directly below surface lane line anchors, and they are on a separate circuit.
- There is adequate acoustical treatment of walls and ceilings of the indoor pool.
- There is adequate overhead clearance for diving.
- Reflection of light from the outside has been kept to a minimum by proper location of windows or skylights.
- All wall electrical receptacles are covered.
- Proper subsurface drainage has been provided.
- An area for sunbathing has been provided and oriented for the outdoor pool.
- Outdoor diving boards or platforms are oriented so that they face north or northeast.
- The outdoor pool is oriented correctly in relation to the sun.
- Wind screens have been provided in situations where heavy winds prevail.
- Lounging for swimmers has been provided for outdoor pools.

Safety and Health

- The pool layout provides the most efficient control of swimmers from showers and locker rooms to the pool.
- Toilet facilities are provided for wet swimmers, separate from the dry area.
- An area is set aside for eating, apart from the pool deck.
- There is adequate deep water for diving that meets U.S. diving rules.
- Required space has been provided between diving boards and between the diving boards and sidewalls.
- Recessed steps or removable ladders are located on the walls so as not to interfere with competitive swimming turns.
- There is adequate provision for life-saving equipment and pool cleaning equipment.
- The proper numbers of lifeguard stands have been provided and properly located.
- All metal fittings are of noncorrosive material. All metal in the pool area is grounded to a ground-fault interrupter.
- Provision has been made for underwater lights.
- The chemical feed systems and containers have been placed in a separate room, accessible from and vented to the outside.
- A pool heater has been included and properly sized.
- Automatic controls for water chemistry have been specified.
- Proper ventilation has been provided in the indoor pool.
- There is adequate underwater and overhead lighting.
- There is provision for proper temperature control in the pool room for both water and air.
- The humidity of the natatorium room can be controlled.
- A fence has been placed around the outdoor pool to prevent its use when the pool is closed.
- Rules for use of the pool been developed and displayed prominently.
- Warning signs are placed where needed and on such equipment as diving boards and slides.
- Starting blocks are placed in the deep end of pool (minimum depth five feet).
- There is a telephone in the pool area with numbers of rescue and emergency agencies.
- Emergency equipment, including a spineboard, has been provided.
- The steps leading into the pool have a black edge to make them visible to underwater swimmers.
- Bottom drain covers are fastened securely to prevent their removal by interlopers.
- The diving stands are equipped with guardrails which extend at least to the water.
- The deck is made of nonslip material.

Summary

This chapter was designed to review current trends in aquatic facilities. In past editions, this section was entitled "Swimming Pools and Natatoria." Since the early 1990s, the aquatic area has expanded to include not just pools, but also a variety of aquatic entertainment centers. Therefore, the chapter was retitled "Aquatic Facilities" to include the increased number of aquatic facilities available to competitors and recreators. The American public loves its opportunities to compete in swimming and to have fun in the water. Water parks have become great family entertainment centers for summer fun.

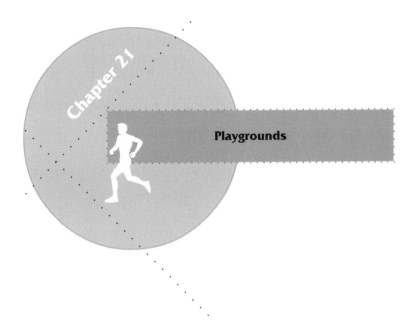

Playgrounds

Donna Thompson, University of Northern Iowa
Susan Hudson, University of Northern Iowa

P laygrounds are an essential part of children's play. These play sites can be found found in a variety of settings, including public parks, schools, child care centers, apartment com-plexes, churches, and commercial establishments. Whatever their settings, all playgrounds should have certain things in common. These include:

- the fostering of a child's physical, emotional, social, and intellectual development, and
- the provision of age-appropriate equipment to meet children's needs.

The use of the word "playgrounds" for this chapter refers to designated areas where stationary and manipulative play equipment is located to facilitate a child's physical, emotional, social, and intellectual development. These areas employ:

- the use of proper surfacing under and around equipment,
- the placement of equipment that allows for easy supervision by adults, and
- the regular maintenance of the equipment and the environment.

This chapter will review trends in playground design, general planning considerations, specific planning steps, installation of the equipment and the surfacing, and on-going maintenance, repair, and inspection procedures.

Learning Objectives

After reading this chapter, the student will be able to

- identify key terms in relation to playground design,
- recognize the trends in playground design,
- understand general planning considerations for playground design,

- identify specific planning steps in a planning a playground,
- understand the procedures for installing playground equipment and surfacing, and
- recognize procedures for maintaining, repairing, and inspecting playground equipment and surfacing.

Trends in Playgrounds

In the 1970s, in response to consumer interest and complaints, the United States Consumer Product Safety Commission (CPSC) initiated a process to develop safety guidelines for playgrounds. The first guidelines were produced in 1981. The guidelines came in two handbooks—one designed to give general information to the public, the other to give technical assistance to the manufacturers of playground equipment. These guidelines were revised in 1991 into one handbook for use by the public. In 1988, the American Society for Testing and Materials (ASTM) accepted responsibility for creating a standard based on the refinement of the technical specifications for playground equipment. The CPSC has maintained its involvement with the technical standards for public use by assisting the ASTM with further development and refinement of these specifications. As a result of these efforts, the first voluntary standard for the playground industry was developed in 1993. This standard, known as F-1487-93 (Standard Consumer Safety Performance Specification for Playground Equipment for Public Use), provided technical specifications for playground equipment, use zones, prevention of entrapments, and maintenance. The standard was revised in 1995 and in 1997. A surfacing standard was created in 1991(F-1292-91). This standard provides for the testing of the impact attenuation of playground surfacing. Specifically, it provides the methodology to assess the amount of surfacing necessary under and around playground equipment to prevent fatal head injuries of children who may fall to the surface off the equipment. This standard has been revised three times (1993, 1995, 1996).

Both the standards and the guidelines by CPSC (which were revised again in 1994 and 1997) have been instrumental in creating safer play environments for children by providing design criteria for surfacing and equipment. Together, they are essential documents needed for designing playgrounds.

Another major regulatory standard now influencing the playground design comes from the United States Access Board. In November 2000, the U.S. Justice Department published the Access Board's guidelines regarding the interpretation of the Americans with Disabilities Act (ADA) and public playgrounds. These guidelines address issues of accessibility to and from play equipment as well as the use of the play equipment by children with disabilities. All new public playgrounds including those found in schools and community parks must conform to these guidelines. If major renovation is done on existing playgrounds, then they also need to comply with the guidelines. It should be noted that whether new or old, all public use playgrounds need to provide access to and from the play equipment. This civil rights regulation has been in place since the passage of the ADA in 1991.

General Planning Considerations

In order to design safe playgrounds, four major elements must be considered. They include:
- the placement of equipment and support structures (i.e., benches), which facilitate the supervision of children in the play area,
- the proper positioning of age-appropriate equipment to promote positive play behavior,
- the selection of appropriate surfacing that will absorb the impact of children falling from the equipment, and
- the consideration of equipment and surface maintenance issues that contribute to the development of safe playground environments.

Supervision Design Considerations

Supervision requires individuals to be able to see and move through the playground area. Thus, design considerations for supervision include separation of equipment, placement of signs, open sight lines, and zones for play.

Age Separation

It is important to divide the playground area into sections appropriate for different ages of the users. Play equipment for children ages two to five is developmentally different from equipment designed for children ages five to 12. Mixing the two types of equipment means that the supervisor will have a difficult time guiding children to use the equipment appropriate for their developmental age level.

Use of Signs

Signs can provide important information to adults concerning both the age separation of equipment and the need for supervision. Figure 21.1 provides an example of playground signs. The use of signs provides adults with a clear indication as to which age group should be on the equipment. It also reminds adults that the equipment will not supervise the children. This is an important consideration for schools whose playgrounds are used before and after the organized school day and in public parks where no formalized supervision is in place. It provides a "good faith" attempt by a sponsoring agency to promote safe supervision practices.

Sight Lines

Open sight lines refer to several angles of visual access for the supervisor. Sight lines must occur through equipment and through natural vegetation. Further, sight lines for play structures should allow visual access to all points of the structure from at least two directions at any one point of observation on the play site (Bowers, 1988, p. 42). Essentially, the ability to respond to emergencies is dependent upon ". . . the ability of the supervisor to approach the structure and get to all the events to provide assistance" using the routes implied by the sight lines (Bruya & Wood, 1997).

Zones for Play

Play sites should also be divided into zones for different activity types. Two types of zones that the designer should pay attention to are activity zones and use zones. Activity zones describe the type of play behavior that children might engage in given the space and equipment that is present. Examples of activity zones include areas for social/dramatic play, fine-motor play, gross-motor play, and quiet play.

Age-Appropriate Design Considerations

Playgrounds should be designed according to the characteristics of the intended user. Therefore, age-appropriate design considerations include selection of the correct size of equipment for children, developmental needs of children, and the physical layout of equipment to support positive play activities.

Correct Size

Size of equipment refers to its height, width, and bulk. The height of the equipment includes the overall distance from the top of the equipment piece to the surface. It also includes the space between various components, such as steps and platforms. Since 70% of reported playground injuries involve falls to surfaces, the height of the equipment becomes a critical factor in designing a safe playground. Experts suggest that equipment for preschool children be no taller than children can reach. Maximum height for most equipment for school-age children should be eight feet (Thompson & Hudson, 1996).

Width of platforms should also allow children to make decisions about how to get on and off equipment safely. A child standing on top of a six-foot slide should have sufficient room to turn around and climb back down the ladder if that child decides not to slide down.

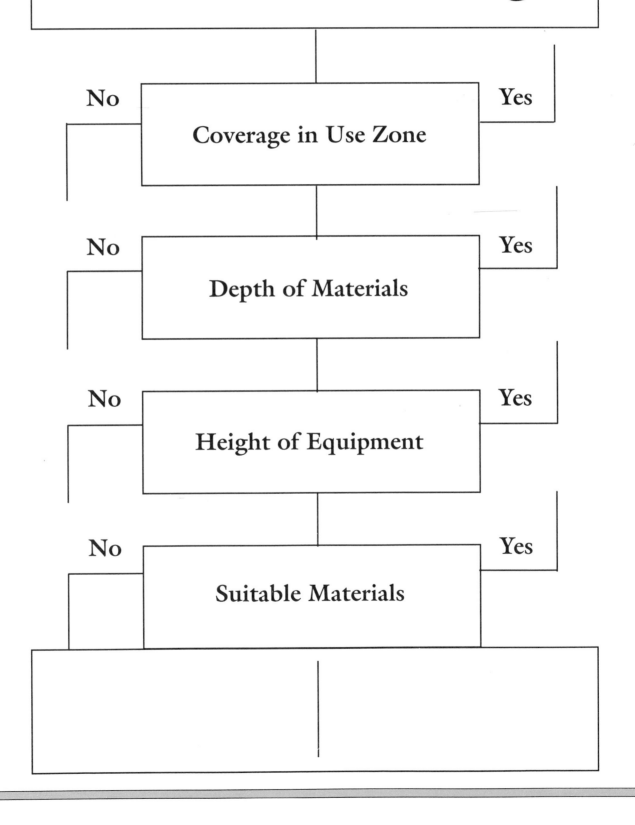

Figure 21.1
Safe Surfacing Decision-Making Model

Bulk is the relationship between the thickness of the material and the grip size of a child's hand. All hand rails, rungs, and other components that children grasp should be between 1 and 1 1/2 inches in diameter.

Developmental Characteristics

Developmental needs of children are also a factor in age-appropriate design. Children grow and develop by stages. The thinking ability of a three-year-old is much different from a seven-year-old. Preschoolers are physically smaller than school-aged children. It is important to consider the developmental needs and abilities of children in planning and designing age-appropriate playgrounds. These needs and abilities include:

- physical (i.e., strength, grip, height, and weight),
- emotional (i.e. risk-taking and exploration),
- social (i.e. cooperation, sharing, and accepting),
- intellectual (i.e., decision-making, inquisitiveness, and creativity), and
- accessibility (i.e., mobility).

These needs and abilities apply to all children. As previously mentioned, even children with limited physical, emotional, social, intellectual and/or mobility have the legal right to use public play areas. Thus, the designer needs to design for the composite "typical/atypical" child if the playground is to be the one where all children can interact successfully.

Physical layout

The physical layout of the playground pieces can limit or enhance the play value and safety of children. An interconnected play area is one in which easy movement throughout the play structure is developed through the inclusion of alternate routes of travel (Bowers, 1998). Shaw (1976) investigated interconnection between parts of the structure, which he came to call the "unified play structure." As a result of the Creative Learning Project, he determined that overall use patterns decreased for separate play modules when compared to the "unified" play space. Thus, by unifying or interconnecting play elements in a play space, overall complexity was increased.

Considerations for Proper Surfacing

Surfacing is the third important general design element. Factors that need to be considered include how much fall

Age Appropriate Design—older elementary children using overhead ladder

Falls to Surfaces—children replacing appropriate surfacing so the depth is proper for the next class.

protection is required, accessibility, management requirements, and costs.

Will this surface provide adequate fall protection?

For the prevention of life-threatening injuries, adequate fall protection needs to be present. The National Program for Playground Safety has developed a safe surface decision-making model to help individuals determine whether or not a playground surface will meet the criteria of adequate fall protection (See Figure 21.1). As can be seen in the model outlined in Figure 21.1, there are four decisions that are involved in the selection of surfaces that will provide adequate fall protection. These include the selection of suitable materials, the height of the equipment, the depth of the materials, and adequate coverage in the use zone.

Suitable Materials

According to the Consumer Product Safety Commission (CPSC, 1997) there are a number of materials that help to reduce the risk of life-threatening injuries. Acceptable materials include sand, gravel, wood chips, engineered wood fibers, shredded rubber, and synthetic surfaces. Hard materials such as asphalt and concrete are unacceptable surfaces under playground equipment. Similarly, earth surfaces such as dirt, soil, grass, and turf are unacceptable, because their shock-absorbing properties vary depending on wear and climatic conditions (CPSC, p. 4).

Height

Equipment height affects the choice of shock absorbent surfacing in two ways. First, some surfaces, such as pea gravel, provide shock absorbency protection for limited heights (i.e., six feet in the case of pea gravel). Second, currently no surface over 12 feet has been laboratory tested. Thus, to date, no one can guarantee the shock-absorbency characteristics for equipment over the height of 12 feet. Because research studies indicate that equipment over six feet in height has double the injury rate of equipment under six feet, the NPPS recommends that the height of playground equipment should not exceed eight feet for school age children and five feet for preschool children.

The CPSC recommendations for the fall heights for various pieces of playground equipment are as follows:
- climbers and horizontal ladders—the maximum height of the structure.
- elevated platforms including slide platforms—the height of the platform.
- merry-go-rounds—the height above the ground of any part at the perimeter on which a child may sit or stand.
- seesaws—the maximum height attainable by any part of the seesaw.
- spring rockers—the maximum height above the ground of the seat or designated play surface.
- swings—since children may fall from a swing seat at its maximum attainable angle (assumed to be 90° from "at rest" position), the fall height of a swing structure is the height of the pivot point where the swing's suspending elements connect to the supporting structure.
- slides—CPSC has no recommendations concerning slide height. Research has shown that equipment higher than six feet have double the injury rate than equipment at lower heights.

It should be noted that equipment that requires a child to be standing or sitting at ground level during play is not expected to follow the recommendations for resilient surfacing. Examples of such equipment are sand boxes, activity walls, playhouses, or any other equipment that has no elevated designated playing surface.

Depth

If the surface does not meet minimum standards for shock absorbency, then it should not be used. Minimum standards are determined through testing procedures as stated in the American Society for Testing and Materials (ASTM) F-1292 standard for Playground Surfacing. However, because of time and cost constraints, many consumers cannot afford to perform this testing. Consequently, as a public surface the NPPS conducted testing of five common loose-fill materials: pea gravel, sand, wood chips, shredded rubber, and engineered wood fiber. The results are provided in chart 21.1. The chart reports the heights at which a life-threatening head injury would not be expected to occur for compressed loose fill materials at three different depths. As can be seen in Chart 21.1, 12 inches of compressed sand, wood chips, shredded rubber and engineered wood fiber can provide shock absorbency for equipment up to eight feet in height. In contrast, the maximum height for 12 inches of pea gravel is six feet. The depth of any loose-fill material could be reduced during use, resulting in different shock-absorbing properties. For this reason, a margin of safety should be considered in selecting a type and depth of material for a specific use. When loose-fill materials are used, it is recommended that there be sections of containment around the perimeter of the use zone (CPSC, 1997).

Use Zone

The final element that helps decide if the appropriate surface is present is the determination of the placement of the surfacing under and around playground equipment. The *Consumer Products and Safety Commission Handbook for Public Playground Safety* defines these areas as use zones. Chart 21.2 presents the requirements for use zones as outlined in the CSPC handbook.

The basic use zone is six feet. However, because children move off swings and slides in different ways than other equipment, the use zone is expanded to provide a larger safety zone. For instance, if a swing beam is eight feet high, then the use zone extends 16 feet in front and 16 feet in back of the swing beam to accommodate children who might jump out of the swing seat while in motion.

How Will Accessibility Be Provided?

The second characteristic that needs to be considered in the section of surfacing is that of accessibility. According

Chart 21.1
Playground Surface Materials

Height of Equipment	Peagravel			Sand			Wood Chips			Shredded Rubber			Engineered Wood Fiber		
	6"	9"	12"	6"	9"	12"	6"	9"	12"	6"	9"	12"	6"	9"	12'
1"	Y	Y	Y	Y	Y	Y	Y	Y	Y	Y	Y	Y	Y	Y	Y
2"	Y	Y	Y	Y	Y	Y	Y	Y	Y	Y	Y	Y	Y	Y	Y
3"	Y	Y	Y	Y	Y	Y	Y	Y	Y	Y	Y	Y	Y	Y	Y
4"	Y	Y	Y	Y	Y	Y	Y	Y	Y	Y	Y	Y	Y	Y	Y
5"	N	Y	Y	Y	Y	Y	Y	Y	Y	Y	Y	Y	Y	Y	Y
6"	N	N	Y	Y	Y	Y	Y	Y	Y	Y	Y	Y	Y	Y	Y
7"	N	N	N	Y	Y	Y	N	Y	Y	Y	Y	Y	Y	Y	Y
8"	N	N	N	Y	Y	Y	N	Y	Y	Y	Y	Y	N	Y	Y

*Based on depth test results conducted by NPPS or manufacturers' literature. Note that the loose-fill results are based on materials tested in a compressed state.

Y = YES, it did meet CPSC recommendations for this critical height.

N = NO, it did not meet CPSC recommendations for this critical height.

Chart 21.2
Use Zones for Equipment

Equipment	Use Zone Requirement
Stationary Equipment	Six feet on all sides of the equipment
Slides	Six feet on all sides. Four feet plus the height of slide in front of slide chute.
Swings	Six feet on each side. Twice the height of the swing beam in front and back of swing.

to the previously mentioned Americans with Disabilities Act of 1990, discrimination on the basis of disability in public accommodations is prohibited. While the entire playground area does not have to be accessible, there must be an accessible pathway to accessible playground equipment. Therefore, a pathway made of an accessible surface material must be provided. At this time, the testing of loose fill materials for accessibility is still in process. However, it is well accepted that sand and pea gravel are not accessible surfaces. Until more testing is done, the only materials that are generally considered accessible under certain conditions are wood fibers and unitary materials, all of which are commercially available. According to a U.S. Department of the Interior advisory, uniform wood fibers tend to knit together to form an accessible surface, while other wood materials (i.e. wood chips, bark, mulch, etc.) do not (McCroy, 1994).

What are the Maintenance Requirements?

The third characteristic, which is often ignored during the selection process, is the maintenance requirements that various surfaces need in order that the shock absorbency characteristics are properly retained. Three elements that should be considered in this area include environmental conditions, soil conditions, and management requirements.

Environmental Conditions

Environmental conditions, such as strong winds, rainy weather, high humidity, freezing temperatures, etc., may influence the appropriateness of the type of surfacing selected. For example, strong winds can erode organic loose-fill materials and sand so that they must be replenished often. Wind and dirt tend to form a hard pan or crust in pea gravel that needs to be broken up periodically. When wet, sand tends to stick together and become almost rigid. Some types of unitary materials are susceptible to frost damage. Thus, the climatic conditions of the playground must be considered when selecting a surface material (Mack, Hudson, & Thompson, 1997).

Soil Conditions

Playgrounds located over poor soil will not drain well, causing pooling of water under equipment. In some areas of the country, the shrink/swell characteristics of clay soil can loosen the foundation of play equipment. Shrink/swell conditions can also cause sinkholes under playground surfaces. This problem can easily destroy a poured-in-place or other unitary surface. One should check with the local soil conservation district or a county extension agent to check the suitability of the soil for playground development.

Finally, the designer must pay attention to the drainage of the site. Normally, one would want water to run down away from the playground. This might mean that the area around the equipment will need to be slightly raised. Since drainage is also dependent on soil type, as mentioned above, the soil composition should be checked prior to the installation of equipment. One should also be aware of what might drain into the playground area. For instance, if a parking lot is located above the play area, grease, oils, and even gasoline may be washed into the play area during a rainstorm. Make sure that there is good drainage at and around the site to avoid problems.

Management Requirements

Consideration must be given as to how the area will be managed. A site that will have high traffic use will require a surface that will be durable without frequent maintenance. Rubber tiles or poured-in-place surfaces, although initially high in cost, may be more appropriate for these types of areas. Loose-fill materials would be more easily displaced, which would have an impact on the overall safety of the site. However, in areas that have controlled use, loose-fill materials may be appropriate.

Maintenance costs and the needs of surfacing materials vary greatly, with loose-fill materials tending to have much higher maintenance needs. In high-use areas, loose materials may need to be raked daily to replace materials that have been pushed or kicked away. Loose-fill materials need to be regularly inspected for protruding and sharp objects such as glass, pop tops, sharp rocks, and metal objects. These surface materials may also have to be tilled periodically to loosen compaction. Sand should periodically be turned over, loosened, and cleaned. Additionally, loads of loose material may need to be added on an annual or semi-annual basis to keep the surface at an appropriate depth.

While not as time-consuming, unitary materials such as rubber mats, tiles, and poured-in-place surfaces also have maintenance needs. Repairs may need to be made to gouges, burns, and loose areas. Unitary materials may also need to be swept frequently to prevent sand, dirt, rocks, or other loose materials from becoming a slip hazard. Finally, rubber surfaces must be washed occasionally to remove spilled beverages, animal excrement, and other foreign matter.

How Much Will it Cost?

Cost factors of the surfacing material should be prorated over the life expectancy of the playground. Materials with low initial cost include sand, pea gravel, wood chips, and bark mulch. However, one should also consider the replenishment costs of these materials along with the initial purchase price. In addition, some method of containment is needed, and the materials cannot be installed over existing hard surfaces, such as concrete and asphalt.

A piece of playground that needs maintenance

Materials with medium initial cost include wood fiber and shredded rubber. Some of these materials are easily installed, while others require professional installation. They may also require a drainage system. Like other loose-fill materials, some type of containment is required, and they cannot be installed over concrete or asphalt.

Unitary materials, such as poured-in-place surfaces, rubber tiles, and rubber mats have a high initial cost when compared to low-cost loose-fill materials. Poured-in-place surfaces are usually the most expensive, with a cost 10 to 15 times higher than common loose-fill surfaces. Rubber mats and tiles typically cost six to 12 times that of the cheaper materials. Installation and site preparation costs should also be considered, because these materials must be professionally installed. Unitary materials also require a hard base. If the existing surface is not concrete or asphalt, then a subsurface must be installed prior to the rubber surface. However, if the current surface is concrete or asphalt, installing a rubber surface will avoid the costs of excavating and removing the existing surface.

Equipment Maintenance Considerations

Considerations about maintenance have to be part of the initial planning process. A poorly built playground is difficult to maintain. Providing good upkeep for a safe play environment begins with planning the playground site. Factors that need to be considered regarding this area include preplanning, materials, inspection, maintenance, and environment.

Preplanning

Prior to any installation of equipment and surfaces, a proper site analysis needs to be conducted. A site analysis addresses natural, manufactured, and aesthetic elements that may affect playgrounds. All of these items will be discussed in greater detail in the next section.

Materials

There is no perfect material for playground equipment. Without good maintenance, wood will splinter, metal will rust, and plastic will crack. Any good maintenance plan should be based on:
- Instructions received from the designer/manufacturer,
- Materials used for equipment and surfaces,
- Age of the equipment and surfaces,
- Given frequency of use on the equipment and surfaces, and
- Environmental factors at a specific location.

Make sure that all instructions from the designer/manufacturer are retained in a file and that the schedule of maintenance is followed. Remember, any modification, deviation, or change from these instructions means that liability issues will reside with the agency, not the designer/manufacturer.

Inspection

Inspect all materials prior to installation. Wood products are aesthetically pleasing but will weather faster than metal or plastic. Plastic materials may not be appropriate in areas of great temperature extremes. Metal materials also tend to absorb heat and cold, which can cause problems in hot and cold climates.

Even newly installed playgrounds should be inspected for hazards. Just because a playground is new doesn't mean that problems cannot occur. This is especially true if the equipment was installed improperly or the overall design and placement of equipment is faulty. On the other hand, older playgrounds do need more regular inspections simply because parts may wear out due to age.

Maintenance Schedule

A well-used playground will need more frequent maintenance than one that is used less often. This is especially true with playgrounds that have loose-fill materials as the surface under and around playground equipment. An agency that schedules only one refilling of these materials a year may find that over half its playgrounds are unsafe, due to the high usage. Each play area may have its own use cycle, and the maintenance schedule should reflect this.

Environmental Factors

Finally, the environmental factors at a specific location are going to determine the required frequency of maintenance. A playground that is located near a shady grove of trees may need to be inspected more frequently because of materials left on the surfacing (e.g., leaves) or other hazards (e.g., overhanging limbs). A playground that is in a wide-open area and exposed to the elements may also experience greater maintenance needs.

It is evident that to maintain a safe playground environment, maintenance practices and procedures need to be thought about at the beginning of the design process. It is also important that these practices and procedures be continually revised and improved.

Specific Planning Steps

The actual planning and design of a playground is accomplished in four distinct phases. They are site analysis, preliminary design, equipment and material selection, and final design.

Site Analysis

Site analysis involves the gathering of information and data about the playground site and adjacent properties. "The purpose of site analysis is to find a place for a particular use or find a use for a particular place" (Molnar & Rutledge, 1986). One of the first things that one should do during the site analysis is an on-site visitation. Personal site visits enable one to see how the area is used and how it relates to surrounding land uses (IPRA, 1995). It allows the planner to mentally visualize the space available for the project.

During the site analysis, step information about environmental elements, manufactured elements, and hazardous conditions is gathered and analyzed.

Environmental Characteristics

Environment that should be considered during the site analysis include soils, geology, drainage, topography, vegetation, and any other physical characteristics that may have an impact on the development process.

Soils and Geology

Soil type is important, because it is directly related to drainage. The playground should be constructed on well-drained soils. A playground constructed on poor soil will be subject to water pooling or standing. It will also tend to erode the foundations of the equipment and cause other problems of equipment stability.

Drainage

In general, water should drain away from the playground. As mentioned earlier, the play area may need to be slightly elevated to accomplish this. One needs to remember that construction of the playground and/or surrounding areas may alter the water movement patterns on the site. If there are questions about preventing or solving water problems, a good source is the local office of the Soil Conservation Service (SACS).

Topography is concerned the general lay of the land. Playground developments work best within a range of slopes. As a general rule, slopes around and beneath playground should conform to the following guidelines:

- Slope between one percent to four percent are most suitable for playgrounds (a one percent slope falls one foot for every 100 linear feet).
- Slopes less than one percent may result in drainage problems.
- Slopes greater than four percent may require site modifications to install and level the equipment (IPRA, 1995).

In addition, slope is an important consideration in providing equal access into the playground for everyone, regardless of physical capabilities. The accessible route into the playground must have a maximum slope of five percent (one foot of fall for every 20 linear feet) and a maximum cross slope of two percent.

Vegetation is another environmental consideration in playground design. Shade should be an essential ingredient for every playground. If trees are not present, it may be necessary to provide man-made shade such as the placement of shelters. While trees, planted along a western and southern exposure may provide the necessary shade, caution must be taken to ensure that overhanging limbs do not interfere with play activities. "In particular, trees planted inside the playground must be carefully located because they may be used for climbing." (IPSA, p.13). In addition, one should avoid planting trees and shrubs, which are messy or likely to attract stinging insects such as bees.

Other environmental considerations include sun orientation, wind patterns, climate, and animal control. Slide surfaces that tend to absorb heat should avoid being placed on a western exposure. The best orientation is north. However, if this is not possible, then natural or manufactured shade needs to be provided.

The direction of the prevailing winds should also be determined. If at all possible, the playground should be located downwind from open fields, farm yards, or areas like unpaved roads where dust from these sites will blow directly into the play area. In addition, if an area is susceptible to strong winds on a routine basis, some type of windbreak should be created.

Climatic conditions that affect playground equipment and surfaces include heat and cold, humidity, and precipitation. As mentioned earlier, temperature extremes have a direct influence on different materials used for equipment and surfacing. In addition, humidity may affect certain loose-fill surfaces, as well as cause the surfaces of equipment to become slippery and hazardous. An area that has constant precipitation may need to have a cover over the equipment as well as excellent drainage.

Manufactured element

The second factor to consider in the site analysis is manufactured elements. These include utilities, roads, buildings, adjacent land use, accessibility, and anything else that could affect or be affected by the playground.

Utilities

As a general rule, playgrounds should not be constructed under utility lines. One needs also to pay attention to unused utility easements. There might be a temptation to use these seemingly open areas, but nothing can stop a utility from using the easement at a later date for power lines. Another utility consideration is the support structures that may be found near the playground site. Power poles and towers can constitute an attractive nuisance in the play area. In addition, guidewires or other supporting cables on these utility structures can create a hazard for children in the area.

Roads

The playground should be located far enough away from roads and parking lots that moving vehicles do not pose a hazard for children. A barrier surrounding the playground is recommended if children may inadvertently run into a street. If fences are used for such barriers, it is recommended that they conform to applicable local building codes (CSPC, 1997). In addition, ASTM has developed a specific standard for fencing around playgrounds (ASTM 300).

Use Zones

Proper use zones need to be maintained in relation to any buildings or structures that may be present on the site. For example, a school playground should be located far enough away from the school buildings so that a child on a climbing structure would be in no danger of falling off the play equipment into the building. In addition, close proximity of the playground to windows may encourage vandalism problems.

Land Use

Neighboring land uses need to be considered because they may affect or be affected by the playground (IPRA, 1995). Railroads, freeways, landfills, streams, and rivers may all contribute to a hazardous environment for children. The long-term effects of some of these items (i.e., waste dumps) may not be determined for years. On the other hand, the location of the playground itself may be seen as a less-than-desirable element within the neighborhood environment. Some people may be upset by the perceived increase of noise, vandalism, and traffic they assume a playground will attract.

Access

Accessibility to and from the site is also a consideration. How will project users get to the playground site? Will it involve children arriving on bicycles, walking, or being brought by cars? The answers to these questions will determine the need for bicycle racks, pathways, and parking lots.

Other considerations

Other considerations may include sources of noise such as airports, railroad lines, roadways, heavy machinery, and factories that can detract from the recreational experiences of playground users. Odors from factories, sewage treatment facilities, and stagnant ponds can have the same effect. Locating a playground adjacent to such detractors should be avoided (IRPA, 1995, p.15).

Hazardous conditions

A variety of hazardous conditions must be considered before determining the site location of the playground. These include visibility and security, crossings, water, and mixed recreation use zones.

Visibility/Security. Visibility and security are primary considerations. Large shrubs (above four feet in height) should not be planted around a playground since they inhibit the ability to observe children at play. In addition, as already mentioned, low tree branches (below a height of seven feet) should be removed to prevent climbing. Any trees that will be seriously affected by the development of the playground should also be removed before they create a hazardous situation.

Crossings. Children should not be required to use unprotected crossings to reach playgrounds. Railroad tracks are a similar hazard. Fencing or natural barriers may be necessary if alternative solutions are not feasible (IPRA, 1995). Another traffic consideration can occur around schools and child care centers where delivery truck routes may pose a potential hazard for children going to and from the play area. Special care should be given to make sure that these routes do not intersect the play area and are not located nearby.

Water. Water is another site element that may pose a hazardous situation. Children are attracted to ponds, streams, and drainage ditches. Cement culverts or ditches are especially dangerous, since their smooth sides may not allow a child easy escape in case of a flash flood. Signage alone will not stop any child from trying to incorporate these areas into their play behavior.

Mixed Use Zones. Mixed recreation use zones can also produce hazardous situations. A soccer field or baseball diamond located too close to a playground is a safety concern because of the chance that errant balls may enter the play area and injure playground users. Locating a playground adjacent to basketball courts, tennis courts, and other similar recreation facilities can also create conflicting access patterns and users.

Preliminary Design

The preliminary design phase is where information about the activity, user, site, and necessary support factors are analyzed and alternative solutions evaluated. At the end of this step, the actual schematic plans will be developed.

Activity Information

What is the purpose of the playground? This fundamental question needs to be answered in terms of performance objectives rather than physical objectives. For instance, if one answers this question by saying the purpose of the playground is to provide slides, swings, and climbing apparatus, then one will limit the possibilities of the play behavior of children. On the other hand, if one answers this question by looking at what children should be able to do, than a different design may result. The philosophical basis for the existence of the play areas must be reflected in the answer to this question. For example, in a school setting, the purpose of the playground should be tied to the educational goals of the total curriculum. Thus, the playground may be designed so that it contributes to a child's understanding of math, language arts, science, and physical education. In a park setting, the playground may reflect the extension of school goals as well as emphasize the physical, emotional, social, and intellectual development of a child. In a child care setting, the play areas should reflect the growth and development of the different ages of young children.

Once the philosophical question about the purpose of the playground is answered, the next step is to decide what experience opportunities should be provided. Experience opportunities are ways that the child will participate in the playground experience. Four different experience opportunities are usually present in the playground environment. They include:

- basic ability level,
- skill improvement,
- program participation, and
- unstructured participation.

Basic Ability

This is especially important in planning play environments for young children. Children do develop in different stages. For instance, in terms of access on play equipment, ramps provide the easiest way for a small child to get onto equipment, followed by stairways, stepladders, rung ladders and climbers. Thus, if one wanted to provide basic skill level opportunities, the design of the play structures would incorporate a variety of ramps and small stairways, as well as be built fairly low to the ground.

Skill Improvement

This allows for children to develop their abilities in incremental steps. For instance, at the age of six, children don't automatically have the upper body strength to control their bodies on overhead ladders. Some intermediate type of equipment is needed between a six-foot-long and a 20-foot-long overhead ladder, where a child can build up the muscle strength and endurance needed to master the higher and longer apparatus without having the fear of falling.

Program Participation

A playground developed on a school site should be designed to complement the academic offerings of the curriculum. Thus, the design of this playground should have specific equipment pieces and shapes that would supplement the academic program (math, science, art, etc.).

Unstructured Participation

This means an area where children are free to roam, explore, discover, and play. Again, this type of experience opportunity demands some specific design considerations, including placement of equipment, open sight lines, and easy access.

Not all playgrounds have to emphasize the same experience opportunities. However, if the designer/planner fails to recognize which opportunities should be present, the playground may become only an area where equipment is randomly placed.

User Information

A brief profile of the intended users is an important aspect of the planning process. Such a profile should include the age distribution of the intended users, developmental and skill levels, known disabilities, and participation time patterns. In addition, information about participation rates per activity period is necessary to determine the design load of the area in terms of needed equipment units, support areas, and services. Seasonal, monthly, and weekly peak participation periods may be additional planning factors in terms of maintenance and operational considerations.

Site Factors

A third consideration in this preliminary design stage is the resource and facility factors that are directly related to the site development. Special requirements, such as the spatial size for the playground area, need to be noted. Preliminary layout of equipment on a grid will allow the planner to visualize traffic flow on and off equipment, relationships of equipment pieces with one another, and space requirements for use zones. Other special requirements may be the location of items such as tree limbs, power lines, and telephone wires that can infringe on air space and cause a hazardous situation.

The solar orientation of the space in relation to the placement of equipment is also an important factor. The primary consideration should be to minimize glare and sun blindness during play and avoid hot surfaces on the equipment.

Support Factors

Items that are auxiliary to the playground but support the area also need to be considered during this preliminary design stage. These items help enhance the overall aesthetic appearance of the area, contribute to the safety of the children, and provide amenities that create an overall positive experience. Trees, bushes, and other vegetation may need to be planted to help provide shade and/or avoid a stark appearance of the playground site. Fencing may be added to keep children safe during play and keep out unwanted animals and others during other times of the day. Benches, water fountains, and shelter areas may provide children and adults with areas to relax and refresh during their visit to the playground. These support factors and others, such as bicycle racks, trash and recycling cans, and security lighting will not suddenly appear unless they are planned for in the preliminary design stage. Furthermore, if they are added later, their placement may not be in congruence with the overall design of the area.

Equipment and Material Selection

Equipment for playgrounds should be designed for public use, be durable, and meet requirements for insurance, standards, warranty, age appropriateness, and use. Any equipment purchased should conform to both CPSC guidelines and ASTM Standard F-1487.

Product Compliance

Always require a certificate of compliance with the CPSC guidelines and ASTM Standard from the manufacturer prior to purchase of the equipment. The same type of compliance with ASTM F-1292 should be secured for any surfacing material. If a manufacturer is unable to produce such documentation or will only provide oral assurances as to compliance, purchase equipment elsewhere. In addition, make sure that any equipment purchased for public-use playgrounds is designed for that purpose. Many times, people with good intentions but limited funds will purchase equipment intended for home use and place it in a public setting. This equipment is neither durable nor strong enough to withstand the constant, heavy use that is found in public sites. In addition, the standard for home-use equipment is quite different from that for public-use equipment.

Product Materials

Playground equipment is usually made out of one of four types of materials: wood, steel, aluminum, or plastic. Each material has its own advantages and disadvantages.

Wood must be treated to prevent rotting by weather or insects. This is especially true when wood is in direct contact with the ground. Any chemical wood preservative used must be approved for contact with humans. Wood is also subject to splitting and checking, which may eventually weaken the structure. Watch out for evidence of splitting in new wood, especially pieces used as support beams and poles. Sanding and other treatments may be required to avoid injuries from splinters. Although aesthetically pleasing, wooden pieces usually have a lifespan of only 10 years.

Steel equipment pieces should be galvanized and have a protective coating that inhibits rust, such as powder coating and painting. Any paint used should not have lead as a component. It should also be noted that scratches and construction defects are subject to rust. Steel also can heat up to dangerous levels with direct exposure to sun. On the other hand, steel equipment pieces are very durable and have a long life span.

Aluminum components are rust resistant and offer lightweight installation. Aluminum is sometimes more costly at purchase, but the reduced maintenance is often worth the extra cost. Shipping charges will be reduced because of the lighter weight. Like steel, aluminum can heat up with direct exposure to sun.

Plastic can be molded, cut, or formed into a wide variety of shapes for playground use. Because of this, it is a favorite material that is used by many playground manufacturers. However, most plastics do not have the strength of natural lumbers and metals and can sag and bend. It is recommended that UV inhibitors be added to the plastic to extend the life expectancy and color. Plastic components must meet safety standards (IPRA, 1995).

Purchase Factors

One should consider at least five factors prior to purchasing any equipment or surface materials. These include product liability insurance, compliance with standards, product warranty, age appropriateness, and public use equipment.

Product liability insurance protects the buyer against any accident caused by the design of the equipment. However, if the buyer makes any alteration or modification or fails to maintain the equipment properly, the insurance will not cover the agency. The equipment vendor should furnish the agency with certificates of insurance and original endorsements affecting the coverage. As with all documentation, make sure the insurance coverage is in writing and on file.

Compliance with standards should also be documented and on file. Do not buy equipment that does not meet CPSC guidelines and ASTM standards F1292 for surfacing and F1487 for equipment. In addition, a certification of proper installation should be obtained from the manufacturer or his representative following the final inspection. Once the manufacturer agrees that the playground is in conformance with its installation recommendations, ask for a sign-off letter stating the date of inspection. Make sure that you keep this document on file. It is extremely important, should an injury occur due to improper design or installation.

Product warranty simply provides the buyer with the length of time for which any products are protected against defects. Many times, the product warranty is a good indication of the product's life expectancy. Again, any modification or repair made without conformance to the manufacturer's guidelines will nullify most warranties.

Age appropriateness of the equipment has already been covered. However, you should notify the manufacturer in writing what the ages of the intended users are to ensure that they have provided you with age-appropriate equipment at the time of purchase.

Public-use equipment is the last item to consider. Not all pieces of equipment are recommended for use in a public playground. The following is a list of equipment to avoid primarily because it fails to meet safety guidelines:

- spinning equipment without speed governors,
- tire swings that do not meet requirements for clearance,
- seesaws that do not meet current safety standards,
- heavy swings (metal, wood, animal-type),
- ropes/cables that are not attached at both ends,
- swinging exercise rings and trapeze bars,
- multiple occupancy swings,
- trampolines, and
- homemade equipment.

Final Design

At this stage, one is ready to put all the components together in a scaled schematic drawing that shows layout, use zones, site amenities, access points, and other construction details. Also, one needs to insure that accessible routes to the equipment are present.

The easiest way to begin this process is to use cutouts or round bubbles to represent the actual equipment and place these items on a scale grid plan. In this way, one can visualize how the equipment pieces fit together and where potential conflicts of use may arise. Any moving equipment, including swings, should be located away from other structures, preferably at the edge or corner of anticipated traffic patterns. In addition, make sure to separate preschool (ages two to five) from school-age (five to 12) equipment.

All equipment has space requirements. By moving the cutouts or squares around, one can make sure that the use zones of the various equipment pieces do not overlap. Remember that these use zones are minimum guidelines. The authors have seen several instances where slide exits were placed directly in front of swing sets. Although the proper use zone was in place, exuberant children who jumped out of the swings landed directly in front or to the side of the slide. Of course, the best way to avoid this situation is not to place these two activities across from one another in the first place.

As mentioned earlier, site amenities should be part of the planning stage. Make sure that the scaled drawings include the placement of benches, bicycle racks, trash cans, etc. If these items are not in the drawings, they will be haphazardly provided later, perhaps at inappropriate spots.

Before finalizing the drawings, make sure that you have considered traffic flow patterns on and off equipment and general access to the area. Every playground should have at least one accessible route to the equipment that will permit children with disabilities the opportunity to be in the playground area and interact with others. Although the final Americans with Disabilities Act regulations have not been finalized, it is important to understand that just getting to the equipment will not be enough to satisfy the law. Once at the equipment, some type of accommodation should be made to allow children on at least some of the equipment as well as to interact with their non-disabled counterparts. Consult the U.S. Access Board for further information on this subject.

Installation

Installation of equipment is an important part of the overall planning process. If equipment and surfacing are installed improperly, the safety of the total play environment will be jeopardized. When dealing with the installation of equipment and surfacing, there are three factors to consider:
- planning of the installation,
- actual installation of the equipment and surfacing, and
- liability issues related to the installation.

Planning of the Installation

Five items need to be considered during the planning of the installation process. These include:
- the manufacturer of the equipment,
- the manufacturer of the surfacing,
- the materials needed,
- who will perform the installation, and
- budgetary factors.

The Manufacturer of the Equipment

This business must be selected carefully. The decision about which manufacturer to use should be made on the basis of the planning committee's criteria. It is critical that the manufacturer chosen produces equipment that meets the ASTM 1487 current standard and the *CPSC Handbook for Public Playground Safety guidelines*. After the tentative selection of the manufacturer has been made, the planning committee should talk with others who have purchased equipment from the potential vendor and check the company's competency. The committee should also find out whether the equipment installation process was understandable and reasonable, and most important, how the equipment held up after being installed.

The Manufacturer of the Surface

As with the equipment manufacturer, the surfacing manufacturer should also be chosen with care. Again, any decision should be based on the criteria established by the planning committee. The surfacing manufacturer must be able to provide testing data from an independent laboratory to show the depth of the product needed proportionate to the height of the equipment purchased. The testing procedure used must be based on the ASTM 1292 current standard. In addition, it is a good idea to talk with others who have dealt with the prospective manufacturer to determine the company's competency and service record.

Materials Needed

A third item that needs to be considered in the planning process for installation is the materials needed. It is easier to obtain materials in some areas of the country than in others. This will affect their costs. In a previous section, weather factors have been discussed, but the time of year that installation will occur also needs to be considered. This is especially critical in relation to surfacing and the setting of cement for footings. It also is a consideration for the drying time of preservatives on wood products.

Who Will Install the Equipment and the Surface?

The determination of the actual installer(s) is the fourth factor. It is possible to use an installer recommended by the company. If that is the decision, the installer should be trained by the company or be a certified installer recommended by the company. A trained installer adds to the overall cost of the equipment. Thus, many times, in an effort to reduce cost, the purchaser will decide to use in-house agency personnel to install the equipment and surface. If this method of installation is chosen, it is important for liability protection to have a company representative observe the actual installation process or direct the process. Either way, an agency should have the company sign off that the installation process has met the company's specifications.

Budgetary Factors

The budget for installation is the last item that needs attention. The budget will be determined by the cost factors associated with who does the installation, the materials needed, and the time it takes to perform the installation. Cutting costs on installation is many times a shortsighted cost savings. As mentioned before, if the equipment is not properly installed or poor materials are used, the playground will cost the agency more money due to increased maintenance and liability issues.

Installing the Equipment and Surfacing

Four factors should be considered in relation to the actual installation of the equipment and surfacing. They are:
- manufacturer's instructions,
- coordination of the installation,
- time needed for the installation, and
- sign-off by the manufacturer.

The Manufacturer's Instructions

According to ASTM F1487, the manufacturer or designer must provide clear and concise instructions and procedures for the installation of each structure provided and a complete parts list (ASTM-F1487-95, 1995). It is important that these procedures be followed during the installation process. In addition, these instructions should be filed, in case any liability issues arise concerning the proper installation of equipment.

Coordination of the Installation

The next step is to coordinate the installation process. Four potential groups need to interact with one another during installation. These groups include the manufacturer, the owner of the site, the organizer for the personnel who will perform the installation, and the vendors from whom products will be purchased.

Time Needed for Installation

Time is also an important issue that needs to be considered. In particular, the amount of time needed for the installation will influence the number of people involved in the actual installation process. One needs to determine whether or not the community will tolerate weekend installation, or if the work must be done during usual work hours or in the evenings. If installation takes a period of time, protecting children from using partially built structures is a priority need.

Manufacturer Sign-off

After the installation is completed, the agency should get the manufacturer of the equipment and surfacing to sign-off that both items were installed according to specifications. This ensures that the structures and the surfacing are safe for children to use.

Liability Issues

Since we live in a litigious society, it is important to protect the agency from being sued. Following appropriate procedures will not prevent lawsuits, but it may reduce the amount of financial responsibility that is imposed, if a suit is upheld. However, the most important thing to remember about following proper installation instructions is not the liability issue, but the safety issue. By following manufacturer's instructions, the agency is being proactive in trying to reduce the potential for children being injured on the playgrounds.

An agency should be concerned with four liability issues regarding the installation of equipment. According to Clement (1988) these are:
- manufacturer's specifications,
- manufacturer's recommendations,
- the posting of manufacturer's warnings, and
- the importance of following manufacturer's instructions.

Manufacturer's Specifications

It is critical that the agency be sure that the installer has followed the manufacturer's specifications for installation. The responsibility for this falls on the manufacturer, if the company performs the installation. If the agency does the actual installation, it assumes the liability and the burden of proof regarding the following of proper procedures.

Manufacturer's Recommendations

Any recommendations by the manufacturer must also be followed. For example, in order to properly deal with the impact attenuation of a surface, it may be recommended that pea gravel be separated from a wood product by use of a fabric. Once installed, it is the agency's responsibility to see that such a separation is continued. Other recommendations may include that bushings on swings be checked annually for wear, or that wood products be covered with a preservative on an annual basis. In each of these cases, it is important that the agency follow the recommendations of the manufacturer.

Posting of Manufacturer's Warnings

The agency must post any manufacturer's warnings that are included with materials. Many manufacturers now place labels on equipment that suggest ages for which the equipment is designed or the proper depth for loose-fill sur-

face materials. In cases where warnings accompany playground equipment, the agency is responsible for replacing the warnings if they become illegible, destroyed, or removed. Diligence on the part of the agency in regard to the posting of the warning label will inform adults about ways to prevent a child from being injured.

Manufacturer's Instructions

Last, following manufacturer's instructions is very important in the installation of equipment. These instructions can include the proper use zone placement of equipment, the installation of the equipment at the proper depths, the correct method of mixing adhesives for surfacing materials, mixing cement in correct proportions with water, and the use of proper tools to lock joints of structures. The agency may need to be able to provide evidence that such procedures were followed.

As adults work with installation, they can conclude that they are dealing literally with the dirt of responsibility, the grit of reality, and the grind of responsibility.

On-Going Maintenance, Repair, and Inspections

The playground area should be perceived as an environment for play that contains many elements including playground equipment (Hendy, 1997). Parking lots, sidewalks, field areas, seating, shelters, and restroom facilities are only a few of the amenities that complement many playground areas. These amenities require maintenance as well. To insure proper long-term maintenance, a comprehensive program must include the total playground environment, not just the equipment.

The basic function of maintenance is to ensure the safety of users by keeping the playground area and equipment in a safe condition. Maintenance also keeps the equipment functioning efficiently and effectively. A track ride is not much fun if the bearings are worn and the mechanism won't glide easily. Maintenance is also performed to keep the area hygienically clean. By keeping an area well maintained, it remains aesthetically pleasing.

A safety audit should be performed when new equipment is purchased and installed to verify that the equipment and installation are consistent with the "Standard of Care" set forth by the agency and the manufacturer. The audit will not need to be repeated unless the Standard of Care changes, the equipment is heavily vandalized, or a natural disaster impacts the equipment.

Inspections

There are basically two types of maintenance inspections that are performed on playground equipment: seasonal (periodic) and daily (high frequency). A seasonal or periodic inspection is one performed two to three times a year. This is an in-depth type of inspection done to evaluate the general wear and tear on the equipment. A daily or high frequency inspection is done routinely to identify rapidly changing conditions due to weather, vandalism, and sudden breakage. It also identifies surfacing problems typically associated with loose-fill surfacing materials.

There is no magic formula for determining the frequency necessary to perform each type of maintenance inspection. How often the playground is used and by what age group are two of the common considerations that will determine frequency of inspection. The vandalism rate in an area will also dictate the timetable chosen to inspect the playground.

The nature of the area and the environment will influence the need for playground maintenance. The soil type and drainage conditions as well as other geographic and climatic conditions will also influence inspection frequency.

Record Keeping

Documentation of inspections, repairs, and maintenance should be recorded regularly. In addition, the agency must establish a system of work requests that will enable maintenance staff to expedite the ordering of replacement parts and repair services. As part of the overall comprehensive program of playground maintenance, it is important to document all inspections and maintenance procedures. A "fail proof" system of follow-up must be established that enables a supervisor to review the inspection forms, noting:

- who performed the inspection;
- items that were corrected on site at the time of inspection;
- hazards that need to be corrected;

- work orders that were issued;
- purchase orders for equipment services, or replacement parts;
- when equipment, parts, or services were supplied or rendered;
- when repair work was completed;
- who performed the repair work; and
- final approval from the supervisor.

Summary

Playgrounds should be an important facility consideration for inclusion in schools, child care centers, parks, and other recreation facilities. By following the systematic design process outlined in this chapter, playgrounds can be safe as well as foster children's physical, emotional, social, and intellectual development. By paying attention to age-appropriate equipment, proper surfacing under and around equipment, the placement of equipment for easy supervision, and the regular maintenance of the equipment and the environment, HPERD professionals will be able to design a play environment that allows children to be playful. It will also provide a setting in which children can increase their ability to take appropriate challenges without fear of taking inappropriate risks.

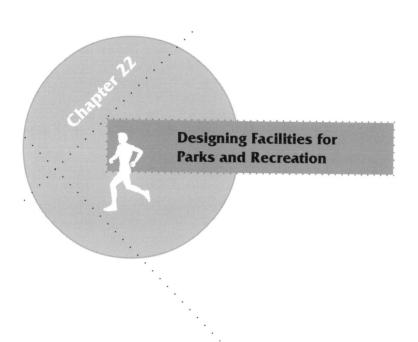

Chapter 22

Designing Facilities for Parks and Recreation

Thomas H. Sawyer, Indiana State University
Michael Hypes, Indiana State University

Park and recreation facilities are experiencing a multitude of trends that are impacting the planning process. Planning principles are not typically subject to change, but inputs to the process are undergoing substantial change.

The late 1990s were characterized by a variety of trends:
- Changing attitudes toward recreation and leisure,
- Changes in employment and in the workplace ("Baby Boomers" beginning to retire),
- A changing population and household composition,
- Marked advances in medical care,
- Dramatic innovations in leisure equipment technology,
- Changing housing patterns,
- Usage of electronic games, cable TV, and computers,
- Changes in world energy,
- Changes in regional economies,
- Unstable political environments, and
- Increased and continuing emphasis on doing more with less.

Facilities and open spaces must clearly be designed to accommodate the dramatic changes of the 1990s. The planning process will continue to need the involvement of the varied public to be served.

Instructional Objectives

After completing this chapter the student should be able to:
Assist architects and planners in designing a functional park for recreation and leisure activities.

A Master Plan Concept (See Chapter 3)

The planning process, regardless of the size of the community involved, typically occurs at three levels. First, there must be a master plan conceptualized at the policy-making level. Second, there is a concept plan which concerns physical matters in that it is site-specific and incorporates factors associated with landscaping, layout, facility mix, and construction. Third is the planning stage, which has a focus on operation and maintenance for facilities, parks, and open spaces. All three levels are critical to sound planning; however, the master plan level is the most important, since it is at the policy-making level where critical initial decisions are made that guide and control all future decisions at the second and third levels of planning.

Community Involvement

In developing plans for new recreation, park, and open spaces, and in proposing improvements to existing facilities and areas, all planning, as suggested within the master plan concept, must reflect the wants and needs of the community. Public cooperation and involvement in the initial planning stages will serve to strengthen community interest, both actively and financially.

There are many ways to involve the public in the planning process. One is the public meeting. Although time-consuming, a series of well-organized public meetings is an effective means of presenting proposed plans.

A survey of leisure behavior and attitudes can be useful in determining the needs and desires of the people within a the planning area. Many users are found in the community at large, outside school populations. Thus, inter-agency agreements for shared use of facilities is on the increase. Also, cooperation between community agencies and organized groups facilitates planning, promotes financial considerations, and assures community involvement.

The field of industrial recreation is developing as a major area of progress in the recreation field. Management and employees are discovering the benefits of industrial fitness programs. Industries throughout the nation are expanding current facilities or establishing new recreational and fitness complexes. Programs such as these range from multi-million dollar facilities with special equipment and a medical and professional staff to programs offered in conjunction with local Y's or school systems.

Again, because industrial recreation/fitness programs encompass such a wide range of opportunities, public and private interests must cooperate to provide the best facilities and programs possible.

Planning Considerations for Urban Areas

As a result of population shifts to urban centers, open space is at a premium within the confines of the urban areas, and there has been a general decline in the environmental quality of these areas. This has led to a growing public concern about recreational facilities and services. Therefore, the following factors must be considered when planning recreational facilities within congested urban areas:

- Lack of open space and often lack of economic resources make it mandatory that all government and public agencies cooperate in planning facilities for maximum use. Recreational use of public housing facilities, social and health care programs in recreational centers, and swimming pools adjacent to or part of fire stations are just a few examples of ways in which the public can maximize facility use.
- Additional or secondary uses of all facilities, both public and private, must be considered. For example, the parking lot of a large industrial plant can be used for recreational purposes on weekends with little or no additional cost if properly planned.
- The mobility of people in dense urban areas is often restricted. Therefore, facilities must be easily accessible to the people.
- Plans should be revised for maximum use of existing facilities. Twenty-four hour use should be considered as a possibility in some areas.
- All facilities need to be handicapped accessible.

Multiple Use

Planning facilities for multiple use is a major consideration in the establishment of playgrounds and other recreational properties. Multiple-use facilities require space that can accommodate varied activities for all age groups during various times of the day, week, month, season, or year. Most activities are associated with specific times and/or seasons. Basketball and hockey are considered winter activities, baseball is played in the spring and the summer, and football is a sport for autumn. Thus, a facility that is planned to accommodate a single use becomes an expensive investment if allowed to stand idle much of the year. Changing recreational preferences requires that indoor and outdoor areas not be restricted with permanent spatial and architectural fixtures designed for specific activities in a set period of time. There must be a flexibility built into indoor and outdoor facilities comparable to the open classroom in the field of education.

The character and location of the population are constantly changing. The ethnic, socio-economic, and demographic features such as age and family size can vary within neighborhoods. With today's mobile population, a community facility that is planned on the basis of a static population soon has many obsolete features.

Eliminating Architectural Barriers

It is essential that all recreational facilities be designed to serve the disabled. Therapeutic recreation services must involve the special members of the population in the planning process to ensure that activities and facilities will serve their needs. Guidelines for the elimination of architectural barriers are detailed in Chapter 7.

Indoor Community Areas and Facilities

Relations among planning units, however, are often changed by physiographic or demographic changes occurring in the planning entity. A new neighborhood might be formed by a significant change in housing or in nationality, or a community might be divided into two neighborhoods by a new expressway. These factors are taken into consideration when defining units.

Use of Planning Units

Population units form the basis for planning programs and activities. The park and recreation agency, in order to plan and manage its services properly, establishes its activities and facilities on the demands of a known population with given economic and ethnic characteristics. The larger the planning and managing agency, the broader the population group with which it will be concerned. An undefined population unit results only in arbitrary allocations of services and provides no accountability or relevancy. Every effort should be made to provide for recreational programs and areas in the most effective and efficient manner.

General Recreational Buildings

Recreational buildings should be planned to meet the needs and interests of all people in the neighborhood or community, regardless of age, sex, or ability. They should provide a safe, healthful, and attractive atmosphere in which every person in the community or neighborhood may enjoy his or her leisure by participating in activities of a social, inspirational, cultural, or physical nature.

Recreational buildings may range from the simple picnic shelter to the complex community recreational building with its variety of special service facilities. They may vary in design from the rustic to the contemporary.

Unlike many of the early structures, present-day buildings provide for adaptability and multiple user. This change from the simple to the complex has stimulated the development of a variety of recreational buildings. These are classified by function and then categorized by size. The size of recreational buildings is usually based on the population to be served and the program to be conducted.

The Neighborhood Center

The facility which is, perhaps, closest to the grassroots service level is the neighborhood center. A neighborhood recreation center is designed to service an area of approximately 8,000 people. Such a building encloses 15,000 to 25,000 square feet. The size will depend also on whether the building is a separate entity or part of a park-school complex where facilities are available in the school.

The neighborhood center usually includes the following facilities:

- Multi-purpose room or rooms
- Gymnasium (if not available in neighborhood school) (see Chapter 13)
- Shower and locker rooms, when a gymnasium is provided (see Chapter 9)
- Arts and crafts room
- Game room
- Kitchen
- Restrooms
- Lounge and lobby
- Office
- Large storage areas

The Community Center

The community recreation center functions beyond the primary purpose of serving a neighborhood. It is designed to meet the complete recreational needs of all the people in the community. The size of the building depends on (a) the number of people to be served, (b) the projected program plan, and (c) whether it is a part of a park-school site or a separate building. This building usually contains 20,000 to 40,000 square feet of space, and is usually located in a major recreational area such as a park-school site or community park.

The community center usually includes the following facilities:

- Multi-purpose rooms
- Gymnasium (see Chapter 13)
- Shower and locker rooms (see Chapter 9)
- Stage and auditorium (sometimes combined with gymnasium)
- Rooms for programs in the arts (art, dance, music, drama)
- Game room
- Kitchen
- Restrooms
- Lounge and lobby
- Office
- Large storage areas
- Clubs or classrooms
- Possible specialized areas as program dictates (racquet courts, gymnastics, weight and exercise room, photography workshop, and so on).

Multi-Purpose Room

The multi-purpose room should be designed to accommodate such activities as general meetings, social recreation, active table games, dancing, dramatics, music, concerts, banquets, and the like. The area of this room should be approximately 2,000 to 3,000 square feet. It should be rectangular in shape, with a minimum width of 40'. The minimum ceiling height should be 16'.

Vinyl flooring is recommended. The floor should have a nonskid surface to prevent many common accidents. It is recommended that the floor also be level to permit multiple use for meetings, dancing, dramatic presentations, and so on.

Gymnasium (see also Chapter 13)

The structure should be at least 90' by 100', with a minimum height of 24'. This size will permit a basketball court of 50' by 84', with additional room for telescopic bleachers seating approximately 325 spectators on one side of the gymnasium.

Provision should be made for a mechanical ventilating system with air-conditioning considered where climate dictates. It is preferable to have no windows in the gymnasium. However, if desired, windows should be placed at right angles to the sun at a height of 12' or more, and they should be equipped with protective guards. The wainscotting, or tile, in the gymnasium should provide clear, unobstructed wall space from the floor to a height of 12'.

Floors with synthetic surfaces have become predominant in recreational gymnasiums. Maple flooring continues to be selected as an alternative to a synthetic surface. If maple flooring is used, the cork spring clip or other type of expansion joint should be installed on all four sides. If suspended apparatus requiring wall attachments is used in the gymnasium, these attachments should be at least seven feet above floor level.

Recessed drinking fountains should be located where they will cause a minimum of interference. Fountains should be hand- or hand-and-foot operated, with up-front spouts and controls. Protective floor covering or drainage at the base of the fountain should be considered to avoid floor damage.

Locker and Shower Rooms

Locker and shower rooms must be provided for physical activities, athletics, faculty, and the like (See Chapter 9).

Stage and Auditorium

A stage and related facilities may be built in conjunction with the gymnasium or multi-purpose room. If space and funds allow, a separate unit is preferred. The stage proper should be about 20' in depth and the proscenium opening should be at least two-thirds the width of the crafts is desirable. However, if this is not possible, at least one club room should be equipped for crafts, with provision for gas, compressed air, and a modern sink with hot and cold water. The sink should have a clay trap.

The approach to the stage from the floor of the main room, should be by inclined ramp with a nonskid surface to facilitate the physically disabled and aging and to accommodate movement of equipment.

The room should be equipped with a modern public address system, permanently installed with matched speakers and outlets for additional microphones and audio-visual equipment. Consideration should be given to a master con-

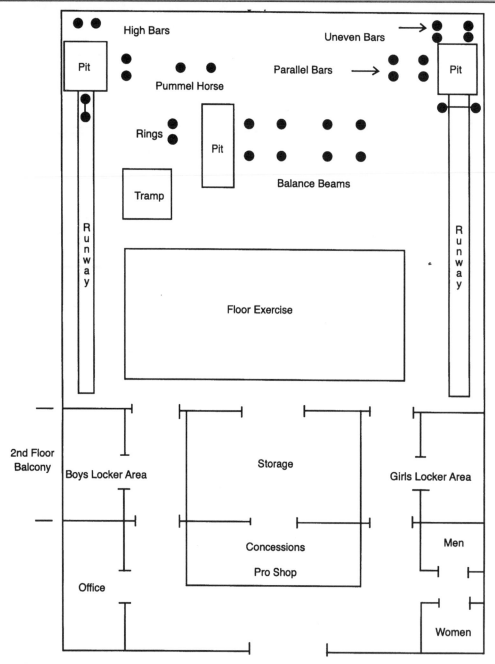

Figure 22.1
Free-standing gymnastics area

Graphic by Meghan Sawyer

trol from the office of the building. All stage lighting should be modern and should be controlled from a dimmer-control cabinet equipped with a rheostat.

The base and wall of the room should be equipped with electrical outlets to accommodate floor and table lamps, motion picture equipment, floodlights, and other electrical apparatus. A heavy-voltage line may be necessary. Provision should also be made for installing television program equipment.

The entrance should contain double doors. Stage doors should be of sufficient width and height to facilitate the movement of scenery It is desirable to have a door at the rear of the stage area to permit the handling of stage properties and

scenery. Adequate exit doors should be provided and should be equipped with panic hardware. Door frames and thresholds should be flush.

Space should be provided for the storage of chairs, tables, and portable staging. This space can be under the stage or in an adjacent storage room provided with dollies having swivel ballbearing fiber or rubber-covered casters.

Acoustics are an important factor in an auditorium and should be kept in mind in the selection of materials for walls and ceilings. Rigid acoustic materials for ceilings are more economical and discourage vandalism better than suspended acoustical tile.

The entrance should contain double doors and should be at the end opposite the stage. Each door should have a minimum unobstructed opening of at least 32 inches, with a removable mullion.

Game Room

The game room, approximately 30' by 64' in size, is designed for a variety of games, including pool and table tennis. In planning this room, sufficient storage space should be provided for the various items of game equipment and supplies.

This room should be close to office supervision and should be acoustically treated. The choice of floor material should be carefully considered because of the heavy traffic anticipated in this room. Windows should be placed high in the walls to reduce glass breakage. A chair rail or wainscotting to prevent the marring of walls should be installed to a height of three feet above the floor. Whenever possible, noncontact (nonmarring) furniture should be used.

The game room should include tables for billiards, table tennis, and other popular table top games.

Kitchen

A kitchen is desirable for most community and neighborhood recreation buildings. If large dinners or banquets are to be served, provision should be made for a full-size kitchen in that room. The kitchen should be located near the club rooms and the gymnasium so it can be used for small gatherings in the club rooms and for large banquets in the gymnasium. The kitchen is often placed between two club rooms and made available to both rooms by the use of aluminum roll-up doors.

Adequate storage space, cabinet space, and electrical outlets for such appliances as the refrigerator, range, dishwasher, and can openers should be provided. Exhaust fans should also be installed.

Arts and Crafts Room

A separate room for arts and conforms to local health regulations and has a free floor space at least 54 inches wide.

Ample storage cabinets, closets, or lockers should be included for the safe storage of craft materials, unfinished projects, and exhibit materials. Base and wall plugs should be provided in all club rooms for the operation of electric irons, sewing machines, power tools, movie projectors, and other equipment. If a kiln is used, it should be equipped with a heavy-duty 220-volt electrical outlet. Bulletin boards and exhibit cases may be used to display completed projects.

Lounge and Lobby

The lobby is located just inside the entrance of the recreation building. The lounge should open off the lobby and, if possible, should be close to the central office and to the multi-purpose room and/or gymnasium. The lounge and lobby are often combined into one room.

This facility should be attractively lighted and should contain a wall-mounted, recessed drinking fountain, a lighted trophy case, and a bulletin board. Provision should be made for public telephones, and at least one telephone should be installed to accommodate a person in a wheelchair. Adequate space, preferably recessed, and electrical and water connections for automatic vending machines should be included.

Lobby entrance doors present a problem from the standpoints of aesthetics, safety, security, and vandalism. Solid-glass panels—from ceiling to floor—and solid-glass doors are quite popular and attractive, but can be easily broken. Good aluminum doors with a minimum of glass are preferable.

Carpet floor covering is desirable for the lounge and lobby area. However, terrazzo, quarry tile, and patio tile are preferred when cigarette damage is a possibility.

Office

The office area, containing approximately 120 square feet, should be located near the main entrance with adequate window space to provide maximum supervision. However, provision must be made to ensure privacy when dealing with disciplinary problems, small meetings, and the like. Secretarial and program offices should be adjacent to the director's office.

An adjoining shower/dressing unit with a floor surface area of not less than 100 square feet is recommended. A storage closet with burglar-resistant door for storing valuable supplies and equipment should adjoin the administrative offices.

Storage Areas

One of the most common errors in planning recreation buildings is lack of sufficient storage space for equipment, maintenance, and custodial purposes. An area adjacent to the gymnasium should be provided for such storage. It should have a six-foot-wide roll up door opening with flush, louvered doors and a flush threshold to permit passage of the most bulky equipment. The minimum size of the storage room should be approximately 400 to 600 square feet. Provision should be made for storage of inflated balls, bats, softballs, and other supplies, either in separate cabinets or a special closet. Appropriate bins, shelves, and racks are suggested. In addition, a recessed alcove for the storage of a piano is desirable.

The maintenance storage room varies in size, depending on the adjacent outdoor space and the size of the building. The room is ordinarily located on the ground level, adjacent to the outdoor areas. An outside entrance should be provided by means of a burglar-resistant door large enough to permit the passage of motorized maintenance equipment. Recessed wall shelving and cabinet storage should be provided for tools, supplies, and equipment. This space should contain hot and cold water, a slop sink, a lavatory, a water closet, and a clothes closet. The floor should be concrete and pitched to a central drain. The junction of the floor and wall should be covered.

A supply closet equipped with a slop sink and space for mops, pails, brooms, and cleaning supplies should be centrally located on each floor level.

Club or Classrooms

Experience indicates the desirability of providing a minimum of 500 square feet of floor space per club room. For community recreation buildings, at least three to five club rooms should be provided for multiple use. At least one large club room should be located adjoining the kitchen.

When windows in club rooms and lounges are placed high in a wall, they are not broken as often as low windows and they also allow more space for furniture, bulletin boards, pegboards, chalkboards, and exhibits. Since broken window glass is a major problem, a nonbreakable type of pane is preferred. Windows may be omitted and sky domes and vent domes used, thus eliminating the need for draperies, Venetian blinds, and curtains—all items subject to vandalism.

A chair rail or wainscotting to prevent the marring of walls should be installed to a height of three feet above the floor. Whenever possible, noncontact (nonmarring) furniture should be used. Floor-level radiant heat in rooms where programs for small children will be conducted should be considered.

Photography Room

A special room can be equipped as a darkroom. Ventilation should be provided through light-proof ventilators. Hot and cold running water, special light plugs (both wall and base), and photographic sinks for developing and washing prints should also be provided. A mixer is desirable to control the water temperatures accurately. A filter should also be provided if the water quality is not good. Doors must be light-proof.

Music Room

The size of the music room should be determined by the potential number in the choral or instrumental group using this facility at any given time. A guide commonly used is to allow 20 square feet for each participant. Provision should be made for the storage of music, instruments, band uniforms, and supplies. Shelves are commonly used for storage of music equipment.

Auxiliary Gymnasium (see also Chapter 13)

The auxiliary gymnasium is for such activities as wrestling, weight-lifting, tumbling, fencing, and apparatus work. Acoustic treatment for this room is desirable. The size of the room and height of the ceiling will depend on the various activities for which this facility will be used. The floor should be treated with material that will withstand the use of such equipment as heavy weights.

At least one well-ventilated storage room will be needed for equipment and supplies used in the auxiliary gymnasium. If the apparatus is to be cleared from this room, an additional apparatus storage room should be provided.

Instructor's Office

If the recreation program is of considerable size, there should be an office for instructors and leaders. It should be approximately 120 square feet in size and should be adjacent to the gymnasium.

A dressing room opening into this office should be provided for the activity leaders. This facility should contain a shower, water closet, lavatory, and clothes closet. Proper ventilation should be provided for all rooms.

Checkroom

The size of the checkroom will depend on the magnitude of the program. This room should open into the lobby and be equipped with a Dutch door, shelves, and portable hanger racks.

Specialized Recreation Buildings

Many cities and communities provide recreation programs that require specialized facilities. While the construction of these facilities can be justified in the majority of cases, care must be taken to provide for maximum year-round use. The specialized centers should be centrally located to serve all the public.

Art Center

In recent years, many cities have constructed a community art center to satisfy the public demand for programs in the arts. The size of the facility will be determined by the number of people to be served and type of art programs to be conducted. Generally, art centers will include work areas for ceramics, sculpture, painting, and sketching. Depending on the interests in the community, a center may also include facilities for woodworking, lapidary, stonecutting, and other arts and crafts. Some art centers include facilities for dance, music, and dramatic classes and programs as well.

Pre-School Center

Pre-school centers for day care, Head Start, and nursery school programs are being built in some communities with the aid of grants or federal funds. These buildings are smaller than neighborhood center buildings, and the design scale is geared to pre-school children. Generally the centers include a large multi-purpose room, small rooms for small-group activities, an office, possibly a kitchen and eating facilities, and ample storage space. Special care should be taken to ensure good acoustic treatment in the center.

Senior Citizen Centers

Senior citizen centers are similar in design to neighborhood recreation centers. However, more emphasis is placed on facilities for the arts, areas for discussion, and rooms for passive games than for large-scale physical activities. While a gymnasium is seldom found in a senior citizen area, a large multi-purpose room is needed for square dance, shuffleboard, and similar activities. The senior citizen center should be a single-floor building, and special care should be taken to eliminate all hazards such as steps and protrusions on walls.

Swimming Pool (Natatorium)

Many neighborhoods and communities have a considerable interest in swimming and demand that a swimming pool be included as part of the recreation building. For maximum year-round use, the indoor-outdoor pool is recommended. The construction cost of this type of pool is greater, but the value of having a year-round rather than a seasonal activity is more important to the community or neighborhood. (See Chapter 20 for complete information on swimming pools.)

Teen Centers

While teen centers have been very popular and continue to be built, the trend today is to construct multi-use centers that will provide opportunities for teen programs along with other activities. For example, a teen office and lounge are provided in many community recreation centers.

When a separate teen center is desired, it should include:
- multi-purpose meeting rooms
- gymnasium
- shower and locker rooms
- rooms for programs in the arts
- restrooms
- game room
- lounge and lobby
- office

Other Specialized Facilities

The planning of any specialized recreation building demands a precise and logical approach. Since a recreation building reflects the unique needs and interests of a neighborhood or community, the specific design will vary, but the preliminary considerations of planning objectives will be the same.

The successful incorporation of accepted planning objectives will ensure maximum use of the building. The initial functional/spatial specification and the continuous reevaluation of the architectural specifications of the building prior to its construction should be considered in terms of the following:

A Check list for indoor recreation facilities

- Has the most effective use of the entire structure been determined?
- Does the preliminary sketch include all the essential facilities necessary to fulfill the program objectives?
- Does the layout provide for flexibility in use and for future expansion?
- Does the floor plan permit convenient access to, and facilitate circulation within the building?
- Does the floor plan provide for ease of supervision and administration of the building?
- Have individual rooms been located to encourage multiple use within safety limits?
- Has the building been designed to ensure opportunity for its use by all members of the community, including the aging and the disabled?
- Does the design encompass accepted aesthetic qualities that relate harmoniously to the surroundings?
- Is the building designed to ensure cooperative use with other public or private agencies?
- Is the building designed to permit economy in construction and subsequent maintenance?

Outdoor Facilities and Open Spaces

Growth projections for the next decade provide evidence that few, if any, metropolitan areas in the United States have sufficient open space to meet the demands of the future. Based on these projections, it is imperative that planning boards and commissions on all levels of government review previous planning philosophies with the intent of revision or, when necessary, the development of new master plans.

As open space becomes less and less available, greater consideration must be given to multiple use of these lands and every measure taken to use them most efficiently. Municipal and school authorities should acquire, plan, and develop areas for joint use. This process calls for professional guidance in the fields of planning, designing, and engineering, and for the advice and counsel of professionals in the fields of education and recreation.

The most efficient and successful planning is accomplished when everyone in the organization, particularly those who will be identified with the finished product, have an opportunity to participate in the planning. Those who are to be served also should have a voice in the planning through community meetings.

Standards

A variety of standards for the size, location, and number of educational and recreational areas and facilities have been proposed over the years by persons with a great deal of experience in the operation of such areas and facilities. These standards are sound when formulated to make possible a program to serve the basic needs of people for physical education and recreation. However, they are not valid in prescribing specific activities or facilities for every neighborhood. While they are a useful guide in the acquisition and construction of a property, standards can seldom, if ever, be applied completely or, without modification because a typical or common situation is seldom found. Standards are formulated to indicate a basis for the intelligent development of local plans. Therefore, the standards for areas and facilities should be reviewed and appraised for each planning unit and modified whenever changing conditions warrant their revision.

Standards for areas and facilities developed by private planning firms, public agencies, and service organizations at the local, state, and national levels have been widely endorsed throughout the United States and have provided the basis for recommendations in scores of long-range plans for school, park, and recreation systems. The proposal that at least one acre of recreation and park space be set aside by urban areas for every 100 of the present and estimated future population has been more widely accepted than any other space standard. However, this standard does not relate to the demographic or physiographic character of particular locales and is becoming obsolete. Professional and governmental authorities, including the National Recreation and Park Association and the National Park Service, have pointed out the desirability of providing an even higher ratio of land-to-population in towns and small cities.

Modification of this general standard has been suggested for all planning entities based upon local requirements for populated cities. Some municipal planning officials believe the development of large outlying properties owned by the municipality will help meet the recognized deficiency in the inner municipality. However, this proposal should be considered as a practicable substitute indicative not just of necessity, but also of feasibility.

Actual studies of recreational behavior patterns verify that people tend to form neighborhood recreational groups with others of similar social backgrounds. The resulting patterns might follow or be divided by arteries, depending on whether transportation is provided.

Previous number standards related to the number of tennis courts or swimming pools per thousands of people and so forth. Such numbers do not take into consideration the land or people and the climatic and geographic locale of the planning entity. The specification and allocation of facilities per thousand are arbitrary. They neither reflect the requirements of the community or neighborhood nor are universally applicable. A planning process of interaction and participation by the public should determine the number of facilities from one end of town to the other.

Recreational acreage should be based on usage. Guidelines for acreage allocations for different park types are only illustrative. Every activity has a public demand. The demand for some activities is often met by the private or voluntary sector. Ski lodges, tennis centers, and other corporations all conduct market studies to ascertain the leisure needs of and probable use by their clientele. Public agencies must conduct comparable studies to analyze demand. If the municipality can ascertain the probable use, turnover, capacity, and low/peak load for each activity, it can compute the number of activity stations and facilities for each activity group. This analysis is comparable to processes used to determine the indoor and outdoor space requirements for a school. The recreational acreage is then computed for actual facilities, for circulating paths and roads, for landscaping, and for other features.

Park and Recreation Areas

The types of outdoor recreation areas described here represent a variety of service units that may be used in programs of athletics, sports, physical education, and recreation. Local conditions will dictate to a large extent which types are to be used in any given locality. Hence, different combinations of areas and facilities will emerge as the solution to the problem of meeting the needs and interests of a particular locality.

There is some controversy over parkland aesthetics as measured by the terms active and passive recreation. Many individuals with inherent interest in recreational or leisure pursuits associated with nature denounce the intrusion into parklands by tennis buffs or ball players. Obviously, these

Photos by Meghan Sawyer

Play apparatus.

Example of outdoor court.

Photos by Meghan Sawyer

**Additional Examples of
Play equipment.**

Celebration Station.

two groups have different attitudes about the character of parklands. Parklands can be designed for active or passive use, or both, without destroying the aesthetic values. The use of parklands should reflect the greatest good for the greatest number and the protection of the health, well-being, and safety of all.

If a community is split over use of parklands, a cost-benefit analysis should be made to ascertain the feasibility and costs of trade-offs. There is no sense in preserving a swamp that was created artificially and lacks any ecological value, but a natural swamp might be found elsewhere and preserved to meet specific needs and interests. There are alternatives in every planning process, and they should be considered. The aesthetic values of a parkland, whether oriented toward play apparatus or floral displays, do not have to be sacrificed because they are termed passive or active.

Abandoned industrial sites, such as strip mines, waste disposal areas, and sand and gravel pits, offer tremendous possibilities for park and recreation development. In many cases, recreational use is not only the most beneficial, but the most economic use of such sites. The recreational planner must not overlook the possibility of obtaining these sites for public use. If possible, cooperative planning should be started while the site is still being used by industry, so landscape features can be developed to make it more appealing for recreational use.

Playlot/Mini-Parks: Location, Size, and Features

A playlot/mini-park is a small recreational area designed for the safe play of pre-school children.

As an independent unit, the playlot/mini-park is most frequently developed in large housing projects or in other densely populated urban areas with high concentration of pre-school children. More often, it is incorporated as a feature of a larger recreation area. If a community is able to operate a neighborhood playground within a one-quarter mile zone of every home, playlots should be located at the playground sites. A location near a playground entrance, close to restrooms and away from active game areas, is best.

The playlot/mini-park should be enclosed with a low fence or solid planting to assist mothers or guardians in safeguarding their children. Thought should be given to placement of benches, with and without shade, for ease of supervision and comfort for parents and guardians. A drinking fountain with a step for tots will serve both children and adults. Play equipment geared to the pre-school child should combine attractive traditional play apparatus with creative, imaginative.

The Neighborhood Park

The neighborhood park is land set aside primarily for both active and passive recreation. Ideally, it gives the impression of being rural, sylvan, or national in its character. It emphasizes horticultural features, with spacious turf areas bordered by trees, shrubs, and sometimes floral arrangements. It is essential in densely populated areas but not required where there is ample yard space at individual home sites.

A neighborhood park should be provided for each neighborhood. In many neighborhoods, it will be incorporated in the park-school site or neighborhood playground. A separate location is required if this combination is not feasible.

A separately located neighborhood park normally requires three to five acres. As a measure of expediency, however, an isolated area as small as one or two acres may be used. Sometimes the functions of a neighborhood park can be satisfactorily included in a community or city-wide park.

The neighborhood park plays an important role in setting standards for community aesthetics. Therefore, it should include open lawn areas, plantings, and walks. Sculpture forms, pools, and fountains should also be considered for ornamentation. Creative planning will employ contouring, contrasting surfaces, masonry, and other modern techniques to provide both eye appeal and utility.

Community Parks and Playfields

This type of recreational area is required in a community where it is not feasible or possible to acquire and develop a community park-school. The community park and playfield, like the neighborhood playground, is designed primarily to provide facilities for a variety of types of organized recreation activities, but it should also have the characteristics of a landscaped park. It usually serves as the playground for the children living in the immediate neighborhood, but its primary service is to a much wider age group. Thus, it supplies a greater variety of facilities and more extensive service than can be justified at the neighborhood playground. The school child, teenager, young adult, hobbyist, senior citizen, and family group all find attractive facilities at the well-developed community park and playfield. Because there is no school building at this area, some type of indoor facility is needed. In many cases, a multi-purpose recreation building is provided to meet this need.

Pagoda

Photos by Meghan Sawyer

Fountain

Covered bridge.

Photos by Meghan Sawyer

Fishing dock.

City-Wide or District Parks

The city-wide or district park serves a district of a large city or a total community of a small city. It should serve a population of from 50,000 to 100,000 with a wide variety of activities. The ideal location for this area is in combination with a high school as a park-school complex. Where this is not feasible, consideration should be given to placing the park as close as possible to the center of the population to be served. The land available will be a determining factor in site selection. While the service zone will vary according to population density, a normal use zone is two to four miles. The size may range from 50 to 100 acres.

Depending on available acreage, topography, and natural features, the city-wide or district park will contain a large number of different components. These would include, but not be limited to, the following:
- Field for baseball, football, soccer, and softball (See Chapter 18)
- Tennis center (See Chapter 17)
- Winter sports facilities (See Chapter 27)
- Day-camp center
- Picnic areas (group and family)
- Cycling paths or tracks
- Swimming pool (See Chapter 20)
- Water sports lake
- Pitch-and-putt golf course
- Recreation building
- Nature trails
- Skating rinks (ice and roller)
- Playlot and apparatus
- Parking areas
- Outdoor theater

The above facilities should be separated by large turf and landscaped areas. Natural areas and perimeter buffers should be provided.

Special-Use Areas and Facilities

Walking Trails

Trails used by walkers and joggers have become very popular. In many locations in the United States, old, abandoned rail lines have been secured from the railroads. In some cases the railroads have salvaged the rails and cross ties. While in other cases they have donated the land, rails, and ties to the government. Once a trail has been established it should easily blend into the environment. The planners need to consider the climate, flora and fauna, topography, local history, and available materials for the infrastructure.

The width of a walking trail should be between three and six feet. When developing a walking trail, the following points should be considered: (1) local community input, (2) initial cost and long-term maintenance costs, (3) interesting attractions featured along the trail, (4) access to public transportation, (5) appropriate signage (e.g., names of plants and trees, distances, grades or elevations, direction of trail, trail layout and map, warnings of hazards, etc.), (6) surface preparation (i.e., asphalt, dirt, gravel, wood chips, saw dust, etc.), (7) fitness equipment along trail, and (8) loops and networks to provide options for the walkers.

A walking trail requires some basic infrastructure: (1) handicapped accessibility (i.e., ramps, handrails), (2) adequate parking at the beginning of the trail, (3) rest stops with benches, drinking water, rest rooms, shelters, and picnic areas), and (4) a trail design to eliminate water drainage problems.

Bicycle Facilities and Pathways

Most of the recommended bicycle programs and facilities will require considerable investments of time and money to bring them to fruition. The development of bicycle paths through urban, residential, and outdoor recreation areas will require costly investments that are not always available from public budgets.

An alternative program might be considered. This program would develop bicycle touring routes in and across the country, using rural and low volume vehicular routes. The only expenses involved in the creation of this system are for initial system planning, printing bikeway maps, and marking intersections. County and city governments together with schools and universities have implemented touring systems. The steps in the development of bicycling facilities are:

- Appoint a committee from interested groups of individuals, including representatives of the school or university and the recreation department.
- Make a survey of county road maps and mark a conceptual bicycle system on a work map. One of the objectives is to create a roughly circular route. "Spoke" routes would radiate from the campus to the peripheral route. Select the safest possible routes. High volume roads and intersections should be avoided. After the road map is finished, the committee should find that it has the framework for an adequate bicycling touring system.
- The next step involves field reconnaissance of the roads marked on the working map. Alternate routes may be selected if the original roads are not appropriate for bicycling. Actual travel by bicycle is recommended for the reconnaissance.
- Following the completion of the field reconnaissance, the next step is the drafting of the final bikeway map. Titles and safety information are also placed on the map. The back of the map may be filled with a variety of information. The bikeway should be marked, especially the abrupt turns. Marking may be done by painting distinctive symbols and arrows on the pavement of the road. Standard highway marking paint may be used, and stencils for the symbols may be cut from heavy gauge linoleum.

Cycle trails require some additional planning beyond the planning needed for a walking or jogging trail. The planners need to include the following additional factors into the design: (1) minimum width of dual path should be 12 feet,

(2) the path should have a safety zone on either side extending five feet clear of all vegetation, (3) the ideal surface material is asphalt for the path and a small gravel or brick clips for the safety buffer, (4) appropriate sight lines will need to be determined for cyclists to avoid hitting walkers on corners, and (5) the cyclists may require bike racks at rest stops.

Bridle Paths and Rings

Horseback riding is popular with all age groups but is generally restricted to the larger park areas because of space requirements. Riding trails are usually a minimum of 10 feet wide to permit riders going in opposite directions to pass in safety. Except on very steep terrain, very little is required in the way of construction. Clearing, a small amount of leveling, removal of large rocks and boulders, and trimming or removal of low-hanging tree limbs constitute the major items. Most small streams can be forded, but an occasional bridge may be required as well as cross drainage on steep gradients. No special surfacing is required except that a gravel base may be needed in wet or boggy areas that cannot be avoided. Tanbark, cinders, and other materials are also used frequently on heavily used trails and in areas of concentrated use around hitching racks and in riding rings.

Stables and adjoining facilities, such as feed racks, holding corrals, riding rings, and hitching racks, should be located at least 500 feet from the nearest public-use area because of the fly and odor problem. The size of these facilities will depend on the number of horses. However, the stable will ordinarily contain a limited number of horse stalls, a feed-storage room, a tack room, a small office, and toilet facilities for men and women. A fenced enclosure, commonly called a holding corral or paddock, into which the horses can be turned at the end of the day, is required. A surfaced riding ring, sometimes encircled with a rail fence, is frequently provided for training novices in the fundamentals of riding.

Finally, horse riding trails (sometimes called bridle paths) are not compatible with walkers or cyclists. The horse trail cannot be of hard surface (e.g., asphalt or concrete) but rather a softer topsoil and clay mixture. The trail needs a good base in order to reduce maintenance costs. The tree limbs need to be cut close to the trunk. It is also necessary to provide good horizontal vegetation clearance (over six feet) and vertical vegetation clearance (over 10 feet). The width of the trail should be between two and six feet.

Exercise Trail

The physical fitness boom of the 1970s and 1980s has inspired a unique total body conditioning program—exercise trails. Marketed commercially under a variety of names including Fitness Trail, Fit-Trail, Lifecourse, and Parcourse, the trail combines cardiovascular development, agility, flexibility, strength, and endurance.

The exercise trail consists of a number of exercise stations located at various lengths along a jogging course. A typical trail could have a 1.5 mile distance with 13 exercise stations. The running intervals and exercises are designed for flexibility, agility, strength, all the while developing the participant's cardiovascular system.

Golf Courses

The design, construction, operation, and maintenance of golf courses is too vast a subject to be covered in detail in this publication. For general information and guidance, write the National Golf Foundation at 200 Castlewood Drive, North Palm Beach, FL 33408 or The American Society of Golf Course Architects, 221 North LaSalle Street, Chicago, IL 60601.

The creation of new golf course facilities throughout the nation continues at a very healthy pace in the '90s despite periodic economic slowdowns and shows no decline throughout the first decade of the new century. As the popularity of the game continues to grow, there is an obvious need to increase the number of golf courses to keep up with demand. Currently, there are over 25 million golfers playing on more than 500 million rounds of golf annually on nearly 15,000 courses. Should new player development continue in the same statistical trends as the past 10 years, the number of golfers and rounds played could increase by 35% between now and the year 2010.

Golf course construction costs vary greatly, but generally planners can count on spending at least $1.6 million. This does not include the cost of the land. A golf course construction budget might look like this:

- construction of 18-hole course
  $1.6 million to $4.5 million*
- Maintenance equipment
  $300,000 to $500,000
- Maintenance building
  $125,000 to $450,000
- Club House
  $750,000 to $1.5 million

Totals
  $2.775 million to $6.95 million

- Includes basic golf course construction, clearing, grading, drainage, construction of tees, fairway and fairway features, greens, sand bunkers, irrigation system, seeding and grassing, shelters, bridges, and cart paths.

It must be emphasized that these cost figures are intended only as a rough guideline and do not include the cost of land, entry road, parking lot, other support facilities (e.g., rest rooms, chemical storage areas, fuel storage, sand and top soil storage areas, golf cart storage space, practice putting green, driving range, and tree nursery), golf course architect, and other necessary professional consulting fees. In addition, maintenance costs usually run between $250,000 and $650,000 annually, plus club operations and golf cart fleets.

Assuming the land is suitable for construction of a golf course, the following space requirements must be taken into consideration:

- For a standard 18-hole course—145 to 200 acres
- For shorter executive courses—75 to 120 acres
- For a standard nine-hole course—70 to 90 acres
- For a nine-hole par three course (including a couple of par four holes)—45 to 60 acres

Some of the most desirable features of the land to be used include rolling hills, interesting landscaping, ravines, creeks and ponds or lake sites, and irrigation resources. The more of these features that can be found on a piece of land, the less the overall construction costs. The planners need to also be concerned about environmental issues (e.g., wetlands), drainage, and quality of the soil. Other key components for site selection are the ease of utility connections and accessibility to the new project.

Where do you begin planning a course?

There are key elements common to both types of developments. Population as well as economic conditions in a given area must be studied to determine the suitability of such a project. Some questions that must be addressed are:

- What is the population within a 20-mile radius of the proposed site?
- Number of public and private courses in the area?
- Projected volume of play and fees?
- Projected operating expenses?
- Have any courses in the area failed? Why?
- Is the area population increasing, at least at an average rate?
- Are employment levels and per capita income at suitable levels?

Marinas and Boat Ramps

America abounds in waterways. The myriad of inland lakes, the rivers and streams, the vast Great Lakes, and the thousands of miles of coastline serve to invite America's citizens to take advantage of this natural resource. Today, boating commands more of the recreational dollar than baseball, fishing, golf, or any other single activity. There is a need for efficient, realistic, and functional planning for facilities to accommodate the present needs and the future growth that this recreational interest will precipitate. The launching, mooring, and storage of yachts and rowboats are the function of a marina that will serve the needs of the recreational boat owner. It is suggested that knowledgeable and experienced personnel be engaged to study the number, types, and sizes of existing boats in the area; the number and size of existing berthing facilities, and the condition of such existing facilities. The survey should also include the potential population growth in the community and surrounding area to determine the future boat ownership. An accurate and comprehensive evaluation of such a study is the first step in planning a marina.

The study will determine the next important consideration in laying out a marina: choosing the correct number of slips of each size that will be required. Based on the needs of the community to be served, planners will determine the necessary number of slips to accommodate boats of various sizes.

Because marinas vary so greatly in their design, function, location, and capacity, it is virtually impossible to arrive at standard conclusions and judgments concerning a model marina. Each planner will be able to apply the general principles to his unique circumstances. From that point, however, he must adapt his marina to the peculiar needs and characteristics of a community.

A marina, since it is a parking lot for boats, will most likely be surrounded by a repair shop, fuel station, dry dock area, and general marine supply shop. Key planning issues include, but are not limited to: (1) environmental impact, (2) local politics, (3) waste management, (4) conservation, (5) quality of construction and compatibility with the environment, (6) financing (i.e., initial cost and long-term maintenance costs), (7) management and safety, (8) size of the project, and (9) monitoring of environmental problems.

A boat ramp is necessary for launching boats into a waterway. The initial task is to locate adequate, safe launching and retrieval facilities. Contrary to popular opinion, suitable locations for boat ramps are hard to find. Planners should consider the following when selecting a suitable location for a boat ramp: (1) protection from severe weather, (2) minimal impact on the surrounding environment, (3) large enough space to accommodate the ramp, and trailer and vehicle parking as well as rigging and maneuvering of trailers, (4) accessibility to the proposed site by an all-weather road, (5) ancillary facilities such as rest rooms, water supply, night lighting, telephone accessibility, wash down area, and waste disposal facility, (6) legal requirements (e.g., requirement for environmental impact study, zoning requirements, etc.), (7) local community input, (8) initial cost and long-term maintenance costs, and (9) water conditions (e.g., wave patterns and currents).

Roller Skating

Roller skating may be permitted on a multi-purpose area or on sidewalks and streets under proper safety controls. If a rink is built, it is suggested that the area be 100 feet by 200 feet. A track for speed skating can encircle the figure or leisure skating area. The track should be banked at the curves, and the interior should be slightly pitched for drainage. Boundaries of the track should be defined with flags, wooden blocks, or pylons. Mark each turn with pylons, and indicate the starting and finishing lines. The rinks should be oriented so that skaters travel in a north-and-south direction (See Chapter 26 for greater details regarding skateparks).

The surface should be smooth wood (wide) or concrete sprinkled with rosin or a similar substance. If the areas for skating are speed rinks or multi-purpose areas, they should be fenced for safety and control.

Ice Skating (see Chapter 27)

Ice-skating facilities are feeling the impact of modern technology in more and more communities each year. With the advent of mechanical freezing, the skating season has been extended from a 20- to 60-day average season to a 140-day season and, depending on climatic conditions, to as much as 240 days.

While natural ice rinks have not gone out of style, artificial rinks are replacing them as central or regional facilities. Natural ice rinks are continuing to serve as a supplemental neighborhood facility in many communities. A considerable number of skaters still prefer the rugged pleasure of an old-fashioned skating experience.

Ice Hockey (see Chapter 27)

Ice rinks may have a sport function as well as providing a recreational service. If ice hockey is to be part of the rink's activity schedule, goals will be needed, and a four-foot-high solid fence, called the dasher, will have to be installed to enclose an area as near 85 by 185 feet as possible. Dasher boards are heavily reinforced to stand the shock of players being pushed against them and are lined on the rink side with either wood or plastic. There is normally a chain link or clear plastic barrier another four to six feet on top of the dashers to enable spectators to view games safely. The dasher board enclosure should have round corners, because square corners present a hazard. A kick board, six to eight inches high, is fastened at the base of the dasher boards and is replaced as often as necessary.

Because dasher boards reflect sunlight and cause melting of the ice, they should be painted a dark color. However, it is difficult to follow the puck if the dasher boards are too dark, so a shade of grey is recommended. If the hockey rink is indoors, the dasher boards can be painted a light color without causing a melting problem.

Information describing the complete ice arena is included in Chapter 27.

Curling

Curling is an ice sport popular in Canada and the northern United States. Sponsored by clubs and leagues, it is played with hand-propelled 42.5 pound stones, referred to as rocks. There are four members on a team, each shooting two rocks. The object is to slide one team's rocks nearest the center of a circle, called the house, at the far end of the rink. The advent of artificial ice has broadened the popularity of curling and extended its geographical interest zone.

Performing Arts Areas

In the past few years there has been increased demand for suitable indoor and outdoor facilities for operas, plays, band and orchestral concerts, pageants, festivals, holiday programs, and civic celebrations. When performed outdoors, such activities usually require a stage or band shell with adjoining amphitheater capable of accommodating large numbers of spectators.

Selection of the proper site for an outdoor theater is of primary importance. It should have good acoustic properties and be located in a quiet place away from the noise of traffic or of groups at play. A natural bowl or depression on a hillside with a slope of 10 to 20 degrees, preferably bordered by slopes or densely wooded areas, provides a fine location.

At some theaters, people sit on the slope of the amphitheater. At others, permanent seats are installed. Terraces with a turf surface are not recommended, because they are too difficult to maintain. Sufficient level space should be provided at the rear of the seating area for the circulation of spectators, and aisles should be wide enough to facilitate the seating of large numbers in a short period of time. Public comfort stations and refreshment facilities are usually provided near the entrance to the amphitheater. Provision for the nearby parking of automobiles is essential, but parking areas must be located where noises and car lights do not disturb the stage action.

The dimensions of the stage are determined by the proposed uses, but rarely should a stage be less than 50 feet in width or 30 feet in depth. The rear of the stage may be a wall or high hedge, or even a planting of trees, and the wings may be formed by natural plant materials. The band or music shell, however, is more satisfactory for projecting voices and sound free from echoes and interference. A vertical rear wall with inclined ceiling is not only the simplest and most economical to construct but affords excellent acoustic qualities.

The band shell usually contains dressing rooms, toilets, storage space, and control centers for amplifying and lighting equipment, although sometimes these facilities are provided in separate structures near the back of the stage. An orchestra pit is generally located between the auditorium and the stage.

Mobile storage units with self-contained lighting and acoustic systems are becoming very popular, because they can be used in many parks instead of restricting programs to one permanent location. Equipped to serve as a band shell, stage, puppet theater, or platform for other performing arts, these mobile units can bring productions to audiences never exposed to such activities. Excellent units can be obtained at a cost less than that required for a permanent band shell.

Archery Range

This sport appeals to a sizable group in most communities. Sufficient space is needed to ensure the safety and enjoyment of the participants. The range should provide shooting distances of 100, 80, 60, 50, 40, and 30 yards. For junior use, target ranges can be from 10 to 50 yards. Targets are 48 inches wide and should be at least 15 feet apart. Generally, the target line is fixed and varying shooting lines are used. The side boundaries should extend 10 yards beyond each end of the range.

In the interest of safety, additional space should be provided beyond the target, free from stones and other substances that might cause the breakage of arrows falling wide of their mark. This space may be protected by an earth bunker or bales of hay and straw piled up to the top of the target.

An archery range should be fairly level. Orientation should be north and south so the archers will not be facing the sun. A fence enclosure is desirable, but not essential. The public should be controlled in some manner, however, so they do not walk through the range.

Storage sheds for butts and other equipment are sometimes a part of the archery range. Some storage rooms have been placed within the earth bunker behind the targets. So the facility may be used by the disabled, it is desirable to design a four-foot-wide, ground-level, hard-surface walk for wheelchair use along the shooting lines. Another walk could extend to the target line (preferably down the center) and perhaps another walkway behind the targets to provide access for extracting arrows. Such walks reduce interference from inclement weather, increase the use of the range, and reduce maintenance costs.

Field archery is a simulation of actual shooting conditions in the field. Up to 28 targets are used on the field course. The site selected for such a course should be heavily wooded and have rolling terrain. It should be fairly well isolated or in an area that can be controlled so the general public will not intrude.

Targets should be mounted on built-up banks or on the side of a hill. Each target has various pins (shooting positions). The farthest target is 80 yards and the nearest is 30.

The target should simulate either animals or concentric circles. The size is dependent upon the distance from the target. The scoring is similar to that for golf-the score is totaled for each target, the grand total giving the score for the complete round.

Clout shooting requires a variation in target size and arrangement. The target face is marked on the ground with white lines. The size of the target is enlarged so that one inch on a regular 48-inch target would equal 12 inches on the ground. The center of the bull's-eye must be indicated by a single-color flag. The range for men is 180 yards; for women and juniors, 120 yards.

The field dimensions for flight shooting are approximately 200 by 600 yards. The field should be roped off on all sides except that from which the archers shoot. A distance of not less than 10 yards behind the shooting line is reserved for the flight shooting space. Officially, the flight must be from a series of colored or numbered pegs set in the ground, usually about six feet apart.

Boccie Ball

A boccie court is 91 feet x 13 feet. Many boccie courts are sunken, with retaining walls constructed out of pressure-treated landscaping timbers. When built above ground, a boccie court needs side and back walls. These can be constructed of wood, lattice, landscape stones, brick, or cinder block.

The boccie court area should include:
- shade trees,
- flowers,
- storage area for equipment,
- lawn chairs, and tables, and
- possibly lights for evening play.

Shuffleboard Area

The shuffleboard court is 52 feet x 5 feet (see Figure 22.2). It is generally laid out on a concrete surface outdoors, and a wooden surface (maple) indoors. The lines are painted with an epoxy paint. Generally there are six to eight courts in one location. These areas are generally lighted for night play.

The shuffleboard court area should include:
- shade trees,
- flowers,
- storage area for equipment,
- wooden score boards,
- lawn chairs, benches, and tables.

Croquet Court

The standard croquet court is a rectangle, measuring 35 x 28 yards (105 feet x 84 feet). Its boundaries shall be marked clearly, the inside edge of the definitive border being the actual boundary. Nylon string (#18) stapled or otherwise affixed to the ground is recommended to be used for the boundary lines. The four corners of the court are known respectively as Corners 1, 2, 3, and 4. The four boundaries are known as South, West, North and East boundaries - regardless of the orientation of the court (see Figure 22.3).

Figure 22.2
Diagram of Shuffleboard Court

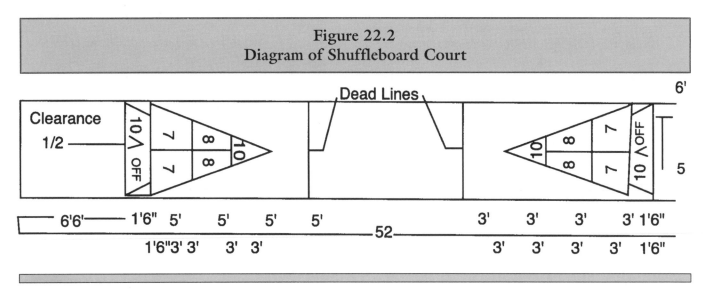

Graphics by Meghan Sawyer

Figure 22.3
Croquet Court

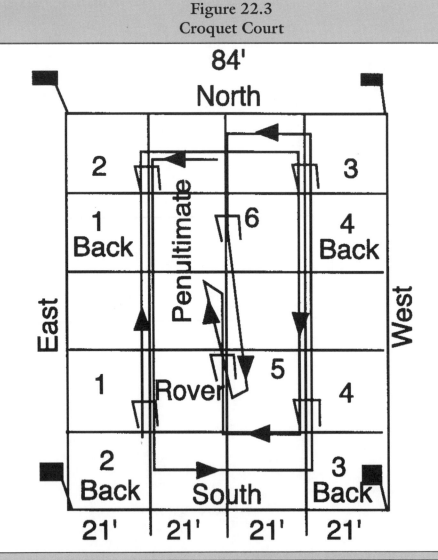

The standard setting of the court has the stake set in the center of the court. The wickets shall be set parallel to the North and South boundaries, the centers of the two inner wickets, 21' to the north and south of the stake, the centers of the four outer wickets, 21' from their adjacent boundaries.

This is the preferred court size and should be the official setting for major tournaments.

The croquet court area should also include:
- shade trees,
- flowers,

- storage area for equipment,
- lawn chairs, and tables, and
- possibly lights for evening play.

Snow Sports (see Chapter 27)

Ski Courses

Skiing has become very popular. If climatic conditions are suitable and desirable topographic features are available, a school or a park and recreation department might look into the possibility of developing the facilities needed to foster this sport. A variety of artificial surfaces simulating real snow has brought skiing instructional opportunities to all sections of the country independent of climate.

The provision of skiing in a school or public recreation system should be approached from an instructional standpoint, the theory being to give participants some basic instruction so they can enjoy it as a leisure-time activity in the resort areas that have more ideal facilities. If the park system contains ideal skiing hills with plenty of room, regular ski courses may be developed. Some of the basic facilities required for skiing instruction include proper topographical features; a headquarters building for rental of equipment, a refractory, and similar purposes; a ski tow; and various slopes for instructional purposes.

Normally, the series of classes is broken into three units—beginners, advanced, and expert. It is the opinion of ski instructors that the beginners' ski class is by far the most important for recreational skiing. Basic instruction in skiing may be conducted in classes not exceeding 25 to 30 beginners. For this group, a gentle and short slope with a relatively large flat run-out area is desirable because it permits a beginner to have complete control of himself and allows him to gain confidence in the use of his skis. In the advanced group, classes are much smaller, and in the expert group, instruction becomes almost individualized. For each successive group, hills become longer and a little steeper.

The following criteria are recommended for the selection of facilities for beginners' classes:
- Flat-top hill area, 50 square feet per skier, 25 skiers per class
- Slope about 75 feet to 100 feet long, drop in grade of 15 feet, or 4:1 ratio
- Starting line at top of slope, 100 feet wide
- Run-out at bottom of slope either flat or uphill
- Slope facing east or northeast
- Instructional area free of stones, woods, and other impediments
- Protective cover, such as trees or brush, around the area

The following criteria are suggested for advanced classes:
- Top of hill about the same as for beginners
- Slope is most important: ratio about 3:1 and length 100 feet to 150 feet
- Width of hill or slope, minimum of 150 feet because of speed and space required for turning movements.

The following criteria are recommended for the selection of facilities for expert classes:

- Either the same hill as advanced classes or, preferably, a longer and steeper hill
- Enough downhill length to permit a minimum of three turning movements—for example, 250 feet on a 3:1 slope
- Greater width than that of slope for advanced classes.

Cross-Country Skiing

The cross-country skiing revival came in the mid-60s, and its popularity has increased dramatically. The rebirth of cross-country skiing, which has become known as ski touring, has attracted many people who cannot afford to keep up with "alpine" or "downhill" skiing price tags, or standing in long lines at the lifts.

Ski touring deserves a place in physical education and recreation programs. One of the attractive features of ski touring is that a successful program can be developed with limited facilities. Unlike downhill skiing, it is not vital to have hilly terrain or several inches of snow base. Such areas as athletic fields, golf courses, parks, and nearby vacant land serve as ideal training courses.

Specially designed skis with rollers mounted on the bottom have made grass skiing possible and this activity is gaining in popularity as a summer activity in parts of Europe.

Coasting, Sleighing, Tobogganing

Often a community has a hill or hills suitable for coasting, which become meccas after every snowfall for children with sleds, toboggans, and other coasting devices. In the absence of a natural coasting hill, some park and public works departments have built such a facility. These hills are usually located in a park safely guarded from the hazards of street traffic.

In developing local sledding (coasting) areas, care should be taken to incorporate adequate safety features. Plenty of room should be provided between sled runs, and up traffic should be isolated from the down traffic. The area should be as free as possible from hazards, such as nearby trees, grills, benches, or other park paraphernalia.

Communities with an extensive response to sledding or skiing may want to counter adverse weather with the use of artificial-snow equipment or improve the activity with a ski lift.

Sleighing is a recreational activity that uses sleighs drawn by horses or oxen. It can take place on roads, trails, or paths.

Tobogganing is a thrilling sport, requiring designed space. Occasionally, natural slopes are used if they are free from obstructions and have a long bottom run-off. The common practice is to choose a hillside with a reasonable steep and even grade. A chute is constructed using a wooden trough. It can be permanent or built in sections.

Snowmobiling

According to a recent survey, snowmobiling ranks as one of the fastest-growing sports in the United States. Assuming snowmobiling will continue to be popular, predictions are that approximately 10 million people will take to the sport by 1995. As with cross-country skiing, areas such as athletic fields, golf courses, parks, and vacant land can serve as ideal training courses for snowmobilers.

Many lake and park areas in the northern United States used previously during summer months have now proven to be a haven for snowmobile enthusiasts.

Areas for Outdoor Education/Recreation

Future historians will surely note the decades following World War II as a time when the outdoors came into prominence as a significant place for both education and recreation. The unprecedented growth of all types of outdoor activities necessitating land areas and facilities can be expected to continue. A growing awareness on the part of educational and recreational leaders that the present generation and those to come are far removed from the land and the rural life of their forebears has caused much interest and concern in the development of outdoor education programs. Because school-age children and many adults know little about the outdoors, programs and facilities must be designed to educate them in, about, and for the outdoors. An ecological approach to outdoor education has both recreational and educational implications.

Outdoor education is a term that refers to learning activities in and for the outdoors. Such activities can be provided in the curriculums of schools, colleges, and universities, as well as in the programs of recreational, camping, and community agencies. Outdoor education has been broadly described as follows:

Outdoor education means learning in and for the outdoors. It is a means of curriculum extension and enrichment through outdoor experiences. It is not a separate discipline with prescribed objectives, like science and mathematics; it is simply a learning climate offering opportunities for direct laboratory experiences in identifying and resolving real-life problems, for acquiring skills with which to enjoy a lifetime of creative living, for building concepts and developing concern about man and his natural environment, and for getting us back in touch with those aspects of living where our roots were once firm and deep.

Outdoor education and outdoor recreation encompass a great variety of activities, many of which can be conducted on a single, large tract of land. With careful planning, facilities, some in or near an urban area and others in more distant places, can be used. An outdoor-education complex on one piece of land or on several plots in close proximity has many advantages in the areas of administration, leadership, equipment, and transportation. Such a site lends itself to wide community use, with responsibilities for leadership and finances shared by several agencies. Obviously, the size and physical characteristics of an outdoor-education complex will depend on the geographic location and the topography of the land.

Some of the facilities and types of site treatment for a complex that would accommodate a broad program of outdoor education and outdoor recreation, and which would constitute an outdoor laboratory or field campus, are briefly described. It is assumed that there will be many areas and facilities, public and private, that can also be used in a comprehensive program.

Considerations in Selecting and Developing Sites

Size

The type of program planned should determine the size of the site. Size alone does not necessarily mean much except that it does affect the numbers of certain species of wildlife that might live in the area. A large area does not necessarily have a diversity of physical features. It may just be level land, harboring only a few species of trees, with no particularly outstanding features. Nevertheless, such an area could be made interesting from an educational point of view, provided good leadership is available.

Many schools, recreation departments, and community agencies already have school sites, parks, and recreational areas that could be developed for outdoor programs. Schools, as well as other agencies, in some sections of the country, also have forest lands that could be developed and used in a broad educational and recreational program.

Site Characteristics

The characteristics of the site are also determined by the type of program planned. If plans call for a resident camp, many more requirements must be met than if the site will be used only on a daily basis. If the land and facilities are to contribute to all aspects of the educational curriculum, or if there is to be special emphasis on science, conservation, and outdoor skills, many characteristics will need to be considered, such as the following:

- A location to give some privacy and solitude
- Year-round accessibility by road
- A minimum of natural and man-made hazards
- Interesting geologic features, such as rock outcroppings, open field, flat terrain, and a variety of soil types
- A variety of native vegetation, including woods
- Wildlife that can be maintained with good management
- A pond, stream, seashore, or large body of water
- Demonstration areas for conservation practices
- Woods for practicing outdoor skills and use of native materials
- Sanitary facilities, including good drainage and good drinking water
- Simple shelters in the event of inclement weather
- Proximity to adequate medical and hospital services

Special Features

Many kinds of developments are found in various types of outdoor education areas. Some of these are appropriate for camps, some for outdoor laboratories or nature centers, and some for outdoor recreation and sport centers. An outdoor education and outdoor recreation complex would include many site plans and facilities not possible in more limited areas. The adaptability of the area to the proposed program, the cost of construction, maintenance problems, aesthetic considerations, and available leadership are all factors in determining what facilities might be developed in a particular land area or cluster of acreages.

Listed below are some of the special developments that might be included in appropriate sites. Some of the features listed are discussed elsewhere in this text and are merely mentioned here. Others, not mentioned in other places, are discussed in more detail.

Grass, shrubs, and trees. They provide shade, prevent soil erosion, provide food and cover for wildlife, serve as windbreaks, mark the boundary of the property, act as a buffer zone to ensure privacy against an adjacent (presently or potentially) populated area, demonstrate principles of plant growth, serve as a resource for ecological studies, and give practice in forest management. A school forest offers many popular activities.

A vegetable garden or a bog garden.

Soil-erosion demonstration areas. Such an area should be rich in vegetation, feature good conservation practices, be situated on inclined terrain, and be located next to a piece of land denuded of its vegetation and also located on an incline. Comparisons can then be made over a period of time to determine what happens to the quantity and quality of soil in both areas.

Snake pit. A variety of reptiles found in the local area could be kept in a circular pit about 20 feet in diameter and constructed of concrete and stone. Concave walls and a water-filled moat surrounding an island will prevent the snakes from escaping.

Wildlife sanctuary. Provide mixed plantings and construct birdhouses, feeders, and bird baths to attract a variety of birds.

Weather station. This is for the study of meteorology and should be located in an area that can be fenced off and locked.

Council ring. This facility provides a place for campfires, for conducting orientations before field trips, and for other special programs. The council ring should be located in a wooded area to ensure a feeling of isolation. Use logs for seats.

Nature trails. Develop, if space permits, a variety of trails, each serving a different purpose. One may be a geology trail, winding its way through an area rich in geologic features. Another trail may emphasize the study of erosion, while still another may lead to an historic spot.

Pioneer living area. Social studies lessons are vividly illustrated in such an area. Dramatize the life of the pioneer, including such activities as making dyes from plants, cooking outdoors, constructing shelters, learning to identify edible plants, and learning other survival practices.

Observation platform. This platform can be used for observing birds and for studying astronomy. It should be located on the highest point of the property.

Outdoor zoo. Animals indigenous to the local area are featured. Be certain that arrangements can be made to care properly for the animals caught.

Miniature gardens. Each garden features a particular grouping of native plants found in the typical setting in which they normally grow.

Plant grafting. A demonstration area that provides interesting studies in genetics.

Animal-baiting area. Put a salt lick and some meat in a cleared area. Spread loose dirt around the baited spot, press it down with the feet, and smooth it out. Animals attracted to the area will leave their footprints, which can then be observed and studied.

Natural preserve. An area could be set aside in which no developments would be made. It would be given complete protection and would provide a spot for the observation of ecological aspects.

Orienteering courses. The development of several courses for map and compass use would stimulate educational and recreational use of the area (See Chapter 34 for details).

Greenhouse. A place for the propagation of plants, some of which may be used for area improvement, is important. A greenhouse would make possible an acquaintance with plants and would be a means of providing projects for study during the off season.

Winter sports area. Places for skating, skiing, and coasting would be desirable in those parts of the country that have sufficient snow and cold weather to make these sports feasible.

Natural play area. An area set aside for children, containing such elements as climbing logs, ropes for swinging across low areas, sandbanks, and hide-and-seek areas, can provide play opportunities different from those found in the city.

Turtle pit. An attractive pit with water and plantings would make possible the study and observation of turtles and other amphibians.

Rifle and skeet ranges. Such an area will provide opportunities for instruction in gun safety as well as for participation in rifle and skeet shooting.

Casting and angling area. Developments for casting and angling would serve both instructional and recreational uses.

Amphitheater. For large-group programs, an amphitheater would be important. It could be used for lectures, drama, music, and a variety of demonstrations.

Astronomy area. A special area for astronomy may be developed on a large open area, waterfront, dock, or even a roof. Seating facilities are desirable, and sometimes a telescope is permanently mounted to facilitate observations.

Bird feeding station.

Historical markers. Sites of old farms, early settlers' homes, Indian trails and village sites, and pioneer roads are illustrations of the kinds of historical sites that might be used for student projects.

Shelters. Adirondack or picnic shelters can serve daycamp and day-use groups during inclement weather.

Tree stump. Locate a fairly well-preserved tree stump. Make a sloping cut, smooth the top by sanding, and treat it with clear waterproofing material, such as fiberglass resin. Much can be learned about tree growth from carefully studying a tree stump.

Herb garden. This garden features food seasoning and medicinal plants and serves as a useful teaching aid for a home economics class.

Photographic blind. Construct a blind near a bird-feeding station for taking pictures of wild birds.

Evergreen tree nursery. Trees can later be transplanted to desired areas.

Field archery. Targets are set up in wooded areas or fields, simulating actual hunting conditions.

Natural areas. Such areas are left relatively undisturbed, and man-made modifications should be avoided as much as possible. These places serve as excellent resources for scientific studies of natural phenomena.

Horse pit.

Photos by Meghan Sawyer

Picnic pavilion.

Picnic shelter.

Picnic site. It is desirable to locate the picnic site on the periphery of the property.

Seashore areas. Communities adjacent to seashores may have areas set aside for study and observation. Developments might include ramps or walks to facilitate observation. Walkways through tidelands may be developed as nature trails. One of the national parks has an underwater nature trail.

Outdoor Laboratories

The term "outdoor laboratory" is used for a piece of land (including wetlands, lakes, and seashores) set aside by a school for learning experiences directly related to land and its resources. It may be located close to an individual school, or it may serve a group of schools. It may be a part of the school grounds or a section of a park-school development. It may consist of only a few acres nearby or of several hundred acres, nearby or many miles away. It may serve individual elementary schools, high schools or universities, or all of them jointly. Because outdoor laboratories are extremely varied in their site possibilities and their purposes, no rigid format for their development is possible.

The term "land for learning" has been applied to the school laboratory. It implies the opportunity of school groups to study, explore, and experiment with land and its resources. Outdoor study, field trips, and experiments with water, soil, plants, and animals constitute its major functions.

Developments may range from nothing more than a few trails, with the area left natural, to nature trails, class and museum buildings, horticultural plots, developed ponds, forest plantations, gardens, and small-farm operations. The creativity of the teacher or outdoor education specialist, the potential of the available site, and funds available may be the only limiting factors in the development of program facilities.

If a laboratory is heavily used, water and toilet facilities might be essential. A storage building for tools and supplies might also be desirable.

Nature Centers

The term "nature center" is used to designate a particular type of development that will facilitate learning in the outdoors and the growth of recreational interests. The establishment of nature centers is being promoted extensively by several science- and nature-related organizations. Several hundred such centers have been developed in the United States in recent years. Children's museums may be considered a part of this development, although some of these museums lack adjacent lands for outdoor education.

Nature centers have been developed principally by three types of financing and management: schools, private associations, and public park and recreation departments.

The Site

Some of the suggestions for the school outdoor education laboratory are applicable here. Nature trails, ponds, bogs, gardens, forest plantings, and the like may provide the variety essential for a rich outdoor education program.

The Building

The building should be designed so as to permit expansion as the program grows and as more funds become available. In its initial stage, the building should contain a minimum space of 2,500 square feet, which is large enough to contain one class adequately. The building should be designed according to the needs set by the program. The following general facilities are recommended:

- Office for staff
- *Toilet facilities.* Access should be provided to the outside as well as to the interior of the building.
- *Large meeting room.* The wall space can be utilized for exhibits. Low cabinets along the walls should be provided for storage of educational aids. A long counter providing work and display space should be constructed on top of the cabinets.
- *Classrooms.* Two classrooms should be provided so that a class may be broken up into smaller groups if necessary.
- *Workroom.* This room would be used for constructing displays and for arts and crafts.
- *Science laboratory.* A room should be equipped with microscopes, soil- and mineral-testing equipment, and other materials necessary for scientific studies.
- *Library.* The large meeting room can contain the library, which would occupy one section of the room. The library should contain reference material, field guides, magazines, and novels concerned with the outdoors.
- *Storage room.* Adequate space should be provided for storage of the many pieces of instructional and janitorial equipment that will accumulate over the years.

It should be emphasized again that it is not essential for one center to have most of the facilities described here. Dynamic leadership is, to a large degree, more important, and not even the ultimate in good facilities can ever satisfactorily replace the need for effective leadership.

Interpretive Centers

Although the name "interpretive centers" might well be applied to the outdoor laboratories and the nature centers mentioned earlier, it has a specific use in describing certain facilities of public parks offered as a service to the general public and, in some cases, to school groups. The National Park Service has the most extensive development of such centers, although state and metropolitan parks have, in recent years, been expanding the number of their interpretive centers. The U.S. Forest Service is beginning to develop information centers that are essentially interpretive centers.

The primary purpose of interpretive centers is to help visitors understand and appreciate the natural, historical, or archeological features of the areas in which the centers are located. Inasmuch as the problems of interpretation of each area are different, facility developments are likewise varied.

Interpretive centers frequently contain a trailside museum or interpretive-center building. This may vary in size from 10 feet by 20 feet to a large, multi-roomed structure.

The size depends on the groups to be accommodated, the interpretive materials available, and the types of programs to be presented. A large building may contain some or all of the following:

- Display rooms with habitat cases and other exhibits
- Office space for staff members
- A laboratory for research and the preparation of display materials
- Meeting rooms for lectures, slides, or movies
- Lavatories and toilets
- A counter for the sale of books and the distribution of pamphlets
- An outdoor amphitheater or campfire area for lectures and movies
- Trails to points of interest (often self-guiding nature trails)
- Parapets or other special observation points, often including mounted telescopes and pointers indicating places of interest
- Interpretive devices at points of interest, including bulletin boards, maps, diagrams, and displays

Parking areas (see Chapter 15)

School groups often visit interpretive centers, usually by school bus on a one-day basis. In some cases, picnic areas are provided for such groups. Work space, where children can work on projects at the center, is often a desirable feature.

School and Community Gardens, Farms, and Forests

Gardens, farms, and forests provide direct experiences with growing plants and, in some cases, with domestic animals. Schools, park and recreation agencies, and a few private agencies have been responsible for the development of facilities. Even when facilities are developed and operated by park and recreation departments or private agencies, some direct relationship with schools is often provided through an instructional program in which the school children are enrolled.

Display Gardens

Gardens of various kinds should be developed to provide for visual, cultural, and educational equipment.

A formal garden may be composed entirely of one type of plant (such as roses), of various types of assorted plant materials, or of a series of individual gardens comprised of single types of plant units. Features such as a water fountain and statuary can be incorporated into the design.

Informal gardens should have long, sweeping lawn areas to serve as a setting for plants and flower beds. Plants may include large specimen trees, flowering trees, shrubs, and vines. The flower borders can be of varied plants. All the plants should be of interest to the average homeowner and should be useful in helping him select plants for his own yard. Attempts should be made to keep abreast of the latest introductions and to display those types of plants that are hardy to the particular region in which the garden is located. This aspect of planting for the homeowner should be stressed in both formal and informal gardens, and demonstrations of plant cultural practice should be provided.

Naturalistic and native, or wildflower, gardens are established in a wilderness location, where the plants native to the region can be assembled in one area so they are easily accessible to the citizens. Developers will probably need an area of varied topography—lowlands, highlands, and prairies—and an area with varied soil conditions—from alkaline to acid—to accommodate the various types of plants.

Tract Gardens

In a tract garden, which is the most common type of school or community garden, a piece of property ranging in size from one to ten acres is divided into small tracts for the use of individuals. A typical plot size may be 10 by 20 feet, but adults and families can use larger gardens. A garden program with 25 plots can be set up on one-fourth acre of land, although more space is desirable. Four acres of land can hold 100 gardeners with plots of varied size and community crops. This size allows space for a service building and activity area. It should be on rich, well-drained soil with water available.

Garden programs may involve instruction, environmental projects, field trips, and science activities. Community projects may include novelty crops, such as a pumpkin patch, gourds, Indian corn, and a Christmas tree farm. Gardening appeals to all ages and is an excellent program for families. Some of the necessary or desirable features of the tract garden are the following:

- Garden building—either a small building for the storage of tools and equipment or a building large enough for class meetings and indoor activities during bad weather
- Toilet facilities adequate to care for the maximum number of participants expected on the garden plot at one time
- Greenhouse for plant propagation
- Ready access to water, with spigots and hoses available for limited irrigation
- Fencing for protection of the garden
- Pathways and walkways to provide easy access to all plots
- A demonstration home yard, with grass, flowers, and shrubs
- Good landscaping

Preferably, the tract garden should be located within walking distance of the homes of the participants. In many cases, gardens are developed on or adjacent to school grounds.

Tract gardens for adults and families have been established in some communities. They are usually intended for people living in crowded urban centers or apartments who would not otherwise be able to garden. In some communities, these gardens are located some distance from homes, and transportation is left up to the individuals concerned.

Farms

Community or school farms are becoming increasingly important, especially near metropolitan centers, and offer opportunities for a rich and varied program. Farm programs include animal care and training and traditional rural activities, such as hay rides, picnics, and nature activities. Model farms are heavily used by families who just want to walk through to see and pet the animals.

Simple barns and pens contain horses, cows, pigs, chickens, sheep, and other domestic animals, which children can help care for and feed. In an urban setting, it is essential that the facility be attractive and well-maintained. There must be water, feed storage, and adequate exercise space for the animals. An office, restrooms, drinking fountain, indoor and outdoor activity areas, and storage space are needed for the people.

In addition to the buildings that are generally found on a diversified farm, there are meeting places and exhibits that make it possible to carry on indoor instruction. Picnic areas, farm ponds, day-camp facilities, campfire circles, and hiking trails are often developed also.

Working farms are sometimes adapted for recreational purposes. This type of facility actually produces, while city residents visit to learn, observe, take part in, and enjoy farming activities. Groups may use the farm on a day basis, and overnight accommodations can be provided. In either case, a large room and open outdoor space are needed for activity and instruction.

Farm camps offer opportunities for a farm-oriented camping experience. The farm camp is a farm not worked for production, but set up for resident programs in environmental education, farm activities, natural history, science, and other outdoor recreation. There may be a large farmhouse converted to a program building and farm buildings converted to cabins. Facilities needed are a kitchen, dining area, sleeping quarters, restrooms, large activity room, and ample storage space. Additionally, barns, farm equipment, and other facilities will be needed. These facilities and animals will be required dependent on program direction.

Forests

Numerous school and community forests can be found throughout the United States. Many of these were acquired from tax-delinquent land, through gifts, or through protection programs for community watersheds. Their use has followed diverse patterns. Some schools have carried on field trips, forest improvement projects, and other outdoor education activities. In general, however, schools have not made the maximum use of such areas.

Many of these forests could be developed as outdoor education laboratories. Some might be suitable sites for nature centers, day camps, or even resident camps.

School and community forests may serve valuable purposes even without extensive development. Water, trails, and toilets may be all the developments need to provide useful educational facilities. Such areas may serve their best functions as places in which to study the ecological changes taking place over a period of years.

Outdoor Skills and Sports Areas

Outdoor skills or sports areas should be included in the outdoor education-recreation complex, but it may be necessary to acquire special sites, depending on the topography of the land. These areas should provide opportunities to learn and practice skills, but they may also be used as outdoor laboratories.

The following are some of the specialized program facilities that might be included in the outdoor skills and sports area:

- Casting and angling—platforms and open, level spaces
- Outdoor shooting range
- Archery range—target field course, archery golf, and other games
- Campcraft skills area
- Overnight camping area
- Outpost camping—Adirondack shelters
- Facilities for water sports, including swimming, canoeing, boating, sailing, skin diving, and water skiing
- Area for crafts with native materials—carving, lapidary, weaving, and ceramics—with a simple structure to provide shelter in inclement weather and to house equipment
- Water sports—ski slopes and tow, ski shelter, tobogganing, and ice-skating rinks

Natural Areas

Natural areas are generally thought of as representative of the original, undisturbed plants and animals of a locale. They may encompass a variety of habitats, such as woodlands, deserts, swamps, bogs, shorelines, or sand dunes.

It is almost impossible today, even in the wilderness, to find undisturbed areas. Most places categorized as natural areas are protected lands that indicate the least disturbance and that, through protection, planting, and development, approximate the original characteristics.

It is characteristic of natural areas that they are protected from nonharmonious developments and activities. Simple access trails, protective fencing, and simple interpretive developments such as entrance bulletin boards are usually acceptable. In designated natural areas, the enjoyment and study of the natural features are encouraged, and uses that detract from the natural features are discouraged.

Schools, parks, and camps are often the agencies that develop, maintain, and protect natural areas. Such areas are valuable assets in environmental education.

Camps and Camping

Historically, the word "camping" signified simple living outdoors and engaging in activities related primarily to the outdoors. Today the term has broadened tremendously and encompasses a wide spectrum of developments for families and children. Resident center, day camps, group camps, family camps, and wilderness camps are the common designations used for the various types of camps.

Camps have been developed by public agencies at all levels of government and by many voluntary youth-serving organizations. The rapidly increasing participation of children and adults in camping necessitates careful consideration of desirable areas and facilities.

Although most organized camping takes place on agency-owned or private property, public land is becoming increasingly involved. Public land is one of the major resources for school outdoor education programs, and many resident centers have been constructed on public property or by public funds. Schools use the facilities during the school year, and park and recreation agencies use them during the summer. The purposes of outdoor education, whether sponsored by park and recreation departments or by schools, are similar in many respects, and cooperative planning is not only necessary in order to get the most from the community dollar but imperative if suitable lands and sites are to be obtained. If adequate facilities are to be provided to meet the needs of both organized camping groups and schools, the facilities must be designed for year-round use.

Program Facilities—What to Expect

Following are some of the facilities used for various camp programs. Specifications and construction details for most are found elsewhere in this book.

Water-related activities are among the most popular in summer camps. During the fall and spring, school groups and other groups may use developments for fishing, canoeing, and boating.

Lakes, ponds, streams, bays, and inlets offer many recreational opportunities. All should be studied in detail with regard to currents, eddies, depth, slope, shoreline, debris, and other factors.

Canoeing, boating, and sailing are activities that may be conducted on a lake, pond, river, reservoir, bay, or other body of water. The water area should have accessory facilities such as floats, docks, markers, or buoys. Various sizes of water bodies are required for different activities and events. For instance, canoe-racing courses are 100, 200, 440, and 880 yards, as well as one mile. Sailing requires a wider body of water because the boats usually finish to windward. The different classes of sailboats, such as Sunfish and Sailfish, require different courses.

Casting is simulated rod-and-reel fishing. Practice casting on a playing field or in a gymnasium is possible the year round. If a pond or lake is nearby, a beach or dock affords an excellent facility for the casting program.

In order to teach all phases of the activity, an area 300 by 100 feet is desirable. A football, soccer, hockey, or lacrosse field is ideal for class instruction.

Casting targets, which are 30 inches in diameter, are easily constructed and can be an excellent project for any woodshop program. It is recommended that at least 10 targets be made. Others can be added as the program expands. Targets for use on the water are also 30 inches in diameter and are made of hollow metal tubing. They float and can be easily anchored.

Other program facilities include campfire circles and council rings, for which most camps develop centers for meetings and evening programs, and craft centers, which can range from canvas-covered areas with provisions for storing tools to extensive and well-equipped craft shops.

Day Camps

A day camp is an area and facility intended to provide a program similar to that of the resident camp, except that campers sleep at home. Many of the considerations of planning for resident camps apply to day camps. However, facility problems are simpler, because day campers sleep at home and usually eat two of the day's meals at home. Provisions, however simple, must nonetheless be made for water, toilets, rainy-day shelters, eating and cooking, refrigeration, first-aid and health, and program supplies. The focus of this section is that of selecting an appropriate day camp facility.

Abundant land for programs is extremely desirable, particularly when the emphasis is on outdoor-related activities. Reasonable isolation and a varied topography with outdoor program possibilities are essential. Natural parks, park-school areas, and community forests often lend themselves for use as day-camp sites. Some communities have developed special day-camp areas; others make appropriate picnic areas available for this special use.

Buses are often used to transport campers to the day camp. If more than half an hour is consumed in daily travel each way, the effectiveness of the program is reduced.

Day-camp groups are divided into units or counselor groups ranging from eight to 20 campers. Most day camps provide simple facilities for each unit, including a fireplace for cooking, storage cabinets, and tables. Some day camps serve a daily meal in a central dining hall, reducing or eliminating the need for unit cooking facilities.

Storage is needed for equipment, food, and program supplies. Some day camps use trailers or trucks for storage, hauling them back and forth each day. Also, a well-equipped first-aid station and a rest-area facility are necessary.

Group Camps

Many public agencies today provide special campsites for small groups, such as scouts, church groups, and school classes. These sites generally accommodate from 10 to 40 persons. In most cases, the groups stay from one to five days. Small units in decentralized resident camps sometimes have facilities that can be used for group camping. Simple fireplaces for cooking, picnic shelters for use in bad weather, toilets, and safe drinking water are necessities.

The great increase in winter camping by small groups often necessitates special developments. Some winter campers live completely outdoors in the cold, even in snow. Usually, however, winterized buildings are used for cooking, sleeping, and evening activities.

Family Camps

At one time "family camping" meant the activity of families pitching tents in natural areas, living and cooking simply, and finding their own interests outdoors. Today the term may include sleeping in tents or living in expensive motor homes, stopping overnight or vacationing in completely equipped resorts with varieties of entertainment.

Overnight or transient camps are usually strategically located for travelers passing by or for those wishing to visit nearby points of interest. These camps need to offer very little—chiefly cleanliness and comfort—for short stays. They generally do not provide natural areas and recreational facilities.

Family resident camps offer complete meal and living accommodations for families or just adults. The facilities may be similar to those of resident camps, except that some of the sleeping quarters may be adapted to families.

Most of the campgrounds in state or federal areas are destination camps. Campers generally stay more than one night and often for several weeks. In recent years, a great many resort camps have sprung up. These resorts, generally privately developed, are more or less complete vacationlands in themselves, offering, frequently under leadership, a recreation program and facilities including swimming pools, recreation buildings, children's playgrounds, special game courts, marinas, horseback riding trails, and the like.

Waterfronts

The use of waterfronts varies with the program offered. The type of program will determine the nature of the waterfront, and yet the environmental situation, such as ocean, stream, or lake, may influence the type and design of the facility. The following categories of use identify the specific areas of the aquatic program:

- Familiarization—Familiarization involves programs acquainting the user with the water.
- Instruction—Instruction involves programs of teaching the user basic activities related to aquatics.
- Recreation—Recreation involves programs that are largely unstructured, for relaxing and refreshing the user, including participating in or watching special events such as synchronized swimming, water shows, and competitive swimming.
- Competition—Competition involves programs of training and competing in swimming and other aquatic activities. The user of a waterfront should be able to participate in a variety of aquatic activities in order to attain the desired objectives. This is especially true in the camp setting, where the camper participates in the constructive fulfillment of inherent attitudes and aptitudes.

Waterfronts for the conduct of aquatic activities are found in children's camps, parks, resorts, marinas, clubs, hotels, residential developments, and other recreation areas. The waterfront, whether it is a beach, floating crib, dock, pond, lake shore, pool deck, or some other area where aquatic programs take place, must be properly located and constructed to insure the health and safety of the public using this facility. The post-World War II years have seen a tremendous development in children's camps in the United States, particularly day camps. Although many of the aspects of this chapter deal primarily with camps; most of the criteria may be applied to beach-front developments as well. In planning the location and construction of natural and artificial waterfront facilities, definite criteria should be established. These criteria should reflect not only the camp program, but also the health and safety requirements.

Planning the Waterfront Location

Criteria for Natural Waterfronts

The natural waterfront site should have certain characteristics to make it desirable for aquatic-program use. The recommended criteria for the selection of waterfront or beach sites are discussed below, and helpful checklists have been provided for the planners.

Water Characteristics

The water content should be of a sanitary quality affording safe usage. The health conditions of a site are primarily judged by a careful examination of both its surrounding environs and its water content. The first is accomplished by a careful field analysis, the second by a laboratory analysis. Both examinations can indicate the bacterial quality and physical clarity of the water.

Checklist:
- Surrounding water source
- Water quality (bacterial content)
- Water clarity (visibility test)

Water-Condition Characteristics

The circulation of the water through the potential waterfront site should be examined. Slow-moving water can produce swampy or built-up mud conditions, while fast-moving water can produce undercurrents and erosive conditions.

The ideal water temperature for swimming ranges from 72% to 78% F, depending upon the air temperature. The American Public Health Association indicates that less than 500 gallons of additional water per bather per day is too small a diluting volume, unless there is sufficient application of disinfection.

Checklist:
- Rate of water flow
- Rate of water turnover
- Water-level fluctuation
- Water constancy
- Availability of water
- Types of currents and undertow
- Outlet for water
- Eddies, floods, waves, or wash
- Weeds, fungi, mold, or slime
- Parasites, fish, animals
- Debris, broken glass, etc.
- Oil slick
- Odor, color, taste

Bottom Characteristics

The waterfront bottom should be unobstructed and clear of debris, rock, muck, mulch, peat, and mud. The waterfront should not be in an area where the channel shifts or silt builds up. The most desirable bottom is white sand with a gradual pitch sloping from the shallow to the deep end. The bottom should not be precipitous, too shallow, nor have holes, pots, channels, bars, or islands.

The bottom should be of gravel, sand, or stable hard ground to afford firm and secure footing. An investigation by taking soundings in a boat, and by making an actual underwater survey should be undertaken before a final decision is made on the location of the waterfront.

Checklist:
- Bottom movement
- Amount of holes, debris

- Slope of subsurface
- Amount of area
- Condition of soil
- Porosity of bottom
- Average depth and various depths
- Bottom color

Climatic Characteristics

Continuous dry spells or numerous rainy seasons will cause the site to have water-retention problems. Dangerous storms, including tornadoes, lightning, hurricanes, and north-easters, create extremely dangerous waterfront conditions. The severity of the winter can also affect the waterfront. Ice and ice movement can cause damage to waterfront facilities and bottom. A south-southeast exposure is ideal so that maximum benefit is derived from the sun and there is least exposure to the wind.

Checklist:
- Number of storms and type
- Prevailing winds
- Amount of ice
- Change of air temperature
- Amount of precipitation
- Fluctuation of temperature
- Sun exposure

Environmental Characteristics

The locale of the waterfront should be carefully examined for all influences on its construction and utilization. Zoning regulations, building codes, insurance restrictions, health ordinances, title covenants, and a multitude of other legal restrictions by the Coast Guard, Conservation Department, Water Resources Commission, public works agencies, and Fire Department should be studied. The arrangement of land uses and their compatibility to the project, transportation, utilities, community facilities, population, and area economics should also be considered.

Checklist:
- Ownership and reparian rights
- Availability of water supply
- Zoning and deed restrictions
- Local, state, and federal regulations
- Adjacent ownerships
- Water patrol and a control agency

Program Characteristics

The waterfront should be so situated that it can be protected by a fence or other controlled access, particularly in a camp, marina, or other small area. It should also be internally segregated (i.e., bathing from boating, boating from fishing, and so on). The site should also have storage room for waterfront equipment, adequate spectator area for use during special events, a safety area near the lifeguard station or post, and ready access to a road.

Checklist:
- Distance of waterfront from other areas
- Access road

- Separation of waterfront activities
- Area for unity of controls
- Space available for adjunct activities

Access Characteristics

The waterfront facility must be accessible by transportation available to the user. There should always be a means of vehicular access for emergency or maintenance use. The site around the waterfront and along its approach should be free of poison ivy, sumac, poison oak, burdock thistle, and other irritating plants.
Check list:
- Location for access road
- Poisonous plants
- Area accessible yet controllable

Area Characteristics

The waterfront bathing area should allow for at least 50 square feet for each user. There should be areas for instruction, recreation, and competition. The depth of the area to be used primarily for the instruction of non-swimmers should not exceed three feet. The area to be used for intermediate swimmers should not exceed 5 1/2 feet (primarily for competition). Smaller or larger swimming areas may be designed if users are divided differently.

The minimum recommended size for a camp swimming area is 60 feet by 30 feet, and the desirable size is 75 feet by 45 feet, providing a 25-yard short course.

Checklist:
- Space for bathing
- Capacity of waterfront
- Water depths
- Division of bathing area into stations
- Size of boating area
- Size of fishing area

Shore Characteristics

The shoreline for the waterfront facility should be free of irregular rocks, stumps, debris, or obstruction. It should be a minimum of 100 feet long for bathing in a camp area and can be many miles long in a park beach.

There should be trees adjacent to waterfront areas to provide shade and wind protection. Large, high trees should be eliminated because they attract lightning, and moldy trees have many decayed overhanging branches. Too many trees of a deciduous nature create mucky shores and water bottoms because of their autumn leaves. There are fewer problems with coniferous trees.

Checklist:
- Surrounding vegetation
- Slope of the shore
- Existing beach
- Extent of clearing
- Amount of debris

Criteria for Artificial Waterfronts

In locating and considering an artificial waterfront, most of the same characteristics as described for natural areas should be examined. Additional criteria that should be considered are outlined below.

Environmental Characteristics

If all available bodies of water are being utilized, then artificial waterfront facilities must be developed. In some cases, waterfront locations are unsatisfactory or unavailable for new camps or resorts. Thus, consideration must be given to utilizing undeveloped sites with sufficient watershed (runoff water), water table (underground water), and water bodies (surface water) for lakes, pools, or impondments.

Water Characteristics

Before any site is selected, the perculation rate and, in particular, the permeability of the soil should be carefully checked in order to be sure that water will be retained. The stability and structure of the soil must also be determined (from test borings and/or test pits) because of the various types of dams, pump houses, dikes, pools, berms, spillways, and other structures that must be built.

Water-Content Characteristics

Unlike natural bodies of water, the content of artificial bodies can be controlled by chlorination and filtration. Runoff water obtained from storms, and contained in a pond or lake, should be collected by diversion ditches and fed to a reservoir and chlorination plant. This water can then be recirculated until potable water is obtained.

Underground water that is obtained from wells or springs can also be contained in a pond. This type of artificial water body usually would have a continuous flow and thus would need only a simple filtration system plus chlorination.

Surface water that is obtained from running streams is usually contained in a bypass pond or in a pond in the stream itself. Both methods require the construction of a dam. These artificial water bodies have continuous running water. However, gate valves and floodgates are required, especially during storms when there is a large flow of water to control. Unless there is a constant turnover or supply of clean water, these impondments will require a filtration and chlorination system.

Climatic Characteristics

Climatic considerations are very important in developing artificial bodies of water and waterfronts. In most cases, natural bodies of water will fluctuate very little because of weather conditions. On the other hand, artificial bodies are solely dependent upon the climate because the water table, runoff, and stream flow depend on the amount and time of rainfall. All other climatic considerations mentioned for natural waterfronts generally apply to artificial waterfronts as well.

Drainage Characteristics

A low-lying area, regardless of its appeal, is not a good location for a pool or pond. Adequate drainage is essential, so that surface and deck water will drain away from the water body, and so that the water body itself can be emptied without pumping. Ground water and frost action resulting from improper drainage can undermine a foundation by causing it to heave and settle.

Waterfront Construction

Criteria for Natural Waterfronts

The natural waterfront facility should have features that make it both safe and usable. The following criteria are suggested as a basis for the construction of such a facility.

Bottom Characteristics

Most swimming facilities around natural bodies of water require the dragging and grading of the bottom sub-surfaces to eliminate hazards. In many cases, where definite improvement of the bottom is required, feed mat, mesh, or plastic sheets have to be laid down on top of muck and staked down. Once these sheets have been laid, sand must be spread over the mat surface. When the bottom is firm, sand can be spread six inches thick on top of ice in the crib area during winter. As the ice melts, the sand will fall fairly evenly over the bottom. This can only be accomplished, however, when the ice does not shift or break and float away.

Shore Characteristics

When a beach is constructed, a gentle slope of from six feet to 12 feet in 100 feet should be maintained. Where the waterfront requires a great deal of construction, a dock shoreline is recommended, rather than trying to maintain an unstable beach. The ground above the water can then be developed with turf, terraces, decks, and boardwalks, depending upon the nature of the project. When the bottom drops off very quickly, the shore can be dug out to the grade desired underwater. This forms a crescent-shaped waterfront with an excellent beach.

Access Characteristics

Access roads and streets around waterfront areas should be acquired by the owner, if possible, to keep the area buffered from conflicting uses. These roads should be durable and be attractively maintained. Access roads should have clear horizontal and vertical vision, so that pedestrian and vehicular conflict can be prevented.

Program Characteristics

The waterfront in small recreation areas, such as camps or resorts, should be completely enclosed by planting or fencing. There should be a central control for ingress and exit. Many facilities require the use of check in-out boards, tickets, and other similar devices for controlling the use of the area. The waterfront bathing, boating, and fishing facilities should be separated, each with its own control.

Criteria for Artificial Waterfronts

Both artificial and natural waterfronts should have certain features that make them safe and usable. In improving and developing an artificial waterfront, most of the same considerations should be rendered as illustrated for the natural waterfront. The following criteria should be carefully considered in providing an artificial waterfront.

Bottom Characteristics

When constructing an artificial beach, the grade should be the same as that recommended for natural shores—six feet to 12 feet in 100 feet. For reservoirs and ponds, there should be a minimum of nine inches of large, crushed stone, then four inches of well-graded smooth gravel to fill in the voids, and then nine inches of washed medium sand. Where the sand beach terminates at a depth of approximately seven feet of water, it is recommended that rip-rapping be established to resist the tendency of the beach sand to move down the slope. The area above the beach should also be ditched where the natural slope of the ground exceeds that of the beach. Thus, the slopes of the beach should be approximately six percent below the water and 10 percent above. For areas in tidal waters, a maximum slope of five for 15 feet can be established for the bottom below-water line.

Shore Characteristics

In creating the shoreline for artificial bodies of water, there should be either a berm or dike if the water is to be confined. A steep slope to eliminate shallow areas is usually required to prevent weeds and other plant materials from growing in the water. If the soil conditions will not allow a steep slope underwater three feet deep to retard water-plant growth, then bulkheads or docks will be required, or only a limited beach can be provided.

Design and Construction of Camp Waterfronts

The camp waterfront is usually composed of either permanent docks or floats to provide safe swimming and boating areas.

Docks and Floats

Permanent structures are usually set on concrete, wood, or steel foundations, or pier piles. The decks should be made in sections of 10 feet to 20 feet for ease in removing for repairs or winter storage. The dock should be constructed with at least a one-foot air space between deck and water. Underwater braces and other cross beams should be limited to prevent swimmers from becoming entangled in them. When water levels change, allowances should be made for the piers to be outside the deck limits so the deck can move up and down on sleeves or brackets. Walkways or decks should be a minimum of six feet wide, preferably eight or 10 feet. They should be cross-planked so swimmers will avoid splinters. The planking should not be less than two inches thick by four inches to six inches wide. Boards should be spaced a maximum of 1/4 inch apart to prevent toe-stubbing. The deck should be treated with a non-creosote-based preservative, since creosote will burn feet, plus a plastic, non-lead paint that is not heat-absorbing. The paint should be white with a blue or green tint to reduce the glare and aid in reflection.

Flotation structures may be made of drums, balsa wood, cork, styrafoam, steel tanks, or other forms of flotation material. There are many innovations that have carried over from war days. Pontoon decks, for example, are sometimes made from surplus bridge parts, airplane fuel tanks, or fuel-oil tanks. All such materials should be treated with red lead after scraping, sanding, and repairing. A frame should be constructed of two inch x eight inch boards to fit over and contain the supporting units. The frame should fit securely, yet be removable at the close of the season. Some flotation materials or devices are just placed in the framing under the floats without any type of anchorage to the frame. Galvanized steel or aluminum straps of 1/8 inches x 1-1/2 inches under the floating units will save time and effort to prevent sinking when these units acquire a leak and fill with water.

The various types of designs employed in waterfronts are shown in Figure 22.4. A typical camp waterfront is shown in Figure 22.5.

Waterfront Equipment

It is important to plan initially for all needed accessory equipment. The amount of equipment required will vary with the size of the waterfront. All necessary safety equipment must be located so as to afford immediate emergency use.

Lifeguard Station

Lifeguard chairs should be placed at a point where the location of beach equipment and sunbathing limit lines do not interfere with the guards' vision of the water areas. Chairs should be a minimum of six feet to a maximum of 10 feet above grade. Usually lifeguard chairs are made of galvanized pipe or wood.

Ladders

In all swimming cribs, there should be a ladder at least two feet in width placed at the sides in order not to interfere with persons swimming the length of the simulated pool.

Log Booms

Logs fastened end to end can form a continuous lifeline around bathing limits in rustic settings and, at the same time, provide the safety to swimmers so necessary at a waterfront.

Lemmon Lines

Lemmon lines are small floats, attached by a nylon or plastic rope or cable, outlining and restricting swimming areas. They can be made of rounded wood, cork, or plastic.

Markers and Buoys

These are floats indicating the limits of areas or channels, or marking underwater obstructions, divers, moorings, and fishing nets. They are usually hollow cans or drums. They can also be flag buoys, a six-inch-square wood block with attached flag, a wooden cross of two inches by four inches with can on top, or a metal ballast with flag.

Figure 22.4
Sample Waterfront Configuations

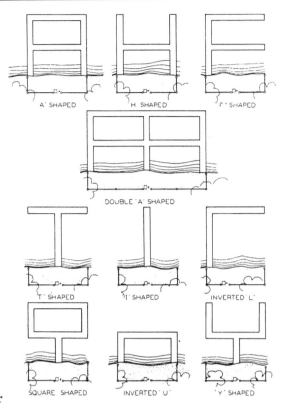

Graphic by Meghan Sawyer

Figure 22.5
Sample Waterfront

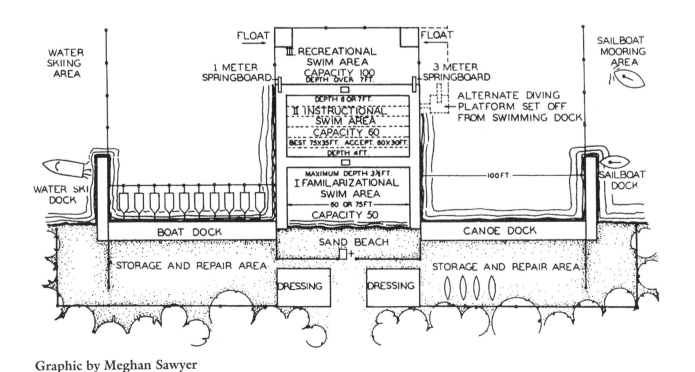

Graphic by Meghan Sawyer

Rescue Craft

Boats should be of the round-bottom or dory type between 12 feet and 14 feet long. There should be lifesaving equipment in the boat at all times. The seats should be removable, and oarlocks should be of a permanent type. A catamaran, surfboards, and, in large beach waterfront facilities, helicopters supplement the lifeboat as a means of patrol.

Kick Rails

A rail for practicing and teaching swimming should be placed at water level. This can be made of galvanized pipe, wood rods, or rope.

Towel Racks

Racks for drying towels and bathing suits should be installed at or near the waterfront.

Miscellaneous Equipment

Life ring buoys should be spaced strategically around the waterfront on racks. These racks are usually in the form of a cross, with the ring suspended from the center and the rope wrapped around the ring from pegs protruding from each end of the cross. Torpedo buoys, bamboo poles, grappling irons, lifelines, shepherd's crooks, stretchers, blankets, microphones, and other such devices should be available to the lifeguards. Numbers indicating depths and the capacities of the crib and other swimming areas should be clearly visible. Kick boards should be available for practice as well as emergency use.

Summary

Park and recreation facilities are experiencing a multitude of trends that are impacting the planning process. Planning principles are not typically subject to change, but inputs to the process are undergoing substantial change.

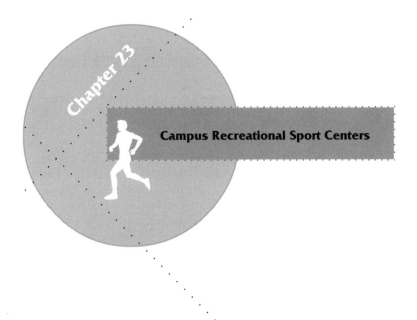

Thomas H. Sawyer, Indiana State University

O ver the past 20 years, a number of recreational sport centers have been constructed on campuses to meet the needs of the student body. These centers have been built for recreational purposes, not instructional or athletic ones. However, recently a number have been built with large aquatic areas (e.g., University of Toledo, Miami University of Ohio, University of Texas, Georgia Tech, University of Michigan, University of Minnesota, and Indiana University) to be used for both recreational and athletic purposes. These centers have been financed primarily with student fees and state and private funds. Most of the facilities include aquatic centers, entrance/lobby area, lounge areas, racquetball/walleyball courts, indoor and outdoor tennis courts, basketball courts, dance exercise areas, indoor running/jogging tracks, strength and cardiovascular training areas, climbing wall, locker rooms, indoor/outdoor rollerblade hockey court, indoor soccer area, administration area, pro shops, concessions, and an area for equipment rental.

This chapter has been designed to provide the planner with an overview of the needs for a campus recreational sport center. The specifics relating to many of the spaces are found in other chapters in this book.

Learning Objectives

After reading this chapter, the student will be able to
- begin planning a new recreational sport center,
- describe indoor activities and facility needs,
- outline outdoor activities and facility needs, and
- describe the security needs for a recreational sport center.

Planning for a New Recreational Sports Center

A common problem is how to secure these new facilities. The following can form the basis from which to justify requests for additional facilities. The initial step in the process of securing any new facility is defining the space requirements. This planning process uses three different types of space used in recreational, intramural, and informal sport programs. The three types, according to Mull, Bayless, Ross, and Jamieson (1977), are described below:

Type A Space

Type A space includes the following areas:

Indoor teaching stations—space requirements: 8.5-9.5 sq. ft. per student (total undergraduate enrollment) including a) gym floors, mat areas, swimming pools, court areas, etc.; and b) location adjacent to lockers and showers and within a 10-minute walking distance of academic classrooms (Mull et al., 1997).

Uses: Recreational, intramural, and informal sports participation for student and faculty recreation.

A1—Large gymnasium area with relatively high ceiling (22 ft. minimum) for basketball, badminton, volleyball, etc. (approximately 55% of Type A space).

A2—Activity areas with relatively low ceiling (12 ft. minimum) for combatives, therapeutic exercises, dancing, weight lifting, etc. (approximately 30% of Type A space).

A3—Indoor swimming and diving pools (approximately 15% of Type A space) (Mull et al., 1997).

Type B Space

Type B space includes the following areas:

Outdoor teaching stations—space requirements including a) sport fields of all types; b) location adjacent to locker and showers, and within a 10-minute walking distance of academic classrooms.

Uses: Recreational, intramural, and informal sports participation for student and faculty for recreation.

B1—Sodded areas for soccer, touch football, softball, etc. (approximately 60% of Type B space).

B2—Court type areas for tennis, volleyball, etc. (approximately 15% of Type B space).

B3—Specialized athletic areas for track and field, baseball, archery, varsity football, golf, camping demonstrations, etc. (approximately 25% of Type B space).

B4—Swimming pools (included in B3 approximation) (Mull et al., 1997).

Type C Space

Type C spaces include the following:

Sport fields and buildings, intramural and general outdoor recreation areas—space requirements, 120-140 sq. ft. per student (total undergraduate enrollment) including playing fields and athletic buildings of all types, softball diamonds, tennis courts, field houses, etc. Too far removed from student lockers, showers, living quarters and academic buildings for use as teaching stations.

Uses: Recreation, intramural, and informal sports for students and faculty recreation.

C1—Sodded areas for soccer, touch football, softball, etc. (approximately 40% of Type C space).

C2—Court type areas for tennis, volleyball, etc. (approximately 10% of Type C space).

C3—Specialized athletic area for track and field, baseball, archery, varsity football, golf, camping demonstrations, etc. (approximately 45% of Type C space).

C4—Swimming pools (included in C3 approximation).

C5—Sports and intramural buildings providing lockers, showers, play space, office space, lounge rooms, etc. (approximately 5% of Type C space) (Mull et al., 1997).

In order to compare a campus with the accepted standards, five steps should be followed: The first step involves the location of existing and potential areas within the boundaries of the campus. This is done by physically canvassing the campus and envisioning the potential of all areas. The initial phase of Step 1 should be the location and identification of all areas that are currently used by recreational, intramural, and informal sport.

The second phase is more difficult and requires more effort and imagination on the part of the observer. Potential areas of expansion are spaces (outdoor and indoor) that can be converted from whatever they are currently being used for to usable recreation areas. Costs of converting each area should be kept at a minimum to further enhance the attractiveness of securing new facilities. For example, the cost of converting a relatively small (50 feet by 100 feet) grassy area to an outdoor volleyball area would only include the installation of two poles and a net. If further funds were available and the sport popular, this area could further be converted to a sand or beach volleyball court at a small additional cost. Providing alternatives or options also enhances the acceptability of the proposal.

Space for conversion should meet the general criteria for Type A, B, or C space before being considered for alteration. For example, an indoor area with an eight-foot ceiling should not be considered for conversion to gymnasium space; however, it could be converted to a dance studio or a karate practice room with the addition of mirrors and mats.

After all available and potential areas have been located, the next step requires computations of the area in square feet. For indoor areas, a tape measure is used; however, for large outdoor areas, a cross-country measuring wheel is most effective.

Multipurpose gym with rounded corners. Central Michigan University. (Photo by Balthazar Korab, Ltd. Courtesy of TMP Associates, Inc.)

Main Street, Student Recreation Center, Central Michigan University. (Photo by Balthazar Korab, Ltd. Courtesy of TMP Associates, Inc.)

When measuring any area, precautions should be taken to allow for a buffer zone of safety around any proposed playing area. An outdoor grassy area measuring 100 yards by 40 yards could theoretically accommodate an intramural football field, but if the boundaries are close to hazards such as chainlink fence poles, trees, or buildings, this area should be considered for some other recreational purpose.

The same precautions apply to indoor space. Most areas considered will be fairly easy to measure. Normally, spaces are either rectangular or square in shape. Odd-shaped areas should not be ignored, and their areas should be estimated to the best of the measurer's ability while still allowing for the safety buffer zone. Odd-shaped areas are also sometimes ignored, because they do not fit the shape of a standard playing field. These areas may, however, accommodate a combination of two or more sports in that area. Any particular space should not be viewed as usable only for football or basketball, but leftover spaces could easily be used for a frisbee golf course or a single table tennis table.

The square footage for all areas considered should next be classified and totaled under one of the three types of spaces. This total figure of space classified according to type can now be compared with the recommended amount of space. Recommended space is computed by taking current enrollment figures and multiplying them by the median figure in the range of each type of space. For example, a university with an enrollment of 15,000 students should have a recommended space requirement for Type A space of 135,000 square feet. The total amount of each type space is then compared with the actual amount to arrive at a figure illustrating the amount above or below recommended standards.

A further breakdown of space within each type into the 12 subclassifications is required to determine the correct "mix" of facilities. This subclassification of space enables the director to specifically locate areas of deficiency.

When standards in terms of square feet per student are used as guides in college or university planning, it is natural to ask where the cut-off begins. Obviously, for a college of 200 students, nine square feet per student of indoor area for sports and athletics would be inadequate. It would not even provide one basketball court. A university or college meeting the space standards for 1,500 students represents the minimum physical recreation space needs of any college institution. As a college or university increases in size, these standards are applicable regardless of enrollment. Also, a ceiling effect applies to some subclassifications of space.

In the beginning phases of planning for recreational facilities, area standards must be developed. A variety of standards relative to size, location, and development of school and recreation areas and facilities has been developed.

The standards provide a useful guide; however, standards can seldom, if ever, be applied completely or without modification. Because a typical or ideal situation is seldom found, standards simply indicate a basis for the intelligent development of local plans.

The third step involves a description of current and potential uses of each area. A description of current uses should be done first. It should include uses by physical education, recreation, intramural sports, and "outside" departments. If a particular area is not being used for any specific purpose, it should be so listed.

Potential uses should be as closely linked to the subclassifications as possible. It is in this phase of the process where the director must make responsible choices as to the development of any given area. A single area must have the potential to be developed into several different types of space. The director must refer to individual program needs and areas of deficiency to make informed decisions as to the development of that particular area. Again, it is important to provide campus planners with options. However, the director should limit the flexibility of the proposal to stay within the most urgent needs of his particular program.

The next step is to determine the cost of converting an area from its current use to its potential use. In some cases, the cost of conversion will be zero. This type of space should be accentuated in presenting the proposal before any board involved with campus planning. Often, cooperation between two departments regarding scheduling can vastly increase facilities available for recreational use at no cost to either program.

Finally, the last step involves defining the availability for use by the major users. If facilities are shared by two or more users, the priority schedule for usage should also be listed. After all, a program may have access to a facility 40% of the total time available, but if those times are at undesirable hours, the facility is not meeting the needs of the program. If no consideration is given to the prime-time needs of students for recreational use, the percentage of availability may be misleading.

After information has been gathered, supporting documents for requesting new facilities must be prepared. The proposal should contain five major parts.

Indoor Recreational, Intramural, and Informal Sport Activities

The following is a partial listing of indoor recreational, intramural, and informal sport activities:

Single Function	Specialized or Multipurpose Function	
Archery range	**Country club**	**Gymnasium**
Badminton court	Golf	Gymnastics
Basketball court	Swimming	Combatives
Billiards	Table sports	Basketball
Bowling alley	Strength training	Volleyball
Combatives room	Tennis	Badminton
Curling rink		Table tennis
Cardiovascular room		
Dance exercise room		
Diving pool		
Electronic games arcade	**Fieldhouse**	**Racquetball club**
Fencing salle	Basketball	Strength training
Gymnastics room	Track	Jogging
Handball	Soccer	
Ice rink	Lacrosse	**Recreation center**
Racquetball court	Jogging	Billards
Rifle-pistol range	Archery	Table sports
Roller skating rink		Table tennis
Rollerblade hockey rink	**Fitness center**	Swimming
Shuffleboard course	Swimming	Gymnasium
Squash court	Strength training	
Swimming pool	Cardiovascular training	
Table sport room	Jogging	
Table tennis room	Combatives	
Tennis court	Dance exercise	
Strength training room		
Wrestling room		
Volleyball court		

Obtaining other costs of conversion generally involves requesting estimates from the physical plant operations staff on campus or from outside contractors. These estimates should be obtained prior to presenting any proposal. Also, the estimates should enhance the flexibility built into the proposal. That is to say, each option should have its own separate estimate. This allows campus planning boards to examine all suggestions in the proposal independently of other suggestions in the proposal.

The first part should state clearly the objectives of the study. It should also list all areas and departments of the campus involved in conducting the study. Finally, it should include limitations or qualifications specific to the institution.

The second part should include brief historical developments of the sponsoring program from both a national and campus viewpoint.

The third section is a statement of the problem. In this section, all forces generating the study should be explained. All major problems affected by changing facility structures should be included, as well as the majority of the information gathered in the aforementioned steps. Listing the standards with the organizations using them will lend national support to the proposal. The relationship between the standard and enrollment is explained next. And, finally, the standards are applied to the specific campus in question. The comparison should emphasize those areas in which critical deficiencies exist, because the largest deficiencies are not always the most critical ones. Section three should conclude with a summary of the work completed on the study and a restatement of those problem areas.

Section four contains recommendations for immediate action and long-term improvements. Flexibility (options) within the overall goals of the organization should be the guiding principle when preparing this section.

Finally, appendices should be prepared to support the proposal. Participation figures may be used in this section; however, the major part of this section should contain a map of the campus with all areas clearly marked. The map should be accompanied by a list of all buildings and rooms investigated. The most precise way of presenting existing and potential areas is according to the following seven-point formula:

- Location,
- Area (structure footage),
- Type of space,
- Current uses,
- Potential uses,
- Cost of conversion, and
- Percentage of use.

Each area should be listed and explained through this format.

Indoor Facilities

In planning new facilities, it should be remembered that substand and facilities usually result in a substandard program. For this reason, official court and field dimensions should be used whenever possible. The following list identifies the types of areas that should be considered in planning indoor facilities for a campus recreational sports center:

- Main gymnasium—regulation basketball, badminton, tennis, and volleyball courts with mechanical divider nets. The divider nets should be constructed of solid vinyl for the first eight feet and the remainder of a mesh material.
- Auxiliary gymnasiums—regulation basketball, badminton, tennis, and volleyball courts, gymnastics area, rollerblade hockey rink, indoor soccer area, suspended track, fencing, batting cages, and dance exercise. The dance exercise area should have hidden mirrors to protect them when the space is used for other activities (i.e., basketball or volleyball), and a retractable instructor's platform. The planners might consider the possibility of locating two gymnasiums side by side with a storage area between to store equipment, audio system, and retractable instructor's platforms. The storage area should be at least eight feet wide.
- Swimming pools—50-meter pool, diving pool, and/or instruction pool.
- Combative room—boxing, martial arts, and judo.

Outdoor Recreational, Intramural, and Informal Sport Activities

The following are common outdoor recreational, intramural, and sport activities:

Airfield	Handball court
Baseball field	Miniature golf course
Basketball court	Motocross course
Beach volleyball	Riding paddock
Bicycle path	Rifle/pistol range
Boat launching ramp	Rollerblade hockey rink
Bocce ball course	Roller skating rink
Bowling green	Shuffleboard
Cross country course	Skateboard/rollerblade course and ramp
Curling rink	Skeet and trap range
Deck tennis	Skiing course
Diving pool	Soccer field
Field hockey field	Softball field
Fishing pond/lake	Speedball
Fitness trail	Swimming pool
Football field	Speedball field
Frisbee golf course	Team handball field
Go-cart track	Tennis court
Golf course	Toboggan slope
Golf driving range	Volleyball
Horseshoe	Lacrosse field
Hydro-slide	Marina
Ice rink	

Indoor soccer/roller hockey.

Photos by Tom Sawyer

Indoor track.

- Strength training area—progressive resistance-training equipment, free-weight equipment, and stretching area.
- Cardiovascular area
- Handball/racquetball/walleyball courts
- Golf room—sand trap, putting area, and driving nets.
- Archery/rifle/pistol range
- Games room—billards, table tennis, table games, shuffleboard.
- Administrative area—offices, storage, conference rooms, and audio-visual room.
- Lounge and lobby area—bulletin boards, trophy cases, control center, and art work.
- Concessions, rental, and merchandise area—concession stand, seating area, rental shop, and pro shop.
- Training room—treatment area only.
- Locker rooms—student and faculty, gender specific, shower rooms, drying areas, locker space, and common spa area (i.e., hydro-tube, sauna, and steam room)
- Equipment and storerooms
- Climbing wall

Outdoor Facilities

The following list identifies the types of areas that should be considered in planning outdoor facilities for a campus recreational sports center:
- Lighted fields—touch/flag football, soccer, field hockey, softball, baseball, handball, and rugby
- Lighted courts—basketball, badminton, tennis, volleyball, handball/racquetball, and horseshoes
- Lighted rollerblade hockey court
- Lighted jogging/running/walking trails and/or track
- Golf course and lighted driving range and practice green
- Lighted skating rink
- Swimming and diving pools
- Bocci field and horseshoe pits
- Storage building(s)
- Tennis practice boards and soccer kicking wall
- Picnic areas with shelters

Security Issues

The campus recreational sports center will quickly become the focus of campus interest. The center will be used heavily throughout the day and evening. The prime times will be 6 to 8 a.m., 11 a.m. to 1 p.m., 4 to 6 p.m. and 7 p.m. to midnight. The planners need to consider providing adequate security, including appropriate outside lighting at all sites, security cameras, alarmed doors (silent and audible), pool alarms, spa alarms, valuable lockers, fire alarms, sprinkling systems, and appropriate signage.

Summary

Recreational sport centers on campuses have become very strong recruiting tools for colleges and universities. Students want to be involved with recreational sports, to relax and play with fellow students. Many colleges and universities are adding new recreational sport centers to their campuses to meet student needs for recreation.

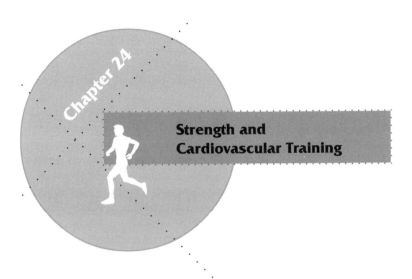

Strength and Cardiovascular Training

Thomas H. Sawyer, Indiana State University

As a strength and cardiovascular facility coordinator, you are responsible for not only knowing how to organize participants for strength and cardiovascular training, but also for knowing how to arrange equipment safely in order to meet the challenge. In some cases you might be responsible for developing a facility. Planning the facility takes many hours of creating and reviewing floor plans and deciding what equipment will be needed, how space may be best utilized, what surfaces are needed in various areas, and other factors. It is worthwhile to contact professionals in other programs who have built a facility and to compile information on specific needs. A committee of people who represent various areas of expertise may be organized to help in the planning of the facility. Such a committee may consist of an administrator, contractor, lawyer, student-athlete, sport coach, instructors who would use the facility, various experts in the field of sport conditioning, and any other people who could give valuable input on design.

This chapter will focus on a discussion of existing facilities and how you might improve and reorganize them to best suit the needs of the philosophy (the ideals and values shaping the program), goals (the desired outcome), and objectives (the individual steps toward a goal) of a program, and what would be needed in a new facility.

Learning Objectives

After reading this chapter, the student will be able to
- assess the needs of an existing or new facility,
- plan and organize an existing or new facility for maximum usage, and
- understand the environmental factors affecting facility development.

Assessing the Needs of an Existing Facility

After defining the program goals and objectives, the facility coordinator should assess existing equipment and the needs of the various sport groups that plan to use the facility. As the coordinator, you will need to answer these questions:
- What are the specific training goals of each group?
- What types of training does each require (e.g., circuits, machines, free weights, platform lifts, plyometrics)?
- What are the seasonal priorities of each group?
- What are the training ages (training experience) of the athletes in the groups?
- When will weight training fit into each group's schedule?
- What repairs, adaptations, and modifications must be made to meet the athletes' needs?
- How should the equipment be placed to best utilize the space in a safe and efficient manner?

Planning the Layout of an Existing Facility

An initial step is to determine who will be using the facility and to develop a list of existing equipment. Prepare a floor plan to (1) visualize the present and potential locations of equipment; (2) organize for safety and the most efficient use of space, exits, and entrances; (3) identify areas of frequent travel; (4) develop facility flow (pathways in the facility); and (5) select supervisor station locations for maximum supervision of the whole facility, especially areas of increased risk (such as the platform area). Safety should always be a priority.

Station all high-risk activities, including platform lifts, squats, overhead presses, bench and incline presses, and exercises that require spotters, away from windows, mirrors, exits, and entrances to avoid breakage of glass, distraction, or collision with the bar or lifter. Place the equipment for these activities in areas that are readily supervised to ensure safety and the execution of proper technique. Supervision is effective only if all areas of the facility can be observed at any given time. Therefore, locate supervisor stations in places with full visibility of all areas of the facility, to allow quick access to participants in need of spotters or immediate assistance.

Arrange the tallest machines or pieces of equipment along the walls, with the shorter, smaller pieces in the middle to improve visibility (as well as appearance) and maximize use of space. Place weight racks enough distance away from bar ends and spotter areas for ease of movement without obstruction. Tall pieces of equipment, such as squat racks, may need to be bolted to the walls or floors for increased stability.

. The following are guidelines suggested by a panel of safety experts at the National Strength and Conditioning Association (NSCA) and the American College Sports Medicine (ACSM) for the safe and efficient use of equipment (Baechle, 1994; Tharrett & Peterson, 1997):

- All weight machines and apparatus must be spaced at least two feet (61 cm) from one another, and preferably three feet (91 cm) apart.
- Platform areas should have sufficient overhead space (at least 12 feet [3.7 m]), which should be free of such low-hanging items as beams, pipes, lighting, and signs.
- The proper spacing of Olympic bars is three feet (91 cm) between ends (12 feet [3.7 m] X 8 feet [2.4 m] = 1 platform lifting area).

Maintain a clear pathway three feet (91 cm) wide in the facility at all times, as stipulated by federal, state, and local laws. Machines and equipment must not be allowed to block or obstruct this flow. Place equipment at least six inches (15 cm) from mirrors and mirrors 20 inches (51 cm) above the floor. Place free-weight equipment well away from exits and entrances to avoid obstruction, give participants ample room for passage, and guarantee safety to the pedestrian and lifter. Organize equipment into "priority sections," such as free-weight areas, machine areas, power training areas, and cardiovascular/aerobic areas. This allows the supervisor to identify and focus on the higher risk areas and keep equipment orderly in the facility.

Organizing the Facility for Maximum Usage

When organizing groups of participants, you should consider the size of the facility and assess the needs of each group in terms of the following:

- specific training needs (e.g., strength, endurance, circuits, and power),
- seasonal priority (i.e., when sports occur, such as football in the fall and baseball in the spring),
- group size and equipment availability (i.e., a football team with 150 members may not be able to use a facility efficiently and safely without being split into groups; other sports groups may have to be scheduled at times other than football groups to ensure sufficient use of the equipment),
- the participant-staff ratio (1:10 to 1:30, depending upon the training group), and

- a minimum space requirement per lifter of 30 feet (2.8 m) and a maximum of 60 feet (5.6m) (Baechle, 1994).

Schedule facility usage so that different groups of participants train in the facility at more or less constant "density" throughout the day; avoid large, congested groups, which increase the potential for injury and inefficient use of equipment. If the facility is designed for high school athletes, groups may be organized through physical education classes that offer beginning, intermediate, and advanced strength and conditioning to the students. Teams may organize facility usage time before or after practice according to seasonal priority.

Assessing Existing Facility Surfaces

Two main surfaces need to be assessed—flooring and walls. The following describes exactly what one should look for when assessing these surfaces.

Flooring

Flooring can be composed of such materials as wood, tile, rubber, interlocking mats, and carpet. The assessor will carefully review the surfaces for the following concerns:

Wooden flooring on platforms must be kept free of splinters, holes, protruding nails, uneven boards, and screws. The boards should run in the direction of the bar so that lifters do not catch their feet against the grain of the wood when widening their stance. This is the safest flooring for Olympic-style lifters.

Tile flooring and anti-static floor should be treated with antifungal, antibacterial agents in the aerobic machine area. The tile should also be resistant to slipping and moisture accumulation and free from chalk accumulation.

Resilient rubber flooring in the free-weight and machine areas should be similar to aerobic flooring. It must be kept free of large gaps between pieces, cuts, and worn spots.

Interlocking mats must be secure and arranged so as not to pull apart or become deformed (with protruding tabs). The stretching area must be kept free of accumulated dust. Mats or carpets should be nonabsorbent and contain antifungal and antibacterial agents.

Carpet must be free of tears. High-use areas should be protected with throw mats. All areas must be swept and vacuumed or mopped on a regular basis. Flooring must be kept glued and fastened down properly. Fixed equipment must be attached securely to the floor.

Walls

Wall surfaces include mirrors and windows, exits, storage areas, and shelves. The assessor needs to carefully look for the following regarding wall surfaces:

- Walls in high-activity areas must be kept free of protruding apparatus (i.e., extended bars and lighting fixtures).
- Mirrors, shelves, and other fixtures must be fixed securely to the walls.
- Mirrors and windows must be located in an area easily reached for repair and cleaning.

- Mirrors, if present in any area, must be attached to the wall at least 50 inches off the floor, and cracked or distorted mirrors should be replaced.

Environmental Factors

Environmental factors that should be considered in helping make the facility safe and effective include noise control, temperature, ventilation, humidity, lighting, electrical cords and outlets, and posted signs. Music can be a form of motivation for many, but it can also pose a problem if the stereo system is not properly managed. Volume should be low enough to allow for clear communication between spotters or instructors and lifters at all times. The stereo system should be controlled by the facility coordinator and qualified supervisors only.

Air temperature should be kept constant at 68° to 72° F (22° to 26° C) to offer a reasonable training environment. If the room is too cold, athletes may become chilled after they finish warming up; if too hot, participants may become overheated or lose motivation to continue. Proper ventilation is important to maintaining air quality and keeping humidity to a minimum (relative humidity should be less than 60%). The ventilation system should provide at least eight to 10 air exchanges per hour and optimally 12 to 15 air exchanges. The result should be no detectable strong odors in the room and equipment free of slickness or rust due to high humidity (Tharrett & Peterson, 1997).

Proper lighting of the facility is important for safety and motivation. A facility is well lighted if it is free of dark areas, and all equipment and areas can be observed from one end of the facility to the other. Bulbs, tubes, and other lighting apparatus should be checked and changed on a regular basis; optimum lighting is 75 to 100 foot-candles. Exit signs should also be well lighted and all exits well marked. All extension cords should be large enough for the electrical load and routed, secured, and grounded. Because some aerobic equipment requires 220 V, both 110 V and 220 V outlets are needed.

All safety, regulation, and policy signs should be posted in clear view, in two or three central places within the facility; more postings may be needed in a large facility.

Procedures for Maintaining Equipment

All strength and cardiovascular facilities, whether they are existing or new, should have a well-planned set of procedures for maintaining equipment in specified areas.

Aerobic/anaerobic fitness area

This space contains rowing machines, bikes, sprint machines, stair machines, skiing and climbing machines. In this area, surfaces that come into contact with human skin should be cleaned and disinfected daily. This not only protects participants from unsanitary conditions, but also extends the usefulness and maintains the appearance of equipment surfaces. The moving parts of the equipment should be properly lubricated and cleaned when needed so that they are not stressed unnecessarily. Connective bolts and screws need to be checked for tightness or wear and replaced if needed. Straps and belts should be secure and replaced if necessary.

Measurement devices such as rpm meters should be properly maintained (this is usually done by the manufacturer, but the life span of the equipment can be extended by wiping off sweat and dirt regularly). Equipment parts such as seats and benches should be easily adjustable.

Machines area

Isokinetic, variable resistance, single-station, multi-station machines are located in this space.

Rehabilitation and special-population machine area

The cleaning and maintenance of both the machines and rehabilitation areas are similar to those processes in the aerobic/anaerobic fitness area. Bench and machine surfaces that come into contact with skin should be cleaned and disinfected daily to provide a clean surface. Padded and upholstered areas should be free of cracks and tears. Moving parts should be cleaned and lubricated (guide rods on selectorized machines cleaned and lubricated two to three times each week). These areas should be free of loose bolts, screws, cables, chains, and protruding or worn parts that need replacing or removal. Pins that were designed for the machines and belts should be kept in stock. Chains and cables should be adjusted for proper alignment and smooth function. Machines should be spaced so that they are easily accessed, with a minimum of two feet (61 cm) on all sides, preferably three feet (91 cm) (Baechle, 1994).

Body weight resistance apparatus area

This area contains sit-up board, pulleys, hyperextension benches, plyometric boxes, medicine balls, climbing ropes, pegboard climb, jump ropes. It should have secured apparatus with well-padded flooring. If mats are used, they should be disinfected daily and be free of cracks and tears. The flooring below plyometric boxes and jumping equipment should be padded to protect the jumper from impact with a hard surface. The tops and bottoms of boxes should have nonslip surfaces for safe use.

Stretching area

Equipment in this area includes mats, stretching sticks, medicine balls, elastic cords, wall ladders. Mats in stretching areas should be cleaned and disinfected daily and be free of cracks and tears. Areas between mats should be swept or vacuumed regularly to avoid the accumulation of dust and dirt. The area should be free of benches, dumbbells, and other equipment that may clutter the area and tear mat surfaces. Medicine balls and stretching sticks should be stored after use, and elastic cords should be secured to a base, checked for wear, and replaced when necessary.

Free-weight area

This area includes bench presses, incline presses, squat racks, dumbbells, and weight racks. Equipment should be spaced to allow easy access to separate areas. All equipment, including safety equipment (belts, locks, safety bars) should be returned after use to avoid pathway obstruction. Benches, weight racks, and standards may be bolted to the floor or walls. In the squat area, the flooring should be of a nonslip surface and cleaned regularly. Equipment such as curl bars and dumbbells should be checked frequently for loose hex nuts. Nonfunctional or broken equipment should be posted with "out of order" signs or, if a long delay in repairs is expected, removed from the area or locked out of service. All protective padding and upholstery should be free of cracks and tears, and disinfected daily.

Lifting platform area

Olympic bars, standards, bumper plates, racks, locks, chalk bins. The cleaning and maintenance of the lifting platform includes ensuring that all equipment is returned after use to prevent obstruction of the area and hazardous lifting conditions. Olympic bars should be properly lubricated and tightened to maintain the rotating bar ends. If standards are used in the area, the base of each should be secure and each standard stored out of the way when not in use. Bent Olympic bars should be replaced and the knurling kept free of debris and chalk buildup by cleaning and brushing occasionally. All locks should be functioning, and wrist straps, knee wraps, and belts should be stored properly. The platform should be inspected for gaps, cuts, slits, and splinters (depending on the type of surface) and properly swept or mopped to remove chalk. The lifting area should be free of benches, boxes, and other clutter to give the lifter sufficient room.

Cleaning supplies should be kept in a locked cabinet located near the office or supervisor station. Supplies should be inventoried and restocked on a regular basis (once or twice each month). These items should be kept in stock (Armitage-Johnson, 1994):
- Disinfectant (germicide),
- Window and mirror cleaner,
- Lubrication sprays,
- Cleaning sprays,
- Spray bottles (about four),
- Paper towels,
- Cloth towels,
- Sponges,
- Broom and dust pan,
- Small vacuum cleaner,
- Vacuum cleaner bags,
- Whisk broom,
- Mop and bucket,
- Shower caps (for bicycle meter equipment), and
- Gum and stain remover (for carpet and upholstery).

Maintenance supplies should be kept in a toolbox located in a locked cabinet. The tool box should contain these items (Armitage-Johnson, 1994):
- File,
- Hammer,
- Pliers (standard and needle-nose),
- Screwdrivers (Phillips and standard),
- Allen wrenches,
- Crescent wrench,
- Rubber mallet,
- Carpet knife,
- Cable splicer parts and appropriate tools,
- Chain splicer parts and appropriate tools,
- Heavy-duty glue,
- Nuts, bolts, washers, nails, and screws in various sizes,
- Transparent tape,
- Masking tape,
- Duct tape,
- Drill and drill bit set,
- Lubricant spray,
- Socket set, and
- Vise grip.

Planning a New Facility

This area will be one of the most popular spaces in the facility. You should expect a mixture of dedicated bodybuilders, recreational weight lifters, dedicated fitness and body tone people, and novices who are just getting interested in strength training. There will be an equal number of men and women involved in strength training programs. Further, this area needs to include space for free weights, strength training machines, cardiovascular and stretching equipment. The designer must consider all these variables and create a room that will fit the needs of all groups.

A strength and cardiovascular training area should provide areas for cardiovascular training, resistance training (divided into free weights and machine weights), and stretching. The design and layout of a facility should provide at least 20 to 40 square feet for each piece of exercise equipment (Tharrett & Peterson, 1997). The exact amount of space is determined by the size of each particular piece of equipment and the recommendations of the manufacturer. Further, "a facility should allow for 20 to 25 sf of space for each person expected to be using the facility at any one time" (Foster & Sol, 1997, p. 51). This is not in addition to the space allocation for equipment previously mentioned.

The designer needs to define the use of the space. This is done by responding to the following questions:
- What programs will be offered, e.g., circuit training, free weights, cardiovascular?
- What is the size of the total membership or the membership registered to use the strength training area?
- What is the approximate peak demand for the area?
- What is the equipment preference (i.e., a mixture of free weights and machines, free weights only, machines only)?
- Is there a high demand for separate or coed areas?
- What type of flooring would be most appropriate?
- Has the equipment been chosen? If yes, who is the vendor, and what are the specific dimensions of the equipment and what is the proposed layout?

Size

The strength training area will include coed free-weight, strength-training, cardiovascular, and stretching areas. A minimum of 9,000 square feet is needed; however, 12,000 square feet is preferred for this space, with at least a 10-foot ceiling. Many new strength and cardiovascular training areas are inadequate when they open, because the designer did not perceive the popularity of the activity during the design stage (Baechle, 1994).

Walls

Three of the walls should be solidly covered with materials that will reduce sound internally as well as externally. The walls should be painted with an epoxy for ease of cleaning. There should be graphics provided to make the walls come alive. Further, numerous mirrors should be placed around the walls. The fourth wall should be constructed of durable glass and face into the lobby/lounge area (with drapes) to further encourage greater use of the area. Each area should have at least one bulletin board (i.e., cardiovascular, weight machines, free weight, and stretching).

Floor

The facility should provide the following types of floor coverings for the strength and cardiovascular training area (Tharrett & Peterson, 1997):

- Cardiovascular area: Anti-static commercial carpet treated with antifungal and antibacterial agents.
- Resistance-training area: A rubber-based resilient floor.
- Stretching area: Nonabsorbent mats or anti-static commercial carpet with antifungal and antibacterial agents.

Platform

In the free-weight area should be at least one platform, 10 feet by 10 feet by 6 inches, constructed of sturdy materials and covered with a rubberized flooring material to be used for heavy weight activities. This platform should be recessed into the concrete slab. Depending on the number of participants, multiple platforms may be needed.

Ceiling

The ceiling clearance needs to be at least 10 feet. The ceiling should be constructed with acoustical ceiling materials. A drop ceiling can be installed for these spaces; however, ceiling panels are more susceptible to damage by objects or individuals and require considerable maintenance. Therefore, it is recommended that a permanent ceiling be considered rather than a drop ceiling.

Electrical

The electrical needs of equipment (i.e., treadmills, stair climbers, computerized bicycles, etc.) in the facility must be considered as well as the equipment layout. There should be numerous receptacles around the perimeter of the room. The designer will need to provide for audio and video needs in the room as well as for computer access.

The lighting in the area should provide at least 50 footcandles of illumination at the floor level. The ideal lighting system has both an indirect and a direct component, throwing surface light on the ceiling to give it about the same brightness as the lighting unit itself. It is recommended that fluorescent lamps be installed since they have the advantage of long life and produce at least two and one-half times the amount of light of incandescent lamps for the same amount of current used.

Sound

The strength and cardiovascular training space by its nature and equipment is a noisy place. Therefore, it is necessary to design the room to accommodate the noise generated. Materials in the walls, on the floor, and in the ceiling should have good acoustical qualities. The sound system should provide equal sound distribution to all areas, not exceeding 90 decibels.

Climate control

When people use weights they generate lots of heat, perspiration, and odor. The designer must consider these problems when designing the mechanical aspects of the room. The three most critical concerns are heating and cooling (68-72° F [22-26° C]), humidity control (55%), and ventilation (8 to 12 exchanges per hour with a 40 to 60 mix outside to inside air). Unfortunately, designers and/or owners neglect these concerns and are extremely disappointed after the facility opens. Climate control can make or break a strength training program.

Security

The room should have provisions for emergency and night lighting.

Special Considerations

The following are special considerations planners should include in the planning process for the strength and cardiovascular training area:

- There should be at least two, 220 volt electrical outlets to service heavy-duty cleaning equipment.
- There should be a provision for a large (40-50 inch) TV with VCR in the cardio respiratory area.
- Commercial structures typically have a 60-pound-per-square-foot load-bearing capacity, but exercise areas need at least 100-pound-per-square-foot capacity.
- The appearance of the room is important. The right ambience entices members to exercise while enjoying their surroundings. Special consideration should be given to the use of mirrors, lighting, carpeting, rubberized flooring, graphics, and skylights.
- Carpeting that extends on the side to wainscoting height serves as an excellent acoustical buffer as a well as protective surface for the free-weight area.
- The color schemes of walls, equipment upholstery, flooring, and ceiling must all be coordinated to appeal to users.

Testing Area

A testing area is a must in any strength and cardiovascular training facility. The testing area should include equipment and space to perform fitness appraisals, such as body composition, functional capacity, strength, flexibility, and/or exercise stress test analysis. The room should be designed according to the testing that will be conducted. The testing protocol will facilitate the determination of the specific space needs.

Size

The testing area includes a fitness testing space (100 to 180 square feet), counseling room (90 to 120 square feet), and seminar room (20 square feet per participant) all with an eight-foot ceiling (Tharrett & Peterson, 1997). There should be adequate space in this area to house two chairs, a desk, a file cabinet, a storage cabinet, a computer station, a bicycle ergometer, a flexibility tester, a treadmill, control console, crash cart, metabolic cart, 12-lead ECG, ECG defibrillator, cholesterol analyzer, examination table, double sink, spine board, and a storage cabinet for equipment such as skinfold calipers, stopwatches, and stethoscope(s).

Walls

Simple drywall construction, epoxy painted with a pleasing color(s), appropriate graphics for the area, and a bulletin board.

Floor

The floors should be carpeted with an antistatic and antifungal commercial-grade carpet, color coordinated with the walls and equipment in the room.

Ceiling

A suspended acoustical panel ceiling is appropriate.

Electrical

The electrical needs of the equipment in the room should be considered as well as the eventual location of the equipment. There should be numerous electrical outlets around the perimeter of the room. The outlets near the sink should be ground fault interrupters (GFI). The recommended lighting for this area is fluorescent units that will produce at least 50 foot-candles of illumination at the floor surface.

Climate control

The mechanical considerations for this space include heating and cooling (68 to 72° F [22 to 26° C]), humidity control (55°), and ventilation (8 to 12 exchanges per hour with a ratio of 40 to 60 outside to inside air). Due to the activities in this room, careful consideration to cooling, humidity control, and ventilation are necessary.

Plumbing

A facility should ensure that every fitness-testing space either has a sink or access to a sink.

Security

There should be emergency lighting and an audible emergency alarm to alert other personnel to a medical emergency in the testing area.

Equipment for the Strength and Cardiovascular Training Area

The International Health, Racquet, and Sportclub Association (IHRSA), National Strength and Conditioning Association (NSCA), and the American College of Sports Medicine (ACSM) recommend that strength and cardiovascular training area planners should consider providing

- a variety of types of equipment for the cardiovascular area, including treadmills, mechanical stair-climbing machines, bicycle ergometers, computerized cycles, rowing ergometers, upper-body ergometers, and total-body-conditioning machines;
- at least one circuit of progressive resistance-training equipment (other than free weights) that includes either a machine or workout station for each of the following muscle groups: gluteus, quadriceps, hamstrings, calves, chest, upper back, lower back, shoulders, triceps, biceps, and abdomen;
- a circuit for resistance-training in a fashion that allows users to train the largest muscle groups first and then proceed to the smaller muscle groups. All compound movement machines should be placed in the circuit before isolated movement machines involving the same muscle(s); and
- a variety of types of free-weight equipment, including a supine bench press with safety pins, incline bench with safety pins, Smith type machine, supine bench, adjustable incline bench, cable crossover system, pull-up or pull-down system, abdominal system, dumbbells, and Olympic-style bar and plates.

Equipment for the Fitness-Testing Area

The NSCA and ACSM suggests that a facility should ensure that its fitness-testing area has the following equipment (Baechle, 1994; Tharrett & Peterson, 1997):

- In the fitness-testing area—a bicycle ergometer, a treadmill or a fixed step device (e.g., a bench) of a desired height, skinfold calipers or other body composition measurement device, sit-and-reach bench on goniometer, tensiometer or other device for measuring muscular strength and endurance, perceived exertion chart, clock, metronome, sphygmomanometer (blood pressure cuff), stethoscope, tape measure, scale, and first-aid kit.
- In the health promotion and wellness area—computer, overhead projector, video system, slide projector, conference table, and chairs.
- In the fitness-testing, health promotion, and wellness area—a system that provides for and protects the complete confidentiality of all user records and meetings.

Cardiovascular Equipment Analysis

Kreighbaum and Smith (1995) analyzed commonly used cardiovascular fitness equipment to determine the advantages and disadvantages of each. The following describes the advantages and disadvantages of cross-country ski simulators, stationary cycles, treadmills, rowing machines, stepping machines, and jumping rope.

Cross-Country Ski Simulators

Advantages

- The potential exists for high-energy expenditure.
- It is a good off-season conditioning method for competition or recreational skiing.
- One can listen to music, converse, or watch TV to divert attention and reduce boredom.
- Simulated skiing is a nonimpact method of exercise that minimizes orthopedic injury.

Disadvantages

- One has to practice the skill required by a specific machine, which may not be similar to actual snow skiing.
- Some machines provide only a relatively easy foot sliding motion with friction control for the arms. For optional training and conditioning, the legs should do most of the work.
- No machine at this time simulates the skating style now used in competition and that of serious recreationalists.
- The energy expenditure value given by one manufacturer (e.g., 600 calories for a 20- minute workout) is unrealistic for the average user. Unrealized expectations from this type of advertising could lead to discouragement.
- Many models have instrumentation to tell how many movement cycles have been completed and/or exercise duration. None have the capability to convert exercise effort into repeatable intensity—a major drawback for the serious exerciser.

Stationary Cycles

Advantages

- They are relatively inexpensive (however, some cost several thousand dollars), compact, and portable.
- One can listen to music, converse, watch TV, or read to divert attention and reduce boredom.
- Cycling eliminates heel-strike forces (only about 0.6 G vs. 3 G while running).
- Some models have meters that display the amount of resistance as well as speed and time. Caloric expenditure can be estimated reasonably well from this information.

Disadvantages

- A "sore behind" can be a problem. Selecting a sex-specific anatomic saddle (broader for females with padding under the "seat bones"), adjusting the seat height properly (almost a straight leg at the lowest pedal position), and using a pressure-reducing seat cover can minimize discomfort. An alternative choice is a model with a chair-like seat (recumbant).
- Many find indoor cycling boring. (However, reading, listening to music, or watching TV can make time pass more rapidly and even profitably if the distraction is entertaining or educational.)

- Cycling only works the legs. Supplemental, upper body, and flexibility exercises are necessary for a balanced program. One model does add some push-pull arm exercise but does not incorporate all muscle groups or use a range of motion to replace stretching.

Treadmills

Advantages

- An exercise session can be precisely controlled by regulating the speed and belt slope- distinct advantage for rehabilitation.
- Heart rate can be monitored by an inexpensive meter or by pulse count. This feature may be a necessity for the person undergoing cardiac rehabilitation, or a nice extra for the serious trainer.
- Once adjusted to walking or running on a treadmill, your stride feels very much like normal walking or running.
- Pace for hills and intervals can be easily set to vary the training session.

Disadvantages

- Cost. Manufacturers have recently entered the home exercise market with scaled-down versions of institutional models. Although these small treadmills cost much less than the larger models, they are still several times the price of an excellent cycle, rowing machine, or ski simulator.
- Size. The home treadmill is small and light enough to be used in a room with a standard ceiling. However, the tradeoffs for small size are little or no elevation capability to simulate hills, a belt width that requires attention to maintain a straight gait, and a short belt length that prohibits safety while running for even an average-sized person. Standard-sized models may be too heavy for house floor supports and require a higher-than-standard ceiling.
- Noise. Laboratories that use treadmills for testing often are isolated to prevent the sound of the machine from bothering others on the same or adjacent floors. There are newer home models with smaller motors and better sound insulation; however, the durability of a smaller motor and light-duty construction may be questionable under prolonged use, or with a heavy person.
- Absence of pleasurable distraction while exercising. Treadmill noise may add either excessive background rumble to music, or cause the listener to turn up the volume to a hazardous level.

Rowing Machines

Advantages

- One uses a larger muscle mass—more than cycling for example.
- One can use more energy per unit of time is than with cycling.
- The use of the hip and back extensors, shoulder horizontal adductors, and arm horizontal extensors makes rowing excellent for posture and possibly may help prevent lower back pain.

- There is no sudden impact stress (as in the foot strike of running).
- Some machines can be folded into a very compact unit for easy storage.

Disadvantages
- Untrained rowers with underdeveloped back, shoulder, and arm muscles may fatigue prematurely due to the limitation of these small muscles.
- The activity may be boring unless attention is distracted (e.g., by listening to music or watching TV).
- The lack of ground impact on the long leg bones may not provide the bone stress necessary to prevent osteoporosis. However, additional weight-bearing exercise such as normal walking could prevent osteoporotic changes.

Stepping Machines

Advantages
- Safety is assured, because no jarring contact occurs as in running or tripping while descending stairs.
- The energy expenditure may be high, comparable to the highest for any aerobic exercise.
- These machines eliminate body-weight loaded lengthening contraction from descending stairs.

Disadvantages
- Many people become bored without diversion (such as listening to tapes or watching TV).
- No upper body or trunk exercise is gained. Climbing should be supplemented with flexibility, trunk, and upper body muscular exercises for a complete program. For example, some devices such as one for wall climbing have been introduced.
- Stepping machines may aggravate knee pain or injury.

Jumping Rope

Advantages
- It is inexpensive. Even the fanciest jumpropes are sold for a nominal price.
- A minimal indoor space requirement or use anywhere outdoors makes rope jumping more convenient than walking, jogging, or running.
- The energy expenditure rate for most adults will be high enough to meet guidelines established by the American College of Sports Medicine.
- In addition to other exercise benefits, some exercise is obtained for the upper body, primarily the shoulders.

Disadvantages
- Rope jumping requires skill. Until sufficiently skilled, you may find exercise intensity too high to maintain; thus rope jumping may be a poor exercise choice for the unconditioned adult.
- Frequent, long jumping sessions (or even infrequent, short sessions if one is overweight) may lead to injury. (Slow, progressive conditioning, proper shoes, and a resilient floor surface can minimize risk.).
- The amount of muscle used jumping rope is less than jogging, which somewhat reduces its overall fitness value.
- Many find rope jumping both difficult and boring, limitations that prevent sufficient frequency and duration to gain significant fitness benefits.

Summary

The development of strength and cardiovascular facilities requires a great deal of specific knowledge about the activities to be carried out within the facility. The planners need to be versed in the programs to be offered and the equipment used in the programs. Finally, the planners need to understand any specific requirements for programs or equipment.

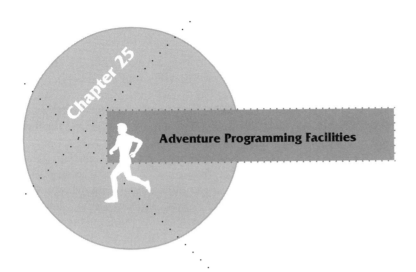

Thomas Horne, United States Military Academy
Ned Crossley, United States Military Academy

There are literally thousands of adventure programs conducted in schools, colleges, summer camps, recreation programs, commercial adventure agencies, YMCA's, and fitness clubs. Adventure programs can be divided into three general categories: (1) Adventure Games, Initiatives Problems and Trust Activities, (2) Adventure-Based Recreation Sports, and (3) Climbing Activities (Ropes Courses and Climbing Walls).

All three categories of adventure activities involve reasonable risk-taking activities designed to foster trust and cooperation, enhance self-image and confidence, and improve physical skills while being fun and exciting. From a facilities standpoint, the least complex and structured category is "Adventure Games, Initiatives Problems and Trust Activities". This category includes simple individual or group games, initiative problems involving group cooperation and innovation, or trust-building activities. "Adventure-Based Recreation Sports Activities" are traditional adventure-based recreation activities like mountain biking, kayaking, canoeing, hiking, skiing, and caving. All of these activities are also appropriate activities to meet adventure program goals; however, neither of these two categories of adventure activities has distinct facilities associated with it. Although these "Adventure Games, Initiative Problems and Trust Activities" and "Adventure-Based Recreation Sports Activities" include popular and effective adventure-oriented activities, they will not be discussed in detail in this chapter since they lack distinctive facilities and utilize a very wide variety of equipment and support materials.

Adventure program activities categorized as "Climbing Activities" usually include challenge ropes courses and climbing walls. There are many variations of climbing walls and a wide variety of both high and low ropes elements. Despite the variety of climbing walls and challenge ropes courses; both have distinctive facility requirements and common features. Climbing facilities may be natural rock climbs, freestanding towers, indoor or outdoor climbing walls, or low bouldering elements that involve lateral climbing. All of these climbing activities involve climbing facilities with handholds, ropes, climbing hardware, and safety equipment. Similarly, ropes courses all have poles or trees as a base and use ropes, wires and wire hardware, pulleys, and safety equipment. This chapter will provide an overview of the common steps in a facility planning process, discuss the structures, equipment and supporting materials needed for climbing walls and ropes courses, and identify safety and administrative considerations for those developing or conducting an adventure program.

Learning Objectives:

After reading this chapter, the student will be able to:
- Discuss the four design and construction planning steps used to develop adventure facilities.
- Identify and compare the three different categories of adventure programs.
- Evaluate selection characteristics for a variety of climbing wall and challenge ropes courses components, such as support poles, ropes, helmets and climbing hardware, handholds, harnesses, and flooring.
- Apply sound safety, risk-management and administrative practices to building and operating adventure facilities.

The Planning Process

The initial step in planning is to establish program goals and determine what type of facility is needed to achieve these goals. In some cases this may require a formal needs assessment. Once a general facility concept is developed, a facility construction strategy is needed. The facility may be self-designed and built, or be designed and built by an outside architect or contractor, or a combination of the two. For example, installing a small bouldering wall (low climbing wall designed for lateral climbing) on an existing wall can be done in-house, but building a large climbing wall or climbing tower is better left to professional climbing wall designers and builders. There are some excellent references that provide detailed information about self-built climbing facilities. For the more complex projects involving outside designers and builders, considerable planning and coordination will be required.

Many schools, colleges, recreation centers, fitness facilities, YMCA's, racquet clubs, commercial climbing centers, and even gymnastics clubs are building adventure program facilities to include ropes courses and climbing walls. Most of these adventure facilities support very popular, highly utilized adventure programs that achieve the goals and objectives of educators and operators. Ask any of the highly successful educators or operators what their secret to success is, and almost every one will mention detailed planning and student-customer-focused programming. In short, they provide a quality product (the adventure facilities) and quality programs (safe, exciting adventure activities).

Whether in a school, community, or commercial setting, building adventure facilities and developing effective adventure programs requires planning. Every parent's guidance, "Do your homework!" is excellent advice for anyone involved in a large project like building and operating an adventure program facility.

Adventure programming is relatively new, so until recently, there weren't many successful adventure programs for novice adventure programmers to use as facility design benchmarks. Today there are many successful adventure programs in operation at schools, fitness clubs, commercial adventure program facilities, and specialized climbing gyms. Lessons learned from both successful and failed programs are valuable planning guidelines for individuals considering developing or improving an adventure program facility.

No two adventure programs are exactly alike, but the planning process for developing and building an adventure facility or other athletic facility is similar. Whether building an indoor or outdoor climbing wall, high ropes course,

low ropes course, comprehensive adventure facility, or any athletic facility, there are common planning steps (See Chapters 3 and 4).

This common recipe for design and construction in Chapters 3 and 4 can be applied to most any athletic facility development project. The exact steps taken and the supporting tasks, coordination, and decisions required will vary with each application. A more detailed description of these planning steps will provide sound guidance on how to proceed with any design process. The next section of this chapter, "Climbing Walls", is written in a facility planning format using the design and development of an indoor climbing wall as an example.

Climbing Walls

The design and constructions steps used in this climbing wall example are similar to the steps that would be followed to design and develop a challenge ropes course or any other athletic facility.

Concept Development and Schematic Design

The initial idea leading to the development of an indoor climbing facility begins with a modest desire to build a simple wall. As the idea is discussed for possible action, it tends to grow. When the idea begins to get serious consideration, the real homework begins by gathering information from as many knowledgeable sources as is feasible. Review recent climbing magazines, contact climbing wall builders, visit other facilities, talk to climbers, check local outdoor climbing sites, and surf climbing and climbing wall web sites. Analysis of existing building codes is advisable at this point to avoid delays

or costly changes. If the climbing wall is part of a multipurpose facility and the architectural engineer is unfamiliar with climbing wall design and construction (most are), the services of a climbing wall or adventure activity consultant may be needed. Most indoor climbing wall and adventure program equipment manufacturers and builders provide these consulting services. Using a professional adventure activities or climbing wall designer often speeds the planning process and results in a more efficient final design.

The motivation to develop a climbing facility is different in each situation, but is often a desire to:

- Use the wall as part of an adventure program.
- Have a climbing facility for personal use or use by a climbing group.
- Include some high-profile architecture (usually in commercial fitness facilities or college recreation centers)
- More efficiently use an underutilized area of the facility (racquetball court, gymnasium wall, hallway, lobby, or storage area)
- Provide a training facility for serious climbers
- Add another fitness development opportunity

Assessing why you want to build a climbing wall helps you determine who will be using the wall and how they will use it. This will guide many of your design criteria decisions. The design concept should meet current needs and provide flexibility for future program growth and development.

The climbing-wall concept will vary greatly, depending on how the climbing wall fits into the overall facility design. The type of wall designed for a commercial indoor climbing gym may be very different from a wall designed for an outdoor adventure program in a public school. Determining how the climbing wall will be integrated into other program and support facilities will also have an effect on the design concept.

The location of the climbing wall in relation to entrances and exits, locker rooms, storage areas, offices, pro shops, water fountains, and other program areas such as the ropes courses, gymnasiums, pools, fitness rooms, racquetball courts, and classrooms will effect design concept decisions. Designers should consider general design criteria like visibility, control, and safety. Also, they need to decide if the climbing wall needs to be near to or isolated from any of the other features. Schematic drawings that show general size, location, and adjacencies will help refine concept development. More than one design option can be explored at this time.

Design Development

The design development phase is decision-making time. If more than one design concept was developed, a decision needs to be made on which design will go to full development. Full development requires the following decisions:

- Scope of the Project—Including budget estimates, funding available, and space allocated for the climbing wall
- HVAC Systems for indoor walls (Heating, Ventilation, and Air-Conditioning)
- Walls, Floor, and Framework—Be sure all the walls and the floor are designed to handle the weight and

live load requirements of a climbing wall. The framework supporting the wall must meet Climbing Wall Industry Standards.
- Wall Surface—Real Rock look, Seamless Cement, Panels, Wood, or doesn't matter
- Wall Height desired
  - Bouldering Wall (12 ft. high or less)—Used primarily for horizontal climbing, normally does not require any top roping, and may require less matting.
  - Commercial Height (25-35 ft.)—High enough to conduct a variety of climbing activities. Climbing walls higher than 35 ft. are more costly and may require longer climbing time and therefore may reduce user capacity and limit climbing opportunities.
  - Competition Walls (May be higher than 35 feet)
  - Training wall—Designed to support military training, rescue training, or other specialized training. (May be higher than 40 feet)
  - Portable walls
  - Climbing treadmills
  - Wall Features—The most important feature is the number, type, and location of handholds.

Other surface features may be built into the wall such as cracks, aretes (corner), depressions, over hangs, caves, ledges, etc. Most of the "real look" type walls have some of these natural features.

- Security—Will the climbing wall be in a self-contained lockable area, or will the wall be in an open area and require some way to limit access to the climbing surface (curtain or other barrier covering the bottom portion of the wall)?
- Flooring—Bouldering walls and walls located in multipurpose locations like gymnasiums often have movable landing mats. Areas used exclusively for climbing usually have specially designed flooring, such as thickly padded carpeting, designed for climbing walls, six inches of rubber pieces, or six inches of gravel. Most new facilities are using the heavily padded carpeting because it provides better protection, is easier to maintain and is cleaner. Current practice calls for protective flooring to extend six feet out from the furthest protrusion of the wall surface.
- Storage—A lot of equipment is required to operate a climbing program (ropes, climbing shoes, harnesses, helmets, carabeners, etc.). The equipment needs to be located near the climbing wall so the storage area for many of the newer climbing walls is built into the back of the wall.

Construction Drawings

Construction drawings are the final detailed drawings used by the construction contractor. Design and construction may be two separate steps. When this is the case, full drawings are completed and approved prior to any construc-

tion. This provides the owner an opportunity to see the entire project in detail, but this may prolong the overall project development time. In other projects, a design-build strategy is used, where the same contractor does the wall design and construction. This approach allows for more flexibility, minimizes the chance of miscommunication between the design architect and the construction contractor, and normally takes less overall development time.

Construction drawings and the supporting narrative descriptions must include all design and material specification. Any significant design changes implemented after the construction drawings are finished may prove to be very costly.

Construction

The most important step in construction is to select a qualified building contractor. If a design-build strategy is used, the contractor selection decision will already have been made. Selecting a contractor with experience in building climbing walls similar to the climbing wall desired is important. Check the contractor's references and visit other facilities built by the contractor if possible.

Once the contractor has been selected, establish a close working relationship with the contractor's construction team. Regular construction meetings should be scheduled to resolve any issues that arise and to provide a formal method of communication.

Planning Summary

Failure to adequately plan (do your homework) and develop a comprehensive project concept often results in a climbing facility that does not have the desired features or meet programming requirements. This may lead to a facility that is unpopular, unsafe, or prematurely obsolete.

Project planners must develop a comprehensive project concept that will guide specific design and operation decisions. Components of a comprehensive project concept for a climbing wall often address the following questions:

- Who are the target facility users? (Who will be climbing on the wall?) The design features for a bouldering facility to teach junior high school students will be

very different from one designed to train lead-climbing mountain guides. Failing to identify the target facility users often results in an inefficient and ineffective climbing facility.
- Will the wall be a stand-alone entity, or will it be used with any other facilities? Climbing walls are often just one element in a comprehensive adventure program.
- What financial resources are available to fund the project?
- How many climbers will use the wall at any one time? (peak load)
- Is this a build new or retrofit of an existing area?
- How much space is available?
- How important are aesthetics? (Is a natural-rock look more important than getting the maximum amount of climbing area?)
- What type of flooring will be best for the facility?
- Do the design features promote safety, minimize maintenance problems, and meet program needs?

Each climbing wall development project is unique and will require design and construction decisions not included in this planning model. This planning model does provide a template to guide the facility planners in developing adventure facilities or any other athletic facility.

Design Features

Building a climbing wall is in many ways like buying a car. Both are sizable investments that involve numerous decisions. Some of these decisions involve selecting which features and options are desired, which are affordable, which will be used, and which will provide the best value. When buying a car, decisions need to be made on the make and model of the car, engine size, color, and a variety of options like trim, floor mats, air conditioning, power steering, antilock breaks, and many others. When building a climbing wall, decisions need to be made on location of the wall (inside or outside), wall surface material, types and quantity of handholds, fixed wall features like overhangs, caves, or cracks, flooring materials, climbing equipment and hardware, and lighting.

Climbing Wall Types

Before selecting individual features of a climbing wall, a decision must be made on what general type of climbing wall is desired. Here is an overview of climbing wall types:

- Homemade—These are usually relatively simple walls made of framing lumber, plywood, paint, and handholds. Individual climbers build homemade walls for their personal use and institutions with limited resources build homemade climbing walls to support their program needs.
- Prefabricated panel system—Prefabricated panels are usually 4'x 8' plywood or fiberglass panels with pre-drilled holes for handholds.
- Portable walls—There are three general types of portable walls: disassemble and reassemble, assembled walls on a trailer, and the portable treadmill type wall.
- Steel structure wall systems—These systems are usually professionally designed and constructed walls with a structural steel frame and plywood surfaces. The surfaces may be coated with a cementitious, fiberglass, or blown synthetic material. Some of the cementitious surfaces have natural features like cracks, ledges, and indentations that are troweled in, while others replicate a real rock-style covering.
- Climbing towers—Towers are usually freestanding wooden towers built outside. They are often just one element of an outdoor adventure course.

The selection criteria most often used in making decisions on the general type of climbing wall to be built are program requirements, funding amounts, space available, and staff proficiency.

Climbing Wall Features and Equipment

Handholds—Most new climbing walls have movable handholds that are attached to the wall with a "T-nut" insert. These "T-nut" inserts may be installed by the contractor as part of the construction, purchased as part of pre-drilled wood or fiberglass panels, or added to climbing panels as part of a homemade project.

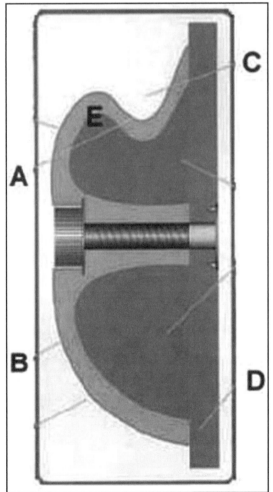

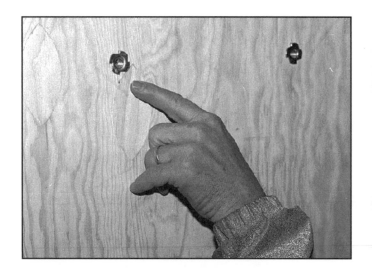

Handholds may be simple wood blocks fixed to the wall surface with epoxy glue, wood screws, "T-nuts", or a combination of these. Wooden handholds are relatively inexpensive, have a forgiving texture, and can be formed in a wide variety of shapes and sizes. Wooden handholds don't duplicate real rock shapes and textures very well. If a real rock shape or texture is desired, then commercially manufactured handholds made of resin and fillers may be the way to go. Serious builders of homemade wall can fabricate handholds from automobile body putty, but this is a technical process not recommended for most wall builders. Most of the commercial handholds are designed for use with a "T-nut" system, but some can be attached to the wall with epoxy cement. There are literally thousands of different types, sizes, and shapes of handholds. Handhold packages are available that includes handholds that replicate natural features in rocks and requires to climbers to use specific grip and foot techniques. Handhold color and texture may attempt to duplicate natural rock, match the existing wall surface, or add color and flare to a climbing wall. Colored-coded handholds may be used to designate specific climbing routes or difficulty levels. Colored or numbered tags can also be attached to the handholds to mark specific climbing routes. The greatest benefit of having movable handholds is that the handholds can be moved, replaced, or simply rotated, providing the climber with an infinite variety of climbing opportunities, route changing.

Climbing Equipment

The size and the scope of the climbing program and climbing wall will determine how much climbing equipment is needed. Magazines and catalogues are filled with a plethora of climbing gear and hardware. Standard equipment for general climbing programs include ropes, harnesses, helmets, belay system, and locking D carabiners. The UIAA (Union of International Associations of Alpinists) certifies that climbing equipment is safe and effective. Purchasing UIAA-certified climbing equipment is a sound practice. The specific selection criteria used to purchase equipment will vary with each application, but the following are general selection criteria for standard pieces of climbing equipment:

- Ropes—Most climbing programs use 11 mm dynamic kernmantle ropes (continuous parallel nylon fibers surrounded by a nylon sheath) as their primary climbing ropes. They provide an excellent combination of strength, stretch, and suppleness. Kernmantle ropes are classified as "dynamic ropes", ropes that stretch so they can absorb some of the shock if there is a fall.
- Harnesses—The harness secures the climber to the climbing rope. Step-in pre-made commercial harnesses are recommended, because they are more secure, comfortable, and convenient than self-made rope or tubular nylon harnesses, but they are more expensive.

- Helmets—Climbing helmets are essential pieces of safety equipment for many climbing and ropes course elements. Purchasing quality adjustable helmets will provide an extra margin of safety, make adjustments easier, and prove to be good investments since they will last longer.
- Belay System—There are numerous types of belay systems, but all are designed to protect the participant from making an uncontrolled fall. Most belay systems are a rope threaded through some hardware (usually two carabiners or a shear reduction devise), or over a belay bar at the top of the wall. One end of the rope is secured to the climber's harness, and the person belaying holds the other end, which is anchored, to the floor.
- Climbing Shoes—Serious climbing programs should have climbing shoes available. Tight-fitting climbing shoes with high-traction rubber soles facilitate good footwork. Climbing shoes clearly make for a better climbing experience. Even when climbing on outdoor all-wood walls or when climbing on novice bouldering walls.
- Locking 11 mm Carabiners—Locking carabiners should be used for climbing and challenge ropes courses activities.

Purchasing, inspecting, and maintaining high-quality climbing gear is very important in protecting climbers from injury and owners and operators from costly litigation.

Climbing Wall Standards

The Climbing Wall Industry Group (CWIG) and the Climbing Gym Association (CGA), both sub-groups of Outdoor Recreation Coalition America (ORCA), have helped establish enforceable climbing wall industry standards. CWIG and CGA standards are not presently required by law or government regulation, but a climbing facility, whether homemade or commercially designed and constructed, should comply with CWIG and CGA technical standards.

The American College of Sports Medicine (ACSM) has also established guidelines and standards for operating climbing facilities (Sol & Foster, 1992). The ACSM guidelines and standards focus much more on program and administrative procedures and less on technical design and construction features. ACSM recommends:

- Climbing wall areas must be supervised at all times by a qualified instructor.
- Supervisors should have CPR and First Aid certification and emergency equipment and supplies must be available.
- Climbing staff should undergo periodic in-service training.
- All policies and emergency procedures must be posted.
- Individuals participating in climbing activities must show proficiency in belay techniques, rope-handling skills, and climbing signals.
- All climbing equipment and facilities must be inspected on a regular basis and appropriate corrective actions taken.
- All climbing ropes must be Union International Association of Alpinist (UIAA) static ropes.
- The climbing wall area must be allotted sufficient space.
- Negative air pressure should be maintained in indoor climbing areas, external air is drawn into the climbing area.
- The surface area of the climbing wall should have a moderately abrasive texture.
- Appropriate temperature (68-70 Degrees Fahrenheit), humidity (60% or less), and air circulation (8-10 changes per hour) should be maintained in indoor climbing areas.
- Mercury Vapor or fluorescent lights are recommended, with a lighting level of 50 footcandles at the surface of the floor.

Government laws and regulations do not currently cover adventure activity design, construction, and program operations. Everyone building or operating a climbing facility should follow CWIG, CGA, and ACSM guidelines. Local laws and regulations that governing zoning, construction, and safety must also be reviewed to ensure compliance.

Climbing Facility Operation

Climbing is an exciting activity that isn't nearly as dangerous as it looks, but certainly is not without risk. Owners and operators of climbing facilities must protect themselves and their organization with insurance. Establishing sound standard operating procedures and conscientiously enforcing them will protect climbing participants and provide some legal protection for owners and operators. Each climbing program and facility will require custommade policies and procedures to maintain a safe and secure climbing environment. The following is a list of recommended policies and procedures for conducting climbing and adventure programs:

- Warn participants that climbing is a potentially dangerous activity. (The participant will then assume at least part of the risk of climbing.) Have climbers sign a waiver of liability form prior to climbing.
- Post appropriate signage with safety warnings, policies, and procedures to be followed, emergency contact numbers, and any facility specific rules.

- Hire highly qualified instructors and staff and keep their training current.
- Conduct regular formal equipment and facility inspections and keep documented records of inspections made and corrective actions taken.
- Supervise climbing activities with a qualified instructor.
- Secure the climbing area when not in use.
- Buy quality equipment and keep it well maintained.
- Train and certify belayers.
- Maintain a written set of policies and procedures, operations manual.
- Keep emergency equipment and supplies available.
- No horseplay should be permitted.
- Warn participants about loose clothing or allowing long hair to hang loose, because they may get tangled in the ropes or hardware.
- Always make a final equipment check before beginning a climb. (A buddy check is recommended.)
- Review communications procedures prior to starting a climb.
- Jewelry, including watches, should not be worn while climbing.
- Students must be given proper training and demonstrate appropriate skills before attempting the more difficult climbs.

This is not a comprehensive list of all risk-management issues associated with climbing, but it does provide guidance on the kinds of issues to be addressed.

High- and Low-Challenge Ropes Courses

As stated earlier in this chapter, adventure programs can be divided into three general categories: (1) Adventure Games, Initiatives Problems, and Trust Activities, (2) Adventure-Based Recreation Sports, and (3) Climbing Activities (Ropes Courses and Climbing Walls). Challenge ropes courses, especially low ropes elements, can be incorporated into any of the three categories of adventure programs, but is most often included as part of "Climbing Activities." This section of the chapter will define ropes courses, discuss the philosophy of adventure programming, describe some high- and low-challenge ropes elements, and provide guidance on how to develop and maintain high- and low-challenge ropes elements for an adventure program.

"A Ropes Challenge Course is a series of individual and group activities designed to foster team-building, group cohesion, cooperation, leadership, problem-solving skills, communication skills, healthy risk-taking, and individual commitment" (Upward Enterprises, 2000). By definition, challenge ropes courses are appropriate to be included in adventure programs. They certainly provide the challenge for the motto "Challenge by Choice," which is the foundation for many of the adventure programs (Rohne, 1989). Ropes courses can develop personal confidence, foster mutual support, and enhance physical agility and coordination while providing a healthy outdoor experience. Although completing high and low ropes elements requires some physical skills, the focus of these challenge ropes courses is to develop the whole individual. The learners must do the challenges:

- Standing alone, "no else but me".
- In pairs, whereby it is "my buddy and me".
- That depend on the entire team for success, "we're in it together".

The personal impact of the journey through the ropes course is much more important than simply completing the course. The personal growth and group satisfaction gained by participating in the challenge ropes elements is why ropes courses are often part of a comprehensive adventure program.

Design and Development of Challenge Ropes Courses

The design and development process for high- and low-challenge ropes courses is the same as described in the previous section on climbing walls. (Concept Development and Schematic Design, Design Development, and Construction.) In an ideal situation, the vision of the desired facility and program would be clearly stated and agreed upon by all. There would be all the funding needed to plan and build the challenge ropes course. In this case, the best course of action would be to contract with an experienced and reputable professional adventure facilities builder to build a ropes course that meets all Association of Challenge Course Technology (ACCT), the recognized agency ropes courses and standards.

Most individuals or groups that build challenge ropes courses don't have an ideal situation. They have to find a suitable location, scratch for adequate funding, promote the adventure facility and program to their leadership, and scramble to find enough qualified people to run the program. Whether in an ideal situation where expert professional advise is available every step of the way, or if the project is going to be a self-designed and homemade project with minimal direct professional help, there are some basic conceptual design and development decisions that need to be made. The ACCT provides industry standards for building ropes courses. Completed ropes courses should meet ACCT certification standards.

One of the first decisions and often relatively easy ones is whether the ropes course will be an indoor course, an outdoor course, or a combination of the two. Many challenge ropes programs are part of a larger outdoor education program, so the most common site for a challenge ropes course is outside.

The next two decisions, site location and supporting base type, are often linked. A decision needs to be made if the ropes course will be tree-based, using natural trees to support the ropes course; pole-based, which uses telephone type poles; or climbing tower-based, where a tower is used as part of the support structure of the ropes course. A tower-based course may also use natural trees, poles, or both for additional support points. The nature of the site available often dictates the type of supporting base used. If there are no trees at the proposed site, then poles or towers must be used. If appropriate trees are available to be used as the challenge ropes course foundation, the amount of rock base, ground slope, erosion potential, natural water, and environmental sensitivity of the area are all factors to consider in selecting the type of supporting base. Using natural trees is less expensive than using poles or towers, so financial considerations may also be a factor in both site location and base support structure. Visiting a highly successful, established challenge ropes course is always a good idea in this early stage of planning. Also, be sure to check on local zoning regulations and building specifications before making the final site and support system selection.

Many of the challenge ropes courses have both low ropes courses and high ropes courses. Low ropes courses are characterized by group challenges that require cooperation, communication, sharing, creativity, and trust. High ropes courses are characterized by "perceived high-risk" activities that require individuals to work through their fears and anxiety, as they negotiate the high challenges. The common learning objectives of the adventure program will be the primary factors for determining if both a low ropes course and a high ropes course are desired. The next sections will provide a more detailed discussion of both high and low ropes courses and the challenge elements typically included in each.

The Common Learning Objectives of Challenge Ropes Courses

- Commitment and respect
- Communication
- Fun, exhilaration, and challenge
- Physical challenge and skill
- Risk taking mentally, physically, and emotionally
- Fear management
- Teamwork, full participation, and common goals
- Leadership and ability to follow
- Problem solving
- Safety education
- Trying to be one's best
- The joy of effort
- Exceeding one's perceived limits
- Trust, cooperation, caring, and compassion
- Physical fitness and coordination

Low-Challenge Ropes Course

The physical distinction between a low ropes course and a high ropes course is that low ropes courses incorporate only challenge elements that are lower than 1.5 meters or five feet, while high-ropes courses include elements that are much higher. Low-ropes elements are generally designed to present group challenges. Each individual is challenged, but an emphasis is placed on group effort and cooperation. Since the elements are relatively low, particants perform most of the spotting and safety procedures. Low-ropes course management is on or near the ground. Low-ropes courses do not require the harnesses, climbing ropes and belayers, or "cowstail" tethers of the high-rope course.

No two low-challenge ropes courses are exactly alike, but most have variations of common low-ropes elements. These general elements are:
- Rope swing on knotted rope
- Spider's web or hanging tire
- Traversing and balancing the swinging log
- Tension traverse on low cable wire with overhead rope
- Traverse the diverging cable wires
- Balance beam traverse

- The low wall
- Higher log beam
- Swinging tires traverse
- Catwalk or twin cable wire feet only traverse

Typical Low Ropes Elements

Despite being called low-ropes courses, many low-ropes courses include non-rope elements, such as tires, logs, walls, nets, trapezes, platforms, and natural features.

High-Challenge Ropes Courses

High-ropes courses are challenge courses that have elements over 1.5 meters (five feet) high. Many high-ropes challenge course elements are from 24-45 feet in the air. Gear is required to negotiate the high-ropes course like climbing harnesses, helmets, climbing ropes, tethers known as "cowtails" or lanyards, and an overhead top rope belay pulley system. Even a challenge vertical wall of eight-14 feet or a suspended log up 10 feet is considered a high-ropes course element. A person could fall from a high-ropes course element and suffer serious injury despite hand-spotting and a prepared landing zone. Due to the danger of falling from these heights, some type of technical fall-protection system that includes positive spotting is essential. Most high-ropes elements use a belay rope strung through an elevated carabiner or shear reduction device. High-ropes courses are usually done by a single person or by small groups with each individual traversing the element followed by the other in the group. Management and supervision of high-ropes course are usually from the ground with students up on the high-ropes elements.

- Vertical rope ladders, cargo nets, or log rungs
- Centipede poles with staples, firecracker ladders
- Inclined log, fidget ladder, or beam
- High- and low-cable bridge traverse
- Balancing beam log traverse
- Zip wire on a pulley
- Trapeze dive
- Pamper pole or high pedestal
- Trapeze or knotted rope swing
- Twin wire cable or rope traverse
- Cable traverse with hanging rings or vertical ropes for hands

operated ropes courses are potentially dangerous, so all participants need to be informed of the potential danger and should sign a waiver of liability form (Assumption of Risk). Other ropes course operation considerations can be divided into Administrative and Staff, Equipment, and Maintenance issues. An overview of these operations issues is provided below. These are by no means complete lists of all operational considerations, but are intended to provide a starting point for ropes course operators.

Ropes Courses Administration and Staffing

- Purchase and maintain liability insurance for the organization and the staff.
- Provide professional training for all staff members.

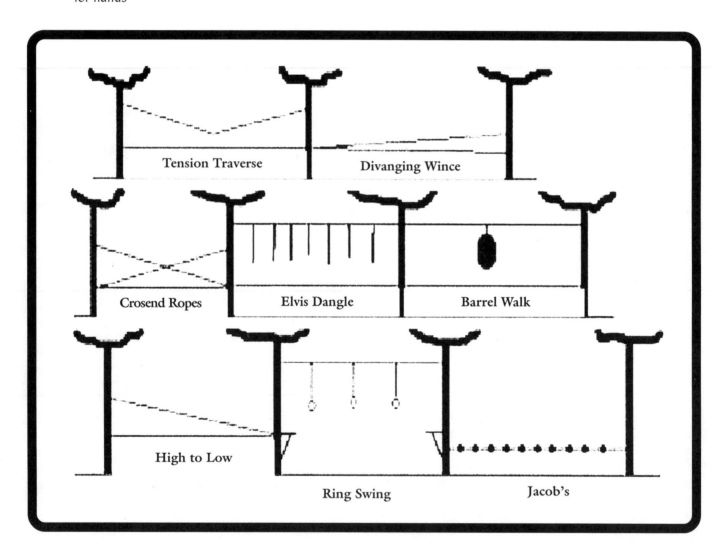

Typical High-Challenge Ropes Course Elements

Ropes Courses Operations

The overall safety record of challenge ropes courses is very good, among the safest of all physical programs (Project Adventure 2001). The Association of Challenge Course Technology (ACCT) has established safety and construction standards to provide guidelines for the safe and efficient operation of challenge ropes courses. Even well-planned and well-

Administrators must provide sufficient funding to ensure that staff are up-to-date on current policies, procedures, and techniques.

- Keep accurate records of staff training, program operations and procedures, maintenance inspections and repairs, liability forms, insurance, student training records, and accident reports.
- Maintain a comprehensive inventory and use equipment sign-out sheets to maintain property accountability.

Ropes Course Maintenance

Inspect the entire ropes course and the supporting equipment on a regular basis. A comprehensive annual inspection should be conducted, preferably by an ACCT-certified inspector.

- Use pressure-treated lumber for outdoors ropes courses. Weatherproof wood parts as needed. (Annually is best if feasible.)
- Use only healthy trees with a solid root system as support trees.
- Use wood chips or bark mulch around the base of trees to protect the soil from compaction.
- Immediately replace dead or insect-infected trees. Tree are susceptible to weather, insects, disease, rotting, and need to be checked regularly.
- Trim and cleared broken or overgrowing limbs.
- Remove splinters and rough edges on all wood parts.
- Replace and repair all rotten or cracked wood.
- Reset protruding nails as necessary.
- Check for rotting of the poles in the ground.
- Use only galvanized metal items such as bolts, cable, cable locks, rapid links, and other metal parts. Cables should be 3/8" wire rope that is 7 x 19 (seven strands with 19 wires per strand).
- Tighten nuts and bolts, turnbuckles, and clamps as required.
- Temporarily cover all frayed cable ends with tape until they can be fitted with a permanent sleeve.
- Inspect cables for smoothness. Cables need to be smooth if a participant's hands or feet will touch the cable.

Challenge Ropes Course Equipment

- Use Union International Association of Alpinists (UIAA)-certified climbing ropes and screwgate locking carabiners. (The same ropes and carabiners used for climbing.)
- Install only stainless steel or galvanized hardware on outdoor ropes courses.
- Have participants wear an adjustable harness. A more secure chest harness is often used instead of the standard waist harness.
- Maintain positive security while on the ropes course using "lobster claws." (Two locking carabiners at-tached to the participant by two shock-absorbing lanyard.) One carabiner is locked onto the new security cable before the other carabiner is unclipped from the previous security cable.
- Minimize rope wear and damage by using a shear reduction device.
- Always have a first-aid kit available.
- Store equipment in a cool, dry place, preferably adjacent to the ropes course.
- Include lightning protection on high-ropes courses.
- Require helmets be worn on high or dangerous elements.
- Use a "gravity break" on a zip-line element. The zip-line pulley system slides to the bottom of a cable arc and then slows to a stop as it rolls up the sloping

cable. A trust break is the alternative where other participants or staff stop the participant on the zip line.

Summary

Adventure programs involve reasonable risk-taking activities designed to foster trust and cooperation, enhance self-image and confidence, and improve physical skills while being fun and exciting. Adventure activities are usually done as games or problems, sports or recreational activities, or as climbing activities. Only programs that include climbing activities tend to have distinct facilities and equipment, climbing walls and challenge ropes courses. The planning, designing, and building process for these adventure program facilities is similar to that of any other athletic facilities. Common design and construction planning steps include creating a schematic design, developing this design, establishing construction drawings, and contracting with a contractor to build the facilities. Throughout this process, many design, construction, and equipment decisions need to be made. Having a comprehensive vision for both the program and the support facilities will guide many of these facility and equipment decisions. Climbing walls and challenge ropes courses are specialized facilities that must be built to industry standards, and building them usually requires the assistance of experienced adventure program facility builders or consultants.

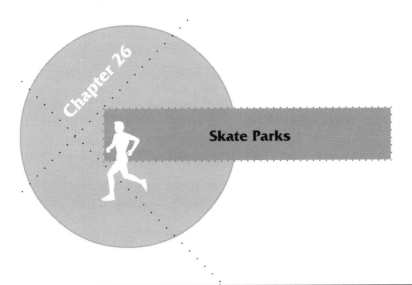

Chapter 26

Skate Parks

Thomas H. Sawyer, Indiana State University

"Just as golfers design golf courses, skaters should design skateparks."

Michael McIntyre, ASLA, Landscape Architect

In the new millennium there continues to be a skate boarding renaissance. Facility develop-ment, equip ment quality, skateboarders' techniques and abilities, and participant attitudes and maturity levels have all reached new peaks. High-performance facilities and equipment for every style of skating are available. The abilities of professional skaters visibly advance each month, seeing athletes (yes, I said athletes) literally reaching new heights. Skaters have become less clique-oriented and more open-minded. All disciplines of skating are now respected.

These changes have made skating more accessible to many different people of varying ages. Presently, there are over 10 million skaters in the United States, making it the sixth largest sport. (National Inline Hockey Association [NIHA], 2000) Skateboarding has become the third-most popular sport among six to 18 year olds. (International Association of Skateboard Companies [IASC], 2001) Further, one in 10 U.S. teenagers owns a skateboard. [IASC, 2001]

The popularity that skateboarding now enjoys is also reflected in the media. Skateboarding is regularly featured on major T.V. networks such as Fox, MTV, TSN, OLN, ESPN's notorious Extreme-Games (X-Games), and NBC's Gravity Games, thus bringing it into today's spotlight. Finally, this coverage, along with skating's appearance in marketing campaigns for Nike, The Gap, The National Fluid Milk Processor Promotion Board, Coca-Cola, and Nintendo, has seen skateboarding appear on billboards, in magazines, and on television. All this exposure has greatly expanded public acceptance of skaters and skating.

Instructional Objectives

The student will be able to:
- develop a plan for a safe skateboard park.

History of Skateboarding

In the 1950s, surfers created skateboarding in order to pass the time when the ocean was flat. Roller-skate mounts and wheels were innocently nailed to 2×4s. This was the birth of the "sidewalk surfer." The earlier skateboard parks in the '50s and '60s reflected the surfer's passion for fluid, wavelike forms, and smooth sensations.

In 1970, the urethane wheel was applied to the skateboard. Skateboard-specific trucks appeared in 1973, which was followed by precision bearings in 1975. Being of higher performance than their predecessors, these new products allowed for an easier, more enjoyable ride. These improvements encouraged advancements in maneuvers, more challenging facilities, and spawned a skateboarding boom that supported massive private skateboard parks across the United States and in Europe. The parks perfected the backyard pools, drainage pipes, and ditches that skaters had taken to riding. However, the demand for parks encouraged the development of poorly designed and constructed parks. This opened the door to insurance and liability problems. As a result, 80% of these parks were bulldozed in 1979, with the rest closing soon afterward. Some public parks remained, but basically skaters were left with nowhere to go, and many simply quit.

Yet during the '80s, the remaining dedicated and innovated skaters continued to push the value of the sport. Many changes took place in the design of facilities and equipment. The wooden backyard half pipe ramps began their evolution, which led to today's modern half pipes.

Presently, there is a resurgence in building skateboard parks. This has occurred because of the demand to remove skaters from city streets and public spaces. Skaters took to the streets because most of the skateparks had closed during '80s, and they developed the "streetstyle" of skating creatively, adapting moves done in a pool or ramp in the deceased parks of the '70s to curbs, ledges, steps, handrails, and walls. Communities became concerned about the skaters, and some considered them rebellious and a public nuisance.

Skateparks have come a long way from the early, unsafe private parks to the well-designed safe public parks of today. The new facilities are larger and safer, and the skaters are using better designed equipment and safety gear. Skateboarding is fast becoming a very safe and exciting sport for young (six-18) males (74%) to spend their spare time perfecting their skills.

Liability

Liability is always a question when dealing with sport in general. Therefore, it is paramount that owners (public or private) carefully plan for a safe facility for participants and spectators. Today most insurance companies do not view skateparks as a high risk for governmental agencies. They are no more dangerous than swings and slides. Yet, it is advisable to make sure the facility is covered with the same blanket plan as the city or town (see Figure 26.1 Summary of Insurance Carriers).

It is further advisable that the agency seriously consider safety when planning the skatepark. Signs should be posted indicating hours of operations, pad and helmet requirements, and the park is used at the participant's risk. The public agency needs to also consider the level of supervision that it should provide. Current common practice with skateparks is to leave the park open to "free play" with no supervision (i.e., similar to playgrounds). This practice will decrease the agency's liability. However, the operator must make sure the area is safe, free of hazards, inspected regularly, and well maintained (i.e., similar to swimming pools at motels/hotels, where legislation protects those who have proper and adequate signage, a fence around the pool, safety equipment available, and the pool is maintained regularly).

The passage of numerous pieces of state legislation has allowed local public agencies to build unsupervised skateparks and post signs requiring safety equipment to be worn while skating. Unsupervised skateparks are very popular with skaters, but care has to be taken to build them in safe locations. If you do not have an ideal location, you may want to consider a supervised park or partnering with a private skatepark or other youth group, such as a church, Boys & Girls Club, or YMCA.

Immunity for Extreme Sports Parks

The Indiana General Assembly provided in Senate Bill 0141 (2001) that public and private owners and operators of extreme sports parks or recreation areas are immune from civil damages for injuries caused by extreme sports if: (1) the extreme sports park or recreation area is designed or maintained for the purpose of extreme sports use; (2) a set of rules governing the use of the facility is clearly posted at each entrance to the extreme sports park or recreation area; and (3) a warning concerning the hazards and dangers associated with the use of the facility is clearly posted at the entrance to the extreme sports park or recreation areas, are immune from civil damages for injuries, if the extreme sports park or recreation area is closed and has a warning against entry posted at each entrance. Other states have similar statutes and it is important for planners to pay attention to the three provisions outlined above when planning a skate park.

Safety Statistics

In 1968, the U.S. Consumer Safety Commission (CPSC) ranked sports & recreation equipment on a mean severity index that ranged from 10 to 2516 (10 being the least severe). Swimming pools were given 335, bicycles 70, and skateboarding 34. There have been three deaths involving skateboarders in the United States since 1970, and these incidents involved motor vehicles. Table 26.1 provides the results of a recent survey conducted by the United States National Electronic Injury Surveillance System.

Of those injured, 33% had been skating less than one week, 20% were people borrowing boards, and 95% had received out-patient care. Most noteworthy is that 50% of the accidents occurred in unsafe areas where the skater struck an irregularity in the riding surface. Therefore, by providing and maintaining a professionally designed skatepark instead of leaving these kids in the street, the above numbers would likely dramatically decrease.

General Planning Criteria

There are many sources of information on skateboard techniques and design of bowls, ramps, and other ancillary facilities. The following information is general in nature and provides the planners a place to begin this type of project.

Figure 26.1
Insurance Carriers

K&K Insurance Company
310-473-2522

Gelfand Newman Wasserman
general liability, participant & event insurance
310-473-2522

Cities Securities Corporation
800-800-2489

International Special Events & Recreation Assoc.
801-942-3000

Joint Powers of Insurance Agency
562-467-8720

Association of Bay Area Pooled Liability Network
510-464-4900

Association of Washington Cities Risk Management
360-753-4137

Table 26.1
Percent of Injuries in Common Sports

Sport	Participants	Injuries	% of Injuries
ice hockey	1,700,000	61,264	3.60
football	14,700,000	409,206	2.78
basketball	29,600,000	761,358	2.57
soccer	10,300,000	146,000	1.42
baseball	36,600,000	437,207	1.26
volleyball	20,500,000	112,120	.54
skateboarding	6,200,000	27,718	.49

Location

The planners should evaluate potential sites by considering the following issues: (1) potential usage of area (i.e., demographic analysis and a needs assessment), (2) size of site (i.e., how big is big enough), (3) access to public transportation, (4) drainage for the site, (5) access to public utilities, (6) nose pollution, (7) nuisance avoidance, (8) spectator seating, (9) parking, and (10) emergency access.

Safety

The following design features address safety issues that need to be considered by planners: (1) safe spectator areas, (2) low-maintenance site, (3) adequate sight lines of the area for supervision as well as viewing activities by spectators, (4) protective netting or barriers to guard against serious falls and to impede flying skateboards, (5) safety lighting, (6) emergency access, (7) exposure to environmental elements such as wind, rain, lightning, or sun, (8) shaded areas, and (9) drinking fountains.

Other considerations

The following are a few additional considerations for planners to think about in the design of the skatepark: (1) adequate lighting for night activities, (2) facilities for skateboarding are suitable for other disciplines such as in-line skating or rollerblading (i.e., recreational speed skating, in-line hockey, and freestyle or aggressive skating), and BMX bikes, (3) noise and light intrusion on neighbors, and (4) north or south orientation rather than an east or west setting.

Consulting Services

The services that are normally provided by consultants (i.e., architect, landscape architect, skaters, and safety experts) in this area include:
- preparing a demographic survey of the local skate community,
- assisting in the site selection.
- determining designs and construction parameters (e.g., wood v. concrete, size, budget, amenities),
- acting as an intermediary between owners and local skaters,
- organizing and establishing a pro-shop, (i.e., contacting vendors, preparing initial orders, etc.),
- preparing of drawings for public venues, and
- developing design specifications for either wood or concrete skateparks.

Design Services

Skateparks are designed of either concrete, steel, or wood. The designs are unique and customized to the specific site, wishes of the local skaters, and the needs of the owners. The park should be designed to provide the skaters with a fun and safe place to skate. Skateparks should include elements for all levels of skating ability, from beginners to advanced with sufficient variety to challenge and keep them coming back for more. Elements are designed with the proper transitions and heights, and the layouts allow flow from one element to the next.

The designer of a skatepark should thoroughly understand skatepark design, site preparation (i.e., surveying, soil testing, etc.), and structural engineering (see Figure 26.2 for listing of builders, consultants, and designers). The designer chosen should be able to provide the following services:
- conducting preliminary consulting services appropriate to design considerations,
- preparing custom concept designs for wood, concrete, or combination of the two,
- developing detailed construction drawings for wood skateparks,
- preparing detailed drawings for concrete parks,
- providing budget estimates (see Figure 26.3),
- preparing detailed specifications for wood park construction,
- consulting with concrete and steel contractors on design elements, and
- producing drawings in various formats using the latest version of AutoCad (See Figure 26.4 Samples of Skatepark Designs http://www.skatedesign.com).

American Ramp Company
fax. 417. 206.6888
www.arc-ramp.com

Ramps R Us
fax. 417. 206.6888

Figure 26.2
Builders, Consultants, and Designers

The following is a listing of builders and designers of skateboard parks:

Anywhere Sports Productions
ph: 310.823.1826 - 949.360.6970
fax. 949.360.7303

Benshoof, Withers,& Sandgren Ltd
818.952.7606
fax. 818.952.7607
www.bwsla.com

BG Consultants Inc
785.749.4474
fax. 785.749.7340
www.bgcons.com

Big Daddy Inc
714.893.5621
fax 714.893.5631
www.bigdaddyinc.com

Cissell Design Group
ph: 203.245.4250
fax. 203. 245.7684
www.cissell-design.com

Dave Duncan Designs
714.960.8636
fax. 714.848.6343

FSU Inc, Functional Sculptures
  Unlimited
1.888.753.2124 - 719.229.7970
kpatterson@fsuinc.org

Grind Co
310.330.0554
fax. 310.330.0409
www.grindco.net

Hirsch & Associates
Chuck Foley
714.776.4340
fax 714.776.4395
www.hha.landarch.com

Land Image Landscape Architects
530.899.1913
fax 530.899.1920

Lawrence R. Moss & Associates
818.248.5200
fx.818.248.6574
www.lrmassoc.com

Mark Podgurski Enterprise
814.349.5633
fax. 814.349.5643
office@woodwardcamp.com

Monkey Manufacturing
530.223.7400
fax. 530.223.7418
johnpfarr@msn.com

Pierce Enterprises
571.633.7583
fax. 517.631.6365

Purkiss Rose Landscape Architects
714.871.3638
fax.714.871.1188
www.skateparkdesigner.com

Ramptech Inc
703-492-2378
fax 703.492.1023
www.ramptech.com

Robo Ramps
ph & fax 909.247.5289

Skateparks Inc
781.544.2020
fax 781.545.6021

Spectrum Skatepark Creations Ltd
604.905.3467
www.mountain-inter.net/spectrum

Spohn Ranc
626.330.5803
fax 626.330.5503
www.spohnranch.com

Suburban Rails
740.593.8145
fax 740.592.5235
www.suburbanrails.com

Team Pain
ph & fax 407. 695.8215
www.teampain.com

Trueride
218.525.2625
fax 218.525 2850
www.trueride.com

Twister Skate Designs
619.226.6241
fax. 619.226.6010

Vertical Consultants
330.782.1456
fax. 330.533.1413

VPI Industries
John Tyson (JT)
ph & fax : 707.537.6803
www.access1.net/vpi

Vertical Skateramps
www.verticalskate.ch

Wally Hollyday Designs
562.438.7122
fax 562.856.5445
www.skatedesign.com

Wormhoudt Landscape
  Architecture Inc
831.426.8424
fax 831.426.8411
www.skateparks.com

Wood Ramp Construction

Wood ramps can withstand many years of abuse by both skaters and the weather. The critical factors are that wood ramps are designed properly, built by experienced carpenters, and constructed of the right materials. The advantages of wood parks is that they are relatively inexpensive, easy to build, and can be placed on an existing concrete or asphalt pad. In addition, most wood equipment can be moved to change the configuration of the park, creating new challenges for the skaters to enjoy. (See Figures 26.5-6 for types of ramps)

Generally specifications for outdoor wood parks include: (http://www.suburbanrails.com)

Figure 26.3
General Information On Skatepark Costs

Portable Parks & Wood Parks—as little as $3,000 and up to $100,000 with the average park being 10,000 sq.ft feet and costing around $25,000 require regular maintenance—surfaces may be masonite, plywood, birch, skatelite or skatelite pro advantages—portable, movable, affordable

Steel Frame Skateparks—steel frame with metal or skatelite surfaces—permanent parks— can be bolted to existing concrete pad some maintenance—more expensive than wood with a 10,000 sq.ft.park starting at around $30,000 advantages—park can be reconfigured, weatherproof, affordable

Concrete Parks—concrete starting as low as $10 sq. ft. averages $16 sq. ft. and as high as $20 sq. ft. depending on excavation, grading, drainage, irrigation,water table etc. average 10,000 sq. ft park $140,000 you must work with qualified builders & designers and make sure the concrete crew is experienced mistakes made in concrete are expensive and permanent and are happening too often 2 bowls ($132,000) were built and the concrete crew brushed the finish making them unskateable advantage—no maintenance, permanent park

Figure 26.4
Skatepark Design

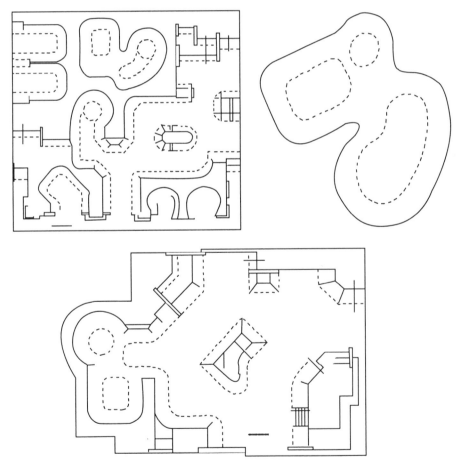

Graphic by Meghan Sawyer

- all wood should be pressured treated,
- 3/4 plywood transition templates, on ends and every 4' or 6',
- 2" x 6" joists, spaced 8" on center, 4' spans/double joists every 24",
- 2 layers of 1/2 plywood sub-surface,
- 3/8 polyboard, 1/4 Skatelite or 12-gauge steel ramp surface,
- 12 ga." x 24" steel for all ramp bottoms,
- 1/4 Polyboard on ramp decks,
- coping, 1.5" or 2" schedule 40 pipe (2" or 21/2 OD)
- ramp joists fastened with #8 x 3" galvanized deck screws
- each layer of plywood is fastened by rust proof decking screws on a 12" pattern, and

- ramp surfaces and bottoms fastened with #10 x 3" sheet metal screws.

Figures 26.5 and 26.6 provide a few examples of ramps. They can be built with varying heights and widths. This list is far from comprehensive.

Concrete Skateparks

Permanent outdoor skateparks are constructed of concrete (see Figure 26.7 for sample concrete park layouts). The material is fluid and allows unlimited shapes to be integrated into the design. Objects can flow from one to another with no interruptions. Long, flowing designs that incorporate soft bumps as well as curbs, ledges, rails, and steps can be easily built to make interesting and challenging runs for skaters of all experience levels. If the owner has the budget, this is the way to go.

Concrete parks are built from the ground up. This allows for a more esthetically pleasing park by incorporating varying elevations, and by integrating grassy knolls, shade trees, flowers, and observation areas. Critical factors in concrete parks are the design and implementation of the transitions and placement of the coping. If a concrete park is poorly designed or built, the owner could be stuck with an area skaters will not skate.

Perfectly installed coping and forms act as guides for templates. The templates then guide a blade, called a fresno, which precisely cuts the concrete to shape. The template is then moved to the end of the trimmed section, and the process is repeated. The concrete used is called shot-crete, which is also used for swimming pools.

A grey coat is recommended for bowls, pools, or anything with transition. Working steeply inclined concrete with floats and trowels makes the concrete slump and compresses the transition, forming a kink. Cutting the concrete, then putting a finish coat on later, allows more control to achieve a precise shape and smoother finish.

Lighting

Most outdoor skateparks require lighting. Chapter 8 provides a great deal of detail regarding exterior lighting. Lighting for the park serves two main functions: to provide light for night skateboarding, and for security when the park is not in use.

Indoor Skateboard Park

There are many locations in the United States that have a combined indoor/outdoor park because of climate. The actual design of the park will be the same, except it will be indoors rather than out. The other components of an indoor structure, such as heating, ventilation, air conditioning, plumbing, electrical, etc. are found in other chapters of this book.

Maintenance

Skateparks are generally constructed of concrete, and repairs are rarely needed. Those that have steel and wooden structures will require regular inspection and maintenance. The facilities are kept clean by skateboarders themselves. They do not want to trip on soda cans or other rubbish.

Figure 26.5

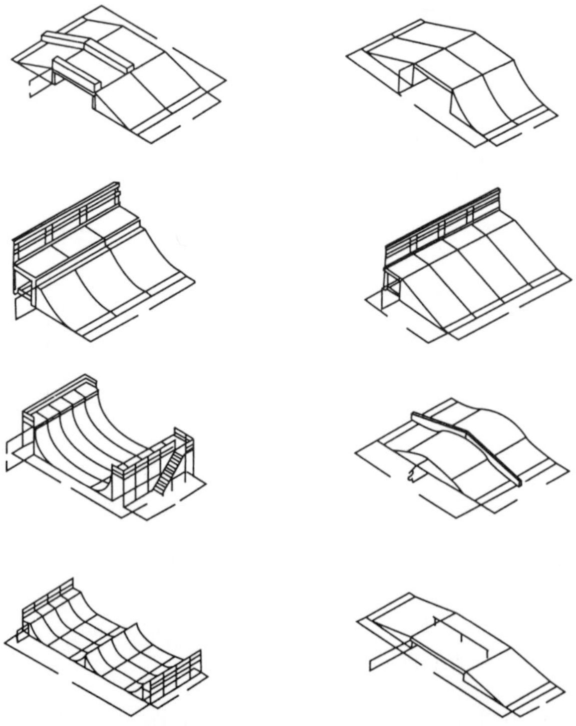

Graphic by Meghan Sawyer

Figure 26.6

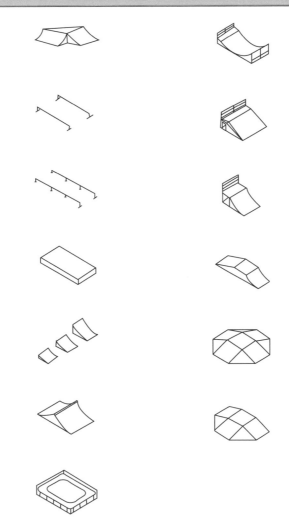

Graphic by Meghan Sawyer

Photo by Michael Hypes

Various Ramps YMCA Skatepark Murfreesboro, TN.

Figure 26.7

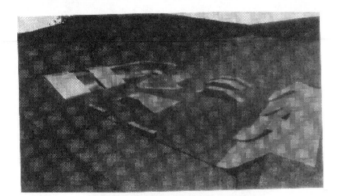

A major maintenance concern with steel is rust and loose bolts and screws. The wooden ramps also have problems with screws loosening and falling out. Weather can take a toll on both steel and wooden ramps. The major concern with concrete is cracks and pooling water areas. The cracks need to be filled prior to winter. Frost can be very destructive to concrete.

Trees and other foliage enhance the visual beauty and provide shade for a park. However, trees require regular maintenance to keep them healthy. Areas around trees require regular cleaning to remove discarded limbs and leaves that could be a safety problem for the park (See Chapter 17 for additional information regarding foliage, trees, and turf).

Other maintenance issues focus on cleaning rest rooms, concession areas, offices, entrance and lobby areas, and the pro shop within the skate house (see Chapter 8 for additional information regarding general maintenance and cleaning). Further, exterior trash containers need to be regularly emptied and cleaned. Finally, the grass areas need to be mowed.

Skateboard Terminology

Air. The act of riding a skateboard in the air, usually in reference to ramps.

Barge. To skate where skating is forbidden.

Backside. The direction of a turn on an incline, in which the backside of the skater's body faces the targeted destination.

Fakie. The backward motion of the board while the skater is in normal operating stance.

Freestyle skating. The act of riding a skateboard through a wide variety of bowls interconnected with channels (or snakes) and featuring vertical walls for continuous movement.

Frontside. The direction of a turn on an incline, in which the front of the skater's body faces the targeted destination.

Flatland. A type of street skating on a flat surface, involving technical board movements.

Grind. To slide on a surface, such as a rail, curb or ramp, using the area of the board between the wheels.

Ollie. To move the skateboard off the ground without using any sort of ramps.

YMCA Skate park
Murfreesboro, TN.

Photos by Michael Hypes

BMX Bike on YMCA
Skatepark Murfreesboro, TN.

Rail. A shortened form of the term "railing." Skaters grind on rails.

Revert. To continue a trick so the board and the skater are going backward.

Slam. An unexpected fall during a trick.

Street skating. The act of riding a skateboard on surfaces and obstacles found in urban environments, such as curbs, benches, ramps, rails, jumps, steps, and platforms.

Tweak. To bend or move the body and board during a trick.

Vert skating. The act of riding a skateboard on surfaces, usually ramps, that take the skateboader in a vertical motion.

Summary

In less than 50 years, skateboarding has become a large sporting industry. It started as a relief to boredom for surfers and has grown into a national pasttime for thousands of young men and women ages six-18.

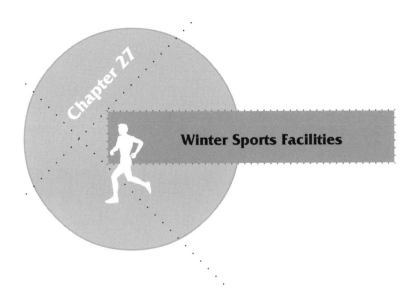

Chapter 27

Winter Sports Facilities

Jack Vivian, JRV, Inc.

With the advent of mechanical refrigeration in the late 19th century, people skated for the first time on ice other than that of a frozen lake, pond, river or canal. From that point forward, mechanically frozen ice was referred to as "artificial ice," and ice frozen by the cold elements as "natural ice."

The main difference between the two is that artificial ice freezes from the bottom up and natural ice from the top down. Artificial ice can be maintained at a fairly close preset temperature. Natural ice will fluctuate over a wide range, depending on the outside ambient temperature, wind velocity, and sun load.

At the turn of the century, there were very few artificial ice arenas; most were located next to a meat packing plant, cold storage warehouse, or block ice plant. Today, almost every small community in Canada and most large cities in the United States have at least one artificial ice arena (Fischler, 1991). Furthermore, there has been an explosion in the number of facilities in recent years, many in the sunbelt regions of the United States. Ice arenas of various types and models are truly becoming a part of the everyday life in the United States.

The purpose of this chapter is to present key considerations when planning a new ice facility. We will look at the types of facilities, refrigeration, and energy consumption aspects, and the general specifications of the various areas in an ice facility as well as the lighting, heating, and ventilation issues of these unique facilities. Although many of the same steps are followed in planning any recreational or sport facility, the special nature of ice alters the process. We will identify the key elements to consider, and the pitfalls to avoid when planning and constructing ice facilities.

Learning Objectives

After reading this chapter, the student should be able to:
- describe various types of ice facilities, dimensions, and uses,
- understand the basic principles of refrigeration and other equipment used to make and maintain conditions in ice facilities,
- learn the design and layout requirements for the overall facility, the team rooms, public assembly spaces, and the mechanical equipment, and
- study the mechanical and energy requirements of ice facilities and look at ways to conserve energy.

Ice Facility Classifications

Most ice surfaces are used for a variety of ice sports, although some are constructed for specific purposes and are of specific dimensions. Usual arena sizes include:

- Hockey

The approved National Hockey League (NHL) arena size is 85 by 200 feet. Radius corners of 28 feet are recommended by both professional and amateur rules (See Figure 27.1). The Olympic and international hockey arena size is 30 meters by 60 meters (approximately 100 by 200 feet). There are many older arenas were the ice surface is 85 by 185 ft. and are still being used. In substandard size arenas, the corner radius should be at least 20 ft. to accommodate the modern resurfacing equipment.

- Figure Skating

Figure skating can be done on a variety of sized arenas. School or compulsory figures were done away with a number of years ago. Freestyle and dance routines are best done on a regular hockey size sheet, but there are shows performed on sheets of ice that are as small as 60 by 100 ft. or less.

- Speed Skating

There are two types of speed skating today, short track and long track. Indoor short track speed skating has traditionally been on hockey-size arenas. Short track speed skaters prefer the Olympic-size sheet, since the 100-foot width

Figure 27.1
Rink Diagram

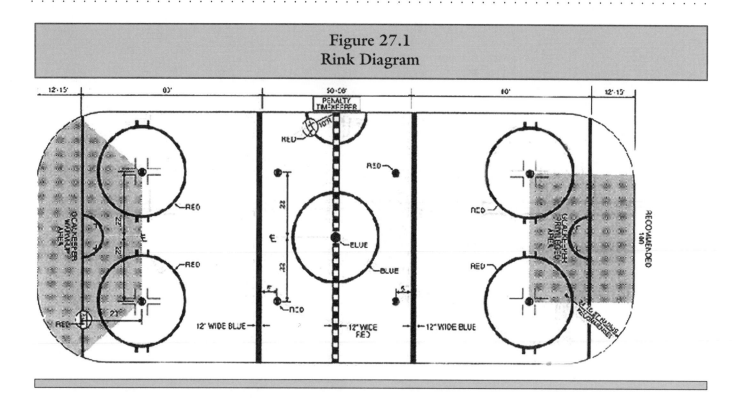

reduces the size of the turning radius and speeds up the track. The most popular outdoor or indoor Olympic-size speed skating track is 400 meters (Figure 27.2). The track size is determined by the distance each skater has to travel to complete one circuit. The standard speed skating distances are 500M, 1000M, 1500M, 5000M, and 10,000 meters. Considering that the 400-meter track has approximately 48,400 square feet of ice surface, which is equal to three standard ice arenas, one can see why there are only a few indoor facilities of this nature in the United States.

- Curling

Regulation surface for this sport is 14 by 146 ft.; however, the width of the ice sheet can be increased to allow for space to install dividers between the sheets, particularly at the circles. The actual curling sheet is 14 ft. by 138 ft. (See Figure 27.3) and the additional four feet in length is provided at each end for storing the curling stones on the ice surface. Curling arenas vary in size from two sheets to 24 sheets under one roof. The most popular sizes are four, six, and eight sheets.

Figure 27.2
400-Meter speed skating track

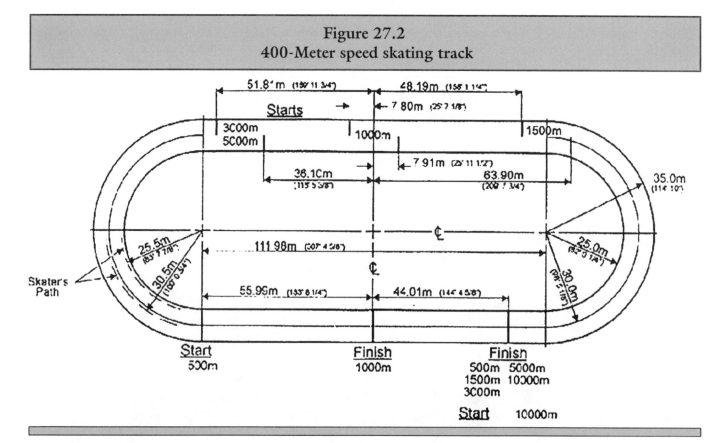

Figure 27.3
Curling Arena

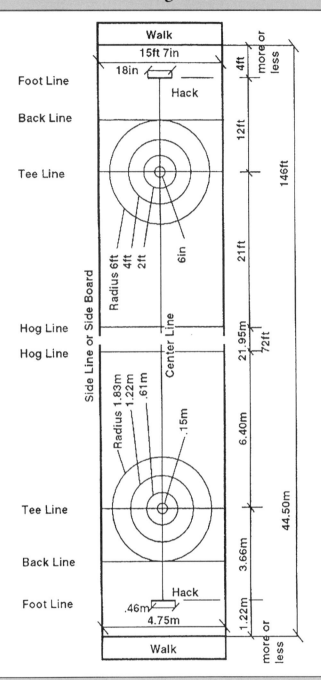

- Recreational skating

Public or recreational skating can be done on any size or shape arena, as long as it is safe. Generally, 25 (per child) to 30 (per adult) square feet is allowed for each person, except when a large number of preteens are skating. An 85 by 200 or 17,320 square foot surface will therefore accommodate a mixed group of about 550 skaters. Public sessions have been conducted on speed skating ovals with over 2,000 on the ice surface at once.

- Public Arenas, Auditoriums and Coliseums

Public assembly and large seating capacity arenas, auditoriums, field houses, and so forth, are designed primarily for spectator events. They are alternatively used for ice sports, ice shows, ice sports, and recreational skating, as well as for non-ice events. The refrigeration system can be designed so that the ice surface can be produced in eight to 12 hours. Many arenas with professional basketball teams, indoor soccer, football, and other shows and concerts, leave the ice in place and hold other events on an insulated floor placed on the ice. While this saves on time and labor, if the ice is to be removed regularly, a specially designed removal system, using the recovery heat from the ice plant, can remove the ice in eight to 12 hours. Many arenas of this type also have removable dasher boards as well.

Keys to Proper Planning

Once the idea of building an ice facility is advanced, there are many questions that need to be answered before planning, designing, and engineering can begin. Some these questions are:

- What is the purpose of the facility? Will it be used mainly for spectator sports or participation activities, or a combination? Will it be used for summer activities as well?
- What population will be served what distance will people travel? How will it relate to existing recreation facilities and schools?
- What sites are available? Are the facts needed for the site selection gathered together? Such things as land cost, drainage, utilities, zoning regulations, and parking requirements need to be considered in the early stages to properly assess the plan.
- What financial sources are available? Will it be necessary to build in stages?
- How will the facility be managed, and what staff will be required for programming and operations?

This chapter is not intended to cover the steps and procedures private owners and communities should follow to determine how many ice surfaces to build, how many seats to include, what amenities to build, or if a proposed facility can be financially and programmatically feasible. We would suggest that these steps be garnered from other chapters in this textbook. Suffice it to say, there have been many new facilities built in recent years only to end up in financial distress shortly after opening. Many of these could have been better planned, designed, and engineered it they followed the proper steps and learned about the features of arenas presented in this chapter. Owners should use every means available to study the market, research the strengths of programs to be offered, and assess the consequences of the high operating cost of ice facilities.

Ice-Making Process or Refrigeration

The freezing of an ice sheet is usually accomplished by the circulation of a heat transfer fluid through a network of pipes or tubes below the ice surface. The heat transfer is predominantly a secondary coolant, such as ethylene or propylene glycol, methanol, or calcium chloride, commonly referred to as brines.

Freon 22 and ammonia are most frequently used for chilling secondary coolant for ice arenas. Due to the phase out of the CFC refrigerants, freon 22 should be evaluated according to its status and availability when equipment is being selected in the future (ORFA, 1992).

There are primarily three types of refrigeration systems used in ice facilities today:

- **Ammonia Brine System**

One of the most popular refrigeration systems in use for ice facilities is the ammonia/brine type system that uses an ammonia refrigeration cycle, cooling the brine and circulating it through the pipes under the ice. Most of these systems use plastic pipe under the ice surface, although some are standard steel pipe or wrought iron.

- **Freon/Brine System**

Freon/ brine systems are the same as ammonia/brine systems except that freon is used as the primary refrigerant.

- **Freon Direct Expansion Arenas**

The freon direct expansion system uses direct expansion with thermal valves or other devices to feed refrigerant into the floor piping. Although forecasted to use less energy (due to not having circulating pumps), some engineers feel this type of system does not guarantee good heat transfer and may lead to patchy and soft ice in certain areas of the arena floor. Due to the phase out of freon, these systems are becoming less popular than they were a number of years ago.

Criteria related to the ice surface—compressors, condenser, chillers, ice floor, subsoil heating systems, and dasher board construction—should meet the following minimum conditions:

Compressors

Two or more compressors should be used in any ice arena system. One compressor should be specified with capacity to maintain the ice sheet under normal loads and operating conditions. When greater capacity is required during the initial installation of the ice surface or under high heat load conditions, the second compressor picks up the load. For arenas with more than one surface, three or more compressors may be required to operate under these same principles. The use of multiple compressors serves as a backup to maintain the ice in the event of compressor failure or a service requirement. Similarly, circulating pumps must be sized and numbered so redundancy is built into the system for emergency purposes.

Condensers and Heat Recovery

Evaporative condensers, air-cooled condensers, and cooling towers are the most common form of condensers used in ice arena applications. Their selections should consider suitable controls to cover the wide range in capacities and protection against freeze-up needed in cold weather.

Heat from the compression can be used for such energy-saving applications as sub-floor heating, melting the ice shavings in the snow-melting pit, domestic water heating, and arena heating. This can be achieved by a heat exchanger on the hot discharge gas side of the compressor (Blades, 1992). There is oftentimes not enough recovery heat available, so sufficient auxiliary back up is generally needed.

Brine Chillers

The brine chiller facilitates heat transfer from the brine to the primary refrigerant. Chiller can be shell-and-tube type or of a plate-and-frame design. Plate-and-frame chillers more expensive, but the benefits of having a smaller refrigerant charge, higher thermal efficiency, and longer life expectancy has made them the popular choice of the future.

The Ice Floor and Dasher Boards

There are two types of ice surfaces floors primarily used today:

- Concrete floors with piping (either plastic or steel) embedded in (Figure 27.4), and

- Sand based with the pipes embedded in the sand (Figure 27.5).

Most indoor arenas have a permanent general-purpose concrete floor so that the floor may be used for other purposes when the skating season is over. The thickness of the floor depends upon what events will be hosted in the arena. Community-sized arenas are normally five inches thick,

Figure 27.4
Arena Logitudinal section cold floor C/W sub-floor heating system

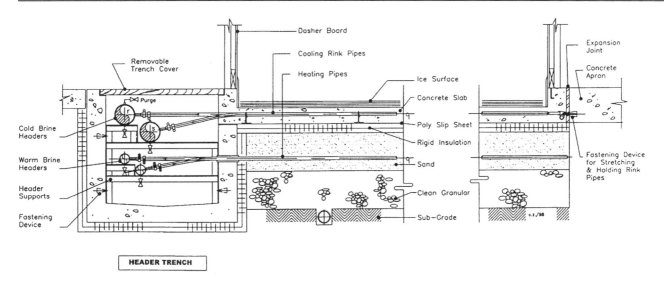

Figure 27.5
Sand Floor Isometric

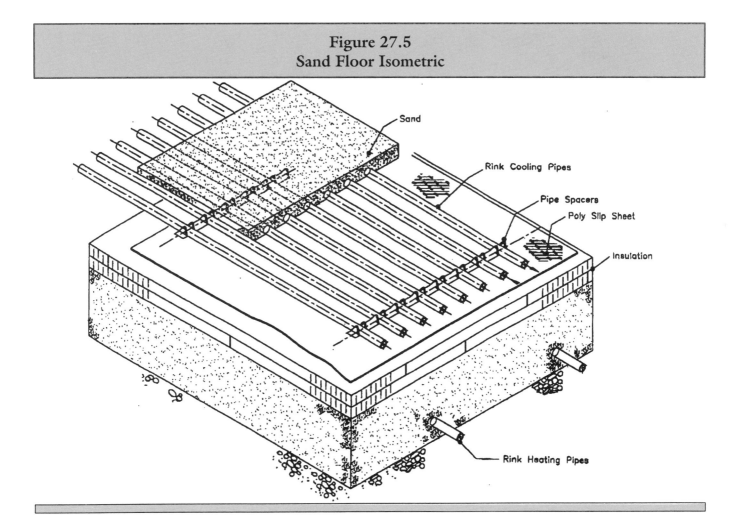

while event facilities use six-inch slabs to support the weight that must be carried on them. The sand-based floor is the least expensive, because the pipes rest on sleeper chairs over a bed of sand. Both of these type floors normally include an insulation layer and a sub-soil heating system to prevent heaving.

The proper design of the floor and selection of the best refrigeration system are the most important consideration when building a facility (Cimco, 1994). The planning of the arena floor begins long before the actual floor construction. Selecting a site with a low water table and good drainage is important. Water must be prevented from entering the sub-soil under the ice. This can be achieved by installing drain tiles, but if the building can be positioned on the site so the water table is sloped to prevent this requirement, there will be considerable savings.

The condition and composition of the soil is important, as clay and non-porous material must be removed so that there is no possibility of holding water pockets under the ice surface. The ideal conditions include 10 to 12 inches of sand that will be compacted once the sub-soil heating lines are installed. When 98% compaction is achieved, and the sand surface is rolled smooth and level, an insulation layer of three to four inches can be installed. On top of that is a vapor barrier of thin plastic on which the piping chairs are laid.

Headers Trench and Piping

Into the piping chairs is laid the piping and connected to a main header line running to the refrigeration system (See Figure 27.6). A well-constructed header trench to house the headers and connections and the sub-floor heating system is essential. Most header trenches are cast into the concrete slab as part of the arena floor. The headers and piping for the sub-floor heating system outside the main floor are usually insulated. Provision must be made for purging air from the arena piping and header system. Purge values are normally located in the perimeter concrete outside the header lines on each side of the arena.

High-flow secondary systems use standard mild steel pipe one or 1.25 inches in diameter or thin-walled polyethylene plastic pipe one inch in diameter. These are placed at 3.5- or four- inch centers on the arena floor. The pipe grid must be maintained as close to level as possible, regardless of the rink piping system used. Headers are schedule 80 steel pipe. The floor is either covered with five to six inches of concrete or the pipes are embedded in sand.

The vapor barrier and insulation will not stop frost penetration into the sub-soil area. That is why the under-floor heating system is required. It has been estimated that frost will penetrate the insulation under normal operating

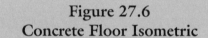

Figure 27.6
Concrete Floor Isometric

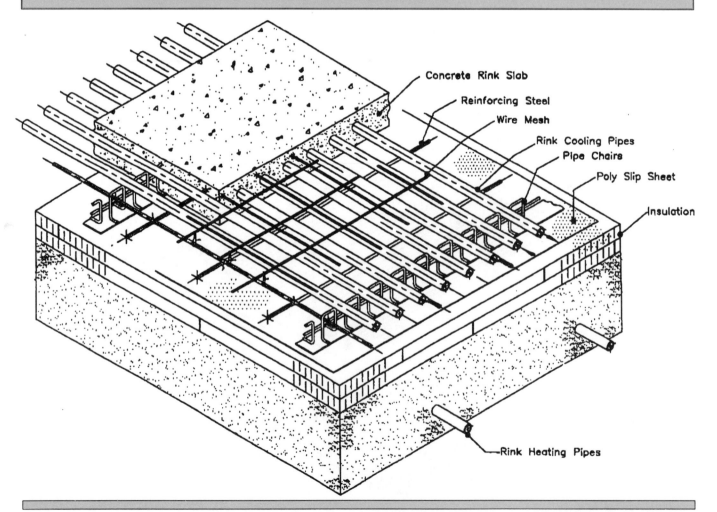

Concrete Rink Slab
Reinforcing Steel
Wire Mesh
Rink Cooling Pipes
Pipe Chairs
Poly Slip Sheet
Insulation
Rink Heating Pipes

conditions in eight to nine months (Cimco, 1994). The solution to this problem can be solved by circulating a warm brine or glycol solution through the piping under the floor. By using the recovery heat from the compressors, this heat is very inexpensive and good insurance against floor heaving. When the temperature in the sub-soil system is below 45 degrees, a sensor in this area calls for circulating the heat, otherwise, it is used for melting the ice shavings in the melting pit or for other domestic water or heating needs.

If a concrete design is selected, it is important to control adverse conditions that may result from an imbalance in the pH. High acid or alkaline conditions can be detrimental and cause corrosion of the piping contained in the floor. The entire rink floor will be one continuous pour with no cold joints; it should be capable of supporting a wide variety of activity loads and equipment, such as tractors and trucks, and should be machine or hand-finished so as not to be slippery. It must be within 1/8" of a true level plane.

The following accessories should be included in the ice floor installation:

- Goal post anchors to be placed at 11 feet (professional) and 15 feet (college) from the end of the rink for optional goal placement.
- Tennis and volleyball net post floor anchor inserts with four bolt-down, inside-threaded anchors welded to the base plate and supplied with flush brass screw plugs.

Dasher Board Systems

The dasher board system should be constructed of lightweight aluminum or steel and should be easy to dismantle and store on stackable dasher board panel and protective-glass carts. The system should use protective tempered glass with end glass heights of six to eight feet and side glass heights of four to six feet. The height of the glass will depend upon the design and location of seating and whether clear monafilament netting is used to protect the spectators and building structure. Many arenas surround the surface with the spectator monafilament netting and receive reduce insurance rates as a result.

The dasher boards should be tightly fastened to the refrigerated concrete slab with a system employing screw-in anchors with flush tops for when the boards are removed. The system should be capable of removing the dasher boards and keeping the ice in by way of an ice dam. This is especially effective for producing skating shows and exhibitions. Player, penalty, score, and goal judge boxes should also be portable and easily stored.

Indoor soccer and lacrosse can be accommodated using the inserts for hockey and by removing sections of the dasher boards. In-line hockey can be played on the concrete or other sport court surfaces using the hockey markings and regular goals.

Energy Conservation for Ice Facilities

To meet today's energy-saving expectations, ice facility owners and operators need to understand how to curb energy without affecting the quality of the ice. Knowledge

about and technology for ice arena refrigeration systems, lighting, and water quality for ice making has improved dramatically in the last few years.

To understand how an ice arena uses energy, it is important to understand the various heat loads and energy needs for making and maintaining ice; for heating, air conditioning, and dehumidifying arena air; for lighting the facility; and for providing water for ice-making.

The refrigeration system in an ice arena consumes the majority of energy used in the building. Since refrigeration is a process of removing heat, the various heat loads in an arena should be closely examined. Most arenas are large metal, block, or brick structures that protect the ice sheet from the effects of weather. All of these conditions have a direct affect on the cost of maintaining the ice surface as well as the climate inside the arena. Table 27.1 shows the sources of the heat loads that affect an arena and the type of energy savings that could be achieved by addressing these sources.

Radiant Loads

One of the most common misconceptions and misapplications in ice facilities and building design is in regard to the insulation of the arena roof, ceiling, and walls. Although some insulation is necessary for building comfort and integrity, the idea of upgrading insulation values to reduce refrigeration plant conductive heat loads is simply incorrect.

Ceiling Radiation

Heat radiating through the ceiling is the largest single heat load in an indoor ice arena. Controlling this source would therefore result in the greatest energy savings. The heat load from the ceiling comes from the sun's infrared energy lighting on the large roof of an arena, as well as from the outdoor air temperature whenever it is above the temperature of the arena.

The amount of heat radiated into the building can be controlled by installing an aluminum and fiberglass fire-resistant barrier called a low-emissivity ("low-e") ceiling. A low-emissivity ceiling is normally installed over cables in the interior roof structure, reducing the radiant heat load by as much as 80 percent (Blades, 1992). In addition, it can reduce ceiling condensation and increase illumination in the building by approximately 15 percent. These savings alone can pay for the cost of the ceiling and its installation in two to three years.

Lighting Radiation

Lighting systems in ice arenas are complex and expensive. To achieve maximum efficiency, both arena designers and operational personnel must anticipate the needs of the programs and activities in the arena. Energy efficient lighting can only be successfully implemented if the objectives of the lighting system are clear when they are installed.

Radiation from lighting, although only seven percent of the total heat load, can be controlled by reducing the number of fixtures installed over the ice. Many older arenas have 40 or more inefficient, 1000-watt metal halide lights. These can be replaced with as few as 28 high-efficient, dual-bal-

Table 27.1		
Load Sources		

Load Source	Approx. Max. Percentage of Total Load (%)	Max. Reduction Through Design & Operation (%)
Radiant loads		
Ceiling radiation	28	80
Lighting radiation	7	40
Convective loads		
Arena air temperature	13	50
Arena humidity	15	40
Conductive loads		
Ice resurfacing	12	60
System pump	15	60
Ground heat	4	80
Headers heat gain	2	40
Skaters	4	0
Total	100	

Source: American Society of Heating, Refrigeration, and Air Conditioning Engineers (ASHRAE), 1992

last fixtures using 400-watt metal-halide bulbs. Lighting levels will be dramatically improved, energy consumption reduced, and the amount of radiant heat on the ice reduced by as much as 40 percent. The new lighting system can be designed to let the facility's management select the proper lighting level for each activity.

Convective Loads

The convective loads placed on an arena's refrigeration system come primarily from the arena's humidity (15%) and temperature (13%). To conserve energy, both the temperature and humidity levels must be properly monitored. When humidity is high, the ice surface becomes a condensation point. This increases the load on the compressors. This condensation can be likened to the moisture that collects on the outside of a glass of ice water on a warm, humid day. In an arena, the ice-making system must work harder to freeze this condensation.

Heating, Air Conditioning and Dehumidification Systems

There are basically three types of heating, air conditioning, and dehumidification systems presently on the market. First, there is the self-contained, air-cooled compressor-type packaged dehumidifier. The second type is the desiccant drier with gas or electric regeneration. The final type is the central heating and air conditioning systems commonly used in most buildings.

The optimum temperature for skating and spectator comfort in an arena is 58° to 60° Fahrenheit. To achieve this temperature without causing excessive loads on the refrigeration system, infrared space heaters or forced-air systems must be directed away from the ice surface. Even when these systems are properly adjusted, a heat load will still affect ice, because skaters' movement circulates arena air toward the ice. According to calculations by ASHRAE, skaters represent four (4%) of the total heat load. These loads cannot be avoided, since skaters' comfort is an important part of doing business.

The central heating and air conditioning systems and space dehumidifiers commonly found in ice arenas operate by collecting and passing humid air over cold coils. This causes the moisture to collect on the cold coils, where it is then removed. Most dehumidification systems have separate compressors to cool the solution used in the coils; some central systems use the ice-floor freezing system for this purpose.

The cooled, dehumidified air is then reheated by passing it over a set of hot coils before it is returned to the arena.

These reheat coils often contain brine or water heated by electricity or gas. Occasionally this air is reheated by heat recovered from the ice-floor compressors.

Desiccant systems dehumidify air without cooling it by passing humid air over a desiccant—a substance that absorbs humidity. Once dehumidified, the air is then returned to the arena. The moisture is removed from the desiccant by using waste heat from the compressors, solar collectors, natural gas, water heaters, or forced-air heaters.

Controlling the humidity in an ice arena is a delicate process. With too much humidity in the air, moisture may collect on the steel building structure. This moisture can drip on the ice as well as damage the structural integrity of the facility (ASHRAE, 1989). Taking too much moisture out of the air, however, can make the ice brittle and crisp, as natural evaporation from the ice will be speeded up. When this happens, the top layer of ice deteriorates in quality. Since humidity represents approximately 15 percent) of the total heat load of a typical arena, arena managers must experiment and determine optimum conditions for their facility.

Sources of Moisture

There are several sources of moistures in an indoor ice rink. Moisture is introduced into the rink environment by: ventilation, infiltration, people, combustion (ice resurfacer, gas heaters), and flood water evaporation. The visible effect of high humidity is fog near the ice surface and condensation on the ceiling. The moisture travels from warm areas to cold areas, since the vapor pressure is lower on a cold surface.

Therefore, the first step in dealing with high humidity in an ice rink is to address each moisture source. For example, the infiltration moisture load can be minimized by keeping the doors to the outside closed as much as possible and installing the proper weather stripping and caulking throughout the building. The moisture created from the combustion processes can be minimized by keeping equipment properly tuned and by operating this equipment only when needed. Flood-water evaporation can be minimized by installing a demineralization system, which uses less flood water and freezes at higher water temperatures, thus resulting in higher overall ice surface temperatures.

Ventilation of outside air represents the greatest source of moisture in a rink. Therefore, ventilation should be the minimum required for the building occupancy load and ice surface area, which still, however, maintains an acceptable indoor air quality. Reducing the moisture produced from these sources will often help eliminate the problem or reduce the capacity and operation of any dehumidification equipment.

Fog on the Ice Surface

Fog is formed when the moisture-laden air at the ice surface is cooled at or below its "dew point" temperature. Dew point is the temperature at which moisture will condense out of the air. Therefore, moisture will condense on anything (boards, glass, speakers, ceiling, flags, etc.) in the rink that has a surface temperature below the dew point. Even the ice surface itself actually acts as a large dehumidifier, condensing moisture from the air. However, this process increases the refrigeration load on the ice-making equipment, which in turn wastes energy.

A far better approach is to use dehumidification equipment. When sized and installed properly, dehumidifiers will virtually eliminate fog near the ice surface, eliminate moisture from forming on the boards and glass, prolong building life, and provide improved comfort conditions.

Ceiling Condensation and Drip

The cold ice surface literally draws the heat out of the ceiling by a process known as radiation. Not only does this process dramatically increase the refrigeration load on the ice-making equipment, but the ceiling surface temperature often falls below dewpoint, and thus condensation and dripping occur.

Low-emissivity ceilings are designed to reduce this radiation effect and raise the ceiling temperature above dew point. Heat that would normally be radiated to the ice now stays up at the ceiling, which raises ceiling temperatures. Furthermore, low-emissivity ceilings will drastically reduce refrigeration loads and energy usage by about 25% (ASHRAE 1994 Refrigeration Handbook, Chapter 33).

Ice-Making Water Temperature

Ice resurfacing represents one of the highest conductive heat loads in ice arena operations. Flooding the ice with water temperatures between 140° and 180° F accounts for about 12% of the total refrigeration requirements (DOE, 1980). While using hot water improves the quality of ice by removing air from the resurfacing water, it causes an additional load on the compressor system. Managers can experiment with lowering the flood water temperature. Lower flood water temperatures may not make much of a difference in most properly dehumidified facilities, but it does mean that the water will freeze faster, thus eliminating wet spots on the ice at the start of the next scheduled use. Furthermore, savings can be realized because the water doesn't have to be heated to as high a temperature.

Ice Temperature Controls

Typically, the refrigeration plant represents about 70% to 80% of the total electrical energy usage in an ice rink (Cimco Lewis, 1994). In the past, inaccurate, cheap, cumbersome and inefficient controls were used to maintain ice temperatures and control the operation of the refrigeration plant. In addition, the control sensor was usually installed in the return brine line (indirect systems) or in the concrete or sand for direct systems. These control strategies made it difficult for the operator to maintain good ice quality for all activities (hockey, skating) and created high energy and operating costs. However, advanced refrigeration control technology has been developed that drastically improves the quality of the ice and helps to reduce operation costs. These products include variable speed pump drive and infrared ice temperature control refrigeration systems.

In the past, control systems for ice rinks tried to control the ice surface by monitoring and controlling from return brine or slab temperatures. As a result, the brine and slab temperatures could be maintained within 2° F to 3° F, but the actual ice surface temperature would vary considerably (4° F to 8° F). In addition, the operator never really knew what the actual ice surface temperature was.

These poor control systems for ice rinks cause the surface temperatures to vary considerably. This variation in ice temperature would also help to explain why many operators are reluctant to set up their ice temperatures during unoccupied periods, skating events, or warm weather. They have experienced soft ice and are concerned about ice quality and losing the ice.

In comparison, the ice surface can be maintained within 1° F of the set point using advanced control and infrared technology, as thermal lag is minimized and brine or refrigerant temperatures can vary to satisfy the magnitude of the actual heat load.

Infrared Ice Temperature Control

Ice temperature control has come a long way from the old brinestat or slab sensor control strategy. Now, it is possible for the operator to monitor and control from the actual ice surface. Operators can now tell exactly what the ice surface temperature is at all times and can easily adjust the set point to match the activity on the ice.

This advanced technology is commercially known as an infrared ice temperature control. Using a state-of-the-art electronic temperature controller and infrared sensor installed above the ice surface, the technology can be used to improve ice quality and reduce operating costs of any direct (ammonia, freon) or indirect (brine, glycol) refrigeration system. Additional savings and benefits are possible when this technology is integrated with a variable speed brine pump control or a computerized building energy management system.

The infrared ice temperature controller can maintain precise ice temperatures based on the set point chosen by the operator. With this type of control system, ice arena operators can take advantage of the tremendous energy savings without the danger of affecting ice quality or losing their ice. The benefits of being able to easily adjust the actual ice surface temperature in response to the various activities on the ice cannot be overstated. Not only does this technology provide improved ice temperature control and quality, but the energy savings can also be substantial.

Conductive Loads

Additional savings and benefits can be achieved by incorporating a variable speed pump drive into the refrigeration system. Variable speed pump drives will help to reduce the cost associated with the operation of the brine pump on indirect systems.

Arenas with indirect refrigeration systems and brine pumps produce pipe-and-pump friction heat loads representing approximately 15% of the total refrigeration load. Most brine systems have one or more pumps driven by 25-horsepower motors. These pumps and motors run continuously, circulating the brine through the ice slab's piping. There are two methods to investigate for reducing these conductive loads:

- Install variable or two-speed brine pumps with high-efficiency motors controlled by the ice temperature. This will reduce the friction loads in the pipes and pumps, especially in the winter when the system does not need to run that much. It will also allow the system to respond to the actual heat loads of the ice surface.

- Develop an automatic or manually controlled system to set the brine temperature higher when the building isn't occupied late at night or in the middle of the day, when the arena is used less (most infrared systems have a computer to help with this process). With the temperature set two to three degrees higher, the compressors, brine pumps, and motors will run less. Care should be taken not to develop a plan that runs the ice compressor system more heavily when peak-demand rates are being charged; this could easily offset the potential savings earned from raising the temperature.

Demineralized Water Systems

Using demineralization technology allows operators to: maintain a thinner ice sheet and higher ice and refrigerant temperatures; use less energy to heat the flood water, and creates a smaller heat load on the refrigeration system. This translates into substantial energy and operating savings for ice rinks.

It is often said that ice is as good as the water it is made from. Anything dissolved in the water resists a phase change. This means that contaminants (organic or inorganic) steadily increase in concentration in the liquid portion of the ice sheet, which is the last to freeze. The ice stratum nearest the surface will always have a higher mineral content than that close to the floor and the effect is cumulative in nature, with successive floods quarantining an increasing salt concentration in the skating surface as the season progresses. The result is slower ice, expensive freezing, reduced hardness, and higher salt content and pH.

Demineralized systems (either reverse osmosis or deionization) are designed to remove impurities from the municipal water source. Both systems also have the affect of forcing air out of the water (the reason for heating the water is to remove air), thus allowing for lower temperature and improves the opacity of the ice. The results are realized in energy savings and better-looking ice with clearer lines and in-ice logos.

Learning about the energy-saving technology and techniques available today is important for ice arena managers. Each facility is unique, so managers need to study their energy-consumption patterns, experiment with various energy reduction methods and techniques, and train their staff on the importance of energy conservation. The savings and benefits will be critical in the years ahead.

Installing Ice

When the refrigeration plant is in operation, the equipment should be operated long enough for a frost to appear on the concrete or sand surface. For sand-based floors, the sand is saturated with water prior to starting the plant. Once the surface shows a sharp frost, the entire surface should be uniformly covered with a fine spray. The process will be repeated until a 0.25 inch thickness of ice is built and the surface is level. After applying a layer of water-based white paint, another 0.125-inch thick layer of ice is built before the hockey markings and logos are painted. These lines and logos need to be covered with a thin layer of ice before flooding with a hose, because the lines will bleed if too much water hits them directly. Most ice facilities will build the ice to 1 to 1.125 inches before allowing skating.

The ice thickness is maintained with the ice resurfacer, putting on water while removing the skate shavings. Hot water (130° to 180° F) is generally used to give harder ice and to remove air bubbles that inhibit the freezing process. Arenas with demineralized flood water are able to reduce the temperature of the water to 90 to 130 degrees Farenheit to reduce energy costs, since this heat must be removed from the system by the ice plant. The reputation for having quality ice is something that every arena manager should cherish and devote attention to doing daily and weekly ice thickness and leveling. Extra thickness ice costs more to maintain, therefore, labor and machine costs can be recovered along with reduced energy consumption.

Designing the Building

The main challenge of designing an ice facility is to create an ideal venue for ice sports that can be converted to accommodate the mix of events hosted in the off-season. The following features should be investigated and included in a state-of-the-art facility. Figure 27.7 shows a two surface program statement space summary of a community-sized ice facility with the following features shown according to square foot requirements.

Main Entrance

The main entrance must be on grade, allowing unobstructed and free access from the exterior and permitting easy, well-lighted conditions for crowd dispersal.

Ticket Sales

The ideal entrance and foyer should provide a direct and obvious path to two or more ticket sales windows to allow free access to the main arena after purchase, without having to cross another line of people. Many arenas have two separate ticket outlets, and several have a ticket outlet for game or event nights, in the central part of the foyer; this allows access from two sides, along with access from the regular windows along the sides of the foyer.

The public skating ticket and sales office is usually adjacent to the arena manager's office. This is more efficient for the staff, who can handle advance ticket sales or provide information easily from a central location. Money-counting areas and cash-handling safes should be out of public view and may double as the safe for concessions, pro shops, and building operation income.

Figure 27.7
Summary of Arena Areas

Lobby and Pre-Function Area		
Main Entrance	400	
Ticket Sales	100	
Lobby and Viewing Area	3,000	
Skate Prep (lockers, benches)	600	
Public Rest Rooms	1,500	
Subtotal		5,600 SF
Arena and Support Areas		
Multi-Purpose Arena	20,000	
NHL arena	20,000	
Seating (300-350 on NHL)	150,000	
Referees' Room	150	
Team Rooms (8 @450 SF ea.)	3,600	
Showers (4 @250 SF ea.)	1,000	
Ice Resurfacer Room	700	
Refrigeration/Electrical/Mechanical	1,250	
Storage and Custodial	750	
Subtotal		197,450 SF
General & Office Areas		
General Office Areas	1,200	
Meeting/General Purpose Room	500	
Skate Rental/Sharpening	750	
Concession & Storage	450	
Pro Shop & Storage	1,000	
Subtotal		3,900 SF
Walls and circulation (15%)		6,185 SF
Estimated Total GSF		213,035 SF

Lobby and Viewing Area

The lobby should have direct visual access to the arena floor, concessions, rest rooms, and have some view of the ice sheet(s). Public telephones should be provided in a prominent position, either near an exit or in the lobby of the arena.

Skate Preparation

This area often serves as a pre-function space for events or concerts as well as an area for putting on skates, storing coats on portable coat racks, and for rental lockers to store valuable items while skating.

The lobby should contain one or two television monitors programmed for providing electronic daily, weekly, and special events schedules, and for playing videotapes. Such monitors can provide good advertising and relieve arena staff from answering many simple questions about schedules and upcoming events. It is also a potential income source as advertising space for local merchants can be alternated with arena information.

Public Rest Rooms and Drinking Fountains

Rest rooms and drinking fountains should be conveniently located throughout the lobbies, concourses, and corridors. The distribution of rest rooms and public pay phones and house phones should correspond to the occupancy load centers they serve, and should be arranged to achieve a balance when the facility is subdivided for multiple uses. These facilities should not be concentrated close to the entrance or skate rental areas, as this will increase congestion at times of heavy traffic. All rest rooms shall provide accessible facilities according to ADA.

Rest room facilities should have high-quality, low-maintenance finishes. Adequate floor drains and nearby custodial closets are desirable.

The lobby should lead directly to the arenas to ease crowd flow at peak periods. The overall design and location of major areas should minimize the distances from one arena to another.

Meeting Room/General Purpose Room

This room can be used for meetings, birthday parties, registrations for conferences and trade shows, and for youth hockey, figure skating, and adult hockey board meetings. The room may have state-of-the art computerized conferencing capabilities and will have an adjacent control and storage room. This room should be capable of being subdivided into smaller areas, each having separately controlled lighting.

Finish Considerations

Floor

The lobbies, public rest rooms, concourses, locker rooms, and corridors should be covered with a rubberized surface to accommodate skate blades. Entry areas should have special flooring to reduce slipping hazards from snow, ice, water, and mud. Where carpet is used, the color, pattern, and texture should be able to withstand the high traffic volume as well as food and beverage spills. Light-colored, monochromatic carpets should be avoided.

Walls

Vertical surfaces should be of materials and finishes that can be easily maintained and resist heavy wear and tear.

Public Address/Score Boards/Safety/Security

A public address system, controlled from the main arena office, should be available throughout for paging, announcements, and background music. The system should be zoned for control during simultaneous events.

Due to the large number of exterior doors required, the variety and broad distribution of valuable items that from time to time are housed in the facility, and the variety of people having access to the facility during activity times as well as attendees during shows, adequate security systems must be incorporated into the facility. The securing of the building perimeter, lobbies, and concourses through the use of a door alarm system, access control systems, and the like must be coordinated with the building administration's operations and staffing. Coordination with local police and fire departments may also be required.

A large scoreboard with advertising panels and a message board should be located so the spectators, the players, and officials in their respective areas can see the clock and perform their duties. A control panel, goal judge system for hockey and soccer, and remote tape deck, plug-in and volume control for figure skaters must also be provided.

Vehicle Access and Maintenance

All corridor and concourses should be wide enough and high enough to permit passage, including turning of light maintenance vehicles, floor scrubber, telescoping ladders, food service equipment, etc.

Electrical outlets should be available throughout the concourse and lobbies for use with janitorial equipment. Custodial closets and other maintenance facilities should be uniformly and conveniently distributed throughout the facility.

Acoustics

Wall and ceiling finishes should provide sound absorption to reduce excessive noise when the lobbies and concourses are crowded.

Main Arena

The architectural design should recognize the intended activities and programmed use of the arena. Arenas of this nature have no windows, skylights, or other openings for outside light. Some new facilities have broken with this tradition, and it is our understanding that natural light has been well received, especially by dry-floor users. If windows or other openings are considered, they must include appropriate devices for blackout to accommodate ice sports and traditional shows with "black box" requirements. If natural light is desired in public assembly and lobby spaces, acoustics must be considered, and outside noise should be prevented from entering the space.

Access

The main arena should have at least one oversized drive-in freight door to allow direct access by semi-tractor trailers to the floor. The door should be approximately 16 feet wide and 12 feet high. If a freight access door to the loading dock is incorporated, it should be 16 feet wide and 12 feet high and should be placed along the dockside of the arena to reduce forklift congestion at the loading dock. Ramps or other changes in elevation needed for drive-in doors should be accommodated outside the facility or in service areas, not within the arena space.

Seating Area

The seating capacity for the typical community-sized arena should be between 350 and 500 seats, depending on design and financial considerations. If possible, these seats should be located along one side of the ice surface, easily accessible for those entering the facility, and close to the dasher boards, as these seats will be primarily scheduled for hockey and figure skating events and small concerts.

Dressing Rooms, Showers, Toilets

There should be a minimum of four dressing rooms per ice surface with two dressing rooms sharing common toilets and showers. Youth and adult hockey associations, along with a successful figure-skating program all impose a heavy demand for dressing room facilities, so when possible, additional large dressing rooms should be provided.

Including coaches and other team personnel, a dressing room can easily attract 24 people or more at one time, and therefore should be designed for 24 players plus coaches. All benches should be made of wood or plastic and supported from the walls to facilitate cleaning of the floors. Lockers are usually only provided in very large arenas or for college or professional teams. Clothing and equipment hooks should be made of steel strapping or rods and secured to the wall or directly to a steel plate that is permanently bolted to the wall. A wooden or metal shelf above clothing equipment hooks is very useful.

The flooring in dressing rooms should be able to withstand skate blades and should be rubberized to protect blade edges. Bare concrete is unsuitable, since it is subject to damage as well as being extremely damaging to skates. Unpainted concrete becomes dirty and unsightly and creates dust.

Doors need to be able to withstand rough use and be wide enough to accommodate players carrying large hockey bags. Steel doorjambs and heavy-gauge steel doors are the most useful and practical.

With a high volume of traffic in and out of the dressing rooms, security is a concern. Some operators provide security by installing heavy-duty hardware (without doorknobs) or hasps with padlocks for team/locker rooms.

Ceilings in the locker area should be plywood, concrete, or other equally durable materials. Acoustic tile or other soft material is not suitable. All ceiling lights should be flush with the ceiling and covered with durable glass or impact-resistant plastic, such as Lexan. There should be no exposed pipes, unless the ceiling is at least ten feet.

Showers and Toilets

It is common to design one shower-toilet area common to two dressing rooms with a doorway leading to the shower-toilet from each room. Most shower rooms have at least six shower heads with 30-second or longer control taps and a mixing valve set to 110° F. Materials resistant to moisture and condensation on the walls and ceiling include ceramic tiling and concrete walls painted with sprayed or epoxy paint. Adequate ventilation to the outside reduces air moisture. By separating or dividing the shower room from the dressing room, a drying area can be provided. The number of toilets and wash basins must be closely calculated to fit the number of users in each area.

Referees' Room

The referees and linemen should have a small dressing room accessible to both ice surfaces, preferably with a single shower, wash basin, toilet, several chairs or a bench with wall hooks, and a mirror. The referees' room should be located away from the locker rooms, the lobby, and, if possible, away from the main entrance. Access for officials to the ice through an ice entrance opposite the players and coach's is desirable.

General Offices/Operation Areas

Properly programmed and effectively designed office suites and workrooms create efficient working relationships among the various user groups and enhance the success of the facility. When office spaces and service areas provide a pleasant environment and a functional setting in which to work, staff members' morale and motivation build, which fosters increased productivity.

Administrative offices should be centrally located with easy access from main entrances. A reception area, controlled by clerical assistants, should be available for guests and for scheduled appointments. It may be advisable, since all of the ice time may not be rented prior to the season, to plan a combined reception office/supervision station close to the ice arena(s) to facilitate working with the users during the weekend and evening hours. This station should have direct sight lines and should contain the lighting and sound controls for the arena's surface.

Administrative office space including spaces for the general office, the general manager's office, two assistant manager's offices, an account clerk's office, and one or two program/marketing offices should be provided. A general storage area could contain space for a copier, a floor safe, and cash-counting area with shelves for office and building promotional supplies.

Food Service/Vending

Concessions or food services are a normal part of every ice arena/events operation, large or small. The only difference between various arenas is in the scale of operation. A large arena may have several outlets as opposed to just one in small arenas. At least one stand should be located in the main lobby, adjacent to the office and skate rental area.

This area will be designed like a "Village of Shops" to give the customer the impression of a sequenced order of the concession, office, and skate rental, but so one person can serve all areas during non-peak periods. Cash registers or computerized point-of-sale systems should be located at strategic service points to facilitate good cash and inventory control.

A well-laid-out food service area can increase food and drink profits, since the time between periods of a hockey game, hockey practice sessions, concerts, trade shows, and conventions is always at a minimum. The concessions should be designed so the soft drink and food sections are convenient to each attendant, eliminating cross traffic and increasing efficiency.

Vending machines supplement crowded concession counters as well as eliminate the need for concession staff during off-peak or low attendance hours. This area should be recessed so it can be closed off when the concession stands are open, and it should be in view of the office, skate rental counter, etc.

Pro Shop

The facility should include a full-service pro shop that would stock a complete line of hockey sticks, tape and protective equipment, athletic supports, mouthpieces, skate guards, laces, tape, etc. The shop would also carry a complete line of figure skates and apparel as well as area university, college and high school products. This area may be leased to an outside vendor or operated by another party, and should have a separate, controlled entrance, ample storage, and a security system.

Skate Sharpening

Management will have a trained skate sharpener and machine available for the immediate skate sharpening needs of their customers. For this to be cost effective, this attendant must be able to work at some other function, such as skate rental or even concessions, during the non- peak periods. The skate-sharpening attendants must develop a reputation of doing the best job in town.

There should be a separate room designated for sharpening, repair, and maintenance of hockey, figure, and speed skates. The skate-sharpening equipment should be equipped with a powerful filtering and vacuum system. Storage space should be provided for extra grinding wheels, skate holders, and blades, as well as work space for blade straightening, eyelet replacement, and repair equipment.

Skate Rental

Most two-surface arenas should have approximately 600 to 800 pairs of hockey and figure skates for rent. This will require a room with proper shelving and a service window. This space must be well ventilated and should be designed to be near the office area, concession stand, and pro shop. One person in low-peak times should be able to serve all of the areas.

The shelves in the skate rental room should be adjustable in height to fit different sizes of skates. Shelves (box-style storage cabinets are not acceptable) must be numbered to coincide with skate numbers and should be able to hold the shoes of the patrons while they have rental skates out. The design should allow the attendant to reach a variety of skate sizes with a minimum of travel.

Mechanical and Electrical

This section of the building must be designed to enclose the electrical control panels and main switch gear in a separate room. The mechanical room must be large enough to contain and provide for maintenance of the hot water tanks and the total building HVAC equipment.

Storage

Storage should be provided in several areas for such general items as chairs, tables, dasher boards (one or two sets), dasher board glass, and hockey, soccer, soccer rug, broomball goals, and tennis nets and posts during the off-season. Some storage must be provided for other equipment, supplies, and the many items that must be stowed from the public in this type of multi-purpose facility.

Ice Resurfacer Room

The building design should provide a secure, well-lit ice resurfacer storage room away from spectators and dress-

**Well organized skate rental area
Api Ski Mountain, NC.**

ing rooms (preferably so that patrons never cross the path of the resurfacers to reach the ice) and able to serve both surfaces. This room must have a snow disposal area and floor drainage close to the ice resurfacer parking. To save energy, the snow-melting pit should be connected to the heat recovery from the compressors. Sufficient head room and width should be provided for front-end as well as side-dump machines. Head room should be at least 14 feet for a front-end dump machine. A side-dump machine requires about 12 feet of horizontal width space with a ceiling height of ten feet. Electricity should be provided for electric ice resurfacers.

The resurfacer room should have a work area for changing the resurfacer's blades and general maintenance. In addition, the room could provide storage space for the ice spuds, scrapers, and hoses used for leveling, cleaning, and flooding the ice.

The temperature of the water used for flooding is important to the final ice surface quality. The water should be between 150° and 180° F for best resurfacing. As much as 180 gallons of hot water will be needed for normal flooding every hour. For ice machines that serve two arenas from different directions, hot water connections are needed on both sides of the resurfacer room, as are floor drains immediately off each ice surface outside the exit doors.

Refrigeration Room

A separate, enclosed, and well-ventilated room should be provided for the ice refrigeration equipment and related items sufficient to serve both ice surfaces. The room must have a gas detector, alarm, and automatic ventilation system to meet code requirements for refrigerant gases. This room is best located at an outside wall with a lift-out wall panel to ease installation and maintenance of the total refrigeration skid. A workbench and a parts storage area should be included. This room should be located as close to the ice resurfacer room as possible to coordinate and reduce piping. It is best located between and at the ends of the two ice sheets.

Figure Skaters Warm up, Exercise, and Dressing Room

A room should be provided adjacent to the ice sheets as a dressing and warm up/exercise area for figure skaters.

This room should have mirrors, a ballet bar, and a videotape recorder/player to allow study of performances and practices. This room can function as a regular locker room for other activities, but it should provide washroom facilities, lockable lockers, and a small lounge for the professional skating staff.

Signboard/Building Signage

Outside the main entrance, there should be a signboard displaying the upcoming events of the facility and large flagpoles. The ideal signboard system would be a computerized board with a control located in the arena office. This would make it easier to change the message and would attract greater attention of people passing the facility. This system also provides opportunities to sell advertising, thus increasing income.

Internal building signage should be uniform, located in strategic areas so patrons can easily find specific locations and seats and easily exit the facility after events. The trend toward computerized internal building signage suggests that this option be investigated during design.

Special Lighting

Provisions for reduced mood lighting for public skating should be included in the original design and wiring of the Olympic arena. Lighting of both ice surfaces should be of a dual ballast, zoned design to reduce energy consumption.

Electrical service should be planned for television cameras, stage lighting for concerts, spotlights for ice shows, and a control sound and lighting area for some concerts. At least one platform for ice show spotlights should be built into the structure of the facility.

Parking (see also Chapter 15)

Visitors' impressions of a facility begin when they first arrive. Clear directions to the building's entry points should be achieved through the use of graphics and marquees. Changeable graphics are desirable to give a clear understanding of the location of each particular event and to give each event to have its own identity.

The drop-off zone should be designed to accommodate large volumes of pedestrian traffic transferring to buses

Outdoor skating rink Appalachia Ski Mountain, NC.

and automobiles. Weather-protected arrival and departure areas should be provided for each entry point. Marshaling areas for buses should be provided. The area should ideally be designed to accommodate peak load conditions and allow the collection, without causing traffic backups, of parking fees (especially if Phase II is completed). Ease of access and departure forms the first and last impressions of a facility in the public's mind and, as such, deserves careful attention in its design. An irrigated, well-landscaped exterior always creates a favorable impression and is relatively inexpensive when one considers the positive image created.

Summary

Ice facilities are very unique and complex facilities to plan and design. To successfully build this type of facility, it is important to understand refrigeration, the technical aspects of making and maintaining ice, and the amenities included in a year-round, state-of-the-art ice facility. Ice facilities operate many hours during the ice season, therefore energy conservation and the use of other modern technologies is critical to the financial success of the venue. Ice facilities are unique to build and operate, therefore learning about these features and techniques prior to building will ultimately save considerable time and money.

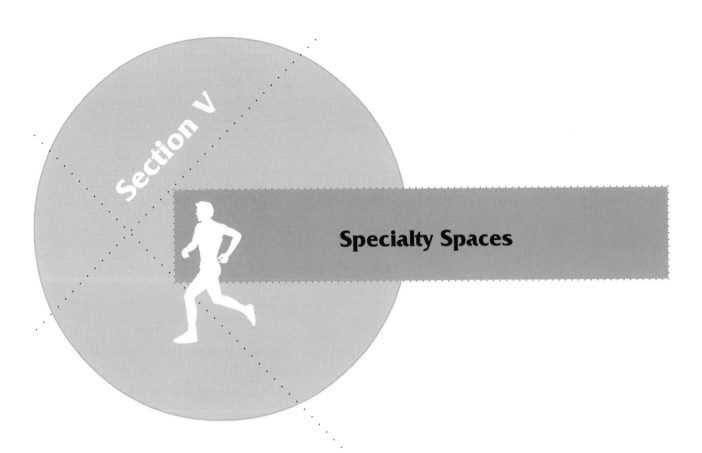

Section V

Specialty Spaces

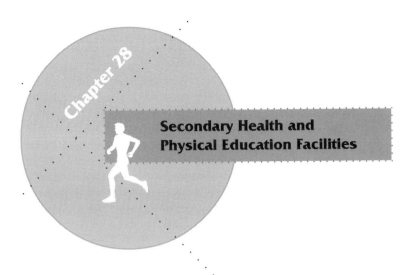

Secondary Health and Physical Education Facilities

Thomas H. Sawyer, Indiana State University
David Hoffa, Lost Creek Elementary Schools
Michael G. Hypes, Indiana State University

Introduction

The unit of primary importance is the room or space where teaching occurs. All other parts of the school plant are, in a real sense, secondary. In physical education, therefore, the determination of the number and character of the teaching stations is basic to the planning process. Further, it is important to locate these facilities in a separate wing for a number of reasons including, but not limited to noise, evening and weekend use, and non-school sponsored uses.

The term "teaching station" is used to identify any room or space where one teacher can instruct or supervise the learning experience of a class or group of students. For instance, a gymnasium would constitute a teaching station and if divided, could provide two or more teaching stations. Swimming pools, auxiliary physical education teaching stations, and dance rooms are examples of other kinds of teaching stations. The number of students accommodated by a teaching station is controlled by the nature of the specific activity, the size of the facility, whether the facility is indoors or out, and accessibility concerns.

The number of teaching stations required is dictated by enrollment, policies pertaining to instructional physical education, average class size, diversity of program, number of periods in the school day, and other uses of the facilities. Folding partitions and combinations of vinyl and mesh curtains can be effectively used for flexibility and to increase the number of teaching stations.

Planners should be aware that indoor facilities for physical education, athletics, and recreation are difficult and costly to expand at some future date. The peak enrollment potential for each space should be known by school planner. The anticipated enrollment five to ten years after completion of construction should serve as a basis for determining the required number of original teaching stations. Long-range planning is imperative to provide for the logical and most economical expansion. The initial design should make provisions for the anticipated construction.

Instructional Objective

The student will be able to:
- consult on the interior design of either an elementary or secondary physical education facility

Common Planning Considerations

There are a number of common planning considerations for physical education facilities in public and private schools. These common planning considerations include surface materials (i.e., ceilings, floors, and walls), sound control and acoustics, electrical systems and service, climate control, security, climbing walls, ropes, and cargo nets, storage, shower and dressing rooms, folding partitions or curtains, and office space for physical education teachers. Each of these common planning considerations are discussed in detail in the following pages.

Surface Materials

The selection of indoor surface materials for ceilings, floor, and walls becomes complicated, because indoor facilities will be subject to hard usage, excessive moisture, and multiple uses. These surfaces must meet minimum standards in terms of acoustical and light-reflecting properties. Geographic location and the availability of certain surface materials are factors to be considered as well (See Chapter 11 for greater details on indoor surfaces).

Floor Surfaces

The best floor surface (see Chapter 11 for greater detail) to use may depend upon the number of different teaching areas. The main gymnasium area should have either a hardwood or synthetic surface. Wood, preferably maple, is an excellent all-around surface, although it lacks the durability and flexibility that might be demanded by extensive community use of the facility. Synthetic surfaces have proven excellent for all normal game-type activities and also can better accommodate events that put additional stress on the floor, such as setting up chairs, tables, booths, etc. In an auxiliary teaching station, carpeting is often used, but not recommend due to the low co-efficient of slippage, which increases the chances of joint injury when quick movements are attempted (i.e., knee and ankle). Tile is also not recommended as a play surface due to the high co-efficient of slippage and the lack of adequate resiliency, which increases the chances of joint injury (i.e., knees and hips).

.There are at least three distinct types of floor surfacing (i.e., hardwood, resilient synthetic, or common surfaces such as tile, ceramic tile, or rug) required in facilities described in this chapter. Floors in service areas such as locker rooms, shower rooms, toweling rooms, and toilet rooms require a surface impervious to moisture (e.g., concrete, or ceramic tile). Classroom, corridor, and office areas may be grouped together for common surfacing (i.e., tile or rug).

Special activity areas require different treatments. For example, a dance gymnasium that is used for instruction in modern dance should have a finished treatment, which will allow dancers to slide or glide across the floor (see Chapter 21 for greater details on dance areas). In other areas, such as basketball courts, the finish should be of a non-slip nature. Careful consideration should also be given to the location of lines for various activities and floorplates for standards or gymnastic equipment.

Flexibility, durability, and cost are three criteria that have been instrumental in seeing synthetic surfaces challenge hardwood floors for installation in activity areas. The most popular synthetic surfacing materials can be classed into two types: plasticized polyvinyl chlorides (PVC's) and polyurethanes. The PVC's are primarily prefabricated, while the polyurethanes are either poured in place or produced in factory-prefabricated sheets that are adhered down on the site. In general, the polyurethanes possess most of the desirable characteristics sought in a floor surface.

Walls

In addition to segregating specific areas, walls should serve as barriers to sound, light, heat, and moisture. In selecting wall surfacing, considerations should be given to the acoustical properties of the material. In general, moisture-resistant walls with good acoustical properties are recommended. Most modern gymnasiums have smooth surfaces on the lower portion of the walls so they may be used as rebound surfaces. Rough-surfaced walls collect dirt easily and are difficult to clean. Recently, there has been a trend to color, use murals, and graphics to add aesthetic appeal. However, in the elementary gymnasium, the need for walls to hold paper, posters, and/or decals need to be considered as well.

In locker rooms, shower rooms, and toilet rooms, where high humidity is often present, it is important to select wall surfacing that is moisture-resistant and has good acoustical properties. Walls serving as barriers between toilet rooms, handball courts, squash courts, and other areas where noise is a problem should have a minimum of sound transmission.

Ceilings

Roof design, type of activity, and local building codes should determine the ceiling construction. Ceilings should be insulated to prevent condensation and should be painted to provide pleasing aesthetics and to enhance light reflection. Acoustical ceiling materials are desirable in instructional and activity areas. Dropped ceiling panels susceptible to damage by objects or individuals will require considerable maintenance. False ceilings with catwalks above them have been effectively designed to permit maintenance and repair of lighting and ventilating systems.

Sound Control and Acoustics

The sonic, or audible, environment is the most difficult phase of the total environment to balance and requires the services of an acoustical engineer. In each room, attention must be given to reverberation time. This is influenced by the absorption and reflection qualities of all surfaces within the room. Hard surfaces reflect sound and produce excessive unwanted reflection and reverberations. Thus, the space may be "noisy." Soft or absorbable surfaces turn the sound into another form of energy and can produce areas that are too "dead." Therefore, most areas must have some materials with sound-absorbing qualities in order to balance the sonic environment for good hearing conditions.

Sound Insulation

Unwanted sound, or noise, may be transmitted into the room by means of ventilating ducts, pipes, and spaces around pipe sleeves. The transmission of sound through ducts can be reduced by the use of baffles, or by lining the ducts with sound-absorbent, fire-resistant materials. The ducts may also be connected with canvas to interrupt the transmission through the metal in the ducts. Pipes can be covered with pipe covering, and spaces in the pipe sleeves can be filled.

Sound can also be transmitted through the walls, floors, and ceilings. This can be reduced to a desirable minimum by the proper structural design and materials. In conventional wall construction, alternate studs can support the sides of the wall in such a manner that there is no through connection from one wall surface to another. This is sometimes known as double-wall construction. The space inside the walls can be filled with sound-absorbing material to further decrease the sound transmission. Sometimes three or four inches of sand inside the walls at the baseboard will cut down the transmission appreciably. Likewise, sound absorption blankets laid over the partitions in suspended ceiling construction can frequently reduce the sound from one room to another.

Machinery vibration or impact sounds can be reduced by use of the proper floor covering and/or by installing the machinery on floating or resilient mountings. "Sound locks," such as double walls or doors, are needed between noisy areas and adjoining quiet areas. Improper location of doors and windows can create noise problems.

It is imperative to pay attention to the acoustical treatment of all areas. Gymnasiums, swimming pools, and dressing locker rooms are frequently neglected.

Materials for Acoustical Treatment

Care must be taken in the maintenance of acoustical materials. Oil paint reduces the sound-absorbent qualities of most materials. Surface treatment for different acoustical will vary. The most common treatment of acoustical-fiber tile is a light brush coat of water base paint. Most acoustical materials lose their efficiency after several applications of paint.

Electrical Systems and Service

All electrical service, wiring, and connections should be installed in accordance with the requirements of the National Electric Code of the National Board of Fire Underwriters, and the state and local building codes and fire regulations (See Chapter 8 for additional information).

The capacity of each individual electrical system should be determined accurately for the obvious reasons of safety and economy. Full consideration should be given to present and future program plans when designing the electrical systems. The increasing use of electrically operated equipment, higher standards of illumination, and special audiovisual equipment should be anticipated.

Illumination

In addition to the amount of light in any given area, the quality of light is of equal importance. Providing efficient illumination is complicated and challenging, and the services of an illuminating engineer are recommended in order to obtain maximum lighting efficiency. Gymnasiums, classrooms, corridors, and other specific areas have distinct and different lighting requirements. Planning for electric illumination requires that each area be considered relative to specific use.

Important Lighting Considerations

In addition to the quantity and quality of light from the various kinds of lighting systems available, additional factors to consider in the selection of an electrical illumination system are maintenance, repair, replacement, and cleaning. The ideal lighting fixture has both an indirect and a direct component, throwing surface light on the ceiling to give it about the same brightness as the lighting unit itself.

There is less need, however, to provide high-ceiling areas with direct-indirect fixtures. In gymnasiums, swimming pools and similar activity areas, an even distribution of light is required to permit the individual to see quickly and distinctly in any part of the room. It is advisable to provide supplementary lighting on such specialized equipment and areas that may be provided in a main or auxiliary gymnasium. Even with careful planning, it is difficult to make adequate provisions without some compromise. In some activities, such as aquatics, the very nature of the activity necessitates a separate facility.

Night lights (sometimes known as safety lights), that burn continually are recommended for gymnasiums, swimming pools, handball courts, squash courts, and other indoor activity areas. Lobbies, corridors, and some classrooms should also be equipped with night lights. These lights are extremely important for safety and security purposes and should have separate controls.

Provisions for outside lighting should be considered. Exit lights must follow the prescribed codes of the local community and the state. Electrically illuminated exit lights, clearly indicating the direction to the exterior, should be provided: over all exit doors from gymnasiums, combined auditorium-gymnasiums, multi-purpose rooms, and other areas as those containing goals or targets, and to place dimmers on the lighting in spectator areas. Supplementary light sources should be shielded from the eyes of participants and spectators in order to provide the proper brightness balance.

Transparent, non-breakable, plastic, protective covers will protect lighting units in activity areas where balls may be thrown. Vapor-proof lighting units are recommended for damp areas, such as toilets, showers, the dressing locker suite, and the swimming pool. Locker room lights should be spaced to the light areas between lockers.

Incandescent, fluorescent, mercury-vapor, sodium-vapor, and metal halide lighting systems are most commonly used in gymnasium buildings. The incandescent light is instantaneous, burns without sound, and is not affected by the number of times the light is turned on or off. Incandescent lights and fixtures are considerably cheaper in initial cost, are easier to change, and the lamp, within limits, may be varied in size within a given fixture.

Incandescent fixtures, however, have excessively high spot brightness and give off considerable heat, a problem when high levels of illumination are necessary. Fluorescent lamps have the advantage of long life; over all exit doors from the building; and at the head and foot of exit stairways. Emergency (white) lighting systems should be provided for exits (including exterior open spaces to which the exits lead) in gymnasiums, multi-purpose rooms, and other places of assembly or large group activity. This lighting should be on a special emergency circuit. All controls should be located so as to be under the supervision of authorized persons, and all other aspects of the installation should meet the specifications prescribed by the Underwriters Exits Code, and state and local fire laws and regulations.

Artificial Lighting System

A variety of trends in lighting systems have developed in conventional structures. One system utilized primarily skylights and is supplemented with conventional artificial light. In such a system, a light sensor assesses the light level coming through the skylight in the working area just above the floor. At this point, the sensor signals that information to the artificial light system to shine from 0 to 100 percent of the wattage capacity, depending upon how much light is coming through the skylights. The sensor in this system can raise or lower the intensity of the artificial light to an acceptable and predetermined candle power dependent on the activity. Installation of skylights plus a light sensor system will add an additional construction cost, but this installation will reward the institution with energy conservation and cost savings. In addition, considering that without the utilization of a light sensor system, a facility's lights would be required to be on full-time whenever the building was occupied. Also, a high percentage of the total kilowatt hours used in a facility are conventionally designed for artificial lighting. A skylight and light sensor system will accrue a significant saving in energy cost. Artificial lights also generate considerable heat, and by reducing the amount of artificial light (heat), a skylight and light sensor system would have a significant impact on saving in air-conditioning cost. Such a system has an approximate theoretical saving projected to reduce air-conditioning costs by one-half and lighting costs by one-third.

Fire-Alarm System

Electrical fire-alarm systems should be separate and distinct from all program-signal or other signal systems and should be designed to permit operation from convenient locations in corridors and from areas of unusual fire hazard. All fire-alarm systems should meet the specifications prescribed by the Underwriters Laboratories and by state and local fire laws and regulations.

Program-Signal System

Gymnasium buildings can be wired for a signal system operated by a master clock or push buttons from the main administrative offices. Secondary controls may be placed in other administrative units of the facility.

Program signals should be independent of the fire-alarm system and should not be used as a fire-alarm system. Program signals usually include: buzzers or chimes in the classrooms; bells in corridors, pool, gymnasiums, fields, and dressing-locker suites; and large gongs on the outside of the building. In many instances, signals placed strategically in corridors rather than in individual classrooms are adequate. Electric clocks should be included in all indoor areas in the program-signal system.

Services for Appliances and Other Electrical Equipment

There are many needs for electrical wiring and connections, which require careful analysis and planning. The following are illustrative:
- Basic construction: motors to operate folding partitions; blowers for heaters and ventilating ducts; exhaust fans in gymnasium ceilings or walls.
- Custodial and maintenance services: receptacles for floor-cleaning equipment and power tools.
- Dressing locker rooms: wiring for hair and hand dryers and electric shavers.
- Lounges, kitchenettes, snack bars, and concessions: outlets for refrigerators, water or soft drink coolers, electric stoves, blenders, mixers, coffee urns, and hot plates.
- Office suites: wiring for individual air-conditioners, business machines, floor fans, and other mechanical and electrical equipment.
- Laundry rooms: wiring for washers, dryers, and irons.
- Pools: provision for underwater vacuum cleaners, pumps, and special lighting.

- Gymnasiums: provisions for special lighting effects, spot lights, and rheostats or controls to lower the illumination for certain activities.
- Health suites: receptacles and provision for audiometers, vision-testing equipment, floor fans, and air-conditioning units.

Climate Control

The engineering design of heating, air-conditioning, and ventilating systems should be based on the technical data and procedures of the American Society of Heating and Ventilating Engineers. The selection of the type of heating, air-conditioning, and ventilating systems should be made with special consideration for economy of operation, flexibility of control, quietness of operation, and capacity to provide desirable thermal conditions. The design and location of all climate control equipment should provide for possible future additions.

Since the number of occupants in any given area of the building will vary, special consideration should be given to providing variable controls to supply the proper amount of fresh air and total circulation for maximum occupancy in any one area. Specially designed equipment and controls are necessary to ensure that climate control in some major areas can be regulated and operated independently of the rest of the facility.

All three mechanical systems—heating, ventilating, and air-conditioning—are interrelated and should be planned together. The services of a competent mechanical engineer should be obtained, not only for design, but also for making inspections during construction and for giving operating instructions to the service department.

Some problems involved in the installation of heating, ventilating, and air-conditioning systems include:
- Maintaining a minimum noise level
- Maintaining separate temperature control for laboratory areas
- Insulating all steam, hot water, and cold water pipes and marking them with a color code
- Exhausting dry air through the locker rooms and damp air from the shower room to the outside
- Providing a minimum of four changes of air per hour without drafts
- Installing locking type thermostats in all areas, with guards wherever they may be subject to damage
- Placing the thermostats for highest efficiency
- Zoning the areas for night and recreational use
- Eliminating drafts on spectators and participants

The geographical location of the proposed facility will dictate to some extent the type of climate control equipment selected for installation. Mechanical ventilation is preferred over open windows. Air-conditioning has been strongly recommended for southern climates, but year-round use of facilities make air-conditioning a desirable building feature in other areas. Special rooms such as locker rooms, shower rooms, swimming pools, and steam rooms need special consideration for moisture and humidity control.

Security

The athletic and physical education complex presents a unique security problem. The facilities and the programs attract large numbers of individuals who move all times during the day and week and through any areas in different directions.

It is reasonable to believe that all students and visitors who come to the building have distinct purpose in coming and should be welcome. This is the type of building, which people enter through many outside doors and disperse to offices, classrooms, dressing rooms, activity areas, and spectator galleries. There should be some plan for pedestrian control and for the handling of visitors.
Security is accomplished in two ways:

- Constructing the facilities according to a plan, which allows for maximum security, and
- Adopting an administrative plan for the direction and control of all persons using the building

The physical layout will facilitate security but will not guarantee it. A good administrative plan will help. However, a good administrative plan cannot completely accomplish effective security if the physical layout does not lend itself to the attainment of such security.

Security Features of Construction

Entrance doors constitute the first barriers against illegal intrusion. Open and descending stairways, walled entries, and deep-set entrances should be avoided. The points of entrance to buildings should be well lighted from dusk until dawn. The corners of the buildings should have floodlights that light the face of the structure. So-called "vandal lights" should be installed and protected to make them vandal proof.

Corridors, which are continuous and straight, providing unbroken vision, add qualities of safety and security to the building, its contents, and its users. Corridors are best lined up with entrance doors, providing a commanding view of the doorway from the corridor, and of the corridor from the entrance door. There should be an attempt to avoid angular corridors and to eliminate niches or cubbyholes.

The use of the night lighting within the building and at its entrances will assist in protection against vandalism and other forms of undesirable conduct. Night lighting will require separate wiring and switches in order to maintain a desirable amount of illumination. Switches for such lighting should be key-controlled to prevent their use by unauthorized individuals. A building chart for day and night "on" and "off" lights should be developed. There should be additional directions for "on" and "off" at every switch, and such directions should be changed according to need. A key-station system for night watch checking is desirable.

Security of the Building

Securing the building and its component rooms against illegal entry is the first and most logical consideration in terms of building protection. Good door framing, substantial doors, and heavy-duty hardware and locks hold up against wear and abuse. In their long life and securing qualities, they constitute a reasonable investment. In reducing replacement costs for materials and labor, the installation of good hardware is economical in the long run.

To reduce loss through breakage and theft, the additional security factor of quality hardware should never be overlooked at any cost.

A lock-and-key system

Developed with the help of experts in the field of building administration, will usually result in a plan, which considers some of the following features:

- A building master plan, including a lock-and-key system;
- The use of electronic locks with cards;
- Lock-tumbler adjustments so that an area may have its own control and authorization;
- Area division (vertical division) by responsibility or usage for key assignment; or "level" division (horizontal division) for key assignment; or a combination of both vertical and horizontal divisions;
- A policy of not lending keys is recommended. The person to whom the key is assigned signs a pledge for no lending. The keys for the facilities should be identified by a distinguishing mark, and a policy should be established with key duplicators in the areas that the duplicators will refuse to duplicate keys carrying such identifying marks; and
- An annunciator system in which outside or other doors of importance, such as swimming pool doors.

Climbing Walls, Ropes, and Cargo Nets

The trend for the last decade has been to involve the elementary students in activities that allow them to develop upper-body strength (e.g., climbing walls (fixed and portable), climbing ropes, and cargo nets). The most recent addition to the elementary gymnasium has been climbing walls and bouldering walls. These walls are either fixed to the gymnasium wall or portable. The fixed versions should have a landing resilient landing base and a safety rope system to protect the students from falls. There are number of reputable companies (see Chapter 25 for a listing of companies and detailed suggestions for construction of a climbing wall).

The traditional rope-climbing activities have not changed a great detail over the years. The important facility and safety issues include how (1) the rope is fixed to the ceiling, (2) it is stored when not in use, and (3) the landing base is established under the rope. Climbing ropes should be attached to a height of 24' and drop to about three feet above the floor. If the ceiling is placed below the structural members, the locations of suspended equipment should be planned and eye bolts provided during construction. Ropes should be placed five feet part, allowing one for each five students in class.

Cargo nets are great fun. The greatest concerns focus on how they secured to the ceiling or wall, and the landing base provided.

Storage area.

Photos by Michael Hypes

Storage

Two types of storage rooms are necessary for every physical education facility. The first is the storage of large pieces of equipment needed in the gym, items such as volleyball standards and officials stands, gymnastic equipment, chairs, mats and score tables, which, if left around the gym floor, are a safety hazard. This room should have easy access to the gym floor through a roll-up door. The room should be planned to provide for current equipment and future expansion and should be equipped with safety lights in case of power failure.

Storage rooms are needed for each of the different instructional areas. The room adjoining the gymnasium should be at least 1,000 to 1,200 square feet, 10' high, equipped with a roll-up door, and should be directly accessible from the gymnasium floor. Consideration must be given to community use of the facility and separate secured storage of related equipment. Ideally, there would be a separate storage room for each of the programs. The storage areas should have adjustable bins, shelves, racks, and hangers for the best utilization of space and the proper care of equipment and supplies. Space to store out-of-season equipment is essential to prevent loss or misplacement between seasons. An outside entrance assists in the handling of equipment that is used outdoors and/or in connection with a summer playground program.

The second type of room needed is for the storage and repair of small equipment and supplies. Special bins, racks, hooks and nets, with a work bench for marking and minor repairs, adds greatly to the efficiency of the room. Ideally this room should be located near faculty offices.

Shower and Dressing Rooms

Although it has been standard practice not to include shower, locker, and dressing room facilities in the elementary school, such facilities are essential if the gymnasium is to be used for intramural-interschool competition and community usage. The size, number of lockers, showers, and toilet facilities will be dependent on the extent of usage (see Chapter 9 for greater detail on these areas). If swimming pools are added as part of the school-community complex, such facilities are a must. Provision for outdoor restrooms is desirable if the general public is involved.

Folding Partitions or Curtains

Folding partitions make possible two or more teaching stations in the gymnasium. They should be power-operated, insulated against sound transmission and reverberation, and installed to permit compensation for building settlement. The control should be key-operated. The design and operation must ensure student safety. Partitions should extend from floor to ceiling and may be recessed when folded. Floor tracks should not be used. A pass door should be provided at the end of a partition. When partitions are installed in gymnasiums with open truss construction, the space between the top of the folding doors and the ceiling should be insulated against sound transmission.

Vinyl/mess combination curtains have become very popular. The curtain is rolled to the ceiling when not in use. The curtains generally are vinyl for the first 6' to 8' with mesh the remaining distance to the ceiling. The vinyl comes in a variety of colors.

Office Space for Physical Education Teachers

The office space for physical education teachers should be in close proximity to the gymnasium and locker room areas. It should range from 150 to 250 square feet and include an attached bathroom and shower facility. The office should have an observation window for the gymnasium and outdoor field spaces. Finally, the office should be designed to include accessibility to a computer and a telephone.

Other General Considerations

It is important for planners to consider other uses of physical education teaching facilities for extra-curricular activities for the students and the community in general at the end of the school day. These considerations include:

- Additional space will be necessary if all students are to be given an opportunity to participate in an intramural and/or interscholastic program.
- It is desirable to have such additional special facilities as dance studios (see Chapter 33), gymnastics areas, swimming pools (see Chapter 20), and

archery ranges in order to expand the offerings of the physical education program. Note: It may be possible for the school to obtain some of these facilities through the cooperative use of existing or proposed facilities owned and administered by some other agency.

- As planning for recreation is considered, the entire school plant becomes a potential space resource, and all units should be scrutinized and planned with recreational adaptability in mind.

Elementary School

The elementary school is defined as follows for this book—kindergarten through fifth grade. These suggestions are based on input from experienced elementary practitioners and the Council on Physical Education for Children.

Indoor Activity Areas

The elementary school physical education program centers around the teaching of fundamental movement patterns, rhythmics or dance, fitness activities, games and sports, gymnastic activities, combatives, self-testing activities, and aquatics. The design and scope of physical education facilities should reflect the activities included the elementary physical education curriculum. Additionally, the planners should refer to the National Association for Sport and Physical Education's Council on Physical Education for Children (COPEC) guidelines for facilities, equipment, and instructional materials in elementary physical education (2001) (See Appendix for the guidelines). Finally, another good resource for planners is Chapter 33, Facilities, Equipment, and Supplies in Pangrazi and Dauer's *Dynamic Physical Education for Elementary School Children*.

A major consideration fundamental to the planning of an elementary school indoor activity area is the anticipated use by the community. Future years are expected to see more and more community use of these facilities.

Several of the standard planning principles apply particularly to the elementary facility. Such planning principles would include establishing priority use for the facility, giving basic consideration to the primary age group using the facility, allowing for use by physically and mentally impaired children, designing for the participants ahead of the spectators, and remembering considerations for maintenance of the facilities.

Location

Elementary schools are often more compact than other schools, and it is desirable to have the activity area apart from the classrooms to reduce noise disturbance. With the increasing use of such facilities by the community, consideration must be given to accessibility from the parking areas. In addition, it should be adjacent to the outdoor play fields. This allows for easier storage of equipment and increases the efficiency of the area to be used as a neighborhood playground in the summer months.

Teaching Stations for Physical Education

Elementary school physical education classes may be organized by a number of methods. The average class size is usually based on the number of pupils in the classroom unit. Because of differences in pupil maturation, physical education periods generally vary from 20 minutes for kindergarten and first grade to 45 minutes for fifth and sixth grades, with the school average (for computation purposes) being 30 minutes per class. The formula for computing the number of teaching stations needed for physical education in an elementary school is as follows:

Minimum number of teaching stations = number classroom of students × number of PE periods/week/class (Total # of PE class periods in a school week)

Example:

- Number of classrooms of students-school contains grades K to 6, three classrooms for each grade level, or a total of 21 classroom units.
- Number of physical education periods per week per class—one period per class for physical education each school day during the week equals five periods per week.
- Total number of physical education class periods in a school week. There are five instructional hours in the school day, and the length of physical education period is 30 minutes. Thus, a total of ten 30-minute periods each school day may be scheduled for physical education, or a total of 50 periods for the five-day school week.

The teaching station needs would be calculated as follows:

Minimum number of teaching stations equals 21 classroom units times five periods per day, 50 periods per week, equals 105 divided by 50 equals 2.1.

In the above situation, if one classroom section was dropped each week (bringing the total to 20) then the need would be two teaching stations. Therefore, requiring physical education five periods per week in the school used in the example would necessitate employing two physical education teachers each hour of the day.

In many school systems, the above situation would be too idealistic. More likely, only one physical education instructor would be available (either a specialist, or the classroom teacher, or a paraprofessional in collaboration with one of the other two). This would then drop the number of sessions per week for each classroom unit from five to an average of 2.5. One teaching station would handle this setup. If only one teaching station can be provided in the elementary school, then preferably it would be a gymnasium, despite the fact that some other type of auxiliary station might prove superior for instruction in the lower grades. The elementary gymnasium remains the preferred facility because of its heavy use by both the upper grades and the community. If the school system and the community were in need of an indoor swimming pool, this would be the choice for a second teaching station.

The next choice is an auxiliary teaching station, sometimes called a playroom. Particularly when heavy community use is anticipated, another alternative is to build a larger gymnasium and allow for dividing it by a folding partition or vinyl/mess curtains. Such a setup would provide four possible teaching stations, two on each side of the divider. This area would also allow for two basketball intramural courts, one basketball inter-school court, three volleyball courts, six badminton courts, and four multi-purpose game circles.

Multi-Purpose, Cafeteria-Gymnasium Combinations, and Self-Contained Classrooms

Multi-purpose rooms and cafeteria-gymnasium combinations have been found to be most impractical for physical education, especially from the standpoint of scheduling. Self-contained classrooms are restrictive in the types of activities that can be offered and have an additional disadvantage. Furniture must be moved whenever activity takes place. But if there is no way to have a separate facility, make sure there is adequate storage space for the tables, chairs, and benches. This storage space should be separate for physical education equipment and for cafeteria equipment. Both spaces should have rollup doors for ease of transfer of equipment between uses.

If used, such classrooms must provide unobstructed area of 450 square feet, be of a nonskid surface, have no dangerous projections, and ideally have direct access to an adjoining terrace, part of which should be roofed for protection against rain. These self-contained classrooms would only be used in the lower grades.

The Gymnasium

In planning the elementary school gymnasium, a minimum of 110 to 150 square feet per pupil and a total of at least 4,860 square feet is recommended. Spectator seating (if provided) and storage rooms (ranging in size from 400 to 600 square feet with rollup doors and a minimum ceiling height of 10') require additional space. Many of the general considerations recommended for secondary school gymnasiums also apply to elementary school facilities.

The specific dimensions of the gymnasium should provide for a basketball court of 42' by 74', with a minimum safety space of six feet around the perimeter. An area of 54' by 90' (4,860 square feet) would be adequate. The ceiling should be at least 22' high. This space is adequate for activities normally included in the elementary school program and will serve the community recreation program. The gymnasium will be of a larger size if the decision is made to use it as a multiple teaching facility and include a folding partition or vinyl/mess curtains as part of the design.

Auxiliary Teaching Stations

If a second indoor physical education teaching area is built, it should be either a swimming pool or an auxiliary instruction room, sometimes called a playroom. Swimming pools are discussed elsewhere in this text (See Chapter 20). The auxiliary teaching station is most practical when the main gymnasium cannot fulfill all of the school's needs for teaching stations.

At least 80 square feet per primary pupil, with a total minimum of 2,000 square feet of space, is suggested for this unit. A ceiling height of 18'-22' in the clear is preferred, although lower ceilings may be used. One wall should be free of obstruction to be used for target and ball games or throwing practice. A smooth masonry wall will provide an adequate rebounding surface. If included, windows should be of breakproof glass or be protected by a shield or grill and located high enough so as not to restrict activities.

The auxiliary unit should be planned to accommodate limited apparatus and tumbling activities, games of low organization, rhythmic activities, movement exploration, and other activities for the primary grades. Often a 30' circle for circle games is located at one end of this room, allowing for permanent or semi-permanent equipment at the other end. The equipment could include such items as climbing ropes and poles, ladders, mats, stall bars, rings, large wooden boxes, horizontal bars, and peg boards. These should be located so as not to interfere with other activities, or so they may be easily moved out of the way. A storage room for equipment and supplies should be included. A section of wall can be equipped with hangers for mat storage.

Electrical outlets are required for the use of sound equipment. This room will, for the most part, be used by the lower grades and should be accessible to those classrooms. If the area is to serve the after-school recreational program for pupils or community groups, toilet facilities should be accessible.

Special floor markings

The elementary gymnasium floor may have additional markings beyond the traditional game markings (e.g., basketball). These other markings may include, but are not limited to, circles of various sizes, and shapes. Floor markings facilitate a variety of activities, but the number of different markings should be limited to reduce confusion. The dominant lines should intersect the non-dominant lines (e.g., game lines should intersect non-game lines). A non-dominant line should be broken (2"), prior to intersecting the dominant line, and lines should be in different colors.

Programming for Construction of a Playroom

Use of Playroom

The area should be suitable for preschool and for grades K-2 or K-3 for fundamental movement activities, including creative games and rhythms, relays, stunts, and climbing and hanging activities.

Size

The area should be a rectangle measuring approximately 50' by 40', providing 2,000 square feet of space.

Ceiling

The ceiling should be acoustically treated, 18 to 22' high (all beams and supports above the minimum height), with suitable fixtures attached to the beams to support hanging equipment.

Walls

Walls below 10' should be free from obstruction. A smooth concrete block sealed with epoxy paint works well.

Above 10' should also be free of obstruction, but made of acoustic or slotted concrete block. A wall free from obstruction will provide practice areas for such activities as kicking, striking and throwing, and a space for the placement of targets and use of visual aids.

Floors

Hardwood maple or synthetic surfaces provide the best floor for general activity use. Both have advantages and disadvantages. The decision should be based on how the floor is to be used. Careful consideration should also be given to the location of lines and the installation of equipment.

Lighting

Fluorescent lighting should supply 35-50 footcandles on the floor, and a switch should be installed at each door. Light fixtures should be guarded to prevent breakage.

Windows

If used at all, windows should be placed on only one side of the room to provide natural light. They should be covered with a protective screen. Window sills should be eight feet above the floor.

Electrical Outlets

Double-service outlets should be installed on each wall.

Equipment Storage Area

At least 400 to 600 square feet should be provided for storage. Cabinets and shelves should be installed. The equipment room should have a double door, so wide equipment may be moved in or out easily. A telephone for emergency use should be placed in the equipment room.

Mirrors

Three full-length mirrors should be placed at one end of a wall, side by side, for visual analysis of movement.

Bulletin Board

Cork board should be hung on the wall near the entrance for posting materials and schedules.

Chalkboard

A chalkboard can be wall-mounted to facilitate teaching if this will not interfere with wall-rebounding activities. Otherwise, portable chalkboards can be used.

Drinking Fountain

One should be placed on a wall in the corridor just outside the door to the playroom.

Speakers

Two matched speakers should be placed high on the wall or in the ceiling. A cordless head set with a mike and sound system should be built into a wall.

Paint

Walls should be painted off-white or a very pale color with epoxy paint. However, murals, accent colors, and designs can be used for aesthetics.

Other Items

If the building is equipped with closed-circuit TV, two outlets should be provided for receiver. There should be a separate entrance for recreational use. The teaching station should be isolated from other parts of the building for evening functions.

Adapted Teaching Station

Local philosophy and state/federal laws vary as to the inclusion of physically and mentally impaired students in regular physical education classes. A separate adaptive teaching station would be an ideal setup, but any special program for such students often has to be accommodated in the regular facilities (see Chapter 7 for further details).

Secondary Schools

A secondary school is defined as the following for this book—either a middle school (6- 8), junior high school (7- 8), and high school (9-12).

Indoor Activity Areas

Teaching Stations

The type and number of indoor teaching stations for a secondary school depends on the number of students and the specific program of physical education and related activities. In all situations, a gymnasium is required. By determining the number of teaching stations essential for the formal program of instruction, planners will have a basis for calculating other needs. Computation of the minimum numerical requirement is achieved by the following formula:

Minimum Number of
$$\frac{700 \text{ Students} \times 5 \text{ Periods per Wk.}}{30 \text{ per Class} \times 30 \text{ Periods per Wk.}} = \frac{3500}{900}$$
Teaching Stations

3500 ÷ 900 = 3.9 Teaching Stations

The fraction is rounded to the next highest number, making four teaching stations the minimum requirement. This number would also afford some flexibility of class scheduling.

In computing teaching station requirements for the secondary school, the desired class size must not be set so low as to require an impossible number of teachers and facilities, nor should it be so high that effectiveness is impaired. An average class size of 30 with daily instruction is recommended. However, if the physical education classes meet only two periods per week, the total number of class periods per week in the formula must be adjusted accordingly.

The next step for planners is to determine the degree to which the number of teaching stations for the program of instruction will meet the needs for voluntary recreation, extramural and intramural activities, and interscholastic athletics for girls and boys, as well as the possible use of facilities by the community. The needs must be based upon the season of the year representing the greatest demand for facilities.

The following guide can be used to determine the number of teaching stations needed for activities other than the formal program of instruction in physical education:

Minimum number of teaching stations, or fractions thereof, needed for interscholastic-team practice at peak load

Plus

Minimum number of teaching stations, or fractions thereof, needed for intramural and extramural activities

Plus
Minimum number of teaching stations, or fractions thereof, needed for student recreation
Plus
Minimum number of teaching stations, or fractions thereof, needed for community recreation
Equals
The total number of teaching stations needed for any specific after-school period.

- Physical education facilities for the middle school should follow the standards for secondary schools.

To illustrate, assume a school has two interscholastic squads, an intramural program, a voluntary recreation group, and no community recreational use of facilities immediately after school during a specific season. The total needs are as follows:

Required Teaching Stations
Equals
2 Interscholastic
plus
1 Intramural
plus
1 Voluntary Recreation
equals
4 Stations

The need for four teaching stations for the after-school program must then be compared to the number necessary for the formal program of instruction in physical education. If the after- school needs are in excess of those for the regular periods of instruction, additional teaching stations should be provided. Careful administrative scheduling results in maximum utilization of facilities.

Variety of Teaching Stations

A wide variety of teaching stations is possible, depending on the number of different activities that would appropriately be included in the physical education program. Among the possible types of indoor teaching stations that might be included are gymnasiums, rhythm rooms, rooms for gymnastics, adapted physical education rooms, wrestling rooms, classrooms, swimming pools, archery ranges, rifle ranges, and racquetball courts.

The problem for some schools is not lack of an adequate number of teaching stations but rather lack of facilities to accommodate the desired variety of activities. For a secondary school with 360 students, a divisible gymnasium will create an adequate number of teaching stations for the program of instruction in physical education but may not meet the peek load requirement for after-school activities. The facility must be planned and designed to serve all program needs as adequately as possible.

Whenever a school's teaching requirements are such that a basic gymnasium is inadequate, planners should consider special purpose stations, such as auxiliary physical education teaching stations, a natatorium, or a dance studio.

Secondary School Gymnasium

The building or portion of the school that houses the gymnasium should be easily accessible from classrooms, parking areas, and the outdoor activity area. This also makes possible use of the facility after school hours or during weekends or holidays without having to open other sections of the school.

Size and Layout

For general purposes, allow a minimum of 125 square feet of usable activity space for each individual in a physical education class at peek load. The space requirements and dimensions of a gymnasium floor are significantly influenced by the official rules governing court games, particularly interscholastic basketball and the extent of spectator seating. The minimum dimensions required of a gymnasium for basketball, however, should be expanded, if necessary, to accommodate other activities. In some instances, an entire gymnasium is not required for an activity. Folding, sound-proof partitions can be used to divide the area and provide two teaching stations.

Walls and Ceilings

The walls of the gymnasium should be of a material that is resistant to hard use, at least to door height. The finish should be non-marking and have a smooth, non-abrasive surface. All corners below door height should be rounded, and there should be no projections into playing areas. Lower portions (10') of the walls should be finished with materials that can be easily cleaned without destroying the finish. An epoxy paint on cement block makes a durable finish.

The ceiling should be 24' to the low side of beams or supports, with fixtures attached to the beams to support hanging equipment. High ceilings are expensive, and a natural method for cutting construction costs is to minimize ceiling height. If this is in the area for basketball, volleyball, gymnastics, badminton, or tennis, it can be a critical error. However, in an auxiliary gym used for wrestling, dance, combatives, weight lifting, or table games, a 15-18' ceiling is acceptable.

All ceilings should be light in color, and, if support beams are below the ceiling, they normally are painted the same color as the ceiling or background. Contrasting colors have been used effectively, but such color contrast may make it difficult to follow the flight of an object.

Acoustical treatment of ceilings and walls is important where teaching is to take place. To get the best results, at least two adjacent surfaces should be treated. Many types of acoustical treatment are available. However, avoid those, which will chip or break when hit with a ball.

Lighting

There are many types of lighting systems that will produce the 35-50 footcandles needed for a good teaching and spectator area. For television, the footcandles should be closer to 200 footcandles, and that requires more sophisticated lighting systems. When selecting a lighting system, compare initial costs, annual replacement costs, and operational or electrical expenses. Some are less expensive to install but very expensive to maintain or operate.

Windows

Windows should generally be avoided. When located to take advantage of the sun for solar heat, the glare may cause serious problems. When windows are on the north side, there is less glare, but the loss of heat may be significant. Vandalism is another disadvantage.

Wall Padding

Generally, at the end of the basketball competition courts, there is padding attached to the wall to protect the students from injury when running into the wall. This is true even when a 10' safety zone is provided at the end of the court. These pads can be permanently installed or made to be portable. They are generally six foot tall and 16' to 24' wide and attached approximately 6" off the floor. The pads can be designed with almost any kind of graphic desired by the school in a wide variety of colors.

Fixed Equipment

If suspended equipment is planned, provision for its attachment should be made before the ceiling is installed. Basketball backstops will need special care in their installation to ensure rigidity and safety. All basketball backstops should be attached to ceilings or walls, and swing- up or fold-up models should be used where the backstops might interfere with other activities. In addition to the main court basketball backstops, provision should be made for other backstops on clear sidewalls. Hinged rims that collapse when grabbed are recommended for baskets used for recreational basketball play.

In the interest of safety, such suspension apparatus as bars, rings, and climbing poles and ropes should be so placed as to allow sufficient clearance from basketball backstops and walls. If wall apparatus is desired in the gymnasium, a strip of metal or hardwood firmly attached to the wall at the proper height is recommended. Wherever necessary, floor plates should be installed for fastening movable equipment such as horizontal bars and volleyball standards. If mats are to be hung in the gymnasium, appropriate hangers placed above head level to avoid any injury must be provided. Rubber-tired mat trucks, which may be wheeled into a storage room, are recommended. For safety reasons, padding should be installed on all walls in back of baskets.

Spectator Seating

The extent of the demand for spectator seating depends upon each school and the community it serves. Modern design uses power-driven folding or rollaway bleachers (see Chapter 13 for greater detail), which require little permanent space. If possible, the outer surface of folding bleachers should create a flat, wall-like surface, so it may be used for ball rebounding.

The width of each seating space should not be less than 18 inches. Rollaway bleachers most commonly allow 22-inch depths for seats. The number of rows available in rollaway bleachers varies, with 23 rows the maximum for standard equipment. In some instances, bleachers with 30 rows can be obtained by special order. Planners should investigate local and state codes.

Balconies can be used to increase the total seating capacity beyond the maximum permitted at floor level. The space at both levels should be considered as activity areas when the bleachers are closed. It may be desirable, in some instances, to provide less than maximum seating at floor level so a balcony will be wide enough to serve as a teaching station for specific activities. Balcony bleachers can be installed to telescope from the back to the front so that in the closed position they stand erect, creating a divider wall at the edge of the balcony. This arrangement affords partial isolation of the teaching station and enhances the safety of participants.

Traffic Controls

Good traffic control should permit the efficient movement of students to and from the gymnasium, locker rooms, and other related service areas. All traffic arrangements for spectators should provide direct movement to and from bleachers with a minimum of foot traffic on gymnasium floors. Spectators should have access to drinking fountains, refreshment counters, and toilets without crossing the gymnasium floor. Steep, high stairways should be avoided. Ramps with non-slip surfaces might be substituted in appropriate places. Local and state building codes and standards of the National Fire Protection Association should be consulted.

Foyers

Where finances and space will allow, foyers should be placed so they will serve as entries to gymnasiums and will guide spectators as directly as possible to seating areas. Toilet facilities for men and women, ticket-sales windows, ticket-collection arrangements, checkrooms, public telephones, a refreshment-dispensing room with counter, and lockable display case should be provided, opening directly to the foyer.

Spectator Rest Rooms

All athletic events that attract spectators require rest room facilities. Rest rooms should be designed for proper light, ventilation, and sanitary care. State health codes will influence the number and location of rest rooms.

Concessions

Concessions have come to be considered a necessary service for public gatherings. Appropriate space and distribution as well as adequate fixtures for concession stands within the fieldhouse should be planned. Since plumbing and electrical services are already available in the field house, the concession stand might be located as a part of or adjacent to the field house. The concessions area will include but not be limited to a double sink, garbage disposal, electric range, microwave, refrigerator, ice maker, popcorn maker, freezer, plenty of counter space, and signage.

Other Factors

Provisions should be made for the installation of electric scoreboards, a central sound and public address system, picture projectors, radio and television equipment, high-fidelity equipment, and cleaning machines. Special consideration should be given to locating floor outlets for scoreboards and public address systems adjacent to the scoring table. Wall outlets should be installed near cupped eyes to permit special lighting as needed. Controls for gymnasium lighting should be conveniently located, recessed, and keyed.

Drinking fountains and cuspidors should be accessible without causing a traffic or safety problem. It may be desirable to provide a drained catch-basin, grilled flush with the floor, to care for splash and overflow.

Cupped eyes can be installed in all walls at approximately 15-foot height and 10-foot intervals for decorating convenience. They may also be used for attaching nets and other equipment to walls at appropriate heights. Bulletin boards and chalkboards should be provided where needed. If wall space is available, such boards may be provided for each teaching station. Three full-length mirrors should be placed at one end of a wall, side by side, for visual analysis of movement.

The Auxiliary Gymnasium

Depending on the demands placed on a facility for classes, after-school athletics, intramurals, and student and faculty recreation, more than one gymnasium may be necessary. Careful program scheduling will determine what is best in each situation. However, most schools need at least one auxiliary gym. Room dimensions should be based on the anticipated uses with special attention to the need to accommodate standard-size wrestling mats.

The other type of auxiliary gymnasium closely resembles the main gym, except there is little or no need for spectator seating, and the floor dimensions may be smaller. A 75' by 90' gym will house two volleyball courts, three badminton courts, three one-wall handball courts, and space for some gymnastic equipment.

The auxiliary gyms can serve a variety of other activities in the instructional, intramural, recreational, or interscholastic program, which cannot all be accommodated after school in the main gymnasium. Some auxiliary gyms are large enough to be divided into two teaching stations. The characteristics of these facilities are similar to those in the gymnasium. A less-expensive type may have a ceiling as low as 18'. Such activities as wrestling, tumbling, calisthenics, self-defense, and fencing may be conducted in such a room.

Adapted Physical Education Area

Federal legislation requires that special considerations be made for the handicapped person. Schools must provide programs which meet their special needs. The adaptive area, therefore, becomes essential (see Chapter 7 for additional information).

Gymnastics Area for the Gymnasium

By planning in detail the equipment layout for gymnastics, attachment hardware for the floors, walls, and ceilings can be included in the original design and construction. The manufacturers of gymnastic equipment will supply details for the attachment of their equipment as well as sug-

gestions for floor plans or layout for the apparatus with proper safety areas. Preplanning results not only in proper installation but also in savings on the cost of doing the work at a later date.

Storage of gymnastics equipment requires special attention, e.g., a room adjacent to the gym with a roll-up door. Equipment left out or stored around the edge of the gym is a safety hazard and will shorten the life of the equipment. Mat storage requires either a mat truck or a hydralic lift to ceiling. The use of light folding mats will, however, alleviate some of the storage problems.

Climbing ropes should be attached to a height of 24' and drop to about three feet above the floor. Apparatus may be attached to the exposed beams. If the ceiling is placed below the structural members, the locations of suspended equipment should be planned and eyebolts provided during construction. Ropes should be placed five feet part, allowing one for each five students in class. The rings should be at least five feet from the walls. End walls at least 35' from the point of attachment will afford safety for the participants. Traveling rings are supported from a height of 18' to 26' and are located seven feet apart along a continuous line. Lines should be provided for drawing ropes and rings not in use to the overhead so as not to interfere with other activities.

High bars require both floor and wall or ceiling attachments. Adjustable bars for class instruction can be arranged in a linear series. Bars vary from six to seven feet in length and require 12' of unobstructed space extending perpendicular to their long axis. Bars for interscholastic competition are commonly located as individual units.

Free-Standing Gymnastics Area

Rarely will a free-standing gymnastics area be found in a secondary school. These facilities are either privately owned or part of a non-profit agency (e.g., YMCA, YWCA, or Boys and Girls Club). The free-standing facility will include:

- entrance area,
- lobby space,
- small pro-shop,
- concessions,
- public rest rooms,
- day care area,
- balcony for spectator seating for 300,
- competition/practice area—boys: runway for vaulting with a landing pit, high bar (2) area with a landing pit, pummel horse area, parallel bars (2) area, rings area, and floor exercise area shared with girls; girls: runway for vaulting with a landing pit, uneven bar (2) area with landing pit, balance beams (3) area with a landing pit, and a shared floor exercise area, (See Diagram 28.1)
- trampoline area with trampoline flush with floor,
- office space, and
- a large storage area at least 600 square feet with a ceiling height of 10' and a roll-up door.

Strength and Cardiorespiratory Area

The current trend in physical education facilities is the addition of a strength and cardiorespiratory area. This area would be used for physical education classes by student-athletes before and after school, and community programming after school hours and on the weekends. The details regarding this space can be found in Chapter 24.

Health Instruction

The purpose of health instruction is to provide health information and experiences that will lead to the establishment of attitudes and practices conducive to the conservation, protection, and promotion of individual, community, and world health. This section of the chapter is concerned with the facilities essential to the conduct of health classes, including first-aid and safety instruction.

Elementary School

For the elementary school, the general principle of the self-contained classroom is accepted. However, in order that there be maximum opportunity for health and safety instruction, it is important to have drinking fountains and handwashing and grooming facilities, and that there be ready access to toilets for the exclusive use of each room in the primary grades. In classrooms for intermediate grades, hand lavatories should be provided. In addition to the central storage space for equipment common to all rooms, each room should have storage space for health teaching aids especially suited to that class. A mobile laboratory table or a resource room equipped with facilities for demonstrations in health and science should be available.

Secondary School

The basic space allotment for the health instruction facilities in the secondary school should be in harmony with generally accepted standards for schoolroom size. However, due to the nature of activities involved in health and safety instructional programs, it is recommended that the space

Diagram 28.1

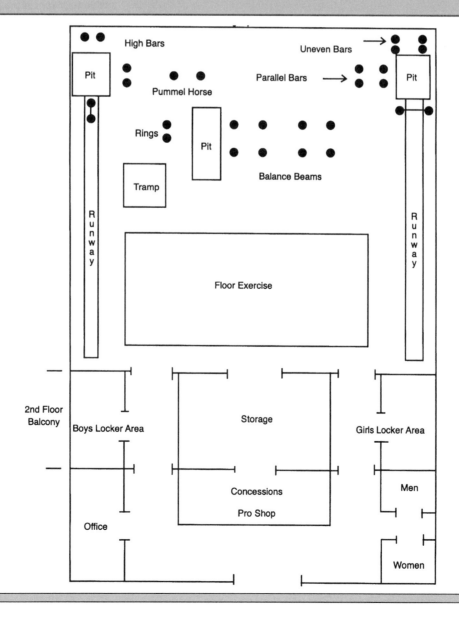

allowed for such instruction be increased approximately 35 percent above requirements for the regular classroom. This will result in a space allotment of 35 square feet per student, including storage space.

The space allotment should be sufficient to allow for such activities as vision and hearing screening, first-aid and safety instruction, and practical demonstrations, and for flexible teacher location. In addition to the conventional teacher's desk, provision should be made for laboratory demonstrations. This indicates the need for a laboratory-demonstration table, which will provide space and facilities for demonstrations. Thus, provisions should be made for water, gas, and electricity, as well as storage space for heating devices, test tubes, flasks, beakers, and other equipment essential to such demonstrations. The diversity of teaching procedures requires that regular classroom arrangements (Chapter 32 for additional information) be used at some times, but at other times floor space be available for practical instruction, such as practice in artificial respiration, splinting, and emergency transportation.

The suggested laboratory method of teaching will require adequate storage space, as well as display areas for charts, mannequins, models, and equipment. First-aid equipment, such as blankets, bandages, splints, and stretchers will also be needed. For instruction in home nursing, such equipment as incubators, roll-away beds, pans, containers, and bedding will be required.

There should be a large amount of display space for the great variety of educational exhibits, literature, and pupil projects inherent in the health education program. This can be provided by allowing liberal space for tables and shelves, and by using all available wall space for bulletin boards and tackboards.

The health instruction laboratory should provide for the optimum use of such additional audiovisual devices as still pictures, slides, motion pictures, radio, and television. This will necessitate a liberal allowance of appropriately located electrical outlets, shades, or curtains that will reduce the outside light, and a screen that may be mounted above the chalkboard behind the laboratory desk.

It may be desirable that there be convenient access between the health instruction laboratory and the health service suite in order that each may augment the total health program. For example, when home-nursing classes are meeting in the health instruction laboratory, there will be times when it is desirable to have free but supervised access to both facilities. Similarly, when there is occasion to have a large number of people using the health service suite, it may be desirable to have access to the health instruction laboratory for seating or other purposes. In some instances, it may be desirable to consider locating the health instruction laboratory near the science laboratories in order to facilitate joint use of equipment and supplies. In other instances, location in the area of the physical education facilities may be desirable.

The secondary school health instruction laboratory should be an example of the ideal classroom environment, with special concern for color of walls, lighting, ventilation, temperature and humidity control, order, and cleanliness (see Chapter 15 for additional information).

Recognition should be given to the desirability of joint planning of school health facilities with public health people and other community groups who might need access to such facilities, thus strengthening the total community health program. Such arrangements can serve to strengthen the program of all who are concerned with health by providing for dual use of such facilities without duplication and with a minimum of expense.

Checklist for Health Instruction Facilities
- Space for 35 square feet per pupil, maximum of 30 pupils
- Flexible teacher location
- Provision for various teaching methods, including laboratory demonstration
- Flexibility of seating
- Hot and cold running water and gas outlet
- Educational exhibit space
- Storage space
- Provision for using audiovisual devices (electrical outlets, window shades, screens)
- Access to health service unit exemplary environmental features
- Adequate handwashing facilities, drinking fountains, and toilets
- Air conditioning
- Accessible to and usable by the disabled
- Planned jointly for community use

Health Services

Health services contribute to the school program by: (1) facilitating learning; (2) encouraging pupils to obtain needed medical or dental treatment; (3) adapting school programs to individual pupil needs; (4) maintaining a healthful school environment; and (5) increasing pupils' understanding of health and health problems. Following the principle that program determines facilities, plans would include accommodations for:
- Appraising the health status of pupils and school personnel,
- Counseling pupils, parents, and others concerning appraisal findings,
- Encouraging the correction of remediable defects and the proper adjustment of those identified as not remediable,
- Assisting in the identification and education of disabled pupils, and
- Helping to prevent and control disease
- Providing emergency service for injury or sudden illness
- Maintaining a cumulative combined health and accident file for each student.

Health service personnel are not only charged with the responsibility for developing policies and procedures, but should also be consulted in planning programs and facilities. Policies and procedures are essential for the attainment of program objectives through the proper utilization of facilities and the protection of school populations under adverse or disaster conditions.

Health Suite

Whether in a small rural or a large urban school building, the health service suite will be used for a variety of activities. It may be the center for emergency care of injuries or sickness and health appraisals by nurses, physicians, dentists or dental hygienists, and psychiatrists or psychologists. Various types of systematized screening tests, such as tests of vision and hearing, may be conducted in this area.

The health suite is the logical place for conferences concerning a pupil's health problems involving the parent, teacher, doctor, nurse, and physical educator. A part of the suite should be used as a dressing room, and another section should serve as a waiting room. Some space should be set aside for the isolation of a pupil when the situation warrants, and accommodations should be provided for pupils on a prescribed rest schedule. The suite will also need to provide space for the health service personnel, plus the necessary space for records and equipment.

The common concerns of school health service personnel and guidance personnel suggest the need for a close, cooperative working relationship. This would indicate the desirability of locating the units in close proximity to each other and the possibility of using a common waiting room.

The school health suite may, in some instances, also serve the community. Thus, the health suite and the adjacent health instruction area may be for well-child conferences and other preschool health activities. They may accommodate classes for expectant mothers and other adult education activities. In those situations where the building and grounds are used for recreation purposes, the unit may serve as an emergency-care and first-aid station for those participating in the recreation program.

The fact that a health service suite is located within the school does not mean that programs for nonschool groups will be administered or manned by school personnel. Usually, these community health activities will be under the direct supervision of the official health agency. If community usage of the health service suite is expected, then those who will provide the service should be involved in the planning.

Location

In locating a health service suite, consideration should be given to the variety of activities that will be carried on therein, and to conditions that will permit those functions to be carried on conveniently and efficiently. Some factors to be considered in the location of a health service suite are:

- It should be located along a corridor near a main entrance to the building so that it may be completely isolated from the remainder of the building, yet conveniently accessible from all parts of the building.
- It should be located on the first or ground floor.
- The location should be in close proximity to the administrative suite. In situations where full-time health service personnel are not contemplated, direct access should be provided between the area and the administrative office, the teacher's lounge, or an adjacent classroom. In the secondary school, advantages will accrue from locating the health classroom and the service suite so that there is convenient access between the two areas. This is especially true when school health facilities are utilized for community health services.
- The location and acoustical treatment should be such that corridor and outside noises are kept to a minimum.
- A maximum amount of natural light should be available.

Rooms

All purposes for which the health service suite is designed may be carried out in one large unit, which may be subdivided into: (1) waiting room; (2) examining room; (3) resting rooms; (4) toilet rooms; (5) counseling room; (6) dental health room; (7) isolation room; (8) special screening areas (e.g., vision and hearing); and (9) office area for health service personnel and records. Depending upon the size of the school and its health policies, various combinations of the above spaces may be planned without affecting the efficiency of the services. For example, in smaller elementary schools, all services may be cared for in one room, provided proper screening is used and the administrative and health service suite are served by a common waiting room.

In larger schools, and especially in high schools, division of the unit into separate rooms is desirable. Thought should be given to the type of wall construction that provides for rearrangement of space allocation, since change in policies and school population will affect the nature and extent of health services. When remodeling old buildings, the same standards that apply to new structures should be maintained.

Guidelines based on accepted standards are recommended below.

Waiting Room

Schools with ten or more classrooms, or enrollments of 300 or more pupils should provide a waiting room, possibly in combination with guidance and/or administrative offices. It should be directly accessible to the corridor and the examining room. The waiting room should be separated from adjacent rooms by a full-height partition.

The decorations and furnishings should be designed to create a bright and cheerful atmosphere. The size is dependent upon enrollment and established health policies of the school (see Table 28.1).

Examining Room

Schools consisting of six or more classrooms, or an enrollment of 180 or more pupils, should include an examining room in the health suite. It should be directly connected with resting rooms and the waiting room, and should have access to toilets, the dental space, and any offices that are provided.

The location should provide for natural light and ventilation. The size and arrangement should be such that an uninterrupted distance of 20' is available for vision testing.

The room should be acoustically treated. If the examining room is to serve as a resting room (in small schools), screened cot areas should be provided. The space should be ample for proper arrangement or storage of the following equipment:

Table 28.1
Recommended Sizes in Square Feet of
Health-Service Facilities for Schools of Various Sizes

ENROLLMENT	200-300	301-500	501-700	701-900	901-1100	1101-1300
Waiting Room	80	80	100	100	100	120
*Examining Room	200	200	200	240	240	240
**Rest room (total area for boys and girls)	200	200	200	240	240	240

Toilets.......... 48 square feet total area (provide one for girls and one for boys)

OPTIONAL AREAS

Dental Clinic	100 square feet for all schools
Office Space	80 square feet for each office provided
Eye examination	120 square feet minimum for all schools

* Examining room areas include 6 square feet for clothes closet and 24 square feet for storage closets.

** For determining the number of cots, allow one cot per 100 pupils up to 400 pupils, and one cot per 200 pupils above 400. Round out fractions to nearest whole number. Allow 50 square feet of floor space for each of the first two cots and 40 square feet for each additional cot.

*** In schools enrolling 901 to 1,100, a three-cot rest room is suggested for boys and a four-cot rest room for girls, and in 1,101 to1,300-pupil schools, a three-cot rest room is suggested for boys and a five-cot rest room for girls.
Note: For larger schools, add multiples of the above areas to obtain total needs.
\# State Department of Education, *School Planning Manual*, school Health Service Section, Vol. 37. November, 1954, Richmond Va.

- desk, chair, computer and possible a typewriter,
- filing cabinets,
- platform scale with stadiometer,
- vision-testing equipment,
- movable spotlight,
- blankets and linens,
- folding screen,
- sterilizer and instrument table,
- cot or couch,
- cabinet for first-aid supplies,
- cup and towel dispensers,
- wastebasket and foot-operated disposal can,
- full-length mirror, and
- audiometric testing devices.

The size of the examining room will be determined by enrollment, the types of activities to be conducted, and the extent of use by medical and other health personnel (see Table 28.1).

Resting Rooms

Resting rooms are essential in all schools. They should be directly connected with the examining room and toilets, or be accessible to them from a restricted hallway. Separate resting rooms should be provided for each sex. A screened cot space may be a necessary arrangement in smaller schools.

The location should be such that natural light and ventilation, and quiet atmosphere are secured. If there are no full-time health service personnel available, the location should be such that supervision of the area may be conveniently provided from the administrative office or an adjacent classroom. Adequate space should be provided for cots (see Table 28.1), bedside stands, wastebaskets, and blanket and linen storage.

Toilet Rooms

A toilet room with stool and lavatory should be directly connected, or be accessible by a restricted hallway, to the resting rooms in all schools with 10 or more classrooms, or with an enrollment of 300 or more pupils. In smaller schools, where the resting rooms are a part of the examining room or other space, provision should be made for convenient toilet facilities. A toilet room with a minimum of 48 square feet should be provided for each sex (see Table 28.1).

Storage Closets

Storage space, opening off each resting room, should be provided for linens, blankets, pillows, etc. In the smaller schools without separate resting rooms, such storage should be provided for in the examining room.

A ventilated cloak closet should be provided for school health personnel. If built-in storage facilities are not feasible, space should be allowed for movable storage cabinets.

Isolation Room

An isolation room as an integral part of the health service suite is desirable to insure privacy when required. It should be directly connected with the examining room, but apart from the resting rooms. A space for one cot and the necessary circulation area is sufficient in most instances.

Vision and Hearing Screening Areas

Such areas should be included as a part of the examining room. An uninterrupted distance of 20' should be provided for vision testing. Audiometric testing will require an acoustically treated room.

Offices

The provision of office space for health service personnel will depend upon the time they spend in the school. If this facility is provided, it should be connected with the waiting room, the examining room, and if possible, the corridor.

The minimum recommended space for two people is 80 square feet. Provision should be made for maintaining health and accident reports.

Counseling Room

Although such space will not be in constant use, a room where the doctor, nurse, teacher, and parent can discuss a pupil's health is an important unit of the total health facility. Space large enough to accommodate a small table and four or five chairs is adequate. It may be used as office space for part-time health service personnel.

General Suggestions

The entire suite should present an informal and pleasant atmosphere. Flooring should be of a material that is non-absorbent, easily cleaned, and light in color. Lavatories used by personnel functioning within the examining room should be operable by the wrist, knee, or foot.

Figures 28.1 and 28.2 are examples of some possible healthsuite arrangements.

Driver Education Areas and Facilities

The program of driver education is generally accepted as a responsibility of the school and, more specifically, as a function of health and safety and physical education departments. The guidelines outlined below are in keeping with approved standards and national recommendations.

Indoor Facilities

For the indoor program, there should be a classroom, a psychophysical laboratory with testing devices, a simulator laboratory, and an office.

Location

All indoor facilities should be on the first floor of the building, near the garage or parking space for the dual-control cars, and near the driving range if one is used.

Classroom

Size

The recommended procedure is to combine the classroom with the laboratory for a combination room of 30'x 40'. Where separate rooms are used, the classroom should be of standard size.

Furniture and Equipment

In addition to the standard classroom facilities and equipment, such as chalkboard, bulletin board, desk, and chairs, the driver education classroom should provide facilities for the following special equipment:
- VCR and monitor
- Bookcases and storage cabinets for video tapes, flip charts, testing equipment, models, etc.
- Demonstration table
- Demonstration equipment, including magnetic traffic board, working models, flannel boards, model signs, and signals

Driver Education Laboratory

The laboratory contains equipment needed to test the student's physical, mental, and emotional qualifications required for safe and skillful driving.

Size

When the combined room is not used, the laboratory should be at least 24'x 30'.

Furniture and Equipment

The needed furniture and equipment will include a demonstration table, chairs, worktables, and spaces to accommodate equipment for testing visual acuity, depth perception, color vision, field of vision, reaction time, steadiness, night vision, etc.

Simulator Laboratory

Driver education simulators are accepted as a means of providing the preliminary steps to behind-the-wheel instruction. Because of the nature of the simulator units, facilities for them should be considered as permanent installations, preferably in a separate classroom.

Size

The size of the simulator laboratory will depend on the number of simulator cars to be installed. A typical eight-car installation will accommodate 450 to 500 students per year, and a 16-car installation will accommodate 960 to 1,000. The room size for eight cars should be 24'x 33'; for 16 cars, it should be 30'x 40'.

Furniture and Equipment

The room should be clear of obstructions that might interfere with the projector beam, and should be provided with the regular complement of chalkboard, bulletin board, tackboard, magnetic board, etc.

Layout

The cars are arranged in a semicircular fashion, with the first row a minimum of 8', preferably 10' to 12', from the screen, and with the outside cars not exceeding an angle of 30° from the screen. The first row should have the lesser number of cars.

Figure 28.1
Health Suite for Elementary School
Seven Classrooms

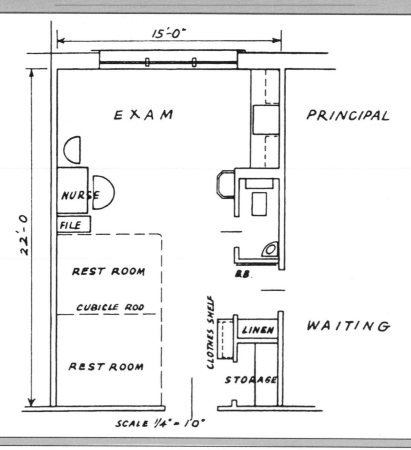

Figure 28.2
Secondary School Health Suite

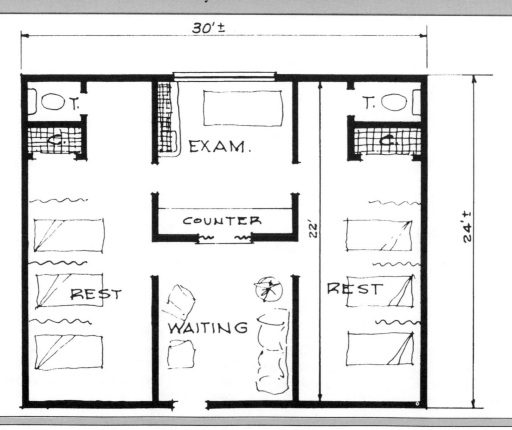

A minimum of 24" should be allowed between the rows, with a 30-inch aisle down each side of the room. Aisle spaces must comply with state safety codes. The projector should be located in the center at the extreme rear of the room, and a 6' x 8' screen should be placed in the front of the room.

Manufacturers' specifications for electrical requirements should be followed. Ordinarily, the standard 120-volt, 60-cycle alternating current is required. It should be supplied through a double outlet located in the vicinity of the recording unit.

Lighting

Amole soft white fluorescent-light tubes recessed in the ceiling with semitranslucent shields to provide 100 footcandles of light at desk height should be installed.

Color

Pastel colors should be used. The woodwork and finishing should be compatible with color used on the walls. A reflection factor of 80 percent is needed for the ceiling, and 60 percent for the walls. The furniture should have a nonglare finish.

Heating and Ventilation

Heating and ventilation should conform to standards required throughout the entire school system.

Outdoor Areas and Facilities

Driving Area

Purpose

Behind-the-wheel instruction provides the skills necessary for safe and efficient driving.

Types

An on-street driving area is recommended for schools where traffic congestion is not a problem. First, driving maneuvers should be conducted in locations such as school driveways where there is no traffic. As ability develops, students get experience driving in situations approximating normal driving conditions, and then, finally, in actual normal traffic situations.

Blocked-off streets are sometimes used when street traffic is too heavy and school driveways are not available to teach the first driving maneuvers. Arrangements should be made with the residents of the area and with police officials. Since advanced driving skills are taught where other traffic is involved, streets should not be blocked off for an undue length of time.

An off-street driving range is recommended where land is available. Ranges should be laid out to simulate most physical situations associated with driving, such as: traffic signs, signals, and other control devices; parallel and angle parking; upgrade and downgrade situations; and simulated emergency situations. Space should allow for needed skill-test maneuvers. Different types of road surfaces should be provided. If night classes are conducted, the area should be lighted. The size of the driving range should be no smaller than 350'x450'.

The multiple-car driving range has the advantage of accommodating several cars simultaneously under the supervision of one teacher, thus reducing the per-pupil cost. With this type of range, communication between the instructor and students is accomplished by means of radio or public-address system (See Figure 28.3).

Recommended Equipment and Facilities

- Curbs for parking practice
- Intersections for various turn maneuvers
- Gravel area for driving and turn maneuvers
- Streets marked properly
- Streets that are both wide and narrow
- All signs-traffic, control signals, stop, warning, yield the
  right-of-way, regulatory, guide, and information
- Upgrade and downgrade roadways
- Simulated road surfaces-concrete, asphalt, and gravel
- Muddy surface for emergency situations
- Signboards found on normal roads
- Stanchions, guide-on, etc., for maneuvers

Points to Remember

- Determine the needs of the student and the objectives of the program.
- Provide as many realistic situations as possible.
- Design the driver-training area equal to the best facilities available.

Summary

The unit of primary importance is the room or space where teaching occurs—the gymnasium. All other parts of the school plant are, in a real sense, secondary. In physical education, therefore, the determination of the number and character of the teaching stations is basic to the planning process for either an elementary or secondary school. Further, it is important to locate these facilities in a separate wing for a number of reasons, including, but not limited to, noise, evening and weekend use, and non-school sponsored uses.

Figure 28.3
Multiple Car Off-Street Driving Range

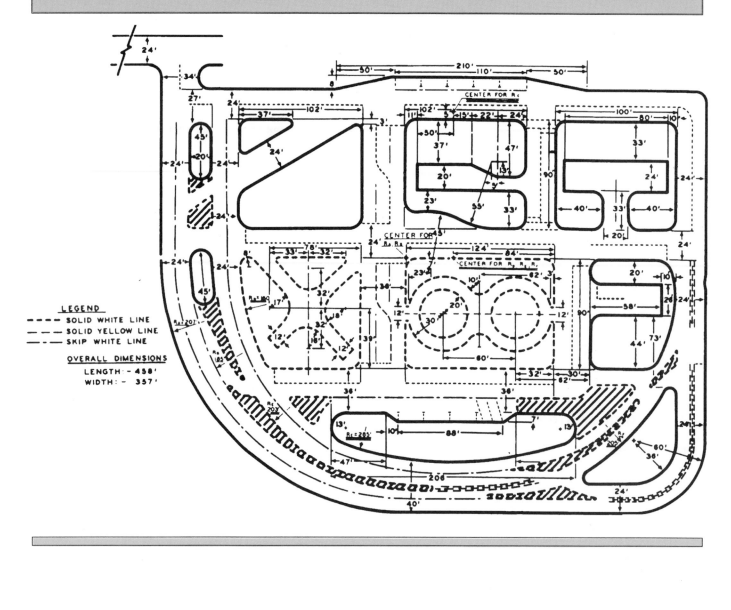

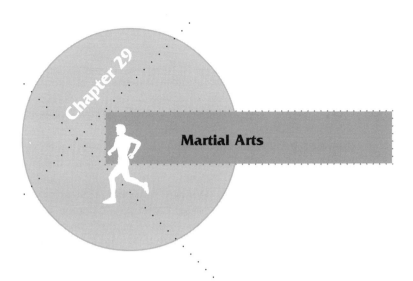

Thomas Horne, United States Military Academy

The martial arts are not merely self-defense techniques designed to make invincible weap-ons of the hands and feet. They are a formulated means by which one can obtain, through diligence and practice, a high level of physical proficiency; a tranquil, yet superior mental discipline, and a measurable degree of spiritual enlightenment (Logan & Petras, 1975).

Participants from Asia tend to emphasize mental and spiritual aspects, while those from the West tend to emphasize competition and physical development. Most of the modern martial arts have roots that go back to the ancient martial arts of Asia. Differing philosophies, interpretations, and interests of instructors and students have produced the wide range of martial arts practiced today.

Building or renovating a martial arts facility requires extensive planning. This chapter will provide information to assist martial arts facility developers with design and construction decisions. Planners and developers of martial arts facilities must understand at least the general nature of martial arts if they are to make informed decisions. The major martial arts are summarized in this chapter to provide this knowledge base. A martial arts web exercise is provided to familiarize readers with web sites that may be helpful in developing a martial arts facility or program. A martial arts facility development case study that details a facility development effort is also included.

Instructional Objectives

After studying this chapter the student will be able to:
- apply general facility planning principles to developing martial arts facilities
- identify the two general types of martial arts facilities
- identify the major martial arts styles and determine which of the two facility types is most appropriate for each style
- list the equipment and key design features for the each type of martial arts facility
- access a number of web sites to get additional information on martial arts facilities
- apply facility development concepts to a martial arts facility case study

Facility Planning Concepts

The goal when constructing or renovating a martial arts facility is to produce a facility that is highly functional, cost effective, aesthetically pleasing, safe, and accessible to all. Failure to adequately plan often results in a facility that costs too much and delivers too little. Participatory planning (seeking information from all interested individuals, especially the representative user group) is the recommended planning strategy (Flynn, 1993). The first step is to conduct a "needs analysis." The needs analysis solicits information from the owners and operators, the target facility users, and staff members. The owner and operator may be a person, a group of people, or an established organization. The owners and operators often provide all or some of the finances for the project, so they expect and deserve the opportunity to influence construction or renovation decisions. They are often the ones to provide a vision for the facility and leadership in organizing and executing both the planning and construction. Staff members provide an excellent source of information on which features should be included in a new martial arts facility. They have practical expertise and experience and can provide many useful recommendations. Gathering information from the target population provides valuable information to determine the demand for martial arts activities and identify which style is most popular. The users, customers, are often the best source of information on the desired support facilities, such as parking areas, locker rooms, concessions, and administrative areas.

Armed with data gathered from the "needs analysis," the next step is to convince higher authority or those providing the funding to support the construction or renovation project. It is important to present the data collected in a professional and persuasive manner. Failing to adequately prepare for this phase of planning could result in a poor presentation and the project being abandoned.

Once a project gets support from higher authority, establish a planning group or a steering committee. This group will stay actively involved during the entire planning and construction process. They will provide guidance, and in some cases make decisions on such issues as:

- renovating an existing facility or building a new facility
- cost limitations and funding sources
- promoting the project
- gathering additional needs assessments data
- site location
- selecting an architectural firm
- approving, rejecting, or modifying architectural firm plans and proposals
- selecting construction contractors
- developing construction schedules and phasing
- specifying material and space requirements
- ensuring code compliance
- identifying and solving design and construction problems
- establishing and implementing maintenance and operation procedures
- determining requirements for support and competition areas

The scope of the project and the complexity of the administrative requirements will determine the magnitude of the planning effort. Whether planning a modest renovation of an existing martial arts room or constructing a new martial arts complex complete with all the support facilities, careful planning will avoid costly mistakes.

Overview of the Martial Arts

Martial arts can be defined as numerous systems of self-defense and offensive techniques that may emphasize sport competition, physical development, mental development, or a combination of these aspects. Initially, most martial arts taught in America were taught in wrestling rooms, gymnasiums, multipurpose rooms, or in the outdoors. This is still the case in most colleges, recreation centers, YMCAs, and other multipurpose facilities. Martial arts facilities, designed specifically for martial arts, are now being included in the design and construction of many of these multipurpose facilities. Many commercial martial arts programs are taught in specialized martial art facilities called dojos (literally translated as "Place where one learns the way").

Whether designing a separate commercial facility or a martial arts area in a larger project, planners must decide if the new martial arts facility will be a general combative facility or a facility designed to accommodate a specific style of martial arts. In either case, a general knowledge of the major martial arts will help planners make important design decisions. There are almost as many types of martial arts as there are types of ball games. There are too many types and styles of martial arts to discuss the facility requirements for each one. Seven of the martial arts represent the major types and styles of martial arts. A brief summary of these seven major martial arts is provided to assist facility planners make informed design and construction decisions (Table 29.1).

Aikido

Aikido (the "Way of harmony") is the art of unarmed self-defense against either an armed or unarmed assailant. Mostly an art of spiritual enlightenment, a main focus of Aikido is to develop a healthy mind, body, and spirit, free from bad habits. Aikidoists attempt to use their unlimited spiritual power called ki, internal energy, to redirect the energy of the attacker in a dynamic circle with joint manipulation and circular throws (Winderbaum, 1977). Most styles of aikido emphasize the art of self-defense and not the sport, so there is neither competition or tournaments. One style of Aikido, the Tomiki style, includes organized competitions (Introduction to Aikido, Internet).

Judo

Judo (the "Gentle way") was adapted from jujutsu by Jigoro Kano. Kano retained the self-defense, flexibility, mental concentration, and self-improvement aspects of jujutsu and discarded dangerous techniques. (Winderbaum, 1977) Judo emphasizes close-contact throwing and grappling techniques that include pinning, choking, arm locks, and striking techniques. Striking techniques are taught in formal instruction but not practiced in the sport aspects of judo.

Karate

Originally, karate was a form of deadly combat, but it is now practiced primarily as a sport. Karate is divided into six major areas, calisthenics, kihon (fundamentals), kata (forms of prearranged movements), kumite (sparring), and weapon training (Karate Terms, Internet). Karate tends to emphasize kicks, punches, and a strong offense as a good defense (Trais, 1973).

Kendo

Kendo, "Way of the sword", is a sport version of Japanese fencing. Contestants wear extensive protective armor and try to hit each other on designated parts of the body with simulated weapons. (Goodbody, 1969)

Kung Fu

The two distinctive styles of kung fu are the "hard style" (Cho-li-fat) and the "soft style" (Sil-lum). The hard style emphasizes power and strength for debilitating offensive maneuvers. The soft style focuses more on speed and agility to deliver an effective attack on vulnerable areas of the body. Kung fu employs both the arms and legs to deliver kicks, blows, throws, holds, body turns, dodges, leaps, and falls. Weapons are used more often in kung fu than karate. Stylized movements are used, and some techniques are derived from animal movements.

Tae Kwon Do

Tae kwon do (the "Way of the smashing foot") is the art and sport of self-defense stressing kicking, aerial, and dynamic circular techniques. Like karate, tae kwon do consists primarily of two components, kata (series of preset movements) and kumite (sparring). With its Olympic recog

Table 29.1
Martial Arts Summary

Art	Aikido	Judo	Karate	Kendo	Kung Fu	Tae Kwan Do	Tai Chi
Meaning	Way of Devine Harmony	The Gentle Way of the Empty Hand	The Way of the Sword	Skill & Effort or Disciplined Technique	The way of Kicking and Jumping	Grand Ultimate Boxing
Country of Origin	Japan	Japan	Okinawa	Japan	China	Korea	China
School	Aikidajo Dojo	Dojo	Dojo	Dojo	Kwoon	Do jang	Kwoon
Uniforms	Judogi	Judogi	Karetegi	Ilendogi	Dark Top, Sash pants & shoes	Dobok	Street Clothes
Competitive	Most forms No	Yes	Yes	Yes	Traditionally No Some Sport Now	Yes	No
Facility Type	Grappling	Grappling	Striking	Striking (Weapons)	Striking (Weapons)	Striking	Striking
Flooring	Sub-Mat with Mat or Tatami	Tatami	Wood/ Synthetic	Wood/ Synthetic	Wood/Mat	Wood/ Synthetic	Wood/ Synthetic

nition and worldwide disbursement, almost all tae kwon do school training now emphasizes the sporting aspects and competition.

Tái Chi

Tái chi is a Chinese soft art that emphasizes the harmony of the mind and the body (Perfetti, Internet). The qualities of slowness, lightness, clarity, balance, and calmness characterize tái chi movements. Never trained competitively, tái chi is the epitome of organized movement and is often practiced by more mature students for health and exercise (Logan & Petras, 1975). The fundamental moves of this graceful martial art can be practiced almost anywhere with little or no equipment.

Types of Martial Arts Facilities

Martial arts facilities tend to be simple structures with areas free from distractions. These training facilities are often called dojos. Most modern-day dojos maintain the standards of simplicity and beauty found in old school dojos (Urban 1967).

There are many different styles of martial arts, and no two martial arts programs require the same type of facility and equipment. The major styles of martial arts emphasize primarily grappling techniques or striking techniques. Grappling martial arts emphasize throws, chokes, joint locks, wrestling, pushing, pulling, trips, and falling. Striking martial arts emphasize kicks, punches, strikes, and weapons.

Martial arts facilities can therefore be divided into two types of facilities: Grappling Martial Arts Facilities and Striking Martial Arts Facilities.

Grappling Martial Arts Facilities

Aikido and Judo are martial arts styles that involve throwing skills, joint locks, and wrestling-type activities. Aikido and Judo require protective floor matting. The requirement of floor matting is the distinguishing characteristic of Grappling Martial Arts Facilities. Grappling martial arts often use traditional wrestling rooms with rubberized wrestling mats and padded walls. These wrestling rooms meet the minimum requirements for grappling martial arts, but a two-layer mat system is recommended for any of the grappling martial arts that require throwing. The standard wrestling mat alone does not provide sufficient protection for high-impact activities like throws. A two-layer mat system with a lower layer of foam-type matting and an upper-layer standard wrestling-type mat is a versatile option. "Tatami" mats, Japanese straw mats (modern tatami mats are made of compressed foam), over a spring-loaded base is ideal for Judo and Aikido.

When designing a dedicated martial arts facility, include specialized matting specifically selected for the intended activity. Most styles of Aikido are non-competitive and only require a firm mat with shock-absorbing properties. The mat should not be slippery or too rough. The competitive Judo mat is a minimum of 14 meters by 14 meters and a maximum of 16 meters by 16 meters. The top layer of matting is

---

Figure 29.1
Judo competition area

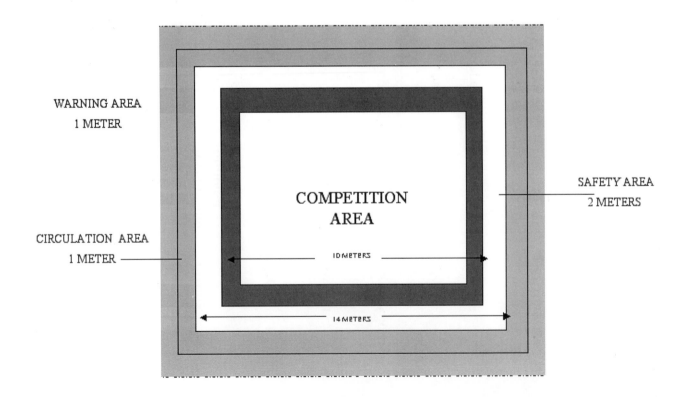

WARNING AREA
1 METER

CIRCULATION AREA
1 METER

COMPETITION
AREA

10 METERS

14 METERS

SAFETY AREA
2 METERS

usually a green-colored "tatami". Judo mats must have a smooth surface without gaps between sections. Competition mats have a competition zone surrounded by a one-meter danger zone marked in red. A three-meter zone on the outside of the danger zone is the safety zone. A resilient wooden platform is the preferred base for judo competitions (Judo Rules, Internet). Competitive judo venues should also include two scoreboards and three timing clocks.

Striking Martial Arts Facilities

Karate, kung fu, tai kwon do, and kendo are martial arts that employ mostly striking techniques (Roth 1974). Karate, kung fu, and tai kwon do all utilize a wide variety of kicks with the feet, punches with the hands, and striking skills with other body parts. The majority of these blows are delivered from the feet with full force and strike into a padded surface or stop just short of a human target. Kata, a prearranged series of skills, is also an important aspect for all of these styles. Normally, only the advanced students participate in contact competitions where they deliver full-contact blows against an opponent. Additional protective equipment is recommended when practicing striking techniques with an opponent and required for full-contact competition. The emphasis in each of these martial arts is body control, striking power, and precise technique. The punching, kicking, and striking techniques are delivered from either a linear or a spinning and turning motion. Wrestling-type mats are not recommended when throwing circular techniques since the anchor foot must rotate freely. Flexible hardwood or smooth synthetic floors are preferred for striking martial arts.

Kendo is predominately a weapon-oriented art that is normally practiced in a striking-type facility. Both karate and some kung fus use weapons on a limited basis. Weapons-oriented martial arts require special protective striking gear and are normally practiced without mats on the floor.

Only a flexible hardwood or smooth synthetic floor is recommended for "Striking Martial Arts." Small area mats may be used on an as-needed basis. Heavy bags and traditional striking posts, "Makiwaras," are usually included in the facility to practice kicking and punching techniques.

Tái chi does not employ either grappling or striking techniques. Most tái chi movements are controlled and are performed in a slow, deliberate manner. Tái chi can therefore be performed in a Grappling Martial Arts Facility, a Striking Martial Arts Facility, or an open outdoor space.

General features for Martial Arts Facilities

While the main distinguishing feature of martial arts facilities is the type of flooring and matting required, facility planners will also have other important facility features to consider.

Wall Coverings

The selection of appropriate wall coverings is critical. All martial arts facilities should have at least a portion of the wall covered with mirrors. Mirrors provide a valuable source of feedback for individuals participating in martial arts. Selecting the best location for the mirrors may be challenging because of conflicting priorities. Placing the mirrors too close to the activity area may result in the mirror being broken. Non-glass mirrors are safer and less likely to get broken, but scratch more easily and tend to give a distorted image. If glass mirrors are to be used, shatter- resistant glass mirrors are recommended. Placing mirrors too far from the activity area may make it difficult for participants to see themselves. Walls that do not have mirrors are often covered with protective wall mats, to a height of six feet.

Water fountains

Martial arts activities are very demanding physically, and martial arts participants will need to keep hydrated. A

Makiwara

Speed bag.

Heavy bag.

recessed water cooler is recommended for all types of martial arts facilities. A recessed water spigot is often desired to make facility sanitation easier. The spigot may be located near or as part of the water cooler.

Ceiling

Martial arts facilities tend to be simple functional facilities with few distractions. The simplest and least expensive ceiling is an open ceiling, the roof or floor above and associated piping, conduit, and ductwork is left exposed. An open ceiling area is normally painted white to give the dojo an open-area feeling. The open ceiling has advantages for activities that involve weapons and throws. The longer weapons, bos and swords, may damage an acoustic tile ceiling. Acoustic tiles used in drop ceilings can be equipped with spring-loaded clips that will allow the tiles to be contacted without being knocked out of place. The open ceiling is not as aesthetic as an acoustical tile ceiling, nor does it have as good of acoustic properties. If the facility is to be used primarily as a teaching station, an acoustic tile ceiling may be the ceiling of choice and worth the extra expense. The mini-

mum ceiling height is 12 feet for martial arts facilities, and a higher ceiling is recommended for a martial arts facility used primarily for weapons-oriented activities.

Lighting

The recommended lighting levels for martial arts facilities are 50 foot-candles. Recessed lights that have some type of protective covering are recommended. If the facility will be used for martial arts demonstrations or shows, equip the lights with a dimmer switch.

Storage

Providing adequate storage space for the martial arts facility is an important planning decision. Like storage space in many other facilities, storage space in martial arts facilities is often overlooked or reduced as soon as finances become an issue. Specific storage needs vary with each martial arts program, but should include at least some storage for personal items and mesh-type lockers to allow stored gear to dry. The size and type of storage facility required depends upon:

- total space available for construction
- budget constraints
- type of facility (grappling or striking)
- class sizes
- whether the mats will need to be taken up and stored or not
- whether the uniforms will be stored or not
- the style of martial arts to be practiced (kendo with its weapons will require more storage space than tái chi)
- Desire to include a trophy case to store and display trophies.

If specific storage needs are not available during the planning phase, allow 8-10 % of the total martial arts facility square footage for storage.

Scoreboard

A scoreboard with a clock is a practical feature for many of the martial arts, especially those that involve competition. The specific features of the scoreboard will depend on which style of martial art will use the scoreboard. If a scoreboard is desired, but funds are not available at the time of design, include the required power source in the plans. Including the power source in the original construction will cost very little and will save both time and money if funds become available to purchase a scoreboard in the future.

Custodial Closet

Martial arts facilities have a lot of skin contact areas that require regular cleaning and disinfecting. Locating a custodial closet in or close to the martial arts facility will facilitate cleaning and sanitation efforts. Rubberized mats require regular cleaning and disinfecting with a liquid disinfectant. A custodial sink is recommended, and a recessed spigot is the minimum source of water for cleaning the martial arts facility. The closet needs to have storage space for mops, buckets, cleaning and disinfecting supplies, and a vacuum cleaner (especially for carpeted facilities).

Summary

Planning and designing a martial arts facility is a difficult task, because there is no template for martial arts facilities. There are numerous types, styles, and variations of the martial arts. No two martial arts programs will have the same facility requirements. Martial arts programs are often conducted in multipurpose combative facilities, which makes the facility planning even more difficult. Facility planners and designers need to gather information from owners and operators, qualified martial arts instructors, staff members, and facility users to accurately determine program needs. Having a basic understanding of martial arts will help planners and designers make informed decisions concerning construction martial arts facilities. Martial arts facilities can be classified as grappling-oriented facilities with matted floors or striking-oriented facilities with flexible hardwood or synthetic floors.

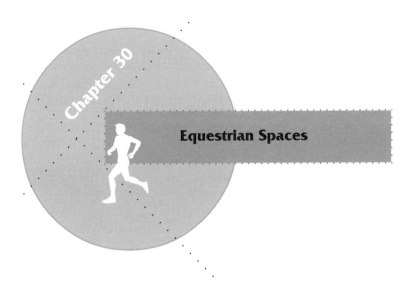

Chapter 30

Equestrian Spaces

Michael G. Hypes, Indiana State University
Julia Ann Hypes, Indiana State University

There are many variables involved in the planning of equestrian facilities. These variables include purpose, budget, image, climate, available material and labor, personal preferences, and future plans, to name a few. These variables make good planning critical to the overall success of the project.

Equestrian facilities incorporate several different components. These components include:
- barns,
- work areas,
- turnout areas, and
- arenas.

Each component serves a specific function in the overall operation of the equestrian program.

Learning Objectives

After reading this chapter, the student will be able to:
- discuss the key components for a stable area;
- describe various types of materials used for construction of a stable;
- identify various safety features to be incorporated in a stable; and
- compare and contrast the different facility needs for the equestrian events;

Barns

"The atmosphere and safety of all activities within a barn are determined by three main barn features: the brightness and placement of lights, the amount of fresh air, and the material and condition of the aisle floor" (Hill, 2000). Although some people prefer their facility to be plain, no frills and practical, others prefer their facility to make a statement. The image you want to portray with your facility can be a preliminary goal in the planning process. This image goal will guide many of the choices made including architectural style, building materials, interior fittings, and equipment.

Site Considerations

A horse barn's site selection should receive careful consideration. The barn's orientation to wind, sun, and shade should be considered. The ideal orientation would utilize summer breezes for cooling effect while avoiding the harsh winter wind. Trees can be used to:
- provide shade,
- serve as wind breaks,
- and to screen private areas.

Good water drainage is necessary to avoid standing water. Standing water or marshy areas could be breeding grounds for insects and disease, thus making it difficult to maintain a healthy stable.

General Construction Issues

A variety of construction materials can be used for barn structures. These materials can range from wood to pre-cast concrete. Whatever choice in materials is made, it is essential that the structure be as fire-resistant as possible.

Many different types or combinations of lighting can be used in a barn. Natural lighting can be used to enhance the overall lighting of the facility through the use of skylights, windows, translucent wall panels, and open doors. Whether incandescent, halogen, fluorescent, or high-intensity discharge lighting is used, it is important to remember that the fixture should be protected from dust and impact. The needed illumination in a given area will dictate the type and amount of fixtures needed.

Another important aspect of any barn is adequate ventilation. Ventilation in barns can be provided by windows, doors, roof vents, and exhaust fans. Adequate ventilation not only keeps barn odor at a minimum, it also helps keep the barn area dry, cool in the summer, and contributes to a healthy environment.

The main aisle in a barn receives a large amount of traffic. The surface in the main aisle should be durable and easy to clean. It is important for the safety of the horse and handler thatthe floor should be relatively smooth and level. The decision as to what type of flooring to use should be based on a balance of your personal preference, cost, availability, maintenance, and durability. Figure 30.1 provides a list of the more common flooring surfaces used in barn structures.

The size and number of components making up the barn will vary not only in relationship to the size of the facility, but also to the requirements placed upon the facility. The following are basic components for a typical barn facility:

- stalls
- feed room
- hay storage
- straw storage/alternative bedding
- feed storage
- wash and cleaning room (drying facilities)
- tack room
- utility stall
- manure disposal
- office
- lavatory accommodations
- equipment storage

The relationship of the components should first be concentrated on the horse. The components should also be considered with respect to other facilities, to the site, surrounding buildings, and to each other. Careful planning and placement of these barn components can minimize movement of heavy materials, feed, and tack, thus maximizing efficiency and safety of the facility.

Stalls

The stall is the indoor living space for the horse. It should be large enough to allow the horse to move about freely, lie down, and get up without hinderance from banging into the walls. Each stall should be large enough to accommodate separate areas for a horse's three main activities: eating, lying down, and defecating/urinating. In addition, stalls can be used for:

- tending to sick horses,
- birthing (foaling),
- sheltering horses from extreme weather, and
- keeping horses clean.

The more time a horse spends in a stall, the larger and more spacious the area should be. Figure 30.2 identifies some common stall dimensions based on the characteristics of the horse.

Stall doors come in a variety of styles. The door size should be sufficient to allow the horse to be led through the door without rubbing the sides and large enough for a cart to be pushed into the stall for cleaning. Stall doors should be a minimum of four feet wide and eight feet high. The edges of the door opening should be rounded to prevent injury. Horse-proof latches should be utilized on all stall doors. Horse-proof latches are out of reach of the horse or are made in such a way the horse cannot open it. Some of the more common latches include spring bolt, turning, and sliding bolt latches. A lower latch can be used to prevent the horse from pushing the bottom of the door out and possibly injuring itself.

A good stall floor will help reduce the amount of bedding needed. The stall floor should be comfortable for the horse, safe, and easy to clean. The flooring should be fairly easy to install, affordable, and able to withstand the abuse from hooves and acid from urine. Natural soil is the cheapest and easiest floor to install. However, over time, it can become uneven from the horse's movements, pawing, and urination. The size of your horse, function of the stall, and amount of stall use will also contribute to the stall flooring decision. Figure 30.3 provides a comparison of different stall floorings.

Flooring can be categorized as a draining or a non-draining surface. A draining floor allows urine to pass through

---

Figure 30.1
Types of Flooring

• dirt	• brick
• wood shavings, chips, shredded bark	• rubber brick
• sand	• rubber tile
• road base	• concrete
• gravel	• asphalt
• wood	• rubber mats

Each type of flooring has distinct advantages and disadvantages. Selection should be based upon your specific needs.

Example of a well-organized
utility area.

Photos by Michael Hypes

| | **Figure 30.2** | |
| | **Common Stall Sizes** | |

Stall Size

Feet	Meters	Suitable for:
10 x 10	3 x 3	Pony: under 14.2 hands Usually under 800 pounds
12 x 12	3.7 x 3.7	Standard Horse: up to 16 hands, 800-1,100 pounds
12 x 14	3.7 x 4.3	Large Horse: 16+ hands, 1,100-1,400 pounds
12 x 16	3.7 x 4.9	Draft Horse: more than 16 hands, over 1,400 pounds
12 x 18	3.7 x 5.5	Foaling Stall: up to 1,400 pound mare with foal

Modified from Hill, C. (2000). *Stablekeeping: A visual guide to safe and healthy horsekeeping.*

holes in the material. A non-draining or solid floor is made of material thatkeeps moisture on top of the flooring, allowing the moisture to be absorbed by the bedding.

Bedding provides a comfortable surface for a horse to lie on. It is used for absorption of urine and as an insulator from cold. Bedding material should be absorbent, soft, dust-free, easyto handle, and nontoxic. A list of possible types of bedding includes:

- straw,
- pine sawdust,
- pine shavings,
- shredded newspaper,
- hardwood chips, shavings, and
- sand.

Feed Room

This room houses the feed for daily use. It should be located close to the stalls. Each type of food should have a separate storage bin. Feed and grain storage bins should be lined with galvanized steel for vermin control. It is essential that the feed room be a dry storage area. Hazardous chemicals, cleaners, and disinfectants should be stored away from feed.

Hay Storage

The hay storage area should be directly accessible from the feed room. The size for this area will depend on the size of the facility and the frequency of feeding. The hay should be stored close to the stalls, usually in the loft, where it can be dropped into cribs in each stall. There should be exterior access to this area for ease of storing hay, either brought in from the field or purchased.

Bedding Storage

A variety of materials may be used for bedding purposes. The type selected may be based on geographical location, personal preference, animal preference, or availability. The area for bedding storage needs to be well-ventilated and dry. Bedding such as straw can be stored in a separate facility to minimize the risk of fire.

Tack Rooms

The tack room should be accessible to all stalls. The exact size and arrangement will be dependent upon the number of horses and the purposes for which the horses are being used.

Figure 30.3
Stall Flooring

Material	Advantages	Disadvantages
Soil (clay, dirt)	Relatively inexpensive Provides good traction and cushion	High maintenance, difficult to clean
Gravel, sand	Inexpensive Good traction and cushion	High maintenance, difficult to clean, danger of colic*
Asphalt	Easy to clean Low maintenance	Cold, hard, and abrasive Can be slippery Hard on legs and feet
Concrete	Easy to clean Good traction** Maintenance-free	Cold, hard, and abrasive Hard on legs and feet Slippery if not textured
Wood	Nice sound Warm	Slippery when wet Difficult to clean and disinfect
Draining flooring	Minimal bedding needed Moisture drains through	Urine accumulates under flooring
Conveyor belting	Easy to clean	Very slippery when wet Difficult to handle and install
Rubber mats	Quiet Good cushion andtraction Easy to clean	Can be difficult to handle and properly install Can gap and buckle

*Sand is not recommended because the horse can ingest the sand and develop colic.

**good traction if textured

Modified from Hill, C. (2000). *Stablekeeping: A visual guide to safe and healthy horsekeeping*

Windows are typically omitted from the tack room, because they take up valuable wall space as well as posing a security risk. The tack room should be designed to fit your needs. Some common elements in the tack room include bridle racks, saddle racks, tack hooks, blanket rods, and shelving for various grooming and veterinary items. If a separate barn office is not available, the tack room may include a refrigerator for storing medications and fireproof file cabinets for storing records. Space should also be allotted for the repair and cleaning of tack.

Many items are common to all horses and should be at hand in all tack rooms. Grooming tools are among the common items. These tools include:

- brushes
- curry combs (rubber and metal)
- electric clippers
- extension cords
- hoof picks

- scissors
- shedding blades
- soft cloths
- sponges
- sweat scrappers

In addition, all tack rooms should have first-aid kits for both horses and people. Depending upon the type of horse stabled, other assorted items are generally stored in the tack room. These include:

- bell boots
- lead ropes
- leg wraps
- longe lines
- ropes
- saddles
- tail wraps

Interior view of stall, feed and water containers.

Photos by Michael Hypes

Space Utilization,
Saint Mary-of-the-Woods
College, IN.

Example of interior stall door.

Example of double door entry.

Example of bedding storage.

Materials and tools for maintaining and repair of tack should also be kept in the tack room. Materials often needed are:

- awls
- hole punch
- knife
- latigo leather
- neats foot oil
- nylon string
- rivets
- saddle leather
- saddle soap
- sheepskin
- waxed linen string

Cleaning

From tack to facilities to horses, cleaning is an important aspect of barn operations. The function will dictate the space and location required. The cleaning area for equipment can be incorporated into a tack room or be a separate area. Large, deep sinks, hot and cold water sources, and washers and dryers aid in the proper cleaning and disinfect-

ing of blankets and other accessories. By placing plumbing for workrooms and horse washrooms adjacent to or near each other, you can help minimize plumbing headaches and costs.

Manure Disposal

The manure disposal area should be positioned well away from the stalls but be easily accessible. It should be located adjacent to a road to facilitate collection and dispersal.

- blankets
- bridles
- cavassons
- chain lead shanks
- crops
- feed bags
- halters
- hobbles

Office

The office space should accommodate a desk, chairs, filing cabinets, and storage space for supplies. An area for a

Tack room,
Saint Mary-of-the-Woods
College, IN.

Photo by Michael Hypes

computer with a dedicated phone line should be considered. The telephone should be fitted with an external bell or extensions, so it may be heard throughout the facility. The office area should be located to provide supervision over the stable yard, deliveries, and arrival of people. The office should be adjacent to toilet and wash room areas. Some facilities have the office adjacent to or located near sleeping areas.

Turnout Areas

All turnout areas should be safe for the horse. These areas are designed to provide limited exercise for the horse. Turnout areas include pens, runs, corrals, and paddocks.

The pen is usually the size of a large stall. A pen is typically 16 by 20 feet. The run is longer, 16 by 60 feet, and allows the horse to get more exercise by trotting. A corral can be a square or round pen. The corral is at least 1,600 square feet. These three areas are usually devoid of grass due to concentrated horse traffic. The paddock area is usually a grassy area from 1/2 acre to several acres and is used for short periods of exercise and grazing.

The turnout areas should have fencing designed for horses. Sturdy five- to six-foot perimeter fences, complete with latched gates, should encircle the area. Types of fencing range from vinyl to recycled rubber. The type best suited

depends on your specific circumstances and livestock type. One of the most practical and inexpensive fences for a horse farm is a five-foot high, 12 1/2 gauge, galvanized 2" x 4" V-mesh. Pipe fences are attractive, easily maintained, and safe when properly constructed.

Competitive Areas

Arenas

Arena sizes vary widely between the disciplines. Working cows and reining typically require the most room. An arena for this purpose should be 100 feet wide by 200 + feet long. Jumping events usually require at least 80 feet wide and 120 feet long and more space is preferable if possible. A large dressage arena is 20 meters by 60 meters (66' x 198') and a small dressage arena is 20 meters by 40 meters (66' x 132').

Roof truss manufacturers use standard dimensions, usually in increments of 10 feet. A standard small covered arena truss is 60 feet wide and spaced 12 feet apart.

A good rule of thumb for commercial riding arenas is to construct bigger than what you think you need. This will allow multiple disciplines to utilize the facility or accommodate multiple riding lessons simultaneously.

Wash room, Saint Mary-of-
the-Woods College, IN.

Photo by Michael Hypes

The proper lighting of arena is an important part of the planning phase. The sheer size of the arena makes it important to plan regarding fixtures, circuit size, and placement.

Jumps

The types of jumps used in Hunter classes are representative of natural obstacles found in the hunt field. These include:

- post-and-rails,
- stone walls,
- Aiken,
- chicken coop,
- brush,
- plank, and
- white gate.

The poles (rails) used in many shows are 12-foot or 14-foot lengths. The longer the pole, the greater the weight and the lesser the tendency to pop out of the cups when hit.

"Fences designed to test for horizontal distances are called spread fences. They may include the oxer, double oxer, hogback, and triple bar. While these obstacles are of different configurations, they can all be raised and lengthened, as for jump-offs." (Price, 1998, p. 245)

The Puissance walls are typically constructed of light plywood with the upper elements able to slide off. Paint is used to create illusions for the horse.

Figure 30.4 provides a summary of the types of fences used in jumping. New variations are appearing all the time; however, these three categories represent most of the jumps currently used.

Indoor arena,
Saint Mary-of-the-Woods
College, IN.

Photos by Michael Hypes

The post-and-rails is a natural rail fence, usually of three cross rails. The chicken coop is a triangular wooden obstacle ranging from perhaps two feet six inches to four feet. The Aiken is a split rail over bushes. (Price, 1998)

All jumps should be constructed with the safety of horse and rider in mind. It should collapse easily to prevent injury. This breakaway characteristic is based upon the types of cups that hold the rails. The inside dimensions of a cup for a four-inch pole must be a minimum of 1 1/2 inches deep and five inches across. The maximum depth must not exceed one-half the diameter of the pole. (Price, 1998)

Summary

A good equestrian facility incorporates many different components. From the smallest stall in a barn to the large areas for competition, careful planning is necessary to ensure both form and function needs are met. Site considerations, general construction issues, and specialized areas are essential parts of a well-conceived equestrian facility plan. The facility purpose, budget, image, climate, available material and labor, personal preference, and future plans are some of the variables in the planning and construction of a facility.

Figure 30.4
Types of Fences

Uprights are fences built vertical to the ground with all parts placed one above the other. These include gates, planks, walls, straight posts and rails.

Spread fences require a horse to jump width as well as height. These include parallels, hogbacks, triple bars, double oxers, wall with rails behind, water ditches, and open water jumps.

Combinations consist of two or more elements placed in front of one another. The combination is usually designed with a single or double non-jumping stride between each part.

The double consists of two fences, which may be of any design. A straightforward distance for non-jumping stride in a double is 7.3-8 meters (24-26 feet). For two non-jumping strides 10-11 meters (33-36 feet).

Trebles consist of three elements of any type of fence or combination of striding.

Modified from Holderness-Roddam, J. (1988). *Competitive riding.* New York, NY: Prentice-Hall.

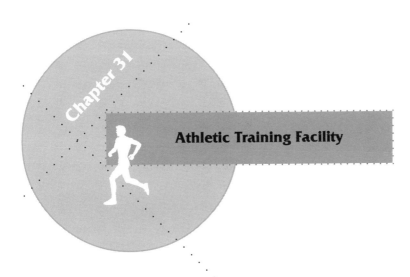

Chapter 31

Athletic Training Facility

Joe Brown, Retired Professor, Austin Peay State University

Athletic training rooms are common features in indoor and outdoor athletic complexes, and their specific purposes depend on the type of activities and facilities they support. For example, in multipurpose recreational facilities, it often serves as a first-aid station for recreational athletes. Conversely, in athletic facilities, it serves as a comprehensive athletic medicine facility for interscholastic, intercollegiate, Olympic, or professional athletes. When housed in a community, the athletic training room may serve the "weekend warrior." Therefore, proper planning, plus an understanding of the essential components of an athletic training room will make it more effective when completed (Ingersoll & Sawyer, 1999). Accordingly, athletic training room planners should regularly consult with staff athletic trainers during the planning phase to ensure the construction of a sound facility for treating and rehabilitating athletes.

While the specific activities performed in an athletic training room are subject to institutional preference along with the availability of financial and facility resources, certain activities are performed in all such facilities. These include team preparation, injury evaluation, injury treatment, injury rehabilitation, and administrative functions. It is important, then, to understand these activities before building, retrofitting, or remodeling an athletic training room (Ingersoll & Sawyer, 1999). To improve the planning process, general considerations for the athletic training room and/or the requirements of organizations concerned with athletic training facilities should be considered.

Learning Objectives

After reading this chapter, the student will be able to:
- Outline the purpose of an athletic training room,
- Describe the various spaces utilized in an athletic training room, and
- List and describe the basic pieces of equipment needed in an athletic training room.

General Considerations for the Athletic Training Facility

Authors in the 1950s (Bevan, 1956; Morehouse & Rasch, 1958), 1960s (Morehouse & Rasch, 1964; Rawlinson, 1961), 1970s (Brown, 1972; Klafs & Arnheim, 1973), 1980s (Forseth, 1986; Penman & Penman, 1982; Sauers, 1985; Secor, 1984), 1990s (Arnheim & Prentice, 1997; (Ingersoll & Sawyer, 1999; Lavoie, 1993; Rankin & Ingersoll, 1995; Ray, 1994), and 2000s (Sabo, 2001) have offered a number of options to be considered when contemplating an athletic training facility. While each author offers his own specific suggestions, there is a common thread associated with each one. Generally, these authors agree that the athletic training room is a place specifically set aside for injury care. It has good lighting and ventilation, a constant temperature range, light-colored walls, ceilings, and floors, easily cleaned surfaces, adequate equipment, and GFI electrical outlets located on all walls. It is easily accessible by being near the dressing room, but is not a part of it, nor is it to be used as a passageway to the dressing room or showers. Moreover, these authors support the importance of a facility set aside specifically for the prevention, treatment, and rehabilitation of individuals who may incur injuries.

It is important, then, for organizations without athletic training facilities to promote the need for an athletic training room. This promotion includes a well-organized plan of action that outlines why the athletic training room is essential to injury care. Basically, the following three reasons should help promote the need for an athletic training facility.
- Minor injuries often are not reported immediately, because there is no one place or person to whom the injured athlete should report. Moreover, the injured person is often reluctant to be treated for these minor injuries in the presence of others. Also, it is difficult to give minor injuries proper attention during the confusion of dressing and undressing.

- Maintaining a sanitary and comparatively private environment is generally helpful for treatment of injuries. Because of the individual's privacy need from a practical and psychological point of view, because of the increased public attention given to sports injury problems, and because injuries affect adversely efficiency, organizations are giving more attention to injury prevention, treatment, and rehabilitation. Thus, the presence of an athletic training facility shows an interest in the welfare of personnel.
- A properly fitted athletic training room's cost is minimal when compared with costs incurred for lost time, uniforms, and other equipment.

Unfortunately, many organizations are not endowed with the money or facilities for the development of an ideal athletic training room. Therefore, it will be necessary to renovate or retrofit present facilities. While these two options do not make it easy, or even feasible, to develop the ideal training room, it is, nevertheless, possible to end up with an athletic training room that is both practical and efficient. The elements to be considered when planning an athletic training room include size, location, traffic flow, and equipment.

Size

LaVoie (1999) indicates the athletic training room designer, the administrative requirements of the athletic training staff, number of athletes, type of equipment, storage needs, and expansion possibilities should be considered in determining the initial size of the athletic training room. Furthermore, he states that a rule of thumb for the size and shape of the athletic training room is unnecessary. Instead, he relies on excellent communication between the designer and the athletic training staff to develop an athletic training facility that will be both productive and efficient. In a way, he agrees with the American Academy of Orthopaedic Surgeons (1991), who maintain that the size and shape of the athletic training room help determine an ability to accommodate large numbers of athletes at one time. Arnheim and Prentice (1997), however, contend that any athletic training room less than 1,000 square feet is impractical. Instead, they recommend that the facility be between 1,000 and 1,200 square feet, with 1,200 square feet being the preferred size. According to them, an athletic training room with this many square feet accommodates large numbers of individuals along with the bulky equipment found in athletic training rooms.

Although minimum space requirements have been suggested, Penman and Penman (1982) provide a specific formula for determining a rough estimate of the minimum space needs for an athletic training room. This formula is based on the assertion that each taping or treatment table is sufficient for 20 athletes and occupies approximately 100 square feet, including the table, work area around the table, and counter and storage space. Thus, the minimum space for the athletic training room can be determined by dividing the number of athletes expected at peak times by 20. This will give the number of treatment and/or taping tables needed. Then, by multiplying by 100, the total square footage can be obtained. The formula follows:

Number of athletes at peak x 100 square feet = Total square footage 20 per table per day

Sabo (2001) agrees that the athletic training room space needs can be determined by using the Penman formula. However, he suggests a more accurate means for sizing the athletic training room is by dividing the facility into eight functional areas: taping/first aid, hydrotherapy, treatment, rehabilitation, offices, physician's examination room, and storage. His specific recommendations for each of these areas follow:

- The taping/first aid area is determined by using Penman's formula. However, Sabo does suggest that the minimum space requirements should be large enough for six taping tables to be used at the same time.
- The hydrotherapy area space is calculated by accessing the space needs of equipment in the area. Whirlpool space is based on the assumption that one whirlpool can accommodate three athletes per peak hour. Thus, the number of athletes who are to be treated during the peak hour is divided by 20 to determine the number of whirlpools needed. This figure is then added to the sum of the square footage of the number of whirlpools needed for the peak load. To get the square footage for the whirlpools, he uses the following guidelines: small whirlpool = 35 square feet, medium whirlpool = 56 square feet, and large whirlpool = 64 square feet.
- The treatment area should be large enough to house six treatment tables, with two of these having privacy curtains. According to Sabo, one treatment table will accommodate three athletes per hour. Consequently, the number of athletes to be treated during the peak hour is divided by three to get the number of tables needed. Then, multiply the required tables by 100 to access the square footage needed in the treatment area.
- The size of the rehabilitation area depends on the amount and kind of equipment housed in this area. The space required for each piece of equipment, working area around the equipment, further expansion, and storage are added together to give approximate space requirements for the rehabilitation room.
- The head athletic trainer's office should not be smaller than 120 square feet.
- The physician's office should be a minimum of 120 square feet.
- The storage area should have at least 100 square feet, but a more accurate measure is the room should be large enough to hold one year's worth of supplies.

The primary purpose of an athletic training room is to provide efficient service to large numbers of athletes at one time. Therefore, when building a new facility with a generous budget, the Arnheim and Prentice recommendation, the Penman and Penman formula, and/or Sabo's guidelines for minimal size should be followed. In retrofitting or remodeling facilities, the athletic training room size will be dictated by a number of factors. Although presented in 1986, but still appropriate, Forseth (1986) lists five general factors of facility development he obtained from Coates that will benefit the athletic training room planner. These general factors for determining the space needed for the athletic training room include:

- Program needs, such as the number of sports and the type of sports offered at the institution;
- Projected institutional enrollment and the stability of the number of participants from one year to the next;
- Space needed for athletic training instruction;
- Cost per square foot estimates to determine what is feasible under the existing economic status; and
- Communication with the architect early in the process assures a functional athletic training room.

Location

In locating the athletic training room, working space and traffic flow is of primary importance. When followed, the guidelines listed below will meet these criteria. Ideally, the athletic training room should be:

- Close to bathrooms;
- Close to dressing rooms, but away from the showers;
- Close to water and drainage;
- Easily accessible for both men and women;
- Easily accessible to emergency vehicle loading zones;
- Near participation areas;
- Adjacent to team locker rooms;
- Located on an outside wall;
- Equipped with a street-level double door that can be operated automatically (similar to a handicapped entranceway); and
- Provided with a janitorial closet that has a large sink, floor drain, and storage area. This janitorial closet should be adjacent to or within the athletic training room.

Traffic Flow

The layout of the athletic training room is designed to maximize the traffic flow of individuals who are using the various services of the athletic training room. Ideally, according to Arnheim and Prentice (1997), individuals should be able to enter and exit the athletic training facilities from an outside doorway and from the men's and women's locker rooms. The design shown in their textbook illustrates an ideal layout. Some of the characteristics of this design are:

- Saves unnecessary footsteps;
- Provides completely unhampered and uncomplicated traffic lanes;
- Places sensitive equipment away from the traffic lanes;
- Positions the athletic trainer's office in the center of the room so he/she can observe all ongoing activities;
- Locates the physician's office in a far corner so there will privacy during the physician's examination; and
- Furnishes the physician's office with a desk and chair, treatment table, sink, refrigerator, and storage space.

Structural Components

To a large extent, structural features will dictate the configuration of the athletic training room. Accordingly, the following structural component guidelines will be beneficial in making the athletic training room as functional as possible.

- Ceilings should be a minimum of 10 feet in the treatment area, so tall athletes can stand as they are being treated. Additionally, the ceilings should be constructed of material that will reflect light and deaden sound. Acoustical tiles are excellent for the athletic training room. For best results, the tiles should be white, ivory, cream, or buff color. These colors tend to reduce glare and provide good light reflection.
- Doors must be large enough to accommodate a wheelchair or a stretcher. Generally, a door 36 inches wide is sufficient for most athletic training rooms. However, if the budget is generous, double doors should be installed in at least one entrance. Figure 31.1 shows the outside double doors leading into the building where the Eastern Kentucky athletic training room is located. These doors have a full glass view and are wide enough for a wheelchair or stretcher to enter or exit through them. Additionally, the surface under the doors is flat, so there will be no problem in moving injured athletes in wheelchairs or stretchers.
- Electrical outlets should be located three to four feet from the floor and spaced at six- to eight-feet intervals. Outlets equipped with ground fault interrupters (GFI) are required in areas where there is moisture. However, it is best if all electrical outlets in the athletic training room are GFI equipped, because there is a possibility that moisture might be present in all areas of the athletic training room.
- Equipment in the athletic training room should be a minimum of a desk and chair, bookcase, lockable file cabinet, one or two visitor chairs, a computer and printer, and a desk calculator. When possible, the computer should be connected to the Internet.
- Floors should be sloped toward a drainage area, covered with a non-slip surface, moisture resistant, and easily cleaned and disinfected. Good materials for the floor include concrete, vinyl tile, ceramic tile, and poured liquid floors.
- Illumination in the athletic training room should provide even and efficient light on the work surface. Fluorescent fixtures with diffusers for elimination of flickering and that produce a minimum of 30 foot-candles four feet above the work surface are good choices. For evaluation and treatment areas, 50 to 60 foot-candles four feet above the work surface is recommended.
- Plumbing should follow all applicable building codes, and the plumbing area must include at least one floor drain equipped with a trap to prevent odors from entering the athletic training room. The plumbing area has a concrete floor covered with a paint that has been modified to prevent slippage, rubber strips, pitted surfaces, or a rubberized liquid coating. The plumbing area should have a back flow device, a

Figure 31.1
Main Entrance to the Eastern Kentucky University Building where the Athletic Training Room is Housed, Automatic Double Wide Doors.

deep sink (preferable a double sink) equipped with hot and cold running water, and at least one whirlpool located in an area with a floor drain. Additionally, all electrical outlets must be GFI rated, and it is recommended that all equipment used in the plumbing area be approved by the Underwriter's Laboratory as safe for use in wet areas.

- Storage facilities are of prime importance, and the storage area should include lockable cabinets, lockers, and closets. For best results, the storage facilities should be near the working space, but out of the traffic flow. Another storage consideration is that the storage area be designed so that it does not require excessive space. An example of efficient utilization of space is the taping and storage table at Austin Peay State University. This taping table shown in Figure 31.2 is 42 inches high, 144 inches long, and 48 inches deep. It will accommodate four to five athletes for taping, and it is located near the entrance to the athletic training room and adjacent to

the Head Athletic Trainer's office. Beneath the table-top are lockable cabinets that are used to store tape and other supplies. Directly across from the taping and storage table is a storage cabinet (See Figure 31.3), which is 42 inches high, 84 inches long, and 26 inches deep, in which gauze, band-aids, alcohol, vaseline, etc. are kept. This cabinet is approximately six feet from the taping table, making it easy for the trainers to get the supplies they need for minor treatment and for preventive taping and wrapping activities. Another good feature of this taping and storage area is its close proximity to the athletic trainer's office and the fact that it meets the primary purpose for preventing waste of materials and supplies while requiring very little square footage.

- Temperature control is provided with heating, ventilating, and air conditioning (HVAC) units capable of maintaining a constant temperature range of 72 to 78 degrees and a humidity range of 40 to 50%. Additionally, the temperature control system must

Figure 31.2
Austin Peay State University Taping Table.

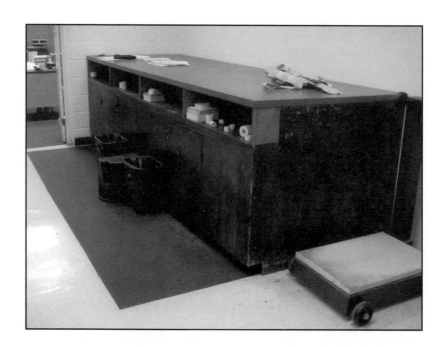

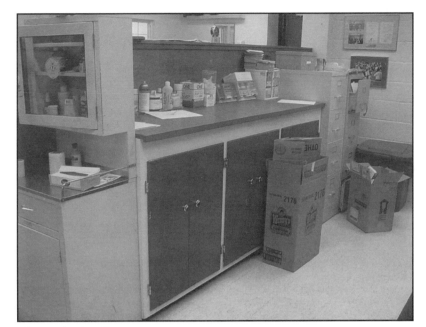

Figure 31.3
Austin Peay State University
Taping Area Storage Cabinet.

Photos by Joe Brown

be sufficient to change the room air eight to ten times each hour, so vapors from the warm water present in the whirlpools and hydrocollators can be exhausted continuously. Moreover, it is recommended, when possible, that the athletic training room temperature control units be separate from the rest of the building's temperature control units.

- Windows should be installed in such a manner that all activities in the athletic training room can be observed, but at the same time maintain the privacy of individuals who may be conversing in the office area. One-way mirrors are good choices when privacy and adequate supervision are of primary importance.

National Athletic Trainers' Association

The most important organization to consult is the National Athletic Trainer's Association (NATA), especially if the athletic training room is in an institution that has a certification curriculum. According to Ingersoll and Sawyer (1999), the Commission on Accreditation of Allied Health Education Programs (CAAHEP) suggests specific guidelines for the development of an athletic training room. In this setting, the athletic training room components include team preparation area, injury evaluation/treatment space, rehabilitation area, wet space, maintenance area, storage space, office area, examination space (office #2), computer/study/conference area, and a classroom (See Chapter 32). The specifications for each of these areas are detailed to assist the planner in developing an appropriate floor plan for the athletic training room.

The team preparation area will have a tile floor with an appropriate number of floor drains; treatment cabinets with Formica tops; a recessed waste receptacle; drawers; and shelves. The ceiling height should be 11 to 12 feet, but not less than 10 feet. Further, fireproof tiles are a requirement for the ceiling. The walls should be constructed of blocks for durability and sound control and painted with an epoxy paint to seal the blocks so they will be easier to clean. A deep, double-basin sink is suggested. The direct lighting should be with fluorescent tubes. Electrical outlets should be located every six feet on all the walls, and those electrical outlets around the sink should be GFI (ground fault interrupter) rated. Finally, this area should have a biohazard waste container and have double doors for entrance and/or exit.

The injury evaluation/treatment area requires different space and equipment needs for performing injury evaluations and treatments. This space has therapeutic modality applications, manual therapy, and treatment activities ongoing at the same time. Typically, this space includes numerous treatment tables that are used to examine body parts, do special tests on joints, and to treat various types of injuries. There should be a suspended curtain system that can, when necessary, be utilized for privacy. Moveable carts between each table are used for transporting therapeutic equipment (e.g., ultrasound machine, muscle stimulator, etc.) and storing supplies (See Figure 31.4). The specific space needs of the injury evaluation/treatment area include:

- A ceiling with a minimum height of 10 feet (11-12 is desirable) that is covered with fireproof tiles;
- Cabinets for storage;
- A deep double-basin, stainless-steel sink;
- Rubberized roll-out sport surface such as Mondo7;
- Block walls covered with epoxy paint;
- GFI-rated electrical outlets at each treatment site and above the counter on either side of the sink;
- Direct fluorescent lighting;
- Biohazard waste containers; and
- Double doors for entering and exiting the area.

The rehabilitation area includes space for therapeutic exercise equipment. This area should be separate from other areas in the complex because of the noise level and the movement of the exercising athletes. The needs of this area include:

- A rubberized roll-out sport floor surface such as Mondo7;
- Free weights;
- Mechanized strength training equipment for exercising shoulders, arms, backs, hips, thighs, knees, and ankles;

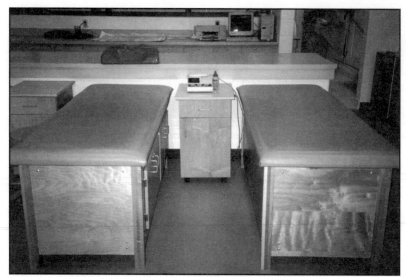

**Figure 31.4
Eastern Kentucky University
Moveable Cart.**

Photos by Joe Brown

- Electrical outlets on all walls spaced every six feet;
- Indirect fluorescent lighting;
- A 10-foot ceiling equipped with fireproof tiles;
- Soundproofing in the epoxy painted block walls;
- Double-door entrance and/or exit;
- Audio and video system; and
- Space for running, jumping, and throwing activities.

The wet space (hydrotherapy) area generally includes whirlpools, ice machines, therapeutic pools, refrigerator, and storage for large drink containers. The area should have:
- Non-slip tiled floor;
- A minimum ceiling height of 10 feet;
- An appropriate number of floor drains;
- Recessed plumbing for whirlpools;
- GFI electrical supply for whirlpools and ice machines;
- Storage area for drinking containers;
- A deep double-basin stainless-steel sink equipped with storage;
- Extra ventilation and humidity control;
- Indirect fluorescent lighting; and
- Close to the athletic trainer's office, so constant visual contact can be maintained.

The maintenance area is where broken equipment is stored and repaired. The area needs are:
- Shelves;
- Work table;
- Concrete floor with a drain;
- Epoxy painted block walls;
- Two eight-feet roll-up internal and external door entrances;
- Fireproof tiled eight-foot high ceiling;
- Enhanced ventilation;
- Deep double-basin, stainless steel sink with storage;
- GFI electrical outlets on all walls and an electrical strip above the workbench;
- Direct fluorescent lighting in the room and over the workbench; and
- Storage space for an electric golf cart and its electrical charger.

The storage space can never be too large. The storage space requirements include:
- Humidity control to protect the stored tape;
- Lockable cabinets;
- Shelves of various heights and lengths;
- Concrete floor;
- Direct fluorescent lighting;
- Epoxy painted block;
- Double-door entrance, or at least a 36-inch door, or a roll door for easy access;
- Located close to the athletic trainer's administrative office area; and
- Close to loading docks and/or delivery areas.

The office area contains all medical records and serves as the administrative hub for the athletic training room. The space should be:
- No smaller than 220 square feet;
- Located adjacent to the wet and storage areas;
- A sight line to all other areas in the facility;
- Electrical, phone, and computer outlets on all walls;
- Lockable file and storage cabinets;
- Carpeted floor;
- Block walls with windows addressing each area of the facility; and
- A fireproofed tiled eight feet ceiling.

The examination space is oftentimes the second office area that is used as a physician's examination room. The space includes those items in the athletic trainer's office area, an examination table, and single sink basin provided with storage above and below it. It should have a lockable door, and it could best be used for record storage, as there is less traffic.

The athletic training students will use the computer/study/conference area. This space should be no smaller than 220 square feet. The space needs include:
- Tables for computers and printers;
- A conference table;
- Shelving for a small library;
- Appropriate furniture for relaxing and studying; and
- Storage lockers for the students' books, coats, etc. located on the outside wall.

The classroom design should include considerations outlined in Chapter 15. More importantly, the classroom must be dedicated for the use of the athletic training curriculum functions. Additionally, this room should have ample storage for instructional equipment and supplies used in athletic training instruction.

The American Academy of Orthopaedic Surgeons

While the NATA is the parent organization for athletic training standards, another good source is the American Academy of Orthopaedic Surgeons. Their publication, *Athletic Training and Sports Medicine* (1991), contains suggestions useful for developing a training room when a curriculum is not a factor. The American Academy of Orthopaedic Surgeons suggests that each organization be obligated to provide athletic training room facilities sufficient for enhancing the athlete's health. Furthermore, this athletic training room facility is to be adequately sized; provided with utilities, supplies, and equipment; and staffed by qualified individuals. The services to be provided include preventive measures, assessment of injuries, first-aid administration, emergency care, routine evaluation and treatment, and rehabilitation of injuries. The academy's specific suggestions follow:

- The size and shape of the athletic training room should accommodate the number of individuals served by the facility.
- The athletic training room should be central to all of the activities provided by the organization. Also, the facility must be equally accessible to both men and women.
- The athletic training room shall be equipped with the basic utilities of electricity, lighting, temperature control, ventilation, and plumbing.
- The walls in the athletic training room shall have a minimum of two electrical outlets.
- The whirlpool area shall have GFI electrical outlets.
- Light fixtures shall produce a minimum of 30 footcandles at four feet above the surface. When illumination varies in intensity, the brightest areas are to be used for evaluation and treatment of injuries or other conditions.
- Because of the use of warm water in the whirlpools and the hydrocollators, super ventilation must be present.
- The ideal athletic training room temperature is between 68 and 70 degrees.
- The basic minimum plumbing requirements include a deep sink with cold and hot water, a whirlpool, and a minimum of one to two floor drains.
- The athletic training room needs a number of lockable storage cabinets and closets. Additionally, a telephone, desk, computer, and file cabinet are necessary.
- The athletic training room traffic flow will be determined by the size and shape of the facility, placement of lighting fixtures, location of electrical outlets, site of phone/computer lines, and position of plumbing fixtures.

The athletic training room traffic-flow problems can be improved by:
- Placing a bench outside a small athletic training room to reduce congestion in the treatment area;
- Locating those services used less often away from the entrance;
- Positioning taping tables nearest to the entrance; and
- Stationing the trainer's desk so all on-going activity can be observed.

Equipment Considerations for the Athletic Training Facility

Athletic training rooms contain a variety of equipment with the extent of the equipment being determined by the availability of financial resources and physical facilities. There are three categories of athletic training room equipment: basic, moderate, and ultimate (well-equipped).

Basic Equipment Needs

Basic equipment for the athletic training room consists of a dry and wet heat source, cold source, rehabilitation source, supply cabinet, treatment cabinet, training table, and whirlpool.

- Heat lamps provide dry heat for treatment of injuries. If a heat lamp is not available, a heating pad is a good substitute. Both these dry heat devices are inexpensive and safe for use in the athletic training room, provided they are used in conjunction with GFI-equipped electrical outlets.
- A refrigerator is necessary for maintenance of an adequate supply of ice for use in treating injuries. A used refrigerator may be purchased in any locality at a reasonable price; just keep in mind that the main feature of this refrigerator is its capacity of making and keeping ice. It is also useful for storing ice bags and cold water.
- A double sink equipped with hot and cold running water, hooked to a trapped drain, and with undersink storage and counter space of two to four feet is strongly recommended. Sinks are relatively inexpensive and can be purchased at home centers. Sinks may also be obtained from salvage yards or obtained when someone remodels their home or business.
- A supply cabinet is an essential piece of equipment for the athletic training room. The supply cabinet may be either metal or wood, and it may be constructed or purchased second-handed. A suitable closet may be used, but it is important that any supply storage area be kept locked to prevent waste and misuse of athletic training materials. Figure 31.5 shows a suitable supply cabinet used in the Austin Peay State University athletic training room. The cabinet is 66 inches high (36 inches on bottom and 30 inches on the top), 18 inches on the bottom section and eight inches deep on the top section, and 30 inches wide.
- The treatment cabinet must have an adequate working surface and space for holding first-aid and other treatment supplies. It should be lockable to prevent

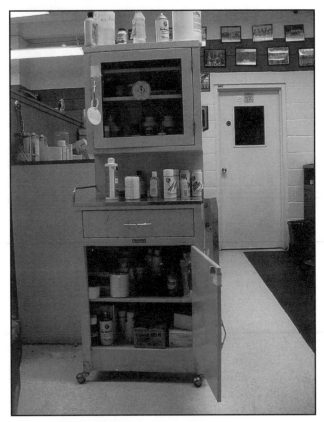

Photos by Joe Brown

Figure 31.5
Austin Peay State University
Supply Cabinet.

misuse of supplies and to keep the supplies sanitary. A set of regular mason jars placed on the cabinet surface is recommended to keep dressing materials clean and available. The size of the treatment cabinet will vary among athletic training rooms, but a treatment cabinet 78 inches high, 18-20 inches deep, and 36 inches wide is adequate for most basically equipped athletic training rooms.

- The training table is the most essential piece of athletic training room equipment as it is used for examining injuries, applying treatment modalities, and applying protective taping and/or wrapping. The training table is usually constructed of heavy wood, and its measurements are 78 inches long, 24 inches wide, and 30 inches high. The top is covered with foam rubber or some other form of padding over which an easily cleaned cloth or other covering is applied. Figure 31.6 shows the pattern for a basic athletic training table.
- The whirlpool is another essential piece of equipment for the athletic training room, for it is used for applying wet, moving heat to athletic injuries. It is important that the whirlpool is on a concrete surface and that the area has adequate drains plus GFI equipped electrical outlets. Figure 31.7 shows a whirlpool setup in the Eastern Kentucky University athletic training room. One way of improvising a whirlpool bath is to take an old bathtub and equip it with a portable agitator. Be sure the improvised whirlpool is properly grounded and connected to GFI electrical outlets.

Austin Peay State University

Austin Peay State University in Clarksville, Tennessee is typical of a moderately equipped athletic training room facility. It was retrofitted from a small athletic training room for football, two locker rooms, three shower rooms, a steam room, a large hallway, a sunken whirlpool and its deck, and an equipment issuing room.

The athletic training room contains 2,138 square feet, and it is divided into seven components: Head Athletic Trainer's office, Assistant Athletic Trainer's office, Team Physician's office, Rehabilitation area, Treatment area, Wet Room, Taping activities, Treatment and Evaluation area, and Storage areas.

Head Athletic Trainer's Office

The Head Athletic Trainer's office has 132 square feet (11 by 12 feet). It was retrofitted from an equipment issuing room, and it has an entrance door from the hallway and a door leading to the taping table. The door leading to the taping table area has glass, so it offers a direct sight line to the taping table area and a partial sight line to the treatment room. Yet, the office design allows for privacy when it is needed. It contains:

- A desk and chair;
- A chair for visitors or consultations;
- A computer connected to the Internet;
- A printer for the computer;
- A telephone;
- A recording machine for voice mail;
- A calculator;
- Two two-drawer and one four-drawer file cabinets;
- A large lockable double-door cabinet that has lockable drawers and file cabinets in it;

Figure 31.6
Athletic Training Table Pattern

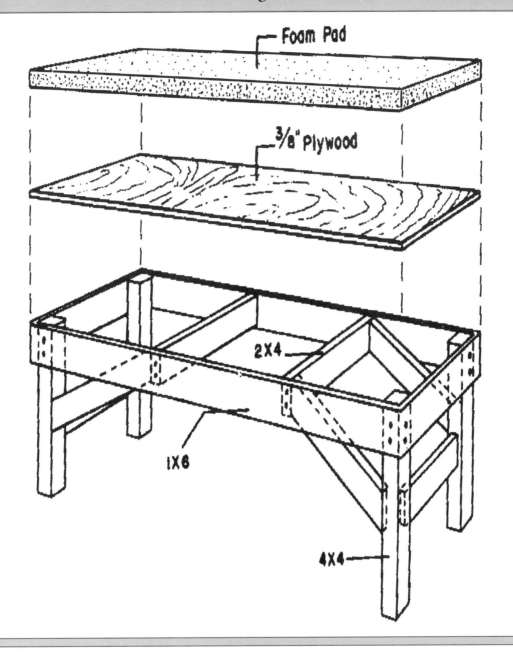

Foam Pad

3/8" Plywood

2X4

1X6

4X4

Figure 31.7
Eastern Kentucky University
Whirlpool Setup.

Figure 31.8
Eastern Kentucky University
Taping/Treatment Area.

Photos by Joe Brown

- A bookcase with adjustable shelves and a lockable cabinet and drawer; and
- A small bookcase with three shelves.

Assistant Athletic Trainer's Office

Two Assistant Athletic Trainers share an office containing 110 square feet (10 by 11 feet). The office was constructed from an area in the rehabilitation area. It has two windows and a glass door with a clear sight line to the rehabilitation activities. This office is equipped with

- Two desks and chairs;
- One computer with Internet connection;
- One printer;
- A small worktable;
- Two file cabinets; and
- Bookshelves along one of the walls.

Physician's Office

The Physician's office has 96 square feet (12 by eight feet) and is located at one end of the treatment area. It has:

- A solid door for privacy;
- A telephone;
- A desk and chair;

- An examination table;
- Lockable storage cabinets along one wall; and
- A sink with hot and cold running water.

Treatment Room

The treatment room is located in a separate room that can be partially observed by the head athletic trainer from his office. It was once a locker room, and it has 345 square feet (23 by 15 feet) of space. It has the following treatment modalities:

- Orthotron KT1 Exercise Table;
- Synatron 500 Electrotherapy CTL CTR;
- Nemectron 2 Ultrasound Therapy Unit;
- Pentium Z Station ZSK-8559;
- Electrotherapy Ultrasound Modality;
- Two Mettler Electronic Stimulators;
- Z Station;
- Treatment Tables;
- Examination Tables;
- A hydrocollator and hydrocollator Tree; and
- A computer with Printer

Figure 31.9
Eastern Kentucky University
Rehabilitation Area.

Figure 31.10
Eastern Kentucky University
Treatment/Therapy Area.

Photos by Joe Brown

Rehabilitation Room

The rehabilitation room was retrofitted from a dressing room. It has 448 square feet (28 by 16 feet) of space in which the following pieces of rehabilitation equipment are located:

- A Nemectrodyn Model V;
- A Nemectrodyn MDL-2 Nerve Stimulator Device;
- An Orthotron II Fitron Cycle-Ergometer;
- A Cybex 2450 Upper Body Exerciser;
- A Lifestep 1000; and
- A Cable Column Rehab Device.

Taping, Wrapping, and Weighing Room

The taping, wrapping, and weighing room has 228 square feet (19 by 12 feet) of useable space. It, like the rehabilitation room and Assistant Athletic Trainer's office, was retrofitted from a room used for dressing and locker space. It has a taping table that is 144 inches long, 42 inches high, and 48 inches deep, a large weight scale, and a storage cabinet that is 84 inches long, 26 inches deep, and 42 inches high. The taping, wrapping, and weighing area is directly to the right of the entrance into the training room and is situated directly adjacent to the head athletic trainer's office. It is separated from the rehabilitation area by a five-inch-thick wooden partition wall that is 60 inches high and 145 inches long. This area is shown in Figures 31.2 and 31.3.

Hydrotherapy Room

The hydrotherapy room was once a shower room. It contains 60 square feet (10 by 6 feet), and it has a full body whirlpool and two extremity whirlpools. It is located adjacent to the treatment area, but it must be entered through a door from the treatment room, making it impossible to supervise its activities from any of the offices or other areas of the athletic training room. It has GFI electrical outlets and excellent drainage. Additionally, the area has a curb that will prevent overflowing water from entering the treatment or storage areas.

Storage Areas

The Austin Peay State University athletic training room has four retrofitted storage areas other than those already mentioned. One of these is a converted shower room containing 84 square feet of useable space (14 by six feet). It houses the ice machine, and it is where all the drinking and ice containers plus crutches are kept.

Another major storage area is located directly across from the hydrotherapy room in what was once a hall leading from the treatment room area to a steam room and a sunken whirlpool. This area contains 240 square feet (16 by 15 feet). It has lockable metal and wooden lockers that are used to store various treatment and rehabilitation supplies and equipment.

Figure 31.11
Eastern Kentucky University
Office Area.

Figure 31.12
Eastern Kentucky University
Treatment/Therapy
Storage Area.

Photos by Joe Brown

The area that was originally a large sunken whirlpool has 255 square feet (17 by 15 feet) including the large whirlpool, the whirlpool deck, and the hallway leading to steam room. The area is utilized mostly for large boxes as well as a variety of protective and preventive equipment.

The former steam room is the most secure storage area, for it has a metal door and is away from any traffic flow. It has 180 square feet (15 by 12 feet). It is used to store old records and sensitive supplies and equipment. The room also has temperature and humidity controls not present in the other storage areas.

Eastern Kentucky University

Eastern Kentucky University's new athletic training room is an example of a well-equipped facility, and it demonstrates what can be done when building a new athletic training room. It is located on the first floor of the 40,000-square-foot Harry Moberly Classroom, Wellness, and Conditioning Building. The first floor of the building houses the physical education activity/laboratory, the weight room, and the athletic training room. On the second floor, there is a wellness center, three large classrooms, human performance and computer laboratories, offices, locker rooms, showers, and dressing rooms. Primarily, the building houses the College of Health, Physical Education, Recreation, and Athletics plus the 16 intercollegiate athletic teams.

The athletic training room is located between the weight room and the physical activity/laboratory. It is entered from the main foyer through glass-enclosed double doors that do not have thresholds. The athletic training facility functional areas follow:

- A taping/treatment area (See Figure 31.8);
- A rehabilitation area (See Figure 31.9);
- A treatment/therapy area (See Figure 31.10);
- Glass enclosed office (See Figure 31.11);
- Treatment area storage (See Figure 31.12);
- Hydrotherapy cooler storage area (See Figure 31.13)
- An in-ground hydrotherapy pool with a treadmill (See Figure 31.14);
- Rehabilitation storage area (See Figure 31.15);
- Treatment storage area (See Figure 31.16); and
- Hydrotherapy room (See Figure 31.17).

In addition to the areas depicted in Figures 31.8-31.17, the athletic training facility has three above-ground therapeutic pools in the hydrotherapy area, x-ray room with accompanying equipment and exposure control measures, and private examination rooms. All office doors have either full glass or partial full-length glass so activities can be observed from the office. There are artificial and natural light sources in all areas.

Figure 31.13
Eastern Kentucky University
Hydrotherapy Cooler
Storage Area.

Photos by Joe Brown

Figure 31.14
Eastern Kentucky University
In-ground Therapy Pool with
Treadmill.

Figure 31.15
Eastern Kentucky University
Rehabilitation Storage Area.

Figure 31.16
Eastern Kentucky University
Treatment Storage Area.

Figure 31.17
Eastern Kentucky University
Hydrotherapy Area.

Summary

The health of athletes and participants is extremely important for a successful athletic program for any organization—amateur, professional, or recreational. The planners for the athletic training room should regularly consult with staff athletic trainers during the planning phase to ensure the construction of a sound facility for treating and rehabilitating athletes.

Acknowledgment:

Special thanks to Bobby Barton Ed.D. (ATC), Head Athletic Trainer, Eastern Kentucky University; Leighton Brown (CSR), NEC, Inc., Nashville, TN; Chuck Kimmel (ATC), Head Athletic Trainer and Assistant Athletic Director, Austin Peay State University; and Jason Kizzee (ATC), Graduate Assistant Athletic Trainer, Austin Peay State University.

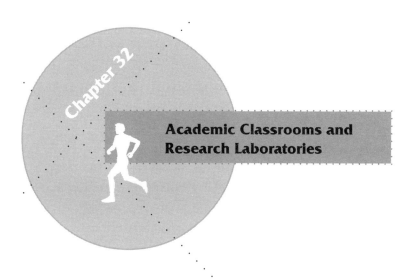

Academic Classrooms and Research Laboratories

Thomas H. Sawyer, Indiana State University

The nature of institutions of higher education and their objectives and functions will determine in large measure the type, number, size, and relative importance of classrooms and teaching/research laboratories. In institutions offering only services courses in physical education, the need for classrooms and teaching/research laboratories will seldom, if ever, be required. However, classrooms, teaching/research laboratories, and testing equipment become integral components for both physical education-teacher education and adult fitness programs.

A lack of appropriate laboratory space and equipment for teaching/research has hampered many institutions of higher education gaining accreditation from the National Council on Accreditation of Teacher Education (NCATE) and the National Association for Sport and Physical Education (NASPE) in the teacher preparation programs and from expanding their program opportunities in non-teaching areas (i.e., adult fitness, fitness, exercise science). Institutions with graduate programs have a greater need for the development of teaching/research laboratories. Such facilities are required not only to provide learning experiences for students but also to attract and retain capable research scholars. Therefore, it is not possible to determine the appropriate square footage for a laboratory space. Each institution and its faculty working together should determine what the need shall be for this space. Yet there are some generic considerations for such laboratories that will be outlined in this chapter.

Learning Objectives

After reading this chapter, the student will be able to
- design a multimedia classroom with distance education capability,
- lay out an exercise physiology laboratory,
- design a biomechanics laboratory, and
- plan a motor development/learning laboratory.

Classrooms

Classrooms need to be designed for multiple uses—from the traditional lecture method aided by multimedia technology to distance education delivery. This requires greater planning and the involvement of multimedia (i.e., sound, video, and graphics) and computer technicians. Classrooms are no longer simple square rooms with adequate lighting, environmental controls, and a blackboard and screen. They have become high-tech instructional spaces.

The ideal classroom is tiered similarly to a theater. The total number of seats will be determined by reviewing typical class sizes over the past five years. Each row should have a counter with the following at each student site—a microphone (for use in televised programming), computer hook-up to mainframe, a 110 V receptacle with appropriate surge protection, comfortable chairs that can be easily accessed, and space for books and paper. The planner needs to consider providing an appropriate number of handicapped seats.

In the rear or on the side of the room there will be a control room. In the front of the room should be a large counter with a built-in TV monitor, overhead projector, and computer, and controls for the audio-visual equipment. Behind the counter will be a combination screen and grease board that is recessed into the wall and can be pulled out when needed. When not in use, the wall will become a backdrop with an appropriate background for telecasting.

Distance Education Classroom System Features

The following features are needed for a distance education classroom system:

- Three color cameras expandable to four with 123 zoom lens 460 lines of resolution;
- Overhead color Elmo camera graphics stand @ 450 lines of resolution;
- Multiple wall-mount monitors for easy student viewing of slides, computer graphics, satellite feeds, and videotape playback;
- One microphone, with expansion capability exceeding 70 microphones, for every two students. This allows student participation in the classroom (16 microphones with 14 for 28 students in classroom, one for instructor, and one for guest);
- Automatic microphone mixing;
- 35 mm slide-to-video conversion for displaying slides locally and at distant locations;
- PC/MAC multimedia computer (minimum 128 mb RAM and 30 gb hard drive with a DVD-RAM, CD-RW, 31/2" disk, and Zip drive) to video converter for PowerPoint and multimedia presentations;
- Computer interface for multimedia such as CD-RW and DVD disks;
- Videocassette for playback with freeze frame capability;
- Multiple VCRs for recording class (one S-VHS VCR playback for presentation, one S-VHS VCR for master record, and five VHS VCR record for library tapes);
- Character generator and video writer for highlighting 35 mm slides, computer graphics, or video stills;
- Sound system for playback of videocassette, CD-ROM or future DVD, computer audio files, audiocassette, and CD player;
- Switching and mixing control of video and audio for all sources;
- Telephone interface for telephone call in or teleconferencing;
- Wireless microphone for instructor;
- Wired microphone for guest;
- Integrated control system for use by instructor and/or for control of videocassette recorders, camera pan and tilt heads, camera lenses, audio, telephone interface, slide to video converter, video source selection, codec;
- AMX integrated control system for simplified operation and full system control;
- Supplemental lighting;
- A system with the ability to use satellite, fiber, codec, or web video and audio as either a source feed or signal distribution for maximum flexibility and adaptability for future technology; and
- A system with room for expansion to accommodate future requirements and technologies.

The Distance Education system consists of six distance education classrooms connected to a central control center. The system designed for each classroom provides multiple local and remote student participation with complete computer, 35 mm slide, videotape, and other multimedia sources. Each classroom has the capability of using satellite, codec, video via fiber, video via the web, or a combination of any of these. Further, the system is designed for video conferencing with two to four people in a room. It has limited capability to expand to either three cameras or two cameras and a single videocassette machine. Finally, each classroom has an option for an overhead graphics camera stand.

Technology is changing rapidly. No matter how well you plan today, it will become outdated in a very short period of time. Therefore, when planning this technical space, consider the importance of upgrading the systems in the future and plan for the capability of upgrading the technical components. This planning should include not only the technical equipment itself, but the spaces in which the equipment is installed.

Computer Classrooms/Laboratories

This is a space that will be outdated weeks and even months before construction is completed, no matter how much futuristic planning is completed. Computer technology changes dramatically about every three months. The space requirements also change fairly rapidly.

Science Laboratories

A number of science laboratories should be considered when planning for HPERD teaching facilities. These include exercise physiology, biomechanics, and motor learning and development. Each of these laboratories has special needs.

Exercise Physiology (Human Performance) Laboratory

This space will be used for laboratory classes, research, and human performance testing for a variety of service programs. The size of the actual laboratory ranges from 400 sf to 2,000 sf. This laboratory can never be too large.

The following components maybe necessary for this space:
- Small office space (200 sf) is needed for the instructor.
- An environmental chamber is needed, with separate environmental controls that are easily accessible for maintenance.
- A hydrostatic pool recessed to floor level should have a service crawl space, a winch on an I-beam to suspend and move the chair, and appropriate outlets for cables from the computer to the sensor attached to the chair.
- The outlets to the computer station should be surge protected.
- The filter area for the hydrostatic pool must be easily accessible to service personnel.
- The floor in the hydrostatic area and locker areas should be tile, and the floor in the exercise areas should be multipurpose synthetic flooring.
- The hydrostatic area and locker rooms should have an appropriate number of drains in the floor to rapidly remove water.
- Two small locker rooms are necessary, with toilet facilities for a maximum of ten people.
- At least one treadmill recessed to floor level is needed (preferably two), with a service crawl space and a ramp to install and remove treadmill.

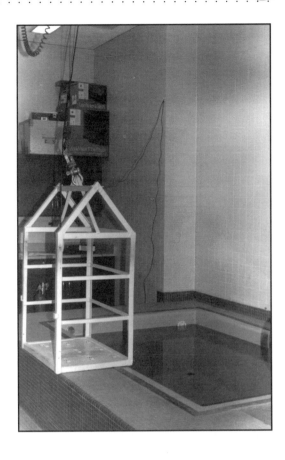

Indiana State University's hydrostatic pool.

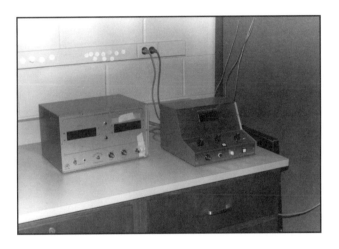

Electronics for hydrostatic weighing,
Indiana State University laboratory.

- The treadmill(s) should have appropriate 110 or 220 wiring in the recessed area.
- Electrical outlets should be located at the floor level for data-gathering machines.
- Both the hydrostatic area and the main laboratory area should have sinks, counter tops, and storage cabinets.
- Additional electrical outlets should be placed around the perimeter of the laboratory to accommodate other exercise equipment that needs surge protected, electricity.
- All electrical outlets near the water supplies must be GFI types.
- All computer stations must be hardwired to the mainframe computer.
- All separate spaces within the laboratory area must be capable of closed-circuit TV.
- Privacy drapes should be suspended from the ceiling for private sections.
- The height of the room with a recessed treadmill will be 10 feet and 14 feet with a treadmill that is not recessed and has a platform constructed around its perimeter.

- If the research conducted deals with taking and analyzing biopsies and blood samples, a small chemical laboratory will have to be constructed separate from the main space.
- Appropriate storage space is necessary.
- The environment in the laboratory must be conducive to exercise—temperature 68-72 degrees Fahrenheit, 60% or less, and 8 to 12 exchanges per hour. (Note: Air exchanges should have an appropriate mix of outside and inside air. This mix is usually 10 percent outside air and 90 percent inside air, though a ratio of 40 to 60, outside to inside, is preferred. The specific ratio of outside to inside air (recirculated air) is most often governed by local engineering codes. These codes should be followed when any air-handling system is installed.)
- Lighting should be indirect to avoid glare on the computer monitors.
- Appropriate security should be provided to protect all computers and equipment.
- A sprinkler system should not be installed in this space. Use an appropriate substitute that will not harm the computers.

Biomechanics (Kinesiology) Laboratory

There are many areas in the field of biomechanics in which research may be conducted. The type of research may range from cinematography to human engineering. The size of the space ranges from 600 sf to 2,000 sf. This space can never be too large.

The following components may be necessary for this space:

- An office space (200 sf);
- A force platform set into the floor in an area where various activities from jumping to running can take place without hindering other activities in the laboratory;
- Ceiling height of at least 16 feet;
- Suspended theater lighting;
- An environment conducive to exercise and cinematography—temperature 68-72 degrees Fahrenheit, 60% or less, and 8 to 12 exchanges per hour;
- Computer stations for laboratory use and digitizing movement;
- All computer stations hardwired into the main frame and all electrical outlets surge protected;
- Possibly a dark room to develop film and appropriate storage space;
- Multipurpose synthetic flooring;
- Nets and background drapes suspended from the ceiling that can be lowered and raised electronically;
- Appropriate storage space;
- Indirect lighting (except for theater lights) to avoid glare on the computer monitors;
- Appropriate security to protect all computers and equipment;
- No sprinkler system, but an appropriate substitute that will not harm the computers.

Motor Learning or Development Laboratory

Much of the research equipment found in exercise physiology and biomechanics laboratories can be used in research in motor learning or development and psychology of sport. However, a separate room or facility is necessary,

at least 600 sf to 1,000 square feet with at least a 12-foot ceiling. The arrangement of the equipment in the room will depend on the research underway at the moment.

The following components maybe necessary for this space:

- An office space (200 sf);
- An environment conducive to movement activities—temperature 68-72 degrees Fahrenheit, 60% or less, and 8 to 12 exchanges per hour;
- Multipurpose synthetic flooring;
- Curtains and nets suspended from the ceiling that can be lowered and raised electronically;
- Four to six telephone-size cubicles with a counter top, chair, light, and electrical outlets;
- Sound proofing and separate environmental controls;
- Counter top spaces around the perimeter of the laboratory with storage below and above;
- A number of computer stations that are directly wired into the main frame and the outlets surge protected;
- No sprinkler system, but an appropriate substitute that will not harm the computers;
- Appropriate storage space;
- Indirect lighting to avoid glare on the computer monitors; and
- Appropriate security to protect all computers and equipment.

Technician's Office and Workshop Area

The science laboratories in HPERD are very technical, and many researchers and teachers are unable to repair equipment when it malfunctions. This means contacting a repair service. The cost of the repair and other customary charges are expensive and the work not always timely. Therefore, serious consideration should be given to hiring a technician to maintain the expensive equipment in all the laboratories. If this option is taken, a technician's office and workshop must be designed.

The following components maybe necessary for this space:

- An office space (200 sf) with computer, phone, cable TV, and electrical outlets;

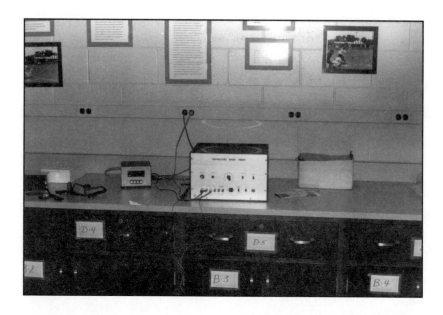

Electronics use in Indiana State University's motor learning laboratory.

- A workshop space (200 sf) with a work bench with multiple outlets, storage cabinets, drawer space, pegboard on wall to hang tools and parts;
- A concrete floor with a painted coarse finish and a floor drain;
- A double-deep sink and cabinets below and above;
- Temperature of 68-72 degrees Fahrenheit, 60% or less, and 8 to 12 exchanges per hour;
- No sprinkler system, but an appropriate substitute that will not harm the computers;
- Appropriate storage space;
- Indirect lighting to avoid glare on the computer monitors; and
- Appropriate security to protect all computers and equipment.

Suggestions for Purchasing Equipment

The manufacture and sale of research equipment has become a very competitive business. As a result, a wide range of the same kind of equipment is frequently available under different brand names. Before purchasing large expensive units, it is worth the time and effort to investigate carefully the various makes. The annual meetings of professional societies generally include exhibits by manufacturers of research equipment appropriate to the particular area of investigation. Consultation with a colleague in the same field who has used the equipment is a good idea before making a purchase.

In considering particular pieces of equipment, determine the following: (a) whether students or trained researchers are to use the equipment; (b) initial and annual servicing cost; (c) whether the equipment is electronically compatible with other equipment now in use or contemplated (often it is more economical to purchase units that match others from the same company so that the responsibility for servicing them rests with one company); (d) what power supply is needed; (e) ease with which the instrument may be calibrated, and whether other equipment is needed for the calibration; (g) what service the company is willing to provide and where the service centers are located; and (h) levels of noise, vibration, and heat generated by the equipment. Unbiased answers to these and other questions can sometimes best be found by having discussions with other researchers who have used such installations.

Exercise Physiology Laboratory Equipment Needs

The equipment for the Exercise Physiology Laboratory includes

- crash cart,
- ECG defibrillator,
- spine board,
- treadmill(s),
- stair climber(s),
- bicycle ergometer(s),
- pneumotachmeter,
- gas meter,
- telemetering apparatus,
- electronic gas analyzer(s), either paramagnetic or electrochemical,

- infrared analyzer,
- multichannel recorder,
- Douglas bags,
- barometer,
- thermocouples,
- face mask with two-way non-rebreathing valve,
- disposable pneumotach,
- one-way, T-shaped non-rebreathing valve with mouthpiece and saliva trap,
- metabolic cart,
- cardiopulmonary diagnostic system,
- cardiotachmeter,
- pedometers,
- telepedometer,
- biomotometer,
- accelerometers,
- actometer,
- caltrac,
- electromyography, and
- computers, monitors, and printers (laser).

Biomechanics Laboratory Equipment Needs

The equipment for the biomechanics laboratory includes:

- force platform,
- other types of force measuring devices,
- high-speed motion picture camera, motor-driven, 50-500 frames per second,
- stroboscopic equipment,
- videotape recorder with two channels and playback capacity,
- oscilloscope,
- electronic counters,
- amplifiers compatible with measuring and recording devices,
- digitizing equipment,
- computers, monitors, printers (laser),
- mirrors, and
- metal storage cabinets.

Motor Learning and Development Laboratory Equipment Needs

Equipment for the motor learning and development laboratory includes:

- multichannel recorders,
- standard electric clocks,
- interval timer,
- steadiness units,
- electronic counters,
- variable power supply,
- electronic kits,
- audio amplifiers,
- microphone,
- audio oscillator,
- oscilloscope,
- telemetry transmitter,
- telemetry receiver,
- voltage stabilizer,
- battery charger,
- seashore test,
- magnetic tape recorder, and
- storage cabinets.

Summary

The key academic spaces for HPERD are classrooms and laboratories. These spaces have become very complicated because of technological advances and increased distance education programming. Further, technological advances are changing faster then are the abilities of institutions to keep pace financially. The key words in designing these spaces are flexibility and upgradability.

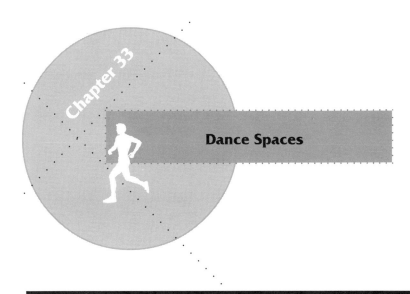

Thomas H. Sawyer, Indiana State University

Dance in education is not a new idea. At all education levels it has existed by virtue of dedicated individuals. In the elementary schools, dance activities under a number of aliases—eurhythmics, rhythms, play party games, singing games, and folk dance—have been offered. Coming into the elementary school curriculum as an offshoot of the playground movement, the dance materials presented were usually happenstance (with a few exceptions in experimental schools). A classroom teacher may have been interested in folk dance or been faced with the necessity to prepare a May Day, a pageant, or a festival.

Within the past few years, many privately administered elementary schools and some public schools have made provisions for dance in the curriculum. By and large, existing physical education facilities are used.

Since the turn of the century, folk dance (usually European in origin) has been offered in physical education classes for girls in secondary schools. When folk dance lessons were first introduced, they were often limited in content and skill, and were, as in the elementary school, an outcome of the playground movement. Toward the end of the 19th century, a few secondary schools in large cities had gymnasiums that were primarily equipped for gymnastics and other sports using limited-size courts. The use of these areas for dance was spasmodic and usually occurred in preparation for special events.

In the 1920s dance in education was materially advanced when Margaret H'Doubler initiated the first dance major at the University of Wisconsin. During this period, clog and tap dance assumed a leading role in dance education, and Henry Ford promoted a return to the formal square dances of an earlier day, such as the Lancers (NDA, 1985).

By the 1930s, the country was sufficiently removed from its pioneer beginnings to acknowledge the joy and value of square dancing. The teaching of social dance was heavily emphasized as a means of implementing the social values of physical education. Modern dance—stemming from natural dance and from the influences of Martha Graham, Doris Humphrey, Charles Weidman, and others—began a slow but steady growth in curricular offerings. In 1931, great impetus was given to dance in education with the establishment of the National Section on Dance within the American Association for Health, Physical Education, and Recreation (NDA, 1985).

The advancement of physical education programs was not without trauma for teachers and administrators. Until World War I, with its emphasis upon fitness and recognition of the recreational needs of service personnel, it was difficult to finance facilities and staff for physical education. Immediately after the war, mobility and better communications enhanced the athletic program and, as the result of athletic needs, more gymnasiums and stadiums were built. The need for a gymnasium in secondary schools was thereby placed on a firm basis. The depression of the late 1920s and early 1930s, however, curbed these programs and the extensive expansion of facilities. World War II not only emphasized fitness and the recreational needs of service personnel but added a new dimension-recreational needs of war workers in factories, shipyards, and munition plants. The Cold War and the possibility of increased leisure time have reiterated the needs for enriched curricula and additional facilities.

Until recently, studios for dance at the secondary school level had dropped in priority behind athletic and aquatic facilities. At the beginning of the 20th century, dance was often better off than were sports in the low-ceilinged basement rooms and narrow hallways. As gymnasiums were built primarily for basketball programs, dance was relegated to a low priority in the use of these facilities both for class and after-school clubs. Moreover, the finish or seal on gymnasium floors made certain dance activities uncomfortable and precluded others. Within the past 10 to 15 years, there has been a growing consciousness of the needs of girls in secondary schools. As dance has proved its worth as a physiologically demanding and aesthetically rewarding activity, consideration is being given to the employment of specialized teachers and the provision of specialized areas for teaching dance at the secondary level.

Gradually, clog and tap dance, natural dance, and later ballroom and square dance as well as modern dance have appeared in the secondary school curriculum. Of significance is the increasing interest of boys in the various forms of dance, especially modern jazz. Frequently, dance programs at the secondary school level are the result of grants from the National Endowment for the Arts (NDA, 1985).

As was true in elementary and secondary schools, facilities for dance education at the college level have developed slowly. The gymnasium dominated the scene, with dance scheduled "catch-as-catch-can" during available hours. As emphasis upon dance in teacher preparation increased and as colleges and universities became more involved in all phases of the arts, auxiliary rooms were planned for dance and related activities.

Learning Objectives

After reading this chapter, the student will be able to
- recognize the basic needs of a general dance facility,
- describe the criteria used to determine dance facility needs,
- outline the construction components for dance areas, including modern dance, ballet, folk dance, social dance, dance production areas, arena stage areas, proscenium stage areas, instructional space, and auxiliary areas, and
- appreciate the differences between elementary, secondary, and collegiate dance facilities.

Basic Dance Facility Assumptions

The essential facilities should be supplied in sufficient quantity and quality to provide for all dance activities in the required and elective curriculums and in extracurricular programs. Particular attention should be given to adequate provision for dance performance, observation, and audience spaces.

Related portions of the activity complex should be provided and meet acceptable standards. These will include (NDA, 1985):
- Box office,
- Construction rooms for costumes, props and sets, and music (composing and recording),
- Costume storage areas,
- Custodial space,
- Laundry, cleaning and drying facilities,
- Listening areas,
- Locker-dressing rooms with make-up areas,
- Office space,
- Parking area,
- Public lavatories,
- Rest rooms (remote from toilets and showers),
- Shower area,
- Storage spaces (props and sets),
- Toilets, and
- Training room.

The following should be provided and meet established standards (NDA, 1985):

- Electrical installation,
- Lighting equipment,
- Acoustics,
- Ventilation,
- Heating,
- Floors,
- Walls,
- Sanitation,
- Safety,
- Drinking fountains,
- Sound systems,
- Filming and taping facilities,
- Installation of fixed equipment,
- Movable equipment, and
- Lines of traffic.

Dance facilities should be designed to serve both genders. Further, the dance facility should be readily accessible to outside entrances and be a unit unto itself even if it is attached to, or a part of, another building. Finally, the dance complex should be constructed, decorated, and furnished in an aesthetically pleasing manner and suitable for the pursuit of dance as an art form.

Criteria for Determining Facility Needs

The following criteria can be used to determine the dance facility needs when planning either a stand-alone dance facility or one for inclusion in a larger complex (NDA, 1985):

Total facilities should be determined according to the amount of emphasis placed on various aspects of the dance curriculum, such as classes needed and areas for individual work and for extracurricular and concert practice.

Based on the design of the dance curriculum, facilities should be considered in terms of:
- Auxiliary space and equipment,
- Classroom space,
- Dance teaching space,
- Office space,
- Performance space,
- Practice space and choreography,
- Rehearsal space, and
- Research space.

Preferably three distinct areas should be provided: one area for folk and social dance, one area for modern dance, and one area for ballet.

Construction of Modern Dance and Ballet Areas

The following information is provided to assist in the development of state-of-the-art modern dance and ballet areas (NDA, 1985):

Dimensions

- A minimum of 100 square feet per person is recommended. An area of 3,000 square feet will accommodate 30 students.

Example of a dance exerciser instructor's elevated platform.

- If an area is to serve as an informal theater and instructional area, it should be between 4,800 and 5,000 square feet to accommodate both the class and the needs of the theater section.
- Ceiling height of 16 to 24 feet is recommended for all dance areas. Full height is essential for large dance areas (over 2,400 square feet) and 16 feet is minimum height for small dance areas. There is a feeling of height when the ceiling is high. Some dancers prefer a height of 16 to 18 feet, but consideration must be given to the total construction in the dance areas. In some instances, any change in the roof line may add prohibitive expense.

Floors

- Dance activities require air space between floor and foundation, and "floating" and/or spring floors for resiliency.
- Floors should be of hardwood (such as maple) of random lengths, and tongue-and-grooved; they should be laid with the grain going in one direction.
- Portable floors (Marly or stage-step) provide flexibility for use when both ballet and modern dance need to be accommodated.
- Floors should be non-slip and constructed for easy cleaning.
- The finish should provide a smooth surface upon which dancers can glide with bare feet or soft sandals. Tung or linseed oil is considered by most to be a satisfactory finish; an alternative might be several coats of wood sealer. No chemical dust mops should be used to clean such floors, only a slightly damp mop.

Doors

There should be wide double doors to permit traffic flow into and out of the room. The sills of such doors should be level with the floor to allow for moving large equipment such as a piano.

Walls

- Walls should be smooth and easily maintained.
- Consideration should be given to having one unobstructed wall of neutral background for filming purposes.
- Stress factors of the walls should be considered to support ballet barres and mirrors.
- Thin walls are inadequate.
- It is desirable to sound-proof walls especially in listening areas.

Lighting

- Incandescent light is preferable to fluorescent light.
- Rheostat lights that also serve as houselights during performances should be controlled from wall switches as well as from the light control board.
- Consideration should be given to natural lighting. Large windows contribute to an aesthetically and psychologically desirable atmosphere. The best location for windows is the north wall to avoid direct sunlight.
- Windows should be curtained so the studio can be darkened for film showing and studio performances.
- When total construction necessitates no windows, the aesthetics may be improved by the use of a pastel color on the walls or draperies serving both aesthetic and acoustical purposes.

Acoustics and Sound Equipment

- When one studio is directly over another or over offices, acoustical treatment is necessary.
- Placement of sound equipment, such as a record player, turntable, microphones, and speakers should be considered in the initial planning in terms of both performance and security.
- An adequate number of speakers, installed in or near ceiling height, should be located so participants can hear both music and instruction.

Ballet bar and mirrors.

- Heavy equipment should be placed on stands of table height equipped with rollers.
- Electrical outlets should be spaced on every wall and located close to where equipment will be used. Four-plex outlets are needed close to the area where most equipment is used (e.g., video-tape recorders, tape deck and amplifiers for performance, and stage manager's desk for cueing lights).

Storage Space

- Locked storage space for sound equipment should be adjacent to the dance area and locked. Storage rooms should have double doors and a flush threshold for easy movement of large equipment, such as a piano.
- Built-in storage space for records, sound equipment, tapes, and musical instruments should be provided.
- A sound-proof area for use of students and instructors in listening to recordings and tapes and viewing videotapes is highly desirable. This area should have adequate acoustics, ventilation, and electrical outlets.

Wiring

- Heavy-duty wiring is essential for all dance facilities. Wiring should be capable of carrying a portable light board as well as phonographs, additional speakers, tape recorders, and projectors. Wall outlets should be plentiful.
- Television conduits should be installed at the time a building is constructed.

Temperature and Ventilation

- Temperature should be maintained at 65° to 72° F (22°-26° C). The thermostat should be located in the studio areas.
- The air should be well circulated, and consideration should be given to the use of natural air. Humidity should be no greater than 95%.

- Mechanisms for heating and circulating of air should be as nearly silent as possible to avoid interfering with the quality of sound and its reception.

Accessories

- Leaf-fold mirrors, which can be folded for protection or curtained during performances, may be installed along two adjoining walls so that movement can be analyzed from two directions. Wall mirrors at least six feet high should be installed flush with the wall and raised 1 or 1 1/2 feet from the floor.
- Ballet barres should be made of wood, preferably oak or aluminum, and be smooth in texture. The minimum length to accommodate one dancer is five feet. Barres from 40 to 42 inches in height may be installed permanently; they should extend six to eight inches from the wall. If feasible, consider double barres—one at 36 inches, and one at 42 inches. If necessary, barres may be placed in front of mirrors. The barre supports may be screwed into recessed floor sockets just in front of the mirror, thus facilitating the removal of the barre and supports when not needed.
- Custom-made percussion cabinets mounted on rollers are a fine accessory. They may have a carpeted top surface, slide-out drawers lined with felt for small instruments, and larger partitions to accommodate cymbals and drums.
- Heavy sound equipment should be built-in or placed on stands of table height equipped with rollers for ease of transportation.
- Since moving affects the tuning of a piano, this instrument should be placed where it will not have to be moved. A piano should be placed on an inside wall where it will not be subject to extreme heat or cold, and be protected by a suitable cover and lock. It should be placed on a heavy-duty dolly if it is to be moved frequently.
- Chalkboards and tackboards are useful accessories.
- Telephone.
- A glass-enclosed exhibit case for photographs, costumes, costume plates, manuscripts, and other items

may be installed near the dance area. A building foyer may be utilized.

- The atmosphere for dance should be conducive to artistic endeavors. Soft colors, clear lighting, and spaciousness are pleasing to both dancers and spectators.

Construction of Folk and Social Dance Areas

The following information is provided to assist in the development of state-of-the-art folk and social dance areas (NDA, 1985):

Dimensions

- An area of 5,400 square feet (54 ft. x 100 ft. is suggested) will accommodate a class of approximately 60 students.
- Dance areas are generally rectangular with a length-width ratio of approximately 3 to 2 (for example, 90 feet x 60 feet).
- Ceiling height should be in proportion to the size of the room but never lower than 12 feet.
- An outside entrance into a main corridor of the building will provide for traffic flow of the relatively large groups using the area.

Floors

Floors as described in the section on ballet and modern dance are necessary. However, an epoxy finish, rather than tung oil, will enable the use of street shoes without damage to the floor.

Lighting and Ventilation

- Acoustics and sound equipment (see above),
- Storage space (see above),
- Wiring (see first point under wiring, above), and
- Temperature and ventilation (see above).

Accessories

- Racks for coats and books should be installed either within the dance area or along the outside corridor wall.
- Tackboards, chalkboards, and display cases are highly desirable.

Dance Production Areas

While a well-equipped theater is the ideal dance performance area, it is not always possible to have such a facility. The alternative is to provide a large area for both instructional and performance activities. The area may be equipped with a balcony for observation of classes and for audience seating during performances. Other seating arrangements such as portable bleachers may also be desirable. A large area may be equipped to provide for arena or proscenium staging, or both.

Arena Stage Area

The planning for an arena stage area should include performance space, seating, lighting, sound equipment, control booths, and wiring. The following describes the specifics needed in each area:

Performance Space

The performance area should contain between 875 and 1,200 square feet (NDA, 1985).

Seating Space

The most desirable seating capacity for performances should accommodate 300 to 500 people. The entire performing area should be visible from all seats. The seating arrangement should be flexible. Seats may be on movable risers so space may be used in a variety of ways. Raked seating is essential. Adequate entrances, exits, and exit lights should be provided for performers and audience in accordance with local fire codes.

The proscenium arch surrounds the stage like a picture frame.

Lighting

Lighting should be available from all directions. It should be possible to use gels on all lighting instruments except house lights. All lights should be on separate dimmers. A sufficient number of electrical outlets should be available. When possible, all lights should be operated from a single console within the control booth.

Sound Equipment

Equipment should be operated from a control booth. Speakers for amplification should be placed so both performers and audience can hear. Backstage monitors should be used.

Control Booths

Provision should be made for control booths or . . . areas with full view of the stage area to operate lights and sound.

Wiring

Wiring should be adequate to carry a portable light board, a phonograph, tape recorder, speaker system, projector, and follow spots (see local electric codes).

Proscenium Stage Area

The planning for a proscenium stage area should include performance space, seating, curtains, teasers, battens, lighting, sound equipment, control booths, and live musicians. The following describes the specifics needed in each area:

Performance Space

The minimum performance area should be 1,200 square feet (30 feet by 40 feet). The two wing areas combined should be equal to the amount of visible stage space. Space should be provided for musicians, chairs, and lighted music stands. Placement of musicians should not interfere with the visibility of the stage or the sound of the music (NDA, 1985).

Seating Space

A balcony with permanently installed raked seating is desirable, with the possibility of portable risers below. The entire performing area should be visible from all seats. The number of seats should be planned for estimated size of audience.

Curtains, Teasers, Battens

Hand control is preferable to a mechanically controlled front curtain. Side curtains (legs) or flats should be provided on both sides of the stage for entrances and exits. Flexible tracks to move the curtain horizontally should be considered. Asbestos teasers and tormentors are needed for safety and masking. Battens to be used for hanging scenery, sky drop, or film screen should be suspended above the visible stage area. Provision should be made for lowering and raising battens for the attachment of scenery. Lines should be attached to a pin rail located at one side of the stage. Metal grids are also usable. The back wall should be free of visible obstructions and painted white for projections. Curtains and flats should be light, absorbent, and of neutral or dark color.

Lighting Equipment

Provision should be made for side lighting, front lighting, and overhead border lighting. Three separate circuits should be provided to be used singly or in combination. There should be front ceiling beam lighting, balcony lighting, or both. Crawl space should be provided in the ceiling above the beams to permit focusing and repair work. It should be possible to use gels on all lights except house lights. All instruments should be on separate dimmers. A sufficient number of electrical outlets should be located in floor pockets or wall spaces in the wings. A low wattage light should be installed for cueing performers and crew members at the side of the front stage. When possible, all lights should be operated from a single console within the control booth.

Sound Equipment

Equipment should be operated from the control booth. Speakers for amplification should be placed so both performers and audience can hear. An intercom should be used to link the backstage, dressing rooms, and control booth. Telephones to handle outside calls should be located in the box office and backstage. The backstage phone should be equipped with a signal light.

Live Musicians

If feasible, space should be allocated for performance appearances.

Control Booths

Control booths for lights, sound, and projections should be centered at the audience end of the facility and should include soundproofing, a large window for viewing the stage, built-in counters and shelves for storing equipment, and an intercom for communication with the backstage area.

Auxiliary Areas

The following auxiliary areas need to be included in the planning process for a dance facility:

Costume Room

A costume room for constructing, fitting, cleaning, and storing should be a minimum of 400 square feet and be equipped with or accessible to:
- Built-in cabinets with shelves and drawers, and racks for hanging and storing costumes.
- Cleaning machine,
- Control room with toilet facilities,
- Cutting table,
- Double door with a flush threshold to facilitate moving costume racks,
- Dress forms,
- Ironing boards and steam irons,

- Laundry tubs and drying facilities,
- Sewing machines,
- Tackboard and chalkboard affixed to one wall,
- Three-way mirror, and
- Washing machine and dryer.

Dressing Rooms

Dressing rooms should be provided for men and women. They should be equipped with costume racks, chairs, wash basins, lighted mirrors, toilets and showers, and a first-aid kit.

Make-up Room

The make-up room should be located between the men's and women's dressing rooms and be furnished with lighted mirrors, built-in shelves, make-up tables, chairs, wash basins, and storage space.

Scene and Prop Room

The scene and prop room should be located as close to the stage area as feasible. It should be a minimum of 400 to 500 sf and have a ceiling height of at least 16 feet, although 24 feet is preferable. The floor should have a paint-resistant surface. Proper ventilation is necessary to avoid fumes from paint and glue. The room should be furnished with built-in bins and shelves for storage of nails, brushes, screws, paints, and glues; a pegboard mounted flush with the wall for hanging tools; a built-in workbench; a wash sink; outlets for electrical tools; and a chalkboard and tackboard. Storage space for props should be a minimum of 500 sf with a 16- to 24-foot ceiling; it should be easily accessible to the backstage area (NDA, 1985).

Box Office (Ticket Booth)

The box office should have locked racks for tickets, a locked drawer for currency, a telephone with an outside line, and an intercom to the backstage area.

Foyer

It is desirable to provide a social area where the audience and performers may meet following a production. It should be situated adjacent to the performing area and include attractive decorations, a comfortable seating arrangement, display cases, and an adjoining small kitchen for preparing refreshments.

Additional Instructional and Laboratory Facility Needs Based on the Size of the Dance Program and Curriculum

Three areas need to be planned for in the dance facility, including teaching space, office space, and auxiliary space.

Teaching Space

The following are planning considerations for dance teaching areas:

- There should be a minimum of one large teaching and performance area. This area should have a 24-foot ceiling and resilient floors, and be equipped with special lighting for performance, sound equipment, a communications media, an observation balcony, and good ventilation and lighting.
- Two additional areas should be provided: an area for ballet and modern dance, and an area for jazz, social, and folk dance.
- Provision should be made for well-designed and well-equipped classrooms and seminar and lecture rooms for instructional use.
- In addition to the performance area, there should be rehearsal space that is somewhat larger than the area designed for performance.
- There should be an area for practice and choreography that is equipped with phonographs, tape machines, and video-tape equipment.
- A library and reference room with an adjoining study area for books, music, records, tapes, and copying machine should be available.
- Provision should be made for a soundproof recording studio large enough to accommodate a piano and small orchestra, turntables and tape recorder. It should have built-in shelves for storage and be not less than 300 square feet.
- Storage space for musical instruments should be provided.

Office Space

The dance facility office space should include the following:

- There should be a centralized office for unified administration.
- A private office and conference space for the director of the dance program should be available.
- There should be office space for faculty members and for technical personnel.
- Supporting space for office equipment and storage should be provided.
- Laboratory space for faculty should be available.

Auxiliary Space

Additional auxiliary space might include the following:

- It is desirable to have a reception-social room (with adjoining kitchen) for use by students, faculty, and community groups on special occasions.
- Locker-shower areas should be available for students and faculty of both genders.
- A faculty conference room should be provided.
- A rehabilitation or therapy room is desirable.

Adaptation of Dance Facilities and Equipment

Since local conditions may demand modification of ideal dance facilities while a dance program is being developed, this section describes some of the adaptations that may be feasible.

Elementary School

Current Practices

Small gymnasiums are used most frequently, with cafeteria-gymnasiums, multipurpose rooms, and auditorium-gymnasiums following in close order. The size of classes ranges from 25 to 70 pupils, with 30 being the average size.

With regard to floor surfaces used for the instruction of dance, hardwood predominates, with linoleum tile running second. The floors in winter should be heated.

As far as equipment was concerned, all elementary schools but one have a record player with convenient electrical outlets, but just over half the schools report having sufficient recordings. The same is true of movable tables with rollers for record players, and of controlled speeds and amplification of recordings. Tape recorders are available in approximately half the elementary schools. There is some evidence of percussion equipment, principally rhythm band instruments, with a few elementary schools having either a Chinese tom-tom or a Gretsch dance drum. Three-fourths of the elementary schools report chalkboards and nearly half of them report bulletin boards in use as teaching aids. Approximately half of the elementary schools cite that storage space is available for recordings and percussion instruments.

Use of Limited Facilities and Equipment

Practically speaking, it is impossible to secure ideal dance facilities in all situations at the elementary school level. Community socio-economic conditions virtually negate such a dream. Lack of ideal facilities and equipment is no reason to omit dance experiences for children. An outstanding authority on children's movement experiences has stated that a multipurpose room is quite adequate for the dance program. Another expert found that children can be taught to move lightweight classroom furniture efficiently so that dance space is available. By constant attention to opportunities for renovations in a school (or a school system), one may ask for use of renovated space, for installation of bulletin boards and electrical outlets, and even for changes in floor surfaces. Teacher initiative is a priority if space for dance is to be acquired.

Recommendations

Dance areas for elementary school children should be large enough to accommodate approximately 30 students. Rooms below ground level are inadvisable, because of possible dampness and lack of adequate ventilation. As increasing numbers of elementary schools are built on a one-floor plan with outdoor exits for individual classrooms, basement facilities will gradually vanish.

Hardwood is advised for dance floors. Tile floors, which frequently are laid directly on cement or concrete, are cold to the touch, often slippery, and conducive to injury. Because tile flooring allows no resiliency for foot action, it can lead to painful shin splints.

There is no answer to the exact type of dance facility that should be provided. Except under unusual circumstances, economics rule out the provision for a dance studio. The combination gymnasium-lunch room is not recommended because of loss of time for classes before, after, and during lunch hours, and the health hazards of dust on food and lunch debris in the activity area. The stage-auditorium, stage-gymnasium, small gymnasium, multipurpose room, or large playroom may be used if adequate electrical outlets and wiring for record players, tape recorders, and minimal stage lighting can be provided.

The rather informal dance programs presented at the elementary school level can often be accommodated by seating the children on the floor and visitors on chairs around three sides of one end of the dance area. Usually storage space for recordings and simple percussion equipment is available in, or adjacent to, such areas. Many physical education items can be used in the dance program. Jumping ropes, balls, boxes, benches, mats, and other play apparatus lend themselves to creative uses.

Dance for children has become an established activity in elementary school programs. It can only take place, however, when space and equipment are provided, time is allocated, and leadership is available.

Secondary School

Current Practices

It is extremely difficult to secure detailed information on dance programs at the secondary school level. The size of areas used for dance varies from extremely small to extremely large, with a rectangular shape being most common. In height, the areas vary from eight feet to 40 feet. Record players and tape recorders are usually available. Percussion instruments, drums predominating, are also in use. Some secondary schools have closet space set aside for costumes and even a full costume room. Ballet barres and mirrors are in use. Wooden floors predominate. One secondary school reports that excellent additional practice space is available, and several schools note that smaller additional space is available, and several secondary schools note that smaller additional space is available only when not in use by other groups.

Use of Limited Facilities and Equipment

Few secondary schools have specialized facilities for dance. One reason is that there has not been adequate emphasis on dance in the secondary school curriculum. There is some indication, however, that specialized concentrations (dance, sports, aquatics, gymnastics) in teacher preparation, and a cultural emphasis upon the arts are beginning to alter this pattern, particularly in suburban areas and in certain consolidated school districts. As these programs begin to establish their value, obtaining facilities will become easier.

Meanwhile, the standard gymnasium can be used. Teachers who are interested in providing dance experiences for their students can plan curricular units, secure a few portable barres, borrow a record player and/or tape recorder from the audiovisual supply room, find storage area for a few percussion instruments, and secure space for a costume closet. The floor with the usual gymnasium seal on it is not ideal but can be used. The battle for time allotments and space assignment is perennial. Interest and effort can perform wonders.

Recommendations

A minimum dance facility should provide 100 square feet per student, one dimension to exceed 60 feet; full-length mirrors at a corner for analysis of skill from two directions; a speaker system designed to distribute sound evenly throughout the room; a control system for record players and microphones; and practice barres on one wall at heights of 34 inches and 42 inches. For modern dance, the floor should be of hard northern maple that has been sealed and then buffed with a fine abrasive. Additional suggestions follow (NDA, 1985):

Equipment. As in the case of the elementary school, physical education equipment such as balls, ropes, and gymnastic apparatus may be used. Stall bars, if available, are an excellent substitute for ballet barres and a fine medium for creative activity.

By wise planning, basic equipment (recordings, percussion instruments, and portable lighting boards) can be floated from school to school for production use.

Portable percussion racks made in an industrial arts department solve the problems of easy storage and efficient class and program use. Portable mirrors, six feet tall and eight feet wide, can be constructed 1 1/2 feet from the floor on rollers and moved into the dance area if wall-mounted mirrors are not feasible. Portable ballet barres of lightweight aluminum are desirable when unobstructed wall space is at a premium.

Floors. Poor floors should be covered by Marly dance flooring rather than a ground cloth.

Areas. Investigation of the following areas may reveal available spaces for dance: adaptive rooms, gymnastic rooms, weight control rooms, recreational game rooms. Careful preplanning of new facilities suggests the possibility of combining two or more of these. Two community resources are feasible-churches and local theater groups. Churches are now interested in dance. Either temporary or permanent use of a large classroom or a church auditorium may be possible. Community theatre groups are adding dance experiences for all age levels to their gamut of activities. It may be possible to arrange for use of their areas during the school day.

The possibility of pooled resources in the performing arts—dance, drama, music—opens wide potential in the development of excellent facilities, economy in their use by several departments, and rich experiences in multimedia.

Performing Arts for Modern Dance or Ballet

The following specific recommendations are made for modern dance and ballet areas (NDA, 1985):

- The stage should be situated at the end of the room that can best provide entrances for the dancers. The dancers' entrances should be out of the audience's view.
- The stage can be formed by curtains or flats.
- A back curtain should have a center opening and be hung at least three feet forward of the back wall to provide crossover space for the performers.
- In the case of a raised stage, the front curtain should be set back about four feet from the raised edge to provide an apron (forestage).
- Side curtains or flats should be provided.
- If curtains cannot be used, an open stage is advisable. The folding mats used in physical education can be set on edge to form entrances and exits. Flats and portable screens are alternative possibilities.

Performing Area for Folk and Social Dance

The following specific recommendations are made for folk and social dance areas (NDA, 1985):

- Roll-away bleachers can be installed at one end of the room.
- Provision should be made for storage of folding chairs, which can be placed along the side walls.
- An auxiliary performing space can be a patio or other outdoor area, such as a dance green or a broad, level surface at the entrance to a school building, which can be adapted for occasional use for dance performances. Marly dance floorings may be placed on the cement surface to protect the dancer's feet and legs.

As in the case of elementary schools, specific dance facilities are not feasible in all secondary schools. Dance is possible, however, depending on the teacher's interest, effort, and ability to adapt to the situation.

College/University

As new facilities have been constructed and older facilities remodeled in the larger colleges and universities, there seems to be little excuse for omission of areas specifically planned for dance. The increasing emphasis upon dance as a major field and the increasing interrelationships among the performing arts have placed dance in a position of importance in college planning.

Summary

Dance facilities are often ignored and the facilities provided are not even close to adequate. This chapter has provided information to assist the planners of HPERD facilities at the elementary, secondary, and collegiate level in properly planning appropriate and adequate dance facilities.

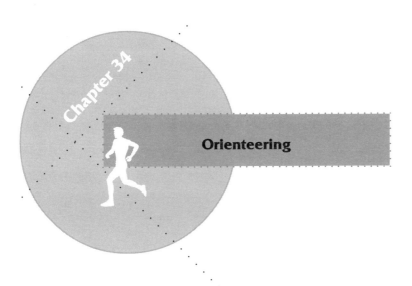

Chapter 34

Orienteering

Thomas Horne, United States Military Academy

Orienteering originated in Scandinavia and was done on both cross-country skis and on foot. Orienteering is an outdoor movement activity that requires participants to find the fastest route between a series of terrain features, using a simple compass and a map as navigational aids. Orienteering, an international sport, has standards and procedures that are well established and formalized. Individuals interested in participating in orienteering activities, but not concerned with formal competition may modify these standards and procedures to meet their individual needs. Orienteers (individuals participating in orienteering activities) decide for themselves whether to focus on wilderness skills, physical training, recreation, winning, or socialization. Even if serious orienteering competition is not the goal, following established basic orienteering procedures will enhance the orienteering activity and make it more enjoyable for the participants.

This chapter will focus on how to organize and conduct orienteering activities. Some technical skills will be covered since orienteering activity organizers do need to know some basic technical orienteering skills to effectively conduct an orienteering event. Adapted and developmental orienteering activities will be covered. An internet web exercise and a case study are included to provide application guidance for implementing an orienteering program.

Instructional Objectives

After reading this chapter the student will be able to:
- describe orienteering and explain the nature of the sport,
- utilize general orienteering concepts to develop customized orienteering activities,
- identify the equipment required to conduct an orienteering competition,
- organize an orienteering competition,
- apply key concepts and principles involved in laying out a safe orienteering course,
- develop support materials and procedures needed to conduct an orienteering program,
- access a variety Internet web sites and get information on orienteering, and
- apply administrative and program concepts utilized in an orienteering case study to develop or enhance an orienteering program.

Orienteering Basics

The primary facility for orienteering is the great outdoors. Most orienteering events are held in wooded or open terrain, with some obvious features such as fields, water bodies, fences and trails. Courses will vary depending on the focus of the orienteering activity, the availability of suitable land, and the age, fitness level, and experience of the participants. A map of the event area is normally provided for each participant. A formal topographic orienteering map is required for serious competitions. A series of check points (controls) are located on the course and recorded on the map. The controls are marked with the standard orienteering control marker (a three-dimensional orange and white marker). Orienteers are given control descriptions (clues) on how to locate the controls that must be visited. Normally, the orienteer who completes the course in the shortest time is the winner.

Activities

Types of Activities

Most orientation activities are conducted using one of two general types of orienteering:

Point-to-Point Orienteering (also called cross-country or route orienteering):

Point-to-point orienteering is used for most formal competitions. Point-to-point orienteering consists of a series of controls (checkpoints) in a specific order to be located by the orienteers. These controls are laid out and numbered sequentially, and their locations are recorded on an orienteering (topographic) map with a circle. Orienteers use a map and compass to locate all the controls in sequence and get to the finish line as rapidly as possible.

Score Orienteering:

Score orienteering is another type of orienteering competition. Similar to point-to-point orienteering, score orienteering participants use a map and compass to locate controls, but the controls are not in a set sequence. Controls blanket the area and are assigned a point value based on distance to the control and how difficult it will be to locate the control. Competition usually lasts a specific time and participants try to earn as many control points as possible in the designated time. Rogaine is a form of score orienteering that originated in Australia. It takes place on a very large course with controls located much farther apart than standard score orienteering. Teams of two or more navigate over often-rugged terrain during competitions that usually last 12 - 24 hours. The clock runs continuously, and the team to earn the most points in the prescribed time is the winner.

Pre-competitive Activities

String Course

A string course is a relatively short and simple orienteering course where a string or rope designates the course. Control points are located on or very near the string line. Participants simply follow the string that leads them to the control points. A simple string-orienteering map is usually employed to show the course and help participants develop basic map-reading skills and familiarize them with orienteering symbols and map colors.

Landmark Hunt (Kjellstrom 1976)

The purpose of the Landmark Hunt is to practice locating landmarks that would typically be used in an orienteering competition. Participants gather at a high point where all the landmarks can be seen. They are then given a short list of landmarks with descriptions that must be located on a map. The first person to correctly locate all the landmarks on the map is the winner. A more advanced version of the landmark hunt requires participants to give the correct compass reading to the landmark.

Map Point Walk (Kjellstrom 1976)

Map Point Walks provide an opportunity for orienteers to practice following a map and locating landmarks on a map. Lay out the course on a map leading through a number of easily identified landmarks. Along the route place small brightly colored streamers in such a manner that each streamer can be seen from the previous one. Major landmarks will be used for control points and will be marked

with a distinct marker such as a standard orienteering marker or a different colored streamer. A north-pointing arrow should be placed at each control point to assist participants in orienting their maps. Participants must locate these landmark controls and mark them on the map. Map Point Walks can be timed if competition is desired. For a Map Point Walk competition, the individual or group to correctly locate all of the landmark controls in the shortest time is declared the winner.

Map Point Reporting (Kjellstrom 1976)

Map point reporting provides an enjoyable way to practice map-reading skills and heightens the awareness of physical features similar to those used in competitive orienteering. Identify six to ten clearly identifiable landmarks on a map. Participants will then attempt to locate as many of these as possible in a set amount of time, the score orienteering format. At each control point, orienteers will be asked to answer questions about the terrain or features around the control. Different points will be assigned for each control based on the accessibility of the control and the difficulty of the question to be answered.

Urban Orienteering

If a wooded or country environment is not available, orienteering activities can be conducted in an urban setting. Standard road maps can be utilized, and there is an abundance of landmarks and features that can be incorporated into the course. Safety is a special concern when orienteering in an urban setting. A theme can be used for controls. For example, have all controls be emergency agencies (police department, fire station, and hospitals). The course must be carefully laid out to maximize safety in such situations as intersections, congested areas, fast-moving traffic, construction sites, and other dangerous areas.

Park Orienteering

Some park managers now have orienteering maps made of their parks, making them ideal sites to conduct orienteering events. The more parks that are mapped for orienteering, the more popular "Park Orienteering" will become.

Levels of competitive orienteering

Orienteering competitions can be informal, loosely organized events or highly structured events that meet sanctioning requirements of the International Orienteering Federation. Formal competitions often have more than one course to accommodate competitors of different ages and experience levels. Orienteering courses include:

White Courses

White Courses are the easiest competition courses and are ideal for younger children, novices, teenagers, and inexperienced adults. They are usually one to three kilometers in length and located on relatively flat terrain. All participants need to know the basic orienteering skills of map reading and using an orienteering compass. Control markers are placed on easily identified features such as trails, junctions, streams, buildings, and large rocks. Younger participants can navigate the course alone, in small groups, or be accompanied by a mature, experienced orienteer.

Yellow Courses

Yellow courses are generally slightly longer than white courses, three to four kilometers. The course should follow easy terrain along distinct features such as trails, fences, and open fields. Control points on yellow courses are usually farther from the main trail and more difficult to locate than those on white courses. Adults and teenagers with some experience on white courses should be able to complete yellow courses solo. Novices and younger children can handle yellow course terrain, but will normally need to have an adult or mature experienced orienteer accompany them.

Orange Courses

Orange Courses are intermediate courses that are longer than White and Orange Courses, four to five kilometers. Orange Courses begin to go off the trails and into the woods. Controls are still located near large or distinct features, but not necessarily on the trail in an obvious location. Orange courses are for the more experienced orienteers with experience on lower-level orienteering courses or other orienteering background. The slightly more challenging terrain and the longer distances require a greater level of fitness to compete successfully at this level. Orange courses are not normally appropriate for younger children, but they may enjoy an occasional outing on an orange course with an experienced adult.

Brown, Green, Red, and Blue Courses (Expert courses)

These expert courses vary in difficulty based on the length of the course (a blue course may be ten kilometers or longer), difficulty of the terrain, and the location of the controls. Successful navigation of a Brown Course (the easiest of the expert courses), Green Course, Red Course, or Blue Course (most difficult expert course) requires considerable experience and a higher level of fitness than that required on the less challenging courses. Expert courses tend to emphasize navigational skills and endurance rather than speed, so adults often excel at orienteering well into middle and advanced age, making orienteering an excellent lifetime fitness activity.

Equipment

Orienteering Maps

A map is a reduced representation of a portion of the earth. A map may be a very simple hand-drawn representation of a specific area or a very detailed, scaled representation identifying a variety of features. A map provides five categories of information, the "five D's" (Kjellstrom 1976).
- Description
- Details
- Directions
- Distances
- Designations

The type of map chosen for an orienteering activity will depend on the objective of the activity, the experience level of the activity organizer and participants, resources available, and type of orienteering. Most formal orienteering activities and competitions require a "topographical" map—from the Greek topes, place, and graphein, to write or draw: a drawing or a picture of a place or area. Topographical maps used for orienteering show landforms, water features, linear features, other artificial features, rock features, and vegetation. The International Orienteering Federation (IOF) has established orienteering map symbols (Figure 34.1) that are generally accepted and used for all sanctioned orienteering competition worldwide.

Another standard for topographic orienteering maps is the color-coding used to identify the different classes of features. Orienteers often read their five-color orienteering maps while on the move, and the color-coding helps them read the map quickly. The IOF standard orienteering map colors are:
- Black—Artificial features, such as roads, trails, buildings, and fences, plus rock features, such as cliffs and boulders.
- Brown—Topographic features, such as hills, valleys, ridges, earth banks, and ditches.
- Blue—Water features, such as lakes, ponds, swamps and streams.
- White (the color of paper)—Normal forest. (This is different from some government maps, which may show fields with white and forest green.)
- Yellow—Clearings and fields
- Green—Vegetation

Topographic maps suitable for orienteering may be available from local sports shops, orienteering clubs, or bookstores. If an orienteering map is not available at one of these sources, numerous commercial orienteering map-making companies are listed on a link from the United States Orienteering Federation home page. IOF symbols and color codes are recommended, even if a hand-drawn or other less formal map is desired. This will make the orienteering event a developmental exercise and avoid confusing individuals who have participated in more formal orienteering events that used the standardized symbols and colors.

The orienteering course is usually displayed on a large master map near the starting line. Orienteers use the master map to copy the route on their personal orienteering map if the route is not printed on their map.

The Orienteering Compass

A conventional compass can be used for orienteering; however, most competitors use an orienteering compass. Orienteering compasses come in two types, the Protractor compass and the NorCompass. The most popular type of orienteering compass is the protractor compass (Figure 34.3). Protractor compasses (also called baseplate compasses) have a clear plastic baseplate with a direction of travel arrow, ruler, and an orienting arrow. The thumb compass attaches to the orienteer's left thumb. (Figure 34.4) Most orienteers find the protractor compass more accurate, but it takes two hands to use it. The thumb compass is not as accurate, but only takes one hand to use. Both compasses are suitable for all levels of

Figure 34.1
Map symbols

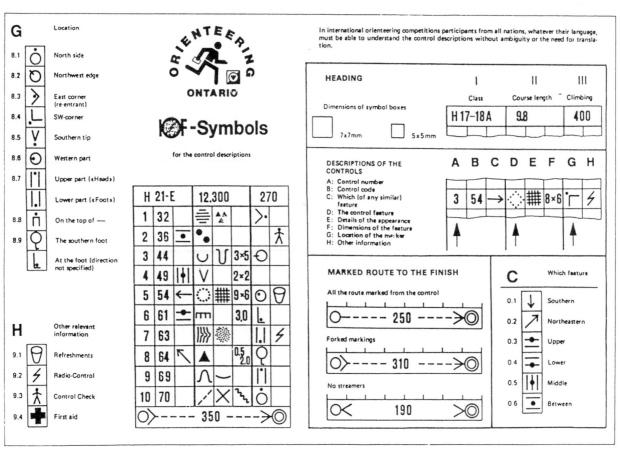

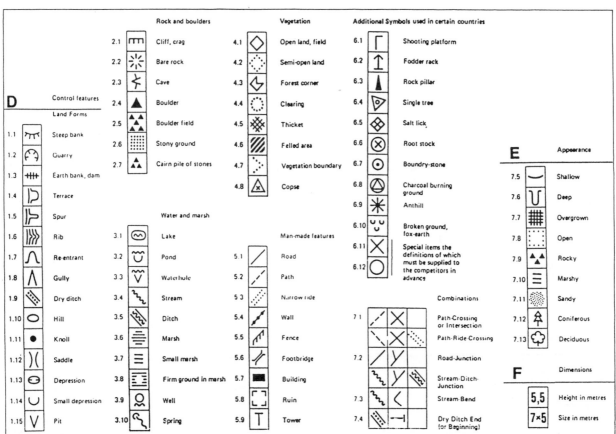

Figure 34.3
Protractor compass

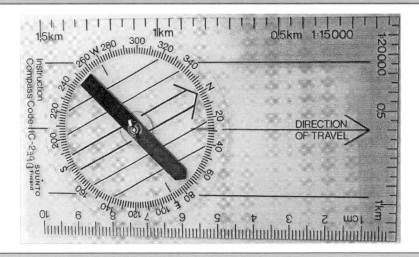

Figure 34.4
Nor compass

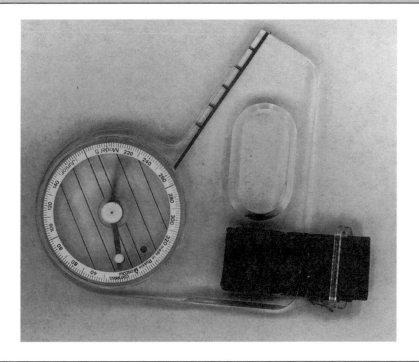

orienteering activities. Most orienteers prefer to use their own orienteering compass for orienteering events. If an orienteering event is designed for novices or individuals with limited orienteering experience, event organizers may provide compasses.

Control markers

Control markers are usually three-dimensional orange and white markers that are designate the location of the control. For less formal events, control markers may be marked with paint, colored ribbons, or other easily distinguished markers.

Official Orienteering Control Marker

Control cards

Orienteers carry a control card with their name, competitive classification, and starting time. Paper control cards have traditionally been carried in a rain- and tear-proof plastic case, but the paper cards are now being replaced by cards made of waterproof rip-stop materials. (Orienteering maps and description sheets are also often carried in the protective case.) The control cards are punched with a distinctive mark to verify the orienteers visit to the control.

Control marker

Control descriptions

Attached to each map is a description sheet with details to help locate the controls. Identifying numbers or letters are placed on the control and the description sheet. Beginners' descriptions may be written out in English. Control descriptions for intermediate and advanced competitions normally use International Orienteering Federation symbols. A comprehensive copy of all IOF symbols can be obtained from the IOF, local orienteering clubs, Internet sites, or a variety of software programs.

Punch

A punch is a tool used to make a distinctive mark on the control card to verify an orienteer's visit to the control. Most formal competitions use punches with pins arranged in a distinctive pattern. The whole pattern left by the pins verifies that orienteer visited the control.

Organizing Orienteering Events

Organizing and conducting orienteering competitions

Orienteering event organizers must decide which type of orienteering competition they will host and how large the event will be. Then they must select a location for the competition and procure orienteering maps. A simple event for a small number of contestants can be conducted with a few experienced volunteers and limited financial resources. Conducting large sanctioned competitions requires an experienced orienteer and considerable planning time, personnel,

and money. Most large orienteering events now use specialized orienteering meet organizing software, but software is available to organizing even relatively small, informal orienteering events. Event organizers must decide:

- the mode of movement
- standard orienteering (on foot)
- ski orienteering (on cross-country skis)
- trail orienteering (vary according to disability)
- the nature of the competition
- individual (participants perform independently)
- relay (two or more team members run consecutive individual races)
- team (two or more individuals collaborate)
- which age groups and experience levels will be offered
- a suitable site location (usually a wooded area with landscape features that will require the use of orienteering skills)
- time of competition
- day (during daylight hours)
- night (at night in the dark)
- type of start
- mass start
- staggered start
- order in which the controls must be visited
- point-to-point orienteering (controls must be visited in a prescribed order)
- score orienteering (visit as many controls as possible in any order)
- the way of determining the competition results
- single race competition

Figure 34.5
Control card

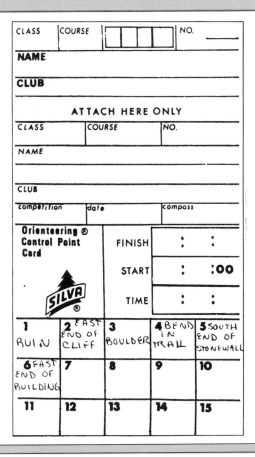

- multi-race competition (combined results of two or more races, held during one day or over several days, are used to determine results)
- qualification race competition (Competitors must qualify for a final race through one or more qualification races. The overall winner is the winner of the final race.)

Once the meet organizers have made these decisions they must develop and distribute invitations and registration forms. Official International Orienteering Federation Registration forms are available on a number of orienteering web sites. Custom-made registration forms should include the above information and:

- exact time and date of the orienteering event
- registration fee schedule
- entry deadlines
- sanction number (if sanctioned)
- host club or organization and event directors (include address and phone number)
- local accommodations and food
- general area of the event and map information
- details on any practice sessions or clinics
- waiver of liability form

Checking the course, also called vetting the course, is an important part of preparing the course for competition. Vetting the course usually takes place the day before the scheduled competition. The event organizer usually marks the location of the controls. Experienced orienteers who are not participating in the competition walk the course to ensure the proposed control points are well located and are designated correctly on the map. Individuals vetting the course should also see if the course is appropriate for the skill level of the participants. Vetting the course minimizes the chance of a control being misplaced or having a course that is too difficult or too easy for the competitors (Schoenstein).

Staffing and equipping an orienteering event requires proper planning. Recruiting and training meet workers is an important task. The number of workers needed will vary with the number of participants and the level of competition. Some individuals will contribute primarily with planning tasks, others will simply work on the day of the competition, while others will assist with both aspects of event management. The exact personnel requirement to staff a competition will vary with each competition, but most competitions will need workers to accomplish the following tasks:

- determine the location of the orienteering course
- lay out the orienteering course
- procure orienteering maps
- produce the master maps and maps for the participants
- prepare meet publicity and registration information
- collect fees and handle finances
- acquire compasses if this service is to be provided
- acquire and place control markers
- produce the control cards

- set up required communications (phones, two-way radios, computer support and fax lines)
- get support materials, such as office supplies, signs, tables, chairs, and clocks
- act as "recorders" (distribute collect and check control cards, record the results on a recording sheet and post results on the results board)
- act as "timers" (record start and finish times on the event cards)
- act as "sitters" (individuals who monitor control points)
- act as "course organizer" (verify correctness of names, finish times, and final scores; posts scores and accounts for all orienteers)
- secure numbered bibs so the competitors can be identified
- purchase trophies or awards
- notify media of the event and report the results

Orienteering software programs are now available to assist competitive orienteering organizers. The features of these programs vary and may includes the ability to print:
- maps
- control cards
- control features
- clue sheets
- the course setting and control locations
- print punch patterns
- individual and team run times and split times
- individual and course statistics.

As demand for computer-assisted orienteering information grows, the availability and the types of information available will continue to grow. Serious orienteering competition organizers will most certainly use these computer software programs to improve the efficiency of competition administration and increase the amount and accuracy of information available.

Safety Considerations

Orienteering event organizers are responsible for providing an orienteering course that minimizes danger. Dangerous areas such as cliffs, swamps, and pits, or mine shafts must be clearly identified on the orienteering map. The course should not cross busy highways, railroads, or other dangerous features.

Figure 34.6
Sample control descriptions

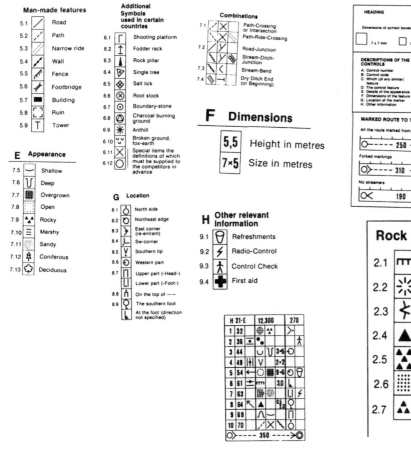

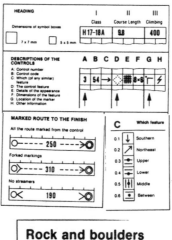

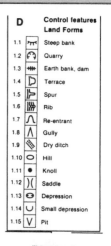

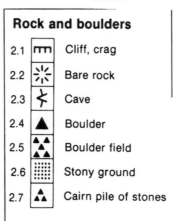

Event personnel should develop and be able to implement an emergency action plan. As a minimum, a first-aid kit and staff trained to use it should be available. Having medical personnel (doctor, nurse, or emergency medical technician) on site for larger events is recommended. Event workers should know how to contact the local hospital, police, rescue squad, or other local emergency response teams.

Adapted Orienteering Competitions

Ski Orienteering

The main idea of ski orienteering is to locate all the controls marked on the map in the correct order, conventional point to point orienteering. The course is organized with cross-country ski tracks (printed in green on the map) connecting the control points. Ski orienteers do not simply follow a single track from control to control. There are numerous tracks that intersect, giving the orienteer the choice of which track to take. The skier must choose the best route based on the length of the route, the track classification and the altitude. They then ski the chosen route as fast as possible. A typical course will have 30-50% continuous lines (wide and narrow), 50-70% broken lines and only 1-2% dotted lines. Most ski-orienteering courses have 10 to 20 controls and up to 200 trail crossings.

The winner is the competitor with the most correct answers on his control card (Figure 34.7). The total time to complete the course is irrelevant in determining the competition winner, as long as the competitor does not exceed the time limit. The course will include a limited number of timed control points. Personnel will staff the timed controls and the time required by the competitor to select the correct control marker will be recorded on the control card. Event organizers will use the cumulative time at these time controls to determine the winner in case of a tie. IOF rules for other orienteering disciplines apply except for the following:

- There will be no classification by disability or gender.
- Requested physical assistance is permitted.
- Any recognized mobility aid is permitted except for combustion-type vehicles.
- No assistance with navigation or problem solving is allowed.
- The course must be accessible to the least mobile.
- Competitors must stay on the tracks or trails. Other areas are out of bounds.
- Course length is usually from 1,000 - 3,500 meters.
- Additional personnel will be required to provide permitted assistance and staff the timed controls.

Classification of tracks

Continuous wide line

- Competition Skiing track
- Width at least 2.5 meters
- Very fast to ski

Continuous thin line

- Skating possible
- Width from 1.5 to 2.5 meters
- Fast to ski

Broken line

- Skating impossible
- Width from 1.0 to 1.5 meters
- Good track to ski

Dotted line

- Width less than 1.0 meters
- Slow to ski, possible dangerous slope

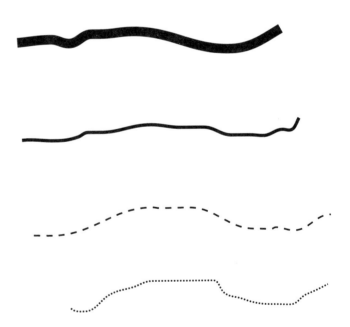

Trail Orienteering

Trail orienteering competitions are open to competitors with some type of functional disability that would prevent them from competing on reasonably equal terms with athletes without disabilities. Trail orienteering is also called control choice, because trail orienteers must locate the control and then determine which of a number of markers is the one located in the center of the control circle on the map.

Other orienteering variations

The orienteering format can be applied to almost any mode of movement. There are already adapted orienteering competitions done on bicycles, horses, and canoes. These forms of orienteering are not as established as standard orienteering and are still developing standard competition rules. Canoe orienteering, horseback orienteering, and bicycle orienteering will continue to develop and other forms of orienteering will be tried. Only time will tell which will become well-established, popular forms of orienteering.

Figure 34.7
Control card.

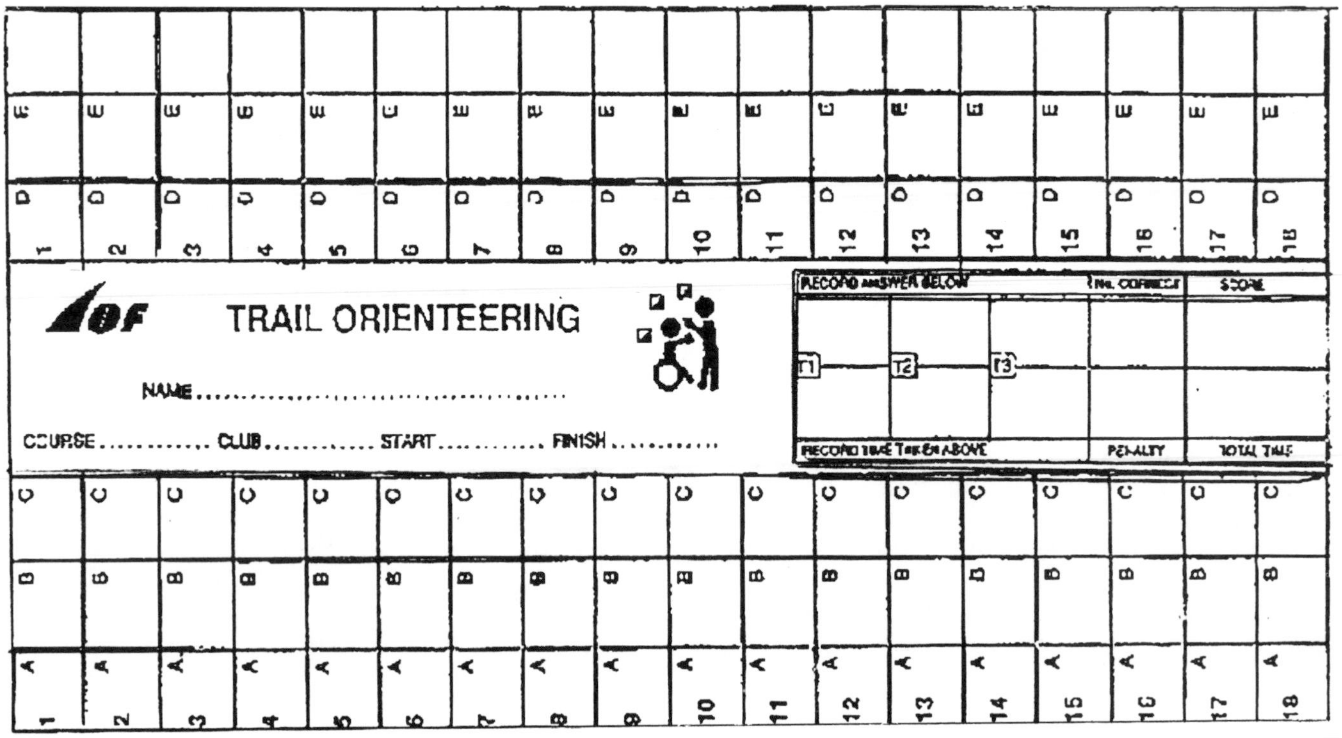

Summary

Orienteering is an outdoor sport movement activity that offers opportunities to develop wilderness skills, improve personal fitness levels, engage in mentally challenging competitions, and enjoy the fellowship and fun of being with others. Participants can select which of these aspects is of most interest to them and participate in orienteering activities that satisfy these interests. Orienteering activities can be highly structured and competitive or very informal and relaxed. Since orienteering requires skill and experience and not just speed, it is suitable for almost any age group. There are adaptations for individuals with disabilities (trail orienteering), lead-up activities for beginners and the very young, and variations done on cross-country skis, horses, bicycles, and canoes.

Orienteering requires very little equipment; a map and compass. All that is needed to conduct an orienteering activity is a few relatively inexpensive pieces of equipment and some open space. Event organizers can follow competition guidelines from the IOF or other orienteering agencies, or they can simply modify the rules to suit their needs. Computer software is currently available to assist orienteering competition organizers conduct efficient competitions and provide an abundance of statistical information.

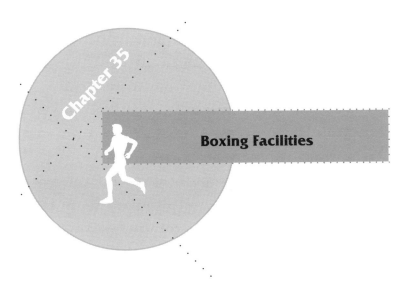

Gordon O. Calkins, Virginia Military Institute
Thomas H. Sawyer, Indiana State University

This section will provide readers with knowledge and information that will allow them to utilize existing space in the physical education building to design a multipurpose boxing facility that meets existing standards for safety and utilization of proper equipment for boxing.

Learning Objectives

After reading this chapter, the student will be able to:
- understand how to utilize the facility as a boxing fitness area, utilizing boxing training activities for the development of physical fitness, and
- understand how to utilize the facility as a training area for the development of basic boxing skills for those interested in learning boxing for self-defense or in competitive boxing.

United States Amateur Boxing Inc. (USA Boxing)

United States Amateur Boxing Inc. (USA Boxing) is the controlling organization for all amateur boxing in the United States. Rules, legislation, and safety regulations are promulgated by USA Boxing and its membership to provide a healthy, safe, and sportsmanlike environment in which young men and women can participate in the sport of boxing throughout the United States.

National Collegiate Boxing Association (NCBA)

The National Collegiate Boxing Association (NCBA) is an umbrella organization under the jurisdiction of USA Boxing that was organized to provide an opportunity for college students to participate in the sport of amateur boxing against other students enrolled in fully accredited institutions of higher learning. Only properly registered students (full-time) from institutions registered with the NCBA may participate in this program, and they may only compete against other full-time college students who meet all the necessary registration requirements. The NCBA is not a member of the NCAA, but is rather an organization of club teams authorized by their respective institutions and registered with both the NCBA and USA Boxing. Numbers of registrations vary from year to year, but there are approximately 30 member clubs (institutions) and over 300 registered participants covering four geographic regions (Northeast, Southeast, Midwest, and Far West). The NCBA conducts educational clinics and annual regional and national championship competitions.

Why a Boxing Facility?

Some may question the use of physical education space for the development of a boxing facility because of boxing's reputation as a violent and potentially dangerous sport. Some of those same people would not think of questioning the use of either outdoor or indoor space for an activity such as football, which is statistically far more dangerous than boxing. While one might argue that boxing (amateur as opposed to professional) is one of the safest of the contact sports, that is not the purpose of this discussion. Rather, it is to describe how a facility can be organized for learning and practicing boxing fundamentals and techniques that are ideal for the development of physical fitness and self-confidence.

Boxing is now widely accepted and utilized as a fitness activity. It is universally known that boxers are among the best conditioned athletes, and that boxing fitness activities (punching drills, bag punching, plyometrics, associated calisthenics, rope skipping, shadow boxing, distance running, and interval training) are excellent conditioners that reduce stress and are fun at the same time. Add to this the potential for learning the fundamentals of self-defense, and you have an activity that is hard to beat.

Considerable media attention has been recently given to "white collar" boxing by young professionals, both male and female. Many of these young men and women have traded their jogging and racquet sport shoes for boxing shoes! It is a relatively inexpensive alternative to many other activities and develops not only aerobic capacity but can also increase strength and muscular endurance. It is also a great opportunity for coed fitness training. Conditioning drills and non-contact offensive and defensive fundamentals can be practiced without regard to gender in an environment that can be designed to push participants to reach beyond their previously self-imposed physical limits.

Finally, a properly designed boxing area can be utilized as a multipurpose facility. If it is set up correctly, a boxing space can easily be turned into an aerobics area, a wrestling or gymnastics room, a practice area for cheerleaders, or a conditioning space for just about any team or activity you can name.

How Much Space Is Necessary?

If the space is to be used for boxing only, any space that is 10' x 10' or larger will suffice. All that is necessary is the proper floor covering, heavy and light striking bags, calisthenic stations, and a small equipment storage area. This area could be categorized as an "all-purpose boxing room" and makes use of almost any available space. The size of a boxing exercise/training area can vary from a large field house, armory, or gymnasium, to a small classroom or similar space suitable for small-group instruction. All that is required for boxing drills/practice is some unobstructed space, adequate ventilation, and sufficient lighting.

If a boxing ring is available, or you desire a multipurpose room, then some additional space will be necessary. A space 20' x 20' is required for the ring setup. A good way to organize such a room would be to divide it into the ring area, a striking bag area (heavy and light), and an exercise section. A 30' x 50' space would be sufficient for this type of room. If you are converting an old swimming pool space (e.g., 20 yds x 10 yds) you should have all the space you need for an excellent boxing/multipurpose exercise room.

Converting such existing space as a swimming pool into a boxing room is worth considering. Many older instructional pools that no longer meet specifications as competitive venues occupy more than enough space for an excellent boxing facility.

Older pools of this type are usually at least 75' x 25' (1,875 sf) with considerable addi- tional space allotted for the pool deck areas. All that is needed is a way to construct a wooden floor over the surface that will support the weight of 25 to 40 participants (100 lbs. per square inch). The buildings and grounds staff of a school along with a local architect can plan and construct this project for less than $10,000.00. (see Diagram 35.1)

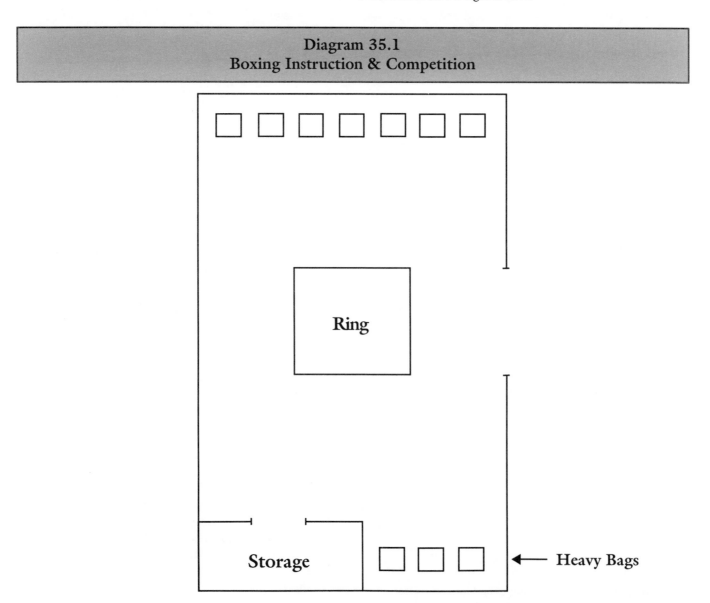

Diagram 35.1
Boxing Instruction & Competition

Materials necessary (other than labor) are:

- 2" x 4" studs,
- 2" x 8" floor joists,
- Wooden bridging pieces,
- 1/2 inch plywood and 5/8 inch particle board (installed on top of the floor joists), and
- Ensolite(r) matting to cover the exercise area.

The Virginia Military Institute (VMI) completed such a conversion in the early 1980s. The space provided has been used continuously since that time as both a boxing facility and a multipurpose room. Any questions regarding construction plans, etc., should be directed to the Physical Education Department, Cocke Hall, Virginia Military Institute, Lexington, Virginia 24450.

What Equipment Is Necessary?

If a ring is used, or if contact drills are used, the ring or floor area must be covered with a one-inch layer of Ensolite(r) AAC or AL closed-cell foam rubber (or a chemical equivalent). The ring padding must be covered with canvas or some similar material, and be tightly stretched and laced securely in place (USA Boxing, 1995). If no contact drills are anticipated, the floor area could be any type surface, but wood is preferable.

Boxing gloves used for sparring or live contact drills must meet the specifications required by USA Boxing Inc. USA Boxing Official Rules (2000, p. 115) require that the padding inside the gloves be "1/2, inch Latex, 3/4, inch PVC (Husitonic), 3/8, inch PVC (Rubitex- 313 V) and V, inch Polyfoam or other products that meet the severity (force of blow) index." For instructional purposes, 16-ounce thumbless or attached thumb gloves are recommended. Remember that the purpose of the gloves (in contact work) is to diminish the impact of a blow and to protect the hands.

The purpose of boxing headgear is to reduce the impact of a blow, reduce/prevent facial cuts, protect the ears, and substantially reduce impact to the head if a fall occurs. Only headgear approved by USA Boxing Inc. should be used (USA Boxing, 2000). Several manufacturers produce headgear to the proper standard.

During any type of contact drills, use of a mouthpiece is mandatory. The mouthpiece reduces the possibility of jaw injuries, cuts to the inside of the mouth, and injuries to the tongue and teeth. A custom-made or individually fitted mouthpiece must be worn by each participant. Examples of the custom-made and individually fitted are the "dentist-molded" and the clear plastic types, respectively (USA Boxing, 2000).

When contact drills are involved, men and women should wear approved groin or chest protection. For men, his means either a foul-proof protection cup or a jock strap cup. Women should wear a well-fitting breast protector (USA Boxing, 2000).

Handwraps are recommended for all types of striking drills, but need not be required (they are mandatory in competition, however). The purpose of the handwrap is primarily to protect the metacarpal bones of the hand. They are not designed or utilized to add force to a blow. Handwraps can be made of cotton gauze, soft surgical gauze or velpeau material. For ease of wrapping, the velpeau type is recommended. Instruction and practice in proper wrapping technique should be given prior to their use.

Heavy bags are vital to the organization of any boxing training facility. They are the single best modality to use for non-contact striking/punching drills and are a must in your training area. They are used to simulate an opponent's body and head, and any number of very useful drills can be done with these bags. Several types and sizes are available (canvas, leather, nylon, vinyl) and they can be filled with foam, water, or rags (depending on the type). An inexpensive way to make up a heavy bag is to use a duffle or "sea" bag filled with sawdust, rags, or a combination of the two.

Light striking bags are used for advanced drills and are a "nice to have" item in your facility, but the heavy bags are much more practical. Light bags are used for developing speed, timing, and coordination. They are much smaller than a heavy bag, but require that a bag "platform" be anchored to a wall in order to be utilized.

A boxing ring is not necessary for boxing instruction, drills, or conditioning exercises. It is, however, an important piece of equipment if any of your participants are interested in competitive boxing. It is also a good way to control the various boxing contact drills or any sparring that is done. Only rings that meet USA Boxing specifications should be utilized. The ring can be either a platform type, elevated about three feet above the floor (not more than four feet), or a floor type, built directly upon the floor or on a slightly raised platform that is laid directly on the floor. The platform type is recommended for competition, but for training purposes, many prefer the floor type. According to USA Boxing Official Rules (2000, p. 17), "the ring must be not less than 16 nor more than 20 feet square within the ropes, and the apron of the ring floor shall extend beyond the ropes not less than two feet." The ring should be equipped with four ropes that are wrapped in a soft material, and all turnbuckles must be covered with protective padding.

Miscellaneous Exercise Stations

Depending on the specific purpose of your room and the needs of the participants, the number and type of exercise stations you develop is unlimited. At a minimum, however, are recommended exercise stations requiring individuals to use their own body weight as resistance. Among these are pullup bars (six to eight), and sit-up and push-up stations. If the floor is not already padded, some type of matting will be necessary at the sit-up station. An area set up for rope skipping and shadow-boxing (two full length mirrors) can also be provided.

Cost of Various Equipment Items

The cost of equipment items for your facility will vary slightly depending on the vendor you use, but the following rough estimates will enable you to establish a budget to get your facility started. The amount of equipment, of course, will depend on the number of participants, but the total costs for this example are based on an expected 25 participants:

Training gloves (16 ounce):
25 pair @ $175/pair $ 4375.00
Bag gloves: 25 pair @ $10.00/pair = $ 250.00
Training head gear: 25 @ $70 each $ 1750.00
Plastic mouthpiece (upper): 50 @ $1.50 each $ 75.00
Groin protection (boxing cups): 25 @ $15.00 each, $ 375.00
Female chest guards (with support bra): 25 @ 45.00 each $ 1125.00
Handwrap: 25@ $5.00 each $ 125.00
Heavy bags (canvas; unfilled): 8 @ $55.00 each $ 440.00
Boxing ring (platform type) $ 6,000.00
Boxing ring (floor type) $ 2,500.00
Total cost (with platform ring) = $14,515.00
Total cost (with floor ring) = $11,015.00

It must be emphasized that these prices may vary from vendor to vendor, and you should shop around for the best price. Your facility does not have to be completely equipped for 25 persons. Depending upon how you organize your exercise /practice sessions, equipment, and exercise stations can be shared and rotated so that you may only have to be equipped for 10 participants or fewer. You may also be able to purchase used equipment, or construct some of your own.

Organization of the Facility

If you intend to set up a boxing room with a ring, remember that a regulation-size ring can be from 16 to 20 feet, inside dimensions of all four sides. Obviously, this means that you will need more space than if you set up the room without a ring. To utilize your available space most efficiently, center the ring on one end of the room, and place heavy bags and light striking bags on the opposite end, thus leaving the space between for drills, calisthenics, plyometrics, or for multipurpose use when the area is not being utilized for boxing. On either end of the room or along the side walls, you can set up permanent pull-up and sit-up stations, using pipe suspended horizontally from the ceiling for the pull-up station and bolted to the floor as an anchor point for feet at the sit-up station. Along one side wall, place full-length mirrors (six by four feet) for shadow boxing and technique drills. This type of arrangement gives you four areas in which to work: a ring area, a bag work area, a calisthenics/conditioning area, and a space in between that can be used as a multipurpose area.

If you decide to set up your facility without a ring, you will save at least 400 square feet of useable space (not to mention the expense of a ring). This will still enable you to set up three areas for specific fitness training, including aerobics and circuit training. It also allows you to design your facility in a much smaller space than is possible with a ring. The number of exercise stations in your circuit is then left up to your imagination and the available space. The perimeter of this fitness training facility should be set up for specific circuit exercises, with the center area left open for multipurpose use.

Any boxing facility that does not have a ring (or the space for one), but is going to be used for self-defense contact drills or sparring, should be set up to ensure that participants are protected from the perimeter walls and any objects that may protrude from those walls, and that the floor surface being used is properly matted. Floor surface matting has already been discussed (one-inch Ensolite™), and its main purpose is to protect against traumatic injuries to the head resulting from falls or knock-downs. Perimeter walls should also be padded with one-inch Ensolite™ to protect against injuries caused by wall contact. When a ring is not available and the perimeter walls are not matted, you can still conduct contact drills and sparring if you organize the session properly. Participants should form a large circle (16-20 foot diameter) and be instructed to act as a "human ring." This ring should be centered in the exercise area and at least six feet from the perimeter walls. Only two participants should spar at a time, and they should begin in the center. Participants on the perimeter of the ring should be instructed to adjust their positions so as to keep the two sparring individuals inside the ring. Any time either of the two boxers makes contact with the ring's perimeter, the instructor should immediately stop the activity and have the participants begin again, in the center. This not only prevents traumatic contact with the perimeter walls, it stops any punching activity when one individual becomes momentarily disadvantaged.

Equipment Storage Concerns

Equipment should be of high quality and meet all published safety standards required by USA Boxing. Properly cared for, boxing equipment will have a long life, and replacement costs will be minimal.

Security of the equipment and, in fact, the entire area is of paramount importance. The entire facility should be locked when not in use and access limited to instructors, coaches, and maintenance personnel.

There should be adequate and assigned storage areas for all equipment that is moveable and used on a regular basis. Boxing gloves and head gear, for example, should be stored in an area that is open to circulating air so that the equipment can dry properly. Gloves and head gear should be stowed in open wire racks, on open shelving, or in lockers with steel mesh fronts that allow the circulation of air. Both should be washed with saddle soap and dried thoroughly each week. Both should also be treated weekly with a commercial disinfectant or with a solution of 10% carbolic acid and 90% sweet oil (Deeter, Rubino, & Simmons, 1950). Handwraps should be allowed to dry after each use and should be washed weekly. Obviously, athletic supporters, groin protectors, athletic bras, and chest protectors should be washed thoroughly on a regular basis and stored in a dry, clean area. Usually, this will be the responsibility of individual participants.

Safety Concerns

If contact drills or sparring are part of your exercise program, then it is mandatory that the boxing gloves and headgear utilized meet the safety specifications of *USA Boxing*. It is also essential that any safety equipment worn be properly fitted to the individual. Protective headgear, especially, should be worn so that it provides the maximum protection possible. All headgear should fit snugly and should not change position on the head if pulled, pushed, or struck. The bottom edge of the padded forehead portion of the headgear should sit just above the top of the eyebrow, approximately 1/2 inch above the hairline of the brow. The participant's ears should fit snugly inside the ear openings on the headgear, and the ears should lie flat against the inside surface. There should be an additional heavily padded area on the rear of the headgear. This should be centered on the back of the head and reach down to the top of the neck. If the headgear has cheek guards, they should fit snugly against the cheeks, tight enough so that they cannot slide up into the eye. Finally, the chinstrap should fit under the chin and be as tight as possible, without causing discomfort.

If plastic mouthpieces (uppers only or doubles) are used, they should be softened and molded to the individual's mouth. This can be done by placing the mouthpiece in a cup of water and then heating it in a microwave oven. When the mouthpiece appears to be softened (flaccid), remove it from the hot water and rinse it with cool water. While it is still soft, have the individual bite down on it until it is "molded" to his or her mouth. This may take a few tries, but it is the most inexpensive way to obtain a fitted mouthpiece.

Handwraps should always be worn when striking drills of any kind are being performed. Cloth (velpeau) handwraps are recommended. Further, it is recommended that commercial handwraps can be applied as follows:

- Place the looped end of the wrap over the thumb,
- Bring the wrap over the back of the hand to the big knuckle of the wrist,
- Go underneath the wrist to the base of the thumb in diagonally across the back of the hand to the big knuckle of the little finger,
- Encircle completely the big knuckles of the hand, wrapping well up toward the middle joints of the fingers,
- Go diagonally across the back of the hand to the outside wrist bone,
- Completely encircle the wrist once, angling the wrap slightly upward, stopping at the base of the thumb,
- Completely encircle the thumb once,
- Following the normal contour of the hand, bring the wrap over across the back of the hand to the joint of the little finger,
- Completely encircle the large knuckles of the hand a second time, Carry the wrapping down diagonally across the back of the hand and around to the base of the thumb,
- Pull it up, completely encircling the thumb for a second time, and
- Finally, bring the wrap diagonally over the back of the hand to the wrist, and encircle the wrist once using a small piece of tape (one inch by six inches) to secure the wrap.

Ensure that participants keep their fingers spread and extended throughout the wrapping process. This will prevent the wrap from being too tight, thus cutting off circulation.

When pairing participants for contact drills, there should be as little weight difference between the participants as possible. A reasonable guideline to follow is to allow no more than an eight-pound differential during any sparring or contact drills. It is perhaps even more important to also pair individuals according to their respective skill/experience levels. If a new skill is being learned, it is a good idea to pair an experienced individual with a beginner. The experienced person can control the action and can also act as an assistant instructor for the beginner. If the activity involves sparring or any competitive situations, then it is usually best to pair the individuals according to size (weight) and relative ability.

During any vigorous activity, there is the possibility of injury. There should be a phone located inside the boxing room with clearly posted numbers of the local emergency squad, the school athletic training staff, and the infirmary. In addition, all instructors should be CPR certified and a first-aid kit should always be on hand. Identifying injuries should be the responsibility of the professional staff, but guidelines for handling suspected head injuries should also be clearly posted inside the room. USA Boxing Inc. has published the following guidelines for recognizing a possible head injury:

Observe the athlete for:
- dizziness or headache lasting more than one hour,
- increasing drowsiness,
- loss of consciousness,
- mental disorientation or confusion,
- unusual or strange behavior,
- restlessness or irritability,
- seizure (convulsion),
- blurred vision or loss of vision,
- repeated vomiting,
- blood or watery fluid from ears or nose,
- inability to control urination or bowel movement, and
- inability to move an arm or leg.

If any of these symptoms occur (or persist), medical personnel should be contacted immediately.

Summary

Designing a boxing room that can also be utilized as a multipurpose facility can be done inexpensively and with a minimum of necessary space. The number of exericse stations and the organization of the facility is limited only by one's imagination and to a much lesser extent, available funding. This type of fitness activity is interesting, a bit different, and most important, pays big dividends in terms of the fitness gains made possible through its proper organization and utilization.

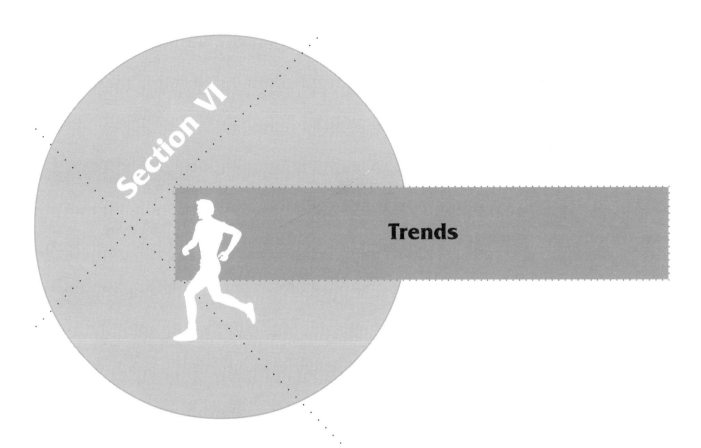

Section VI

Trends

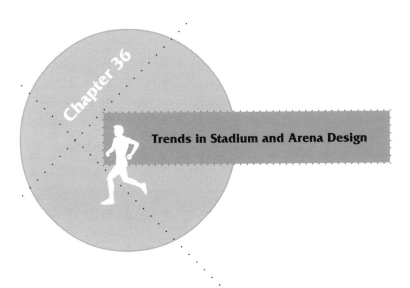

Chapter 36

Trends in Stadium and Arena Design

Todd L. Seidler, University of New Mexico

This chapter will present an overview and analysis of certain recent trends and innova-tions in stadium and arena design. It is by no means a complete look at these unique sports facilities; many others are covered in other parts of this book. This chapter will merely try to high-light certain significant trends and concepts that should not be overlooked.

Learning Objectives

After reading this chapter, the student will be able to:
- be familiar with the concept of the retractable roof stadium and understand its advantages,
- identify the three main types of fabric structures and list the advantages and disadvantages of each,
- describe the importance of designing luxury suites and club seats in new spectator facilities,
- identify the advantages of wooden domes, and
- identify the new arena design features intended to speed the change-over from one event to another.

A New Breed of Facilities

The fundamental purpose and design of stadiums and arenas has changed radically in the last decade. These changes are so dramatic that many facilities have become obsolete, and even young ones 10 to 20 years old are facing the wrecking ball. The basic idea behind this change is that modern arenas and stadiums are no longer just places to watch an event, but are now designed to provide a total entertainment experience.

Historically, most large arenas and stadiums have been funded by city or state governments, or by colleges and universities. Recently these entities have experienced tighter budgets and, more than ever, must rely less on public funding. The current trend is more toward private funding (Jewell, 1992). In order to maximize return on such a large investment, every effort must be made to ensure that the facility be able to accommodate as many events and different kinds of

activities as possible. Recent design improvements have focused on optimally supporting each event and being able to change over from one event to another as quickly as possible. Whereas some older facilities would rely on eight to 10 football games or 40 basketball games per year as their main source of revenue, some facilities now schedule from 250 to 600 events per year, including sporting events, concerts, conventions, trade shows, rodeos, monster truck shows, and professional wrestling. It is not uncommon for older facilities to require up to a full day for a crew to change the set-up from one event to another, whereas a well-designed facility can be transformed in a matter of hours. Not only can this provide a significant cost savings in manpower, but it also often means that more than one event can take place in the same day. Several aspects of design that allow a facility to accommodate a wide variety of events and also to quickly alter the set-up for different events include:
- Versatile lighting and sound systems that can adequately handle the wide variety of events.
- Heavy-duty lighting grids that can be lowered to the floor in order to enhance the placement of sound and lighting equipment for concerts.
- Loading ramps that allow semi-trucks to back all the way onto the floor. Even better, some facilities provide floor access for two or more trucks at a time so that one can be loading after a show while another is unloading for the next.
- Versatile, moveable sections of seats that can quickly change the configuration of a facility.
- Fixed, pre-wired camera positions that allow for quick and easy set-up for television broadcasts. Many new arenas are constructed with a full television production studio, which permits a television network to broadcast a game without bringing in their semi-trucks full of production equipment.

Many sport organizations have made a shift in their fundamental mission and have gone from primarily trying to put a winning team on the court/field to providing a great family entertainment experience. This change in thinking has led to many design changes in the arenas and stadiums being constructed today. In general, this has caused a move toward more upscale facilities and greater service, entertainment, and convenience for spectators. Some aspects of this trend include the following:

- Providing more rest rooms. In the past, many spectator facilities provided only enough rest rooms to satisfy the local code requirements. This often resulted in long lines and frustration on the part of the spectators. Many facilities are now being designed with more than twice as many rest rooms as the minimum required. Since some events may draw a disproportionate number of men or women, consideration should be given to designing some rest rooms that can serve either gender simply by changing the sign on the door. Family rest rooms are also becoming common in new stadiums and arenas.

- *Taking into consideration the requirements of customers with disabilities.* With the advent of the Americans With Disabilities Act, full accommodation of the needs of people with disabilities is now federal law. Recent lawsuits have established new standards for the placement of handicapped seating. All wheelchair-accessible seats should now be located so that users can see over the heads of the spectators in front of them even when the spectators stand.

- *Building larger concourse areas and adding separate concourses to serve different levels.* Improved access and less crowding make these areas more attractive. Some concourse areas are being designed to resemble a mini-mall by offering many different choices of food, novelty items, and entertainment opportunities. Some concession areas are designed so that customers standing in line still have a direct view of the field while others place closed-circuit televisions so that patrons will not miss the action while spending their money. Opportunities for amusement are becoming more common. These include things such as batting cages, merry-go-rounds, museums, and many types of electronic games. Many facilities strive to provide the atmosphere of an amusement park.

- *One of the most significant trends in stadium and arena design is adding luxury suites and club seating.* Luxury suites are small, private rooms opening toward the court or field that are usually leased to individuals or companies who desire a semi-private lounge area, typically large enough to accommodate 12 to 20 guests. Suites are normally leased on multi-year contracts and are often furnished and decorated by the tenant. The prevalence of these luxury suites is growing rapidly, primarily because they are such good revenue producers. The Palace of Auburn Hills is a good example of how important suites have become to the economics of this type of facility. The original plans called for 100 luxury suites to be built as part of the arena. About one-third of the way through construction, all of the suites had been leased. Some quick design changes by the architect produced an additional 80 suites, which were also leased by the time the Palace opened. Total construction cost was about $63 million, and the income from the lease of the suites alone was almost $12 million per year (Gordon, 1990).

This incredible increase in revenue can make a big difference in the profitability of a team and can be a huge advantage over other organizations that do not have it. It also has become an essential part of the equation for financing a new facility. The Palace generated enough revenue just from leasing the suites to pay for the facility in less than six years. That is not including revenue from ticket sales, food, concessions, parking, etc. Luxury suites have become a significant design feature and not only make the construction of future arenas and stadiums more economically feasible, but are becoming a necessity for many sports organizations to remain financially competitive.

Club seats are usually exclusive seating areas where the right to buy tickets may be purchased through a permanent seat license (PSL). Club seats are typically larger, more comfortable, and have more leg room than regular seating and include special considerations such as a wait staff who take orders and deliver food right to the seat. Income from PSL's and club seats can be significant and an important source of revenue.

Innovations in Materials and Methods of Construction

Recent innovations in the methods of enclosing large areas without support pillars and posts that interfere with spectator sight lines are providing many more options for the construction of stadiums and arenas. Stadiums with retractable roofs, tension fabric structures, air-supported fabric structures, wooden domes, and cable domes are examples of building designs that have been successfully used to enclose large sports facilities.

Retractable Roof Stadiums

One of the biggest innovations in stadium design is the concept of having a stadium that is open to the elements when the weather is nice but can be quickly covered when needed. The first attempt at a retractable roof stadium was Olympic Stadium in Montreal, built for the 1976 Olympic Games. The original plan was to build a huge concrete mast next to the stadium that would support a fabric roof supported by steel cables. The roof was supposed to have the ability to be lifted off the stadium and suspended from the mast, thereby becoming an open-air stadium (Holleman, 1996). The roof could then be lowered back on top of the stadium to enclose it again when desired.

The design has never worked correctly, but this ambitious idea eventually led to the successful designs we are seeing today. It is estimated that adding a retractable roof to the design of a new stadium will increase the cost between $30 and $70 million.

Examples:

- SkyDome—Located in Toronto, Ontario, SkyDome was the first stadium to have a fully retractable roof. Opened in 1989, SkyDome can completely open or close the entire steel-trussed roof in 20 minutes. This is accomplished by three movable roof sections, two of which slide and another that rotates. The stadium seats 50,600 for baseball, 53,000 for football, and has different seating arrangements for concerts ranging from 10,000 to 70,000. It also contains 161 luxury SkyBoxes, a 348-room hotel and health club, full broadcast facilities, underground parking, and a 110 by 33 foot state-of-the-art video screen. Original estimates of the cost for SkyDome were $184 million (Canadian), but it ended up costing about $585 million. Typically, the roof only has to be closed for about four or five games a season due to inclement weather (Gordon, 1990).

- BankOne Ballpark—Opened for the 1998 season, BOB is the home of the Arizona Diamondbacks. Located in downtown Phoenix, it was the first retractable-roof stadium to be built since SkyDome. This air-conditioned, retractable-roof stadium is designed primarily for baseball and seats 48,500. It has a natural grass field and was built for a cost of $349 million with 68% coming from public financing. With a total of 69 private suites, six party suites and 5,592 club seats, there is something for everybody, including 350 bleacher seats that are sold for $1 per game. As with many of the new stadiums, it is more than just a place to watch a ballgame. BOB contains two micro-breweries and two 10,000-square-foot beer gardens, a mini hall of fame fashioned after Cooperstown, a 4,000-square-foot team store, 110 picnic tables, 212 concession stands and a swimming pool just beyond the outfield fence.

Toronto Skydome

Photo courtesy of Ellerbe Becket

BankOne Ballpark

Photo courtesy of Ellerbe Becket

- Enron Field—The new home of the Houston Astros, Enron Field was completed in time for the 2000 baseball season. Built for a very inexpensive $248 million, it seats approximately 42,000 and has a fully retractable steel roof. The roof covers 6.25 acres when closed and is made up of three moveable sections that can be opened in less than 20 minutes. The moving roof panels contain over 5,000 tons of steel as well as an acre of glass to allow for spectacular views even when the roof is closed. Also, the roof has been designed to withstand hurricane-force winds. Special amenities within the stadium include a children's play area, batting cages, more than 60 private suites and 4,850 club seats, a café, retail space, and even has a 65,000 lb. full-size locomotive that moves along an 800 ft. section of track after game highlights. The new stadiums are meant to provide a quality entertainment experience, not just a place to watch a game.

Other examples include:

- Milwaukee Miller Park
- Seattle Safeco Field

At the time of this writing, several other teams are planning or considering construction of retractable-roof stadiums. It appears that the retractable-roof stadium is now coming into its own, and we will probably see many new examples in the coming years.

Fabric Structures

A fairly recent development in the area of physical education, recreation, and athletic facilities is the concept of fabric structures. The fabric used most commonly is a Teflon-coated fiberglass material. The fiberglass fabric is, pound for pound, stronger than steel and is also less expensive. It can be designed to allow either a large amount or very little natural light to penetrate. The fabric can withstand temperatures of 1300 to 1500 degrees Fahrenheit and is not adversely affected by cold or the ultraviolet rays of the sun. Fabric structures offer a number of potential advantages and disadvantages when compared with standard construction.

Advantages

- Lower initial cost—Initial costs are usually lower than with conventional construction. Several factors contribute to this, the primary one being weight. A fabric roof is 1/30 the weight of a conventional steel-truss roof. This reduced weight means that the walls, footings, and foundations are not required to be nearly as strong as in a conventional building.
- Less construction time—The amount of construction time is directly related to the initial cost of the structure. The total time necessary to build a fabric structure is usually less than for a conventional roof.
- Natural lighting—Since the fiberglass fabric material that is used is translucent, it results in a large amount of interior natural lighting. Without using artificial lights during the day, the light intensity inside can vary anywhere from 100 to 1,000 foot-candles, depending on weather conditions, design,

and choice of fabric. The interior light is considered to be of high quality, because it is non-glare and shadow-free.

- Possibly lower energy costs—In some climates or regions, energy costs may be substantially reduced by the fabric's translucency. The large amount of natural light may reduce or eliminate the need for artificial light during the daytime. This may also reduce the need for air-conditioning required to overcome the heat generated by the artificial lights.
- Less maintenance—The non-stick characteristics of Teflon allow the fabric to be washed clean each time it rains.
- Full utilization of space—Depending on the fabric structure's configuration and support, the area that can be enclosed is almost limitless.

Disadvantages

- Life span—The fabric envelope in use today has a life expectancy of up to 25 years, with longer-life materials being tested. All other items such as the foundation, flooring, and mechanical equipment have the life span of a conventional building.
- Poor thermal insulation—In cold climates, there may be an increase in energy costs when compared with conventional construction due to lower insulating properties of the fabric roof. The insulating value of a typical fabric roof is about R-2, but can be increased substantially (see Lindsay Park Sports Centre). The cost of heating is a significant factor and should be evaluated against that for a conventional building over time. During winter months when the heat is required to melt the snow or to cause it to slide off, a safe level of temperature will have to be maintained at all times, which has an impact on heating costs. If the bubble is not to be heated during inactive hours, it will have to be supervised constantly for the dangers of unexpected snowfall. In the summertime, the heat gain of the air-supported structure may pose a cooling problem.
- Acoustic problems—The curved shape of the air-supported structure produces a peculiar acoustic environment. This large, reflective surface magnifies crowd noise and can create undesirable noise conditions.
- Restriction due to wind—In winds of hurricane velocity, many codes require that the fabric structure be evacuated.

There are three basic types of fabric structures in use: tension structures, air-supported structures, and cable domes. Tension structures are made by stretching the fabric between rigid supports and/or steel cables. Air structures are sealed buildings that, through the use of fans, maintain a positive internal air pressure that supports the roof. These structures are actually inflated like a balloon and must maintain the positive air pressure to remain inflated. Cable domes are the newest type of fabric structure. The cable dome is actually a modified tension structure that uses a complex network of cables and supports to suspend and support a fabric roof.

Tension Structures

Some projects lend themselves more naturally to tension structures than to air-supported structures or cable domes. Some of the conditions in which tension structures may be more favorable are as follows:

- When free and open access from the sides is desirable or required.
- A unique design, or aesthetics, are of importance.
- The facility will be largely unattended or not monitored.
- Possible deflation of an air structure would constitute a severe operational or safety problem.
- A retrofit to an existing building or structure such as a swimming pool or an outdoor stadium is desired.

Examples

- La Verne College—La Verne College in La Verne, CA, contains the first permanent enclosed fiberglass structure in the United States. The tent-like struc-

ture covers 1.4 acres, with the fabric roof having been erected in just three days. Called the Campus Center, it contains a gymnasium that seats 900 people, men's and women's locker rooms, offices, the campus bookstore, and lecture areas. A smaller, separate tension structure houses the drama department. This facility was completed in 1973.

- Knott Athletic, Recreation & Convocation Center— Located at Mount Saint Mary's College in Emmitsburg, MD, the Knott Center is a unique combination of standard construction and a fabric tension structure. Completed in 1987, most of the facility is built with standard brick construction, with the tension-structure field house connected onto one side of the building. The fabric roof covers 30,000 square feet of activity space, including a multiple-court set-up and a 10-lap-per-mile running track. Rising to a height of 40 feet, the double-layered roof allows for almost exclusive use of natural light during the day. Also included within the facility are four racquetball courts, locker rooms, and a 25-yard pool.

**Photo courtesy of Bohlin Cywinski & Jackson
Photo by Matt Wargo**

Knott Center - exterior.

Knott Center - interior.

**Photo courtesy of Bohlin Cywinski & Jackson
Photo by Matt Wargo**

- Lindsay Park—The Lindsay Park Sports Centre in Calgary, Alberta, Canada, houses a 50-meter pool, a diving pool, a fully equipped 30,000-square-foot gymnasium, and a 200-meter running track. The roof is unique in that it was designed with insulation that is rated at R-16. This compares with a typical fabric roof that has about an R-2 rating. Despite the great improvement in insulating qualities, the fabric roof is still translucent enough to allow for an interior illumination of about 200 foot-candles. This facility was completed in 1983.
- McClain Athletic Training Facility—Completed in 1988, this field house is located at the University of Wisconsin at Madison, WI. Due to site restrictions, this $9.5 million facility contains a 90-yard football field instead of a full-size field. Most of the field is covered by a 42,000-square-foot fabric-tension roof that admits up to 750 foot-candles of natural light into the structure. When comparing the fabric roof to standard construction, it is estimated that the increased cost for heating and the reduced cost for artificial lighting result in an overall saving of about $21,000 per year. Below the synthetic turf field lies a full 64,320-square-foot basement that contains locker rooms for football, track, and coaches; weight room; training facilities and therapy pool. The therapy pool is 15 by 40 feet and goes from four to seven feet in depth. Also included in the facility are an auditorium, six meeting rooms, and a film room.

Air-Supported Structures

There are two basic types of air-supported structures: large, permanent structures and smaller, more portable structures.

Air-supported fabric roofs are held up by a positive air pressure within a totally enclosed building. These facilities are actually inflated with positive air pressure that is produced by a group of large fans. In conventional buildings, the foundation, walls, and internal columns must support a roof weight of between 10 and 40 pounds per square foot. In air-supported structures, a roof weight of about one pound per square foot is transmitted directly to the ground by the increased air pressure. This increased pressure of about four or five pounds per square foot greater than ambient pressure is usually unnoticed by the building's occupants. Some of the instances when an air structure may be preferable to a tension structure or standard construction are:

- When column-free spans of greater than 150 feet are desired,
- When large, column-free spans are desired at a cost that is greatly reduced compared to conventional structures. In fact, cost per unit area usually decreases as the size of the span increases, and
- When a low silhouette is desired.

Examples

- Dedmon Center—Located at Radford University in Radford, VA, the Dedmon Center was constructed for a cost of $6,750,000 and opened in 1982. Encompassing 110,000 square feet, it has 5,000 temporary seats for basketball. Used for physical education, athletics, and recreation, the center provides five full basketball courts, weight room, pool, locker rooms and offices.
- Thomas E. Leavey Activities Center—This physical education and athletic complex is located at the University of Santa Clara in Santa Clara, CA. It contains a 5,000-seat arena for basketball and volleyball along with racquetball courts, wrestling, gymnastics, weight training and conditioning areas, conference rooms, staff offices, and a 25-meter swimming pool. The pool is covered by a separate air-supported fabric roof that can be removed in the summertime, converting it into an outdoor pool. This facility was completed in 1978.
- DakotaDome—Located at the University of South Dakota in Vermillion, SD, the DakotaDome contains five basketball/volleyball courts, two tennis courts, an eight-lane 200-meter track, four racquetball courts, a six-lane 25-meter pool, locker rooms, classrooms, and the offices for the athletic department. The main floor is a synthetic surface that is used for most court activities and has an artificial turf foot-

Dedmon Recreation Center

Photo courtesy of Sasaki Associates

ball field that can be rolled out for football, soccer, and other field events. When the facility is set up for football, there is seating for 12,000 spectators. The entire facility was built for the bargain price of about $51 per square foot in 1978.

- Carrier Dome—The Carrier Dome, located in Syracuse, NY, is the home of Syracuse University athletics. The stadium seats 50,000 for football and over 30,000 for basketball. Also a great bargain, total construction cost was $27,715,000, which figures out to $554 per seat. This is very inexpensive when compared to conventional covered stadiums. This facility was completed in 1980.

- Silverdome—The Silverdome, located in Pontiac, MI, has the largest capacity of any indoor stadium in the world. Opened in 1975, the Silverdome has permanent seating for over 80,000 spectators for football and has accommodated over 90,000 for special events. The inflated fabric roof covers an area of 10 acres and is maintained at a height of 202 feet above the playing surface. The Silverdome is owned by the city of Pontiac and is currently the home of the Detroit Lions. At the time of this writing, the Lions were building a new stadium in Downtown Detroit and should move soon after 2001.

Other examples:

- Steve Lacy Field house—Milligan College, Milligan, TN, 1974,
- Uni-Dome—University of Northern Iowa, Cedar Falls, IA, 1975,
- Metrodome—Minneapolis, MN, 1982,
- B.C. Place Amphitheater—Vancouver, B.C., Canada, 1983, and
- RCA Dome—Indianapolis, IN, 1984.

Since the concept of fabric structures is still quite new, not all the problems have been resolved. However, each new fabric structure appears to have fewer problems and to be an improvement over those built previously. In spite of the many advantages of the large air-supported structures, their days may be numbered. The primary disadvantage of air-supported structures is the need for the constant positive air pressure. Since this positive pressure is what supports the roof, if there is even a temporary loss of pressure, the fabric will hang down on the supporting cables. Although this alone should cause no damage to the facility, this is when the structural system is the most vulnerable. Even light winds, snow, or rain may cause extensive damage to a fabric roof in the deflated position. These facilities must be constantly moni-

Photo by Todd Seidler

Pontiac Silverdome

MetroDome

Photo courtesy of Geiger Engineers

tored and all precautions must be taken to ensure that all systems are functioning properly. Cable domes appear to have the same advantages as the large air-pressure structures but with fewer problems. It is entirely possible that we have seen the last large air-supported structure that will ever be built (see Cable Domes).

Combining Air-Supported and Tension

A recent development in the construction of fabric structures is the idea of combining both an air-supported roof and a tension roof in the same building. An example of this concept is the Stephen C. O'Connell Center. This physical education, recreation, and athletic complex is located at the University of Florida at Gainesville. This was the first structure to combine both air-supported and tension roofs in one building. The center or main arena is covered by a large, air-inflated roof, while the outer areas of the building are the tension-covered spaces. The main arena has an indoor track and can seat 10,400 spectators for basketball. Located under the tension-supported areas are a gymnastics area, dance studio, weight room, locker rooms, offices, and a 3,000-seat, 50-meter natatorium. Like most fabric structures, this facility was a bargain. The total construction cost was $11,954,418, which comes out to about $49 per square foot. This facility was completed in 1980.

The Sun Dome at the University of South Florida in Tampa is based on a very similar design. Following the same plans as the O'Connell Center, the Sun Dome initially was built with only the air-supported fabric-roof main arena. It was not until several years later that the outer areas were enclosed by a tension roof and the building was completed.

Temporary Air Structures

This section will outline the merits of the smaller and more portable air structures. Air structures work well as environmental covers placed over existing recreational areas and, for many organizations, the "bubble" is the answer to an increasing need for large, covered activity areas at a nominal cost. Cost savings are in proportion to the size of the space to be covered. Spaces over 300 square feet usually bring a cost savings when compared to conventional roofing. Heat gain seems to present a more severe problem than heat loss and must be considered in warmer climates. There are numerous playing fields within communities and around schools and colleges that lend themselves easily to enclosure by a fabric air structure. Some of the additional advantages and disadvantages of using small air-supported structures are as follows:

Advantages:

- Speed of erection—Once in place, the actual erection of the structure usually takes only one or two days. However, additional time is required for the ground work, site services, foundation, anchorage, flooring, and installation of mechanical and electrical equipment needed in the initial installation. Only minimal field labor is needed.
- Ease of deflation, inflation, and repair—Deflation and inflation of the fabric bubble usually does not require skilled labor.

- Portability—When deflated and packed, the fabric envelope can be stored in a small space or easily transported elsewhere for storage or use. Depending on the size of the dome, deflation and packing usually require one or two days.
- Adaptability for temporary functions—For temporary use, the air-supported structure has definite physical and financial advantages over a conventional building.
- Long-span and high-ceiling features—Clear and unobstructed spaces are an inherent feature of the air-supported domes. Conventional long-span and high-ceiling structures are much more expensive.
- Integrated heating, ventilation, and air-pressure system—The integrated heating, ventilation, and air-pressure system is simple and less expensive than conventional systems. Lengthy duct work is not required.

Examples

- Memorial Stadium—A portable inflatable fabric bubble is used to cover the entire football field at the University of Illinois in the winter. First erected in 1986, it was purchased for $1.5 million. With an average inside winter temperature of 55 degrees, the field is used heavily by several departments across the campus. The concept of a portable dome over the game field adds extra use to a facility that would otherwise sit empty much of the year.
- University of Santa Clara—The swimming pool at the Thomas E. Leavey Center is covered by a portable air structure. It is removed for use as an outdoor pool in the summer months and then re-inflated for the winter to transform the pool for indoor use.
- Numerous tennis centers, golf driving ranges, pools and fitness centers.

Cable Domes

Cable domes are the most recent innovation in fabric structure technology. Through a complex system of cables and girders, very large spans can be inexpensively covered by a fabric roof without the need for columns or fans to maintain integrity. Engineers predict that the cable dome concept is feasible for spans of at least 1,000 feet. Cable domes incorporate most of the advantages of fabric structures when compared to standard construction, and fewer of the disadvantages. Many experts in fabric roof technology believe that cable domes will replace the air-supported structure as the fabric roof design of choice for the future. There will probably not be any more large air structures built because of the inherent advantages of the cable dome. Some of these advantages are as follows:

- Huge column-free spans can be covered.
- There is no need for expensive, energy-consuming fans.
- A passive system means there is no need for someone to constantly monitor the facility.
- The structure has an extremely low silhouette.

Examples

- Redbird Arena—Opened in 1991, Redbird Arena is on the campus of Illinois State University in Bloomington-Normal, IL. This multipurpose arena can seat 10,500 spectators for basketball, with the ability to provide an additional 1,500 seats on the floor for concerts or commencement. The lower sections of seats are portable bleachers that can be removed to provide 36,000 square feet of space on the main floor. Built for a cost of $20 million, Redbird Arena was the first cable dome to be constructed on a college campus, but probably won't be the last.

- Tropicana Field—Tropicana Field is located in St. Petersburg, Florida and was opened in 1990. This multipurpose stadium was designed primarily for baseball, yet with the flexibility to accommodate football, basketball, soccer, and tennis, as well as concerts and trade shows. In addition to 50 private suites, a variety of seating arrangements allows the facility to function as an 18,000-seat arena or a 43,000-seat stadium for baseball. The unique movable grandstands contain built-in concession stands and public toilets. The fabric roof is 688 feet in diameter and was constructed on a tilt of 60 degrees. This tilt is designed to allow more clearance for the trajectory of fly balls and allows the roof to reach a height of 225 feet in front of home plate. The cable truss roof system is capable of supporting 60 tons of lighting and sound equipment for concerts, yet weighs a mere six pounds per square foot. Tropicana Field was built for a cost of $132 million and is the home of the Tampa Bay Devil Rays.

- Georgia Dome—Located in downtown Atlanta, Georgia, the Georgia Dome was completed in August 1992. This $210-million structure was the site of both the Super Bowl and the Olympics in 1996. The Teflon-coated fabric roof covers 8.6 acres, weighs 68 tons, and incorporates 11.1 miles of steel support cables. This multipurpose facility seats 70,500 for football and is the home of the Atlanta Falcons. A total of 202 luxury suites are located on different levels around the stadium that range in price from $20,000 to $120,000 per year for a 10-year lease. During the planning process, it was estimated that changing the design from an open-air stadium to a fabric-covered dome increased the cost of the project by only 20% or less.

Redbird Arena

Photo by Todd Seidler

Tropicana Field

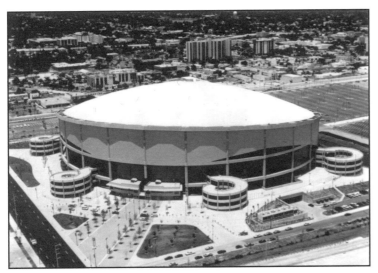

Photo courtesy of HOK, Inc.
Photo by George Cott

Georgia Dome - exterior.

Photo courtesy of Heery Architects & Engineers

Georgia Dome - interior roof.

Photo by Todd Seidler

Wooden Domes

Another recent development in encapsulated spaces is the wooden dome. These spherical wooden structures have several advantages over conventional structures. Column-free spans of up to 800 feet are possible, and they are generally easier to build. There are several wooden dome structures around the country, ranging from high school gymnasiums to very large stadiums. Some of the advantages of wooden domes when compared with standard construction may include:

- Efficient construction of huge column-free spans,
- Lower initial cost when compared with conventional construction,
- Less construction time,
- Full utilization of space, and
- Good insulation and acoustical properties.

Examples

- Round Valley Ensphere—Located in Eager, Arizona, this wooden dome is the only high school domed football stadium in the world. Opened in 1991, it was built for a total project cost of only $11.5 mil-

lion and is unique in many respects. The 113,000 square feet of unobstructed floor space provides a full-size synthetic turf football field with seating for 5,000; a six-lane, 200-meter, synthetic-surface running track with 100-meter straight away; seven combination basketball, volleyball, or tennis courts; a softball field; as well as offices, training room, and four full locker rooms. The wooden roof is insulated to a value of R-28 and is very energy and acoustically efficient. One of the most interesting features of the dome is that it contains a large skylight in the center of the roof. This skylight is made of clear Lexan and provides good illumination of the activity areas even on overcast days. At an elevation of over 7,000 feet, the Round Valley area experiences extremes in weather, including snow-packed winters. During these colder months, the skylight also acts as a solar collector, helping to make the Ensphere very energy efficient.

- Walkup Skydome—This laminated wood dome is located in Northern Arizona University in Flagstaff, Arizona. Opened in 1977, the Skydome is 502 feet across and covers 6.2 acres. It contains a full-size,

Round Valley Ensphere - exterior.

Photo courtesy of Rossman, Schneider, Gadberry & Shay

Round Valley Ensphere - interior.

Photo courtesy of Rossman, Schneider, Gadberry & Shay

roll-up synthetic football/soccer field, a professional-sized ice hockey rink, a 1/5-mile running track, a portable wood basketball court, and has seating for more than 15,000 people. The total construction cost was $8.3 million, or about $620 per seat.

- Tacoma Dome—The Tacoma Dome in Tacoma, Washington, was opened in 1983. This $44-million multipurpose complex is 530 feet across, and for eight years was the largest wooden dome in the world. It can seat 20,722 for football and 25,138 for basketball and contains a full-size permanent ice rink.

- Superior Dome—Constructed on the campus of Northern Michigan University in Marquette, Michigan, this state-owned wooden dome was opened in the fall of 1991. With a diameter of 533 feet, the 14-story, $21.8-million structure was envisioned in 1985 as an Olympic training center. It has a 200-meter track, a full-size football field and is home to the NMU football team, with seating for 8,000 spectators. Designed to be constructed in phases as funding becomes available, the facility will eventually include an additional 5,000 seats; an ice rink for hockey, speed skating, and figure skating; locker rooms; sports medicine facilities; and public use areas.

Summary

The fundamental purpose and design of stadiums and arenas has changed dramatically in the last decade. These changes are so radical, that many facilities built in the last 20 years have become obsolete. The basic idea behind these changes is that modern arenas and stadiums are no longer just places to watch an event but are now designed to provide a total entertainment experience.

Superior Dome

Photo courtesy of TMP Associates, Inc.
Photo by Balthazer Korab, Ltd.

Superior Dome

Photo courtesy of TMP Associates Inc.
Photo by Balthazar Korab, Ltd.

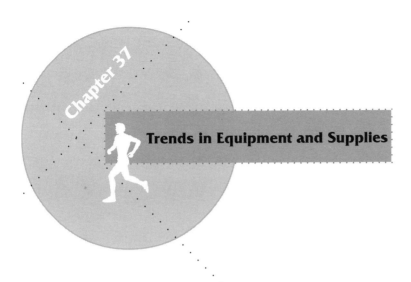

Trends in Equipment and Supplies

Jeffrey C. Petersen, Loras College

In the process of building a new facility or completing major renovations of an existing facility for physical activity or sport, the planning process typically focuses on the building itself. At times, the focus may shift to major building systems, such as the electrical, HVAC, plumbing, or structural. While these areas are an important aspect of the building or renovation process, the needs of facility users must be the greatest consideration. Although the facility itself needs to be a high priority, in the building process it is also crucial that the equipment and supplies required within the facility are carefully considered and selected. The equipment and supplies are just as vital as the building itself if the facility is to fully serve its intended purposes for the users.

Consider, for example, a very basic health and fitness center. While a physical space for this center must be created, the space alone will never meet the expectations of the facility users without the procurement of the necessary equipment and supplies.

As the demand for these sport and recreation facilities increases, so does the demand for necessary supplies and equipment. When considering the competitive nature of sport organizations (interscholastic, intercollegiate, and professional) as well as the pressure on fitness centers and health clubs to attract and maintain a customer base, it is not surprising that new equipment and supply innovations are regularly entering the sport marketplace. Each athletic program wants to provide the latest equipment innovation that may help their athletes or programs become more successful. Similarly, leaders in the fitness industry search to find the next "must have" exercise machine. Identifying trends becomes crucial for success, because of the large capital investments in equipment and the competitive nature of the fitness and sport market. Of course, predicting future trends is just as difficult as predicting a moneymaking stock or predicting which team will win the Super Bowl. It is more typical to identify equipment or supplies that are experiencing rapid growth in use and popularity. The purpose of this chapter is to examine selected trends impacting the selection and use of equipment and supplies within several venues. The dis-

cussion of various products should in no way be considered a blanket endorsement, because each facility operator or manager must develop her own selection criteria based on the wants and needs of the consumers.

Learning Objectives:

After reading this chapter, the student will be able to:
- differentiate between the terms equipment and supplies.
- Analyze the balance between the user needs and the equipment costs.
- Identify selected equipment trends for stadiums, arenas, and gymnasiums and the causes of those trends.
- Identify selected equipment trends in fitness venues.
- Describe the impact of "extreme sports" on facilities and equipment.
- Identify selected supply trends.
- Describe storage options available for supplies and equipment.
- Estimate space needs for storage of equipment and supplies.

Supplies and Equipment Defined

A case of athletic tape, a soccer uniform, hockey mouthpieces, football helmets, a case of tennis balls, portable bleachers, a baseball pitching machine, basketballs, wrestling mats, towels, and a pole vault landing pit are all items that might be necessary in a facility used for physical activity and sport. Which of these would be considered a supply, and which would be equipment?

According to *Miriam Webster's Collegiate Dictionary*, equipment is defined as all the fixed assets other than land and buildings of a business enterprise. A fixed asset is often considered an item with a worth or value above a pre-established dollar value. Equipment could also be defined as durable goods, i.e., items used repeatedly over a period of years.

Items that have a short duration of use, typically one year or less, are classified as supplies. Many supplies have a "one-time-only" use, while others may be repeatedly used but do have a relatively short functional life. Equipment, on the other hand, will have a minimum of over one year of useful service.

The cost per item or unit is another method of differentiating between equipment and supplies. Items with higher costs are usually considered equipment. Therefore, something as large as a scoreboard and something as small as an external heart monitor are both considered to be equipment. Depending on the established policies of the organization, be it governmental, school, or private enterprise, a price standard may be set to distinguish between supplies and equipment. This may be set at the low end of perhaps $100 per item, or at higher levels such as $250, $500 or even $1,000 per item. Items designated as equipment are more closely monitored through item tagging and annual inventory processes. Therefore, the two major considerations in differentiating between supplies and equipment are the cost of the item and the duration of its use.

Cost Considerations

The cost of supplies and equipment is a major consideration in both the initial creation and annual operation of facilities for physical activity and sport. When considering the costs for equipment and supplies, a balance must be maintained between the ultimate wants of the users and the total cost. There is usually a very significant portion of the project cost that should be allocated to properly equip and furnish a facility for sport or recreation. Without taking this into consideration, a beautiful facility could be constructed, but it would be useless without the necessary equipment and supplies.

Consider, for example, a fitness center. The greatest equipment cost factor for a new fitness facility would be the cost of the cardio and strength training equipment desired. According to a compilation of data from six recently completed facilities compiled by Kevin Stubbs of RDG Sports, a leading architectural firm, the fitness center equipment costs vary greatly (see Table 37.1). There was a rather large range of cost ($20 to $51.44 per square foot for equipment) depending on the specific requirements of the clients, but the average of the selected projects was found to be just over $30 per square foot. Note that these estimations only include the exercise equipment itself, and a facility of this type would require other furnishings and operational supplies as well.

Equipment Trends for Stadiums, Arenas, and Gymnasiums

With the 1990s being a decade of unprecedented growth in professional sport venues in the U.S., it is not surprising that many colleges have also seen this prosperous economic climate as a time to build or expand facilities. With such a high rate of growth in spectator sport venues, several equipment trends have emerged. Most of the trends described in this section focus on enhancing the spectator comfort, the spectator sensory experience, or the use of creative management to reduce direct equipment expenses for the owner or operator.

The development of a myriad of seating options has been one major trend in large spectator facilities, both indoor and outdoor. Gone are the days of standard bleachers with the minimal 18-inches-per-person seating width allowance. The current trends are expanding not only the seat width, but also the leg room (tread depth) available. Stadium seating now commonly includes various seat back options, different levels of cushioning, custom color schemes, logo or graphic incorporations, arm rests, and even cup holders.

Consider as an example, the new Broncos Stadium in Denver. This new facility has an official seating capacity of 76,125 with a total facility size of 1,717,000 square feet. The previous home stadium of the Broncos had an official capacity of only two less spectators at 76,123, but the total size was less than half the total of the new stadium at only 850,000 square feet. This increase of total square footage cannot be completely blamed on seating upgrades. The old stadium had an average seat width of 18 inches and leg room of 31 inches, while the new facility has a 19-inch minimum seat

Table 37.1 Fitness Equipment Costs from Six Recent Building Projects		
Facility Area (sq. ft.)	**Equipment Cost**	**Equipment Cost per sq. ft.**
1,200	$24,000	$20.00
2,000	$48,000	$24.00
2,500	$100,000	$40.00
6,000	$125,000	$20.83
7,270	$374,000	$51.44
15,000	$360,000	$24.00

K. Stubbs (personal communication, January 18, 2001)

width and 32-33 inches of standard leg room. The club seating area in the stadium boasts 20-inch-wide padded seating with 33 inches of tread depth. The new stadium seating also provides the added amenity of cup holders for every seat, regardless of the seating section.

The continued trends of both luxury boxes and club seating areas also cater to the increased desire to provide "creature comforts," such as food and beverage catering services, television monitors, and full climate control. There has also been increased emphasis in high-quality sound systems to enhance the live sport experience.

While watching a sporting event live at the venue was once considered the best place to view sports, television's use of instant replay (begun in the 1960s) has added a great deal to the viewing experience. Replays allow the spectator at home to see again plays that may be spectacular or controversial in nature. Spectators attending an event at the stadium or arena may completely miss key parts of the game due to lapses in concentration or their distance from an actual play. However, the installation of big-screen LED (light emitting diode) panels that serve as large video or television monitors can solve these viewing problems. The use of this video equipment now allows the spectators at the venue to view both the live action and have access as a whole to the replays, game statistics, close-up images, and other video information broadcast on the LED big screens.

The number of LED screen installations in sport venues increased enormously throughout the 1990s and this growth is likely to continue. LED displays are not the only video technology available, but other systems such as projection, liquid crystal display (LCD), and cathode ray tube (CRT) are at a significant disadvantage compared to LEDs. First, the power consumption for LED is lower than the previously mentioned systems. The second major advantage to LED displays is that they will typically operate for 100,000 hours before dropping to 50% of the original brightness (Dahlgren, 2000). The LED systems are also much lighter than the CRT display options, making them easier to suspend or mount. The major drop in production cost of the blue and green LEDs has also allowed the price for full-color

displays to drop and become more affordable for collegiate programs, and minor league professional venue use. The LED displays have even entered the high school market with installations now in place at Emerald Ridge High School in Puyallup, Washington, and at Cicero North Syracuse High School in Cicero, New York.

Another reason LED video boards are expanding in use is that three different types of display manufacturing have been developed, each with its own specific applications. The lamp LED method uses a combination of reflector cups and epoxy lenses to intensify and focus the light. These are typically the brightest systems and can be used outdoors where more light intensity is needed. The surface-mounted lamp method utilizes a metal reflector frame that is mounted directly to the board. This method provides a higher resolution and allows for viewing from a wider range of angles. The drawback to the surface-mounted lamp LED display is that it lacks the brightness necessary to provide an optimal image outdoors. The chip on the board method places the LED directly on the board without any type of reflection or lens system. Of course, this method is the least expensive, but it is the least light efficient of the three, and it is often harder to maintain. The full-color displays in all three manufacturing options are obtained by the blending of light from the combination of red, blue, and green LEDs to create up to 16.7 million colors. The red LEDs continue to be the least costly to produce, so many scoreboard or marquee sign applications of LED technology continue to use red as the primary color.

A major factor in the growing popularity of the LED video display would be the competition between colleges and professional sports organizations. Each venue attempts to either keep up with or become the leader with the biggest or the best video displays available for their patrons. The inclusion of large video display screens is almost considered standard in new large-scale venue constructions. Another advantage of the LED screens is that older venues can easily add the displays to upgrade the facility. This can have a major impact on spectators' impressions of the facility. The wide range of size options (from 6' x 8' at the small end to the 27'

Figure 37.1 Indoor LED video display at Nationwide Arena in Columbus, Ohio featuring four 9' x 16' video screens.

Photo courtesy of Diamond Vision Corporation

**Figure 37.2
Outdoor application of LED
video technology at Spartan
Stadium at the campus of
Michigan State University in
East Lansing with a video
display size of 21' x 27'.**

Photo courtesy of Diamond Vision Corporation

x 96' mammoth screen being installed in the new Denver Broncos stadium) allows each stadium to create a more customized fit for its particular needs.

Another trend impacting equipment in spectator venues is contracting and outsourcing portions of the typical functions associated with the venue. According to Peter Bendor-Samuel, considered a leading outsourcing authority, outsourcing occurs when an organization transfers the ownership of a business process to a supplier. The key aspect is the transfer of control. Outsourcing differs from contracting, where the buyer retains control of the process and tells the supplier how to do the work. It is the transfer of ownership that defines outsourcing and at times makes it a challenging process. In outsourcing, the buyer does not instruct the supplier how to perform its task. The buyer clearly communicates the desired results and leaves the process decisions for accomplishing those results with the supplier.

Within stadiums and arenas, typical operational aspects that may be outsourced include services such as: concessions, laundry, and facility maintenance. One of the advantages of outsourcing can be significant savings in major equipment expenditures. When organizations or teams owning or operating these facilities outsource, then the equipment and supplies required can be significantly reduced. For example, at a venue where concessions are outsourced, only a space allocation with water and electrical supply would be provided. The outsourced supplier for concessions would provide all the necessary equipment for the preparation, storage, and sales of all products. Of course this would create a significant decrease in equipment and supplies expenditures in this aspect of operation. According to the Outsourcing Research Council (Raiford, 1999) operations and facilities outsourcing had an 18% growth rate in 1999 in the corporate sector. This trend will continue to impact the equipment needs for major venues in the future. The needs for equipment will not decrease, but outsourcing will shift the responsibility of equipment search research/selection, purchase and maintenance on the outsourcing supplier.

Gymnasiums are facilities in secondary schools throughout the country that serve as both a primary activity space for physical education as well as a primary spectator venue for interscholastic sports. As spectator venues, gymnasiums require safe and ample seating, while as a teaching

and practice area, the need is for maximum useable floor space. The most common solution to these two needs has been the telescoping bleachers unit. Most gyms have these seating structures, but current requirements in the Uniform Building Code (UBC) and the Americans with Disabilities Act (ADA) are most likely not met if bleachers were installed before 1990. The replacement of older models of bleachers has become a growing trend in the renovation and improvement of gyms.

The older-model bleachers have some serious deficiencies in regard to safety and risk management. Many old bleacher models have an open space area between the seat and the foot rest or tread area. This is a space that small children can often fit through to fall under the structure, or where an adult could slip a foot or a leg into and be injured. Additionally, many old units lack designated aisles, and require that the seating area itself double as an access route up and down the bleachers. The rails on many older units consist of a single or double bar that has a large open area where children could fall. Most older bleacher units also require manual operation to open and close, which can expose workers to the risk of injury during the process.

Because of the significant issues with many older bleacher units, it is not surprising that bleacher replacement is becoming more popular. Steel remains the primary structural component of the units, but seats can be made of wood, vinyl-coated metal, or of molded plastic for standard seating. Tip-up seating with chair backs either padded or unpadded is another option for telescoping bleacher units. The price for new bleachers ranges from the entry-level $90 to $100 per gross seat to as much as $350 per seat if fold-up padded seating with chair backs is selected (Kocher, 1996).

The specific UBC regulations impacting bleacher seating begin with row limitations. A maximum of 16 rows is allowed if the bleachers load only from the top or only from the bottom. No row limitations exist if the bleacher section can load from both the top and bottom. Whenever there are more than 11 rows of seating, aisles are required, and no more than 20 seats can separate each aisle. Aisle steps cannot exceed nine inches without providing an intermediate step, and since the typical bleacher rise between rows is more than nine inches, these intermediate steps are almost always required. A minimum aisle width of 42 inches is necessary if servicing seating on both sides, or 36 inches wide if seating is only to one side. When considering railings, the aisles require discontinuous rails that allow spectators to move laterally as well as up and down the aisle. These rails must also have an intermediate rail 12 inches below the top of the rail for shorter spectators (Scandrett, 1998). These "P-shaped" railings usually attach to the riser face in the center of the aisle and must be attached and removed each time the units are moved. The end railings prevent falls and must have no gaps greater than six inches.

The ADA requirements also specify that the seating areas provided for those with wheelchairs be spread throughout the facility, rather than all congregated together. The number of wheelchair spaces should be reviewed carefully to maintain ADA compliance. For example, facilities with a capacity of over 500 spectators must provide one wheelchair location for every 100 seats over the initial 500, plus six. So a gymnasium with a seating capacity of 5,000 would necessitate 51 wheelchair locations (Scandrett, 1998).

Bleacher replacement (see Chapter 13) can improve a gymnasium facility not just by improving the facilities compliance with ADA and UBC but also by creating an improved facility appearance. Many models have color options to enhance the aesthetics image of the facility. The use of mechanical opening and closing greatly reduces the injury risk for personnel in facility set-up and teardown. The risk management benefits ADA compliance associated with bleacher replacement help make this improvement not only a desired trend, but in many cases a necessity.

Equipment Trends for Fitness Venues

In 1999 a survey by the National Sporting Goods Association ("NSGA study," 1999, March) found that 46.45% of over 5,000 survey participants indicated a desire to increase their level of participation in activities utilizing exercise equipment. With this great desire of individuals to use exercise equipment, public and private institutions continue to focus efforts on meeting these fitness needs with their selection of exercise equipment.

One major consideration in the selection of fitness equipment is the cost. Table 37.2 identifies the average cost of 12 selected weight machines. While cost is one major factor in equipment selection, the needs and wants of the users cannot be overlooked. According to the Fitness Products Council (*Trend Setting*, 1999), four of eight major fitness trends identified related directly to equipment. One of the most significant trends is the explosive growth of aerobic exercise equipment. A 63% increase in use for Americans was noted from 1987 to 1997 with 67.3 million people reporting regular workouts with cardio equipment. Within this increased use of cardio machines, the treadmill was still the highest used piece of equipment with 36.1 million regular users in 1997. The use of weight training among American women has increased by 127% from 1987 to 1997 to a total of 16.8 million. There can also be significant variance in the equipment preferences based on the demographic traits such as age and gender. This is evident in the results of a survey of

Table 37.2
Total-Body Weight Workout Sample Equipment Cost Sheet

Weight Equipment	Average Cost Per Unit
Lower Body	
Leg Press	$4,783
Seated Leg Curl	$2,459
Leg Extension	$2,388
Multi-Hip	$2,406
Mid Section	
Abdominal	$2,394
Lower Back	$2,729
Upper Body	
Arm Curl	$2,081
Triceps Extension	$2,256
Chest Press	$2,546
Shoulder Press	$2,414
Rowing	$2,281
Lat Pulldown $2,044	
Total Cost	$30,781

(Hasler & Bartlett, 1995)

nearly 1,200 collegiate recreation providers (see Table 37.3). The top preference of males at these colleges was free weights, while the female top preference was treadmills.

Weight training has a variety of equipment options, from free weights to plate-loaded machines, to selectorized (weight stack and pin) machines. While novice lifters typically prefer the selectorized machines, there continues to be a significant amount of growth in the use of free weights as well as the plate-loaded systems. One trend within all of the strength-training modes is a continued focus on safety and risk management. Some selectorized systems have incorporated shrouds that cover much of the weight stack and many moving parts to reduce to risk of injury

Table 37.3 Collegiate Fitness Center Preferred Equipment		
Choice of Equipment	Males	Females
First Choice	Free Weights	Treadmills
Second Choice	Bikes	Steppers
Third Choice	Treadmills	Elliptical
Fourth Choice	Steppers	Bikes

(Patton 1999, August)

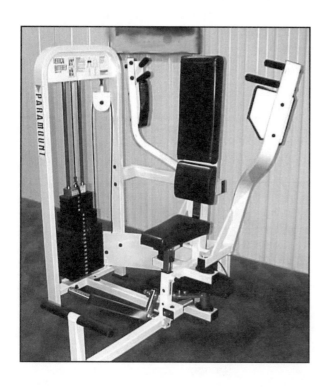

Figure 37.3
Butterfly chest press as a
typical selectorized weight machine.

Figure 37.4
Plate loaded Smith machine.

(see Figure 37.5). On the free weight side, changes in the plate designs, such as the addition of openings for hand holds and/or the addition of flat surfaces on the circumference have been made to reduce the number of accidents due to dropped or rolling plates (note Figure 37.6). Another major trend in weight-training equipment is the continued integration of computer-chip technology on many selectorized systems. For example, some systems are able to read users' swipe cards or other input devices and can set resistance levels and record results based on a prescribed workout routine from a personal trainer.

The increasing use of aerobic or cardio machines is another current trend. Since walking may be the most popular of all forms of aerobic exercise, it is not surprising that the treadmill is still a very popular piece of exercise equipment. Cycling machines have also been a mainstay of cardio exercise machines, but have continued to diversify. Cycling equipment now includes many options, such as such as the traditional exercise cycle, air resistance cycle, spin cycle, and recumbent cycle (see Figures 37.7-37.9). Additional innova-

tions, such as steppers and elliptical machines are also popular cardio options that offer non-impact based aerobic training. While some cardio equipment users may exclusively train on one type of machine, other users tend to enjoy using a variety of machines to avoid stagnation or boredom in their exercise programs. Because of the varied use of aerobic exercise equipment, it is difficult to know what machine might become the next top machine, but it is almost certain that there will be other creative innovations.

The integration of computer technology within cardio machines is also a trend that should continue to expand in the future. The use of direct pulse monitoring while using the cardio machines is not such a new innovation, but the development of computer programming that can alter the speed or resistance level of the machine to keep the person exercising within a specified target heart rate in definitely a great step forward in customizing workouts. The computerized workout routines that focus on optimal fat-burning pulse zones or optimal cardiovascular benefit zones are becoming common options on many cardio machines. At the same time,

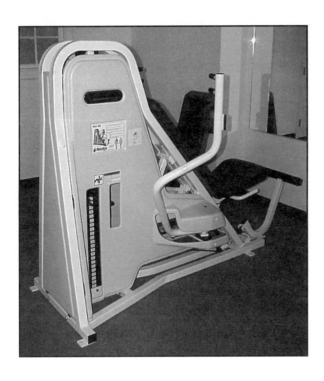

Figure 37.5
Selectorized weight machine with shroud providing protection from many moving parts during use.

Figure 37.6
Free weight plates designed with risk management features.

**Figure 37.7
Typical exercise cycle with
electronic control panel.**

**Figure 37.8
Recumbent cycle with a
high backed seat.**

there are users of these machines who simply wish to get on and workout at a steady rate or pace without using these programming options. For those types of users, the manual operation options are also available to allow a very basic workout.

The entertainment of individuals using exercise equipment is a current trend that will likely continue to expand in the future as well. Cardiovascular exercise areas in the past may have provided reading material, a room-wide stereo system, and perhaps a television. More recent trends involve the use of multiple video display screens and FM band audio programming for individual headset listening of either the video programming or music. Numerous video monitors coupled with audio broadcasting units systems are now trademarked as comprehensive systems, such as Cardio Theater and Broadcast Vision. These systems meet users' needs by allowing them to select their own programming in news business or entertainment. In addition to the standard or large-screen video systems, there are also small-scale equipment mounted systems that provide small video screens in combination with cassette and CD players. The video portion of these systems can play network or cable programming, or they can play specific workout motivational or educational programming.

In addition to the expansion of audio and video entertainment options while exercising, computers have been modified for ease of use while using many cardio machines. Computers and display monitors have been modified to allow for operation while exercising on a treadmill, stepper, or elliptical trainer. This technology allows the exerciser to access the Internet via a touch screen or modified mouse. These technology trends allow for an increase in individual choice in the entertainment options while exercising, and market forces will likely continue to drive an expansion of these trends.

Figure 37.9
Spin cycle typically used
in group classes.

Figure 37.10
The treadmill is still one of the
most popular cardio machines.

Figure 37.11
Typical stepper with electronic controls.

Figure 37.12
Elliptical machine providing a
non-impact cardio workout.

Extreme Sports

Adventure-oriented sports continue to grow in popularity and bring unique requirements for facilities and equipment. The media exposure of the extreme sports through competitions such as ESPN's X Games and numerous other network imitations continues to help fuel interest in and give creditability to these activities. Although some of the events such as street luge may have limited appeal to mass participation, activities such as rock climbing and skating (skateboarding and in-line skating) have high levels of participation. In fact, these activities are attracting so many participants, that instead of being viewed as "extreme sports," it might be better to consider them extremely common.

The number of participants in skateboarding according to the SkatePark Association of the United States of America (SPAUSA) tops more than nine million regular users. There are approximately 650,000 serious climbers and perhaps millions of people starting the sport annually. Add to this in-line skating, which has over 75,000 members within the USA Hockey Inline with at least 2.5 million playing inline hockey informally (Ahrweiler, 2001). Including the vast number of inline skaters for cardiovascular exercise and recreational street and skatepark skating, there is a significant population with sporting and recreational needs in this area.

Skateboarding and inline skating opportunities can be enhanced through the creation of skateparks, designated areas developed for safe, supervised, and exciting riding. More than 300 public skateparks were constructed in 1999, with double that number expected in 2000 (Ahrweiler, 2001). While some skateparks are elaborate concrete build-in-place systems, there are also modular park components available. These components could be considered necessary equipment to create a skatepark from an available asphalt or concrete space. The modular components can be made out of concrete, wood, or a combination steel framing, polyethylene, and zinc plating. These components combine elements such as angled and curved ramps, rails, curbs, and bumps to create fairly comprehensive parks suitable for both skateboard and inline skate use. The modular components have even been assembled into portable units such as the "Flip Side" in Caledon, Ontario. This portable system of seven ramp structures and grind rails is transported to various locations throughout the summer in this Toronto suburb.

Inline hockey has allowed the expansion of the traditionally "northland" sport of hockey to be adapted to sunbelt states without the requirement of ice. Inline hockey can be played indoors or outdoors, and the facility space can often be converted for modified soccer use. Equipment needed to create a usable facility includes the dasherboards, goals, and a smooth base surface. The dasherboards are commonly constructed from wood, fiberglass, or plastic. One change is that the Plexiglas upper portion of the boards seen in ice hockey is often replaced with coated fencing or netting for inline hockey. The preferred surface is smoothly finished concrete, but portable vinyl tiling systems, such as Sport Court or other similar products, can also provide a good playing surface.

The over 300 dedicated climbing gyms and the multitude of fitness clubs and recreation centers with climbing wall components have their own unique equipment requirements. The equipment required for the use of a climbing structure might consist of a variety of mountable holds (fiberglass or resin fixtures for hands or feet), belay systems (safety harness), ropes and rope hardware, helmets, and climbing shoes. Most climbing structures are "custom built" walls or free-standing structures, but in some instances, existing wall space of adequate height and structural soundness can be adapted into a functional climbing surface. Of course, the custom climbing areas are much more impressive in appearance and in realistic climbing features. Regardless of the climbing wall type, the ability to alter the holds creates immense flexibility for the climbing wall to be configured for both novice and experienced climbers. This changeability also helps to keep climbers motivated and interested in the climbing experience.

Supply Trends

It is far more difficult to trace supply trends within sport facilities and sport and fitness organizations. Changes in the market for particular supplies, be it towels, athletic tape, or basketballs, would be more likely to be researched by the manufacturers and those practitioners in the field than those in the facility-planning process. The specific supply needs also vary greatly, based on the nature of the organization. A tennis club has far different supply needs than an arena league football team. Similarly, the maintenance department for a major stadium has far different supply needs than the baseball team that plays at the stadium.

One innovation that can now greatly influence the selection and purchase of supplies regardless of the program or department is the explosive growth of the use of the Internet. The Internet can be used to research products, obtain price quotes, and even place orders for almost any supply needed in the realm of sporting and recreation. The use of standard search engines can be used to locate supplies, but the development of sport-specific supply websites can also be effective. Athleticsearch.com can be used to research product information from a multitude of suppliers, as well as access to articles from trade magazines and other sources. The bidding and purchasing process can be facilitated through sites like Athleticbid.com that contact multiple vendors to allow them to place bids on your specified needs.

Supply and Equipment Storage

The storage space necessary for supplies and equipment is often one of the most overlooked areas in the facility-planning process. An examination of the programs operating within a facility can help to determine the storage needs. It is important to gather input from those administrators, teachers, managers, coaches, and others who will have to deal with the storage of equipment and supplies.

The arrangement of the storage space should also be considered. One option is to have one large, centralized storage area. This type of storage is advantageous to large-scale programs that may have a full-time equipment manager and staff. With this arrangement it may be easier to control the issuing, returning, and maintenance of equipment and supplies. One possible problem with the creation of a large, centralized storage area is that it may become a target for renovation into a classroom, lab, office space, or other possible uses.

A second option is to have small, separate storage areas. These storage spaces would be located near to the individual team or program activity spaces. An advantage to this system is that individual coaches or program leaders would control their own access to equipment. This arrangement may allow for equipment to be stored closer to its point of use. The disadvantage to this system is that control of access to the multiple areas can be difficult to monitor.

In many instances, facilities do not have enough storage space, or have outgrown their existing storage space. Utilization of "just-in-time" purchasing and delivery is one option to reduce the amount of storage space required. For example, rather than ordering and receiving your facility cleaning supplies in bulk for the year, the items could be purchased in bulk but delivered on a monthly or bi-monthly schedule. This would reduce the amount of storage space that would need to be dedicated to these types of supplies. This form of purchasing, however, does not work well with large equipment or non-consumable items.

Regardless of whether the storage space is arranged in a large, centralized space or in smaller, "point-of use" areas, the total amount of space available must be adequate for the proper storage equipment and supplies. Proper storage would include keeping equipment secure and protecting it from inappropriate use or theft. Proper storage is also necessary to reduce liability for the facility operators and owners. In addition, proper storage should include adequate temperature and humidity controls for equipment that could be adversely impacted by environmental extremes. The use of overhead roll-up also can help maximize use and access of storage space.

How much storage space for equipment is enough? That is a question with no simple answer, but there have been a number of facility studies conducted over time that have tried to approach this question in a systematic manner. Some of these studies have relied on the opinions of expert panels, while others have relied upon data collection from selected facilities and input from facility administrators.

Table 37.4 traces the development of these recommendations over a period spanning more than 60 years. These recommendations provide an excellent starting point for consideration of storage space needs. Once an appropriate guideline has been selected for the proper level and facility, the recommendation for storage space can be tested with the actual and projected needs specific to the programs to be served by the storage.

Summary

Supplies are typically items that are used only one time or that have a lifespan of a year or less. Equipment has a lifespan of one year or longer, and because of the fact that it is a type of durable good, the cost is often higher than most supplies. For each purchase of equipment or supplies, facility administrators must balance the wants and needs of the users or programs with the costs of the desired items. The product quality level must be considered, as well as the need to remain within the budgetary constraints of the organization. A primary influence on trends in spectator venues is the comfort and entertainment of the spectators. These trends include upgraded seating options in gymnasiums, stadiums, and arenas, the addition of video and audio systems and the use of contracting or outsourcing.

Table 37.4
Equipment Storage Space Recommendations – a selected chronology

Date	Researcher(s)	Recommendation	Source & Level
1938	Evenden, Strayer & Englehardt	400-square foot apparatus storage room	Expert Panel for collegiate facilities
1961	Sapora & Kenney	40% of total activity space dedicated to all ancillary areas including lockers, showers, drying areas, equipment storage, supply rooms & offices	Research of Big 10 Conference Universities
1967	National Facilities Conference	35% of activity area for all ancillary areas including lockers, showers, drying areas, equipment storage, supply rooms & offices	Expert Panel for collegiate facilities
1968	College & University Facilities Guide	250-330 square feet of storage space for each exercise area	Expert Panel for collegiate facilities
1969	Berryhill	35% of activity area for all ancillary areas including lockers, showers, drying areas, equipment storage, supply rooms & offices	Research of one high school with expert panel input
1988	Strand	20-30% of all ancillary space within the facility	Research of Big10 Conference Universities
1989	Walker	20-22% of all ancillary space within the facility	Research of 18 small colleges from two conferences
1997	Petersen	20-22% of all ancillary space within the facility	Research of 40 high schools

(Adapted from Walker & Seidler, 1993)

Compliments of Athletic Business, National Collegiate Athletic Association, and the National Federation of State High School Associations

Appendix A

FACILITY SPECIFICATION GUIDE

(The information contained in this guide, based on information provided by various associations and governing organizations, is intended merely as a guide and is not applicable to all situations. Contact the appropriate organization for further information.)

FACILITY SPECIFICATION GUIDE
BASEBALL

LEGEND
- BASE LINES, BATTER'S BOX, CATCHER'S BOX, FOUL LINE, PITCHER'S PLATE, COACH'S BOX
- ON-DECK CIRCLE
- BASE LINES
- GRASS LINES

(Reprinted with permission of the NCAA.)

YOUTH LEAGUE

200' OPTION

180' RADIUS

60'   46'

SANDY KOUFAX (AABC) AND PONY LEAGUE

300' OPTION

250' RADIUS

75'   54'

BABE RUTH AND SENIOR LEAGUE

335' OPTION

300' RADIUS

90'   60'

ALSO:
MICKEY MANTLE
CONNIE MACK
JUNIOR LEGION
HIGH SCHOOL
    310' RADIUS
    360' OPTION

HOME PLATE

17''

8½''

8½''

PITCHER'S PLATE

24''

6''

(Diagrams courtesy of USA Baseball.)

For more information contact:

USA Baseball
Hi Corbett Field
3400 E. Camino Campestre
Tucson, AZ 85716
(520) 327-9700
Fax: (520) 327-9221
www.usabaseball.com

American Amateur Baseball Congress
118 Redfield Plaza
P.O. Box 467
Marshall, MI 49068
(616) 781-2002
Fax: (616) 781-2060
www.voyager.net/aabc

National Collegiate Athletic Association
6201 College Blvd.
Overland Park, KS 66211-2422
(913) 339-1906
www.ncaa.org

FACILITY SPECIFICATION GUIDE

BASKETBALL

PROFESSIONAL COURT

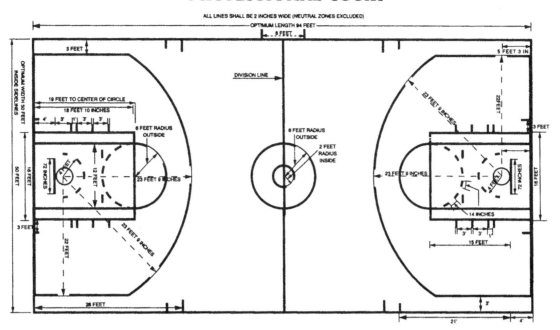

HIGH SCHOOL & COLLEGE COURT

Note: The optimum length of the high school court is 84 feet. If court is less than 74 feet long, it should be divided by two lines, each parallel to and 40 feet from the farther end line.

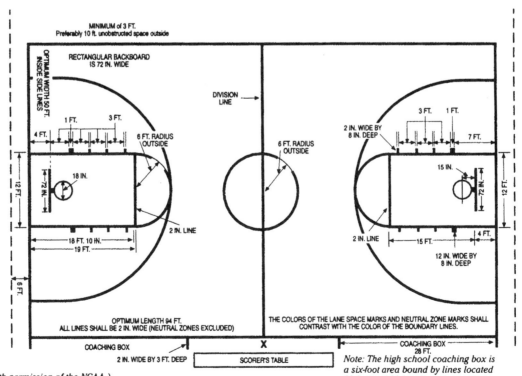

(Reprinted with permission of the NCAA.)

National Basketball Association
Olympic Tower
645 Fifth Ave.
New York, NY 10022
(212) 826-7000
www.nba.com

National Federation of State High School Associations
P.O. Box 20626
Kansas City, MO 64195-0626
(816) 464-5400
Fax: (816) 464-5571
www.nfhs.org

National Collegiate Athletic Association
6201 College Blvd.
Overland Park, KS 66211-2422
(913) 339-1906
www.ncaa.org

FACILITY SPECIFICATION GUIDE
HOCKEY

PROFESSIONAL

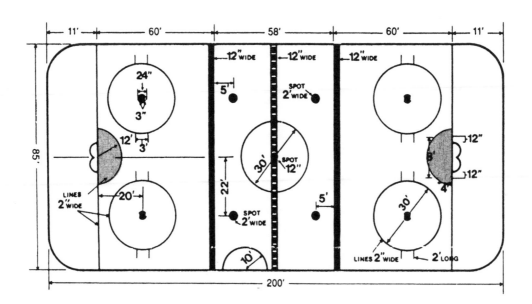

COLLEGE AND HIGH SCHOOL

Commercial, institution or conference logos
and/or names are allowed in the ice only in the
nuetral zone.

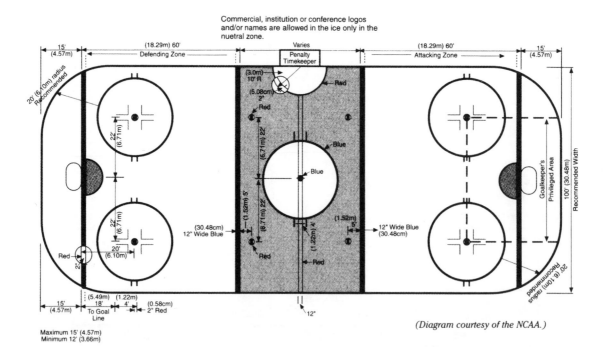

(Diagram courtesy of the NCAA.)

Maximum 15' (4.57m)
Minimum 12' (3.66m)

For more information contact:

National Hockey League
75 International Blvd., Room 300
Rexdale, Ontario M9W 6L9
(416) 798-0809
Fax: (416) 798-0819
www.nhl.com

**National Federation of State High
School Associations**
P.O. Box 20626
Kansas City, MO 64195-0626
(816) 464-5400
Fax: (816) 464-5571
www.nfhs.org

**National Collegiate Athletic
Association**
6201 College Blvd.
Overland Park, KS 66211-2422
(913) 339-1906
www.ncaa.org

FACILITY SPECIFICATION GUIDE

RACQUETBALL/ HANDBALL

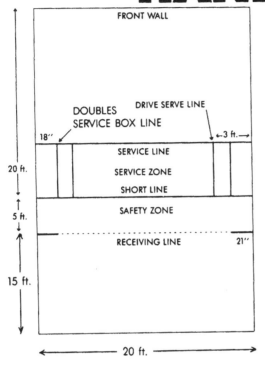

FRONT AND
SIDE WALL
HEIGHT: 20'0''

REAR WALL
HEIGHT:
AT LEAST 14'0''

For more information contact:

United States Racquetball Association
1685 W. Uintah
Colorado Springs, CO 80904-2921
(719) 635-5396
Fax: (719) 635-0685
www.racquetball.org

SQUASH

NORTH AMERICAN COURT   INTERNATIONAL COURT   DOUBLES COURT

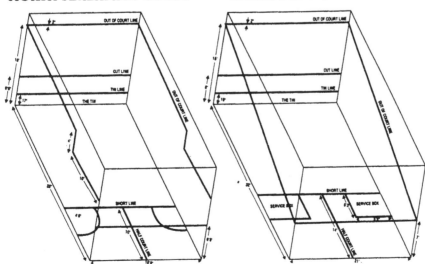

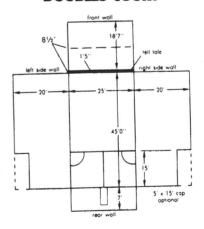

For more information contact:

United States Squash Racquets Association
23 Cynwyd Road, P.O. Box 1216
Bala-Cynwyd, PA 19004
(610) 667-4006
Fax: (610) 667-6539
www.us-squash.org/squash

FACILITY SPECIFICATION GUIDE

WOMEN'S LACROSSE

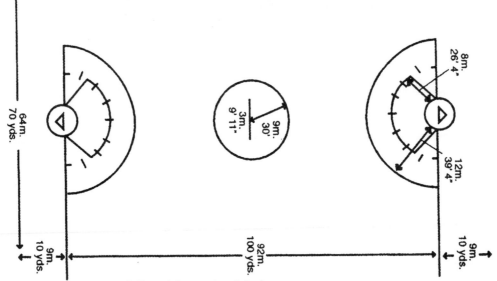

(Diagram courtesy of the U.S. Women's Lacrosse Association.)

For more information contact:

U.S. Women's Lacrosse Association
35 Wisconsin Circle, Suite 525
Chevy Chase, MD 20815
(301) 951-8795
Fax: (301) 951-7082
www.USWLA.org

US Lacrosse Inc.
113 W. University Pkwy.
Baltimore, MD 21210
(410) 235-6882
Fax: (410) 366-6735
www.lacrosse.org

MEN'S LACROSSE

1997
The Lacrosse Field of Play

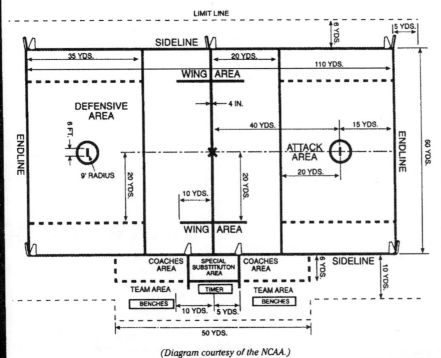

(Diagram courtesy of the NCAA.)

For more information contact:

US Lacrosse Inc.
113 W. University Pkwy.
Baltimore, MD 21210
(410) 235-6882
Fax: (410) 366-6735
www.lacrosse.org

National Collegiate Athletic Association
6201 College Blvd.
Overland Park, KS 66211-2422
(913) 339-1906
www.ncaa.org

FACILITY SPECIFICATION GUIDE
TRACK & FIELD

POLE VAULT LANDING AREA DETAIL

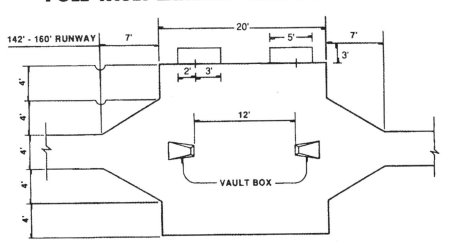

LONG JUMP/TRIPLE JUMP PIT PLAN

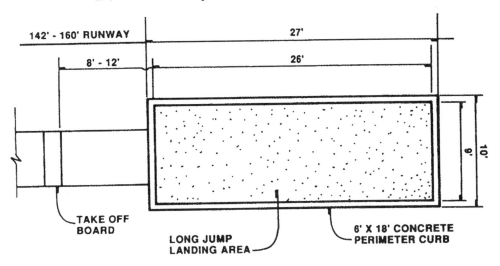

HIGH JUMP DETAIL

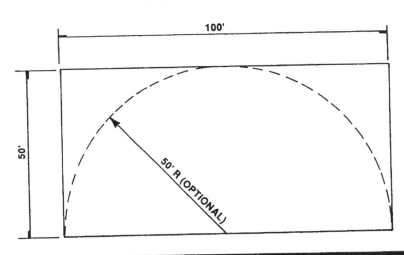

All diagrams reprinted with permission
of the USTC&TBA.

For more information contact:

**U.S. Tennis Court and
Track Builders Association**
3525 Ellicott Mills Drive, Suite N
Ellicott City, MD 21043-4547
(410) 418-4875
www.ustctba.com

FACILITY SPECIFICATION GUIDE
TRACK & FIELD

Dimensions for track and field events appearing in the following diagrams are based on requirements set forth by the National Federation of State High School Associations (NFHS). There are variations of requirements for facilities governed by the National Collegiate Athletic Association (NCAA), USA Track and Field (USAT&F) or the International Amateur Athletic Federation (IAAF). Please consult the appropriate governing body or the U.S. Tennis Court and Track Builders Association (USTC&TBA) for specific information.

TRACK USE ONLY

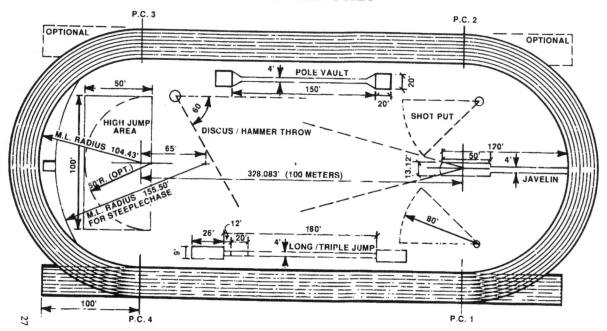

400 METER EVENTS

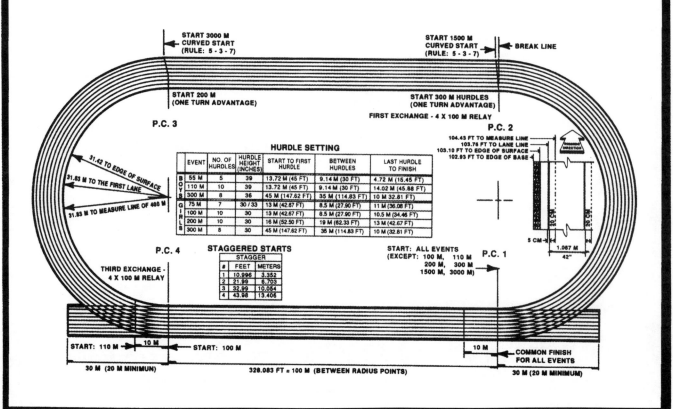

HURDLE SETTING

	EVENT	NO. OF HURDLES	HURDLE HEIGHT (INCHES)	START TO FIRST HURDLE	BETWEEN HURDLES	LAST HURDLE TO FINISH
B O Y S	55 M	5	39	13.72 M (45 FT)	9.14 M (30 FT)	4.72 M (15.45 FT)
	110 M	10	39	13.72 M (45 FT)	9.14 M (30 FT)	14.02 M (45.88 FT)
	300 M	8	36	45 M (147.62 FT)	35 M (114.83 FT)	10 M 32.81 FT)
G I R L S	75 M	7	30 / 33	13 M (42.67 FT)	8.5 M (27.90 FT)	11 M (36.08 FT)
	100 M	10	30	13 M (42.67 FT)	8.5 M (27.90 FT)	10.5 M (34.46 FT)
	200 M	10	30	16 M (52.50 FT)	19 M (62.33 FT)	13 M (42.67 FT)
	300 M	8	30	45 M (147.62 FT)	35 M (114.83 FT)	10 M (32.81 FT)

STAGGERED STARTS

	STAGGER	
#	FEET	METERS
1	10.996	3.352
2	21.99	6.703
3	32.99	10.054
4	43.98	13.406

FACILITY SPECIFICATION GUIDE
TRACK & FIELD

STEEPLECHASE HURDLES

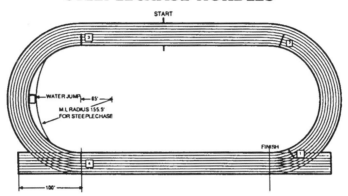

WATER JUMP
85'
M.L RADIUS 155.5'
FOR STEEPLECHASE

100'

Distance for Junior
Events—2,000m

SHOT PUT PAD (HIGH SCHOOL)

THROWING SECTOR
9' RADIUS

1/4" STONE CHIPS
12" DEPTH

TOE BOARD

2" WIDE PAINTED STRIPE OR
3/4" RECESSED CIRCLE

1/8" SAWCUTS

4" REINFORCED CONCRETE
SLAB WITH
LIGHT BROOM FINISH

1/8" SAWCUTS

10'

10'

NOTE: INSTALL 1/8" SAWCUTS ON
RECESSED CIRCLE ONLY

DISCUS CAGE (HIGH SCHOOL)

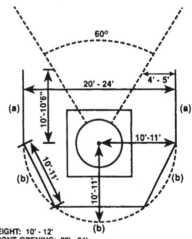

60°

20' - 24'

4' - 5'

(a)

(a)

10'-10'6"

10'-11'

(b)

(b)

10'-11'

10'-11'

(b)

HEIGHT: 10' - 12'
FRONT OPENING: 20' - 24'
4' - 5' : DISTANCE CORNER
POST TO SECTOR LINE
10' - 11' : DISTANCE CENTER
OF CIRCLE TO FENCING

JAVELIN THROW

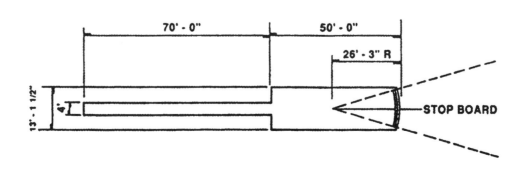

70' - 0"

50' - 0"

26' - 3" R

13' - 1 1/2"

STOP BOARD

FACILITY SPECIFICATION GUIDE
SWIMMING & DIVING

INTERNATIONAL AND NATIONAL COMPETITION

There are a number of sanctioning organizations for national and international amateur competition. Included here are the facility standards of FINA (the Federation Internationale de Natation Amateur) and one of its U.S. affiliates, United States Swimming Inc.

FINA STANDARDS
• Length—50m. When touch panels or electronic timing devices are used, the pool must be of such length that ensures the required distance between the panels.
• Width—25m preferred.
• Depth—1m minimum.
• Number of lanes—8. For Olympic Games and World Championships, 10 lanes are required.
• Width of lanes—2m minimum with spaces of 0.2m outside first and last lanes. A lane rope must separate these spaces from the first and last lanes.

U.S. SWIMMING STANDARDS
• Length—Long course, 164'½" (50m); short course, 82'¼" (25m) or 25 yds.
• Width—Eight lanes, 8'2½" (2.5m) minimum (centerline to centerline), with approximately 1'6" (0.45m) outside first and last lanes.

• Water depth—For national championships and international competition, 6'7" (2m) throughout the course. Minimum water depth for racing starts during competition and practice shall be measured for a distance 3'3½" (1m) to 16'5" (5m) from the end wall. Starting requirements and height of starting blocks shall be as follows: (1) In pools with water depth less than 3'6" (1.07m) at the starting end, the swimmer must start from the deck or from within the water; (2) In pools with water depth 3'6" (1.07m) to less than 4' (1.22m) at the starting end, starting platforms shall be no more than 18" (0.46m) above the water surface; (3) In pools with water depth 4' (1.22m) or more at the starting end, starting platforms shall meet the following height requirements: A. Long course: The front edge of the starting platforms shall be no less than 1'8" (0.50m) nor more than 2'5½" (0.75m) above the surface of the water. B. Short Course: The front edge of the starting platforms shall be not higher than 2'6" (0.762m) above the surface of the water.

NOTE: Local, state and municipal statutes, ordinances, rules and regulations may have depth limitations in conflict with the above. The LSC and all member clubs should check for this at all times.

For more information contact:

United States Swimming Inc.
One Olympic Plaza
Colorado Springs, CO 80909
(719) 578-4578
Fax: (719) 575-4050

STANDARD DIMENSIONS FOR PUBLIC SWIMMING POOLS

The following are the currently recommended standard dimensions for Class B and Class C public swimming pools, not designed for sanctioned competition.

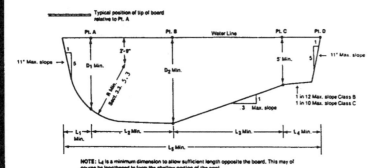

MINIMUM DIMENSIONS FOR DIVING PORTION OF CLASS B AND C POOLS
(This drawing does not show the shallow portion of the pool)

NOTE: L4 is a minimum dimension to allow sufficient length opposite the board. This may of course be lengthened to form the shallow portion of the pool

| POOL TYPE | RELATED DIVING EQUIPMENT | | MINIMUM DIMENSIONS | | | | | | | | MINIMUM WIDTH OF POOL AT: | | |
	MAX. DIVING BOARD LENGTH	MAX. BOARD HGT. OVER WATER	D₁	D₂	R	L₁	L₂	L₃	L₄	L₅	PT. A	PT. B	PT. C
VI	10'	26" (¾ meter)	7'-0"	8'-6"	5'-4"	2'-6"	8'-6"	10'-6"	7'-0"	28'-0"	16'-0"	16'-0"	18'-0"
VII	12'	30" (¾ meter)	7'-6"	9'-0"	6'-0"	3'-0"	9'-0"	12'-0"	6'-0"	30'-0"	16'-0"	20'-0"	20'-0"
VIII	16'	1 Meter	8'-6"	10'-0"	7'-0"	6'-0"	10'-6"	15'-0"	2'-0"	31'-6"	20'-0"	22'-0"	22'-0"
IX	16'	3 Meter	11'-6"	12'-0"	8'-6"	6'-0"	10'-6"	21'-0"	0	37'-6"	22'-0"	24'-0"	24'-0"

L2, L3 and L4 combined represent the minimum distance from the tip of the board to pool wall opposite diving equipment.

For board heights exceeding 3 meters, see Article 3.5.4.

* NOTE: Placement of boards shall observe the following minimum dimensions. With multiple board installations minimum pool widths must be increased accordingly.

Deck level board to pool side ....8'
1 meter board to pool side ....10'
3 meter board to pool side ....11'
1 meter or deck level board to 3 meter board....................10'
1 meter or deck level to another 1 meter or deck level board ....8'
3 meter to another 3 meter board ....10'

DEPTH
• Swimming—In Class B and C pools, water depths at the shallow end of the swimming area shall be 3' minimum with 3'6" minimum for racing pools. Exceptions may be made in a recessed area of the main swimming pool, outside of the competitive and/or swimming course, when the pool is of an irregular shape with the permission of the state or local authority.
• Diving—Class B and C pools intended for diving shall conform to the minimum water depths, areas, slopes and other dimensions shown in Article 4.7 and shall be located in the diving area of the pool so as to provide the minimum dimensions as shown in Article 3.6.1. Competitive diving equipment shall not be installed in Class B and C pools.
There shall be a completely unobstructed clear vertical distance of 13' above any diving board, measured from the center of the front end of the board. This area shall extend horizontally at least 8' behind, 8' to each side and 16' ahead of point A. (See diagram.)
According to a spokesperson for the National Spa and Pool Institute (NSPI), this standard has been approved by the American National Standards Institute. American National Standards, once approved, may be revised at any time. Make sure that you have the latest edition of this standard by ordering the NSPI-1 Standard for Public Swimming Pools from the NSPI.

For more information contact:

National Spa and Pool Institute
2111 Eisenhower Ave.
Alexandria, VA 22314-4678
(703) 838-0083
Fax: (703) 549-0493
www.poolspaworld.com

FACILITY SPECIFICATION GUIDE

SWIMMING & DIVING

The following are NCAA standard pool dimensions. These are recommended dimensions for collegiate competition only, and specifications are subject to annual review and change.

POOL CROSS-SECTION

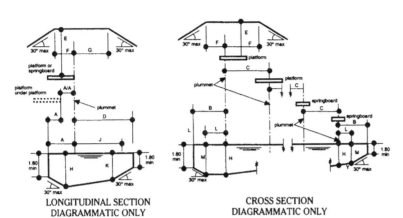

LONGITUDINAL SECTION
DIAGRAMMATIC ONLY

CROSS SECTION
DIAGRAMMATIC ONLY

DIVING CHART

NCAA Recommended Dimensions for Diving Facilities	Dimensions are in Feet	SPRINGBOARD		PLATFORM		
		1 Meter	3 meters	5 meters	7.5 Meters	10 Meters
Revised to March 3, 1991	LENGTH	16'	16'	20'	20'	20'
	WIDTH	1'8"	1'8"	5'	5'	6'7"
	HEIGHT	3'4"	10'	16'5"	24'8"	32'10"
		Horiz. Vert.	Horiz. Vert.	Horiz. Vert.	Horiz. Verth.	Horiz. Vert.
A From plummet BACK TO POOL WALL	Designation	A-1	A-3	A-5	A-7.5	A-10
	Minimum	5'	5'	4'2"	5'	5'
	Preferred	6'1"	6'1"	4'2"	5'	5'
A/A From plummet BACK TO PLATFORM plummet directly below	Designation			A/A5	A/A7.5	A/A10
	Minimum			2'6"	2'6"	2'6"
	Preferred			4'2"	4'2"	4'2"
B From plummet to POOL WALL AT SIDE	Designation	B-1	B-3	B-5	B-75	B-10
	Minimum	8'3"	11'6"	10'8"	14'	17'3"
	Preferred	8'3"	11'6"	12'4"	14'10"	17'3"
C From plummet to ADJACENT PLUMMET	Designation	C-11	C-331	C-531	C-7.5531	C-107.55531
	Minimum	6'7"	7'3"	7'5"	8'3"	9'1"
	Preferred	7'1"	8'3"	8'3"	8'3"	9'1"
D From plummet to POOL WALL AHEAD	Designation	D-1	D-3	D-5	D-7.5	D-10
	Minimum	29'7"	33'8"	33'8"	36'2"	44'4"
	Preferred	29'7"	33'8"	33'8"	36'2"	44'4"
E On plummet from BOARD TO CEILING	Designation	E-1	E-3	E-5	E-75	E-10
	Minimum	16'5"	16'5"	10'8"	10'8"	13'2"
	Preferred	16'5"	16'5"	11'6"	11'6"	16'5"
F CLEAR OVERHEAD behind and each side of plummet	Designation	F-1 E-1	F-3 E-3	F-5 E-5	F-7.5 E-7.5	F-10 E-10
	Minimum	8'3" 16'5"	8'3" 16'5"	9'1" 10'8"	9'1" 10'9"	9'1" 13'2"
	Preferred	8'3" 16'5"	8'3" 16'5"	9'1" 11'6"	9'1" 11'6"	9'1" 16'5"
G CLEAR OVERHEAD ahead of plummet	Designation	G-1 E-1	G-3 E-3	G-5 E-5	G-7.5 E-7.5	G-10 E-10
	Minimum	16'5" 16'5"	16'5" 16'5"	16'5" 10'8"	16'5" 10'8"	19'9" 13'2"
	Preferred	16'5" 16'5"	16'5" 16'5"	16'5" 11'6"	16'5" 11'6"	19'9" 16'5"
H DEPTH OF WATER at plummet (minimum required)	Designation	H-1	H-3	H-5	H-7.5	H-10
	Minimum	11'	12'	12'2"	13'6"	14'10"
	Preferred	11'6"	12'6"	12'6"	14'10"	16'5"
J-K DISTANCE AND DEPTH ahead of plummet	Designation	J-1 K-1	J-3 K-3	J-5 K-5	J-7.5 K-7.5	J-10 K-10
	Minimum	16'5" 10'10"	16'5" 11'10"	19'9" 11'10"	26'3" 13'2"	36'2" 14'
	Preferred	16'5" 11'2"	19'9" 12'2"	19'9" 12'2"	26'3" 14'6"	36'2" 15'7"
L-M DISTANCE AND DEPTH each side of plummet	Designation	L-1 M-1	L-3 M-3	L-5 M-5	L-7.5 M-7.5	L-10 M-10
	Minimum	5' 10'10"	6'7" 11'10"	19'11" 11'10"	12'4" 13'2"	14'10" 14'
	Preferred	9'11" 11'2"	8'3" 12'2"	11'6" 12'2"	14'10" 14'6"	17'3" 15'7"
N MAXIMUM SLOPE OF REDUCE DIMENSIONS beyond full requirements	Pool depth Ceiling Ht.	30 degrees 30 degrees	Note 1: Dimensions C (plummet to adjacent plummet) apply for Platforms with widths as detailed. For wider Platforms increase C by half the additional width(s). Note 2: All dimensions rounded up, even if only fractionally greater than the enxt lowest inch.			

Reprinted with permission of the NCAA.

LONG COURSE SWIMMING POOL

- Preferred—The racing course should be 164'1⅛" (50m, 2.54cm) in length by 75'1" (22.89m) in width, providing for eight 9' (2.74m) lanes with additional width outside lanes 1 and 8. A minimum water depth of 7' (2.13m) is desirable for competition. Optional markings: nine 8' (2.44m) lanes or ten 7' (2.13m) lanes.
- Acceptable—The racing course may be 164'1⅛" (50m, 2.54cm) in length by 60' (18.29m) in width, providing for eight 7' (2.13m) lanes with additional width outside lanes 1 and 8. The water depth may be no less than 4' (1.22m) at the starting end of the racing course and no less than 3'6" (1.07m) at the opposite end. However, a water depth of no less than 4' (1.22m) is recommended throughout the entire length of the racing course.

SHORT COURSE SWIMMING POOL

- Preferred—The racing course should be 75'1" (22.89m) in length by at least 60' (18.29m) in width, providing for not less than eight 7' (2.13m) lanes with additional width outside lanes 1 and 8. A minimum water depth of 7' (2.13m) is desirable for competition.
- Acceptable—The racing course may be 82'1¼" (25m, 2.54cm) in length by at least 45' (13.72m) in width, providing for six 7' (2.13m) lanes with additional width outside lanes 1 and 6. The water depth may be no less than 4' (1.22m) at the starting end of the racing course and no less than 3'6" (1.07m) at the opposite end. However, a water depth of no less than 4' (1.22m) is recommended throughout the entire length of the racing course.

DIVING POOL

- Preferred—The diving facility should be 60' (18.29m) in length by 75'1" (22.89m) in width. It should be equipped with two 1-meter and two 3-meter springboards and a diving tower, providing takeoff platforms at 5, 7.5 and 10 meters. Recommended dimensions for diving facilities are specified in the table on the left.
- Acceptable—The diving facility may be separated from or incorporated with the swimming pool. Recommended dimensions for diving facilities are specified in the table on the left.

Note: The above dimensions may be incorporated in "L," "T," "Z," and "U" shaped pools.

For more information contact:

National Collegiate Athletic Association
6201 College Blvd.
Overland Park, KS 66211-2422
(913) 339-1906
www.ncaa.org

FACILITY SPECIFICATION GUIDE

TEAM HANDBALL

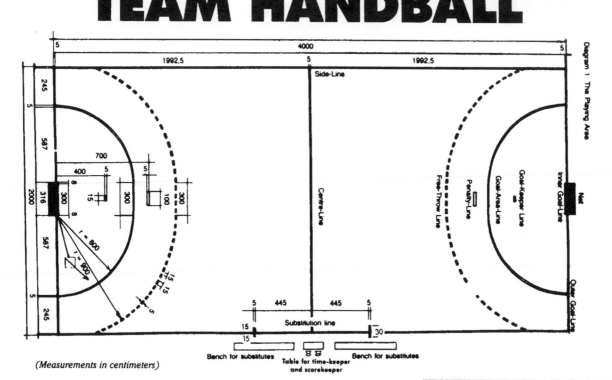

(Measurements in centimeters)

For more information contact:

United States Team Handball Federation
1903 Powers Ferry, Suite 230
Atlanta, GA 30339

FIELD HOCKEY

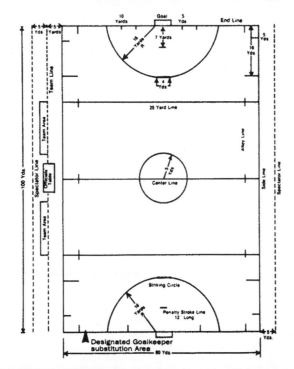

For more information contact:

National Federation of State High School Associations
P.O. Box 20626
Kansas City, MO 64195-0626
(816) 464-5400
Fax: (816) 464-5571
www.nfhs.org

FACILITY SPECIFICATION GUIDE

TENNIS

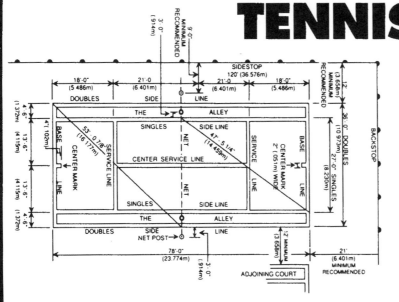

TRUE PLANE
SLOPE
REQUIREMENTS:
SIDE TO SIDE → *(preferred)*
END TO END
DIAGONAL

The recommended court slope should be:

Fast Dry:
Minimum 1" in 30' (0.28%) (preferred)
Maximum 1" in 24' (0.35%)

Hard Courts:
Minimum 1" in 10' (0.833%) (preferred)
Maximum 1" in 8.33' (1%)

○ MARKER FOR SINGLES STICKS OR SINGLES NET POSTS

LINE WIDTH 2" 5CM
4" 10 CM
NOTE BASE LINES CAN BE 4" WIDE

(Reprinted with permission of the USTC&TBA.)

Lines should not vary more the 1/4" (.64cm) from exact measurement.

For more information contact:

U.S. Tennis Court and
Track Builders Association
3525 Ellicott Mills Drive, Suite N
Ellicott City, MD 21043-4547
(410) 418-4875
www.ustctba.com

United States Tennis Association
70 W. Red Oak Lane
White Plains, NY 10604
914/696-7000
www.usta.com

BADMINTON

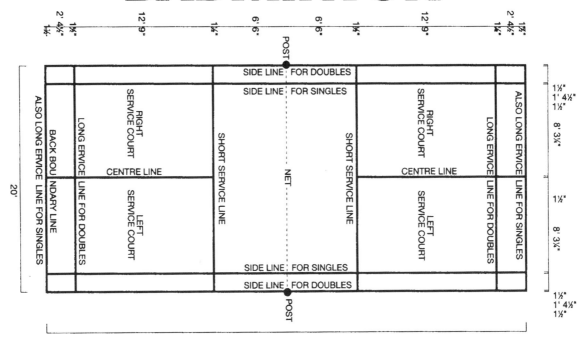

1½"
1' 4½"
1½"

8' 3½"

1½"

8' 3½"

1½"
1' 4½"
1½"

For more information contact:

USA Badminton
One Olympic Plaza
Colorado Springs, CO 80909
(719) 578-4808
Fax: (719) 578-4507
www.usabadminton.org

Note: Court can be used for both singles and doubles play.
Dimensions determined by the International Badminton Federation.

FACILITY SPECIFICATION GUIDE

SOCCER

LAW I. — THE FIELD OF PLAY
The Field of Play and appurtenances shall be as shown in the following plan:

Note: For players under 16 years of age, the size of the field of play, as well as the width between the goal posts and the height of the cross-bar may be modified.

OUTDOOR FIELD

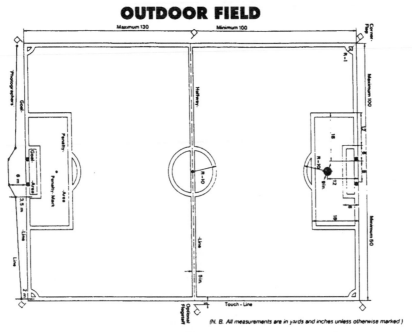

(N. B. All measurements are in yards and inches unless otherwise marked.)

Note: The length of the touch line must be greater than the length of the goal line.

INDOOR FIELD

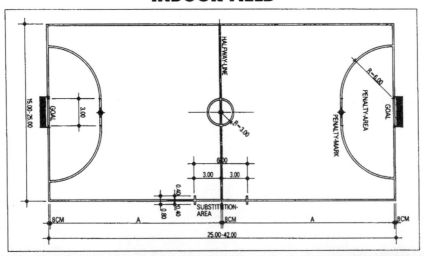

For more information contact:

United States Soccer Federation
1801-1811 S. Prairie Ave.
Chicago, IL 60616
(312) 808-1300
www.us-soccer.com

American Youth Soccer Organization
5403 W. 138th St.
Hawthorne, CA 90250
(800) USA-AYSO
Fax: (310) 643-5310
www.ayso.org

US Youth Soccer
899 Presidential Drive, Suite 117
Richardson, TX 75081
(800) 4-SOCCER

FACILITY SPECIFICATION GUIDE
SOFTBALL

OFFICIAL DIMENSIONS FOR SOFTBALL DIAMONDS

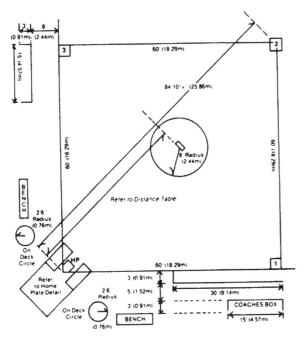

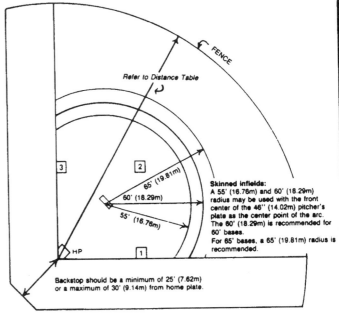

Skinned infields:
A 55' (16.76m) and 60' (18.29m) radius may be used with the front center of the 46'' (14.02m) pitcher's plate as the center point of the arc. The 60' (18.29m) is recommended for 60' bases. For 65' bases, a 65' (19.81m) radius is recommended.

Backstop should be a minimum of 25' (7.62m) or a maximum of 30' (9.14m) from home plate.

(Diagrams courtesy of the Amateur Softball Association of America.)

DISTANCE TABLE

ADULT

GAME	DIVISION	BASES	PITCHING	FENCES Minimum	FENCES Maximum
Fast Pitch	Women	60' (18.29 m)	40' (12.19 m)	200' (60.96 m)	250' (76.20 m)
	Men	60' (18.29 m)	46' (14.02 m)	225' (68.58 m)	250' (76.20 m)
	Jr. Men	60' (18.29 m)	46' (14.02 m)	225' (68.58 m)	250' (76.20 m)
Modified	Women	60' (18.29 m)	40' (12.19 m)	200' (60.96 m)	
	Men	60' (18.29 m)	46' (14.02 m)	265' (80.80 m)	
Slow Pitch	Women	65' (19.81 m)	50' (15.24 m)	265' (80.80 m)	275' (83.82 m)
	Men	65' (19.81 m)	50' (15.24 m)	275' (83.82 m)	315' (96.01 m)*
	Co-Ed	65' (19.81 m)	50' (15.24 m)	275' (83.82 m)	300' (91.44 m)
	Super	65' (19.81 m)	50' (15.24 m)	325' (99.06 m)	No Max
16 Inch Slow Pitch	Women	55' (16.76 m)	38' (11.58 m)	200' (60.96 m)	
	Men	55' (16.76 m)	38' (11.58 m)	250' (76.20 m)	
14 Inch Slow Pitch	Women	60' (18.29 m)	46' (14.02 m)		
	Men	60' (18.29 m)	46' (14.02 m)		

YOUTH

GAME	DIVISION	BASES	PITCHING	FENCES Minimum	FENCES Maximum
Slow Pitch	Girls 10-under	55' (16.76 m)	35' (10.67 m)	150' (45.72 m)	175' (53.34 m)
	Boys 10-under	55' (16.76 m)	35' (10.67 m)	150' (45.72 m)	175' (53.34 m)
	Girls 12-under	60' (18.29 m)	40' (12.19 m)	175' (53.34 m)	200' (60.96 m)
	Boys 12-under	60' (18.29 m)	40' (12.19 m)	175' (53.34 m)	200' (60.96 m)
	Girls 14-under	65' (19.81 m)	46' (14.02 m)	225' (68.58 m)	250' (76.20 m)
	Boys 14-under	65' (19.81 m)	46' (14.02 m)	250' (76.20 m)	275' (83.82 m)
	Girls 16-under	65' (19.81 m)	50' (15.24 m)	225' (68.58 m)	250' (76.02 m)
	Boys 16-under	65' (19.81 m)	50' (15.24 m)	275' (83.82 m)	300' (91.44 m)
	Girls 18-under	65' (19.81 m)	50' (15.24 m)	225' (68.58 m)	250' (76.02 m)
	Boys 18-under	65' (19.81 m)	50' (15.24 m)	275' (83.82 m)	300' (91.44 m)
Fast Pitch	Girls 10-under	55' (16.76 m)	35' (10.67 m)	150' (45.72 m)	175' (53.34 m)
	Boys 10-under	55' (16.76 m)	35' (10.67 m)	150' (45.72 m)	175' (53.34 m)
	Girls 12-under	60' (18.29 m)	35' (10.67 m)	175' (53.34 m)	200' (60.96 m)
	Boys 12-under	60' (18.29 m)	40' (12.19 m)	175' (53.34 m)	200' (60.96 m)
	Girls 14-under	60' (18.29 m)	40' (12.19 m)	175' (53.34 m)	200' (60.96 m)
	Boys 14-under	60' (18.29 m)	46' (14.02 m)	175' (53.34 m)	200' (60.96 m)
	Girls 16-under	60' (18.29 m)	40' (12.19 m)	200' (60.96 m)	225' (68.58 m)
	Boys 16-under	60' (18.29 m)	46' (14.02 m)	200' (60.96 m)	225' (68.58 m)
	Girls 18-under	60' (18.29 m)	40' (12.19 m)	200' (60.96 m)	225' (68.58 m)
	Boys 18-under	60' (18.29 m)	46' (14.02 m)	200' (60.96 m)	225' (68.58 m)

Note: The only difference between college and high school is the pitching distance.

high school	fast pitch male	...........46'
	slow pitch male	...........46'
	slow pitch female	..........46'
	fast pitch female	..........40'
college	....	.43'

For more information contact:

Amateur Softball Association of America
2801 N.E. 50th St.
Oklahoma City, OK 73111
(405) 424-5266
www.softball.org

FACILITY SPECIFICATION GUIDE
FOOTBALL

PROFESSIONAL

(Diagram courtesy of the NFL.)

COLLEGE

DIAGRAM OF FIELD

GOAL POST DETAIL

PYLON DETAIL

RECOMMENDED YARD-LINE NUMBERING

END ZONE DETAIL

(Diagrams courtesy of the NFHS.)

For more information contact:

National Football League
410 Park Ave.
New York, NY 10022
(212) 758-1500
www.nfl.com

National Collegiate Athletic Association
6201 College Blvd.
Overland Park, KS 66211-2422
(913) 339-1906
www.ncaa.org

FACILITY SPECIFICATION GUIDE

FOOTBALL

HIGH SCHOOL

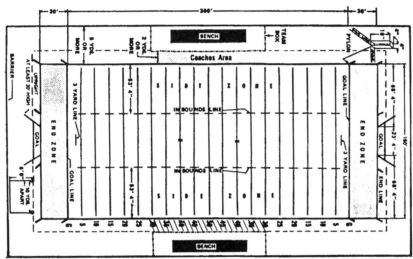

(Diagram courtesy of the NFHS.)

Note: Both team boxes may be on one side between the two 45- and 20-yard lines. End lines and sidelines should be at least 4 inches wide. Other field dimensions should be 4 inches wide.

Note: Recommend the area between team boxes and sidelines be solid white or marked with diagonal lines.

Note: Inbounds lines should be 24'' long and 4'' wide.

Note: Recommend the field slope from center to each sideline at 1/4-inch per foot.

Note: A 4-inch wide broken restraining line may be put around the entire field, 2 or more yards from boundaries.

For more information contact:

National Federation of State High School Associations
P.O. Box 20626
Kansas City, MO 64195-0626
(816) 464-5400
Fax: (816) 464-5571
www.nfhs.org

VOLLEYBALL

Note: NFHS rules require standards to be 3' (1m) outside the court.

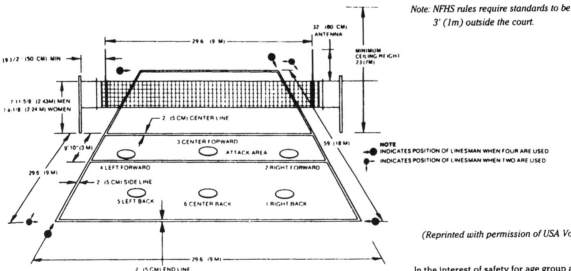

(Reprinted with permission of USA Volleyball.)

In the interest of safety for age group and scholastic competition, the height of the net shall be that specified for male competition. This height requirement shall not be modified.

The following net heights are currently in practice for the below indicated age groups and scholastic levels of competition:

AGE GROUPS	GIRLS	BOYS/COED
18 years and under	2.24m (7'4⅛")	2.43m (7'11⅝")
16 years and under	2.24m (7'4⅛")	2.43m (7'11⅝")
14 years and under	2.24m (7'4⅛") or 7'0"	2.24m (7'4⅛")
12 years and under	2.10m (7'0") or 6'6"	2.10m (7'0") or 6'6"

SCHOLASTIC LEVELS	GIRLS	BOYS/COED
Grades 1 thru 6 (Elementary School):	1.85m (6'1")	1.85m (6'1")
Grades 7 and 8 (Middle School):	2.24m (7'4⅛")	2.24m (7'4⅛")
Grades 9 thru 12 (Sr. High School):	2.24m (7'4⅛")	2.43m (7'11⅝")

For more information contact:

USA Volleyball
3595 E. Fountain Blvd.
Colorado Springs, CO 80910-1740
(719) 637-8300
www.volleyball.org

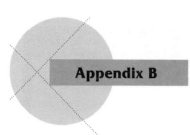

Planning Checklist for Outdoor Spaces

The following is an abbreviated list of items to be considered during the planning process:

Circulation

- Types: Vehicle (cars, trucks, buses, maintenance, etc.); pedestrians (handicapped, different teams); participants (different teams, players, coaches, officials, etc.); main entry; secondary entries; control and security points, etc.
- Roadway: Type of vehicles (trucks, cars, buses, etc); quantity of traffic (conduct survey); type of roadway system (single or two directional); roadway width (vehicle size and number of lanes); surface systems (materials); protection devices (bollards, guard rails, etc); etc.
- Parking: Type of vehicles (trucks, cars, buses, etc.); quantity of vehicles; sizes (length and width) of vehicles; drainage (surface or subsurface, water collection/detention areas); snow removal (storage areas); protection devices (bollards, guard rails, tire bumpers, etc.)
- Walkways: Type of use (pedestrian and/or vehicle); walkway widths; surface system (materials); elevation changes (walks, ramps, stairs and lifts); railings.

Activity Areas

- Landscaping: Type of surfaces (grass, etc.); type of plantings (ground cover, shrubs, plantings, etc.); etc.
- Game Standards: Applicable Association regulations for each sport; etc.
- Activity Configuration: Areas (separate or combined activity); orientation; flexibility; etc.
- Surfaces: Type (natural, synthetic, or combination); grading and drainage (surface and subsurface); etc.

Sports Areas

- Diamonds: Type of sport(s); type (game and/or practice); size; quantity; etc.
- Courts: Type of sport(s); type (game and/or practice); size; quantity; etc.
- Fields: Type of sport(s); type (game and/or practice); size; quantity; etc.
- Ranges: Type of sport(s); type (game and/or practice); size; quantity; etc.

Structures

- Tickets: Type (fixed or portable); surfaces for portable types (pads); utilities; quantity of units (location on site); etc.
- Security: Type (fixed or portable); surfaces for portable types (pads); utilities; quantity of units (location on site).
- Medical Treatment: Type (fixed portable); surfaces for portable types (pads); utilities; quantity of units (location on the site); etc.
- Storage: Type (fixed or portable); Surfaces for portable types (pads); utilities, quantity of units (location on site); type of storage (equipment and tools); etc.
- Communications: Type (fixed or portable); utilities (supplemental); quantity of units (location on site); type of systems; etc.
- Concessions: Type (fixed or portable-owner or vendor-supplied); surfaces for portable types (tent pads, trailer pads, etc.); utilities; quantity of units (location on the site); etc.
- Seating: Type (standing and/or seats); persons (spectators, teams, officials, etc); natural (beams, sloped areas, etc.); artificial (prefabricated bleachers, type of seat, guard rails, etc.); etc.

Signage

- Vehicle: Type (direction, information, safety, etc.); etc.
- Pedestrian: Type (direction, information, safety, etc.); etc.
- Activity: (by sport, area, etc.); etc.
- Scoreboard: activity (single or combined use); type (manual or electronic); size; etc.

Barriers

- Vehicle: Type (sound, visual, safety, etc.); natural (plantings, berms, depressed areas, etc.); artificial (walls, fending, railings, etc.);
- Person: Type (sound, visual, safety, etc.); natural (plantings, berms, depressed areas, etc.) artificial (walls, fencing, railings, etc.) etc.
- Security: Type (gates, juxtaposition, or open); etc.

Utilities

- Power: Site lighting (pedestrian and vehicle); activity lighting; structures (tickets, security, storage, communications, concessions, etc.); etc.
- Water: Irrigation; sanitary; drinking fountains (hot and cold), etc.
- Sanitary: Type of units (fixed or portable); etc.
- Storm Drainage: Type (surface and subsurface); etc.
- Communications: Scoreboards; team sidelines to observation booth; public address for game; telephones for public and private use; broadcasting for television and radio; portable communications for security personnel; emergency; etc.

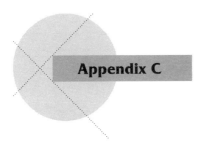

Surface Selection Process

A systematic approach must be followed to conduct a search to determine the appropriate surface. The following guidelines will assist in the decision-making process:

- **Definition:** Define the characteristics required to meet specified needs. These characteristics should be material, system, and activity-specific, such as, the effects of sunlight on synthetic materials, the internal filtration of water through the system, or the bounce of a ball on the surface, respectively. This task may seem research-intensive, but it usually isn't since many of these questions already have been addressed by the manufacturers in their literature.

- **Solicitation:** Don't allow a cost limitation to prevent review of all available systems. Request information from as many manufacturers as possible to obtain literature. The information contained in the literature will provide you with a broad knowledge of different systems, a basis to compare systems, and instill a curiosity to question system design. Project costs as well as material estimates should be obtained. References, list of installers, and locations of systems should be furnished with the literature.

- **Comparison:** Review and compare each system after receiving the manufacturers' literature. Categorize the information by type and desirable qualities, such as natural versus synthetic or resiliency, etc. A table of desirable attributes is most helpful in comparing the systems.

- **Visitation:** After the type of products has been narrowed to a few systems, the sports professional should plan to visit various sites to inspect the products, as well as discuss the performance and maintenance factors with the users.

- **Selection:** Select a system based on research to this point. Although this may be the system eventually purchased, other factors still have to be considered and may influence the final selection.

- **Quality:** Defining the quality of a system may become difficult since several systems may be very close in design. Quality refers to the materials as well as the installation of the system.

- **Manufacturers:** What type of reputation does the manufacturer have? Ask for references, but don't be surprised if they give the manufacturer and the installer high marks. Some manufacturers have provided products to clients at reduced rates in exchange for their marketing assistance. How many years has the manufacturer been in business? What type of technical support is available through the manufacturer and the local representative? Ask for information regarding the manufacturer's method of monitoring quality control in the plant as well as in the field.

- **Installer:** The installer should be recommended by the manufacturer to be assured that the installer is familiar with the products and installation. The installer should be asked questions similar to those asked of the manufacturer.

- **Maintenance:** Since maintenance can be a considerable portion of the operating budget, it is important to define the extent of the system. Questions, such as these will help with planning: What type of maintenance is required? What is the frequency of each type of maintenance?

- **Initial Cost:** What is the "total" initial cost of the system? Ask if two systems are considered the same, then why is one system more costly than the other? It may be that the quality of the materials or the system or both are the reason for the cost reduction. In some instances, the product name will increase the cost of the system, or hidden costs will be identified by the low bidder after the work has been awarded.

- **Life Cycle Cost (LCC):** This is a comparative analysis of each type of surface which considers the initial cost, the operation and maintenance cost, the operation and maintenance cost, and the replacement cost, if necessary, during an established time period. The figures generated from the analysis provide the anticipated total costs. Generally, the more expensive systems (initial cost) will be comparable to the less expensive systems when all factors are considered.

- **Bidding:** When the owner is required to conduct competitive bidding for products or services, attention should be directed to the written specifications, to insure that the products and methods of installations are clearly and accurately described. Too often the specifications make assumptions which permit systems of lesser quality to be considered as equals and therefore acceptable.

- **Installation/Installer:** Up until this point, the owner has had control over the selection process. However, this phase is where additional expertise will be required. It is in the owner's interest to require the manufacturer to perform periodic on-site supervision of the installer to insure compliance with the manufacturers' specifications.

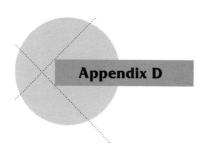

Indoor Activity Dimensions

Activity	Play Area in Feet	Safety Space in Feet*	Total Area in Feet	Minimum Ceiling Height
Archery 5 3 60	15e	5 3 75	12	
Badminton	20 3 44	6s, 8e	32 3 60	24
Basketball				
Jr. High instructional	42 3 74	6s, 8e		24
Jr. High interscholastic	50 3 84	6s, 8e		
Sr. High interscholastic	50 3 84	6s, 8e	62 3 100	
Sr. High instructional	45 3 74	6s, 8e	57 3 90	
Neighborhood E. Sch.	42 3 74	6s, 8e	54 3 90	
Community Junior H.S.	50 3 84	6s, 8e	62 3 100	
Community Senior H.S.	50 3 84	6s, 8e	62 3 100	
Competitive— College & University	50 3 94	6s, 8e	62 3 110	
Boccie	18 3 62	3s, 9e	24 3 80	
Fencing, competitive	6 3 46	9s, 6e	18 3 52	
instructional	4 3 30	4s, 6e	12 3 42	12
Handball	20 3 40			
Racquetball	20 3 40			20
Rifle (one pt.)	5 3 50	6 to 20 e	5 3 70 min.	20
Shuffleboard	6 3 52	6s, 2e	18 3 56	12
Squash	18.5 3 32			12
Tennis				
Deck (doubles)	18 3 40	4s, 5e	26 3 50	
Hand	16 3 40	41/2s, 10e	25 3 60	
Lawn (singles)	27 3 78	12s, 21e	51 3 120	
(doubles)	36 3 78	12s, 21e	60 3 120	
Paddle (singles)	16 3 44	6s, 8e	28 3 60	
(doubles)	20 3 44	6s, 8e	32 3 60	
Table (playing area)			9 3 31	
Volleyball				24
Competitive and adult	30 3 60	6s, 6e	42 3 72	
Junior High	30 3 50	6s, 6e	42 3 62	
Wrestling (competitive)	24 3 24	5s, 5e	36 3 36	

*Safety space at the side of an area is indicated by a number followed by "e" for end and "s" for side.

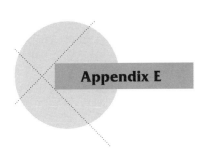

Indoor Activity Area Planning Checklist

Checklist for Planning and Designing Indoor Activity Areas

A checklist has been prepared to aid those responsible for planning facilities for athletics, physical education, health and recreation. The application of this checklist may prevent unfortunate and costly errors.

General

_____ 1. A clear-cut statement has been prepared on the nature and scope of the program, and the special require ments for space, equipment, fixtures, and facilities have been dictated by the activities to be conducted.

_____ 2. The facility has been planned to meet the total requirements of the program, as well as the special needs of those who are to be served.

_____ 3. The plans and specifications have been checked by all governmental agencies (city, county, and state) whose approval is required by law.

_____ 4. Plans for areas and facilities conform to state and local regulations and to accepted standards and practices.

_____ 5. The areas and facilities planned make possible the programs that serve the interests and needs of all the people.

_____ 6. Every available source of property or funds has been explored, evaluated, and utilized whenever appropriate.

_____ 7. All interested persons and organizations concerned with the facility have had an opportunity to share in its planning (professional educators, users, consultants, administrators, engineers, architects, program specialists, building managers, and builder)—a team approach.

_____ 8. The facility will fulfill the maximum demands of the program. The program has has not been curtailed to fit the facility.

_____ 9. The facility has been functionally planned to meet the present and anticipated needs of specific programs, situations, and publics.

_____ 10. Future additions are included in present plans to permit economy of construction.

_____ 11. All classrooms and offices are isolated from background noise.

_____ 12. Ample numbers and sized storage areas are built-in flush with walls at all teach stations.

_____ 13. No center mullions or thresholds are on storage room doorways.

_____ 14. All passageways are free of obstructions; fixtures are recessed.

_____ 15. Storage areas are well ventilated, dry, and cool.

_____ 16. Buildings, specific areas, and facilities are clearly identified.

_____ 17. Locker rooms are arranged for ease of supervision.

_____ 18. Offices, teaching stations, and service facilities are properly interrelated.

_____ 19. Special needs of the physically handicapped are met, including a ramp into the building at a major entrance.

_____ 20. All "dead space" is used.

_____ 21. The building is compatible in design and comparable in quality and accommodation to other campus structures.

_____ 22. Storage rooms are accessible to the play area.

_____ 23. Workrooms, conference rooms, and staff and administrative offices are inter-related.

_____ 24. Shower and dressing facilities are provided for professional staff members and are conveniently located.

_____ 25. Thought and attention has been given to making facilities and equipment as durable and vandal-proof as possible.

_____ 26. Low-cost maintenance features have been considered.

_____ 27. This facility is a part of a well-integrated Master Plan.

_____ 28. All areas, courts, facilities, equipment, climate control, security, etc., conform rigidly to detailed standards and specifications.

_____ 29. Shelves are recessed and mirrors and supplies are in appropriate places in restrooms and dressing rooms.

_____ 30. Dressing space between locker rows is adjusted to the size and age of students.

_____ 31. Drinking fountains are placed conveniently in locker room areas or immediately adjacent areas.

_____ 32. Special attention is given to provision for locking service windows and counter, supply bins, carts, shelves, and racks.

_____ 33. Provision is made for repair, maintenance, replacement, and off-season storage of equipment and uniforms.

_____ 34. A well-defined program for laundering and cleaning towels, uniforms, and equipment is included in the plan.

_____ 35. Noncorrosive metal is used in dressing, drying, and shower areas, except for enameled lockers.

_____ 36. Antipanic hardware is used where required by fire regulations.

_____ 37. Properly placed house bibbs and drains are sufficient in size and quantity to permit flushing the entire area with a water hose.

_____ 38. A water-resistant, covered base is used under the locker base and floor mat and where floor and wall join.

_____ 39. Chalkboards and/or tackboards with map tracks are located in appropriate places in dressing rooms, hallways, and classrooms.

_____ 40. Book shelves are provided in toilet area.

_____ 41. Space and equipment are planned in accordance with the types and number of enrollees.

_____ 42. Basement rooms undesirable for dressing, drying, and showering, are not planned for those purposes.

_____ 43. Spectator seating (permanent) in areas that are basically instructional is kept at a minimum. Rollaway bleachers are used primarily. Balcony seating is considered as a possibility.

_____ 44. Well-lighted and effectively displayed trophy cases enhance the interest and beauty of the lobby.

_____ 45. The space under the stairs is used for storage.

_____ 46. Department heads' offices are located near the central administrative office which includes a well-planned conference room.

_____ 47. Workrooms are located near the central office and serve as a repository for departmental materials and records.

_____ 48. Conference area includes a cloak room, lavatory, and toilet.

_____ 49. In addition to regular secretarial offices established in the central and department chairmen's offices, a special room to house a secretarial pool for staff members if provided.

_____ 50. Staff dressing facilities are provided. These facilities also may serve game officials.

_____ 51. The community and/or neighborhood has a "round table" for planning.

_____ 52. All those (persons and agencies) who should be a party to planning and development are invited and actively engaged in the planning process.

_____ 53. Space and area relationships are important. They have been considered carefully.

_____ 54. Both long-range and immediate plans have been made.

_____ 55. The body comfort of the child, a major factor in securing maxmum learning, has been considered in the plans.

_____ 56. Plans for quiet areas have been made.

_____ 57. In the planning, consideration has been given to the need for adequate recreational areas and facilities, both near and distant from the homes of people.

_____ 58. Consoles for security, information, and checkout have been ideally located.

_____ 59. Every effort has been exercised to eliminate hazards.

_____ 60. The installation of low-handing door closers, light fixtures, signs, and other objects in traffic areas has been avoided.

_____ 61. Warning signals—both visible and audible—are included in the plans.

_____ 62. Ramps have a slope equal to or greater than a one-foot rise in 12-feet.

_____ 63. Minimum landings for ramps are five-by-five feet, extend at least one foot beyond the swinging arc of a door, have at least a six-foot clearance at the bottom, and have level platforms at 30-foot intervals on every turn.

_____ 64. Adequate locker and dressing spaces are provided.

_____ 65. The design of dressing, drying, and shower areas reduces foot traffic to a minimum and establishes clean, dry aisles for bare feet.

_____ 66. Teaching stations are related properly to service facilities.

_____ 67. Toilet facilities are adequate in number. They are located to serve all groups for which provisions are made.

_____ 68. Mail services, outgoing and incoming, are included in the plans.

_____ 69. Hallways, ramps, doorways, and elevators are designed to permit equipment to be moved easily and quickly.

_____ 70. A keying design suited to administrative and instructional needs is planned.

_____ 71. Toilets used by large groups have circulating (in and out) entrances and exits.

_____ 72. All surfaces in racquetball, handball, and squash courts are flush.

_____ 73. At least one racquetball, handball, or squash court has a tempered glass back and side wall.

_____ 74. All vents in racquetball, handball, and squash courts are located in the back one-third of the ceiling.

_____ 75. Standard size doors are utilized on racquetball, handball, and squash courts.

_____ 76. All aspects of safety are planned carefully for the weight areas.

_____ 77. Racks are provided for all lose plates, dumbbells, and barbells in weight areas.

_____ 78. Special attention is paid to acoustical treatment in weight areas.

_____ 79. Ample walk areas for traffic flow are planned around lifting areas in weight rooms.

_____ 80. Concession areas are planned for and built flush with existing walls.

_____ 81. Adequate numbers of concession areas are planned.

_____ 82. Concession stand cash-handling methods have been planned carefully.

_____ 83. Storage and maintenance has been planned for concession areas.

_____ 84. Classrooms are planned by instructors, students, and maintenance staff.

_____ 85. Classrooms are planned for the numbers of users and the styles of teaching to be utilized in the room.

_____ 86. Careful attention has been paid to storage areas in classrooms.

_____ 87. Faculty offices should be private and secured.

_____ 88. Storage areas and windows are planned in faculty offices.

_____ 89. Laboratories need to be planned for both teaching and research utilization.

_____ 90. Ample space and subdivisions within laboratories are planned carefully.

Climate Control

_____ 1. Provisions made throughout the building for climate control—heating, ventilating, and refrigerated cooling.

_____ 2. Special ventilation is provided for locker, dressing, shower, drying, and toilet rooms.

_____ 3. Heating plans permit both area and individual room control.

_____ 4. Research areas where small animals are kept and where chemicals are used have been provided with special ventilating equipment.

_____ 5. The heating and ventilating of the wrestling gymnasium has been given special attention.

_____ 6. All air diffusers adequately diffuse the air.

_____ 7. Storage area ventilation is planned carefully.

_____ 8. Humidity and ventilation are balanced properly in racquetball, handball, and squash courts.

_____ 9. Thermostats are located out of the general users' reach and/or are secured.

_____ 10. The total energy concept has been investigated.

Electrical

_____ 1. Shielded, vapor-proof lights are used in moisture-prevalent areas.

_____ 2. Lights in strategic areas are key-controlled.

_____ 3. Lighting intensity conforms to approved standards.

_____ 4. Adequate numbers of electrical outlets are placed strategically.

_____ 5. Gymnasium and auditorium lights are controlled by dimmer units.

_____ 6. Locker room lights are mounted above the space between lockers.

_____ 7. Natural light is controlled properly for purposes of visual aids and to avoid glare.

_____ 8. Electrical outlet plates are installed three feet above the floor unless special use dictates other locations.

_____ 9. Controls for light switches and projection equipment are located suitably and are interrelated.

_____ 10. All lights are shielded. Special protection is provided in gymnasium, court areas, and shower rooms.

_____ 11. All lights must be easily accessible for maintenance.

_____ 12. The use of metal halide and high pressure sodium lighting has been investigated.

_____ 13. All areas have been wired for television cable and computer hookups.

_____ 14. Indirect lighting has been utilized wherever possible.

_____ 15. All teaching areas are equipped with a mounted camera, 25-foot color monitor, and tape deck securely built-in flush with the existing walls.

Walls

_____ 1. Movable and folding partitions are power-operated and controlled by keyed switches.

_____ 2. Wall plates are located where needed and are attached firmly.

_____ 3. Hooks and rings for nets are placed (and recessed in walls) according to court locations and net heights.

_____ 4. Materials that clean easily and are impervious to moisture are used where moisture is prevalent.

_____ 5. Shower heads are placed at different heights; four feet (elementary) to seven feet (university) for each school level.

_____ 6. Protective matting is placed permanently on the walls in the wrestling room, at the ends of basketball courts, and in other areas where such protection is needed.

_____ 7. Adequate numbers of drinking fountains are provided. They are properly placed (recessed in wall).

_____ 8. The lower eight feet of wall surface in activity areas is glazed and planned for ease of maintenance.

_____ 9. All corners in locker rooms are rounded.

_____ 10. At least two adjacent walls in dance and weight areas should have full-length mirrors.

_____ 11. Walls should be treated acoustically 15 feet and above.

_____ 12. Walls are reinforced structurally where equipment is to be mounted.

_____ 13. Flat wall space is planned for rebounding areas.

_____ 14. Walls should be flat with no juts or extruding columns.

_____ 15. Pastel colors are utilized on the walls.

_____ 16. Windows should be kept to a minimum in activity areas.

Ceilings

_____ 1. Overhead support apparatus is secured to beams that are engineered to withstand stress.

_____ 2. The ceiling height is adequate for the activities to be housed.

_____ 3. Acoustical materials impervious to moisture are used in moisture-prevalent areas.

_____ 4. Skylights are gymnasiums, being impractical, are seldom used because of problems in waterproofing roofs and of controlling sun rays.

_____ 5. All ceilings except those in storage areas are acoustically treated with sound absorbent materials.

_____ 6. Ceilings should be painted an off-white.

Floors

_____ 1. Floor plates are placed where needed and are flush-mounted.

_____ 2. Floor design and materials conform to recommended standards and specifications.

_____ 3. Lines and markings are painted in floors before sealing is completed (when synthetic tape is not used).

_____ 4. A cove base (around lockers and where all and floor meet) of the same water-resistant material that is used on floor is found in all dressing and shower rooms.

_____ 5. Abrasive, nonskid, slip-resistant flooring that is impervious to moisture is pro-vided on all areas where water is used (laundry, swimming pools, shower, dressing, and drying rooms).

_____ 6. Floor drains are located properly, and the slope of the floor is adequate for rapid drainage.

_____ 7. Hardwood floors are utilized in racquetball, handball, and squash courts.

_____ 8. Maintenance storage is located in areas with synthetic floors.

_____ 9. Floors should be treated accoustically when possible.

_____ 10. Hardwood floors should be utilized in dance areas.

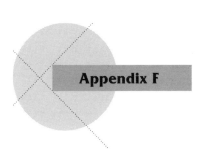

Metric Conversion Formulas

Converting from Metric to English:

	To Obtain	Multiply	By
	Inches	Centimeters	0.3937007874
	Feet	Meters	3.280839895
	Yards	Meters	1.093613298
	Miles	Kilometers	0.6213711922

Converting from English to Metric:

	To Obtain	Multiply	By
	Centimeters	Inches	2.54
	Meters	Feet	0.3048
	Meters	Yards	0.9144
	Kilometers	Miles	1.609344

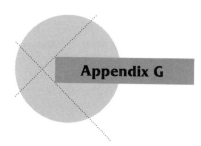

General Resources for Planning Facilities

Books and Guides

Council of Educational Facility Planners (CEFP), International. (1985). *Guide for planning educational facilities.* Columbus, OH: Council of Educational Facility Planners.

DeChiara, J., & Callendar, J. H. (1990). *Time-Saver standards for building types* (3rd ed.). New York: McGraw-Hill.

Gillis, John (Ed.). (1992). *National Federation court and field diagram guide.* Kansas City, MO: National Federation of State High School Associations.

Gonsoulin, Sid (Ed.). (1988). *Outstanding sports facilities.* Corvallis, OR: National Intramural-Recreational Sports Association.

National Collegiate Athletic Association Rules and Interpretations Guides, Overland Park KS:
- —Baseball
- —Basketball
- —Illustrated Basketball
- —Football
- —Ice Hockey
- —LaCrosse
- —Rifle
- —Skiing
- —Soccer
- —Swimming & Diving
- —Track & Field/Cross Country
- —Water Polo
- —Wrestling

Sol, Neil, & Foster, Carl. (Ed.). (1992). *The American College of Sport Medicine's Health/Fitness Facility Standards and Guidelines.* Champaign, IL: Human Kinetics Books.

Periodicals

Athletic Business. Published monthly by Athletic Business Publications, 1842 Hoffman Street, Suite 201, Madison, WI 53704, (608) 249-0186.

Athletic Management. Published bimonthly by College Athletic Administrator, Inc., 438 West State Street, Ithaca, NY 14850, (607) 272-0265.

Club Industry. Published monthly by Sportscape Inc., Framingham Corporate Center, 492 Old Connecticut Path, Third Floor, Framingham, MA 01701, (508) 872-2021.

Fitness Management. Published monthly by Leisure Publications, Inc., 3923 West 6th Street, Los Angeles, CA 90020, (213) 385-3926.

Journal of Physical Education, Recreation and Dance. Published monthly except in July by American Alliance for Health, Physical Education, Recreation and Dance, 1900 Association Drive, Reston, VA 22091, (703) 476-3400.

Parks and Recreation. Published monthly by National Recreation and Parks Association, 3101 Park Center Drive, Alexandria, VA 22302, (703) 820-4940.

The Physician and Sports Medicine. Published monthly by McGraw-Hill Co., 4530 W. 77th Street, Minneapolis, MN 55435, (612) 835-3222.

Recreation Resources. Published monthly by Lakewood Publications, 50 South Ninth Street, Minneapolis, MN 55402, (612) 333-0471.

Sports Medicine Digest. Published monthly by PM, Inc., P.O. Box 10172, Van Nuys, CA 91410, (818) 997-8011.

Tennis Industry. Published monthly by Sterling Southeast Inc., 3230 West Commercial Blvd., Fort Lauderdale, FL 33309, (305) 731-0000.

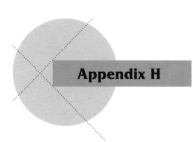

Associations Pertinent to Planning Recreation, Sport, and Physical Education Facilities

Aerobics & Fitness Association of America
15250 Ventura, Suite 310
Sherman Oaks, CA 91403, (818) 905-0040

American Alliance for Health, Physical Education, Recreation and Dance (AAHPERD)
1900 Association Drive
Reston, VA 22091, (703) 476-3400

American Amateur Racquetball Association
815 North Weber, Suite 101
Colorado Springs, CO 80903, (719) 635-5396

American Association of Cardiovascular and Pulmonary Rehabilitation
7611 Elmwood Avenue, Suite 201
Middleton, WI 53562, (608) 831-6989

American Athletic Trainers Association and Certification Board, Inc.
660 W. Duarte Road
Arcada, CA 91006, (818) 445-1978

American College of Sports Medicine
P.O. Box 1440
Indianapolis, IN 46206-1440, (317) 637-9200

American Council on Exercise
6190 Cornerstone Court East, Suite 202
San Diego, CA 92121

American Heart Association
7320 Greenville Avenue
Dallas, TX 75231, (214) 373-6300

American Massage Therapy Association
1130 West North Shore Drive
Chicago, IL 60626

Association for Fitness in Business
310 N. Alabama, Suite A100
Indianapolis, IN 46204, (317) 636-6621

Athletic Institute
200 Castlewood Drive
North Palm Beach, FL 33408, (408) 842-3600

Illuminating Engineering Society of North America
345 E. 47th Street
New York, NY 10017, (212) 705-7926

International Council for Health, Physical Education and Recreation (ICHPER)
1900 Association Drive
Reston, VA 22091, (703) 476-3400

International Dance Exercise Association (IDEA)
6190 Cornerstone Court East, Suite 204
San Diego, CA 92121, (800) 999-IDEA

International Racquet Sports Association
253 Summer Street
Boston, MA 02210, (800) 228-4772

Maple Flooring Manufacturers Association
60 Revere Drive, Suite 500
Northbrook, IL 60062, (708) 480-9138

National Archery Association
1750 East Boulder Street
Colorado Springs, CO 80909, (719) 578-4576

National Association of Concessionaires
35 East Wacker Drive, #1545
Chicago, IL, 60601, (312) 236-3858

National Collegiate Athletic Association
6501 College Blvd
Overland Park, KS 66211-2422, (913) 339-1906

National Employee Services and Recreation Association
2400 S. Downing Avenue
Westchester, IL 60154, (708) 562-8130

National Institute for Occupational Safety and Health
944 Chestnut Ridge Road
Morgantown, WV 26505

National Intramural-Recreation Sports Association
850 Southwest 15th Street
Corvallis, OR 97333-4145 (503) 737-2088

National Recreation & Park Association
3101 Park Center Drive
Alexandria, VA 22302 (703) 820-4940

National Rifle Association
1600 Rhode Island Avenue, N.W.
Washington, DC 20036 (202) 828-6000

National Strength & Conditioning Association
P.O. Box 81410
Lincoln, NE 68501 (402) 472-3000

National Swimming Pool Foundation
10803 Golfdale, Suite 300
San Antonio, TX 78216 (512) 525-1227

National Wellness Association
University of Wisconsin
Stevens Point, WI 54481

President's Council on Physical Fitness and Sports
450 5th Street, N.W., Suite 7103
Washington, D.C. 20001 (202) 272-3421.

Sporting Goods Manufacturers Association
200 Castlewood Drive
North Palm Beach, FL 33408 (407) 842-4100

United States Badminton Association
920 "O" Street, Fourth Floor
Lincoln, NE 68508 (402) 438-2473

United States Fencing Association
1750 East Boulder Street
Colorado Springs, CO 80909 (719) 632-5737

U.S. Golf Association
P.O. Box 708
Far Hills, NJ 07931 (201) 234-2300

U.S. Gymnastics Federation
Pan American Plaza, Suite 300
201 South Capitol Avenue
Indianapolis, IN 46225 (317) 237-5050

U.S. Handball Association
930 North Benton Avenue
Tucson, AZ 85711 (602) 795-0434

U.S. Squash Racquets Association
P.O. Box 1216
Bala-Cynwyd, PA 19004 (215) 667-4006

U.S. Tennis Court and Track Builders Association
720 Light Street
Baltimore, MD 21230 (301) 752-3500

U.S. Volleyball Association
3595 East Fountain, Suite 1-2
Colorado Springs, CO 80910-1740 (719) 637-8300

Wellness Council of America
7101 Newport Avenue
Omaha, NE 68152 (402) 572-3590

YMCA of the USA
726 Broadway, 5th Floor
New York, NY 10003 (212) 614-2827

YWCA of the USA
101 North Wacker Drive
Chicago, IL 60606 (312) 977-0031

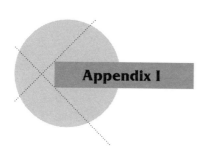

Associations Pertinent to Planning for Accessibility

**American Coalition of
Citizens with Disabilities**
1346 Connecticut Avenue,
NW, Room 814
Washington, DC 20036
(chapters in states)

American Council of the Blind
1211 Connecticut Avenue,
NW, Suite 506
Washington, DC 20036
(chapters in states)

Arthritis Foundation
1212 Avenue of the Americas
New York, NY 10036

**Association for the Aid of
Crippled Children**
345 East 46th Street
New York, NY 10017

Disabled American Veterans
3725 Alexandria Pike
Cold Spring, KY 41076
(state and local units)

**International Society for the
Rehabilitation of the Disabled**
219 East 44th Street
New York, NY 10017

**Muscular Dystrophy
Association of America**
1790 Broadway
New York, NY 10019

National Association of the Deaf
814 Thayer Avenue
Silver Spring, MD 20910
(local chapters)
**National Association of the
Physically Handicapped**
76 Elm Street
London, OH 43140
(local chapters)

**National Congress of Organizations of
the Physically Handicapped**
6106 North 30th Street
Arlington, VA 22207

**National Easter Seal Society for
Crippled Children and Adults**
2023 West Ogden Avenue
Chicago, IL 60612

**National Foundation for
Neuromuscular Diseases**
250 West 57th Street
New York, NY 10019

National Multiple Sclerosis Society
257 Park Avenue South
New York, NY 10010

National Paraplegia Foundation
333 North Michigan Avenue
Chicago, IL 60601
(state and local chapters)

Paralyzed Veterans of America
4330 East West Highway, Suite 300
Washington, DC 20014
(state and local chapters)

United Cerebral Palsy Association, Inc.
66 East 34th Street
New York, NY 10016

Track and Field Layouts

OVERALL DIAGRAM OF FIELD EVENTS

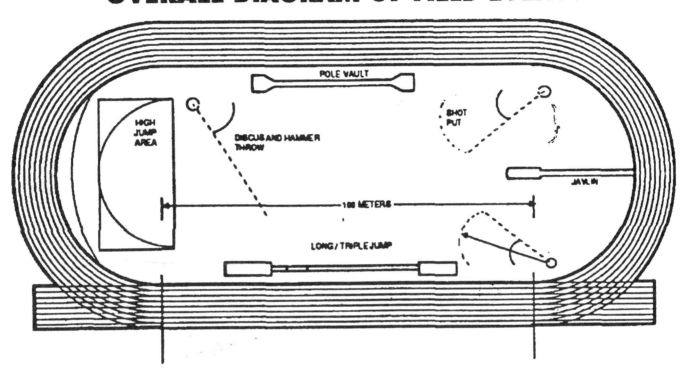

STANDARD 400M TRACK

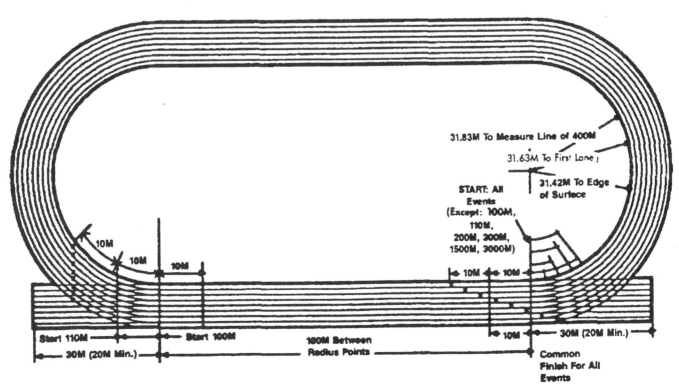

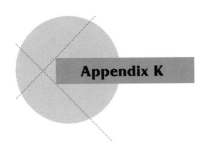

Retrofitting or Replacing Facilities

Renovation, Retrofitting, or Replacing

The practice of buying-using-discarding has become an unacceptable practice today. This not only applies to paper, aluminum cans, and glass, but to facilities as well (CEFP, 1985). Due to the high cost of new construction, upper level administration, whether it be in the private sector, at a university, municipal agency, or in a public school system, has the responsibility of making the wisest use of existing buildings. In meeting this obligation, it is necessary for administrators, with input from knowledgeable resource persons, to consider the feasibility of either renovating or retrofitting an existing building, or of constructing a new facility.

By definition, the renovation of an existing facility is the rehabilitation of the physical features of that building, including the rearrangement of spaces within the structure. Retrofitting, on the other hand, is the addition of new systems, items, features, materials, and/or equipment to a facility which were not installed at the time the building was constructed. These changes may be minor, or they could be significant to the point of changing the primary function of the facility.

To accurately ascertain whether renovation, retrofitting, or new construction is the most prudent alternative, administrators have a myriad of factors to consider. One of the more important is the effect that the construction process has relative to ongoing programs. Consideration must be given to program modifications and adaptions that may occur during the construction process. A close scrutiny of the advantages and disadvantages of both the present and the possibility of a new building should be undertaken. The following is an adequate representation of the factors to consider:

Cost Considerations
- What is the cost of new construction to provide comparable space?
- What is the cost of construction needed to bring the existing facility up to compliance with safety codes/accessibility?
- Does the cost of renovation or retrofitting exceed 50 percent of the cost of new construction?
- Will the increased cost of maintaining an older building justify renovation instead of constructing a new facility?
- Could the existing facility be sold or leased to a private entity to help defray the cost of new construction?
- If the amount of construction time becomes critical, which method, renovation or new construction, could be completed in the least amount of time?

Site Considerations
- Is a site available, and how effectively does the site meet the agency's immediate and long-range goals?
- Is the location of the present structure easily accessible?
- Is the parking adequate at the present site?
- How efficient is the sewer and storm water control?
- How is the soil-bearing performance of the present site?
- What is the general condition of the grounds?
- Is there sufficient area for all program activities?
- Are vehicular drives well located for safe ingress and egress?
- Are the existing utilities on or near the site adequate to provide the needed services?

Architectural and Structural Considerations

A certified architect and engineer should be sought to determine the following structural factors:
- Is the present facility aesthetically appealing and structurally sound?
- Does the existing facility meet current and long-range program goals and, if not, would renovation or retrofitting realistically elevate the facility to acceptable standards?
- What is the availability of utilities?
- How energy efficient is the present facility? Does it meet all updated energy codes?
- Are there signs of deterioration of footings, foundations, or piers?
- Are structural members adequate and in serviceable conditions?
- Is the exterior masonry sound? Are there structural cracks, water damage, or defective mortar?
- What is the condition of the roof and roofing surfaces, roof drains, and skylights?

- What is the condition of flashing, gutters, and downspouts?
- What are the conditions of doors and windows?
- What are the conditions of door hardware and panic devices?
- What are the locations, numbers, types, and condition of plumbing fixtures?
- What is the condition and capacity of the present water supply, sewage lines, and drainage systems?
- Is the present HVAC System adequate and energy efficient? Does it meet updated codes?
- What is the condition and adequacy of lighting and power distribution systems?
- Do the existing light fixtures provide adequate illumination in all areas?
- Are stairways, circulation patterns, and exits safe and adequate in number?
- What is the present condition of fire alarms and inter-communication systems?

Educational Considerations

- Is the building now meeting the agency's program?
- What is the current inventory of rooms and their sizes?
- Are laboratories adequately served by all required utilities?
- Is the library adequate to house the required book collection and to provide media and related services?
- Are food service facilities adequate to meet present and projected needs?
- Are physical education, recreation, and athletic areas usable or capable of being retrofitted if required?

Community Considerations

- Will the renovation of the building be consistent with present zoning requirements and policies?
- What are the plans for the area served by the program as projected by city or area planning agencies?
- Is the building on or eligible for placement on the National Register of Historic Places?
- Will a new facility constitute a political problem with businesses in the private sector?

Before deciding on the wisdom of renovation, retrofitting, remodeling, or replacing, factors concerning the existing and proposed facilities should be evaluated in detail, both individually and collectively. It also would be beneficial for administrators to project a reasonable life expectancy of the facility, taking into account factors such as:

—increased or decreased populations served by the programs within the facility,

—growth and development of areas surrounding the facility, and

—the potential reorganization, community re-zoning, or consolidation of schools in the district.

A decision on whether renovation or retrofitting is advantageous over new construction then should be rendered, based on a composite of all the factors. (Figure 1)

Figure 1
Facility Evaluation (Permission to print by the
Council of Educational Facility Planners, International)

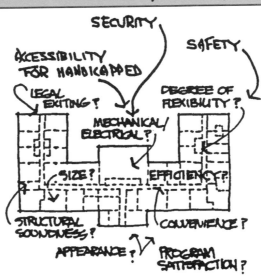

FACILITY EVALUATION

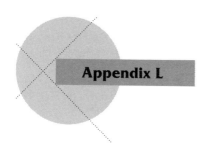

Sample ASHRAE Standard

ANSI/ASHRAE/IESNA 90.1-1989—Published standard
Addenda 90.1b-1992, 90.1c-1993, 90.1d-1992, 90.1e-1992, 90.1f-1995, 90.1g-1993, 90.1l-1993, 90.1m-1995 to ASHRAE/IESNA 90.1-1989 (Addendum 90.1n-1997 approved for publication by ASHRAE BOD 97/07/03 [Publication pending])

Energy Efficient Design of New Buildings Except Low-Rise Residential Buildings

1 PURPOSE

1.1   The purposes of this standard are to: new buildings so that they may be constructed, operated, and maintained in a manner that minimizes the use of energy without constraining the building function nor the comfort or productivity of the occupants;

(a) provide criteria for energy efficient design and methods for determining compliance with these criteria; and

(b) provide sound guidance for energy-efficient design.

1.2   This standard shall not be used to circumvent any safety, health, or environmental requirements.

2 SCOPE

2.1   This standard sets forth design requirements for the efficient use of energy in new buildings intended for human occupancy. The requirements apply to the building envelope, distribution of energy, systems and equipment for auxiliaries, heating, ventilating, air conditioning, service water heating, lighting, and energy managing.

ASHRAE Standard

2.2   This standard applies to all new buildings or portions of buildings that provide facilities or shelter for human occupancy and use energy primarily to provide human comfort, except single- and multi-family residential buildings of three or fewer stories above grade.

2.3   This standard does not apply to:

(a) areas of buildings intended primarily for manufacturing or commercial or industrial processing:

(b) buildings or separately enclosed identifiable areas having an combination of dedicated space heating, service water heating, ventilating, air-conditioning, or lighting systems whose combined peak design rate of energy usage for these purposes is less than 3.5 Btu/(h · ft2) of gross floor area; or

(c) buildings of fewer than 100 ft2 of gross floor area.

2.4   Where specifically noted in this standard, certain other buildings or elements of buildings may be exempt.

Standing Standard Project Committee 90.1 (Project Committee originally authorized 83/01/23 and changed to standing committee 83/09/16) (TPS revised 97/07/02)

Maintenance and revision of ASHRAE/IESNA 90.1 with revised TPS.

Energy Standard for Buildings Except Low-Rise Residential Buildings

1 PURPOSE. The purpose of this standard is to provide minimum requirements for the energy-efficient design of buildings except low-rise residential buildings.

2 SCOPE.

2.1   This standard provides:

ASHRAE Standard

(a) minimum energy-efficient requirements for the design and construction of:

1. new buildings and their systems,

2. new portions of buildings and their systems, and

3. new systems and equipment in existing buildings.

(b) criteria for determining compliance with these requirements.

2.2   The provisions of this standard apply to:

(a) the envelope of buildings provided that the enclosed spaces are:

1. heated by a heating system whose output capacity is greater than or equal to 3.4 Btu/h · ft2 (10 W/m2), or

2. cooled by a cooling system whose sensible output capacity is greater than or equal to 5 Btu/h · ft2 (15 W/m2);

(b) the following systems and equipment used in conjunction with buildings

1. heating, ventilating, and air-conditioning,

2. service water heating,

3. electric power distribution and metering provisions,

   4. electric motors and belt drives, and

   5. lighting.

2.3 The provisions of this standard do not apply to:

  (a) single-family houses, multi-family structures of three stories or fewer above grade, manufactured houses (mobile and modular homes),

  (b) buildings that do not use either electricity or fossil fuel, or ASHRAE Standard

  (c) equipment and portions of building systems that use energy primarily to provide for industrial, manufacturing or commercial processes.

2.4 Where specifically noted in this standard, certain other buildings or elements of buildings shall be exempt.

2.5 This standard shall not be used to circumvent any safety, health or environmental requirements.

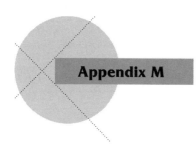

Leadership in Facilities and Equipment since 1920

The following professionals have been the council since 1920:

Leaders in Facilities, Equipment, and Supplies

1920-23	George L. Meylan
1924-27	Harry A. Scott
1927-28	A.R. Winters
1928-45	Prettyman
1928-45	Caswell M. Miles

Chairpersons of the Council on Equipment and Supplies [CES]

1954-56	Thomas E. McDonough
1956-59	Charles Heilman
1959-60	D.K. Stanley
1960-61	Robert Weber
1961-62	James C. Loveless
1962-63	John A. Friedrich
1963-64	William Theunissen
1964-65	John Fox
1965-66	Maurice A. Clay
1966-67	Wayne Brumbach
1967-68	Richard B. Westkaemper
1968-69	Joseph M. Pease
1969-70	John Nettleton
1970-71	James Delamater
1971-72	Alexander Petersen
1972-73	O.N. Hunter
1973-74	Ghary M. Akers
1974-75	Richard B. Flynn

Chairpersons of the Council on Facilities, Equipment, and Supplies (CFES)

1975-76	James E. Sharman
1976-77	Edward Coates
1977-78	James Mason
1978-79	Marty McIntyre
1979-80	Margaret Waters
1980-81	Mike Collins
1981-82	Robert L. Case
1982-83	Edward T Turner
1983-84	Ernest A. White
1984-85	Dan Gruetter
1985-86	Jack Lynn Shannon
1986-87	Larry Horine
1987-88	Armond Seidler
1988-89	Harvey White
1989-90	David Stotlar
1990-91	Maureen Henry
1991-92	Todd Seidler

Chairpersons of the Council on Facilities and Equipment [CFE]

1992-93	Brad Strand
1993-94	Marcia Walker
1994-95	Richard J. LaRue
1995-97	Thomas H. Sawyer
1997-99	Robert Femat
1999-2001	Bernie Goldfine
2001-2003	Michael G. Hypes

The CFES or CFE Award Winners
Honor Award

1979	Richard B. Flynn
1980	Edward Coates
1981	Edward Shea
1982	Martin McIntyre
1983	Margaret H. Aitken
1994	Armond Seidler
1995	James Mason
1996	Harvey White
1997	Todd Seidler & Marcia Walker
1998	Edward Turner
1999	Thomas H. Sawyer
2000	Hervy LaVoie

Professional Recognition Award

1994	Edward Turner
1995	Larry Horine
1996	Alexander Gabrielsen
1997	Arthur Mittelstaedt
1998	Alison Osinski
1999	Dave Stotlar
2000	Rick LaRue
2001	Todd Seidler

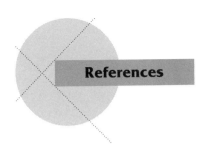

References

Ackerman, R. K. (1997). Television cable provides wireless communications. *Signal, 51*(8), 21-23.

Adaptive Environments. (1995). *Checklist for readily achievable barrier removal.* [On-line]. Available: http://www.usdoj.gov/crt/ada/checkweb.htm

Adventure Unlimited, Inc. [On-line]. Available: http://www.adventureropes.com

Agron, J. (2001, April). Dwindling support. *American School & University: Facilities, Purchasing and Business Administration, 24,* 26-28, 30, 32.

Agron, J. (2001, April). Rising to the challenge. *American School & University: Facilities, Purchasing and Business Administration,* 50b, 50d, 50f, 50h.

Ahrweiler, M. (2001, January/February). Extremely mainstream. *Recreation Management,* 12-17.

AJJF Kata Contest Rules. [On-line]. Available: http://www.ajjf.org.rules.html

Alpine Towers International. [On-line]. Available: http://www.alpinetowers.com

American National Standards Institute. [On-line]. Available: http://www.ansi.org

American Institute of Architects. (1990). *Selecting the building team.* Washington, D.C.: Author.

American Institute of Architects. (1992). *Guidelines for construction documents and the bidding process.* Washington, D.C.: Author.

American Society for Testing and Materials. (1993). *Standard consumer safety performance specification for playground equipment for public use.* (F 1487). West Conshohocken, PA: Author.

American Society for Testing and Materials. (1995). *Standard consumer safety performance specification for playground equipment for public use.* (F 1487). West Conshohocken, PA: Author.

American Society for Testing and Materials. (1991). *Standard specification for impact attenuation of surface systems under and around playground equipment.* (F 1292). West Conshohocken, PA: Author.

American Society for Testing and Materials. (1993). *Standard specification for impact attenuation of surface systems under and around playground equipment.* (F 1292). West Conshohocken, PA: Author.

American Society for Testing and Materials. (1995). *Standard specification for impact attenuation of surface systems under and around playground equipment.* (F 1292). West Conshohocken, PA: Author.

American Society for Testing and Materials. (1996). *Standard specification for impact attenuation of surface systems under and around playground equipment.* (F 1292). West Conshohocken, PA: Author.

American Society for Testing and Materials. (2000). *Standard consumer specification for playground equipment for public use.* (F 1487). West Conshohocken, PA: Author.

American Society for Testing and Materials. (2000). *Standard guide for fences and barriers for public, commercial, and multi-family residential use outdoor play areas.* (F 2049). West Conshohocken, PA: Author.

Americans with Disabilities Act. (1990). United States Access Board, Washington D.C.

Anonymous (1998). Making indoor air quality work for you. *P.M. Public Management, 80*(8), A10.

An overview of mechanical engineering at Berkeley. (1998). [On-line]. Available: http://www.me.berkeley.edu/overview.html

Appenzeller, H. (1998). *Risk management in sport: Issues and strategies.* Durham, NC: Carolina Academic Press.

Appenzeller, H. (1993). *Equipment and facilities: Managing sports and risk management strategies.* Durham, NC: Carolina Academic Press.

Armitage-Johnson, S. L. (1994). Equipment maintenance. In T. R. Baechle (Ed.), *Essentials of strength training and conditioning.* Champaign, IL: Human Kinetics.

Arnheim, D. D., & Prentice, W. E. (1997). *Principles of athletic training* (Ninth ed.). Boston: WCB/McGraw Hill.

ASHRAE. (1994). *1994 handbook-refrigeration, systems and applications.* Atlanta: American Society of Heating, Refrigerating, and Air Conditioning Engineers, Inc.

ASHRAE. (1989). *Ventilation for acceptable indoor air quality.* ANSI/ ASHRAE Standards 62-1989.

ASLA (1998). Landscape Architecture. [On-line]. Available: http://www.asla.org/asla

Association for Challenge Course Technology (ACCT). *Standards Manual* [On-line]. Available: http://www.acctinfo.org

Athletic Business Journal. [On-line]. Available: http://www.athleticbusiness.com/

Author. (1990). *Americans with Disabilities Act, Public Law 336 of the 101st Congress.* Washington, D.C.: United States of America. [On-line]. Available: http://www.usdoj.gov/crt/ada/pubs/ada.txt

Author. (1992). *The Americans with Disabilities Act: Your personal guide to the law.* Washington, D.C.: Paralyzed Veterans of American.

Author. (1992, September). Protecting our clean water. *Energy Ideas,*1(3), 2-11.

Author. (1992, October). Sealing the envelope. *Energy Ideas,*1(4), 1-6.

Author. (1992, November). Blowing hot air. *Energy Ideas,* 1(5), 1-7.

Author. (1992, December). Air conditioning and the earth's sunscreen. *Energy Ideas,* 1(6), 2- 5.

Author.(1993, February). It's a small world after all. *Energy Ideas*, 1(8), 6-8.

Author. (1993, March). Sports vs. efficiency (OT). *Energy Ideas*, 1(9), 8-9.

Author. (1993). *The Americans with Disabilities Act Title III Technical Assistance Manual*. Washington, D.C.: United States Department of Justice, Civil Rights Division, Public Access Section. [On-line]. Available: http://www.usdoj.gov/crt/ada/taman3.html Yearly Supplements [On-line]. Available: http://www.usdoj.gov/crt/ada/taman3up.html

Author. (1995). *ADA handbook: Statutes, regulations and related materials*. Cincinnati, OH: Anderson Publishing.

Author. (1998). Las Vegas hotel & casino parking. *Parking Today*, 3(4), 28-31.

Author. (2000, August). Sports facilities of the year. *Recreational Sports & Fitness* 2(5).

Baechle, T. R. (Ed.). (1994). *Essentials of strength training and conditioning*. Champaign, IL: Human Kinetics.

Baker, J. [On-line]. Available: http://ourworld,compuserve.com/homepage/james_baker/html

Bardeen, J., Renner, M. P., Ediger, R., Lemons, B., Parks, S., Petrucelli, J., & Rauch, T. W. (1992, November). Precision tracks. *Athletic Business*, 16(11), 49-56.

Barkely, J. T. (1997). Surfacing. *A Fitness, Recreational Facility and Parks and Recreation Web Magazine*. [On-line]. Available: http://www.sanfordgroup.com/ editoriall...library/fitness_ facilitysurfacing.html

Bast, J. L. (1998, February 23). *Sports stadium madness: Still ripping off taxpayers*. [On-line]. Available: http://www.heartland.org/studies/sports/madness-ps.htm

Batchelder, J. (1997, March/April). Creating an ADA facility master plan. *Facility Management Journal*.

Bauer, R. L. (1986). *Facilities planning*. New York: American Management Association.

Bedini, L. A. (1995, March-April). Campers with disabilities: Encouraging positive interaction. *Camping Magazine*, 21-21.

Berg, R. (1994). Unsafe. *Athletic Business*, 18(4), 43-46.

Bevan, R. (1956). *The athletic trainer's handbook*. Englewood Cliffs, NJ: Prentice-Hall, Inc.

Bishop, W. (1997). Athletic Flooring. *Cornerstones: A Fitness Recreational Facility and Parks and Recreation Web Magazine* [On-line]. Available: http://www.sandford group.com/editoriall...thletics_library/athletic_flooring.html

Blades, R. W. (1992). *Modernizing and retrofitting ice skating rinks*. Atlanta, GA: American Society of Heating, Refrigerating & Air-Conditioning Engineers, Inc.

Body, D., & Johnston, R. (199#). *Design and Construction Overview*. Athletic Business Conference Workshop.

Bower, M. (1980). *Foil fencing* (4th ed.). Dubuque, IA: William C. Brown.

Bowers, L. (1988). Playground design: A scientific approach. In L.D. Bruya (Ed.), *Play spaces for children: A new beginning* (pp. 22-48). Reston, VA: AAHPERD.

Brady, E., & Howlett, D. (1996, September 6). Economics, fan ask if benefits of building park outweigh costs. *USA Today*, C13-C14.

Brickman, H. (1997, November). Helping hardwood perform. *Athletic Business*, 67-70, 72.

Brown, B. J. (1972). *Complete guide to the prevention and treatment of athletic injuries*. West Nyack, NY: Parker Publishing Company.

Bruya, L., & Wood, G. (1997). Why provide supervision on the playgrounds. In S. Hudson, & D. Thompson (Eds.), *Playground safety handbook* (pp. 38-48). Cedar Falls, IA: National Program for Playground Safety.

Canadian Electrical Associates. (1992). *Potential electricity savings in ice arenas and curling rinks through improved refrigeration plant*. CEA No. 9129 U 858, Marbek Resource Consul Book.

Carpenter, L. J. (2000). *Legal concepts in sport: A primer* (2nd ed.). Champaign, IL: Sagamore Publishing, Inc.

Chernushenko, D. (1994). *Saving money by saving energy, facilities operation: Going further with less, greening our games*, (pp. 13, 173-185). Ottawa, Canada: Centurion Publishing.

Cimco, L. (1994). *Things you should know about ice rink construction and operation*. [Brochure]. Toronto, Ontario: Cimco Refrigeration.

Clement, A. (1988). *Law in sport and physical activity*. Indianapolis, IN: Benchmark Press.

Climbing Gym Association. [On-line]. Available: http://www.orca.org

Climbing Magazine. [On-line]. Available: http://www.climbing.comwww.climbing.com

Climbing Sports Group. [On-line]. Available: http://www.orca.org

Climbing Wall Industry Group. [On-line]. Available: http://www. www.orca.org

Cocco, A. F., & Zimmerman, J. C. (1996, March). Guide to conducting a compliance review of the Americans with Disabilities Act. *The CPA Journal*, 44 +.

Cohen, A. (2000 December). House of Cards. *Athletic Business*, 12, 121-130.

Cohen, A. (2000). You just don't understand. *Athletic Business*, 24(8), 83-87.

Colette Urquhart, S. (1989). *Mock rock, the guide to indoor climbing*. New Orleans, LA: Paper Chase Press.

Competition Rules for International Orienteering Federation (IOF) Events. [On-line]. Available: http://www.orienteering.org/Publications/Int Rules.html

Council of Educational Facility Planners (CEFP), International. (1991). *Guide for planning educational facilities*. Columbus, OH: Author

Council on Physical Education for Children (COPEC). (2001). *Guidelines for facilities, equipment, and instructional materials in elementary physical education*. Reston, VA: National Association for Sport and Physical Education.

Dahlgren, S. (2000, December). 20th annual facilities of merit. *Athletic Business* 24(12) 42-59.

Dahlgren, S. (2000, November). Making the Grade. *Athletic Business*, 77-78, 80- 82.

Dahlgren, S. (2000, September). Leading the way. *Athletic Business*, 73-81.

Dahnke, H., Jones, D., Mason, T, & Romney, L. (1971). *Higher education planning and management manuals.* Boulder, CO: Western Interstate Commission for Higher Education and American Association of Collegiate Registrars and Admissions Officers.

de Booji, M., & al-Harbi, K. (1993, October). Managing maintenance operations by computer. A professional seminar paper on Total Maintenance System Engineering conducted by Future Engineering, Riyadh, Sau. Ar.

Di Pilla, S. (2001, April). Minimizing slip & fall. *Facilities Design and Management,* 48.

Docherty, D. (1996). *Measurement in pediatric exercise science.* Champaign, IL: Human Kinetics, Inc.

DOE. (1980). *Energy conservation in ice skating rinks.* Prepared by B. K. Dietrich & T. J. McAvoy. U.S. Department of Energy.

Dresner, S. (1998). Just pick up your computer and dial. *Communication News,* 35(2), 42-43.

Driscoll, T. I. (2000, October). Cushion Extends Life. In J. Goodman, *Facilities Design and Management,* (pp. 54, 56).

Eldorado Wall Company. [On-line]. Available: http://www.eldowalls.com

Entre Prise. [On-line]. Available: http://www.ep-usa.com

Evenden, E. S., Strayer, G. D., & Englehardt, N. I. (1938). *Standards for college buildings.* New York: Teachers College, Columbia University

Fabel, B. K. (1996). Airing out the facts on HVAC energy recovery. *Consulting- Specifying Engineer,* 20(3), 36.

Fenton, B. C. (1997). Super sound. *Popular Mechanics,* 174(5), 44-46.

Fleming, J., Honour, H., & Peusner, N. (1999). *The Penguin dictionary of architecture and landscape architecture.* New York: Penguin Books.

Flynn, R. B. (Ed.). (1985). *Planning facilities for athletics, physical education and recreation* (seventh ed.). Reston, VA: American Alliance for Health, Physical Education, Recreation and Dance.

Flynn, R. B. (Ed.). (1985). *Planning facilities for athletics, physical education, and recreation.* Reston, VA: The Athletic Institute and American Alliance for Health, Physical Education, Recreation, and Dance.

Flynn, R. B. (1993). *Facility planning for physical education, recreation, and athletics.* Reston, VA: The Facilities Council of the Association for Research, Administration, Professional Councils and Societies.

Flynn, R. B. (Ed.). (1993). *Facility planning for physical education, recreation, and athletics.* Reston, VA: American Alliance for Health, Physical Education, Recreation, and Dance.

Flynn, R. B. (Ed.). (1993). *Planning facilities for athletics, physical education, and recreation.* Reston, VA: Athletic Institute and American Alliance for Health, Physical Education, Recreation and Dance.

Flynn, R. B. (Ed.). (1993). *Planning facilities for athletics, physical education and recreation* (eighth ed.). Reston, VA: American Alliance for Health, Physical Education, Recreation and Dance.

Flynn, R. B. (Ed.). (1994). *Planning facilities for athletics, physical education and recreation.* Reston, VA: The Athletic Institute and American Alliance for Health, Physical Education, Recreation and Dance.

Flynn, B., & Schneider, R. (1997). Energy audit. *Athletic Business,* 21(8), 51-52.

Fogg, G. E. (1986). *A site design process.* Chicago: National Recreation and Park Association.

Franke, A. H. (1994, September-October). The academic accommodation of disabled students. *Academe,* 96.

Fischler, S. (1991). *Great book of hockey: More than 100 years of fire on ice.* Lincolnwood, IL: Publications International, Ltd.

Fitzemeyer, T. (October 2000). Airing it out. *American School & University: Facilities, Purchasing and Business Administration,* 20, 22, 25.

Forseth, E. A. (1986, Spring). Consideration in planning small college athletic training facilities. *Athletic Training.* 23-25.

Frequently Asked Questions. [On-line]. Available: http://www.rain.org/ ~ ssa/judofaq.htm

Future trends in fitness equipment. (1997, November). *Joe Weider's Muscle & Fitness.* 26.

General Rules for Trail Orienteering [On-line]. *Available:* http://www.orienteering.org/publishing/TrailORules.html

Goodman, J. (October 2000). Cushion extends life. *Facilities Design & Management,* 54, 56.

Green, F. P., & de Coux, V. (1996, Winter). Inclusion of students with disabilities in campus recreational sports programs. *NIRSA Journal,* 34-37.

Giometti, A. (1997, October 10). Healthy buildings/IAQ 1997 reports. [On-line]. Available: http://204.7184.20/about/iaqwrap2.htm

Goldberger, D. J., & Jessop, P. (1994). *Profiting from energy efficiency,* pp. 25-29, International Council for Local Government Initiatives, Toronto, Canada.

Goldman, J. D. (1995, May/June). A sense of timing: Electronic timing and scoring takes meet management to new level. *Aquatics International,* 12-13.

Goodbody, J. (1969). *The Japanese fighting arts.* South Brunswick, NY: A. S. Barnes and Company.

G.R. Climbing Handholds. [On-line]. Avaialble: http://www.grholds.com

Groperz Handholds. [On-line]. Available: http://www.groperz.com

Hackensmith, C. W. (1966). *History of physical education.* New York: Harper & Row.

Hall, K. (1993, May). Sound. *Fitness Management,* 42-44.

Hall, K. (1991, May). Aerobics sound. *Fitness Management,* 34-36.

Hamar, D. (2000, November). Making the grade. *Athletic Business,* 77-78, 80-82, 84.

Hamer, J. M. (1988). *Facility management systems.* New York: van Nostrand Reinhold Company.

Handley, A. (1991, December). The new club: The Americans with Disabilities Act: What your club needs to know. *Club Industry,* 49-56.

Hanford, D. J. (1998, March). What's going down. *Building Operating Management* [On-line]. Available: http://www.facilitiesnet.com/NS/NS3b8ch.html

Hasenkamp, T, & Lutz, B. (2001, March). The dash for splash. *Athletic Business*, 55-56, 58, 60.

Hasler, A. E., & Bartlett, M. (1995, September). Equipped for exercise. *Athletic Business*, 47-54.

Head-Summit, P., & Jennings, D. (1996). *Basketball fundamentals and team play* (2nd ed.). Dubuque, IA: Brown and Bench-mark.

Hebrard, M. (2001). Show off your hidden talents. *SportsTurf*, 17(5), 18-23.

Hendy, T. (1997). The nuts and bolts of playground maintenance. In S. Hudson, & D. Thompson (Eds.), *Playground safety handbook* (pp. 60-70). Cedar Falls, IA: National Program for Playground Safety.

Herbert, D. L., Esq. (1992). *The Americans with Disabilities Act: A guide for health clubs and exercise facilities*. Canton, OH: Professional Report.

High 5. [On-line]. Available: http://www.high5adventure.org

Hill, D. (2000). Pre-construction. *Facility Manager*, 16(6), 13-16.

Hill, C. (2000). *Stablekeeping: A visual guide to safe and healthy horsekeeping*. Pownal, VT: Storey Publishing.

Holderness-Roddam, J. (1988). *Competitive riding*. New York, NY: Prentice-Hall.

Holzrichter, D. (2001, January). Gymnasium Makeovers. *Athletic Business*, 59- 60, 62-65.

Howard, D.R., & Crompton, J. L. (1995). *Financing sport*. Morgantown, WV: Fitness Information Technology, Inc.

Howe, D. K. (2000, March/April). Nine trends of the 1990s. *American Fitness*, 12-13.

Hudson, S., & Thompson, D. (1998). *SAFE playground handbook*. Cedar Falls, IA: National Program for Playground Safety.

Hughes, D., Jr., & Higginbotham, J. S. (1996). *Systems for success*. Cedar Rapids, IA: Dwight Hughes Systems, Inc.

Hunsaker, S. (1998). Getting pool light right. *Athletic Business*, 22(3), 51-54.

Hyder, M. A. (1999, November/December). Have your students climbing the walls. *JOPHERD*.

Innovation by consensus: ASTM's first century. (1998). [On-line]. Available: http://www.astm.org/ANNIVER/ consensus.htm

Illinois Park & Recreation Association. (1995). *A guide to playground planning*. Winfield, IL.: Author.

Index of Products. [On-line]. Available: http://www.hand-crafted.cim/index.html

Indiana State University. (1996). *Construction documents for ISU Music Rehearsal Building*. Terre Haute, IN: Author.

Indiana State University. (1995). *Construction documents for ISU John T Meyers Technology Building*. Terre Haute, IN: Author.

Indoor Climbing. [On-line]. Available: http://www.indoorclimbing.com

Ingersoll, C., & Sawyer, T. (1999). Sports medicine and rehabilitation. In *Facilities planning for physical activity and sport. Guidelines for development* (Ninth ed.). Dubuque, IA: Kendall-Hunt.

International Association of Skateboard Companies. [On-line]. Available: http://www.iasc.com

International Orienteering Federation Address Book. [On-line]. Available: http://www.orienteering.org/AddressBook/Nations.htm#United States

Introduction to Aikido. [On-line]. Available: http://www.ii.uib.no/~kjartan/akiidofaq/b_section01.html

Introduction to Ski Orienteering. [On-line]. Available: http://www.helsinki.fi/~jkleemol/skio/int/introd.html

Jewell, D. (1992). *Public assembly facilities*. (2nd ed.). Malabar, FL: Krieger Publishing Co.

Johnson, D. K., & Patterson, D. S. (1997, December). Window and Curtain Walls: Out With the Old? *Building Operating Management*. [On-line]. Available: http://www. facilitiesnet.com/ NS/NS3b7lb.html

Jones, T. E (1990, April). Choosing Court Colors. *Athletic Business*, 70-71.

Judo Rules. [On-line]. Available: http://www.ijf.org/02-03-00.html#chap1

Judo Rules. [On-line]. Available: http://www.rain,org/~ssa/rules.html#2

Kaplan, D. (1998). ABS: A new way to pay. *Sport Business Journal*, 1(1), 3.

Karate Glossary. [On-line]. Available: http:/www.europa.cs.mun.ca/~johnt/glossery.html

Kennedy, M. (2000, October). A Well-Grounded Plan. *American School & University: Facilities, Purchasing and Business Administration*, p. 30, 32, 34.

Kirkpatrick, S. A. (1997). Parking systems. In *Facilities management: A manual for plant administration* (3rd ed.) (p. 949-966). Alexandria, VA: The Association of Higher Education.

Kjellstrom, B. (1976). *Map and compass: The orienteering handbook* (4th ed.). New York: Charles Schribner's Sons.

Klafs, C. E., & Arnheim, D. D. (1973). *Modern principles of athletic training* (Third ed.) (pp. 33-42). St. Louis, MO:

Kocher, E. (1996, April). Gymnasium facelifts. *Athletic Business*, 39-42.

Kreighbaum, E. F., & Smith, M. A. (1995). *Sports and fitness equipment design*. Champaign, IL: Human Kinetics, Inc.

LaVoie, H. (1993). Ancillary Areas. In R. B. Flynn, (Ed.), *Facility planning for physical education, recreation, and athletics*, (pp. 147-148). Reston, VA: The Facilities Council of the Association for Research, Administration, Professional Councils and Societies: An Association of the American Alliance for Health, Physical Education, Recreation, and Dance.

Leavitt, R. (1991). Home climbing walls. *Climbing Magazine*. [On-line]. Available: http://www.climbing.com

Leibrock, C. (1994). Dignified options to ADA compliance. *Facilities Design & Management*, 13(6), 56 + .

Lewis, W. (1994). Weeding out unwanted growth: Weed problems on athletic fields can be nipped in the bud by implementing a total week management program. *Athletic Management*, 6(3), 28.

Logan, W., & Petras, H. (1975). *Handbook of the martial arts and self-defense*. New York: Funk and Wagnalls.

Lowery, R., & Sidney, K. (1989). *Orienteering: Skills and strategies* (3rd ed.). Willowdale, Ontario, Orienteering Ontario.

Lumpkin, A. (1998). *Physical education and sport: A contemporary introduction* (4th ed.). Boston: WCB/McGraw-Hill.

Lundin, B. L. V. (1997). Floor plans. *Building Operation Management*. [On-line]. Available: http://www.facilitiesnet.com/NS/NS3b7ce.html

Lyberger, M. R., & Pastore, D. L. (1998). Health club facility operators' perceived level of compliance with the Americans with Disabilities Act. *Journal of Sport Management, 12*, 139-145.

Mack, M. G., Hudson, S., & Thompson, D. (1997, June). A descriptive analysis of children's playground injuries in the United States 1990-1994. *Journal of the International Society for Child and Adolescent Injury Prevention, 3*, 100-103.

Mack, M. G., Sacks, J. J., & Thompson, D. (2000, June). Testing the impact attenuation of loose-fill playground surfaces. *Injury Prevention, 6*(2), 141-144.

Macomber, B. A. (1993). Outdoor facilities. In R. B. Flynn (Ed.), *Facility planning for physical education, recreation and athletics* (2nd ed.). Reston, VA: American Alliance for Health, Physical Education, Recreation and Dance.

Maloy, B. P. (2001). Safe environment. In D. J. Cotten, J. T. Wolohan, & T. J. Wilde (Eds.), *Law for recreation and sport managers*, (pp. 105–118). Dubuque, IA: Kendall/Hunt Publishing Co.

Maloy, B. P. (1993). Legal obligations related to facilities. *Journal of Physical Education, Recreation, and Dance, 64*(2), 28-30, 68.

Mazzola, G. (1998). Turn your turf into a field of dreams. *Scholastic Coach and Athletic Director, 67*(10), 36-38.

McGovern, J., Esq. (1992). *The ADA self-evaluation: A handbook for compliance with the ADA by parks and recreational agencies.* Ashburn, VA: National Recreation and Parks Association.

Merriam-Webster. (Eds.). (1995). *Webster's New American dictionary.* New York: Smithmark.

Metolius Climbing Products. [On-line]. Available: http://www.metoliusclimbing.com

Miller, L. K. (1997). *Sport business management.* Gaithersburg, MD: Aspen Publishers, Inc.

Miller, C. A. (1992, October). Equal access under the law: Removing barriers opens opportunities for the disabled. *Recreation Resources, 18.*

Minnesota Building Codes and Standards Division. (2001). Print-outs: *Bleacher seating.* [On-line]. Available: http://www.admin.state.mn.us/buildingcodes/printouts/bleachers.html

Molnar, D., & Rutledge, A. (1986). *Anatomy of a park* (2nd ed.). New York: McGraw-Hill.

Montoye, H. J., Kemper, H. C. G., Saris, W. H. M., & Wasshburn, R. A. (1996). *Measuring physical activity and energy expenditure.* Champaign, IL: Human Kinetics, Inc.

Moran, B. (1999, June). Mission essential: NIRSA conference highlights recreation's power to recruit and retain. *Recreational Sports & Fitness, 14-18.*

Moravek, J. (1996). Preventing future shock in today's buildings. *Consulting Specifying Engineer, 20*(5), 28-32.

Morehouse, L. E., & Rasch, P. J. (1964). *Sports medicine for trainers* (Second ed.) (pp. 214-223). Philadelphia: W.B. Saunders Company.

Morehouse, L. E., & Rasch, P. J. (1958). *Scientific basis of athletic training* (pp. 216-224). Philadelphia: W.B. Saunders Company.

Morrissey, P. (1993). *The educator's guide to the ADA.* Alexandria, VA: American Vocational Association.

Morrow, J. R. Jr., Jackson, A. W., Disch, J. G., & Mood, D. P. (1995). *Measurement and evaluation in human performance.* Champaign, IL: Human Kinetics, Inc.

Moussatche, H., Languell-Urquhart, J., & Woodson, C. (2000 September). Life-Cycle costs in education: Operations & maintenance considered. *Facilities Design & Management, 20*, 22.

Mueller, P., & Reznik, J. W. (1979). *Intramural-recreational sports: Programming and administration* (5th ed.). New York: John Wiley & Sons.

Mull, R. F., Bayless, K. G., Ross, C. M., & Jamieson, L. M. (1997). *Recreational sport management* (3rd ed). Champaign, IL: Human Kinetics.

Munson, A. L., & Comodeca, J. A. (1993, July). The act of inclusion. *Athletic Management, 14 + .*

Murphy, N. (1998, April 17) Biological effects of lighting: Shouldn't all you designers know about this? In IESNA Public Forum [On-line]. Available: http://www.iesna.org

Myers, C. (1997). Intelligent buildings require a smart pitch. *Facilities Design, 16*(9), 52-55.

Myers, J. N. (1996). *Essentials of cardiopulmonary exercise testing.* Champaign, IL: Human Kinetics, Inc.

National Dance Association. (1985). *Dance facilities.* Reston, VA: American Alliance for Health, Physical Education, Recreation, and Dance.

National Electronic Injury Surveillance System. [On-line]. Available: http://www.neiss.com

National Facilities Conference. (1962). *Planning facilities for health, physical education, and recreation.* Chicago: The Athletic Institute.

National Facilities Conference. (1966). *Planning facilities for health, physical education, and recreation.* Chicago: The Athletic Institute and the American Association of Health, Physical Education and Recreation.

National Facilities Conference. (1966). *College and university facility guide.* Washington, D.C.: The Athletic Institute and the American Association of Health, Physical Education and Recreation.

National Inline Hockey Assocation (USA). [On-line]. Available: http://www.niha.com

NewsOK.com. [On-line]. Available: http://www.ascm.org

NCAA Guides. Overland Park, KS: National Collegiate Athletic Association.

NCAA Men's and Women's Illustrated Basketball Rules Book (2001).

NCAA Rule Books for Baseball, Football, Soccer, and Lacrosse. (2000). Indianapolis, IN: National Collegiate Athletic Association.

NFHS Rule Books for Baseball, Football, Soccer, Softball, and Field Hockey. (2000). Indianapolis, IN: National Association for State High School Associations.

Neville, W. (1994). *Serve it up: Volleyball for life.* Mountain View, CA: Mayfield Publishing.

Newton, N. T. (1971). *Design on the land: The development of landscape architecture.* Cambridge, MA: Belknap Press of Harvard University Press.

Nicros. [On-line]. Available: http://www.nicro.com

Occupational Safety & Health Administration. [On-line]. Available: http://www.osha.gov

O-Equipment, Services, Software. [On-line]. Available: http://www.us.orienteering.org/cimmercial/index.html

Ontario Recreation Facilities Association Inc. (ORFA). (1992). *Refrigeration and Ice Making.* Aylmer, Ontario: The Aylmer Express Ltd.

Orienteering Clue Symbols. [On-line]. Available: http://www.williams.edu:803/Biology/orienteering/clues.html

Orienteering Map Symbols. [On-line]. Available: http://www.williams.edu:803/Biology/orienteering/legend.html

Orienteering. [On-line]. Available: http://ourworld.compuserve.homepages/magnus/orient.htm#WhatisO

Outdoor Network. [On-line]. Available: www.outdoornetwork.com

Outdoor Recreation Coalition of America (ORCA). [On-line]. Available: http://www. www.orca.org

Page, J. A. (1988). *The law of premises liability.* Cincinnati, OH: Anderson Publishing Co.

Pangrazi, R. P., & Dauer, V. P (1998) *Dynamic physical education for elementary school children* (10th ed.). New York: Macmillian Publishing Company.

Patton, J. D. (1999, April). Fitness in flux. *Athletic Business,* 51-54.

Patton, J. D. (1997). Mission control: A host of passive and active control measures bring security and comfort within the grasp of recreation facilities. *Athletic Business, 21*(8), 63-68.

Patton, W., Grantham, W. C., Gerson, R. F., & Gettman, L. R. (1989). *Developing and managing health/fitness facilities.* Champaign, IL: Human Kinetics Books.

Penman, K.A., & Penman, T.M. (1982, September). *Training rooms aren't just for colleges. Athletic Purchasing and Facilities.* 34-37.

Perfetti, R. & Ch'uan, T. C. [On-line]. Available: http://www.maui.net/~ táichi4u/overview.html

Petersen, J. C. (1997). Indoor activity space and ancillary space analysis for New Mexico high schools. Unpublished doctoral dissertation, The University of New Mexico, Albuquerque.

Petrogrips. [On-line]. Available: http://www.users.penn.com/petro

Piper, J. (1998, March). Complete performances. *Building Operation Management,* [On-line]. Available: http:www.facilitiesnet.com/NS/NS3b8ci.html

Piper, J. (1997). Restroom planning and design: Form meets function. *Building Operation Management,* [On-line]. Available: http://www.facilitiesnet.com/NS/NS3b7cg.html

Popke, M. (2000). Taking Root? *Athletic Business, 24*(9), 53-62.

Popke, M. (2000, October). Skate nation. *Athletic Business,* 67-74.

Poros, J. (1999, June 24). Renovating older schools reusing older schools. [On-line]. Available: http://www.edi.msstate.edu/olderschools.html#topolder

Practice Guidelines. [On-line]. Available: http://www.maui.net/~ táichi4u/practice.html

Price, S. D. (Ed.). (1998). *The whole horse catalog.* New York: Simon & Schuster, Inc.

Project Adventure. [On-line]. Available: http://www.pa.org

Puhalla, J., Krans, J., & Goatley, M (1999). *Sports fields: A manual for design, construction, and maintenance.* Ann Arbor, MI: Ann Arbor Press.

Pusher. [On-line]. Available: http://www.pusher.com

Rabin, J. (1993, July). Locker room bulletin board: Light years ahead. *Athletic Management,* 6.

Raiford, R. (1999, June) Into uncharted territory: Outsourcing redirects the future of business for facilities professionals. *Buildings,* 40-42.

Ramsey, T. (1998). *Building your own climbing walls.* Montana: Falcon Press.

Rankin, J., & Ingersoll, C. (1995). *Athletic training management: Concepts and applications.* St. Louis, MO: Mosby.

Rawlinson, K. (1961). *Modern athletic training.* Englewood Cliffs, NJ: Prentice-Hall, Inc.

Ray, R. (1994). *Management strategies in athletic training.* Champaign, IL: Human Kinetics.

Recreation: Sports:Martial Arts. [On-line]. Available: http://www.yaho.com/Recreation/Sports/Martial Arts

Regan, T. (1997). Financing facilities. In M. L. Walker, & D. K. Stotlar, (Eds.), *Sport facility management.* Sudbury, MA: Jones and Bartlett Publishers.

Rice, E. A., Hutchinson, J. L., & Lee, M. (1958). *A brief history of physical education* (4th ed.). New York: The Ronald Press Company.

Rice, E. A. (1926). *A brief history of physical education.* New York: A.S. Barnes and Company.

Roberts, E. (1996). Maintenance. In G. John, & K. Campbell (Eds.), *Handbook of sports and recreational building design: Vol. 2 indoor sports* (2nd ed.). (pp. 22-23). London: The Sports Council.

Robillard, P., & G. Todesco. (1992). *Potential electricity savings in ice arenas and curling rinks through improved refrigeration plant.* Canadian Electrical Association report No. 9129 U 858. Montreal, Quebec.

Rock and Ice Magazine. [On-line]. Available: http://www.rockandice.com

Rogers, J. (1996). Light. *Athletic Business, 20*(5), 51-54.

Rogers, J. (1994). Bright prospects: Proper field lighting can bring a sunny outlook to every night game on the gridiron. *Athletic Business, 18*(12), 53-56.